Ariel Feldman and Liora Goldman
Scripture and Interpretation

Beihefte zur Zeitschrift für die alttestamentliche Wissenschaft

Edited by
John Barton, Reinhard G. Kratz
and Markus Witte

Volume 449

Ariel Feldman and
Liora Goldman

Scripture and Interpretation

Qumran Texts that Rework the Bible

Edited and introduced by
Devorah Dimant

DE GRUYTER

ISBN 978-3-11-055268-3
e-ISBN 978-3-11-030305-6
ISSN 0934-2575

Library of Congress Cataloging-in-Publication Data
A CIP catalog record for this book has been applied for at the Library of Congress.

Bibliographic Information published by the Deutsche Nationalbibliothek
The Deutsche Nationalbibliothek lists this publication in the Deutsche Nationalbibliografie; detailed bibliographic data are available on the Internet at http://dnb.dnb.de.

© 2017 Walter de Gruyter GmbH, Berlin/Boston
This volume is text- and page-identical with the hardback published in 2014.
Printing and binding: CPI books GmbH, Leck

♾ Printed on acid-free paper
Printed in Germany

www.degruyter.com

Contents

Abbreviations —— VI
Abbreviations of Frequently Cited Works —— VIII
DJD Volumes Quoted in the Present Work —— X
Preface —— XII

Devorah Dimant
Introduction: Reworking of Scripture at Qumran —— 1

Ariel Feldman
Rewritten Scripture: Narrative and Law —— 12
    1Q19–1Q19^{bis} (Book of Noah) —— 14
    4Q370 (Admonition on the Flood) —— 42
    4Q577 (Text Mentioning the Flood) —— 73
    4Q422 (Paraphrase of Genesis and Exodus) —— 83
    4Q464 (Exposition on the Patriarchs), 4Q464^a, and 4Q464^b —— 130
    2Q21 (Apocryphon of Moses?) —— 159
    4Q368 (4QApocryphal Pentateuch A) —— 164
    4Q377 (4QApocryphal Pentateuch B) —— 195
    1Q22 (Words of Moses) —— 225

Liora Goldman
Rewritten Scripture: Law and Liturgy —— 263
    The Qumran *Apocryphon of Moses* (4Q375, 4Q376, 1Q29, 4Q408): General Introduction —— 265
    4Q375: The Identification of True and False Prophets —— 267
    4Q376: The Rules Regulating Permitted Wars —— 288
    1Q29: Law and Ceremony —— 305
    4Q408: Prayers —— 323
    General Conclusion: The Nature of the *Apocryphon of Moses* —— 351

Indices —— 359

Abbreviations

AB	Anchor Bible
ABD	*Anchor Bible Dictionary* (ed. D. N. Freedman; New York: Doubleday, 1992), 6 vols.
BDB	F. Brown, S. R. Driver, and C. A. Briggs, *Hebrew and English Lexicon of the Old Testament* (Oxford: Clarendon Press, 1975).
Bib	*Biblica*
BibOr	Biblica et orientalia
BJS	Brown Judaic Studies
BZAW	Beihefte zur Zeitschrift für die alttestamentliche Wissenschaft
CC	Continental Commentaries
DCH	*Dictionary of Classical Hebrew* (ed. D. J. A. Clines; Sheffield: Sheffield Academic Press, 1993–2011), 8 vols.
DJD	Discoveries in the Judaean Desert
DSD	*Dead Sea Discoveries*
DSS	Dead Sea Scrolls
EJL	Early Judaism and Its Literature
FAT	Forschungen zum Alten Testament
FCB	Feminist Companion to the Bible
FRLANT	Forschungen zur Religion und Literatur des Alten und Neuen Testaments
HALOT	L. Koehler and W. Baumgartner, *The Hebrew and Aramaic Lexicon of the Old Testament* (ed. and trans. M. E. J. Richardson et al.; Leiden: Brill, 1994–2000).
HSS	Harvard Semitic Studies
JBL	*Journal of Biblical Literature*
JHS	*Journal of Hebrew Scriptures*
JSJSup	Supplements to the Journal for the Study of Judaism
JSOT	*Journal for the Study of the Old Testament*
JSOTSup	*JSOT* Supplement Series
JSP	*Journal for the Study of the Pseudepigrapha*
Leš	*Lešonenu* (Hebrew)
Meghillot	*Meghillot: Studies in the Dead Sea Scrolls* (Hebrew)
MT	Masoretic Text
Neot	*Neotestamentica*
NIV	New International Version
NJPS	The New Jewish Publication Society translation of the Holy Scriptures (Tanakh)

OTP	*Old Testament Pseudepigrapha* (ed. J. H. Charlesworth; Garden City: Doubleday, 1983), 2 vols.
PTSDSSP	Princeton Theological Seminary Dead Sea Scrolls Project (ed. J. H. Charlesworth; Tübingen/Louisville: J. C. B. Mohr/Westminster John Knox, 1994–2011), 7 vols.
RevQ	*Revue de Qumrân*
SBL	Society of Biblical Literature
SBLEJL	Society of Biblical Literature Early Judaism and Its Literature
SBLSCS	Society of Biblical Literature Septuagint and Cognate Studies
ScrHier	Scripta Hierosolymitana
Shnaton	*Shnaton: An Annual for Biblical and Ancient Near Eastern Studies* (Hebrew)
STDJ	Studies on the Texts of the Desert of Judah
TDOT	*Theological Dictionary of the Old Testament* (ed. G. J. Botterweck and H. Ringgren; Grand Rapids: Eerdmans, 1974–2006), 15 vols.
ThWQ	*Theologisches Wörterbuch zu den Qumrantexten* (ed. H.-J. Fabry and U. Dahmen; Stuttgart: Kohlhammer, 2011–2013), 3 vols.
VT	*Vetus Testamentum*
VTSup	Vetus Testamentum Supplements
WUNT	Wissenschaftliche Untersuchungen zum Neuen Testament

Abbreviations of Frequently Cited Works

BDB
> F. Brown, S. R. Driver, and C. A. Briggs, *Hebrew and English Lexicon* of the Old Testament (Oxford: Clarendon Press, 1975).

DCH
> D. J. A. Clines, ed., *Dictionary of Classical Hebrew*. Sheffield: Academic Press, 1993–2011, 8 vols.

DSSR
> *The Dead Sea Scrolls Reader* (ed. D. W. Parry and E. Tov; Leiden: Brill, 2004–2005), 6 vols.

DSSR²
> *The Dead Sea Scrolls Reader: Second Edition, Revised and Expanded* (ed. D. W. Parry, E. Tov, in association with G. I. Clements; Leiden: Brill, 2013), 2 vols.

DSSSE
> F. García Martínez and E. J. C. Tigchelaar, *The Dead Sea Scrolls Study Edition*. (Leiden: Brill, 1997–1998), 2 vols.

DSSNTr
> M. O. Wise, M. Abegg, and E. Cook, *The Dead Sea Scrolls. A New Translation* (rev. ed.; New York: HarperCollins, 2005).

Ginzberg, *Legends*
> L. Ginzberg, *Legends of the Jews* (Philadelphia: The Jewish Publication Society, 2003), 2 vols.

HALOT
> L. Koehler and W. Baumgartner, *The Hebrew and Aramaic Lexicon of the Old Testament* (ed. and tr. M. E. J. Richardson et al.; Leiden: Brill, 1994–2000).

Jastrow, *Dictionary*
> M. Jastrow, *A Dictionary of the Targumim, the Talmud Bavli and Yerushalmi, and the Midrashic Literature* (New York: Judaica Press, 1982).

Joüon-Muraoka, *Grammar*
> P. Joüon, *A Grammar of Biblical Hebrew*. Translated and revised by T. Muraoka (SubBi 14/II; Rome: Editrice Pontifico Instituto Biblico, 1996).

Kugel, *Traditions*
> J. Kugel, *Traditions of the Bible* (Cambridge, Mss.: Harvard University Press, 1998).

Kutscher, *Isaiah Scroll*
> E. Y. Kutscher, *The Language and Linguistic Background of the Isaiah Scroll (1 Q Isa)* (Leiden: Brill, 1974).

Milik, *Books of Enoch*
: J. T. Milik, *The Books of Enoch: Aramaic Fragments of Qumran Cave 4* (Oxford: Clarendon Press, 1976).

Preliminary Concordance
: R. E. Brown et al., *A Preliminary Concordance to the Hebrew and Aramaic Fragments from Qumran Caves II–X*. Published privately, Göttingen, 1988, 5 vols.

PTSDSSP
: Princeton Theological Seminary Dead Sea Scrolls Project. J. H. Charlesworth, ed. Tübingen/Louisville: J. C. B. Mohr/Westminster John Knox, 1994–2011, 7 vols.

Qimron, "A Grammar of the Hebrew Language"
: E. Qimron, "A Grammar of the Hebrew Language of the Dead Sea Scrolls." Ph.D. diss. The Hebrew University of Jerusalem, 1978 (Hebrew).

Qimron, *Hebrew of the DSS*
: E. Qimron, *The Hebrew of the Dead Sea Scrolls*. HSS 29. Atlanta: Scholars Press, 1986.

Qimron, *The Dead Sea Scrolls*
: E. Qimron, *The Dead Sea Scrolls: The Hebrew Writings*. Between Bible and Mishnah. Jerusalem: Yad Ben-Zvi Press, 2010–2013, 2 vols.

Sokoloff, *Dictionary of Jewish Palestinian Aramaic*
: M. Sokoloff, *A Dictionary of Jewish Palestinian Aramaic*. Ramat-Gan: Bar Ilan University Press, 1990.

TDOT
: G. J. Botterweck and H. Ringgren, eds. *Theological Dictionary of the Old Testament*. Grand Rapids: Eerdmans, 1974–2006, 15 vols.

ThWQ
: H.-J. Fabry and U. Dahmen, eds. *Theologisches Wörterbuch zu den Qumrantexten*. Stuttgart: Kohlhammer, 2011–2013, 3 vols.

Tov, *Scribal Practices*
: E. Tov, *Scribal Practices and Approaches Reflected in the Texts Found in the Judean Desert*. STDJ 54; Leiden: Brill, 2004.

Wacholder-Abegg, *Preliminary Edition*
: B. Z. Wacholder and M. G. Abegg, *A Preliminary Edition of the Unpublished Dead Sea Scrolls*. Washington, D. C.: Biblical Archaeology Society, 1991–1995, 3 vols.

DJD Volumes Quoted in the Present Work

DJD I
Qumran Cave 1 (ed. D. Barthélemy and J. T. Milik; DJD I; Oxford: Clarendon Press, 1955)

DJD III
Les 'petites grottes' de Qumrân (ed. M. Baillet, J. T. Milik, and R. de Vaux; DJD III; 2 vols.; Oxford: Clarendon Press, 1962)

DJD IV
The Psalms Scroll of Qumrân Cave 11 (11QPs^a) (ed. J. A. Sanders; DJD IV; Oxford: Clarendon Press, 1965)

DJD V
Qumrân Cave 4.I (4Q158–4Q186) (ed. J. M. Allegro with A. A. Anderson; DJD V; Oxford: Clarendon Press, 1968)

DJD VII
Qumrân grotte 4.III (4Q482–4Q520) (ed. M. Baillet; DJD VII; Oxford: Clarendon Press, 1982)

DJD IX
Qumran Cave 4.IV: Palaeo-Hebrew and Greek Biblical Manuscripts (ed. P. W. Skehan, E. Ulrich, and J. E. Sanderson; DJD IX; Oxford: Clarendon Press, 1992)

DJD X
Qumran Cave 4.V: Miqṣat Maʿaśe ha-Torah (ed. E. Qimron and J. Strugnell; DJD X; Oxford: Clarendon Press, 1994)

DJD XI
Qumran Cave 4.VI: Poetical and Liturgical Texts, Part 1 (ed. E. Eshel et al.; DJD XI; Oxford: Clarendon Press, 1998)

DJD XII
Qumran Cave 4.VII: Genesis to Numbers (ed. E. Ulrich et al.; DJD XII; Oxford: Clarendon Press, 1994)

DJD XIII
Qumran Cave 4.VIII: Parabiblical Texts, Part 1 (ed. H. Attridge et al.; DJD XIII; Oxford: Clarendon Press, 1994)

DJD XIX
Qumran Cave 4.XIV: Parabiblical Texts, Part 2 (ed. M. Broshi et al.; DJD XIX; Oxford: Clarendon Press, 1995)

DJD XX
Qumran Cave 4.XV: Sapiential Texts, Part 1 (ed. T. Elgvin et al.; DJD XX; Oxford: Clarendon Press, 1997)

DJD XXV
Qumran Cave 4.XVIII: Textes hébreux (4Q521–4Q528, 4Q576–4Q579) (ed. É. Puech; DJD XXV; Oxford: Clarendon Press, 1998)

DJD XXVIII
Wadi Daliyeh II: The Samaria Papyri for Wadi Daliyeh; Qumran Cave 4.XXVIII: Miscellanea, Part 2 (ed. D. Gropp; E. Schuller et al.; DJD XXVIII; Oxford: Clarendon Press, 2001)

DJD XXIX
Qumran Cave 4.XX: Poetical and Liturgical Texts, Part 2 (ed. E. Chazon et al.; DJD XXIX; Oxford: Clarendon Press, 1999)

DJD XXX
Qumran Cave 4.XXI: Parabiblical Texts, Part 4: Pseudo-Prophetic Texts (ed. D. Dimant; DJD XXX; Oxford: Clarendon Press, 2001)

DJD XXXIII
Qumran Cave 4.XXIII: Unidentified Fragments (ed. D. M. Pike and A. Skinner; DJD XXXIII; Oxford: Clarendon Press, 2001)

DJD XXXVI
Qumran Cave 4.XXVI: Cryptic Texts; Miscellanea, Part 1 (ed. S. J. Pfann; P. S. Alexander et al.; DJD XXXVI; Oxford: Clarendon Press, 2000)

DJD XXXIX
The Texts from the Judaean Desert: Indices and an Introduction to the Discoveries in the Judaean Desert Series (ed. E. Tov; DJD XXXIX; Oxford: Clarendon Press, 2002)

DJD XL
Qumran Cave 1.III: 1QHodayot^a, with Incorporation of 4QHodayot^{a-f} and 1QHodayot^b (ed. H. Stegemann, E. Schuller, and C. Newsom; DJD XL; Oxford: Clarendon Press, 2009)

Preface

The present volume embodies the results of a research project on various small rewritten Scripture texts found in the Qumran library that have received little attention until now. The initiative for this research was prompted by the impact of many hitherto unknown Qumran texts of this type that have appeared in print for the first time over the past three decades. The fruits of this enterprise are presented in this volume. Such a demanding undertaking could not have been carried out and brought to completion without the generous support of several institutions. A four-year grant (No. 190/05) provided by the Israel Science Foundation (ISF) permitted Ariel Feldman and Liora Goldman to conduct the necessary investigation under my direction. Our gratitude is conveyed to the ISF for choosing to support this project. As the theme of this investigation was closely related to the research project I conducted with Reinhard Kratz from the Georg-August-Universität in Göttingen, we considered it as part of our own enterprise. Within the framework of our own project, which was supported by the Deutsche Forschungsgemeinschaft (DFG), it was therefore possible to meet the production expenses of the present volume. For this much-appreciated help, the authors and I are grateful to the DFG and to our friend and colleague Reinhard G. Kratz for his assistance in the matter. Our thanks go also to the University of Haifa for providing a suitable setting and the material support needed for conducting the research. Janice Karnis has expertly edited the English version and performed the copy-editing. Thanks are also due to the editors of the Beihefte zur Zeitschrift für die alttestamentliche Wissenschaft, John Barton, Reinhard G. Kratz, and Markus Witte, for accepting the volume into their series.

Devorah Dimant
Haifa, June 2014

Devorah Dimant
Introduction: Reworking of Scripture at Qumran

The discovery of the Qumran scrolls opened up unsuspected vistas on the literary and religious scene in the land of Israel during the Second Temple era. One of the many new phenomena revealed by these documents is the adaptation of the Hebrew Bible as a major tool for producing new literary creations. Of particular prominence are the texts that rewrite and rework the Hebrew Bible in a sustained manner. Known in certain non-Qumranic compositions before the discovery itself, the Qumran library considerably augmented the number of works that fall into this category. The first scholar to draw attention to the importance of this form of biblical reworking was Geza Vermes, who labeled this type of texts as "rewritten Bible." The label has had significant impact on subsequent discussion. Not a few articles devoted to the subject start by quoting his definition of such texts as "a narrative that follows Scripture but includes a substantial amount of supplements and interpretativets."[1] In Vermes's definition, the emphasis is already placed on the narrative form. Indeed, the majority of the specimens he considered as belonging to this category retell stories from the Pentateuch, with *Jubilees* and the *Genesis Apocryphon* occupying the central position.[2] Although Vermes included other, non-Qumranic, works in the list of "rewritten Bible" compositions, such as the *Biblical Antiquities* and the *Martyrdom of Isaiah*, the narrative rewriting of the Pentateuch remained the central feature of the "rewritten Bible" texts discussed in later surveys. In his contribution, "Retelling the Old Testament," Philip Alexander analyzed four such texts that in his view should be labeled "rewritten Bible": *Jubilees*, the *Genesis Apocryphon*, *Biblical Antiquities*, and the section of Josephus' *Jewish Antiquities* that reworks the biblical sources.[3] Alexander follows Vermes in assigning to the group works that have not been transmitted in Hebrew: the Aramaic *Genesis Apocryphon*, the Greek *Jewish Antiq-*

---

[1] Cf. e.g. P. Alexander, "Retelling the Old Testament," in *It is Written: Scripture Citing Scripture; Essays in Honour of Barnabas Lindars* (ed. D.A. Carson, H. Godfrey, and M. Williamson; Cambridge: Cambridge University Press, 1988), 99–121 (99); G.J. Brooke, "Rewritten Bible," *EDSS* 2:777–81 (777); M.J. Bernstein, "'Rewritten Bible': A Generic Category Which Has Outlived its Usefulness?," *Textus* 22 (2005): 169–96 (172–73). The quotation is from G. Vermes, "Biblical Midrash," in E. Schürer, *The History of the Jewish People in the Age of Jesus Christ (175 B.C.–A.D. 135)* (ed. G. Vermes, F. Millar, and M. Goodman; Edinburgh: T & T Clark, 1986), 3:308–41 (326).
[2] Cf. Vermes, ibid.
[3] Cf. Alexander, "Retelling the Old Testament."

uities, and the *Biblical Antiquities*, preserved only in a Latin translation. He also retained Vermes's basic definition by stating that "Rewritten Bible texts are narratives, which follow a sequential chronological order."[4] The selection of texts defined as "rewritten Bible" was narrowed significantly in the following treatments. In her monograph devoted to these texts, Sidnie White Crawford restricts herself to works found among the Qumran scrolls. Having adopted this perspective, she added to previous lists 4QReworked Pentateuch, the *Temple Scroll*, and 4QCommentary on Genesis A while dropping non-Qumranic compositions from her treatment. By attaching the *Temple Scroll* to this category, an important subject matter prone to be reworked, the biblical law, was added to the narrative specimens.[5] Another contemporary survey of this type of texts by Daniel Falk devoted its analysis to only three texts: the *Genesis Apocryphon*, 4QReworked Pentateuch, and 4QCommentary on Genesis A–D.[6] The most recent monograph-length treatment of the subject by Molly Zahn is confined to 4QReworked Pentateuch, the Samaritan Pentateuch, and the *Temple Scroll*.[7]

Limiting the discussion to a small number of compositions that rework the biblical narrative and law of the Pentateuch has resulted in a restrictive definition of the rewritten Bible texts. Thus, Moshe Bernstein ends up by defining them as "comprehensive or broad scope rewriting of narrative and/or legal material with commentary woven into the fabric implicitly...."[8] Such a view seems to be based on the fact that the works discussed, such as *Jubilees*, the *Genesis Apocryphon*, 4QReworked Pentateuch, and the *Temple Scroll*, survived in relatively long and well-preserved versions that permit detailed and comprehensive analysis. In addition, comparing rewritten narratives to their biblical models is a relatively straightforward operation due to the clear sequential outline that is characteristic of such passages.[9] However, taking the sequential line as the point of departure

---

[4] Alexander, ibid., 116.
[5] Cf. S. White Crawford, *Rewriting Scripture in Second Temple Times* (Grand Rapids: Eerdmans, 2008). For the reworking or retelling of law, see M. J. Bernstein and S. A. Koyfman, "The Interpretation of Biblical Law in the Dead Sea Scrolls: Forms and Methods," in *Biblical Interpretation at Qumran* (ed. M. Henze; Grand Rapids: Eerdmans, 2005), 61–87 (66–70).
[6] D. K. Falk, *The Parabiblical Texts: Strategies for Extending the Scriptures in the Dead Sea Scrolls* (New York: T & T Clark, 2007).
[7] M. M. Zahn, *Rethinking Written Scripture: Composition and Exegesis in the 4QReworked Pentateuch Manuscripts* (STDJ 95; Leiden: Brill, 2011).
[8] Cf. Bernstein, "Rewritten Bible," 195.
[9] This characteristic is implied by Zahn's statement: "Compositional techniques can be identified by comparison of rewritten text with its scriptural source." Cf. eadem, *Rethinking Written Scripture*, 14.

tends to present divergences between the reworked texts and their biblical sources in quantitative terms. Indeed, arranging rewritten Bible texts along a continuum from works with "small" changes to texts with "large" ones became the central organizing principle in White Crawford's presentation.[10] This approach has been criticized rightly for, in the absence of precise tools for measuring quantitative differences, results obtained by such an analysis are limited and at times one-sided.[11] Moreover, such an approach is ill-suited for charting more complex adaptations of biblical elements that cannot be defined in quantitative terms. In an attempt at a more precise characterization of the rewritten Bible technique, Molly Zahn introduced the analytical distinction between "Compositional Techniques," that is the content elements of a given rewritten Bible text, what it wishes to say, and the form it employs to say it, namely, how the text is doing so.[12] As methods employed by these compositional techniques, Zahn enumerates procedures well known from previous research, such as additions, omissions, and alterations.[13] The terms introduced by Zahn bring to the fore a useful distinction, but using it in a systematic fashion also involves quantitative elements that are not always applicable to nonsequential complex forms reworking the Bible. This is seen clearly when analyzing adaptations of biblical law and the Prophets.[14]

The adoption of a restrictive definition of rewritten Bible texts, a "minimalist" one, as it is labeled by Daniel Machiela,[15] has left aside many fragmentary texts and more intricate ways of reworking the Hebrew Bible. Little has been said, for instance, on the reworking of biblical books beyond the Pentateuch, and that of other narrative, poetic, and wisdom passages. Thus, the historical, prophetical, and wisdom biblical books were rarely considered in the context of rewritten Bible texts.[16] In contrast, George Brooke has examined the problems involved in rewritten Bible texts from a wider perspective. He adopts a broad definition

---

10 Cf. White Crawford, *Rewriting Scripture*, 11–14.
11 Cf. Zahn, *Rethinking Rewritten Scripture*, 7–11; D. A. Machiela, "Once More, with Feeling: Rewritten Scripture in Ancient Judaism—A Review of Recent Developments," *JJS* 61 (2010): 308–20 (312–13).
12 Cf. Zahn, *Rethinking Rewritten Scripture*, 12–17.
13 Zahn, ibid., 17–19.
14 For the law, see the examples analyzed by Bernstein and Koyfman, "The Interpretation of Biblical Law." For prophecy, see D. Dimant, "Hebrew Pseudepigrapha at Qumran," in *Old Testament Pseudepigrapha and the Scriptures* (ed. E. J. C. Tigchelaar; BETL 270; Leuven: Peeters, 2014), 89–103.
15 Cf. Machiela, "Once More, with Feeling," 309.
16 On the reworking of biblical Joshua, see recently A. Feldman, *The Rewritten Joshua Scrolls from Qumran* (BZAW 438; Berlin: de Gruyter, 2014). On the reworking of Ezekiel in the Qumranic *Pseudo-Ezekiel*, see Dimant, "Hebrew Pseudepigrapha at Qumran."

of the term and it permits him to include the Prophets and Wisdom literature in the category.[17] In line with this approach, and following other treatments of this category, Brooke also designates Aramaic texts as falling under his definition.[18]

The various approaches to the rewritten Bible texts sketched above betray the difficulty in defining them. Appearing in a wide range of contexts and forms while at the same time sharing similar features, the rewritten Bible texts cannot be easily delineated. The difficulty is also reflected by the debate on whether the rewritten Bible texts constitute a distinctive literary genre. Adopting a flexible definition of genre, Molly Zahn answers in the affirmative.[19] Espousing a similar point of view, George Brooke speaks of "evolution and instability of genres,"[20] which permits him to broaden the category. He also stresses the need to include texts other than narratives in the definition.[21] A narrower approach is adopted by Michael Segal.[22] Concerned with differentiating between a proper biblical text and a rewritten one, Segal typifies a rewritten Bible text as one that does not include its biblical model in its entirety, accords a new narrative framework to its creation, and alters the biblical narrative third person voice to a different one, often the first person voice of the narrator.[23] This perspective leads him to exclude non-Hebraic works from his definition.[24]

Another useful distinction between rewritten Bible texts and proper biblical manuscripts is adduced by Tov and White Crawford. They note that in texts considered biblical, including in the harmonistic Proto-Samaritan biblical manuscripts, the alterations and additions are always composed of elements found elsewhere in the Bible, whereas rewritten Scripture texts supply new, nonbiblical

---

[17] Cf. Brooke, "Rewritten Bible," 778. See also idem, "Genre Theory, Rewritten Bible and Pesher," in *Reading the Dead Sea Scrolls: Essays in Method* (Atlanta: SBL, 2013), 115–35 (126–29).
[18] Brooke, "Rewritten Bible," 779–80. See also idem, "The Rewritten Law, Prophets and Psalms: Issues for Understanding the Text of the Bible," in *The Bible as Book: The Hebrew Bible and the Judaean Desert Discoveries* (ed. E. D. Herbert and E. Tov; London: The British Library, 2002), 31–40.
[19] Cf. M. Zahn, "Genre and Rewritten Scripture: A Reassessment," *JBL* 131 (2012): 271–88 (277, 281).
[20] Cf. Brooke, "Genre Theory," 346–48.
[21] Ibid, 339–40.
[22] Cf. M. Segal, "Between Bible and Rewritten Bible," in *Biblical Interpretation at Qumran* (ed. M. Henze; Grand Rapids: Eerdmans, 2005), 10–28.
[23] Segal, "Between Bible and Rewritten Bible," 20–23.
[24] In an earlier contribution, Segal analyzed 4Q158 along these lines and showed that due to the exegetical character of several of its passages it is closer to *Jubilees* than to a biblical text. Cf. M. Segal, "Biblical Exegesis in 4Q158: Techniques and Genre," *Textus* 19 (1998): 45–62 (62).

additions.²⁵ While these are important distinctions, they are again based mainly on straightforward sequential narrative reworking of the Pentateuch. However, even when following the main narrative outline, some texts that rework Pentateuch passages present a composite elaboration of the biblical base story, as is evident from the texts considered in the present volume. Moreover, the above distinctions offered by Tov, White Crawford, and Segal were motivated by the need to differentiate between proper biblical texts and rewritten ones. This issue arises from discussion essentially unrelated to the literary character of the rewritten Bible texts as such, namely, the plurality of textual forms of the Hebrew Bible.

This plurality is one of the important new facts to emerge from the study of biblical manuscripts found at Qumran. It is now known that the final text and literary forms of many biblical books took shape following a long process of re-edition. With the discovery of a large group of rewritten Bible texts that adopt the stance of the biblical authors and reshape the biblical text, the relationship between the textual fluidity of the biblical models and their rewritten creations became a critical issue. Of particular weight in this context has been the fact that various procedures used in editing biblical texts, such as harmonization, are also displayed in the rewritten Bible works.

Viewing the rewritten Bible texts within the context of the textual fluidity of the Hebrew Bible introduced into the discussion the problem of authority. Many scholars take the view that the appropriation by rewritten Bible texts of biblical garb confers biblical authority on their new creations. Thus, Emanuel Tov employs the notion of authority to distinguish between biblical and nonbiblical rewritten Bible texts. According to him, the former are authoritative, whereas the latter are not.²⁶ However, the term "authority" itself is vague and problematic. It is drawn from the circumstances of the later scriptural canon, which appeared as a closed and sacred collection of writings only from the 2nd century, and thus is irrelevant to the situation prevalent during the last centuries prior to the destruction of the Second Temple in 70 CE. Indeed, the plethora of forms and versions evidenced among the Qumran biblical scrolls attest to this reality. So a "canonical" authority in the proper sense did not exist in the last centuries of the Second Temple era. Recent discussion has attempted to reflect this distinction by replacing the nomenclature "rewritten Bible" by "rewritten Scripture" in order to avoid

---

25 Cf. E. Tov, "Between Bible Compositions and Biblical Manuscripts, with Special Attention to the Samaritan Pentateuch," *DSD* 5 (1998): 334–54 (352, 354); White Crawford, *Rewriting Scriptures*, 13.
26 Cf. Tov, "Between Bible Compositions and Biblical Manuscripts," 334.

anachronism.²⁷ However, the change of term does not clarify the nature of authority accorded to certain biblical books before the final canonization of the entire collection. That the Torah, the Prophets, and some sections of the canonical Psalms²⁸ occupied an authoritative position may be gathered from the fact that they are cited and interpreted in Qumran documents and other contemporary works beyond Qumran.²⁹ But less certain is the status accorded to the remaining biblical books of the Writings section.³⁰ Altogether problematic is the attempt by some scholars to attribute scriptural authority to rewritten Scripture works. It has been so particularly in the case of *Jubilees*, firstly because of the pseudepigraphic attribution of the book to Moses, and secondly because it is allegedly quoted by the *Damascus Document* (CD XVI, 3–4).³¹ However, pseudepigraphic framework as a literary device was widely used in contemporary Jewish literature without investing authority in every case in which it was employed. Moreover, it is questionable whether *Jubilees* is quoted in the *Damascus Document*.³² Equally gratuitous is the claim that the high number of copies of *Jubilees* at Qumran reflects its authoritative standing there.³³ The Aramaic *Book of Giants* survived in ten copies at Qumran, a relatively high number, but no one claims that this work had authoritative standing among the Qumran sectaries. Moreover, despite its Bible-like style and the incorporation of long scriptural passages, as in other rewritten Scripture works, *Jubilees* did not aim at replacing its biblical model, a fact stressed by all scholars who addressed these issues.³⁴ Why assume, then, that these works were invested with an authority resembling that of their biblical models? More plausible, and according better with the literary facts, is the view that *Jubilees* and similar rewritten Scripture texts strove to confer authority on the interpretation of their biblical sources rather than on their specific literary text and form as such. In any case, as noted by Michael Segal, authority is a

---

27 Cf. e.g. White Crawford, *Rewriting Scriptures*, 9–10; Zahn, *Rethinking Rewritten Scripture*, 1–2. The term Rewritten Scripture will therefore be used in the following.
28 See Brooke, "Rewritten Bible," 779.
29 See the survey of evidence by J. C. VanderKam, *The Dead Sea Scrolls Today* (2nd ed.; Grand Rapids: Eerdmans, 2010), 179–86.
30 But note the quotation of Prov 15:8 in CD XI, 21–22.
31 For criteria for attributing authority to a given text, see the proposals of VanderKam, *The Dead Sea Scrolls Today*, 191–92, followed by White Crawford, *Rewriting Scripture*, 8–9.
32 See D. Dimant, "Two 'Scientific' Fictions: The So-Called *Book of Noah* and the Alleged Quotation of *Jubilees* in the *Damascus Document* XVI, 3–4," *History, Ideology and Bible Inter-pretation in the Dead Sea Scrolls: Collected Studies* (FAT 90; Tübingen: Mohr Siebeck, 2014), 353–68 (363–68).
33 Cf. White Crawford, ibid., 9.
34 Cf. e.g. Alexander, "Retelling the Old Testament," 116–17; Brooke, "Rewritten Bible," 780; Segal, "Between Bible and Rewritten Bible," 11.

sociohistorical issue.³⁵ It therefore cannot be defined on the basis of literary data, neither should it be used for outlining the genre and literary character of a given text.³⁶

The foregoing survey of scholarship on rewritten/reworked Scripture texts emphasizes the complexity of the issues at stake and the variety of approaches taken to elucidate them. It has been pointed out that the discussion on the pertinent data has tended to concentrate on Pentateuch narrative and law as they appear in long and well-preserved compositions. The present volume aims at reviewing shorter Qumran documents that rework the Pentateuch that belong, at least partly, to the corpus of rewritten Scripture texts, but which have remained outside the discussion on the subject.³⁷ As is shown in the detailed examination of the texts, despite their adherence to Pentateuch narratives and laws, retaining their general sequence, they are not straightforward sequential rewriting but instead present more elaborate and complex ways of adapting Scripture. Admittedly, the texts assembled here are fragmentary remains of larger compositions now lost, a fact that limits the scope and validity of the observations extracted from these pieces. Nevertheless, there is much to be gained from a close study of these remains of a rich Hebrew literature reworking the Hebrew Bible that once thrived in the land of Israel.

Small as it is, the group of texts analyzed here illustrates well the wide range of techniques applied to reworking and interpreting Hebrew scripture, some of them known from the well-studied longer specimens. However, several scrolls discussed here rewrite various biblical passages in a freer manner than specimens such as the *Temple Scroll* and *Jubilees*. Although attached to particular biblical sections, they do not follow closely the biblical sequence and therefore their method of reworking their models cannot be measured by a quantitative yardstick. Perhaps the most prominent feature to emerge from a survey of all the

---

35 Cf. Segal, ibid., 17.
36 For instance, as done by VanderKam (*The Dead Sea Scrolls Today*, 187–93) and White Crawford (*Rewriting Scripture*, 8–9).
37 ⁷ The research project, which forms the basis of the present volume, was originally intended to cover also texts that rewrite the biblical historical books, such as the *Apocryphon of Joshua* (now published by Feldman in a separate volume; see n. 16 above), but time and resource constraints imposed restrictions on its scope. In its final form, the project has been confined to short reworked Pentateuch texts; the longer *Pseudo-Jubilees* has also been excluded from the volume for this reason. It was edited separately and commented on by Atar Livneh in a doctoral dissertation, "The Composition *Pseudo-Jubilees* from Qumran (4Q225; 4Q226; 4Q227): A New Edition, Introduction, and Commentary" (Ph.D. diss., University of Haifa, 2010), now being prepared by her for publication.

texts edited here is the addition of new nonbiblical material to rewritten biblical passages. So each text has to be analyzed on its own terms.

Prominent in the group of texts considered here are those that treat various aspects of Moses' career. The text labeled 4QApocryphal Pentateuch A (4Q368) appears to contain some of the most sustained rewriting of Scripture passages of the type known from the *Temple Scroll* and *Jubilees*. Thus, frg. 1 reproduces, with small changes and additions, Exod 33:11–18, while frg. 2 reworks Exod 34:11–22. However, the scroll seems to possess a narrative framework serving to introduce episodes from the life of Moses (see 4Q368 1 2, 4; 4 2; note frg. 3 7), exhortation (frg. 2 3–8), and various laws (frg. 2 9–17). While all these sections are based more or less on biblical sources, frg. 10 i offers a nonbiblical pericope, perhaps a paraenetic discourse by Moses to Israel (see the address in the second person plural in frg. 10 i 6–7).

Moses is also the central figure in 4QApocryphal Pentateuch B (4Q377). Here, various episodes from the desert period are retold in a narrative third person style (see frgs. 2 i; 11). It therefore seems that the work survived in these fragments contained a narrative framework. The story is interspersed with various discourses, for instance by Israel (frg. 2 i 10–11) and by an unknown figure, Elibaḥ (frg. 2 ii 3–10). The speech by Elibaḥ is of particular interest since it summarizes the Sinai revelation in a highly poetic style, based on various biblical texts. As characteristic of many Qumran rewritten Bible texts, the author of this text associates different verses that share similar themes and formulations. At the same time, it supplies nonbiblical additions that reflect an advanced interpretation of the biblical material. This is illustrated, for instance, by the angel-like sanctification of Moses, based on his sojourn on Mount Sinai (in frg. 2 ii 10–12).

A different method of reworking Scripture is exemplified by the *Words of Moses* (1Q22). The literary structure of this text is borrowed from Moses' admonitory addresses in Deuteronomy. Built on the opening scene and concluding admonitions in Deuteronomy, frg. 1 contains divine instructions to Moses (col. i 1–11), and Moses' exhortation to Israel (cols. ii 11–iv 11). The text reshapes the biblical farewell exhortations into a new literary creation, fashioning it as a tapestry of phrases and expressions relevant to the theme but taken from various sections of Deuteronomy and other biblical books. Yet nonbiblical ideas are interwoven into this seemingly biblical exhortation. An example of this is the proleptic presentation of the admonition as a legal warning to Israel, which serves to justify subsequent divine punishment on future transgressions (col. i 4–5). Of special interest is the addition announcing that Israel "will f[orget statute, and appointed time, and mo]nth, and Sabbath, [and jubilee,]and covenant" (col. i 8). The formulation is strikingly similar to statements to this effect in sectarian texts (CD III, 14–15) and works related to the sectarian ideology (*Jub.* 1:14; 4Q390 1 7–8). In this way,

1Q22 presents a rewritten Scripture text that betrays links to sectarian ideas; in this respect it resembles both the *Temple Scroll* and *Jubilees*. The partly preserved cols. iii and iv produce a string of laws, of which only those concerning the Sabbatical Year and the Day of Atonement have survived. Evident here is the method of combining details pertinent to the same theme but occurring in different biblical books. For the Sabbatical Year, mainly Leviticus 25 and Deuteronomy 15 are brought together, while the precepts related to the Day of Atonement are based on Leviticus 16 and Num 29:7–11. The exhortation occupying the first two columns seems to serve as an introduction to the laws cited subsequently. A similar configuration may be suggested by the admonitory tone of the first surviving column of the *Temple Scroll*.

In several respects, the picture emerging from the *Words of Moses* (1Q22) resembles that imparted by the *Apocryphon of Moses* (4Q375, 4Q376, 1Q29, and 4Q408). The *Apocryphon* is characterized by a unique reworking of laws from Deuteronomy that stress the role the high priest plays in elucidating and deciding on legal issues, the biblical basis being Deut 17:8–11. One of the issues addressed in this complex work is the identification of true and false prophets (4Q375 i–ii), reworking and interweaving three Deuteronomy passages, 13:1–6, 18:15–20, and 30:2–10, together with phraseology from other biblical texts. In addition, this work treats several other laws: one prescribes a procedure for deciding whether to engage in a permitted war, another one lays down how to establish that the person who refuses to accept the high priest's authority is a "prophet who speaks rebellion." The novel legal elements in the work are particularly clear in the description of an unknown procedure whereby the priest inquires via the Urim (4Q375 ii; 4Q376 i). Here, too, there is no close adherence to the biblical sources but a free reworking of various biblical laws in order to create new ones. At the same time, the composition includes a nonbiblical prayer of praise to the Creator of the light and luminaries (4Q408 3). It seems to suggest a metaphorical link between the light of the celestial entities and the light that shines through the Urim while the priest officiates in the temple. The reworking of the biblical sources seems to assign the *Apocryphon of Moses* to the category of rewritten Scripture, but that of a special type. It is therefore interesting to note that some of its aspects are closely linked to sectarian nomenclature and theology. This is particularly true of the prayer (4Q408 3), which betrays several terminological and thematic affinities to the sectarian liturgy. In addition, the preoccupation with the issue of true and false prophets is related to a matter of concern to the community, since it considered itself heir to the true prophets, charging its opponents of being false prophets.

2Q21 may have been similarly selective. The single surviving fragment of significant size lists the names of Aaron's sons, Abihu and Eleazar, taken from the biblical lists (cf. e.g. Exod 6:23; 28:1; Num 3:2; 26:60). It perhaps relates to the sin of Nadav and Avihu, two of Aharon's sons (Leviticus 10; Num 3:4). The second section of the fragment records a prayer, probably of Moses, perhaps pronounced in the wake of the sin committed by his brother's descendants.

Other texts assembled here furnish free reworking of themes from Genesis and Exodus. The first column of 4QAdmonition on the Flood (4Q370) reworks the biblical record of this event. However, while it follows the main outline of Genesis 6–9, 4Q370 summarizes the narrative in a poetic style, borrowing expressions from other biblical books. Thus, for example, the author resorts to poetic pictures from the Song of the Sea (Exod 15:10) and Isa 24:18–20 (in 4Q370 i 3–4) to describe the tumult of the natural elements brought by the flood. In addition, it intertwines aggadic motives into its presentation. For instance, the notion known from rabbinic midrash that the antediluvian generations were blessed with bountiful produce but were ungrateful and rebellious and therefore punished by the flood is advanced here (4Q370 i 1–3). Another motif appearing in the passage, referring to the giants who perished in the flood (4Q370 i 6), is known from *1 Enoch* 6–7 and other ancient Jewish sources. This account of the flood, embellished by various biblical allusions and new additions, is discontinued in the second column. Here, an unknown admonition appears. Formulated in biblical phraseology, it is nevertheless a nonbiblical creation that ties up with didactic comments in the first column (see 4Q370 i 2–3, 6). Interestingly, the present text displays links to other pieces found at Qumran, 4Q185 1–2 i and the apocryphal *Hymn to the Creator* (11QPs[a] XXVI).

In a similar vein, 4QParaphrase of Genesis and Exodus (4Q422) gives poetic summaries of major biblical episodes. Preserved chiefly in a large fragment containing three columns, the first column summarizes the creation of man and the sinful eating from the Tree of Knowledge (Genesis 1–2), the second one reworks the flood story (Genesis 6–9), while the third column outlines the story of the Ten Plagues in Egypt (Exodus 1–12). Typical of this type of reworking is the poetic style, drawing upon other biblical sources such as the paraphrase of the plagues story in Psalm 78. The fact that these far-removed episodes are compressed into three consecutive columns betrays the abridged form of the stories. The didactic tenor of the depiction (see cols. i 11–12; ii 8–9; iii 7, 11) is similar to that of 4Q370. Therefore, 4Q422 may be described as an anthology of biblical episodes, composed for edifying purposes.

The next work to be considered, 4QExposition on the Patriarchs (4Q464), is preserved in several fragments and indicates a text that reworks Scripture. Thus, frgs. 1, 3, and 6 deal with episodes from the life of Abraham, frgs. 7–8 concern Jacob, frg. 10 probably alludes to Joseph, and frg. 12 refers to the Israelites' servitude in Egypt. However, the fragments are too small for a meaningful estimate of their literary character and technique. Perhaps the original work contained a selection of reworked biblical events in the vein of 4Q422.

4Q577 is another scroll that has survived in several small fragments. Frg. 1 4 mentions the flood and frg. 7 i–ii also seems to deal with this topic. However, the fragments are very small and do not afford any impression of their wider context and form.

The last manuscript to be discussed, 1Q19, presents a special case. Although frgs. 1–3 deal with antediluvian times and seem to follow the general outline of the biblical account, the details they provide of the relevant episodes are taken from nonbiblical descriptions. Frgs. 1 and 2 depict the corruption of the earth in antediluvian times and the reaction of the archangels to the evil done there. These details parallel the story in *1 Enoch* 7–9. Frg. 3 refers to the miraculous birth of Noah, a story found in *1 Enoch* 106–107 and cols. II–V of the *Genesis Apocryphon*. The original work appears to have contained additional nonbiblical materials, as may be inferred from frg. 13, which contains remains of a nonbiblical song of praise. Whether this text can be classified accurately as rewritten Scripture is a question that must be dealt with elsewhere. However, its inclusion in this volume provides further evidence of the various ways in which biblical materials were reworked during the Second Temple times.

In conclusion, a note must be added regarding the relationship of the rewritten Scripture texts discussed in this volume to the particular literature of the Qumran community. One of the questions that prompted the research project, the fruits of which are presented here, was whether the rewritten Scripture texts have any bearing on the particularistic views and formulations of the Qumran community.[38] The major examples of this group, such as the *Temple Scroll* and *Jubilees*, share ideas with the sectarian literature but not its style or nomenclature. The present analysis indicates that a similar situation may be observed in the *Apocryphon of Moses* (in particular 4Q408 3) and perhaps also in 4QWords of Moses (1Q22 i 4–5). However, the issue merits further study.

---

38 In my recent re-edition of the classification of the Qumran scrolls, all the manuscripts contained in the present collection are included in the Hebrew nonsectarian texts. See D. Dimant, *History, Ideology and Bible Interpretation in the Dead Sea Scrolls: Collected Studies* (FAT 90; Tübingen: Mohr Siebeck, 2014), 48–50.

Ariel Feldman
Rewritten Scripture: Narrative and Law
with contributions by Devorah Dimant

1Q19–1Q19ᵇⁱˢ (Book of Noah)*

Literature

J. T. Milik, "1Q19–1Q19ᵇⁱˢ. Livre de Noé," in *Qumran Cave I* (ed. D. Barthélemy and J. T. Milik; DJD I; Oxford: Clarendon Place, 1955), 84–86, 152; D. Dimant, "'The Fallen Angels' in the Dead Sea Scrolls and in the Apocryphal and Pseudepigraphic Books Related to Them" (Ph.D. diss., The Hebrew University, 1974), 132–37 (Hebrew); idem, "1 Enoch 6–11: A Fragment of a Parabiblical Work," *JJS* 53 (2002): 223–37 (236–37); idem, "Two 'Scientific' Fictions: The So-Called *Book of Noah* and the Alleged Quotation of *Jubilees* in CD XVI, 3–4," in *History, Ideology and Bible Interpretation in the Dead Sea Scrolls: Collected Studies* (FAT 90; Tübingen: Mohr Siebeck, 2014), 354–62; J. A. Fitzmyer, *The Genesis Apocryphon of Qumran Cave 1: A Commentary* (3rd ed.; Rome: Biblical Institute Press, 2004), 258–60; K. Beyer, *Die aramäischen Texte vom Toten Meer* (Göttingen: Vandenhoeck & Ruprecht, 1984), 1:229, 236–37, 250; F. García Martínez, *Qumran and Apocalyptic* (STDJ 9; Leiden: Brill, 1992), 42; L. T. Stuckenbruck, *The Book of Giants from Qumran* (TSAJ 63; Tübingen: Mohr Siebeck, 1997), 219–20, 232; idem, *1 Enoch 91–108* (CEJL; Berlin: de Gruyter, 2007), 612, 626, 629; idem, "The Lamech Narrative in the Genesis Apocryphon (1QapGen) and Birth of Noah (4QEnochᶜ ar): A Tradition-Historical Study," in *Aramaica Qumranica* (ed. K. Berthelot and D. Stökl Ben Ezra; STDJ 94; Leiden: Brill, 2010), 253–75 (254–55); S. Bhairo, *The Shemihazah and Asael Narrative of 1 Enoch 6–11* (AOAT 322; Münster: Ugarit-Verlag, 2005), 4–5; D. Peters, *Noah Traditions in the Dead Sea Scrolls: Conversations and Controversies of Antiquities* (SBLEJL 26; Atlanta: SBL, 2008), 132–34; C. Batsch, "1Q19–1Q19bis," in *La Bibliothèque de Qumran: Torah: Genèse* (ed. K. Berthelot, T. Legrand, and A. Paul; Paris: Cerf, 2008), 249–55; C. Pfann, "A Note on 1Q19: 'The Book of Noah'," in *Noah and His Book(s)* (ed. M. Stone et al.; SBLEJL 28; Atlanta: SBL, 2010), 71–76; E. Eshel, "The Genesis Apocryphon and Other Related Aramaic Texts from Qumran: The Birth of Noah," in *Aramaica Qumranica*, 277–97 (283–84).

The fragmentary scroll 1Q19–1Q19ᵇⁱˢ was first published by Józef Milik in DJD I. The text of the first two fragments has an affinity to the tale of the birth of the giants (Gen 6:1–4) in *1 Enoch* 6–11, while the story of Noah's birth, related in the third fragment, is similar to *1 Enoch* 106–107 and *Genesis Apocryphon* II–V. Given the literary links of the Qumran fragments to *1 Enoch* 6–11 and 106–107, and the prevalent view that these *1 Enoch* passages belong to a lost *Book of Noah*,[1] a book

---

* This a reworked version of my earlier article "1Q19 (The Book of Noah) Reconsidered," *Hen* 31 (2009): 284–306.
1 For the research history and a critique of this theory, see Dimant, "Two 'Scientific' Fictions," 354–62. For a recent defense of this theory, see M. E. Stone, "The Book(s) Attributed to Noah," *DSD* 13 (2006): 4–23, reprinted in *Noah and His Book(s)* (ed. M. E. Stone and A. Amihai, and V. Hillel; SBLEJL 28; Atlanta: SBL, 2010), 7–25.

mentioned in several contemporary writings,² Milik estimated that the present fragments recover some of it. Accordingly he labeled them "Livre de Noé."

Various aspects of 1Q19 were discussed by several scholars (see literature above), but since its first publication in 1955 this scroll has never been treated in its entirety. Moreover, due to the editorial policy adopted in the first volumes of DJD, it was published without a commentary. Thus, a detailed discussion of 1Q19 is long overdue.³

The Manuscript

The DJD edition contains twenty-one fragments written in a Herodian hand.⁴ At the time of the publication, the color of the fragments was dark red. Since then, many of them have darkened and become virtually illegible (frgs. 9–12, 17–21). Frg. 2 (= 1Q19^{bis}) is in private hands.⁵ Frgs. 1 and 3 are in the possession of the Department of Antiquities of Jordan.⁶ The rest (frgs. 4–21) are preserved by the Israel Antiquities Authority.⁷

---

2 See 1QapGen V, 29; *Jub.* 8:11; 10:12–14; 21:10; *T. Levi* 18:2 (addition in Ms. E). See M. de Jonge, *The Testaments of the Twelve Patriarchs* (Leiden: Brill, 1978), 47.
3 Some notes are supplied by Batsch, "1Q19–1Q19bis."
4 On the paleographic dating of 1Q19, see J. T. Milik, "The Dead Sea Scrolls Fragments of the Book of Enoch," *Bib* 32 (1951): 393; Beyer, *Die aramäischen Texte*, 1:29. A similar dating of frgs. 1–11 has been proposed by Stephen Pfann (quoted in Pfann, "A Note on 1Q19," 73). He dates frgs. 13–21 to the second quarter or mid-first century CE. On Pfann's attribution of frgs. 13–21 to a different scribal hand, see below.
5 Until his death, this fragment was in the possession of A. Y. Samuel. Its photograph appears in the supplement to A. Y. Samuel's book, *Treasure of Qumran* (Philadelphia: Westminster Press, 1966). It seems to be identical to the photograph published by J. C. Trever, "Completion of the Publication of Some Fragments from Qumran Cave I," *RevQ* 5 (1964–1966): 323–42 plate VII. A digitized copy of this photograph was provided to me by The Ancient Biblical Manuscripts Center of the Claremont School of Theology. I thank the Center's staff for their assistance. Frg. 2 was rephotographed for the Princeton Theological Seminary Dead Sea Scrolls Project. However, I was not able to secure a copy of this image. Recently, a new set of photographs of frg. 2 was made available by the West Semitic Research Project of the University of Southern California (http://www.inscriptifact.com/; accessed on 13 October 2011). A reference to one of them, ISF DO_37152, is made below.
6 In addition to the PAM photographs of these fragments (40437; 40536; 43753), I have used the recently prepared images, AWS 4a–b, available on http://www.inscriptifact.com/.
7 I inspected the fragments at the premises of the Israel Antiquities Authority several times during the years 2006–2007.

A close examination of the scroll reveals that the script of frgs. 7, 8, 11, 13, and 15–21 is smaller and more compact than that of frgs. 1–6, 9–10, 12, and 14. This led some scholars to conclude that the DJD edition of 1Q19 contains fragments that belong to several scrolls. In their opinion, this conclusion is supported by the differences in content between frgs. 1–3 and 13–15.[8] However, an examination by Ada Yardeni confirms Milik's conclusion that all of them seem to have been written by the same scribe.[9] The aforementioned differences, noted also by Milik, are perhaps due to the inscription having taken place at different times or under different circumstances. As to the differences in content, the discussion below will demonstrate that they are not so obvious and the fragments in question may well belong to the same composition.

Text and Comments

Frg. 1

ויֹהֹי[ ] הוֹאׄ[	1
[ם גברו בֹּארץ וֹ[	2
א[ת דרכו עֹלֹ הארֹץֹ[	3
צעק[תֹםׄ לפֹני אל וֹ[	4
]אׄם אׄ[	5
]אׄ לֹ[	6

Notes on Readings
L. 1 The word הוא is preceded by a letter-sized lacuna, unnoted by Milik.

---

8 Dimant, "Enoch 6–11," 236; Pfann, "A Note on 1Q19," 71–76. Pfann suggests that frgs. 13–21 were inscribed by another hand. She further quotes Stephen Pfann's observation that frg. 12 may belong to yet another manuscript (p. 73 n. 6). While the difference in the height of the letters, rightly emphasized by Pfann, is obvious, the variations in the shapes of *alef*, *bet*, *waw*, *yod*, *dalet*, and medial *kaf* may not be as pronounced as she indicates, especially in view of the variations in their shapes that are observable in frgs. 1–11 (see table in idem, 74).
9 Private communication. Yardeni also suggests that 1Q19 seems to have been written by a prolific scribe, whose works were recently discussed by her in "A Note on a Qumran Scribe," in *New Seals and Inscriptions, Hebrew, Idumean, and Cuneiform* (ed. M. Lubetski; Hebrew Bible Monographs 8; Sheffield: Sheffield Phoenix Press, 2007), 287–98. I wish to thank Dr. Yardeni for examining the fragments and sharing her observations with me.

L. 2 בֿארץ. The convergence of the vertical stroke and base line of a *bet* are visible on the photographs (PAM 40437, 43753, AWS 4a), and therefore Milik's reading בֿארץ is preferable to that of Bhairo,]ארץ[.[10]

L. 4 צע[קתֿמֿ. Traces of two letters before the lacuna are clearly visible on PAM 40437, 43753, and AWS 4a. Of the first letter, a short horizontal stroke with a short oblique serif is extant and it may be read, with Milik, as the upper bar of a *taw*. It is followed by a horizontal stroke descending to the left with a long thick serif at its left end. Here, it is read with Milik as a final *mem* (cf. final *mem* in אם [line 5]) rather than Beyer's reading of a *taw*, which is also possible.

L. 5 אם[. The editor read here ם‎י[, but on photograph AWS 4a the angular join of an oblique stroke with the left stroke of *alef* can be seen.

Translation
1. and it] came to pass [ ]he [
2.]. they became dominant on the earth and[
3.]its way on the earth[
4.]their c[ry] before God .[
5.].. .[
6.]. .[

Comments
L. 1]הוא[ ] יֿהֿ[י. The first two letters are restored, with Milik, as a 3rd masc. sg. *Qal wayyiqtol* of היה. Given the fragmentary state of this line, it is difficult to determine who is implied by a 3rd masc. sg. demonstrative pronoun הוא. See Discussion.

L. 2]וֿ בארץֿ גברו ם[. גברו is a 3rd pl. *Qal qatal* of גבר, meaning "to be strong, to prevail, to increase."[11] Since the following line implies that all those living on earth corrupted their ways (cf. Gen 6:5; *Jub.* 5:3, 19), the present expression גברו בֿארץ appears

---
10 Cf. Bhairo, *Shemihazah and Asael*, 4.
11 BDB, 149; HALOT, 175. The translation "became dominant" follows that of J. Maier, *Die Qumran-Essener: Die Texte von Toten Meer* (Munich: E. Reinhardt, 1995), 210; *DSSR*, 3:581. Milik rendered here: "se sont multipliés." He is followed by *DSSSE*, 1:25.

to describe those responsible for such a phenomenon.[12] Milik assumed that the line deals with the giants, the descendants of the Watchers, and proposed to restore here בני עירי[ן] or רשעי[ם] with *1 En.* 7:6.[13] Following him, Dimant suggested that the scroll alludes here to Gen 6:4 and restored: גברי[ם] גברו בארץ.[14] Beyer interpreted גברו as referring to the wicked generation in general (cf. *1 En.* 8:2).[15] See Discussion.

L. 3 **א[ת דרכו עֹל הארץֿ]**. The phrase א[ת דרכו עֹל הארץֿ is borrowed from Gen 6:12. One may perhaps restore here with Milik: כי השחית כל בשר א[ת דרכו עֹל הארץֿ. Dimant proposed that the author interpreted Gen 6:12 as referring to giants.[16] Yet, the quotation from Gen 6:12 tallies well with Beyer's suggestion that line 2 refers to the wicked generation as a whole, as in 1 En. 8:2.

L. 4 **צעק[תֹםׁ לפׁני אל**. Milik, whose reading is followed here, assumed that this line refers to the cry of the victims of violence (cf. *1 En.* 8:4) and restored it according to the biblical idiom: ותבוא צעק[תֹםׁ (cf. Gen 18:21; Exod 3:9; 1 Sam 9:16).

Frg. 2 (= 1Q19[bis]**)**[17]

א[ל הֹשמֹ]ים	1
מש[פֹטנו לפֹ]ני	2
[ולא נחתך]	3
מיכ[אל וגבריאל]	4
אדונ[] אדונים וגב[ור גבורים	5
[עלמֹי]ם	6

Notes on Readings

L. 1 **א[ל הֹשמֹ]ים**. The traces of the first letter are difficult to decipher. Milik read and restored it as קֹ[דוש]י. This reading is supported by the recent photographs of

---

[12] Gen 7:18–20, 24 employs a similar expression, ויגברו/גברו על הארץ, to depict the rising waters of the flood. However, the present locution cannot refer to this event for it would create an illogical sequence of events, according to which the sins alluded to in line 3 would come after the reference to their punishment by the flood in line 2. Thus also Peters, *Noah Traditions*, 194.
[13] Milik, "Livre de Noé," 85. Cf. idem, *The Books of Enoch: Aramaic Fragments of Qumran Cave 4* (Oxford: Clarendon Place, 1976), 59.
[14] Cf. Dimant, "The Fallen Angels," 133. Thus also Peters, *Noah Traditions*, 193.
[15] Beyer, *Aramäischen Texte*, 1:229 n. 1, 236.
[16] Dimant, "The Fallen Angels," 133.
[17] Frg. 2 was published in a supplement to DJD I, 152.

the fragment (esp. ISF DO_37152). Yet, on the photograph published by Trever, faint traces of *lamed* are visible, which may be restored as א[ל.[18] On both images, next to *shin* there is a trace of ink (unnoted by the editor), which may belong to the right bottom curve of medial *mem* (as read here) or *nun*.

L. 3 **נחתך**. The DJD edition reads תחתך. The shape of the first letter as it appears on Trever's image and on ISF DO_37152 is consistent with a medial *nun*. There are no traces of an upper bar and right vertical stroke, which would justify the reading of a *taw*.

L. 4 **[אל**. Based on Trever's photograph, the reading is certain (thus Milik's reading), so there is no justification for its omission in Bhairo's edition.[19]

Translation
1. t]o the heav[ens
2.]our ca[se] bef[ore
3.]and had not been determined [
4. Mich]ael and Gabriel [
5. Lord] of Lords and Mig[hty one of Mighty ones
6.]fore[ver

Comments
L. 1 **א[ל הֿשֿמֿ]ים**. Since line 2 quotes the complaint of the victims, the phrase א[ל הֿשֿמֿ]ים ("t]o the heav[ens") may depict their cry ascending to the heavens, as in *1 En.* 9:2.

L. 2 **מ[ש]פטנו לפֿ]ני**. This line quotes the victims' request. The wording is reminiscent of Num 27:5, but the theme is that described in *1 En.* 9:3: "Bring our suit before the Most High."[20] Dimant suggested, plausibly, הביאו מש[פטנֿו with the Greek (εἰσαγάγετε) and Ethiopic (*'abə'u*) versions of *1 En.* 9:3.[21] The restoration

---
18 See Trever, "Completion," plate VII.
19 Bhairo, *Shemihazah and Asael*, 5.
20 M. A. Knibb, *The Ethiopic Book of Enoch* (Oxford: Clarendon Press, 1978), 82.
21 Dimant, "The Fallen Angels," 135. The Aramaic version of this verse has not been preserved. The Greek translation of *1 Enoch* found in Codex Panopolitanus and in the Chester Beatty-Michigan Papyrus is quoted here from M. Black (ed.), *Apocalypsis Henochi Graece* (Leiden: Brill, 1970). The passages from the *Chronography* of George Syncellus are cited from A. S. Mosshammer, *Geor-*

לפ֯]ני אל, as in frg. 1 4, should also be considered. Less plausible is Milik's reconstruction, גלו מש[פטנו לפ֯]ני, since the locution גלה משפט is not attested in the ancient Hebrew sources.

ולא נחתך[. The verb נחתך is a 3rd masc. sg. *Nif'al qatal* of חתך. It occurs both in the Hebrew Bible (Dan 9:24) and in the Qumran scrolls (4Q252 I, 2), where it denotes "to be determined."[22] It perhaps refers here to the "judgment" (משפט) mentioned in line 2. If so, the phrase ולא נחתך may imply that God had not yet determined the judgment of the sinners. According to several ancient Jewish sources, a similar postponement of a judgment is implied in Gen 6:3, where God's decree to shorten human life to 120 years can be interpreted as a delay in the judgment meted out to the antediluvians in order to allow them to repent.[23] Note the use of the verb חתך in 4Q252 I, 2 when rewriting Gen 6:3: ויחתכו ימיהם ("and their days were determined").

L. 4] מיכ[אל וגבריאל. The theophoric ending]אל[and the *waw* attached to the word גבריאל suggest that the first word is also the name of an angel. *1 En.* 9:1 lists the names of four archangels: Michael, Sariel (Greek: Uriel),[24] Raphael, and Gabriel. Milik restored, therefore, מיכאל ואוריאל רפ[אל וגבריאל. However, the context indicates that line 4 is not totally identical to *1 En.* 9:1. Line 2 quotes the complaint found in *1 En.* 9:3. Line 4 contains the archangels' address to God, parallel to *1 En.* 9:4. Thus, it seems that the scroll mentions the names of the angels (at least of two of them) before their prayer, as is done also in the Aramaic version of *1 En.* 9:4: ועללין ר[פאל ומיֹכֿ]אל עיריא (4Q202 1 iii 13).[25] The tentative reconstruction [מיכ אל וגבריאל takes up the names of the two angels frequently mentioned together in ancient sources.[26]

---

gii Syncelli Ecloga Chronographica (Leipzig: Teubner Verlagsgesellschaft, 1984). For the Ethiopic translation, the editions prepared by R. H. Charles, *The Ethiopic Version of the Book of Enoch* (AO; Semitic Series 11; Oxford: Clarendon Press, 1906), Knibb, *Enoch*, and Bhairo, *Shemihazah and Asael*, were consulted.

22 HALOT, 364. See further S. Luggassy, "New Verbal Roots and New Verbal Patterns in the Dead Sea Scrolls" (Ph.D. diss., Ben-Gurion University, 2004), 42–43 (Hebrew). In the rabbinic literature, the *Nif'al* of חתך is used in a legal context. See *b. Sanh.* 108a (cf. also *Meg.* 15a); Jastrow, *Dictionary*, 513.

23 Cf. Philo, *QG* I, 91; Aramaic Targums to Gen 6:3 (*Tg. Onq.*; *Tg. Ps.-J.*; *Tg. Neof.*; *Frg. Tg.*); *Mek. Beshalaḥ* [*Shira*], 5; *Mek. R. Shim. Bar Yoḥai, Beshalaḥ* (to Exod 15:6); *Tanh. Beshalaḥ,* 15. See Kugel, *Traditions*, 208–09, 212–16.

24 The name Sariel appears in the Aramaic version of *1 Enoch* (4Q402 1 iii 7).

25 See further Milik, *Books of Enoch*, 171–72.

26 Gabriel and Michael are mentioned also in the biblical Daniel (8:16; 9:21; 10:13, 21; 12:1).

L. 5 ‏אדון] אדונים וגב]ור גבורים‎. The parallel text from *1 En.* 9:4 suggests that both titles belong to the doxology that opens the angelic address to God. The title ‏אדון [אדונים‎, restored by Milik and followed here, takes up the formulation of the above Enochic verse. The title is known from the Hebrew Bible in a double plural form (‏אדני האדנים‎; Deut 10:17; Ps 136:3), and it also appears once in this form in a Qumran text (‏אדני האדונים‎[; 4Q381 76–77 14). The second title, ‏גב]ור גבורים‎, restored by Milik on a similar pattern, is unattested by these two literary corpora and *1 Enoch*, but it is obviously influenced by biblical parlance.[27] For the adjective ‏גבור‎ as a title of God appears both in the Hebrew Bible (Jer 32:18; Neh 9:32) and in Qumran texts (e.g. 1QM X, 1; 4Q372 1 29; 4Q381 76–77 14).

L. 6 ‏עלמי]ם‎. The word appears to continue the chain of doxologies of the Deity that open the angels' address to God, which are partly preserved in the preceding line. The parallel verse in *1 En.* 9:4 has the similar titles, θεὸς τῶν αἰώνων,[28] corresponding to ‏אל עולמים‎, and βασιλεὺς τῶν αἰώνων,[29] corresponding to ‏מלך עולמים‎ (note the similar title ‏מלך כול עלמים‎ in 1QapGen II, 7). Alternatively, it may correspond to an expression found in the Aramaic version of *1 En.* 9:4: ‏וכורס[א יקרך‎ ‏ל{כל}] דר דריא די מן עלמ]א‎ (4Q202 1 iii 15; cf. ‏דרות עולמים‎ [Isa 51:9])[30] or to the phrase preserved in the Greek: καὶ εὐλογητὸν εἰς πάντας τοὺς αἰῶνας, corresponding to ‏ומבורך לכל עולמים‎.[31]

Frg. 3

]◦[ ]שׁ◦[	1
]◦תן השתנ]ו	2
ג]בור הולד כי נכבדים [	3
אביהו וכאשר ראה למד] [אֹתֹ]	4
ויא]ר את חדרי הבית כחדודי השמש [	5
]ל לבעת את [	6
]◦[ ]◦[ ]◦◦[	7

---

27 It is known from later sources. See *Kerovah* to Gen 14:1 by Yannai: ‏לך מיוסדת הקדושה גדול גדולים גיבור גיבורים‎ ("to you is established the holiness, great of the greats, mighty of the mighty ones"). Z. M. Rabinovitz, *The Liturgical Poems of Rabbi Yannai* (Jerusalem: Bialik Institute, 1985), 1:133 (Hebrew).
28 Attested by the short version of Syncellus.
29 Thus Codex Panopolitanus.
30 Cf. Milik, *Books of Enoch*, 171–72.
31 Thus all the Greek versions. Compare *'Abot R. Nat.* (A), 31: ‏יהא שמו הגדול מבורך לעולם ולעולמי עולמים‎ ("Let His great name be blessed for ever and ever").

Notes on Readings

L. 1]∘[]∘שׁ̇[. The DJD edition reads]∘∘א[. The traces of the first letter are more consistent with *shin* than with *alef* (cf. *shin* in ו]השתנ [line 2]).

L. 2 ת̇ה̇∘[. Milik reads here ∘ה̇∘[. However, the long vertical stroke visible after the *taw* in PAM 40536 and AWS 4a may belong to a final *nun*.

ו]השתנ̇. In his preliminary publication, Milik read]השתנ̇.[32] Indeed, the vertical stroke slanting to the left and curving to the right at its lower part, seen on PAM 40536 and AWS 4a, better suits a medial *nun* (cf. *nun* in נכבדים [line 3]) than a medial *mem* (cf. *mem* in למך [line 4]). Therefore, Milik's reading in his preliminary edition is to be retained and is followed here rather than his correction in DJD, השתמ]מו.[33] Milik's second reading is also to be rejected on account of its defective orthography, which is unlike the plene spelling used for such *Hithpolel* verbs in the Hebrew Bible (Isa 59:16; Ps 143:4; [also Sir 43:24]; the present scroll follows the MT orthography), and also the Qumran texts (1QIsa[a] XLVIII, 9; LI, 1).[34]

L. 3 ג[בּ̇ור. Traces of an upper stroke and a base line, suiting a *bet* or medial *kaf*, are visible on PAM 40536, 43753, and AWS 4a. Given the context, the reading proposed is בּ̇ור[, rather than Milik's early [35]ה[ניר or later ב[כּ̇ור in the DJD edition. Beyer has בּ̇יר,[36] which is closer to the above reading.

הולד. Since *waw* and *yod* in 1Q19 are frequently indistinguishable, it is also possible to read here היל (as read by Beyer).[37]

כי. Thus Milik. Beyer reads בו.[38] The base line of *bet* in this scroll usually projects beyond its vertical stroke. However, this is not the case here. Therefore, Milik's reading should be retained.

L. 5 וא[ר̇. The editor suggested no reading for the tiny trace of ink appearing at the beginning of the line. It may perhaps be read as the left extremity of an upper bar of *resh* (cf. *resh* in the word חדרי [line 5]).

השמש. The lacuna after this word is unusually large, so it is probably part of the left margin of the column. Consequently, the entire fragment comes from the left section of the column.

---

32 Milik, "Fragments of the Book of Enoch," 394.
33 A reading ו]השתנ was proposed by Eshel, "The Genesis Apocryphon," 287 n.23.
34 See Qimron, "A Grammar of the Hebrew Language," 199.
35 Ibid.
36 Beyer, *Aramäischen Texte*, 1:250.
37 Ibid.
38 Ibid.

Translation
1.   ]..[ ].[
2.   ].. change[d
3.] the child [is a mig]hty one, since glorious [
4.   ]his father and when Lamech saw [ ] the[
5. and he illumina]ted the rooms of the house as the rays of the sun [
6.   ]. to terrify the [
7.   ]..[ ].[ ]..[

Comments

L. 2 וֹ]נְשׁתֹּנוּ. The verb is restored here as a 3rd pl. *Hithpaʻel qatal* of שנה. The *Hithpaʻel* occurs in Sir 43:8(B) with the meaning of "change" (מה נורא בהשתנותו; "how terrible it is in changing," said of the sequence of the months[39]). This sense fits the depiction here, apparently as a reaction to the extraordinary birth of Noah. In the preliminary edition, Milik connected this verb to Noah's physical appearance,[40] but none of the parallel descriptions of Noah's wondrous birth refers to such a detail. Perhaps, as proposed by Fitzmyer, ו]נשתנ describes a change in Lamech's facial expression.[41] According to 1QapGen II, 12, while confronting his wife with a question regarding whether Noah is an offspring of a Watcher, Lamech's "disposition has changed" (אשתני אנפי עלי); see also col. II, 16–17 and the similar expression in Dan 3:19 (note also Dan 7:28). In the rabbinical literature, the phrase השתנו פניו expresses shame, bewilderment, and anger.[42]

L. 3 גֹ[בוֹר. The surviving letters may be restored as גֹ[בוֹר ("strong, mighty one").[43] Gen 6:4 calls the offspring of the sons of God "הגבּרים" (see also 4Q180 1 8; 4Q370 i 6). According to 1QapGen II, 1, Lamech feared that Noah was one of them, sired by one of the sinful angelic Watchers. Thus the reading גֹ[בוֹר fits the story of Noah's birth better than Milik's בֹ[כור. The fact that Noah is the firstborn son of Lamech is not mentioned in *1 Enoch* 106–107 or in 1QapGen II–V.[44]

---

39 Cf. *DCH*, 8:498.
40 Milik, "Fragments of the Book of Enoch," 398.
41 Fitzmyer, *Genesis Apocryphon*, 258.
42 See *b. Beṣah* 15b; *b. ʻArak.* 16b; *b. Soṭah* 35a.
43 BDB, 150; *HALOT*, 172.
44 Eshel, "The Genesis Apocryphon," 287, proposes to read here כור הילד[, a Hebrew parallel of the Aramaic כור הורתי, employed in a similar context in 1QapGen II, 1. However, this is a difficult Hebrew construction, unattested by any other source.

הולד. הולד may be read as הַוָּלֵד, "offspring, child" (Gen 11:30; 4Q396 1 2, 3),[45] or as a 3rd masc. *Hof'al qatal* of ילד, yet this form of the verb is otherwise unattested in the Hebrew Bible and in the Qumran texts.

כי נכבדים. The conjunction כי suggests that the following sentence explained why the newborn is called ג]בור. The following word is a pl. masc. *Nif'al* participle of participle of כבד, נכבדים. Since this participle is used with reference to angels in some scrolls (1QH[a] XVIII, 10; 4Q400 2 2 [= 4Q401 14 i 8]; 3 ii + 5 9), Milik proposed that it refers here to the Watchers.[46] However, in both the Hebrew Bible and the Qumran texts, this participle is often used in the general sense of "honored/esteemed ones" (see Isa 23:8; Ps 149:8; 1QpHab IV, 2; 1QM XIV, 11). So perhaps it may be assumed with Dimant that נכבדים here refers to Noah's face, as is reported in *1 En.* 106:5: "and glorious is his [Noah's] face" (cf. also *1 En.* 106:2).[47]

L. 4 **אביהו וכאשר ראה למך [אֹתוֹ].** The use of a 3rd per. *qatal* verb, ראה, a 3rd per. possessive pronoun in אביהו, and the name למך, indicates a 3rd per. narrative style, and not a 1st per. autobiographic account narrated by Lamech, as is the case in 1QapGen II. However, it is unclear what Lamech actually saw. It must have been something unusual in the appearance of Noah and the illumination of the house, as is implied in lines 3 and 5.

L. 5 **ויא[ר את חדרי הבית כחדודי השמש].** The sentence depicts the light illuminating the house, apparently, with Noah's birth. The first word is restored here as a 3rd masc. sg. *Hif'il wayyiqtol* of אור, ויא[רֹ ("was illuminated").[48] The said illumination is compared to the sunlight, but a peculiar collocation, חדודי שמש, is employed. The plural form of the noun חדוד occurs in Job 41:22 in the phrase חדודי חרש, describing the giant Leviathan.[49] In Mishnaic Hebrew, חדוד denotes a

---

45 *HALOT*, 260.
46 Milik, "Fragments of the Book of Enoch," 394; idem, "Livre de Noé," 85. He is followed by Peters, *Noah Traditions*, 195. Batsch, "1Q19–1Q19bis," 253, suggests that these might be either the Watchers or their gigantic progeny.
47 Dimant, "The Fallen Angels," 135. A similar interpretation is suggested by Eshel, "The Genesis Apocryphon," 287. In the ancient sources, the motif of glorious face is frequently associated with Moses (LXX to Exod 34:29, 30, 35; *Tg. Onq.*, *Tg. Neof.* and *Sam. Tg.* to Exod 34:29; *L. A. B.* 12:1; 2 Cor 3:7). See also Stuckenbruck, *1 Enoch*, 638.
48 Batsch, "1Q19–1Q19bis," 252, also proposes (on contextual grounds) that the scroll might have read here a *Hif'il* form of אור.
49 *HALOT*, 292, renders it as "pointed scales." See further M. Kister, "Continuity and Oblivion in Postbiblical Hebrew Vocabulary," *Leš* 56 (2007), 15–22 (19–20) (Hebrew).

"pointed projection, prong."⁵⁰ So Milik rendered the phrase in the present fragment as "rays," but Qimron suggests that 1Q19 reflects here the understanding of the unusual חדוד חרס in Job 41:22 as חִדּוּדֵי חֶרֶס, "sunrays," replacing the rare word חֶרֶס with the more familiar one, שמש.⁵¹ The preposition *kaf* in כחדודי indicates that the illumination was a simile, and not caused by the true sunlight. In a similar manner, David is said to "have shone like the light of the sun" (ואור כאור השמש) in the apocryphal psalm about David (11QPsᵃ XXVII, 1). In the parallel depictions of Noah's birth found in *1 En.* 106:2, 5, 10 and 1QapGen V, 12, the source of the light is Noah's eyes.⁵²

L. 6] **לבעת את**[. Milik interpreted לבעת as a *Pi'el* infinitive of בעת, "to terrify, to frighten" (1 Sam 16:14; 2 Sam 22:5; Job 7:14).⁵³ According to *1 En.* 106:4, 6, 12 and 1QapGen V, 7, Lamech was frightened by Noah's wonderful appearance and strange behavior. If the same situation is implied here, the subject of this verb is Noah and the object, marked by the את, is Lamech. Indeed, Beyer more appropriately restores here such a context: הח[ל] [ ]לבעת את [למד ("beg]an to frighten [Lamech").⁵⁴

Frg. 4

]אֹת הל[

Frg. 5

1]יֹהֹ[
2]ת כל הֹ[
3]לo

---

50 See *m. Kelim* 2:5, 4:1, 3. Jastrow, *Dictionary*, 451.
51 E. Qimron, "'His Underpart is Jagged shards' (Job 41:22)," *Leš* 37 (1973): 96–98 (Hebrew); idem, "Biblical Philology and the Dead Sea Scrolls," *Tarbiẓ* 58 (1988–1989): 297–315 (313) (Hebrew). A similar interpretation of Job's language is found in *Pesiq. Rab Kah., Parasha Aḥeret*; b. Ḥul. 67b. Cf. also Rashi's comment on Job 41:22.
52 According to the rabbinic tradition, when Moses was born the whole house was filled with light (*b. Soṭah* 12a; *Exod. Rab.* 1:20). On the motive of light, see further Kugel, *Traditions*, 146, 157.
53 *HALOT*, 147.
54 Beyer, *Aramäischen Texte*, 1:250 (Beyer inserts the Hebrew line of the present text into his edition of the Aramaic *1 Enoch* 106–107). However, Beyer translates the verb לבעת with an intransitive expression (251), but such a rendering is in contrast to the following preposition את, a marker of a direct object attached to a transitive verb.

Notes on Readings

L. 1]ה̇י̇[. Milik read here]ה̇ ○[, but the vertical stroke slanting to the left may be read as *waw* or *yod*. The upper bar of the following letter projects beyond its left vertical stroke, as is usual in *he* but not in *ḥet* (cf. the *ḥet* in חדרי and חדודי [frg. 3 15]). A close examination of the fragment reveals that there is no space between the two letters.

L. 3]○ל[. The DJD edition reads]○ ל[. However, there is no space between the letters.

Frg. 6

]פ̇ם○[1
]○ש[2
]○ ○[3

Notes on Readings

L. 1]פ̇ם○[. Milik read here ○ים[. However, in PAM 40536, the traces of *pe* are clearly visible. The two letters are written without an intervening space.

L. 3]○ש[. According to the editor, the second letter is a *taw*. Yet, the tiny vertical stroke visible on the photographs is too small to propose a reading. Perhaps the fragment was in a better state when Milik examined it, enabling him to propose a reading.

Frg. 7

[אז דב̇ר]

Translation

]then he spoke[

Comments

The adverb אז suggests that דב̇ר is a 3rd masc. sg. *Pi'el qatal* of דבר (cf. Josh 10:12). Alternatively, one may restore here [מ]אז דב̇ר[(cf. Josh 14:10).

Frg. 8

1 ו[יֹעֲבֹו]ר
2 [מתושל]חֹ
3 [ ]לֹ[

Notes on Readings

L. 1 ו[יֹעֲבֹו]ר. The DJD edition reads]עֲבֹם ○[but Milik later corrected it to]וֹיֹעֲבִ[.[55] Given the difficulty in distinguishing between *yod* and *waw* here, both readings are possible. The third letter should be read as *bet*, since the vertical stroke descending to the right and meeting the long curving base, observed on PAM 40536, belongs to this letter. It is certainly not the right vertical stroke of a final *mem*, as read in DJD. See Comments.

Translation

1. and] he passe[d
2. Methusel[ah
3.].[

Comments

L. 1 ו[יֹעֲבֹו]ר. The reading of this verb as the 3rd masc. sg. *Qal wayyiqtol* of עבר accords well with the general context of the passage and may refer to Methuselah's journey to Enoch, mentioned in *1 En.* 106:7–8 and 1QapGen II, 23. Milik's reading and restoration, ם]וֹיֹעֲבִ[, a masc. pl. form of עבה, "thick," supposedly referring to Noah's thick hair, mentioned in the Greek translation of *1 En.* 106:2, is less likely.[56] The Hebrew noun שׂער ("hair") is never used in the plural, but always in the singular.

L. 2 [מתושל]חֹ. The explicit mention of Methuselah confirms that the topic of this fragment is the story of Noah's birth.

---

[55] Milik, *Books of Enoch*, 209.
[56] The Greek text reads οὖλος, "thick, woolly" (H. G. Liddell and R. Scott, *Greek-English Lexicon* [Oxford: Clarendon Press, 1996], 1270). This detail is absent from the Ethiopic version. The Aramaic original of this verse has not been preserved.

Frg. 9

[ומלחׄ]

Notes on Readings

ומלחׄ[. Milik read here]ימל ׄ◦[. Since *waw* and *yod* are frequently indistinguishable in 1Q19, it is also possible to read the first letter as *waw*. A vertical stroke preserved at the end of the line may belong to *he* or *ḥet*. There is no space between the last two letters.

Comments

The preserved letters may be restored as ומלח]מה[("and war").

Frg. 10

[ג[

Frg. 11

[ל בני] 1
ע[ל הקיׄוׄ] 2

Notes on Readings

L. 1]ל בני[. The distance between *lamed* and *bet* is short and so it may be read as]לבני[.
L. 2] ע[ל הקׄיׄוׄ. Milik read ל הקׄיׄדׄ[ש. The letter added above the line may be read as *waw* or *yod*. According to PAM 40444, the last letter is certainly *waw* or *yod* and is followed by a blank space.

Translation

1.] sons of[
2. o]n the measuring line [

Comments

L. 2] ע[ל הקוֹ. The second preserved word is the noun קו ("a measuring line").[57] Orthographically it is difficult to determine whether the line reads קיו or קוו. However, since the usage of "וו" for a consonantal *waw* is very rare in the scrolls,[58] it may be assumed that the scribe wrote קיו, like the orthographic representations of the words חיו (cf. CD XIX, 12) and (1QpHab X, 10, 11[59]). For the phrase על הקו, see 1QH^a IX, 30; XIV, 29; 4Q437 2 i 5. Cf. also Sir 44:5.[60]

Frg. 12

]ויפן[

Notes on Readings

Milik read]וַיִפְּךְ[but according to PAM 40476 the last vertical stroke should be read as a final *nun* rather than a final *kaf*.

Translation

]and he turned[

Frg. 13

1   ]וֹכיכבוֹד זוֹך ○[   ]○ [לכבוד אל ב]
2   [נִ]שׂא בהדר כבוד ותפארתֹ]
3   ]○[יכבד בתוך [

Notes on Readings

L. 1 וֹכיכבוֹד[. Milik read here]○ כי כבוד[, but PAM 40444 shows that a *waw* (or *yod*) stands at the beginning of the line, and that the words וֹכי and כבוֹד were written

---

57 *HALOT*, 1081.
58 According to Qimron, "A Grammar of the Hebrew Language," 52, the only certain example is עווֹל in 11Q13 2 11.
59 As read by E. Qimron, "The Psalms Scroll from Qumran: A Linguistic Survey," *Leš* 35 (1975): 99–116 (107 n. 25) (Hebrew); idem, "A Grammar of the Hebrew Language," ibid.
60 On the passage from Sirach, see M. Kister, "Notes on the Book of Ben-Sira," *Leš* 47 (1983): 125–46 (142) (Hebrew).

without an intervening space.⁶¹ The following letter is certainly a medial *kaf* (thus Milik), and not *bet*, as was suggested by Beyer.⁶²

וֹזָךְ. Thus Milik. Beyer and Stuckenbruck read וֹאך.⁶³ However, Milik's reading of a *zayin* as the first letter is to be retained since, represented by a curving downstroke open to the left, it does not have the hook-shaped top typical of *waw*. The second letter is a vertical stroke that does have a hook-shaped top, so it is a *waw*. The hook is slightly longer than usual perhaps due to an unwarranted move of the writing implement.⁶⁴

]ב○[. The DJD edition reads]ב ○ but there is no space between the letters.

Ll. 2–3 Milik joined frg. 14 here, but the spaces between the lines in the two fragments are different (frg. 13: 1.1 cm; frg. 14: ~0.7 cm). Therefore, his placement should be rejected.⁶⁵ García Martínez suggested joining the first line of frg. 15 to the end of line 3, obtaining the following text: ויכבד בתוך [בח]ירי כי אל כונן[.⁶⁶ However, the shapes of the edges of these two fragments do not fit together and the resulting text is problematic.⁶⁷

Translation
1.]and because the glory of your splendor[ ] to the glory of God in[
2. h]e will be elevated in majesty of glory and splendor[
3.]. he will be honored in [

Comments
L. 1 וֹלִיכְבוֹד זוֹךְ[. כבוד זוֹךְ derives from the nonbiblical expression כבוד זיו, with זיו standing with the possessive suffix. Since further on God is referred to as אל, the

---

61 For attaching short words, including כי, in Qumran scrolls, see Qimron, "A Grammar of the Hebrew Language," 121–27.
62 Beyer, *Aramäischen Texte*, 1:229 n. 1.
63 Beyer, ibid.; Stuckenbruck, *Book of Giants*, 232.
64 It seems that the scribe tried to rectify the damage by turning its bottom section into the downstroke of a final *kaf*.
65 Thus also García Martínez, *Qumran and Apocalyptic*, 42.
66 Ibid.
67 The difficulty lies in that it is not clear who is implied by the 1st sg./pl. possessive suffix in [בח]ירי. The most plausible interpretation would be that it refers to God. However, as was noted by Stuckenbruck (idem, *Book of Giants*, 232 n. 7), God is referred to in the 3rd masc. sg., כי אל כונן, further on in the obtained text.

2nd sg. suffix of זוּךְ points to somebody else, perhaps to Noah (compare God's address to Noah in 1QapGenVII, 5: יקר ואגרו אנה משלם לך ["honor and reward I am paying to you"][68]). This detail is perhaps related to the radiance that filled the house when Noah was born, depicted in frg. 3 3, 5.

זוּךְ. זוּךְ is to be understood as the noun זִו (written defectively) with the 2nd sg. possessive suffix (thus Milik).[69] Less likely is parsing the word as the noun זֹךְ ("purity"), since this word is attested only in late sources.[70] זִו occurs in the Aramaic section of Daniel (defective [4:33] and plene [2:31; 5:6, 9, 10; 7:28]), meaning "radiance, brightness, fresh complexion."[71] In the Qumran documents, it appears mainly in the Aramaic texts (4Q212 1 iv 18 [defective]; 4Q531 13 4 [plene]), but also in the Hebrew scroll 4Q462 1 16: ותשנה בזיוה (see the Aramaic זיוהי שנוהי, וזיוהי שנין עלוהי in Dan 5:6, 9).

לכבוד אל. The phrase לכבוד אל occurs in 1QS X, 9 (= 4Q258 IX, 8; cf. also CD XX, 26). If זוּךְ refers to Noah, then the line states that his glorious appearance honors God. Milik assumed that this fragment preserves a canticle by Methuselah.[72] While the identity of the speaker is by no means clear (Lamech?), the style of the passage indeed suggests a song of praise.

L. 2 י[נ]שא בהדר כבוד ותפארֹתֹ]. The first word נשא[is restored here with Milik as a 3rd masc. sg. *yiqtol* of נשא in *Nif'al*, "to be elevated,"[73] in parallel with יכבד (line 3). The nouns הדר ("splendor, majesty")[74] and כבוד, which may be taken as a construct collocation, occur together in the Hebrew Bible and in the Qumran scrolls (Ps 8:6 [הדר כבוד הודך], 145:12 [וכבוד הדר מלכותו]; 1QH^a XX, 18 [הדר כבודכה]). תפארת ("glory, splendor, radiance")[75] appears in the phrase כבוד ותפארת in Exod 28:2, 40.[76] All three nouns occur in Ps 96:6. Given this background, it seems

---

68 The Aramaic text and translation are taken from E. Eshel, "The Noah Cycle in the Genesis Apocryphon," in *Noah and His Book(s)* (ed. M. E. Stone et al.; SBLEJL 28; Atlanta: SBL, 2010), 81.
69 So also *DSSSE*, 1:26; *DCH*, 3:101.
70 For instance, in Yannai's *Kerovah* to Gen 26:1: ולקחת זוך זרע[י]ם לזכרון זה (Rabinovitz, *Liturgical Poems*, 2:177).
71 *HALOT*, 1864. In 1 Kgs 6:1, 37, זו occurs as the name of a month.
72 Milik, "Livre de Noé," 85.
73 *HALOT*, 726.
74 Ibid., 240.
75 Ibid., 1772.
76 C. H. T. Fletcher-Louis, *All the Glory of Adam* (STDJ 42; Leiden: Brill, 2002), 44–45, suggests that 1Q19 alludes here to Exod 28:2, 40, describing the garments of the high priest. He proposes that this hints at the tradition in which priestly functions are attributed to Noah. However, since the fragment reads בהדר כבוד ותפארת, one can hardly regard it as an allusion to Exodus 28.

more fitting to apply the verb יִ[נשׂא to God (note Isa 6:1; Ps 94:2) rather than to Noah.

L. 3 **יכבד**. יכבד בתוך is a 3rd sg. *yiqtol* of כבד in *Nifʿal*, "to be honored, to appear in one's glory."[77] The subject of this verb is uncertain. It may have either God (cf. the use of ונכבדתי בתוכך in Ezek 28:22) or Noah[78] as its subject.

Frg. 14

```
                                    ]ר[      1
                                  ]ו ס∘∘[    2
```

Notes on Readings

Ll. 1–2 Milik joined this piece to frg. 13 2–3. However, as noted above, the join is problematic (see frg. 13, Notes on Readings).

L. 2]ו ס∘∘[. The editor read and restored here בני שׁ[מֹים ו] but the reading of the two letters preceding the final *mem* is difficult. A vertical stroke is visible before this letter in PAM 40541, resembling a *waw* or *yod*, but it has no characteristic hook-shaped top. An illegible trace of a letter can be seen at the bottom right corner.

Frg. 15

```
                                      ]אֹ[           1
                              ב[חירו כי אל כוננ]     2
                          ]ס לכלֹ]  ]∘∘לֹ∘[          3
```

Notes on Readings

L. 1]אֹ[. Traces are seen in PAM 40500 that are perhaps the oblique and right strokes of an *alef* (cf. *alef* in יִ[נשׂא [frg. 13 2]).

ב[חירו. The DJD edition has ב[חֹירי but according to PAM 40500 the reading of *het* is certain. *Waw* and *yod* are sometimes indistinguishable in 1Q19 but it is suggested to read here a *waw* to fit with the context.

---

77 *HALOT*, 455.
78 Thus Peters, *Noah Traditions*, 195.

Translation
1.].[
2. his [ch]osen one. For God established[
3.]....[ ]. for all[

Comments

L. 1 ב[חירו כי אל כונן]. Given the similarity between yod and waw in 1Q19, one may read here בחירי/רי or בחירו/ר(י)ו. If the possessive suffix refers to God, then a reading בחירו/ר(י)ו should be preferred (cf. 4Q374 2 ii 5), for God is referred to here in the third person: כי אל כונן. The verb כונן is a 3rd masc. sg. *Polel qatal* of כון ("to establish").[79] Frgs. 13 and 15 are distinguished by their small and condensed script. This and the color of their leather indicate that they come from the same sheet. While the context is lost, the physical similarities between the two fragments may suggest that frg. 15 also dealt with the story of Noah's birth. The noun בחיר is not applied to Noah in the stories of his birth recorded in *1 Enoch* 106–107 and 1QapGen II–V, but he is pictured there as God's chosen one.[80] As to the phrase כי אל כונן, in the Hebrew Bible such expressions as כונן ארץ/שמים (Isa 45:18; Prov 3:19), כונן כסא (2 Sam 7:13; Ps 9:8), and כונן צדיק (Ps 7:10) occur.

Frg. 16

[בֿכל ο]

Frg. 17

[ο ο]   1
[ל]   2

Frg. 18

[ל מο]

---

79 *HALOT*, 464.

80 Scholars tend to identify Noah as the figure described as "the chosen one" in the Aramaic text 4Q534 1 i 10: בחיר אלהא הוא (cf. e.g. J. A. Fitzmyer, "The Aramaic 'Elect of God' Text from Qumran Cave IV," *CBQ* 27 [1965]: 348–72; García Martínez, *Qumran and Apocalyptic*, 42). But see Dimant's criticism of this identification (idem, "Scientific Fictions," 360–61).

Frg. 19

]א[

Frg. 20

]ח̇[

Frg. 21

]לא[

Notes on Readings

Milik read here]ולא[. A straight vertical stroke interpreted by Milik as a *waw* is more likely the vertical stroke of a *lamed*. If so, the other two letters, לא, are a supralinear addition.

The Connections between 1Q19, *1 Enoch* 6–11, 106–107, and 1QapGen II–IV

Since its publication, the students of 1Q19 have been concerned primarily with the relation of 1Q19 to *1 Enoch* and the *Genesis Apocryphon*. While most scholars agree that there is an affinity between the three texts,[81] its precise nature is disputed. Since this issue has a bearing on the understanding of the literary character of 1Q19, it deserves a detailed analysis.

1Q19 1–2 and *1 Enoch* 6–11

Let us first consider the relation of 1Q19 to *1 Enoch*. The first of the 1Q19 fragments quotes Gen 6:12 (line 3). In line 4, it mentions the cry of the victims of the wrong done on earth, a theme elaborated by *1 En.* 7:10, 8:4, and 9:10. So the relationship

---

[81] A dissenting position has been adopted by Siam Bhairo (idem, *Shemihazah and Asael*, 4–5), who suggests that the fragmentary state of the material precludes any conclusions regarding their relation to *1 Enoch* 6–11. However, note the critique of his readings in the *Notes on Readings* to frgs. 1–2.

between the present fragment and the account of *1 Enoch* has been defined in various ways. Milik proposed that it parallels *1 En.* 7:3–6.[82]

1Q19 1	1 En. 7:2–6
	"And they conceived and bore to them great giants. And the giants begot Nephilim, and to the Nephilim were born Elioud. And they were growing in accordance with their greatness. They were devouring the labor of all the sons
1. and it] came to pass [ ]he [	of men, and men were not able to supply them.
2.]. they became dominant on the earth and[	And the giants began to kill men and to devour
3.]its way on the earth[	them. And they began to sin against the birds and beasts and creeping things and the fish, and to devour one another's flesh. And they drank the blood. Then the earth brought accu-
4.]their c[ry] before God .[	sation against the lawless ones."

According to this suggestion, one has to assume that the two texts deal with the same account of the giants' misconduct, yet relate it differently. Thus, both passages describe the atrocities committed by the giants, based on Gen 6:12. However, while frg. 1 3 quotes this verse verbatim, *1 En.* 7:3–5 expands it considerably to fit in with its own the narrative outline.[83] Furthermore, the complaint is presented differently. Frg. 1 4 seems to mention the cry of the victims, whereas *1 En.* 7:6 speaks of the earth's complaint.

Dimant compared frg. 1 to *1 En.* 7:2–8:4:[84]

1Q19 1	1 En. 7:2–8:4[85]
	"And they conceived and bore to them great
1. and it] came to pass [ ]he [	giants. And the giants begot Nephilim, and to
2.]. they became dominant on the earth and[	the Nephilim were born Elioud. And they were
3.]its way on the earth[	growing in accordance with their greatness.
	They were devouring the labor of all the sons

---

82 Milik, *Books of Enoch*, 59.
83 The description of the giants' deeds in *1 En.* 7:3–5 reworks Gen 6:11–12. The list of the living creatures against whom the giants sinned (7:4–5) is based on the biblical כל בשר. See, further, G. W. E. Nickelsburg, *1 Enoch: A Commentary on the Book of 1 Enoch. Chapters 1–36; 81–108* (Hermeneia; Augsburg: Fortress Press, 2001), 186.
84 Dimant, "The Fallen Angels," 133–34.
85 The translation of 1 Enoch here and elsewhere in this chapter follows that of Nickelsburg, 1 Enoch.

1Q19 1	1 En. 7:2–8:4[85]
	of men, and men were not able to supply them. And the giants began to kill men and to devour them. And they began to sin against the birds and beasts and creeping things and the fish, and to devour one another's flesh. And they drank the blood. Then the earth brought accusation against the lawless ones. Asael taught men to make swords of iron and weapons and shields and breastplates and every instrument of war. He showed them metals of the earth and how they should work gold to fashion it suitably, and concerning silver, to fashion it for bracelets and ornaments for women. And he showed them concerning antimony and eye paint and all manner of precious stones and dyes. And the sons of men made themselves and for their daughters, and they transgressed and led the holy ones astray. And there was much godlessness on the earth, and they made their ways desolate. Shemihazah taught spells and the cutting of roots. Hermani taught the sorcery for the loosing of spells and magic and skill. Baraqel taught the signs of the lightning flashes. Kokabel taught the signs of stars. Ziqel taught the sins of the shooting stars. Arteqoph taught the signs of the earth. Shamsiel taught the signs of the sun. Sahriel taught the signs of the moon. And they began to reveal mysteries to their wives and to their children. (And) as men
4.]their c[ry] before God .[	were perishing, the cry went up to heaven."

Like Milik, Dimant assumes that frg. 1 2–3 parallels *1 En.* 7:3–5. However, she also notes the similarity between the descriptions of the cry in frg. 1 4 and *1 En.* 8:4. As the quotation from Gen 6:12, corresponding to *1 En.* 7:3–5, and the cry of the victims, parallel to *1 En.* 8:4, appear in consecutive lines in frg. 1, she proposes that it did not contain Asael's story (*1 En.* 8:1–2) and the list of the sinning angels (*1 En.* 8:3).[86]

In a later publication, Dimant suggested that frg. 1 may correspond to a brief description of the giants' misbehavior in *1 En.* 9:9–10, belonging to the archangels' prayer:[87]

---

[86] Dimant, "The Fallen Angels," 52, 133–34.
[87] Dimant, "Enoch 6–11," 236.

1Q19 1	1 En. 9:9–10
1. and it] came to pass [ ]he [2.]. they became dominant on the earth and[3.]its way on the earth[4.]their c[ry] before God .[	"And now look, the daughters of men have borne sons from them, giants, half-breeds.<And the blood of men is shed on the earth,> And the whole earth is filled with iniquity. And now look, the spirits of the souls of the men who have died make suit, and their groans come to the gates of heaven."

This suggestion is based on a general similarity between the two passages. Thus, while *1 Enoch* utilizes the language of Gen 6:11 to describe the giants' deeds, frg. 1 3 quotes Gen 6:12. In addition, the description of their misconduct in *1 En.* 9:9 seems to be shorter than the parallel passage in frg. 1 2–3.[88]

Milik and Dimant assumed that frg. 1 depicts the acts of the giants and their consequences. However, it is equally possible that frg. 1 2–3 deals with human wickedness (see *Comments* on frg. 1 2–3). Beyer suggested that it may correspond to the description of human corruption in *1 En.* 8:2, alluding, as does frg. 1 3, to Gen 6:12:[89]

1Q19 1	1 En. 8:1–4
1. and it] came to pass [ ]he [2.]. they became dominant on the earth and[3.]its way on the earth[	"Asael taught men to make swords of iron and weapons and shields and breastplates and every instrument of war. He showed them metals of the earth and how they should work gold to fashion it suitably, and concerning silver, to fashion it for bracelets and ornaments for women. And he showed them concerning antimony and eye paint and all manner of precious stones and dyes. And the sons of men made themselves and for their daughters, and they transgressed and led the holy ones astray. And there was much godlessness <u>on the earth</u>, <u>and</u> they made <u>their ways</u> desolate. Shemihazah taught spells and the cutting of roots. Hermani taught the sorcery for the loosing of spells and magic and skill. Baraqel

---

88 The nature of the phrase found in the longer version of Syncellus, "and the blood of men is shed on the earth," remains unclear. For the arguments supporting its originality, see Nickelsburg, *1 Enoch*, 202–04. Bhairo, *Shemihazah and Asael*, 174, argues that it is secondary.

89 Beyer, *Aramäischen Texte*, 1:229 n. 1, 236. In fact, he proposed that frg. 1 in its entirety is a Hebrew version of *1 En.* 8:2 (see *Notes on Readings* on frg. 1). That frg. 1 2 parallels *1 En.* 8:2 (or 9:1) was suggested recently also by Stuckenbruck in "The Lamech Narrative," 254.

1Q19 1	1 En. 8:1–4
	taught the signs of the lightning flashes. Kokabel taught the signs of stars. Ziqel taught the sins of the shooting stars. Arteqoph taught the signs of the earth. Shamsiel taught the signs of the sun. Sahriel taught the signs of the moon. And they began to reveal mysteries to their wives and to their children. (And) as men were perishing, the
4.]their c[ry] before God .[	cry went up to heaven."

Accordingly, the phrase וי[הֺ] הוא̊[from frg. 1 1 may refer to Asael, who is mentioned in 1 En. 8:1, while the cry of the victims in frg. 1 4 would parallel that of *1 En.* 8:4. If correct, this proposal leads to the conclusion that frg. 1 did not contain the list of the disobedient angels found in *1 En.* 8:3 since the space in lines 3–4 would not suffice for it.[90]

The deteriorated state of the fragment precludes any firm conclusions regarding its relationship to *1 Enoch* 7–9. However, the last suggestion, linking frg. 1 to *1 En.* 8:2–4, has the advantage of being based on parallel phrases found in *1 En.* 8:2, 4.

The second fragment of 1Q19 quotes the victims' petition and an angelic address to God. The parallel passage is found in *1 En.* 9:3–4.[91] A comparison of the two texts brings forth their similarities but also their differences. While the complaint in lines 1–2 corresponds to *1 En.* 8:4 and 9:10, not so the expression ולא נחתך (line 3), perhaps alluding to Gen 6:3. Also, the doxological address to God that introduces the angelic prayer in *1 En.* 9:4 includes no parallel expression גב]ור גבורים (admittedly largely reconstructed). Thus, frgs. 1–2 of 1Q19 present a version of the giants' misdeeds that is close to but also different from *1 Enoch* 6–9.

1Q19 3 and *1 Enoch* 106–107

The third fragment of 1Q19 relates the story of Noah's birth. It displays several parallels to *1 Enoch* 106–107, in particular regarding Noah's birth (106:2–4, 5–7, 10–12). The similar details are the illumination of the house, Noah's glorious face, the sunrays metaphor used to describe the illumination, and Lamech's fear of the

---

[90] Dimant, "The Fallen Angels," 52, showed the independent character of this unit.
[91] Thus Milik, "Livre de Noé," 152; Dimant, "The Fallen Angels," 134–35; Beyer, *Aramäischen Texte,* 1:37; Stuckenbruck, "The Lamech Narrative," 255.

newborn.⁹² However, there are also differences here, for the words הֻשְׁתַּנִּ[י and ג]בּוֹר have no parallel in *1 Enoch* 106. Also, frg. 1 3–6 connects the appearance of Noah to Lamech's reaction, while *1 Enoch* presents them separately.

There are other fragments that seem to be related to the story of Noah's birth,⁹³ such as frg. 8, which mentions Methuselah. Frgs. 13 and 15 are also possibly related, for the phrases כָּבוֹד זוֹ (frg. 13 1) and ב]חירו (frg. 15 1) may refer to Noah. However, the text produced by these fragments, perhaps forming a song of praise, has no parallel in *1 Enoch* 106–107.

The above comparison between 1Q19 1–3 and *1 Enoch* 8–9, 106 also reveals important differences. It thus rules out the possibilities that 1Q19 preserves a Hebrew version of *1 Enoch* as argued by Beyer,⁹⁴ that it was one of the sources of *1 Enoch* as suggested by Milik,⁹⁵ Dimant,⁹⁶ and Knibb,⁹⁷ and that 1Q19 is influenced by *1 Enoch* as proposed by Nickelsburg.⁹⁸ More plausibly, both works rely on a common exegetic tradition that has been reworked in different ways.

This conclusion has bearing on the question of the relation of 1Q19 to the alleged existence of a *Book of Noah*, to which belong several passages in *1 Enoch* and *Jubilees*.⁹⁹ Milik saw in 1Q19 a remnant of this *Book of Noah*, because the affinities of this Qumran fragment fall precisely in *1 Enoch* 6–11 and 106–107, both

---

92 See the detailed discussion of these features in A. Amihai and D. A. Machiela, "Traditions of the Birth of Noah," in M. Stone et al. (eds.), *Noah and His Book(s)* (SBLEJL 28; Atlanta: SBL, 2010), 53–69 (61–62).
93 Beyer, *Aramäischen Texte*, 1:229 n. 1, 259, suggested that frgs. 11, 13, and 15 belong with the Hebrew copy of the *Book of Giants*. However, as was demonstrated by Stuckenbruck, *Book of Giants*, 220, this proposal is untenable.
94 Ibid., 229, 250.
95 Milik, "Livre de Noé," 84, initially identified 1Q19 with the *Book of Noah* and assumed that it was a source used by the author of *1 Enoch*. Later, he proposed that both 1Q19 and *1 Enoch* 6–11, 106–107 depend on the Aramaic *Book of Noah*. See J. T. Milik, "Écrits prééséniens de Qumrân: d'Hénoch à Amram," in *Qumrân: Sa piéte, sa théologie at son milieu* (ed. M. Delcor; Paris-Gembloux: Duculout, 1978), 95; idem, *Books of Enoch*, 55. Milik's conclusion was recently restated by Eshel, "Birth of Noah" (though without adopting Milik's view that the *Book of Noah* was composed in Aramaic).
96 Dimant, "The Fallen Angels," 136–37; idem, "Enoch 6–11," 234–37, suggests that *1 Enoch* 6–11 is based on a Hebrew composition that reworks the Hebrew Bible. She assumes that 1Q19 is close to this composition or represents another stage in its literary growth.
97 Knibb, *Enoch*, 2:7 n. 2.
98 Nickelsburg, *1 Enoch*, 77.
99 In addition to sources listed in note 3, several passages from *1 Enoch* (6–11, 39:1–2a, 54:7–55:2, 60, 65–69:25, 106–107) and *Jubilees* (7:20–29, 10:1–15) are commonly identified with the *Book of Noah*. Also, several Qumran texts are attributed to the *Book of Noah*: 1Q19, 1QapGen VI–XVIII, 4Q534–4Q536, 6Q8 (see frg. 1 4–6). See García Martínez, *Qumran and Apocalyptic*, 27–28.

of which have been assigned to the said *Book of Noah*. However, Milik's identification met with criticism,[100] and his identification of 1Q19 as part of the *Book of Noah* has been rejected.[101] This study questions another of Milik's suppositions, namely that 1Q19 was a source of *1 Enoch*, thus providing another reason for abandoning its identification with the alleged *Book of Noah*.

1Q19 3 and 1QapGen II–V

Finally, let us briefly discuss the relation of 1Q19 to the *Genesis Apocryphon*. The fragmentary state of both 1Q19 3, 8, 13, 15 and 1QapGen II–V, which relate the story of Noah's birth, makes their comparison difficult. Despite this, cols. II–V provide some parallels to 1Q19 3, such as a change in Lamech's facial expression (col. II, 12), sun-like light (col. V, 12), and Lamech's fear (col. V, 7). In its present state, 1QapGen II–V does not contain a song of praise, as frgs. 13 and 15 seem to do.[102] Given the paucity of surviving text, it is difficult to evaluate the relative weight of the similarities and differences between the two works. Yet, it seems that, as in the case of *1 Enoch*, one should posit here a common tradition that developed in different ways.[103]

---

100 See Dimant, "The Fallen Angels," 122–40; idem, "Two 'Scientific' Fictions," 354–62; Stone, "The Book(s) Attributed to Noah," 8 (with regard to *1 Enoch* 106–107).
101 Dimant, "The Fallen Angels," 137; M. E. Stone, "The Axis of History at Qumran," in *Pseudepigraphical Perspectives* (ed. E. Chazon and M. E. Stone; STDJ 31; Leiden: Brill, 1999), 133–49 (138–39); F. García Martínez, "Interpretations of the Flood in the Dead Sea Scrolls," in *Interpretations of the Flood* (ed. F. García Martínez and G. P. Luttikhuisen; Themes in Biblical Narrative 1; Leiden: Brill, 1998), 86–108 (89); Stuckenbruck, *1 Enoch*, 612.
102 One may note that a blessing is mentioned at the end of col. V: מברך למרה כולה (col. V, 23). Also, in 1QapGen IV, 11, the phrase חזית למעבד דין appears, though it is difficult to determine whether these are God's words or an address to God.
103 For the relationship between *1 Enoch* 106–107 and 1QapGen II–V, a topic that lies beyond the scope of the present study, see D. Machiela, *The Dead Sea Genesis Apocryphon* (STDJ 79; Leiden: Brill, 2009), 9–13. In a recent discussion, Stuckenbruck, "The Lamech Narrative," 253–72, suggested that while *1 Enoch* 106–107 may be earlier than 1QapGen II–V in some respects, it also contains late elements and that both texts seem to have relied on the same (apparently, oral) tradition, yet developed it in different ways. For a similar conclusion, see Amihai and Machiela, "Traditions of the Birth of Noah," 69. In this case, 1Q19, *1 Enoch*, and 1QapGen preserve three different versions of this tradition.

Conclusion

The foregoing discussion emphasizes the fact that 1Q19 is a work in its own right, and not a translation or a source for *1 Enoch*. Yet its affinity to *1 Enoch* 6–11, 106–107 and *Genesis Apocryphon* II–V is notable. Both *1 Enoch* and the *Genesis Apocryphon* rework Gen 5:28–29 and 6:1–4 by incorporating extensive exegetical additions into the biblical text. Thus, it may be assumed that 1Q19 preserves a composition that reworked biblical passages employing similar exegetical techniques.[104] Furthermore, close links between the Hebrew 1Q19 and the Aramaic *1 Enoch* and *Genesis Apocryphon* testify to the fact that both Hebrew and Aramaic Jewish literatures of the Second Temple period drew from a common pool of exegetical traditions.

---

104 Thus Dimant, "The Fallen Angels," 137.

4Q370 (Admonition on the Flood)

Literature

C. Newsom, "An Admonition Based on the Flood," *RevQ* 13 (1988): 23–43; idem, "370. 4QAdmonition Based on the Flood," in DJD XIX, 85–97; F. García Martínez, "Interpretations of the Flood in the Dead Sea Scrolls," in *Interpretations of the Flood* (ed. F. García Martínez and G. P. Luttikhuisen; Themes in Biblical Narrative 1; Leiden: Brill, 1998), 86–108; M. J. Bernstein, "Noah and the Flood at Qumran," in *The Provo International Conference on the Dead Sea Scrolls: Technological Innovations, New Texts, and Reformulated Issues* (ed. E. Ulrich, D. W. Parry; STDJ 30; Leiden: Brill, 1999), 199–231; G. Barzilai, "Offhand Exegesis: Passing Allusions to Interpretation of the Book of Genesis, as Found in the Dead Sea Scrolls" (Ph.D. diss.; Bar-Ilan University, 2002), 191–213 [Hebrew]; idem, "Incidental Biblical Exegesis in the Qumran Scrolls and Its Importance for the Study of the Second Temple Period," *DSD* 14 (2007): 1–24 (5–8); A. Feldman, "The Reworking of the Biblical Flood Story in 4Q370," *Hen* 29 (2007): 31–50; D. M. Peters, *Noah Traditions in the Dead Sea Scrolls: Conversations and Controversies of Antiquity* (EJL 26; Atlanta: SBL, 2008), 212–17; T. Legrand, "Homélie sur le Déluge," in *La Bibliothèque de Qumrân: Torah: Genèse* (ed. K. Berthelot et al.; Paris: Cerf, 2008), 283–89; A. Jassen, "A New Suggestion for the Reconstruction of 4Q370 1 i 2 and the Blessing of the Most High (*Elyon*) in Second Temple Judaism," *DSD* 17 (2010): 88–113; D. Dimant, "The Flood as a Preamble to the Lives of the Patriarchs: The Perspective of Qumran Hebrew Texts," in *Rewriting and Interpreting the Hebrew Bible: The Biblical Patriarchs in the Light of the Dead Sea Scrolls* (ed. D. Dimant and R. G. Kratz; Berlin: De Gruyter, 2013), 101–31 (126–29); A. P. Jassen, "Admonition Based on the Flood," in *Outside the Bible* (ed. L. H. Feldman, J. L. Kugel, L. H. Schiffman; The Jewish Publication Society, 2013), 1:263–71.

The Manuscript

Museum Inventory plate 341, on which 4Q370 is currently displayed, contains two fragments, with the larger one preserving remains of two columns. A smaller fragment appears near the ink traces in col. I line 10 of the first fragment. This small piece contains the word ישראל, a bottom margin and a vertical line, probably a right margin ruling.[1] However, while the leather and script of the two fragments are similar, they may have been copied by different hands.[2] In light of this, the small fragment is treated here as belonging to a different scroll. The hand of the larger fragment is a late Hasmonean semiformal one. However, the letters

---

[1] On PAM 43369, the latest photograph of 4Q370 in the PAM series, the small fragment is placed at the bottom of 4Q370 i. This photograph appears in the DJD edition of 4Q370 (Plate XII) yet neither this nor other editions of 4Q370 mention the fragment.
[2] So Ada Yardeni (personal communication).

in col. ii are slightly larger (2–3 mm, at times 4 mm) than those in col. i (1.5–2 mm, occasionally 3 mm), are spaced less tightly and are inscribed more evenly. Moreover, in col. i the scribe combined some words (כלנפש [line 1], כ̇[כ]ל̇דרכיהם [line 3], בי̇ע̇ב̇ר [line 5], עלכן [line 6]). In addition, an interchange between medial and final forms of *mem* can be observed in this column (שמ [line 2], סוסדי [line 4], סטר̇ [line 5]). These phenomena do not occur in col. ii. However, the handwriting of both columns is very similar and is best explained as the work of a single scribe.[3] The slight differences in script may be due to the use of a different writing instrument or to a change in the time and circumstances of the scribal work. The first column reworks the biblical flood story (Genesis 6–9). The second column contains an admonitory discourse.

Text and Comments

Col. i

top margin

יוכלו וישבעו

1 [ו]יעטר̇ הרים תנ[ובה וש]פ̇ך אכל על פניהם ופרי טוב השביע כלנפש כל אשר עשה רצוני אמר י̇[ה]וה

2 ויברכו̇ את שמ [עליו]ן̇ והני הם אז עשו הרע בעיני אמר יהוה ויאמרו אל במ[עלי]ליהם

3 וישפטם יהוה כ̇[כ]ל̇דרכיהם ו̇כמחשבות יצ̇ר̇ לבם ה̇[רע]וירעם עליהם בכח[ו וי]נ̇עו כל

4 סוסדי אר̇ץ ומ̇[י]ם נ̇בקעו מתהמ̇מ̇ת̇ כל ארבות השמים נפתחו ופצו כל תהמו̇ת מ̇[י]ם אדרי̇ם

5 וארבות השמים ה̇[רי]קו סטר̇ו וא̇בדם במבול ו[ל] ב̇[מ]ים כלם בי̇ע̇ב̇ר] ה[

6 עלכן נ̇[מחו] כל אש̇[ר ב]ח̇רבה ו̇[מ]ת̇ האדם ו̇[הבהמה וכל]צפר כל כנף והג[בור]ים לוא נמלטו

7 ו̇[ ] ב̇[נ]י̇ו̇ בתב̇[ה] ויעש אל [וא]ת קשתו נתן̇[ ]בענן ל[מען יזכור]ברית

8 [ ] [מי המבול ל]ו̇ ולוא יפ[תחו המון מים ע̇[שו]

9 [ ]ם̇ ושחקים [ ] [למים]

10 [ ]ו̇[ ]ooo[

---

[3] So Ada Yardeni (personal communication).

Notes on Readings

L. 1 **ותנ]ובה וש[פך**. As read by Strugnell.[4] Newsom reads תנ̇וֹ[בה ו]שׁ̇פך, but the fragment and the photographs (PAM 40601; 41865; 42506; 43369) show no traces of a *waw*.

L. 2 **ע̇[ליו]**. The DJD edition has [קדש]ׄ. Jassen reads ע̇[ליו][5], which better fits the ink traces and is confirmed by PAM 42506.

L. 3 **בׄ[כ]לׄדרכיהם**. Written without a space.

L. 5 **במבולׄ[ ]לׄ[**. The editor reads במבול ○[, but a tiny trace of ink may be observed in PAM 40601 above the lacuna, apparently of the vertical stroke of a *lamed*.

ב[מ̇ם̇. The DJD edition has [○ים. However, a short vertical stroke descending to the right (PAM 40601; 43369) seems to belong to a medial *mem* before the *yod*.

L. 6 **כל אש̇[ר**. Newsom reads כלאש̇[ר. However, there is a space between *lamed* and *alef*, as may be seen on the fragment and its photographs.

ו̇[הבהמה. The DJD edition reads וׄה̊[בהמה, but there are no traces of a second letter on the fragment and the photographs (PAM 40601; 42506; 43369).

L. 7 **ב̇נ̇י̇ו̇**. Newsom has ה̊○[. The upper part of a vertical stroke visible right after the lacuna is consistent with the vertical stroke of a medial *nun*. It is followed by two hook-shaped vertical strokes (PAM 40601). These are *yod* and *waw* (cf. *waw* in מחשבות and *yod* in עליהם [line 3]).

בת̇בׄ]ה. The editor suggests ב̇ת̇○ but in PAM 43369 a vertical stroke is visible after the *taw*. The context suggests the vertical stroke of a *bet*. If so, the space between בת̇בׄ]ה and the following ויעש is slightly larger than the usual practice in this fragment. But note the large intervals between בעיני אמר (line 2) and מתהמׄ̇וׄתׄ כל (line 4).

---

[4] *Preliminary Concordance*, 4:1910.
[5] Jassen, "The Reconstruction of 4Q370 1 i 2."

Translation[6]

1. [And] he crowned the mountains with pr[oduce and po]ured out food upon them. And with good fruit he satisfied every creature. "Let all who do my will <eat and be satisfied>," said the L[o]rd,
2. "And let them bless the name of [the Most Hig]h." "But look! Then they have done what is evil in my eyes," said the Lord. And they rebelled against God in their d[ee]ds.
3. And the Lord judged them according to [al]l their ways and according to the thoughts of the [evil] inclination of their heart. And he thundered against them with [his] might. [And] all
4. foundations of the ear[th] [q]uaked. [And wat]ers broke forth from the depths. All the windows of the heavens were opened, and all the depth[s] were overflowed [with] mighty waters.
5. And the floodgates of the heavens p[ou]red forth rain.[So] he destroyed them in the flood[ ] [ ] all of them [in wa]ter. For he passed [   ].
6. Therefore, everyone wh[o was on] the dry ground was [wiped out]: man and [cattle and every]bird, every winged thing, died. And the str[ong on]es did not escape.
7. And[   ]his [son]s in the ar[k] and God made [and] his bow he set[in the cloud s]o that he may remember the covenant.
8. [   ]waters of the deluge [and] the multitude of waters [would not be ope]ned.
9. [   ] <did?>and heavens [   ]to water [   ]
10. [   ] [   ] [   ]

Comments

יוכלו וישבע

Ll.1–2 ‏[עליו]ן שם את ויברכו ה]י אמר רצוני עשה אשר כל. These lines are of particular significance since they define the moral obligation of gratitude and recognition owed by the antediluvian mankind to God for the bounty he accorded them. The understanding of the phrase is therefore crucial. Some scholars place the supralinear addition יוכלו וישבעו after the word רצוני and thus obtain the reading אשר כל וישבעו יוכלו רצוני עשה ("all who do my will eat and are satisfied").[7] Others suggest

---

[6] The translation follows that of Newsom with slight alterations, reflecting the different readings and interpretations.
[7] *DSSSE*, 733; M. O. Wise, "A Sermon on the Flood. 4Q370," in *DSSNTr* 419; Barzilai, "Offhand Exegesis," 205.

that the supralinear words should precede the word כל, obtaining the sequence: יוכלו וישבעו כל אשר עשה רצוני ("will eat and be satisfied all who do my will").[8] The second alternative is preferable as the Qumran scribes usually wrote supralinear additions directly above the place they should have stood in the running text (cf. the additions in col. I lines 4 and 9)[9] or slightly afterwards,[10] but as a rule not before it, as posited by the first reading. So if the scribe wished the words יוכלו וישבעו to be inserted after the word רצוני, he would have written them above the space between רצוני and אמר or a little to the left.[11] Moreover, the second alternative fits the syntax of the whole passage, for the author of 4Q370 imitates biblical syntax by frequently placing a verb at the beginning of a clause (cf. col. i: [ו]יעטר [line 1], וישפטם, ונעו[י] [line 3], ופצו [line 4], וי[מ]ת [line 6]; col. ii: יצדיק [line 2], ויטהרם [line 3], ותשמח [line 8]).[12] The verbs יוכלו וישבעו appear in the divine direct speech and thus may be read as jussives (cf. below). This reading is also supported by the fact that in the biblical Hebrew a jussive in an optative sentence is usually placed before the subject.[13] If so, it appears that the scribe refrained from writing the addition above the space between the words כלנפש and כל because of the two *lamed*s found in these words (Newsom).[14] Since the addition is relatively long, the scribe wrote it a little further to the left.[15] The three verbs יוכלו, וישבעו, ויברכו draw on Deut 8:10a: ואכלת ושבעת וברכת את יהוה אלהיך על הארץ הטבה אשר נתן לך ("When you have eaten and are satisfied, praise the Lord your God for the good land he has given you").[16] The author of 4Q370 rewrote this verse as God's generous invitation to eat, become satisfied and bless his name, changing the mood of the verb into a jussive. He also replaced the biblical יהוה אלהיך with the expression שמ[עליון]. The construction ברך שם עליון is found both in the Hebrew Bible (Gen 14:19–20) and in the Scrolls (4Q222 1 4–5 [= *Jub.* 25:11]; cf. 11Q14 1 ii

---

8 Newsom, "4QAdmonition Based on the Flood," 91.
9 Tov, *Scribal Practices*, 226. See, for instance, 1QH[a] XII, 34; 11QT[a] LXI, 11.
10 Compare 11QT[a] LXVI, 4.
11 In such a case, the scribe also could have written in the space between the columns, as did the scribe of 1QIsa[a] in cols. XXX and XXXIII. Cf. Tov, *Scribal Practices*, 226–27.
12 Joüon-Muraoka, *Grammar*, 579, § 155 k.
13 Joüon-Muraoka, *Grammar*, 580, § 155 l.
14 In some Qumran scrolls, the presence of a *lamed* did not alter the placement of the supralinear addition. In similar cases, scribes wrote the addition above the *lamed* (11QT[a] XLVIII, 3), very close to the vertical stroke of the *lamed* (1QH[a] XII, 34), or on both sides of the vertical stroke of the *lamed* (11QT[a] XXIII, 6). At times, the added word is split into two, with the first section written on the right side of the vertical stroke of the *lamed* and the second section on the left of it (11QT[a] LXI, 8). Obviously, the scribe that wrote 4Q370 chose a different technique.
15 A similar case, but without any relation to a *lamed*, is found in 11QT[a] LXVI, 4.
16 Newsom, "4QAdmonition Based on the Flood," 93; Barzilai, "Offhand Exegesis," 205.

2–5; note also its usage in the Aramaic 1QapGen ar XII, 17; XX, 12–13; XXII, 15–16). This construction is used in *Jub.* 22:6 (with reference to blessing God after a meal) reworking Deut 8:10.[17]

L. 1 ‏ויעטר הרים תנ[ובה‏]. Col. i offers a description of an abundance of food enjoyed by the antediluvians, but the abrupt presentation suggests that the beginning of the composition was copied in the preceding columns that are not preserved. The string of 3rd per. verbs in the past tense (ויעטר, ושפך, השביע) indicates a narrative description, which takes up with ויאמרו at the end of line 2. The text between these two sections represents a quotation of divine speech, mostly formulated with jussives. The expression עטר הרים תנובה is not attested in the Hebrew Bible but the imagery of mountains overflowing with an abundance of agricultural produce is reminiscent of several biblical passages (cf. Ezek 36:8; Joel 4:18; Amos 9:13; Ps 72:16, 104:13, 147:8–9). However, the precise locution appears, with slight variations, in an apocryphal psalm from Qumran, the "Hymn to the Creator" (11QPs[a] XXVI, 13) with reference to God's creative acts: מעטר הרים תנובות אוכל טוב לכול חי ("He crowns the mountains with produce, good food for all the living" [line 13]).[18] So one may be dependent upon the other, or both may rework an unknown common source.[19]

ויעטר[‏]. The lacuna before ‏יעטר[‏ can accommodate one letter. Newsom's restoration ויעטר[‏] is in line with the frequent use of *wayyiqtol* forms in this passage (cf. וירעם, וישפטם [line 3], ויעש [line 7]). In biblical Hebrew, the verb עטר in *Pi'el* usually means "to crown" (Ps 8:6, 103:4; Song 3:11;[20] cf. also Sir 6:31 [= 2Q18 2 12]; 4Q372 3 8; 11Q5 XIX, 7). The verb ויעטר[‏] refers to God, as do all the 3rd masc. sg. verbs in the passage.

וש[פך אכל על פניהם. The phrase depicts the abundance lavished by God on antediluvian mankind. The bounty of food is stressed by the choice of the verb וש[פך,

---

17 As noted by Jassen, "The Reconstruction of 4Q370 1 i 2," 107.
18 The Hebrew text is cited according to the edition of J. A. Sanders in DJD IV, 47, 90. The English translation is that of *DSSSE*, 1179, with slight changes.
19 Newsom, "4QAdmonition Based on the Flood," 91–92, suggests that 4Q370 is dependent upon the "Hymn to the Creator." She is followed, among others, by García Martínez, "Interpretations of the Flood," 97–98; Barzilai, "Offhand Exegesis," 193 n. 495; E. G. Chazon, "The Use of the Bible as a Key to Meaning in Psalms from Qumran," in *Emanuel: Studies in Hebrew Bible, Septuagint and Dead Sea Scrolls in Honor of Emanuel Tov* (ed. S. M. Paul et al.; VTSup 94; Leiden: Brill, 2003), 85–96 (94). While noting that Newsom's analysis is plausible, M. J. Goff, *Discerning Wisdom: The Sapiential Literature of the Dead Sea Scrolls* (VTSup 116: Leiden: Brill, 2007), 258 n. 147, cautiously suggests that in this case no definite conclusion can be reached.
20 BDB, 742–43; *HALOT*, 815.

a 3rd masc. sg. *qatal* of שפך, which has God as subject. שפך is used of liquids, meaning "to pour, pour out" (Gen 9:6; Deut 12:16; 1 Sam 7:6), or of a quantity of material, in the sense of "heap up" (2 Sam 20:15; 2 Kgs 19:32; Isa 37:33).²¹ The second meaning applies to the present context, although the locution שפך אוכל is not biblical.

פניהם. The 3rd masc. pl. possessive pronoun of פניהם refers to living beings rather than to the "mountains" (הרים), for the following parallel phrase mentions "every being" (כל נפש). The following words in this line also speak of humans in the 3rd masc. pl.: ויברכוֹ ... ויבעו.

ופרי טוב השביע כלנפש. The phrase echoes Ps 145:16: פותח את ידך ומשביע לכל חי רצון ("You open your hand and satisfy the desire of every living thing"). Note that the biblical generalized formulation כל חי, referring to all living creatures, is replaced in 4Q370 with the expression כל נפש, also carrying the same general sense. נפש is used here in the sense of a living creature, probably drawing on the Genesis creation story (e.g. Gen 1:20, 24). The expression ופרי טוב השביע is, perhaps, influenced by Ps 104:13, 28.

יוכלו. A phonetic spelling יוכלוּ (vs. MT: יֹאכְלוּ) with a drop of a quiescent *alef*.²²

אמר י[ה]וה. This formula serves to mark the divine direct speech in lines 1–2. It is notable that while replacing the biblical Tetragrammaton in the reworked Deuteronomic reference mentioned above, 4Q370 employs it here and elsewhere (cols. i 2–3; ii 2, 7), as well as the term אל (col. i 2, 7).

L. 2 **והני הם אז עשו הרע בעיני אמר יהוה**. The line continues the divine speech and defines the offence of ancient humanity. The adverb והני emphasizes the dissonance between the behavior expected of humans who enjoyed God's kindness and their actual ingratitude (for a similar usage of והנה, see Isa 22:12–13).²³ The phrase עשה רע בעיני אלוהים occurs frequently in the Hebrew Bible (e.g. Num 32:13; Deut 4:25), as well as in the Scrolls (4Q390 1 4, 9, 12; 2 i 8; 4Q393 1 ii–2 2). However, in the present context, the formulation appears to allude specifically to antediluvian sins, as formulated by Gen 6:5.

והני. The unusual orthography והני (MT: והנה) is explained by the well-attested usage of *yod* as a *mater lectionis* for *ṣere* in Qumran Hebrew.²⁴

---

21 *HALOT*, 1629–30.
22 Qimron, *Hebrew of the Dead Sea Scrolls*, 20.
23 For הנה/והנה in the Hebrew Bible, see B. K. Waltke, M. O'Connor, *An Introduction to Biblical Hebrew Syntax* (Winona Lake: Eisenbrauns, 1990), 678.
24 Qimron, *Hebrew of the Dead Sea Scholls*, 20.

ויאמרו אל במ[על]יהם. In style and subject matter, the phrase belongs to the narrative content of the fragment and is not part of God's direct speech, as some scholars suggest.[25] For the preceding quotation of the divine words is phrased in the 1st sg. (בעיני, רצוני), whereas here God is referred to in the 3rd sg. and is designated by אל. Moreover, ויאמרו is a *wayyiqtol* verbal form, characteristic of the narrative part of 4Q370 i (וירעם, וישפטם [line 3]). In contrast, God's direct speech in lines 1–2 employs jussive verbal forms (ויברכוׂ, וישבעו, יוכלו). Hence, the phrase ויאמרו אל במ[על]יהם should be understood as part of the following narration rather than the preceding divine speech.[26]

ויאמרו אל. Here, again, the choice of vocabulary clearly expresses the author's attitude toward the sinners. The verb ויאמרו is a 3rd masc. pl. *wayyiqtol* of מרה in the *Hif'il*, "to behave rebelliously."[27] In the biblical perspective, the verb articulates the emblematic revolt of Moses and Aaron for which they were barred from entering Canaan (Num 20:24; 27:14). In Ps 78:17 (למרות עליון בציה), which obviously influenced the formulation of this line, the verb designates the revolt of all the Israelites during their desert wandering. All these biblical contexts employ the verb מרה to indicate the rebellion against divine commandment or will. The Ps 78:17 reference is particularly relevant since it is linked to the feeding of the Israelites in the desert, a reference stated in the following verse (וינסו אל בלבבם לשאל אכל לנפשם; Ps 78:18). This is an allusion to the episodes of the manna (Exod 16) and the quails (Exod 16:13; Num 11:31–32). So, by using this specific verb, 4Q370 may be correlating the provision of food for the Israelites in the desert with that for antediluvian humanity, and is comparing the sinful ingratitude of both. In this way, 4Q370 is also defining the ingratitude of antediluvian mankind as disobedience to the divine directive specified in line 2 (Dimant).

ויאמרו. In the MT, this verbal form is spelled as וַיַּמְרוּ (Ps 78:56). The addition of *alef* in 4Q370 may be explained as a *mater lectionis* for the vowel "*a*."[28] The verb מרה occurs once more in 4Q370 ii 9: אׇל תׇמׁרו דבר[י יהוה.

במ[על]יהם. The noun *מעללים (with or without pronominal suffix) is usually spelled in the MT without a *yod* between the two *lameds*, except for a

---

25 See *DSSSE*, 2:733; Wise, "A Sermon on the Flood," 419.
26 This is also the understanding of Newsom, as reflected in her translation, "4QAdmonition Based on the Flood," 91.
27 *HALOT*, 632–33.
28 See E. Qimron, "Medial *Alef* as a *Mater Lectionis* in the Hebrew and Aramaic Documents from Qumran in Comparison with Other Hebrew and Aramaic Sources," *Leš* 39 (1975): 133–46 (134–35) [Hebrew]; idem, *Hebrew of the DSS*, 22.

Ketiv ומעליליכם in Zech 1:4 (*Qere* ומעלליכם).²⁹ Since the lacuna may contain three letters, Newsom restored במ[עלי]ליהם (cf. also מ[עליל]ם; 4Q381 46a + b 6). The basic meaning of *מעללים in the Hebrew Bible is neutral, "deeds."³⁰ However, at times, it is used there in a negative sense, "wicked deeds" (Isa 3:8; Ps 106:29), as is the case in 4Q374 2 ii 3 and here.

L. 3 [רע]ה̇ לבם יצ̇ר ובמחשבות ב̇[כ]לדרכיהם יהוה וישפטס. This phrase opens the depiction of the divine judgment of antediluvian mankind and its punishment by the flood (lines 3–6). The formulation takes up Gen 6:5, 12. ב̇[כ]לדרכיהם refers to Gen 6:12 (for the locution לשפוט כדרכו, see Ezek 7:3, 8; 18:30), while מחשבות יצ̇ר לבם ה̇]רע is taken from Gen 6:5.

וירעם עליהם בכח]ו. The verb וירעם is a 3rd masc. sg. *Hifʿil wayyiqtol* of רעם, "to thunder" (2 Sam 22:14; Ps 29:3).³¹ For the construction הרעים על, see 1 Sam 7:10 (in the context of God's miraculous aid to Israel in the battle against the Philistines). The locution רעם בכח does not occur in the Hebrew Bible but a similar expression, ירעם אל בהמון כוחו, is found in 1QHᵃ XI, 35.

וי[נֹעו כל סוסדי א]רץ. The verb וי[נֹעו, as it is restored by Newsom, is a 3rd masc. pl. *wayyiqtol* of נוע, "tremble, shake," in *Qal*.³² The phrase וי[נֹעו כל סוסדי א]רץ is built on Isa 24:18–20 וירעשו מוסדי ארץ...נוע תנוע ארץ כשכור ("And earth's foundations tremble ... The earth is swaying like a drunkard"). Significantly, Isa 24:18c itself depicts the cosmic upheaval of the final judgment in analogy with that of the ancient deluge, for it employs the phrase ארבות ממרום נפתחו, clearly taken from the flood story (cf. Gen 7:11). So 4Q370 presents the reverse process, describing the flood in terms of the final cataclysm.

Ll. 4–5 **ופצו כל תהמו]ת מ̇ים אֹדֹרי̇ / וארבות השמים ה̇]רי[קו סטר**. The lacuna found before the word מ̇ים can accommodate more than one letter and is restored accordingly following the locution פוץ מ... in Zech 1:17, עוד תפוצינה ערי מטוב (thus Newsom). (ו)פצו, parsed as a 3rd pl. *qatal* of פוץ in *Qal*, is used in the biblical parlance with the sense "to spread," "disperse," and "overflow."³³ It is the last meaning that suits best the present context (note Prov 5:16). The fragment obviously reworks the scene described in Gen 7:11b, as is evident from the context and

---

29 On this *Ketiv*, see D. L. Petersen, *Haggai and Zechariah 1–8* (OTP; Philadelphia: Westminster Press, 1984), 127 n. b.
30 *HALOT*, 614.
31 *HALOT*, 1267.
32 *HALOT*, 681.
33 *HALOT*, 919.

the use of the expression ארבות השמים, a marker of the flood story in that verse. But 4Q370 also draws here on other biblical depictions of rain and mighty waters. Thus the phrase מ]ים אַדִּרִי°ם is borrowed from the Song of the Sea (Exod 15:10; cf. also Ps 93:4). Note that in this case the scroll uses a defective orthography, אדרים, while the MT reads אדירים. As for the restoration, הֹ[רי]קו is a 3rd masc. pl. *Hif'il* of רוק "to pour out."[34] It is proposed by Newsom on the basis of Eccl 11:3: גשם על הארץ יריקו (cf. 4Q422 ii 6). The rain is described here using the word מטר, which is found in the flood story only as a participle of the same root, ממטיר (Gen 7:4). The actual Genesis depiction of the rain employs גשם (Gen 7:12). But note the combination of the two words in Job 37:6 וגשם מטר.

L. 4 ומ[י]ם נׂבקעו מתהֹמֹוֹת כל ארבות השמים נפתחו. This description of the flood waters is based on Gen. 7:11a.

L. 5 [וֹ]אָבדם במבול [ ]לֹ[ ] בֹ[מ]ים כלם בֹּיׁעֹבׂר] ה[. This line describes the destruction of the wicked in the flood. The verb וֹ]אָבדם], referring to God, is a 3rd masc. sg. *qatal* of אבד in *Pi'el*, meaning "to destroy."[35] While the noun מבול occurs several times in Genesis 6–9 (6:17; 7:7, 10, 17; 9:11, 15, 28), the expression אבד במבול is not biblical.

בֹ[מ]ים כלם. Newsom interpreted the word כלם as a 3rd masc. sg. *qatal* of כלה in *Pi'el*, "to destroy" (Exod 32:10; 33:3; 1QpHab V, 3),[36] with an attached 3rd masc. pl. object suffix, כִּלָּם (for this form, see Lam 2:22; 4Q434 1 i 5). If her interpretation is accepted, this line may be restored as: וֹ]אָבדם במבול] כֹּ[ל]ם וב[מֹים כִּלָּם ("and he destroyed all of them in the flood and in waters annihilated them"). Alternatively, one may read here כֻּלָּם in the defective form given other defective spellings used in this manuscript (אכל [col. i 1], כל [col. i 1, 4], אדרים, תהמות, ארבות [col. i 4, 5]), in distinction from the usual plene orthography, כולם, preferred by other Qumran texts (1QS VIII, 9; 1QM VII, 3; 1QpHab VIII, 6; yet cf. 4Q372 3 6; 4Q448 ii 7). If so, the phrase may also be restored וֹ]אָבדם במבול] וּכֹ[ל]ה בֹ[מֹ]ים כֻּלָּם ("and he destroyed them in the flood and annihilated in waters all of them").

בֹּיׁעֹבׂר. The two words כי עבר are written as one, as in the similar cases כלנפש (col. i 1), עלכן (col. ii 6). The lacunae make it difficult to ascertain the context and meaning of this expression. The editor suggests that the scroll alludes here to Isa 28:15; note also Isa 28:18: שוט שוטף כי יעבר ("When the sweeping flood is passing

---

34 *HALOT*, 1228.
35 *HALOT*, 3. The use of אבד is interesting in view of the allusion to Deut 8:10–14 in lines 1–2. Deut 8:19–20 describes the punishment of the ungrateful Israelites using forms of אבד.
36 *HALOT*, 477.

through") and 1QH³ XIV, 38: ובעבור שוט שוטף. The locution שוט שוטף ("sweeping flood"³⁷) links this verse to the flood story. Accordingly, Newsom proposes to restore כיעבר] שוט שוטף היבש[ה, but the restoration is too long, for the lacuna consists of about ten character-spaces.

L. 6 עלכן נ̇[מחו] כלאשׁ[ר ב]ח̇רבה ו̊[מ]ת̇ האדם ו̇]הבהמה וכל [צפר כל כנף. Taking up the general formulation of Gen 7:22, this line details the types of living beings that perished in the flood besides mankind, animals (restored) and birds.

והג̇[בור]ים לוא נמלטו. The scroll may allude to the wording of Jer 46:9: אל ינוס הקל אל ימלט הגבור ("The swift will not run away, the warrior will not escape") or of Amos 2:14: ואבד מנוס מקל וחזק לא יאמץ כחו וגבור לא ימלט נפשו ("Flight shall be lost for the swift, the strong shall find no strength, and the warrior shall not save his life"). The inclusion of "the strong ones" (הג̇[בור]ים) in the list of creatures that perished in the flood is an addition to the biblical picture. This is undoubtedly a reference to the "strong ones" (הגברים), the offspring of the sons of God and the daughters of men, mentioned in Gen 6:4 (cf. 4Q180 1 8). In several Second Temple sources they are the mighty giants (CD II, 20; Sir 16:7; *1 En.* 7:2; *3 Macc.* 2:4). For the translation "the strong ones" see note 52 below.

L. 7 [ב̊[נו̇ בת̇ב̊[ה]נו̊[. The lacuna preceding]נו̊[is of about eighteen letter-spaces. So perhaps it contained part of Gen 7:23: וישאר אך נח ואשר אתו בתבה ("Only Noah was left, and those with him, in the ark"). If so, 4Q370 replaces the biblical general phrase ואשר אתו with the explicit mention of Noah's sons, as in Gen 6:18 (cf. Gen 7:13; 8:16, 18).

ויעש אל [ ] וא[ת קשתו נתן] בענן ל[מען יזכור ברית. The wording here clearly depends on Gen 9:13–15. Perhaps one may restore here with Gen 9:12, 13 ויעש אל [אות ברית. For the expression עשה אות, see Exod 4:30; Judg 6:17; Ps 86:17.

L. 8 מ̇[י המבול ל] ולוא יפ[תחו המון מים. In the previous line, the covenant is mentioned that God concludes with all living creatures, and this line describes its content. Therefore, the first unpreserved section of this line reworked the list of those included in this covenant, as found in Gen 9:15a (cf. also Gen 9:9–10, 12, 16, 17). Since the expression מי המבול is taken from Gen 9:11, the scroll may have followed Gen 9:11 here: מ[י המבול ל]עולם. But the following words are composed from various verses. ולוא יפ[תחו contrasts with the beginning of the flood in Gen 7:11: וארבת השמים נפתחו. The locution המון מים is borrowed from Jer 10:13 (= 51:16).

---

37 *HALOT*, 1441. See further S. Poznański, "Zu שׁוֹט שֹׁטֵף," *ZAW* 36 (1916): 119–20.

L. 9 [ ]למים[ ] ם[ושחקים]
[עשו

L. 9 [ ]למים[   ] ם[ושחקים. The supralinear addition, if consisting of only the word עשו, should be inserted before the word ושחקים (cf. Comment on line 1). The word שחקים is not attested in Genesis 6–9.

Col. ii

top margin

1 מ]עון ידרשו מ[
2 ש]יצדיק יהוה [
3 [ויטהרם מעונם
4 [רעתם בדעתם בי
5 יצמחו וכצל ימיהם ע̊[ל ה]ארץ
6 [ועד עולם הוא ירחם
7 גבורת יהוה זכרו נפל]אות
8 מפני פחדו ותשמח נפ[שכם
9 משניכם אל תמ̊רו דבר̊[י יהוה

Translation
1. from iniquity, they will seek [
2. the Lord will justify [
3. And he will purify them from their iniquity [
4. their wickedness in their knowing [
5. they will spring up and like a shadow are their days o[n the earth
6. and forevermore he will have compassion [
7. the might of the Lord, remember the won[ders
8. on account of the fear of him and [your] soul wil[l] rejoice [
9. your enemies. Do not rebel against the word[s of the Lord

Comments

L. 1 מעון ידרשו מ[. The occurrence of the same noun עון in the locution ויטהרם מעונם in line 3 favors the reading here מֵעָוֹן ("from iniquity", with Newsom) rather than the noun מָעוֹן ("a dwelling"). But it is unclear how מֵעָוֹן is connected to the following word ידרשו, a 3rd masc. pl. of the verb דרש, meaning "investigate, supplicate, question."[38] Since the two words cannot be combined they should be separated and the verb ידרשו/י is to be read as opening a new clause.

---

38 *HALOT*, 233.

ידרשו. This is a 3rd masc. pl. *Qal yiqtol* of דרש, although, given the similarity between *yod* and *waw* in this manuscript, the reading ודרשו cannot be ruled out.

L. 2 **יצדיק יהוה ש]**. The verb יצדיק, a 3rd masc. *Hifʿil yiqtol* of צדק, has God as its subject (for a similar usage, cf. Exod 23:7; 1 Kgs 8:32 [= 2 Chr 6:23]). The reading וצדיק יהוה is also possible (cf. Ps 11:7; Dan 9:14).

L. 3 **ויטהרם מעונם]**. Since the verbs preserved in the first two lines are *yiqtol* forms, one may also read here ויטהרם, namely a 3rd masc. sg. *yiqtol* of טהר in *Piʿel* with 3rd masc. pl. pronominal suffix. The expression טהר מעון occurs both in the Hebrew Bible (Jer 33:8; Ezek 36: 33) and in the Scrolls (1QS III, 7; 4Q424 2 2; 11QPsᵃ XIX, 14). The subject of ויטהרם is most probably God, while the 3rd masc. pl. pronominal suffix refers to the same group of people referred to by the verb ידרשו. Most likely, they are also the object of the verb יצדיק in the previous line.

L. 4 **רעתם בדעתם בי]**. The 3rd masc. pl. possessive suffixes attached to רעתם and בדעתם refer to the same group referred to in the previous lines. Newsom restores בדעתם בי]ן טוב לרע ("in their knowledge [how to distinguish]bet[ween good and evil]") on the basis of the biblical locution ידע בין טוב לרע (Deut 1:39; 2 Sam 19:36; note 1QSa I, 10–11). It designates the ability to distinguish between good and evil, which denotes maturity and the capacity to assume moral responsibility.[39] However, the restoration goes beyond what may be conjectured on the basis of the surviving letters.

Ll. 5–6 **ועד עולם הוא ירחם]**. The formulation is reminiscent of Ps 103:15–17 (cf. also Isa 54:8).

L. 5 **יִצְמְחוּ וכצל ימיהם עָ]ל האר֯ץ**. The surviving words seem to associate two biblical images depicting the short and ephemeral human life, that of a plant and that of a shadow. The 3rd. masc. pl. *Qal qatal* יִצְמְחוּ points to the imagery of a plant that grows up and quickly withers (Isa 40:6–8; Ps 103:15; note Job 14:1, 2) while the expression וכצל ימיהם draws on 1 Chr 29:15: כצל ימינו על הארץ ("our days on earth are like a shadow"). Accordingly, the locutions are completed with the appropriate restoration. In its depiction of the short and ephemeral human life, frgs. 1–2 i 9–13 of the Qumranic sapiential composition 4Q185 also associate the image of a small

---

[39] See G. W. Buchanan, "The Old Testament Meaning of the Knowledge of Good and Evil," *JBL* 75 (1956): 114–20; R. Gordis, "The Knowledge of Good and Evil in the Old Testament and the Qumran Scrolls," *JBL* 76 (1957): 123–38.

plant with that of a passing shadow: [וְ]הוּא כְצֵל יָמָיו עַל הָאָ[רֶץ] (lines 9–10);[40] וְאַתֶּם בְּנֵי אָדָם א[ין כח [כִּי הִנֵּה כְחָצִיר יִצְמָח (line 13).[41]

יְמֵיהֶם. In accordance with the entire passage, the biblical יָמֵינוּ, borrowed from 1 Chr 29:15, is replaced by יְמֵיהֶם, probably referring to the group mentioned by the previous verbs. However, here as with other verbs, it is difficult to ascertain whether mankind in general is being referred to or just a specific group.

L. 7 **גבורת יהוה זכרו נפל]אות**. In lines 7–9, the 3rd sg. and pl. verbs of the previous lines are changed into 2nd pl. in admonitory style. Due to the fragmentary state of the column it is impossible to know who is the speaker and to whom the discourse is addressed. However, the general tenor and the formulations follow various biblical passages. Syntactically, it is possible to take the constructed nouns גבורת יהוה as the object of the verb זכרו,[42] but the context here of praise of God's marvelous acts suggests that נפל]אות is the better-suited object, since it functions as such in the similar biblical formulation and context of Ps 105:5 (= 1 Chr 16:12), which influenced the 4Q370 wording. For several elements assembled in this psalm and in Ps 106 are combined in 4Q370. Among "the mighty acts of God" (גבורות יהוה; Ps 106:2), the psalm lists events related to Exodus (Ps 106:7–11) and defines them using the term נפלאותיך (Ps 106:7). Both גבורות יהוה and נפלאות appear in the present phrase. In the Hebrew Bible, נפלאות frequently designates also the events surrounding the Exodus (Exod 31:10; Judg 6:13; Mic 7:16; Ps 106:7, 22; Neh 9:17). So perhaps also 4Q370 refers here to Exodus, as does the parallel text from 4Q185 1–2 i 14–15: וְחָכְמוּ מִן [גְ]בוּרַת אֱלֹהֵינוּ זִכְרוּ נִפְלָאֹם עשה / במצרים ומופתיו בְּ[ארץ חם].[43]

זכרו. This form should be parsed as pl. imperative זִכְרוּ rather than the *qatal* זָכְרוּ, since it better suits the admonitory tone of lines 8–9 (cf. אַל תָּמְרוּ).

---

40 Newsom, "4QAdmonition Based on the Flood," 96, restores this line according to the parallel text of 4Q185: כי הנה כחציר [יצמחו]. By the same token, she restores other lacunae in this column utilizing the parallel texts of 4Q185. However, in view of the differences between the extant texts of 4Q370 and 4Q185 (see below), this procedure has been avoided.
41 4Q185 is quoted from H. Lichtenberger, "Der Weisheitstext 4Q185 – Eine neue Edition," in *The Wisdom Texts from Qumran and the Development of Sapiential Thought* (ed. C. Hempel, A. Lange and H. Lichtenberger; Leuven: Leuven University Press, 2002), 127–50 (130).
42 For placement of the object before the verb in biblical Hebrew, see T. Muraoka, *Emphatic Words and Structures in Biblical Hebrew* (Jerusalem: Magnes Press, 1985), 38–39.
43 The third letter of the first word is clearly a medial *kaf*, as is evident in PAM 43514. The word should, therefore, be read וְחָכְמוּ, rather than Allegro's תָּמוּ (in DJD V, 85), Strugnell's חכמו (cf. J. Strugnell, "Notes en marge du volume V des "Discoveries in the Judaean Desert of Jordan," *RevQ* 7 [1970]: 270), or Lichtenberger's יִהְמוּ (cf. Lichtenberger, "Der Weisheitstext 4Q185," 135).

גבורת יהוה. For this expression, see Ps 71:16, 106:2; 1QM I, 11, 14; 11Q17 VIII, 5.

L. 8 **מפני פחדו ותשמח נפֿ]שכם**. The 3rd masc. sg. possessive suffix of פחדו in the locution מפני פחדו refers to God, as is clear from the source of this expression in Isa 2:10, 19, 21, מפני פחד ה', in the context of the future judgment. A similar formulation is found in 4Q185 1–2 i 15–ii 1: נ[פשכם   ועשו רֹצ̇]ונו / ויֹערץ לבבכֹם מפֹנֹי פחדוֹ בחסדיו הטבים. For the phrase שמח נפש, cf. Ps 86:4; 1QH[a] XIX, 33; 11QPs[a] XXII, 15.

L. 9 **משניכם אל תֹמֹרו דבר֯]י יהוה**. The noun משניכם can be parsed as a plural of מִשְׁנֶה. In the Hebrew Bible, מִשְׁנֶה denotes "a subordinate,"[44] either with reference to one's age (1 Sam 17:13) or to one's position (Neh 11:9; cf. 1QM II, 1; 11QT[a] XXXI, 4). Newsom does indeed derive משניכם from מִשְׁנֶה, and interprets it temporally: "those who follow you." She supports her interpretation by adducing 4Q185 1–2 ii 2: שארית לבניכם אחריכם (compare the usage of משנה in 4Q405 11 2–3) as a possible parallel. But this sense and usage of מִשְׁנֶה are not attested. Alternatively, משניכם may be a phonetic spelling of משנאיכם ("your enemies"), a pl. *Pi'el* participle of שנא, "to hate,"[45] used in the Hebrew Bible with the meaning "enemy" (e.g. Deut 32:41; Ps 44:8; for the dropping of an *alef*, cf. 4Q511 18 ii 7 [שנתי instead of שנאתי]; in 1QS IV, 24 ישנא appears to have been written initially with a *he*).[46] If so, this word should not be connected to the following text but should be read instead as the end of the previous sentence. The following negative imperative אל תֹמֹרו would, then, open a new phrase. The verb תֹמֹרו is a 2nd pl. jussive of מרה in *Hif'il*. The *Hif'il* of this verb occurs also in col. I, 2: ויאמרו אלבמ]עלי[ליהם. Compare the phrase המרו דבר ה' in Ps 105:28 (cf. also Ps 105:40, 107:11; 4Q299 3 ii 8).

Unidentified Fragment

[ישראל]   1
bottom margin

---

44 BDB, 1041; *HALOT*, 650.
45 BDB, 971.
46 Qimron, *The Dead Sea Scrolls*, 1:216.

Discussion

As with many other pieces of the Scrolls, these two fragmentary columns elude a clear-cut definition due to the distinct character and subject of each column. The first column employs a narrative style and depicts the episode of the flood, while the second column is predominantly an admonitory address. The best-preserved first column offers an interesting example of the reworking of the outline of a single main text, in this case the flood account of Genesis 6–9, while interweaving formulations from other biblical books, as well as themes and ideas taken from nonbiblical sources.

Use of the Hebrew Bible in col. i

4Q370 i	Hebrew Bible
[וֹ]יְעַטֵּר הרים תנ[וֹבה וש]פֹּך אכל על פניהם ופרי טוב השביע כלנפש (line 1)	Ps 145:16
יוכלו וישבעו כל אשר עשה רצוני אמר יֹ[ה]וה / ויברכוֹ את שם [עליוֹ]ןֹ (lines 1–2)	Deut 8:10
והני הם אז עשו הרע בעיני אמר יהוה (line 2)	Gen 6:5a
וישפטם יהוה כֹ[כֹ]לֹדרכיהם וֹכמחשבות יצֹר לבם הֹ[רע] (line 3)	Gen 6:5b, 12
וֹ[נֹ]עו כל / סוסדי ארֹ[ץ (lines 3–4)	Isa 24:18–20
ומ[ים נֹבקעו מתהמֹוֹת כל ארבות השמים נפתחו ופצו כל תהמוֹת מ[יֹם / אֹדֹריֹ^ם	Gen 7:11b;
וארבות השמים הֹ[רי]קוֹ סטרֹ] (lines 4–5)	Exod 15:10
עלכן נֹ[מֹחו] כל אשֹ[ר ב]חֹרבה וֹ[מֹ]תֹ האדם וֹ[מֹ]ת הבהמה וכל [צפר / כל כנף והג[בור]ים לוא נמלטו (lines 6–7)	Gen 7:22–23; 6:4
ב[נֹוֹ בתבֹ]ה (line 7)	Gen 7:23b
ויעש אל [אות ברית וא]ת קשתו נתן[בענן ל]מען יזכור ברית (line 7)	Gen 9:12–15
ולוא יכרת כל בשר עוד מ[מי המבול ל]עֹולם ולוא יפֹ[תחו המון מים (line 8)	Gen 9:15

This catalogue shows that essentially 4Q370 draws on the flood story and follows the main stages of the biblical sequence: the antediluvians' sin (Gen 6:5, 12), the floodwaters (Gen 7:22a), the destruction of the wicked (Gen 7:22a), the salvation of Noah and his household (Gen 7:22b), and the covenant with Noah (Gen 9:12–15). Allusions to these biblical verses provide the outline of the reworked story. Yet the reworking of Genesis 6–9 is selective; it does not mention Noah's righteousness, the construction of the ark, the gathering of the animals, boarding the ark, the stages of the flood, the landing of the ark, the sending out of the birds and Noah's disembarking. Similarly, the scroll seems to omit all the chronological data found in Genesis 7–8. However, while omitting details from the Genesis narrative, 4Q370 incorporates references to other sources, biblical as well as nonbiblical. This method is illustrated in each of the reworked episodes.

Use of Genesis 6–9

The central topic in col. i, the flood story, is introduced by the reworking of verses mainly from Genesis. This is done by summarizing the biblical narrative and by using its vocabulary. 4Q370 i, 1–2 makes use of the few general biblical terms that describe the sins that brought about the punishment of the flood. The expression "they have done what is evil (הרע) in my eyes" (line 2) seems to allude to "man's wickedness" (רעת האדם) in Gen 6:5. Line 3 adds another detail from the Genesis story: "And the Lord judged them according to [al]l their ways and according to the thoughts of the [evil] inclination of their heart." The phrase "according to [al]l their ways" (כ̇[כ]ל֯דרכיהם) echoes Gen 6:12 (השחית כל בשר את דרכו), while the formulation "and according to the thoughts of the [evil] inclination of their heart (וכמחשבות יצר֯ לבם ה̊[רע]) is taken from Gen 6:5 (וכל יצר מחשבת לבו רק רע).[47] However, their use in 4Q370 is unique in several respects. First, the verb וירא ("and saw") that appears in both verses is replaced in 4Q370 with the verb וישפט ("and judged"). One may suggest that the mention of the judgment in 4Q370, which explicates the reason for the divine verdict ("according to"), serves to justify the severe punishment of the antediluvians. In addition, the biblical locution יצר מחשבת לבו,[48] which is a construct chain, is rephrased in 4Q370 with the noun מחשבת as a *nomen regens* and יצר and לבם as *nomina recta*.[49] This reworking emphasizes the word מחשבות.[50] While several other extrabiblical sources state

---

47 These two verses, which are related to each other in content, are reworked also in the Flood story as recorded in *1 En.* 8:2 and *Jub.* 5:3 (cf. also 4Q422 II, 1).
48 This locution appears also in 1 Chr 29:18 (ליצר מחשבות לבב עמך) and, in an abbreviated form, in 1 Chr 28:9 (וכל יצר מחשבות).
49 On this phenomenon, see C. Yalon, *The Language of the Scrolls From the Judaean Desert* (Jerusalem: Kiryat-Sefer, 1967), 85 [Hebrew]; Y. Avishur, "The Reversed Construct Structure in the Bible, Qumran Scrolls and in Early Jewish Literature," *Leš* 57 (1993): 279–88 (282–83) [Hebrew].
50 The same alteration is attested in other texts from Qumran, predominantly those assigned to the sectarian literature: CD II, 16 [= 4Q270 1 i 1]; 1QS V, 4, 5; 4Q286 7 ii 7–8; 4Q417 1 ii 12. Cf. J. Hadot, *Penchant mauvais et volonté libre dans la Sagesse de Ben Sira* (Brussels: Presses universitaires de Bruxelles, 1970), 51.

that God judged the antediluvians,[51] 4Q370 seems to stress that they were judged not only for their wicked deeds, but also for their evil thoughts (for the notion of divine retribution based on one's ways and heart, see 1 Kgs 8:39). However, the main stress is laid on the sin of ungratefulness, which is not found in the biblical narrative (cf. below). Interestingly, the description of the flood itself (lines 3–5) consists mostly of formulations taken from biblical sources other than Genesis. The only exception is the locution ארבות השמים ("the windows of the heavens"), which is taken from Gen 7:11.

The same technique of condensing the biblical account but retaining its vocabulary is evident in the reworking of Gen 7:22–23, which list those who perished in the flood (line 6): "Therefore, everyone wh[o was on] the dry ground was [wiped out]: man and [cattle and every]bird, every winged thing, died. And the str[ong one]s[52] did not escape." In rewriting these verses, the author summarizes their content and reduces the number of repetitions. In reworking v. 23, he replaced the phrase עוף השמים ("birds of the sky") with a synonymous expression, [כל] ציפור כל כנף ("[every] bird, every winged thing"), borrowed from Gen 7:14. However, he dropped one category of animals included there, רמש ("creeping things"). The list also contains a significant addition not found in the Bible, namely the "strong ones" (גברים), who also perished in the flood. This addition is discussed below.

The covenant with Noah, which reworks Gen 9:12–15a, is treated in the same way. Most of the observable changes were introduced in order to adapt the quotation of the biblical divine speech in 1st sg. to the 4Q370 narrative style in the 3rd sg. In addition, the author of 4Q370 tends to create parallelisms, for instance ויעש אל [   ] וא[ת קשתו נתן] בענן. The replacement of the biblical double use of the verb נתן with the pair נתן/ויעש is clearly motivated by stylistic concerns. This literary tendency is evident throughout the column.

---

51 See *Jub.* 5:11, 20:5; *1 En.* 65:10–11; Philo, *QG*, II,16. This is also the tradition of the Palestinian Targums (*Tg. Ps.-J.*, *Tg. Yer. I*, *Tg. Neof.*) to Gen 6:3. See J. Schlosser, "Les jours de Noé et de Lot," *RB* 80 (1973): 13–36 (15–16).
52 Newsom, "4QAdmonition Based on the Flood," 91, translates "giants." Since the relation between הג[בור]ים mentioned here and the הגברים of Gen 6:4, described in the Second Temple writings as giants, has to be established first, it is suggested to render הג[בור]ים as "the strong ones" (see BDB, 150; *HALOT*, 172). Cf. the discussion in the following section.

Use of Biblical Verses Other than Genesis 6–9

Occasionally, the author interlaces the Genesis outline with allusions to verses from Exodus, Deuteronomy, Isaiah and Psalms. This technique is apparent from the first lines of col. i. Since the Genesis account of the antediluvians' sins is laconic (Gen 6:5, 11) and is used only sparingly by 4Q370, lines 1–2 introduce an altogether novel motif, the abundance of food generously provided by God to all the living (col. i, 1), which was not thanked for by mankind living at the time. The depiction of bounty is borrowed from Ps 145:16 and, perhaps, the Qumranic "Hymn to the Creator" (11QPs[a] XXVI, 13). Yet, in reworking this detail, 4Q370 hints at other elements from the Genesis story that are not connected to the flood. For, according to 4Q370, beside "food," designated by the general noun אכל,[53] the antediluvians were nourished by תנובה ("produce"), namely produce of the fields (תנובת השדה; cf. Deut 32:13; Ezek 36:30) and פרי טוב ("good fruit"). This is in line with Gen 1:29–30, where mankind is given "every seed-bearing plant" and "every tree that has seed-bearing fruit" for food. The eating of flesh was allowed only after the flood (Gen 9:3). Thus, 4Q370 appropriately does not include it in the antediluvians' diet.

Yet the careful choice of terms is aiming at another matter; it subtly emphasizes the divine grace using particular formulations. Thus, God did not just cause plants to grow but he "crowned" the earth with produce. He did not simply provide food but "poured it" out; the food consisted of "good fruits" and not just "fruits." These details strongly emphasize the divine bounty, which is further enhanced by the statement that God generously provided for "every creature" and as a result every living being was satisfied. The phrase השביע כל נפש ("he satisfied every creature") alludes to Ps 145:16, which depicts God as providing sustenance to all his creatures: "You give it openhandedly, feeding (ומשביע) every creature (לכל חי) to its heart's content (רצון)." This psalm echoes Deut 8:10: ואכלת ושבעת וברכת את ה' אלהיך ("when you have eaten and have been satisfied you must bless the Lord your God"). The following line of 4Q370 hints at both: "Let all (כל) who do (עשה) my will (רצוני) eat and be satisfied." The noun רצון[54] in Ps 145:16 may be interpreted as referring to God's favor and goodwill.[55] Still, some ancient and modern com-

---

53 HALOT, 47.
54 For a general discussion of רצון in the Hebrew Bible, see TDOT, 13:625–29; cf. HALOT, 1282–83.
55 The Vulgate translates it as a blessing. Rashi interprets it as appeasement, reconciliation. Cf. also translations by M. Dahood, *Psalms III: 101–150* (AB; Garden City: Doubleday, 1970), 335; H.-J. Kraus, *Psalms 60–150* (CC; trans. H. C. Oswald; Minneapolis: Augsburg Fortress Press, 1993), 546.

mentators interpret it as referring to the desire of all living beings that is satisfied by God.[56] This second meaning of רצון is attested in the same psalm, v. 19: "He fulfills (עשה) the wishes (רצון) of those who fear Him." It appears that the author of 4Q370 also understood the word רצון in Ps 145:16 as a "desire," yet reworked it as referring to the will of God himself. Thus, in reworking the Torah injunction of Deut 8:10a ("Let all who do my will eat and be satisfied ... And let them bless my [hol]y name"), 4Q370 makes it clear that in order to enjoy God's generosity one should acknowledge it and be thankful for it, thus expressing submission to the divine will.

In his adaptation of Deut 8:10a, the author of 4Q370 changed the biblical direct speech into jussives and replaced the phrase יהוה אלהיך ("the Lord your God") with the expression שמ [עליו]֯ ("the name of [the Most Hig]h"). But by adapting the Deuteronomic formulation to the circumstances of the flood, 4Q370 projects the Torah directive of Deut 8:10a to pre-Sinaitic times. This seems to indicate that he viewed the command to bless God for the provision of food as an eternal principle, a position adopted by Jubilees in regard to other Torah precepts.[57] The importance assigned in the scroll to blessing the creator for sustenance may reflect the practice of reciting the benediction after the meal that was practiced already at the time of the author.[58] However, the allusion to Deut 8:10 functions in a specific way: it suggests that the antediluvians defied the Deuteronomic injunction and warning "Take care lest you forget the Lord your God ... beware lest your

---

56 Thus in the Peshitta, the Targum to Psalms and the medieval Jewish commentators Kimḥi and Ibn Ezra. Cf., e.g., L. C. Allen, *Psalms 101–50* (WBC; Waco: Nelson, 2002), 366.

57 Jubilees (2:18; 6:18–19; 7:1–3; 32:2–15) applies the same principle to several major Torah commandments, such as the Sabbath, tithes and festivals, all celebrated before the giving of the Torah.

58 *Jub.* 2:21 and *Jub.* 22:6 (adduced by Jassen, "The Reconstruction of 4Q370 1 i 2," 107) allude to Deut 8:10 and may also reflect this practice. Moreover, according to M. Weinfeld, "Grace after Meals in Qumran," *JBL* 111 (1992): 427–40 (428–29), the inclusion of Deut 8:5–10 in 4QDeut[j] (4Q37) V, 1–12 and 4QDeut[n] (4Q41) I, 1–8 may testify to the practice of blessing God after meals. He also suggested ("Grace," 427–40) that 4Q434 2 preserves a text of a grace after a meal in the house of a mourner (for a slightly different interpretation, see A. Shmidman, "A Note Regarding the Liturgical Function of DSS Document 4Q434," *Zutot* 5 [2008]: 15–22). Furthermore, Josephus, *J. W.* ii, 131, reports on the Essene practice of saying a blessing before, as well as after, the communal meal. In the rabbinic tradition, the obligation to recite a blessing after a meal is derived from Deut 8:10 (*t. Ber.* 6:1; *Mek., Bo* on Exod 13:3; *b. Ber.* 48b). This verse is included in the traditional Jewish benediction after meals. See L. Finkelstein, "The Birkat Ha-Mazon," *JQR* 19 (1928–1929): 211–62. For a discussion of the rabbinic sources, see M. Benovitz, "Blessings before the Meal in Second Temple Period and Tannaitic Literature," *Meghillot* 8–9 (2010): 81–96 [Hebrew]. Yet, Benovitz dismisses the evidence provided by 4Q370 and *Jubilees* (84 n. 8, 86 n. 11) and claims that the Second Temple sources refer only to the blessing before the meal.

heart grow haughty and you forget your Lord your God" (Deut 8:11–14; cf. Deut 32:15). Note that in reworking the Deuteronomistic directive, Neh 9:25–26 use the verb מרה: "They ate, they were filled, they grew fat; they luxuriated in your great bounty. Then, defying you, they rebelled (וימרו)." The use of this verb in 4Q370 is influenced by the formulation in Nehemiah; the author probably chose to use it in order to emphasize the rebellion of the antediluvians.[59]

The biblical account does not mention the actual judgment of the antediluvians, but only their punishment.[60] But 4Q370 1 i 3 notes specifically the judgment (וישפטם). The description of the punishment, namely the flood, follows the judgment: "And he thundered against them with [his] might. [And] all foundations of the ear[th] [t]rembled" (frg. 1 i 3–4). While God's thunder and the trembling of the earth are absent from the biblical flood story, both elements are common in biblical theophanies (e.g. 1 Sam 7:10; Ps 29:3; 68:9; Job 37:5).[61] They appear also in the descriptions of God's future war against all the nations (Isa 24:18–20; 29:6). Hence, it is not surprising that in the Second Temple writings God's thunder and the tottering of the earth appear frequently in the eschatological war descriptions (cf. *As. Mos.* 10.4; *Sib. Or.* 3.669, 675), such as that found in *Hodayot* (1QH^a XI, 35–36): "For God thunders with the powerful roar ... and the eternal foundations shall melt and quake."[62]

The phrase וי[נ]עו כל מוסדי א]רץ ("[And] all foundations of the ear[th] [sh]ook") is based on the formulation in Isa 24:18: וירעשו מוסדי ארץ ("and the foundations of the earth will shake"). The Isaianic passage depicts the upheavals of the future punishment.[63] Significantly, it combines this phrase with another description taken from the Genesis flood story (verse 18): "for the floodgates are opened from heaven" (כי ארבות ממרום נפתחו), which echoes Gen 7:11. So Isa 24:18 describes the future catastrophe in terms of the flood catastrophe, while 4Q370 interweaves

---

59 Although both Neh 9:25–26 and 4Q370 i 2 are based on Deut 8:10–14, it is precisely the use by 4Q370 of מרה, not found in Deut 8, but prominent in Neh 9:26 (וימרו וימרדו בך) that attests to the dependence of 4Q370 also on Nehemiah. Compare the use in Sir 16:7 (המורים; ms. A) of the same verb when speaking of the giants' offence.
60 As was noted also by García Martínez, "Interpretations of the Flood," 97. N. M. Sarna, *Genesis: The Traditional Hebrew Text with New JPS Translation and Commentary* (Philadelphia: JPS, 1989), 47, notes that the verb וירא, occurring in Gen 6:5, 12, implies investigating the facts and acting accordingly.
61 On theophany in the Hebrew Bible, see T. Hiebert, "Theophany in the OT," in *ABD*, 6:505–11.
62 כיא ירעם אל בהמון כוחו...ויתמוגגו וירעדו אושי עולם. The translation is that of C. Newsom in DJD XL, 156, with slight alterations.
63 Isaiah 24 is usually attributed to the apocalyptic chapters of this book (24–27). See O. Kaiser, *Isaiah 13–39* (trans. R. A. Wilson; OTL; London: SCM Press, 1973), 190–91; H. Wildberger, *Isaiah 13–27* (trans. by T. H. Trapp; CC; Minneapolis: Fortress Press, 1997), 445–46.

into its flood story elements of the eschatological war.[64] It is possible that the explicit reference to the judgment in the scroll is also related to the depiction of the flood in terms of the eschatological events, since the judgment of the wicked is an important element in the future Day of the Lord in the Hebrew Bible (Joel 4:12; Dan 7:26) and in writings from the Second Temple period. In the *Apocalypse of Weeks* (*1 En.* 93:4; 91:15), the two events are placed in clear parallelism. The analogy between the flood and the eschatological judgment and reward is also apparent in the future beatific life of the righteous, the depiction of which concludes the flood story in *1 En.* 10:16–11:2.[65] In *Jub.* 5:12, also, the postdiluvian conditions are outlined in terms of the eschatological new creation. The analogy between the antediluvians' dissolute conduct serves in the Gospels as a warning to those living in the last generation (Matt 24:37–39; Luke 17:26–27).[66] In 2 Pet 2:5–6, 9, the flood is used as an example of God's ability to save the righteous and to punish the wicked, which will be demonstrated on a larger scale in the future judgment. The analogous character of the flood and the final judgment is also highlighted in the rabbinic[67] and patristic sources.[68]

The author of 4Q370 introduces God's thunder and the trembling of the earth before the reworking of Gen 7:11b: "On that day all the fountains of the great deep burst apart and the floodgates of the sky broke open." The adapted text suggests that it is the thunder of God, directed against the wicked, that opens the floodgates of the sky, while the shaking of the earth causes the great deep to burst

---

[64] This tendency may also be reflected in other ancient sources that rework the biblical flood story. Thus, the description of the flood in *1 En.* 89:4, 8 introduces mist and darkness (cf. Joel 2:2; Zeph 1:15), while along with darkness and God's thunder *Sib. Or.* 1.217–220 depict the flood also with hurricanes (cf. Isa 29:6; Mic 1:3; Zech 9:14). Cf. P. Tiller, *A Commentary on the Animal Apocalypse of 1 Enoch* (EJL 4; Atlanta: Scholars Press, 1993), 267.

[65] For a discussion, see L. Hartman, "An Early Example of Jewish Exegesis: 1 Enoch 10:6–11:2," *Neot* 17 (1983): 16–26 (16–23); G. W. E. Nickelsburg, *1 Enoch* (Hermeneia; Minneapolis: Fortress Press, 2001), 226–28.

[66] See Schlosser, "Les jours de Noé," 15–25.

[67] See the flood of fire tradition in the Second Temple writings (Philo, *Moses* 2.263; Josephus, *Ant.*, i, 70–71) and in the rabbinic midrashim (e.g. *t. Ta'anit* 2:13; *Mek.* on Exod 18:1; *b. Zebaḥ.* 116a, See L. Ginzberg, "The Flood of Fire," *Ha-Goren* 8 (1912): 35–51 (Hebrew); idem, *Legends of the Jews* (2nd ed.; Philadelphia: The Jewish Publication Society, 2003), 1:139; W. J. van Bekkum, "The Lesson of the Flood: *Mabbul* in Rabbinic Tradition," in *Interpretations of the Flood* (ed. F. García Martínez and G. P. Luttikhuizen; Themes in Biblical Narrative 1; Leiden: Brill, 1998), 124–33 (127–29).

[68] J. Daniélou, *From Shadows to Reality: Studies in Biblical Typology of the Fathers* (trans. W. Hibberd; London, Burns & Oates, 1960), 69–112.

apart. Thus, the two elements that are foreign to the biblical flood narrative are interwoven into its rewritten version.

The adaptation of Gen 7:11b in lines 4–5 is also interesting from several points of view. First, this biblical passage is rewritten here twice:

Gen 7:11b   נבקעו כל מעינת תהום רבה   וארבת השמים נפתחו

4Q370 i 4–5   ומ[ֹיֹם נֹבקעו מתהמֹוֹת   כל ארבות השמים נפתחו
              ופצו כל תהמו[ת מ[ֹמֹים אֹדֹריםֹ וארבות השמים הֹ]רי[קו סטרֹ

The double reworking of Gen 7:11 could have been employed here to emphasize the tremendous volume of waters gathered to punish the wicked. Notably, the first reworking of this text employs the vocabulary of the verse itself, while the second introduces expressions taken from other biblical books. The phrase מים אדרים ("mighty waters") is borrowed from the Song of the Sea (Exod 15:10[69]). While in 4Q370 the waters of the flood are described using a locution taken from the Song of the Sea, an opposite case is found in Isa 51:10. There, the prophet employs the language of the flood story to allude to the Israelites crossing the Red Sea. In referring to the miraculous passage through the Red Sea, Isaiah employs the expression תהום רבה ("the great deep"[70]) used only in the flood account (Gen 7:11). In fact, both stories describe God's punishment of the wicked by water and the miraculous deliverance of the chosen ones. This notion of water being used as the divine instrument of punishment is further indicated by the use of the expression מֹים אֹדֹריםֹ (i, 4).

In sharp contrast to the wicked antediluvians punished in the flood, the scroll describes the salvation of the ark dwellers: "]his [son]s in the ar[k" (line 7), with whom God established his covenant mentioned in line 7: "s]o that he may remember the covenant," promising that "the multitude of waters [would not be ope]ned" (line 8). This promise is the last explicit reference to the biblical flood story in the extant text of the first column.

---

[69] במים אדירים ("in mighty waters"). See also Ps 93:4. It is possible that the replacement of the biblical expression תהום רבה with the word תהמות, occurring twice in the reworked version of this verse, is also influenced by the language of the Song of the Sea (תהמות appears in Exod 15:5, 8). On the other hand, it may also be related to the frequent use (14 times) of the plural of תהום in the Hebrew Bible (see Deut 8:7; Isa 63:13; Ps 106:9). Cf. a similar locution in Prov 3:20: בדעתו תהמות נבקעו ("By his knowledge the depths burst apart").

[70] The original meaning, with which the phrase תהום רבה may have been invested, has no bearing on this discussion. See C. Westermann, *Isaiah 40–66* (OTL; London, SGM Press, 1969), 240–43; J. Blenkinsopp, *Isaiah 40–55* (AB; New York: Doubleday, 2002), 330–33.

Use of Nonbiblical Traditions

In comparison with the relatively elaborate description of the flood itself (4Q370 i, 3–6), only few details pertaining to mankind's sin and revolt before the flood are noted (4Q370 i, 1–2). The biblical account also has meager information on this subject. However, extrabiblical literature of the Second Temple period abounds with data about these sins. The juxtaposition of the pericope on the sons of God who fathered giants by the women (Gen 6:1–4) with the reference to the corruption before the flood (Gen 6:5) generated many postbiblical elaborations on the precise nature of the antediluvian sins. They all view these sins as rebellion against God[71] since they break the cosmic laws laid down by him for the created world.[72] The very act of desiring the women and fathering offspring with them constitutes a transgression of the boundaries set by God between immortal angels and mortal humans, and entailed the defilement of the sinful angels. This is made clear by several Enochic writings assembled in *1 Enoch*.[73] The actual corruption, referred to in Gen 6:11, was generated according to some traditions by the giant offspring of that unlawful union, due to their pugnacious and bellicose character and actions. These giants are said to have plundered and killed humans before turning on each other.[74] A variant tradition attributes the corruption created on earth to the angels themselves, who unlawfully taught humans corrupting arts such as magic, cosmetics and weaponry.[75] However, other contemporary sources attribute the revolt against God to antediluvian humanity in general. But they neither specify the manner in which it was carried out nor its causes.[76]

---

71 See Barzilai, "Offhand Exegesis," 196–97.
72 See D. Dimant, "'The Fallen Angels' in the Dead Sea Scrolls and in the Apocryphal and Pseudepigraphic Books Related to Them," (Ph.D. diss., The Hebrew University, 1974), 55–56 (Hebrew).
73 See the *Book of Watchers* (= *1 En.* 6:2–6; 7:1; 15:4), *Animal Apocalypse* (= *1 En.* 86:2–3), and the *Appendix on Noah* (= *1 En.* 106:13–15). Cf. Dimant, "The Fallen Angels," 81–92. The *Genesis Apocryphon* version of the birth of Noah (1QGenApoc II, 3–12) also implies that the antediluvian sin was related to the unlawful contact between angels and women. See the comments of J. A. Fitzmyer, *The Genesis Apocryphon of Qumran Cave 1 (1Q20): A Commentary* (3rd ed.; BibOr 18/B; Rome: Pontifical Biblical Institute, 2004), 124–25.
74 Cf. the *Book of Watchers* (= *1 En.* 7; 15:11–12), the *Animal Apocalypse* (=*1 En.* 86:4–6).
75 Cf. the *Book of Watchers* (=*1 En.* 7:1; 8:1, 3); the *Book of Parables* (=*1 En.* 54:6).
76 One of the traditions adduced by *Jubilees* (5:2, 3) states that all living beings corrupted the course prescribed for them by the Creator. See the comments of M. Segal, *The Book of Jubilees: Rewritten Bible, Redaction, Ideology and Theology* (JSJSup117; Leiden: Brill, 2007), 135–37. The notion of rebellion underlies Josephus' description of the antediluvians as "no longer rendering to God His due honors" (*Ant.* i, 72; cf. i, 100).

Interestingly, 4Q370 does not mention any of the foregoing sins, but introduces instead a motif that is rare in this literature, that of mankind's ingratitude for the abundance of food lavished on it by divine grace.[77] The description is built on the contrast between the ingratitude and the abundance.[78] So, in 4Q370, the particular sin of the antediluvians is linked to the beneficial state prevailing before the flood. The theme is constructed chiefly of elements from Deut 8:10, Ps 145:16, and the Qumranic "Hymn to the Creator" (11QPs^a XXVI, 13). Yet, the combination as a whole is not biblical. This nonbiblical motif is not found in other contemporary compositions of the Second Temple period, with the exception of Philo's writings,[79] but it was popular in later rabbinic midrashim.[80] Thus, 4Q370 is the oldest known source to record this motif and is a witness to its early origin.[81]

Yet, having referred to the sin of ingratitude, 4Q370 1 i 2–3 attaches to it the general formulations of Gen 6:5: "'And they did evil in my eyes' ... And the Lord judged them according to [al]l their ways and according to the thoughts of the

---

[77] Newsom, "4QAdmonition Based on the Flood," 88–89, suggests that the description of abundance and that of frg. 1 as a whole is influenced by Ezek 36:19–33. However, the proposal is gratuitous since none of the locutions adduced to support this proposal is unique to Ezekiel 36, and the subject matter of the two texts is quite different.

[78] Newsom, "4QAdmonition Based on the Flood," 92; García Martínez, "Interpretations of the Flood," 97–98, interpret 4Q370 i 1–2 as a telescoped account of human history from the creation to the flood. This interpretation is based on the assumption that the description of prosperity in 4Q370 is based on the "Hymn to the Creator" (11QPs^a XXVI, 13). Since the parallel text appears in this hymn in the context of creation, it is assumed that the profusion of food in 4Q370 i 1 also describes an act of creation. However, 4Q370 clearly juxtaposes the abundance to the flood and therefore this link better fits the context.

[79] Philo, *Moses* 2.53; *QG* i 89, 96. Note also a tradition preserved in *Ps.-Clem. Homilies* 8:15 (4th century C. E.), according to which the giants born to the daughters of men (Gen 6:1–4) were nourished by God by means of manna rained down on them from above (referred to by Newsom, "4QAdmonition Based on the Flood," 93).

[80] Noted also by Newsom, "4QAdmonition Based on the Flood," 93. See *t. Soṭah* 3:6; *Gen. Rab.* 34, 1; *Num. Rab.* 9, 24 and the discussion by Ginzberg, *Legends of the Jews*, 1:138–41 (n. 15).

[81] The rabbinic exegesis of the antediluvians' prosperous life and rebellion is frequently derived from Job 21:7–15, which describe the well-being of the wicked yet their open defiance of God. See, for instance, *Mek. Beshalaḥ* on Exod 15:1; *Gen. Rab.* 36, 1; 38, 1; *Lev. Rab.* 4, 1. This exegetical tradition is expressed characteristically by the rabbinic saying (*Gen. Rab.* 26, 7): "If Job had come only for the purpose of spelling out the things that the generation of the flood did, that would have been enough." See J. Neusner, *Genesis Rabbah: The Judaic Commentary to the Book of Genesis: A New American Translation* (BJS 105; Atlanta: Scholars Press, 1985), 1:288; E. Slomovic, "The Book of Job and the Midrash on the Flood and Sodom-Gomorrah Narratives," *Proceedings of the Rabbinical Assembly* 61 (1979): 167–80 (171–74). However, 4Q370, at least the portion that has survived, does not associate the description of the prosperity and rebellion with the Job passage. Hence, the link to Job 21 in the rabbinic sources may be a later development.

[evil] inclination of their heart" (כ[כ]לדרכיהם וּבֹמחשבות יֹצֹר לבם הֹ [רע]; עשו הרע בעיני). So, according to 4Q370, the evil described in Genesis is specifically the ingratitude.

Nevertheless, the clause (ויאמרו אל במ[עלי]ליהם) suggests that the author may have been aware of other sinful activities not explicated here but elaborated on in other contemporary extrabiblical works. This possibility is conveyed by another significant addition in the list of creatures that perished in the flood. As shown above, it rewrites Gen 7:22–23 with one exception, the inclusion of "the str[ong ones]" (הג[בור]ים). Since humanity is labeled in this list as האדם, one may conclude that the group called הג[בור]ים does not refer to humans. Undoubtedly, it stands for the offspring of the "sons of God" and "daughters of men," named הַגִּבֹּרִים in Gen 6:4. The syntax of 4Q370 suggests that its author wanted to emphasize their death in the flood. For, instead of simply mentioning them in the list, he added a separate clause והג[בור]ים לוא נמלטו ("and the strong ones did not escape").

Based on the reference in Gen 6:4, Second Temple writings usually consider the "strong ones" (הגברים) to be giants.[82] Some of them make a distinction between humans and the giants and note that the giants died because of their internal strife (*1 En.* 10:9; *Jub.* 5:9); other sources speak of their destruction in the flood (CD II, 19–21; Wis 14:6–7; 3 Macc 2:4). The *Animal Apocalypse* (= *1 Enoch* 85–90) combines the two traditions and notes that the giants died first by sword and later those who survived were destroyed in the flood (*1 En.* 88:2; 89:6). Another tradition reports of giants who survived the flood.[83] It is apparently related to the biblical stories about giants that populated ancient Canaan (Num 13:33; Deut 1:28; 9:2; Josh 11:22; 14:12).

So, while using another motif to describe the antediluvian sin, the reference to the "strong ones" suggests that the author of 4Q370 was familiar with the tradition of their destruction in the flood. Indeed, he may have been familiar with several Enoch writings, copies of which were preserved in the Qumran library. However, 4Q370 does not separate mankind from the giants and includes both in the list of the flood victims. According to one opinion, the mention of the "strong ones" reflects the polemic in 4Q370 against the tradition that claimed that not all

---

82 CD II, 19; *1 En.* 7:2; *Jub.* 5:1; Bar 3:26; Josephus, *Ant.* i, 72.
83 Cf. *Pseudo-Eupolemus* in Eusebius, *Prep. Evang.* 9.17.2–3; 9.18.2. Cf. C. R. Holladay, *Fragments from Hellenistic Jewish Authors* (JBL Texts and Translations 20: Pseudepigrapha Series 10; Chico: Scholars Press, 1983), 1:157–58. See L. T. Stuckenbruck, "The Origins of Evil in Jewish Apocalyptic Tradition: The Interpretation of Genesis 6:1–4 in the Second and Third Centuries B. C. E.," in *The Fall of the Angels* (ed. L. T. Stuckenbruck and C. Auffarth; Themes in Biblical Narrative 6; Leiden: Brill, 2004), 93–98. The tradition is attested also in the rabbinic literature. Cf. *Tg. Yer. I* to Gen 14:13; Deut 3:11; *b. Zebaḥ.* 113b; *b. Niddah* 61a. See Barzilai, "Offhand Exegesis," 207–13.

the giants died in the flood.[84] While this is possible, the reference may be better understood in the context of 4Q370 using the traditional depiction of "strong ones" as rebels against God who trusted in their own might.[85] Thus, for instance, Sir 16:7 (MS A) depicts them as: נסיכי קדם המורים עולם בגבורתם (MS A; "the princes of old[86] rebelling against their yoke [המורים עולם] in their might").[87] The unique locution המורים עולם (note the use of מרה, as in 4Q370 i 2) may be read הַמּוֹרִים עוֹלָם ("rebelling against their yoke"),[88] while the yoke here refers to God's sovereignty.[89] Stating emphatically that the strong ones did not escape, 4Q370 makes it clear that the height and strength of these rebels did not prevent their death in the flood. As noted above, the phrase "and the str[ong one]s did not escape (נמלטו)" seems to refer to Jer 46:6 ("The swift cannot get away, the warrior [הגבור] cannot escape [ימלט]") or to Amos 2:14 ("Flight shall fail the swift, the strong shall find no strength, And the warrior [וגבור] shall not save [ימלט] his life"), declaring that even the strong ones will not escape God's punishment (cf. also Ps 33:16, 17). Given the similarities between the depiction of the flood in 4Q370 and the descriptions of the eschatological war in the Hebrew Bible, it is not coincidental that these verses appear in the context of God's war against the nations (Jer 46:10)[90] and his future punishment of the wicked ones among his own people (Amos 2:16).[91]

---

84 Barzilai, "Offhand Exegesis," 207–13.
85 CD II, 20–21; Wis 14:6; 3 Macc 2:4.
86 The Greek and Latin Bible versions render נסיכי קדם as "giants."
87 Translation by P. W. Skehan, A. A. Di Lella, *The Wisdom of Ben Sira* (AB; New York: Doubleday, 1987), 268, adapted to the reading proposed here. MS B reads here: המורדים בגבורתם ("rebelling in their might").
88 Thus Dimant, "The Fallen Angels," 141–44. Cf. the expression פרק עול ("to throw off the yoke") attested in the rabbinic literature (see Jastrow, *Dictionary*, 1050). Dimant estimated that the reading of MS B: המורדים בגבורתם ("rebelling in their might") is secondary since it replaces the more difficult reading of MS A. But Kister has proposed to read the text of MS B as הַמּוּרָדִים ("those thrown down"). Cf. M. Kister, "A Contribution to the Interpretation of Ben Sirah," *Tarbiz* 59 (1990): 327–28 [Hebrew]. Dimant's reading of MS A avoids emending the text, e.g. מעולם, proposed by Lévi and Segal. I. Lévi, *L'Ecclésiastique* (Paris: E. Leroux, 1898), 115. M.-Z. Segal, *The Complete Book of Ben-Sirah* (Jerusalem: Mosad Bialik, 1997), 89 [Hebrew].
89 Note the similar formulation of the antediluvians' offence in *2 En.* 34:1.
90 On Jer 46:10 and its setting, see R. P. Carroll, *Jeremiah* (OTL; London: SCM Press, 1986), 759–65 (763); W. L. Holladay, *Jeremiah 2* (Hermeneia; Minneapolis: Fortress Press, 1989), 318, 320.
91 On Amos 2:14 and its context, see J. L. Mays, *Amos* (OTL; London: SCM Press, 1969), 43–45, 54; S. M. Paul, *Amos* (Hermeneia; Minneapolis: Fortress Press, 1991), 76, 95–97.

The Admonition (col. ii)

The second column does not refer to the flood story at all. It preserves a fragment of an admonition and accordingly it draws on different biblical passages. While lines 1–6 are phrased in the third person (singular to God, plural to humans), lines 7–9 contain admonitory remarks formulated in the second person plural. Although there are differences in style and content between the two columns, the textual evidence shows that col. ii follows col. i For the difficult combination מעון ידרשו at the beginning of line 1 of the second column, it appears to continue a sentence from col. i, now lost, rather than open a new composition.[92] Also, there is a certain affinity between the two columns. The way in which the Genesis story is reworked, and how the additions are inserted into it, with their emphasis on sin and punishment, convey a didactic purpose.[93] In fact, the second column pursues the similar theme of sin and justification, and admonishes against rebellion against God, taking up the Hebrew verb מרה (אל תֹּמרו [col. ii 9]) that was used for the antediluvians in the first column (ויאמרו [col. i 2]).[94] Perhaps the admonition in col. ii elaborates on the lessons gained from the reworked flood account in col. i and the calamitous consequences of the rebellion against God. Perhaps the Flood generation is introduced as a prototype of the wicked in the first column, and the way of the righteous is indicated in the second column.[95]

4Q370 presents an interesting case of literary affinity between two nonsectarian Qumran texts that adapt biblical materials. This sort of literary connection is found in both columns. Line 1 of col. i presents a formulation similar to the "Hymn to the Creator," found in the Psalms scroll from cave 11 (11QPsª XXVI, 13).

---

92 In several Qumran biblical scrolls, different biblical books are copied in the same column, with several vacant lines separating them (Tov, *Scribal Practices*, 165–66), but this is obviously not the case in 4Q370.
93 Thus also Newsom, "4QAdmonition Based on the Flood," 86–89; Barzilai, "Offhand Exegesis," 204–07; M. Bernstein, "Contours of Genesis: Interpretation at Qumran: Contents, Context, and Nomenclature," in *Studies in Ancient Midrash* (ed. J. L. Kugel; Cambridge: Harvard University Press, 2001), 57–85 (75–76); idem, "The Contribution of the Qumran Discoveries to the History of Early Biblical Interpretation," in *The Idea of Biblical Interpretation* (ed. H. Najman and J. H. Newman; JSJSup 83; Leiden: Brill, 2004), 215–38 (230–31).
94 Also, one may observe that while the first column reworks Genesis 6–9, the second column alludes to the exodus story (line 7). Although this is an allusion, and not a detailed reworking, it may point to the same didactic method of using past events for didactic purposes.
95 Thus Dimant, "The Flood as a Preamble," 120.

Use of Nonbiblical Traditions

The admonition in col. ii (4Q370 ii 5, 7–9) displays affinity with a longer passage of the didactic address found in 4Q185, as shown in the following table.[96]

4Q185 1–2 i 9–ii 3	4Q370 ii 5–8
	i
9 ואתֿםֿ בני אדם א[י]ן כח [כי הֿנֿה	1 מעון ידרשו מ[
10 כחֿצֿיר יצמח וֿפֿאֿרֿתֿו יפרח כציץ חסדו נשב[ה בו] רוחו	2 יצדיק יהוה ש[
11 ויבש עֿגזו וציצו תשא רֿוח עד אֿיקום לעֿמֿ[ד]ו מלֿ[בֿד	3 ויטהרם מעונם [
12 [ו]יבקשוהו ולא ימצאהו ואֿין מקוה vacat ולא ימצא בֿי רוח	4 רעתם בדעתם בי[ן
13 והוא כצל ימיֿו עֿל הארֿ[ץֿ] ועתה שמעו נא עמי והשכילו	5 יצמחֿו וכצל ימיהם עֿ[ל הארץ
	6 ועד עולם הוא ירחם [ ]
14 לי פתאים ׄׄשֿיֿׅׄׄוֿתֿומֿו מן [גֿ]בורת אלהיֿנֿוֿ וזכרו נֿפֿלֿאֿׄיֿםֿ עשה	7 גבורת יהוה זכרו נפלֿ[אות
15 במצרים ומופתיֿו בֿ[ארץ חם] וֿיֿערץ לבבכֿםֿ מֿפֿנֿי פחדֿוֿ	8 מפני פחדו ותשמח נפֿ[שכם
	ii
1 ועשו רֿצֿ[ו]נו נֿ[פשכם כחסדיו הטבים חקרו לכם דרך	9
2 לחיים ומסלֿהֿ[ ]סשארית לבניכם אחריכם ולמה תתנו	
3 [לבב]כֿם לשח[ת מ]שֿפט שמעוני בני וֿאֿל תמרו דברי יהוה	משניכם אל תמרו דברֿ[י יהוה

A comparison of the two texts reveals a close similarity between the language of 4Q370 ii 5, 7–9 and that of 4Q185 1–2 i 13–ii 3. Only lines 1–4 of 4Q370 ii have no parallel in 4Q185. But in spite of their similarity there are also differences between the two texts. Thus, for instance, the comparison of human life to that of a plant is

---

96 The text is quoted from the re-edition of Lichtenberger, "Der Weisheitstext 4Q185." On the contents and genre of 4Q185, see T. H. Tobin, "4Q185 and Jewish Wisdom Literature," in *Of Scribes and Scrolls* (ed. H. W. Attridge et al.; Lanham: University Press of America, 1990), 145–52; D. J. Harrington, *Wisdom Texts from Qumran* (London: Routledge, 1996), 36–39; S. White Crawford, "Lady Wisdom and Dame Folly at Qumran," in *Wisdom and Psalms* (ed. A. Brenner and C. R. Fontaine; FCB 2; Sheffield: Sheffield Academic Press, 1998), 205–17 (213–15); Goff, *Discerning Wisdom*, 122–45.

more developed in 4Q185 (lines 9–13) than in 4Q370 (line 5). Also, the admonition found in 4Q185 1–2 ii 15–iii 3 is longer than that appearing in 4Q370 ii 8–9. On the other hand, the phrase ועד עולם הוא ירחם, occurring in 4Q370 ii 6, has no parallel in 4Q185. Hence, the two texts do not present an identical reworking of the same biblical texts. Still, it is not possible to establish whether they depend on each other or whether both scrolls are based on a source that has been lost.[97]

---

97 Newsom, "4QAdmonition Based on the Flood," 89–90, avoids defining the relation between the two scrolls, as does Tobin, "4Q185 and Jewish Wisdom," 149. See Goff, *Discerning Wisdom*, 143; D. J. Verseput, "Wisdom, 4Q185, and the Epistle of James," *JBL* 117 (1998): 691–707 (698, n. 24).

4Q577 (Text Mentioning the Flood)

Literature

É. Puech, "577. 4QTexte mentionnant le Déluge," in idem, *Qumrân Grotte 4, XVIII. Textes Hébreux* (DJD XXV; Oxford: Clarendon Press, 1998), 195–203; T. Legrand, "Interprétations sur le thème du Déluge," in *La Bibliothèque de Qumrân 1: Torah: Genèse* (ed. K. Berthellot, T. Legrand, and A. Paul; Paris: Cerf, 2008), 291–97.

The Manuscript

One of the fragments assigned to 4Q577 mentions the flood, which thus led to its inclusion in the title of the entire text.[1] The official edition of 4Q577 contains eight fragments written in an early Hasmonean script. The leather on which frg. 8 was inscribed differs from that of the rest of the fragments.[2] But since its script resembles that of frgs. 1–7, Puech assigned it to another sheet of the present scroll.

Text and Comments

Frg. 1

] ∘∘[	1
]ובארץ[	2
]חקוקים[	3
]ד̊ ∘[ ]∘[	4

Notes to Readings

L. 1]ד̊. Puech read the last letter of this line as a final *mem*, but noted that it may also be read as a *dalet*, as preferred here. An examination of PAM 41677 confirms this reading as the vertical stroke of this letter reaches beyond its upper horizon-

---

[1] The first editor, Émile Puech, therefore entitled it "4QTexte mentionnant le Déluge." Initially, this manuscript belonged to Jean Starcky's lot and he did the preliminary work on it. The final stage of his work is reflected in PAM 43605. Puech's edition was utilized by Thierry Legrand, who published it with a French translation accompanied by a brief commentary. Cf. Legrand, "Interprétations sur le thème du Déluge."

[2] One may add that the space between lines 2–3 in this fragment is larger than usual in 4Q577.

tal stroke, as is usually the case with *dalet* in 4Q577 (cf. *dalet* in]עדני[in frg. 8 1) rather than *mem* (compare the final *mem* in חקוקים in line 3).

Translation
1.].. [
2.]and in the land [
3.]inscribed [
4.].[ ]. .[

Comments
L. 1]ובארץ[. The editor suggests that the scroll might have read ובארץ [בשמים; for this expression, see Deut 3:24; Joel 3:3; Ps 113:6.

L. 3]חקוקים[. חקוקים is a masc. pl. *Qal* passive participle of חקק ("to carve, to inscribe, to decree").[3] This verb is used in several Qumran scrolls to express the idea that the course of history was predetermined by God (1QS X, 1; 1QH[a] IX, 26; 1QpHab VII, 13, 14; 4Q266 2 i 3 [= 4Q268 1 5]; 4Q468dd 1–2).[4] See Comments on frg. 4 3.

Frg. 2

[ו̇כתב̇] 1
[ר כיי̇ו̇ל] 2
[ל̇עשות מש̇]פט 3

Notes on Readings
L. 1]ו̇כתב̇[. *Waw* and *yod* in 4Q577 are sometimes indistinguishable. Thus, one may also read here, with Puech,]י̇כתב̇[.

L. 2]ר כיי̇ו̇ל[. The DJD edition reads]ר כי יו̇י[. However, the space between כי and the second *yod* is equal to the interval between two adjacent letters. The diagonal vertical stroke at the end of the line is that of a *lamed*, as seen in PAM 41677 (cf. *lamed* in]כבול[in frg. 4 6), and also noted by Puech.

---

[3] *HALOT*, 347.
[4] *DCH*, 1:303–04.

Translation
1.]and he wrote[
2.]. since ...[
3.]to do jus[tice

Comments

L. 1]וֹכתֹבֹ[. The surviving letters may be read either as the noun כְּתָב or as a *Qal qatal* of כתב with a *waw* conjunctive (thus translated). The writing mentioned here is perhaps related to the term חקק in frgs. 1 and 4.

L. 2 כיוֹלֹ[. The scribe attached the conjunction כי to the following word, which seems to be a verbal form of ילד : יולד(ו) (cf. Gen 6:1), יוֹליד(ו) (cf. Gen 5:28), or יֻלַּד(ו).[5] If the fragment deals with the flood story, there are two verses that employ the verb ילד in the biblical flood story, the birth of Noah (Gen 5:28) and the birth of the Nephilim (Gen 6:1, 4).

L. 3 לעשות משֹׁפֹּט]. This is a common biblical locution (e.g. Deut 10:18; 1 Kgs 3:28, 8:59) and here it may refer either to God (cf. Gen 18:25; CD I, 2 [4Q266 2 i 7]; 4Q268 1 10) or to humans (cf. Mic 6:8; 4Q372 1 23). If the fragment deals with the flood, it is perhaps concerned with the judgment on the antediluvians (compare the use of שפט in 4Q370 i 3).

Frg. 3

1 [וֹא יקבלֹ]
2]ᵒᵒ[

Translation
1.].. will receive[
2.   ]..[

---

[5] On attaching כי to the following word, see Qimron, "A Grammar of the Hebrew Language," 123.

Comments

L. 1 ‏]וֹא יקבל‏[. ‏יקבל‏ is a 3rd sg. (or pl. if restored as ‏ו]יקבל‏) *Pi'el yiqtol* of ‏קבל‏. This verb does not appear in Genesis 6–9, so its connection to the flood account is difficult to establish. Puech restored: ‏ל]וֹא יקבל[‏. Alternatively, it may be restored ‏ה]וֹא יקבל[‏.

Frg. 4

1 ‏[מבול]‏
2 ‏[אדו]נ֗י אשר מלטם‏
3 ‏כו]ל אשר היה חק[וק‏
4 ‏א[ת הכול א]‏
5 ‏[ה ויצו]‏
6 ‏[כ]כ֗ול א[שר‏

Translation

1.]flood [
2. the Lor]d who rescued them [
3. al]l that was decr[eed
4.] all .[
5.]. and he commanded [
6.]according to all th[at

Comments

L. 1 ‏מבול[‏. The noun ‏מבול‏ confirms that the fragment deals with the flood story.

L. 2 ‏מלטם.אדו[נ֗י אשר מלטם‏ is a 3rd masc. sg. *Pi'el qatal* of ‏מלט‏ ("to rescue"),[6] ‏מִלְּטָם‏. The 3rd masc. pl. pronominal suffix apparently refers to the ark dwellers who were saved from the flood. If Puech's reading and restoration of ‏אדו[נ֗י‏ are correct, the language of the fragment may point to Ps 41:2, which speaks of the divine rescue of the wretched from harm. If correct, 4Q577 appears to have replaced the Tetragrammaton with ‏אדוני‏, a practice attested also in other Qumran scrolls.[7]

---

6 *HALOT*, 589.
7 See 1QSb II, 22; III, 1 (cf. Num 6:25, 26); 1QHª XVI [VII], 28 (cf. Exod 15:11); 4Q225 2 i 3, 5 (cf. Gen 15:2, 4); 4Q434 1 i 1; 4Q437 1 1 (cf. Ps 103:1, 2, 22; 104:1, 35). For a discussion, see M. Rösel, *Adonaj – Warum Gott "Herr" genannt wird* (Tübingen: Mohr Siebeck, 2000), 212–15.

L. 3 כו[ל אשר היה חק]וק. Puech restores the possible חק]וק, a masc. sg. *Qal* passive participle of חקק. In Qumran sectarian writings, this verb designates the deterministic view of history (see also frg. 1). The notion that the events of history have been inscribed on the heavenly tablets from the very beginning is entertained by both Qumranic and non-Qumranic writings.[8]

L. 5 ויצו. This 3rd masc. sg. *wayiqtol* perhaps applies to Noah, echoing the biblical references to divine commands given to this patriarch (Gen 6:22; 7:5, 9, 16).

L. 6]בֿכול א[שר. This is perhaps related to Gen 6:5, 22, which note that Noah did as he was commanded. See also frg. 7 i 5.

Frg. 5

]הֿ∘[	1
]וֹנֿשאה[	2
]אֿהֿ∘[	3

Notes on Readings

L. 1]הבי∘[. Puech read and restored]הבי[ל. However, he did not note the undecipherable trace of ink visible at the beginning of the line in PAM 43605.

L. 2]וֹנֿשאה[. The editor read here]שאה ∘[ם but an oblique stroke descending to the left is visible at the beginning of the line in PAM 43605; its shape and position identify it as the hook of a *waw* or *yod*. Next to it, the vertical and base strokes of a medial *nun* are clearly identifiable on this photograph.

Translation
1.]....[
2.]and it was carried[
3.]...[

---

[8] For Qumran, see 4Q177 1–4 12; 4Q180 1 3 (discussed by Dimant, "Pesher on Periods," 388). For non-Qumranic works, see *1 En.* 93:2, 103:2–4, 106:19–107:1 (also 81:1–2, 108:7); *Jub.* 5:13–15, 16:9, 23:32, 24:33 (also 32:21–22). For חקק as "to engrave," see Isa 22:16; Ezek 4:1, 23:14. Cf. F. García Martínez, "The Heavenly Tablets in the Book of Jubilees," in *Studies in the Book of Jubilees* (ed. M. Albani, J. Frey, and A. Lange; TSAJ 65; Tübingen: Mohr Siebeck, 1997), 243–60 (247–50); C. Werman, "The Torah and the *Te'udah* on the Tablets," *Tarbiz* 68 (1999): 473–92 (Hebrew).

Comments

L. 1]‏הבי‏∘[. The surviving letters may be interpreted as a verbal form of ‏בוא‏ in *Hif'il* ("to bring"). In the biblical flood account, this verb is applied to both bringing the flood (Gen 6:17) and bringing the animals into the ark (Gen 6:19) (as proposed by Puech).

L. 2]‏וֹנִֹשֹׂאה‏[. Given the context, the word should be read here as ‏וְנִשְׂאָה‏, a 3rd fem. sg. *Nif'al qatal* of ‏נשא‏ ("was carried"). In Gen 7:17, the verb ‏נשא‏ appears with the feminine noun ‏התבה‏ ("the ark") as its object, which also may be the case here.

Frg. 6

```
[ל̊]                    1
[ ]להׄ[שחית           2
[ש̊ לברי̊ת             3
[ב̊]                    4a
```

Notes on Readings

L. 2] ‏לה[שחית‏. A dark dot is visible at some distance from the fourth letter *taw* on the fragment and in PAM 43605. Puech read it as a *waw*,]‏שחיתו‏[. However, if it is indeed a trace of ink, it seems to belong to the next word, but no definite reading may be offered.

L. 3 ‏ש̊[לברי̊ת‏. It is proposed to read the convex vertical stroke that is visible at the beginning of the line as the left vertical stroke of a *shin*. Puech read it as a left vertical stroke of *ḥet* (cf. *ḥet* in ‏חק[וק‏ in frg. 4 3) but neither the fragment nor its photograph (PAM 43605) display the upper horizontal stroke of a *ḥet*.

L. 4a]‏ב̊[. According to Puech, this letter was a supralinear addition.

Translation

1.   ].[
2.   to cor]rupt [
3.   ]. to a covenan[t

Comments

L. 2 ‏לה[שחית‏. The surviving letters are restored as the *Hif'il* infinitive of ‏שחת‏, which occurs in Gen 6:11, 12, and 13 with reference to the sins of antediluvian humanity. However, given the mention of the covenant in the next line, the term may allude to God's promise never to send a flood again. The biblical formulation of this promise in Gen 9:11, 15 employs the same verb. A *Hifʿil* of שחת occurs also in frg. 7 2.

L. 3 שׁ֗ לבריֿ]ת. The word לברי]ת may refer to the covenant with Noah (Gen 17:7, 13, 19).

Frg. 7 i–ii

	ii		i	
			מאד[ם ועדֿ]	] 1
			[השחיתו	] 2
	] ○		[לוֿ וכול	] 3
			ב]ני האדם	] 4
			לע[שׁ֗וֿת ככול	] 5
			[○ת̊]	] 6

Notes on Readings
The trace of ink to the left of the phrase [לוֿ וכול in line 3 (PAM 41438, 43605), which was not noted by the editor, belongs to the following unpreserved column. However, the fragment preserves an intercolumnal margin.

L. 3 לוֿ[. The editor read לה̊[. A stroke descending obliquely to the left, resembling the hook-shaped top of a *waw* or *yod* rather than the upper horizontal stroke of *he* as suggested by Puech, is seen next to *lamed* in PAM 41438.

A small scrap of leather has been joined to the beginning of this line. Its placement there is highly doubtful for the shape of its edges does not fit with that of the main fragment. Therefore it was placed lying on its left side (see PAM 41438; 43605). Traces of several letters are still visible on it:

]○[1
]ת̊○[2

L. 5 לע[שׁ֗וֿת. Puech read]שחית but PAM 41438 contains nothing between *shin* and *waw* (Puech reads a *yod*).

ככול. The editor read כול, but two medial *kaf* letters are visible in PAM 43605.

L. 6]ת̊○[. The DJD edition has]ת̊א̊[. A tiny vertical stroke is visible before *taw* in PAM 43605, but it cannot be identified as a specific letter.

Another small scrap of leather containing two letters has been placed at the bottom right corner of the fragment. In PAM 43605 it appears lying on its left side. Puech suggests that it complements line 5. However, this is doubtful as the shape of its edge does not fit that of frg. 7. The letters]שׁב֯[can be read on this little fragment.

Translation
1. [from a m]an to[
2. [   ](they) corrupted
3. [   ]to him and all
4. [hum]an beings
5. [   ]to do according to all
6. [   ]..[

Comments

L. 1]מאד֯[ם וע. Given the context, the locution appears to rework Gen 6:7, in which God promises never again to annihilate all living creatures, "men together with beasts, creeping things, and birds of the sky" (מאדם עד בהמה עד רמש ועד עוף השמים). This understanding and restoration is better suited to the sequence and allusions in the fragment than Puech's restoration לעול[ם ועד].

L. 2]השחיתו[. This is perhaps a reference to Gen 6:12. A *Hif'il* of שחת appears also in frg. 6 2.

L. 4 ב[ני האדם. This collocation, בני אדם/האדם, does not appear in the flood narrative (Genesis 6–9), which employs only אדם (Gen 6:5–7). The expression appears only once in Genesis, in the story of the tower of Babel (Gen 11:5).

L. 5 לע[שׂ֯ות ככול. The fragment may allude to Gen 6:22: "Noah did so; just as God commanded him, so he did" (ויעש נח ככל אשר צוה; cf. also Gen 7:5).

Frg. 8

1 [עדנ֯י]
2 [לפנ]יכה ונשמע֯
3 [ה אשר֯ ○ה]

Notes on Readings

L. 2 לפנ]יכה. A close examination of the fragment and its photographs (PAM 41438, 43605) indicates that *yod* is the first extant letter in this line.

Translation

1.   ] the bliss of[
2.   befor]e you and we will obey[
3.   ].. which[

Comments

L. 1]עֲדָנִ֯[. This word may be read as a plural form of the noun עֵדֶן ("bliss"; Jer 51:34; Ps 36:9),[9] constituting the first governing noun (*nomen regens*) of a construct pair, in which the second governed noun (*nomen rectum*) has not been preserved. The noun appears in several Qumran texts with the sense of "luxury, delight" (e.g. 1QS X, 15; 1QH^a V, 34; XVIII, 26).[10] If the scroll indeed read]עדנו[, it could be parsed as a *Hitpaʿel* form of the verb עדן, denoting "to live a life of luxury" (Neh 9:25),[11] and restored as either]עדנו(הת)[or]עדנו(ו)ית[.[12]

L. 2]לפנ[יכה ונשמע. The attached 2nd masc. sg. pronominal suffix, -כה, suggests that this line contains a second person address. The verb ונשמע, standing in 1st pl. *Qal yiqtol* of שמע ("to hear, to obey"), indicates that the addressee is God, while the identity of the speakers is unclear. In any case, one may restore here in line with a recurring biblical phrase: לפנ]יכה ונשמע[בקולכה (cf. נשמע בקול ה' אלהינו [Jer 42:6]).

Discussion

The name assigned to the present scroll, "Text Mentioning the Flood," is not an accurate description of its extant contents. Perhaps it should be entitled "Text about the Flood," since the text does not merely "mention" the flood (frg. 4), as the readings and reconstructions proposed above demonstrate, but deals with

---

9 *HALOT*, 792.
10 Cf. *DCH*, 6:283.
11 *HALOT*, 792.
12 For this verb with the sense "be luxurious, luxuriate," see *DCH*, 6:282.

various aspects of this story, such as the destruction of humanity (frg. 7 2), Noah's obedience (frgs. 4 4–6; 7 5), the flood itself (frg. 5 2), the rescue of the ark dwellers (frg. 4 2), and the covenant with Noah (frg. 6 3). In addition to the phraseology borrowed from Genesis 6–9, the scroll also employs terms not found in the biblical account. Of particular interest is the use of the verb חקק since in Qumran sectarian writings it belongs to the terminology used for describing the predetermined character of history. So perhaps the author of 4Q577 held the view that the flood formed a part of the divine predetermined plan.

One of the fragments (frg. 8) seems to contain an address to God. If this fragment indeed belongs to 4Q577 (see The Manuscript, above), this prayer might have been attributed to one of characters of the flood story, for example, Noah.

4Q422 (Paraphrase of Genesis and Exodus)

Literature

T. Elgvin and E. Tov, "422. 4QParaphrase of Genesis and Exodus," in *Qumran Cave 4. Parabiblical Texts, Part 1* (ed. H. Attridge et. al.; DJD XIII; Oxford: Clarendon Press, 1994), 417–41; T. Elgvin, "Admonition Texts from Qumran Cave 4," in *Methods of Investigation of the Dead Sea Scrolls and the Khirbet Qumran Site: Present Realities and Future Perspectives* (ed. M. O. Wise et al.; Annals of the New York Academy of Sciences 722; New York: New York Academy of Sciences, 1994), 179–96 (186–88); idem, "The Genesis Section of 4Q422 (4QParaGenExod)," *DSD* 1 (1994): 180–96; idem, "How to Reconstruct a Fragmented Scroll: The Puzzle of 4Q422," in *Northern Lights on the Dead Sea Scrolls* (ed. A. K. Petersen et al.; STDJ 80; Leiden: Brill, 2009), 223–36; E. Tov, "Biblical Texts as Reworked in Some Qumran Manuscripts with Special Attention to 4QRP and 4QParaGen-Exod," in *The Community of the Renewed Covenant: The Notre Dame Symposium on the Dead Sea Scrolls* (ed. E. Ulrich and J. VanderKam; Christianity and Judaism in Antiquity 10; Notre Dame: University of Notre Dame Press, 1994), 111–34 (120–22); idem, "The Exodus Section of 4Q422," *DSD* 1 (1994): 197–209; idem, "A Paraphrase of Exodus: 4Q422," in *Solving Riddles and Untying Knots: Biblical, Epigraphic, and Semitic Studies in Honor of Jonas C. Greenfield* (ed. Z. Zevit, M. Sokoloff, and S. Gitin; Winona Lake: Eisenbrauns, 1995), 351–63; T. Elgvin and E. Tov, "4Q422 (4QParaphrase of Genesis and Exodus)," *DSSR* 3:570–72; A. Feldman, "The Flood Story according to 4Q422," in *The Dynamics of Exegesis and Language at Qumran* (ed. D. Dimant and R. Kratz; FAT 2/35; Tübingen: Mohr Siebeck, 2009), 57–77; idem, "The Reworking of the Exodus Story in 4Q422," *Meghillot* 8–9 (2010): 373–91 (Hebrew).

The Manuscript

The extant fragments of the scroll 4Q422 rework the biblical stories of creation, Adam's sin, the flood, and the exodus. Entrusted to John Strugnell for publication,[1] it was finally edited by Torleif Elgvin and Emanuel Tov as "Paraphrase of Genesis and Exodus."[2]

---

[1] Strugnell's preliminary readings are embedded in Brown, *Preliminary Concordance*. Prior to its final publication, this scroll was known as "Traditions on the Fathers" (Wacholder-Abegg, *Preliminary Edition*, 2:245).

[2] Elgvin-Tov, "Paraphrase." Elgvin was responsible for the fragments concerned with the book of Genesis, while Tov edited the fragments reworking the book of Exodus. The fragments were initially published by Elgvin, "Admonition Texts," 186–88; idem, "The Genesis Section of 4Q422"; and Tov, "Biblical Texts as Reworked in Some Qumran Manuscripts," 120–22; idem, "The Exodus Section of 4Q422"; idem, "A Paraphrase of Exodus: 4Q422." Elgvin also dealt with some aspects of this scroll in idem, "How to Reconstruct a Fragmented Scroll."

Since its publication, this scroll has been studied by several scholars. Moshe Bernstein, in his review of DJD XIII, proposed several new readings.[3] Some of these were incorporated in the revised edition of 4Q422 i–ii published subsequently by Elgvin.[4] The reworking of the flood story in 4Q422 ii was explored by Florentino García Martínez,[5] Moshe Bernstein,[6] and Dorothy Peters.[7] The literary genre of 4Q422 and its relation to other Qumran writings were discussed by George Nickelsburg,[8] Esther Chazon,[9] Moshe Bernstein,[10] and Eibert Tigchelaar.[11]

The DJD edition of 4Q422 contains thirty-three fragments.[12] Eleven of them (frgs. 1–6, 10a–e) were placed into three consequent columns (i–iii).[13] The approx-

---

[3] M. J. Bernstein, "Review of *Qumran Cave 4, VII: Parabiblical Texts, Part 1*, by Attridge, H., et al. Discoveries in the Judaean Desert XIII. Oxford: Clarendon Press, 1994," *DSD* 4 (1997): 102–11 (111).
[4] *DSSR* 3:570–72. The French edition of 4Q422 by J.-C. Dubs follows the DJD edition closely. See idem, "Paraphrase de Genèse-Exode (4QParaphrase of Gen and Exod)," in *La Bibliothèque de Qumrân 2: Torah: Exode-Lévitique-Nombres* (ed. K. Berthelot and T. Legrand; Paris: Cerf, 2008), 73–79.
[5] F. García Martínez, "Interpretations of the Flood in the Dead Sea Scrolls," in *Interpretations of the Flood* (ed. F. García Martínez and G. P. Luttikhuisen; Themes in Biblical Narrative 1; Leiden: Brill, 1998), 86–108 (93).
[6] M. J. Bernstein, "Noah and the Flood at Qumran," in *The Provo International Conference on the Dead Sea Scrolls: Technological Innovations, New Texts, and Reformulated Issues* (ed. E. Ulrich and D. W. Parry; STDJ 30; Leiden: Brill, 1999), 199–231 (211–13).
[7] D. M. Peters, *Noah Traditions in the Dead Sea Scrolls: Conversations and Controversies of Antiquity* (SBLEJL 26; Atlanta: SBL, 2008), 139–44.
[8] G. W. E. Nickelsburg, "Dealing with Challenges and Limitations. A Response," *DSD* 1 (1994): 229–37 (230–33).
[9] E. G. Chazon, "The Creation and Fall of Adam in the Dead Sea Scrolls," in *The Book of Genesis in Jewish and Oriental Christian Interpretation* (ed. J. Frishman and L. Van Rompay; Traditio Exegetica Graeca 5; Leuven: Peeters, 1997), 13–24 (16–18, 21–23).
[10] M. J. Bernstein, "Pentateuchal Interpretation at Qumran," in *The Dead Sea Scrolls after Fifty Years* (ed. P. W. Flint and J. C. VanderKam; Leiden: Brill, 1998), 1:128–59 (139); idem, "Contours of Genesis: Interpretation at Qumran: Contents, Context, and Nomenclature," in *Studies in Ancient Midrash* (ed. J. L. Kugel; Cambridge: Harvard University Press, 2001), 37–85 (74–75); idem, "The Contribution of the Qumran Discoveries to the History of Early Biblical Interpretation," in *The Idea of Biblical Interpretation* (ed. H. Najman and J. H. Newman; JSJSup 83; Leiden: Brill, 2004), 215–38 (229–30).
[11] E. J. C. Tigchelaar, "Eden and Paradise: The Garden Motif in Some Early Jewish Texts (1 Enoch and Other Texts Found at Qumran)," in *Paradise Interpreted* (ed. G. P. Luttikhuizen; Themes in Biblical Narrative 2; Leiden: Brill, 1999), 37–62 (53–54).
[12] The DJD edition counts thirty-four fragments. However, the small fragment that was joined to frg. 10e (= col. iii, 8–9) was edited both as part of col. iii and as Unidentified Fragment P.
[13] The revised edition of col. ii (Elgvin, *DSSR*, 3:571) includes also frg. 7. This fragment was joined to col. ii also in the present edition. Thus, the three columns, as presented here, contain twelve fragments.

imate line length in col. iii is 16 cm (approximately eighty-five letter-spaces). All three columns were probably written on the same sheet of leather. The stitches in the left margin of col. iii indicate that it was followed by another sheet, which did not survive. According to Elgvin's calculations, this sheet contained only one column. In his opinion, the approximate length of 4Q422 was 70 cm.[14]

According to the editors, in addition to cols. i–ii, three more fragments belong to the section of 4Q422 concerned with the book of Genesis. These were numbered as frgs. 7–9. The DJD edition also contains nineteen "unidentified" fragments.[15] Of them, only eleven may be seen today on Museum Inventory plate 165.[16] The location of the other eight fragments is unknown.[17] When transcribing these fragments, the editors based their findings on the photographs. Additional fragments associated with 4Q422 appear on these photographs but they are absent from Mus. Inv. plates 165–166 and were not included in the DJD edition of 4Q422; perhaps they also disappeared. Here they are edited as frgs. U and V. The script of 4Q422 is dated to the Hasmonean period.

As to the relation of 4Q422 to the literature produced by the Qumran community, Tov notes that the third column reflects no ideological or exegetical links to the sectarian literature.[18] However, in his preliminary edition of the Genesis section, Elgvin mentions four factors that point to a certain affinity between 4Q422 and the writings of the Yahad:[19] 1. The usage of the phrases מועדי רוח קודש, יום ולילה, and דורות עולם (cols. i 7; ii 10–12); 2. The substitution of the Tetragrammaton with the title אל (cols. ii 5, 9; iii 11); 3. The interchange ירוק>ירק (col. iii 11) attested also in 1QIsa[a]; 4. Affinities to the sectarian composition, *Instruction*, displayed in parallel expressions[20] and in the interpretation of the creation and human destiny on earth.[21] Yet, none of the aforementioned phrases belongs to the terminology peculiar to the Qumran sectarian writings.[22] Also, the change

---

14 See Elgvin–Tov, "Paraphrase," 420; Elgvin, "How to Reconstruct," 223–28.
15 The DJD edition includes twenty unidentified fragments. But, as mentioned above, frg. P was joined by the editors to frg. 10e (= col. iii 8–9). The term "unidentified" is somewhat misleading for, like frgs. 7–9, the contents of frgs. C, D, G, N, and O are related to cols. I–III. The editors have mentioned this fact in their comments on these fragments.
16 Frgs. A–D, F–H, J–L, N.
17 Frgs. E, I, M, O, Q–T. The editors suggested that they may have been assigned to other Qumran manuscripts. However, the wording of these fragments cannot be identified in other published Qumran texts.
18 Tov, "Exodus Section," 197.
19 Elgvin, "Genesis Section," 196.
20 יצר רע (col. i 12) // מחשבת יצר רע (4Q417 1 ii 12), המשילו (col. i 9) // המשילכה (4Q423 1–2 2).
21 See Elgvin, "Admonition Texts," 186–87.
22 See *Comments* on the respective passages.

in the nominal pattern (if it indeed occurs here; see *Comments* on col. iii 11) is a linguistic phenomenon that is characteristic of the Qumran corpus in general. Similarly, the avoidance of the Tetragrammaton is not a distinctive marker of sectarian provenance, for this scribal convention was also practiced by other Second Temple circles.[23] Finally, the affinity to *Instruction* is of a general character and may not signal the sectarian provenance of 4Q422. Therefore, I concur with Tov that 4Q422 should be considered a nonsectarian composition, even if the scroll itself was copied at Qumran, as the editors suggest.[24]

Text and Comments

The first column of 4Q422 as reconstructed by the editors deals with the creation story and Adam's sin (Genesis 1–3). The editors identify a single fragment that belongs to this column. The shape of its bottom section matches that of frg. 3, which contains some of the words of col. ii 6–12. The editors concluded, therefore, that this fragment contains the remains of lines 6–13.[25]

Col. i (Frg. 1)

שמים וכול [צבאם עשה בדבֿרֿ]ו	6
אש[ר עשה ורוח קודשֿ]ו	7
נפ[שׁהחיה והֿרמש]	8
זורע זר[ע המשילו לאכול פר]ֿי	9
[ֿלֿ]ב[ֿ]לתי אכול מעץ הדֿ[עת טוב ורע	10
הֿקים עליו וישכחו[ן]	11
[ֿלֿ[ ]בֿיוצר רע ולמֿעשֿ]ֿי	12
[שלהֿ∘]ֿ	13

---

23 D. Dimant, "The Qumran Manuscripts: Contents and Significance," in *Time to Prepare the Way in the Wilderness* (ed. D. Dimant and L. H. Schiffman; STDJ 10; Leiden: Brill, 1995), 29 n. 15.
24 See Tov, "Exodus Section," 198–99; Elgvin–Tov, "Paraphrase," 420. This assumption relies on the orthography of 4Q422. See further Tov, *Scribal Practices*, 277–88, 337–43. In his latest statement on the issue, Elgvin, "How to Reconstruct," 233–34, stresses the "universalist features of cols I and II," although the manuscript was copied by a Yahad scribe.
25 Elgvin–Tov, "Paraphrase," 418–19.

Notes on Readings

L. 8 נפ[שׁהחיה. Elgvin reads הנפ[שׁ החיה, but the *shin* and *he* are very close to each other. The photographs (PAM 40966, 41478, 41856) show that the left stroke of *shin* touches the right vertical stroke of *he*. The two words seem to have been written with no space between them (a similar phenomenon occurs in בלירא[ה in col. iii 9).

] והֹרמשׁ. The editor read and restored והרמשׁ[ת, but PAM 41856 shows that the *shin* is followed by a blank space, indicating that it is the last letter in this word.[26]

זר[ע. Elgvin read and restored הארץ[. At the beginning of this line one may see a convex vertical stroke with an oblique stroke joining it from the left. These are the remains of an *'ayin*, as was proposed by Strugnell[27] (cf. the *'ayin* and *ṣade* in מעץ in line 10).

L. 11 הֹקים[. The vertical stroke visible at the beginning of this line is straight with the upper part leaning to the right (PAM 42820) and so is consistent with a *he* (cf. המשילו in line 9) rather than with a *yod* (usually represented by a convex stroke open to the left in the present scroll), as read by the editor, ויקום[. The third letter may be read either as a *waw* or a *yod*.

L. 12 בֹּיוצר רע[. Thus the DJD edition. Strugnell suggested בייצר, namely the noun יֵצֶר with two *yods*.[28] From the paleographic point of view, both readings are possible. However, since the usage of double *yod* is not attested in the Qumran Scrolls, Elgvin's reading is followed here. The scribe of 4Q422 wrote a few words without an intervening space. Thus, one may also read here בֹּויצר רע[, namely בו יצר רע (see Comments).

שׁלהֹ○[. The editor proposes שׁלומֹ[. However, Wacholder and Abegg (perhaps following Strugnell) suggest that the third letter is a *he*.[29] Indeed, the vertical stroke read by Elgvin as a downstroke of *waw* is, in fact, the right vertical stroke of *he*. Its left vertical stroke, as well as the upper horizontal stroke, is visible on all the photographs (especially PAM 40966 and IAA 375678). The short oblique stroke crossing the upper horizontal stroke of *he* is difficult to decipher. Perhaps, it may be read as the right vertical stroke of a final *mem* (compare the final *mem* in

---

[26] Given the full orthography of the present scroll, if its author had wished to write רמשׁת, he would have written רומשׁת. Compare וקודשׁ[(col. i 7); נוח][(frg. G 3); ארובות (col. ii 6); כול (cols. ii 7; iii 8).
[27] *Preliminary Concordance*, 3:1356.
[28] Ibid., 2:845.
[29] Wacholder–Abegg, *Preliminary Edition*, 2:247.

the word הֹ֯קִים[in line 11). In this case, one would read here]שלהֹ֯ם[(a possessive pronoun used frequently in rabbinic Hebrew).

Translation

6. [the heavens and all] their hosts he made by [his] word[
7. [whic]h he had done. And [his] holy spirit[
8. [the living [creat]ures and the creeping things [
9. [sowing see]d he set him in charge to eat the fru[it
10. [   ]that he shoul[d n]ot eat from the tree of know[ledge of good and evil
11. [   ]he imposed upon him and they forgot [
12. [   ].[ ]in evil inclination and to deed[s
13. [   ]....[

Comments

L. 6 [צבאֹ֯ם וכול] עשה בדברו. שמים וכול. The scroll reworks here Ps 33:6. The author of 4Q422 rewrote the passive נעשו of the biblical verse as an active עשה.[30] The phrase וכול [צבאֹ֯ם occurs also in Gen 2:1.

L. 7 [ו]אש[ר עשה ורוח קודשֹ֯. The words עשה אשר appear to mark the end of a clause that is now almost completely lost. The formulation is taken from Gen 1:31 and 2:2, summarizing God's activities during the six days of creation. The expression ורוח קודשֹ[ו] ("[his] holy spirit") opens a new clause. This expression (occurring in Isa 63:10; Ps 51:13; CD II, 12; 4Q504 XVIII, 16) may refer to the divine spirit in general, which was the instrument of creation (cf. Ps 33:6 and 4QNon-Canonical Psalms B [4Q381] 1 7[31]). Alternatively, it may allude more specifically to the divine spirit hovering above the waters of Gen 1:2. Other contemporary Jewish sources interpret רוח אלהים as referring to angels (*Jub.* 2:2)[32] or to a wind (Josephus, *Ant.* i, 27).[33]

---

[30] Ps 33:6 is employed in a similar context in 4Q381 1 3 (cf. also 2 Bar 21:4). For a creation by means of speech, cf. Jdt 16:14; Sir 42:15; Wis 9:1; *Jub.* 12:4; Heb 11:4; 2 Pet 3:5.
[31] 4Q381 1 7: [ובכל באדמה אלה בכל למשל העמידם וברוחו ("and with his spirit he instated them to rule on all these on earth and on all["). See further Elgvin, "How to Reconstruct," 232.
[32] See Kugel, *Traditions*, 50; J. van Ruiten, *Primaeval History Interpreted: The Rewriting of Genesis 1–11 in the Book of Jubilees* (JSJSup 66; Leiden: Brill, 2000), 25.
[33] See T. W. Franxman, *Genesis and the Jewish Antiquities of Flavius Josephus* (Rome: Biblical Institute Press, 1979), 39 n. 7; L. H. Feldman, *Judean Antiquities 1–4: Translation and Commentary* (Flavius Josephus: Translation and Commentary 3; Leiden: Brill, 2000), 10. A similar interpretation is reflected in targumic tradition (*Tg. Onq.*, *Tg. Ps.-J.*, *Frg. Tg.*, and *Tg. Neof.* ad loc). See

L. 8] **נפ[שׁהחיה והרמש**. The phrases נפש (ה)חיה and (ה)רמש occur separately several times in Genesis 1. However, the combination נפ[שׁהחיה והרמש is peculiar to 4Q422. Perhaps it is based on Gen 1:28, which links the living creatures with the creeping ones: ורדו בדגת הים ובעוף השמים ובכל חיה הרמשת על הארץ ("and rule the fish of the sea, the birds of the sky, and all the living things that creep on earth").[34] This tallies well with the description of human rule over every plant and tree in the following line. The Qumranic phrase may also borrow from the related verses, such as Gen 1:24.[35]

L. 9 **זורע זר[ע המשילו לאכול פר]י**. The expressions זר[ע and לאכול פר]י are borrowed from Gen 1:29, according to which God gives humans all edible trees and plants as food. Yet, while the biblical verse employs the verb "I give" (נתתי), 4Q422 uses here a *Hif'il* of משל, most likely, under the influence of Ps 8:7: ותמשילהו במעשי ידיך ("You have made him master over Your handiwork"). The scroll seems to have understood this act of giving as extending human dominion to both fauna and flora. The language of Ps 8:7 is used in a similar way also in 4Q381 1 7: וברוחו העמידם למשל בכל אלה באדמה ובכל [("And by his breath [or "spirit"] he made them stand, to rule over all these on earth and over all"). However, while 4Q381 has העמידם (with a 3rd masc. pl. pronominal suffix; cf. Gen 1:26, 28, 29), 4Q422 prefers המשילו (with a 3rd masc. sg. pronominal suffix). By way of this choice, 4Q422 may focus on Adam alone (cf. הֹקים עליו[in line 11; see also Wis 9:2–3). Alternatively, it may be influenced by Gen 2:7–9, 15, which state that God appointed Adam as a ruler over every tree before Eve was created. Compare formulations of this notion in other Qumran scrolls: ובאשר באֹרץ המשילו ("and over what is in the earth he gave him dominion" [4Q301 3 6]); בג[ן עדן אשר נטעתה המשלתֹ]ה אותו ("in the gard]en of Eden, which you had planted You have made [him] govern" [4Q504 I, 5–6]). Cf. also *Jub.* 2:14 and 4Q423 1–2 i 2.

M. L. Klein, *The Fragment-Targums of the Pentateuch according to Their Extant Sources* (Rome: Biblical Institute Press, 1980), 2:3 n. 3; B. Grossfeld, *Targum Neofiti 1: An Exegetical Commentary to Genesis* (New York: Sepher-Hermon Press, 2000), 57. See also b. Ḥag. 12a; Gen. Rab. 2, 4. For other interpretations, see L. Ginzberg, *Die Haggada bei den Kirchenvätern und in der apocryphischen Litteratur* (Berlin: Calvary, 1900), 14–15; idem, *Legends*, 1:7, n. 15.

34 As suggested by E. Chazon (quoted by the editor in DJD XIII, 423, n. 8). Elgvin (ibid.) proposes that the expression refers to the creation of the animals during the fifth and sixth days of creation by employing phraseology found in Gen 1:20–21, 24–25.

35 Compare the addition of the word ובחיה in the reworking of Gen 1:28 in *Jub.* 2:14 (= 4Q216 VII, 17), perhaps under the influence of Gen 1:24, 25. See further Van Ruiten, *Primaeval History*, 46.

L. 10 [‏.‏[ל]ל[ב]לתי אכול מעץ הד]עת טוב ורע. The fragment refers here to the divine prohibition against eating from the Tree of Knowledge in Gen 2:17. The locution ל[ב]לתי אכול is drawn from another verse, Gen 3:11, depicting the transgression of the interdiction. By formulating the initial prohibition employing a detail from its subsequent transgression, the author indicates that humans will disobey the divine commandment.[36]

L. 11 [‏.‏הֹקים עליו וישכחון[. The verb הֹקים is to be parsed as a 3rd masc. sg. *Hifʻil qatal* of קום but the construction להקים על is not attested in the Hebrew Bible.[37] In the Qumran texts, it is used with the meaning "to impose something on someone, to adjure" (4Q504 I, 8; 4Q508 2 3; cf. also CD XV, 6;[38] 1QS V, 8).[39] The 3rd masc. sg. עליו accords well with Gen 2:16–17, where Adam alone receives the command regarding the Tree of Knowledge (compare 4Q504 I, 8: ‏ו]תקם עליו לבלתי ס[ור ["and You imposed on him not to tu[rn away"]). However, since Eve was also familiar with the prohibition (Gen 3:2–3), the fragment goes on to say: וישכחו, 3rd pl., referring to both Adam and Eve.

L. 12 ‏לֹ[ ]] ‏בֹּיוצר רע ולמֹעשֹ]י. The reading ‏בֹּיוצר[is preferred on the basis of orthographic considerations but the possible reading ‏בויצר[= בּוֹ יֵצֶר is also noted (see *Notes on Readings*). In this case, the preposition בּוֹ would refer to Adam. The word ‏ביוצר may be understood as the noun יצר (יֵצֶר in the MT) in the nominal pattern *qutl*, יוֹצֶר.[40] That this is a noun, rather than a participle of the same root, is supported by the adjective רע describing it. This nominal form occurs also in 1QS

---

[36] Thus Chazon, "Creation and Fall of Adam," 16–17, 22. She notes that this is one of the parallels between 4Q422 and 4Q504 (a copy of the *Words of the Luminaries*). She prefers to interpret them as pointing to the literary dependence of the *Words of the Luminaries* on 4Q422, but the general character of their similarities suggests rather the second possibility she mentions, namely, that both rework the same motifs employing similar exegetical methods (ibid., 22, 23).

[37] See, however, the similar expression ‏לקיים על ("to impose something on someone") in Esth 9:21, 27, 31. Cf. *HALOT*, 1087. See also Num 30:14, 15.

[38] See L. Ginzberg, *An Unknown Jewish Sect* (New York: Jewish Theological Seminary of America, 1976), 295; L. H. Schiffman, *Sectarian Law in the Dead Sea Scrolls: Courts, Testimony, and the Penal Code* (Chico: Scholars Press, 1983), 70 n. 80.

[39] Also Bernstein, "Review of DJD 13," 111, understood 4Q422 as employing the expression ‏להקים על but restores it ‏ו[יקים עליו. However, this restoration is problematic since in Qumran Hebrew the 3rd masc. sg. *Hifʻil wayyiqtol* of קום is always a short form: ויקם. See Qimron, "A Grammar of the Hebrew Language," 183.

[40] For a discussion of the *qutl* pattern, see Kutscher, *Isaiah Scroll*, 396–98; Qimron, ibid., 118–21, 277–81.

XI, 22: יוצר יד ("one shaped by hand"). In the Hebrew Bible[41] and in the Qumran texts,[42] יֵצֶר may denote "something made into a shape" (e.g. Isa 29:16; Hab 2:18; 1QH[a] IX, 23; XII, 30) or an "inclination" (Gen 6:5, 8:21; Deut 31:21; 1QH[a] X, 16; 1Q18 1–2 3 [= *Jub.* 35:9]). The doctrine of two inclinations, good and bad, is well known from the rabbinic literature.[43] It has been noted that in Second Temple literature, including the Qumran Scrolls, a certain development of the biblical concept of יצר towards the later rabbinic doctrine may be observed.[44] However, given the fragmentary state of the present line, it is difficult to ascertain whether this is the case here, as Elgvin and Vermes suggest.[45] Chazon suggested that this line links the creation story and Adam's fall to the flood story, for the noun יצר occurs for the first time in the Hebrew Bible in Gen 6:5.[46] However, as will be shown below, this biblical verse seems to be reworked in the first line of the second column, in connection with the flood. Thus, it is not impossible that the scroll is still dealing here with Adam's sin, as Elgvin suggests. One may note that Sir 15:14 uses the noun יצר to describe the heart inclination of Adam (or, for that matter, of the entire humankind), which could be good or bad, according to his choice.[47]

---

41 BDB, 428; *HALOT*, 429.
42 *DCH*, 4:270–71. For surveys and discussions, see R. E. Murphy, "*Yeṣer* in the Qumran Literature," *Bib* 39 (1958): 334–44; J. Hadot, *Penchant mauvais et volonté libre dans la Sagesse de Ben Sira* (Brussels: Presses Universitaires de Bruxelles, 1970), 47–55; G. H. Cohen Stuart, *The Struggle in Man between Good and Evil* (Kampen: J. H. Kok, 1984), 94–100; M. Kister, "Body and Purification from Evil: Prayer Formulas and Concepts in Second Temple Literature and Their Relationship to Later Rabbinic Literature," *Meghillot* 8–9 (2010): 243–69 (Hebrew).
43 See F. C. Porter, "The *Yecer Hara*: A Study in the Jewish Doctrine of Sin," in *Biblical and Semitic Studies* (New York: Charles Scribner's Sons, 1901), 108–35; S. Schechter, *Aspects of Rabbinic Theology* (3rd ed.; New York: Schocken, 1969), 242–92; E. E. Urbach, *The Sages: Their Concepts and Beliefs* (Jerusalem: Magnes, 1969), 415–27 (Hebrew); Cohen Stuart, *The Struggle in Man*, 242–92.
44 See Kister, "Body and Purification," 264–69.
45 Elgvin-Tov, "Paraphrase," 423; G. Vermes, *The Complete Dead Sea Scrolls in English* (London: Penguin Press, 1997), 446.
46 Chazon, "Creation and Fall of Adam," 17. This possibility is also discussed by Elgvin-Tov, "Paraphrase," 423.
47 Ms. A reads: אלהים מבראשית ברא אדם וישתיהו ביד חותפו ויתנהו ביד יצרו ("God from the beginning created Adam [or "humankind'] and he put him in the hand of his [or "their"] kidnapper and he placed him [or "them"] in the hand of his [or "their"] inclination." The understanding of יצר here as referring to a freedom of choice seems to be implied by the LXX rendering, διαβούλιον, "design, plan" (cf. T. Muraoka, *A Greek-English Lexicon of the Septuagint* [Louvain: Peeters, 2009], 149). Compare its usage in LXX Ps 10:2, Sir 44:4, and Hos 11:6. It was also understood in this way by M. Z. Segal, *The Complete Book of Ben Sirah* (Jerusalem: Bialik Institute, 1997), 97 (Hebrew); Hadot, *Penchant mauvais*, 103; P. Skehan and A. A. Di Lella, *The Wisdom of Ben Sira* (AB; New

ולמׄעשֵׂ]י. Elgvin restored ולמׄעשֵׂ]י רשעה. However, this locution is not attested by the Hebrew Bible or the Qumran Scrolls. Perhaps the fragment employed one of the following expressions: מעשי רשע (1QS V, 5), מעשי רע (1QH^a V, 20), מעשי עולה (1QH^a X, 5), מעשי נדה (4Q522 18 ii 7), to mention but a few.

Col. ii (Frgs. 2–7)[48]

]top mar[gin

			[רבה וׄ[	1
			]ב את ה[	2
	א[תׄו אל חיה]	]הׄ דׄלׄ[	ב[דׄורו עׄ]	2a
	עׄ[ל הארץ כיאׄ]	לה[יׄות הׄ[	[נצלו לׄ[	3
[את בניו א[ת אשתו ואת נשי בניו [אל התב]ה מפני [מי המבול ומ]ן הבהמה הטהורה				4
כול	]ׄ ○ [	[לׄ]וׄ[ב את ה]עׄליו צו [ ] ○ [	והעׄ]וף ויס[גור אל בעדם]	5
וגשם הרי[קו על הארץ	נפׄ[תׄ]וׄ חׄ]ם	[אׄרׄוׄבׄוׄת השמי]ׄם [○	אשר בחרבה כלא[שר	6
ארבעים [יום וארב]עים	לה[עׄ]לות מׄיׄםׄ על הׄאׄרׄ]ץ		תחת כול השמי]ׄם	7
למען [טהׄר חיט ולמען	המיׄ[ם גב]רׄו [עׄלׄ] הארץ		לילה היה העׄ[ל]גשם הארץ	8
[הגׄיש לפניו	[אתׄ]		דעתׄ כבוד עלׄ]יון	9
לׄ[המה] [אות לדורו]ת	הא[רׄצ וא]		ויאׄר על [ה]שׄמׄ]יׄם	10
	לוא עוד[היות מבׄוׄלׄ] לשחת הארץ		עׄ]וֹלם לחדא[	11
	עׄ[ל שׄמׄיׄםׄ וארׄ]ץׄ		[מו]עׄדׄי יום ולילה]○	12
	הכוׄ]ל נתן לאדם		[הארץ ומׄ]לׄ[וׄ]אׄהׄ]	13

Notes on Readings

The DJD text of 4Q422 ii comprises frgs. 2–6. The corrected edition of 4Q422 ii also includes frg. 7, placed in lines 4–5.[49] It reads as follows (with some corrections, elaborated below):

York: Doubleday, 1987), 271–72; J. J. Collins, "Interpretations of the Creation of Humanity in the Dead Sea Scrolls," in *Biblical Interpretation at Qumran* (ed. M. Henze; Grand Rapids: Eerdmans, 2005), 29–43 (35). The phrase וישתיהו ביד חותפו is most likely a later addition. See further A. A. Di Lella, *The Hebrew Text of Sirach: A Textcritical and Historical Study* (The Hague: Mouton, 1966), 119–25. See also the discussion of Kister, "Body and Purification," 259 and n. 82.

48 I have discussed 4Q422 ii in A. Feldman, "The Flood Story according to 4Q422," in *The Dynamics of Exegesis and Language at Qumran* (ed. D. Dimant and R. Kratz; FAT 2/35; Tübingen: Mohr Siebeck, 2009), 57–77. The present page format does not permit a precise representation of the size of the lacunae between the six fragments that constitute col. ii, as calculated by Elgvin–Tov, "Paraphrase," 425.

49 Elgvin in DSSR, 3:570.

[ה דֿלֿ◦]
1   לה[יׄות ה]
2   [אׄל התב]ה

Frg. 7 is placed here in lines 2a, 3, and 4. This placement positions the letters]◦דֿלֿ הׄ[in line 2a and places the expression]אׄל התב[ה into the reworked text of Gen 7:7 in line 4.

L. 2a]◦דֿלֿ הׄ[. An examination of frg. 7, where these letters appear as a supralinear addition to line 1, reveals that *he* is written on a tiny scrap of leather joined to this fragment.[50] Given its small size, this letter might have indeed belonged to an addition written above the line. However, the shape of this tiny piece of parchment hardly fits that of frg. 7. Yet, even if this placement is accepted, the resulting intervening space between *he* and *dalet* is larger than usual. Thus Elgvin's DJD reading,]◦דֿלֿ הׄ[, is to be preferred to the corrected one,]וֿדֿלֿהׄ[. Still, while he takes the final letter to be a *waw*, the vertical stroke appearing after *lamed* is open to other interpretations (e.g. *yod*, *he*, *resh*, or *taw*).

א[תׄוׄ. DJD reads here]◦ו[. However, on frg. 4 and its photographs (PAM 40966, 42820), a vertical stroke with a short base line, resembling the left vertical stroke of *taw*, is discernible.

חיה [. The DJD reading חיה was later corrected by Elgvin to חי. However, upon scrutiny of frg. 4, it appears that *he* is a genuine letter and not the imprint of a letter written on another layer of the scroll.[51]

L. 3] נצלו ל◦[. The DJD edition reads here]נצלו עׄלׄ[. Indeed, the evidence for a *lamed* is clear. On frg. 6, as well as in PAM 41478, the vertical and horizontal strokes of this letter are visible. In addition, Strugnell's preliminary transcription has a *lamed* here.[52] However, no clear traces of a letter preceding the *lamed* can be detected, but rather those of a following letter. However, only the bottom section of its vertical stroke remains, and therefore it is impossible to identify the letter.

לה[יׄוֹת. The editor read the first extant letter as an *alef*,]את. However, a vertical stroke, curving slightly to the left, with a hook on its top is a *waw*. The short diagonal stroke preceding it (seen on PAM 41856, 42820) is the hook of a *yod*, as

---

50 I examined the fragments of 4Q422 at the Israel Museum in the spring of 2007.
51 Several fragments of 4Q422 are translucent and in some cases the imprints of letters written on the upper layer of leather are visible. See Elgvin–Tov, "Paraphrase," 417–18.
52 *Preliminary Concordance*, 1410.

suggested here. A *waw* is also possible graphically but it does not accord with the reading of the entire word.

L. 4 ‏את[‎. The DJD edition reads ‏וֹאת[‎. However, both frg. 6 and its photographs (PAM 41478, 42820) show no trace of ink before the *alef*. The black spot visible on PAM 42820 is a hole in the leather.

L. 5 ‏הֹ[עליו‎ צו. Elgvin read here ‏וֹעליו[‎. However, the preserved vertical stroke of the first letter turns slightly left at its top and curves and slants down to the left (PAM 40966, 41478, 47478), which is consonant with the left vertical stroke of a *he* in this manuscript (cf. the *he* in ‏חיה‎ and ‏היה‎ [lines 2a, 8]). The left edge of the horizontal stroke of this letter is discernible on PAM 41478.

‏אֹת כֹ[וֹ]ל[‎. The DJD edition reads here ‏יֹתֹן[ ]לֹ[‎, but in PAM 41478 the first letter is certainly an *alef*. The *taw* is followed by a letter-sized space. The editor read the following vertical stroke as a final *nun*. However, given the preceding space that marks a new word, this reading is precluded. A trace of an upper horizontal stroke is visible on the same photograph, probably that of a medial *kaf* (cf. *kaf* in ‏כול‎ [line 7]).

L. 6 ‏בחרבה כֹֿלֹ[אֹ]שר‎. The editor reads here ‏בחר בה‎. However, the space between the *resh* and *bet* is too short to be that occurring between adjacent words. On PAM 41856 and IAA 375678, traces of two supralinear letters are visible following ‏בחרבה‎. Although it is difficult to decipher them, it is proposed to read them as a medial *kaf* and a *lamed* (cf. *lamed* in ‏כול‎ [line 7]), suggested by the form of the surviving traces.

‏נפֹ[ת]חֹו‎ ○ [‏אֹרֻבֹוֹת השמיֹ[ם‎]. Elgvin reads ‏אֹרֻבֹוֹת השמיֹ[ם‎]נפֹ[ת]חֹו [, as if the words ‏השמיֹ[ם‎ and ‏נפֹ[ת]חֹו‎ are separated by a single letter-sized lacuna. However, the locution ‏אֹרֻבֹוֹת השמיֹ[ם‎ is found in the last line of frg. 4. Moreover, the word ‏נפֹ[ת]חֹו‎ appears in the first line of frg. 3 preceded by a letter-sized lacuna, indecipherable letter, and another lacuna that may contain two or three letters: ‏נפֹ[ת]חֹו‎ ○ [. These features are not represented by the DJD transcription.

L. 8 ‏הֹ[גשם הארץ‎ ע֯לֿ. In the photographs (esp. PAM 41478), a supralinear *'ayin* is visible to the left of the *he* of ‏הֹ[גשם‎. It differs from the other supralinear additions in this scroll as the letter appears to be inscribed vertically, and not horizontally. Above the *'ayin*, there appears a trace of a possible *lamed*, which was unnoticed by the editor. Both letters are missing from the fragment itself and are visible only on the photographs. Given the vertical placement of this addition, the possibility that this is an imprint of letters inscribed on an upper layer of the scroll cannot be ruled out.

טֹהֲר[. DJD reads]○○ור[. Two vertical strokes and a trace of a horizontal stroke preceding *resh* fit well the shape of *he* as it is written in this scroll (cf. *he* in עשה [col. i, 2]). Before the *he*, a tiny vertical stroke that curves to the right can be seen on PAM 40966. Given the context, it is proposed to read it as a *ḥet*.

חיט. The editor proposed two readings: חוט and חיט. Whereas the second letter may be read as a *waw* or a *yod*, the context favors reading חיט as suggested by Strugnell and adopted here (see Comments).[53]

L. 10]וא. The DJD edition reads]וא [ֹלֹ[but also proposes]ואל in the notes. In the corrected edition, Elgvin read וא[ד]ֹם. An examination of frg. 3 reveals no trace of ink after *alef* and thus one should read here]וא.

]לְהֲמֹה[. The DJD edition has here]מֹהֲ[ר, but in the notes Elgvin suggests the reading]וֹמֹהֲ[ר. On PAM 41478, a vertical stroke and a horizontal stroke that curves downward, typical of *he*, are visible before the medial *mem* (cf. הגיש [line 9]). As to the third letter, its right vertical stroke that slants down to the right seems to fit better with a *he* than a *ḥet* (compare the *ḥet* in חיט [line 10]). The space between]לְהֲמֹה[and the following word is too narrow for the insertion of another letter.

L. 11]לחדא[. The DJD edition reads לחרא. A revised edition has לחדא. The third letter may be read as either *dalet* or *resh*. However, given the context, it is more appropriate to read it, with Strugnell, as a *dalet*.[54]

Translation
1.   ] great and .[
2.   ]. The .[
2a.   ] his generation [   ] ....[with] him God kept alive[
3.   ] they were saved ..[to b]e the[o]n the earth because[
4.   ] his sons, [his wife and his sons' wives] to the ar[k because of]the waters of the flood, and o[f the pure animals
5.   and (of) the bir[ds. And] God [sh]ut behind them [   ].[command]ed him a[l]l[ ]..[all
6.   that was on the dry land ᵃˡˡ t[hat   ]the sluices of heav[en].   were op[en]ed ..   [and] they [pou]red out [rain] on the earth
7.   under all the heave[ns   to cause]water to rise upon the ea[rth forty] days and for[ty]

---

53 Ibid., 713.
54 *Preliminary Concordance*, 1111.

8. nights there was r[ain]on[the earth   the water]s prevail[ed]on[the earth in order to] cleanse sin and in order
9. to make known the glory of the Most [High   ]the[   ] he presented before him
10. And he shined upon [the] heave[ns   the ea]rth and .[for] them [ ]a sign for generation[s] of
11. eternity greatly[and never more] will a flood[destroy the earth
12. [the s]et times of day and night .[o]n heaven and ear[th
13. [the earth and]its [fu]ll[ne]ss   everythi]ng he gave [to mankind

Comments

L. 1]∘רבה[. The word רבה ("great") occurs twice in Genesis 6–9, once in Gen 6:5a, referring to the great wickedness of man, and in 7:11, describing the "great deep." However, since the outpouring of the flood is depicted further on in lines 6–8, the first verse seems to be alluded to here.

L. 2a ב[ד̇ורו ע]. Apparently this is a reference to Noah being blameless in his age (Gen 6:9). The scroll uses the singular ב[דורו instead of the plural בדרתיו in Gen 6:9. This understanding may have been influenced by God's address to Noah in Gen. 7:1: "for you alone have I found righteous before me in this generation (בדור הזה)"; cf. LXX and *Tg. Neof.* (marginal variant) to Gen 6:9 and also *L. A. B.* 3:4. See the Comments on frg. G line 3.

א[ת̇ו אל חיה]. The DJD edition reads the phrase אל חיה as אֶל חַיָּה ("to an animal"). While the term חַיָּה is indeed current in the Genesis flood story (see Gen 7:14, 8:1, 17, 19), it is better to read אֵל ("God") and חיה as a 3rd masc. sg. *qatal* of חיה in *Pi'el*, חִיָּה ("to preserve/keep alive").[55] Here it is proposed to read the phrase א[ת̇ו אל חיה ("with him God kept alive") in light of the divine command to Noah in Gen 6:19, using the similar phrase לְהַחֲיוֹת אִתָּךְ (a parallel command in Gen 7:3 employs לחיות). But also the restoration או[ת̇ו אל חִיָּה ("him God kept alive") is possible.

L. 3]∘ל נצלו[. This verb is to be parsed as a 3rd pl. *qatal* of נצל in *Nif'al*, "to be rescued."[56] נצל does not occur in the flood story of Genesis 6–9, but it appears in Ezek 14:14–16 with reference to Noah.[57] The subject of this plural verb is most

---

55 *HALOT*, 309.
56 Ibid, 717.
57 As noted by Bernstein, "Review of DJD XIII," 111.

probably the inhabitants of the ark. On the use of the *qatal* form depicting their rescue as something that has already taken place prior to the detailed description of the flood, see *Discussion*.

לה[ה]יׄות ה[ ]**עׄ[ל הארץ כיאׄ]**. Given the context, the *Qal* infinitive of היה, לה[יׄות, may refer to the flood survivors. Thus the restoration לה[ה]יׄות ה[שארית ע]ל הארץ ("to b]e the[remnant o]n the earth"), similar to Sir 44:17: בעבורו היה שארית ("Because of him [of Noah] there was a remnant"), may be proposed. One may also consider a restoration לה[ה]יׄות ה[מים ע]ל הארץ כיאׄ] (proposed by Dimant). The expression על הארץ ("upon the earth") occurs frequently in Genesis 6–9 (e.g. 6:17; 7:4, 19).

L. 4 **[את בניו א]ת אשתו ואת נשי בניו] אל התב]ה מפני [מי המבול**. Most of the elements of this line are taken from Gen 7:7.

Ll. 4–5 **ומ]ן הבהמה הטהורה [והע]וף**. The proposed reconstruction relies on the wording of Gen 7:8 since line 4 reworks Gen 7:7. The editor's restoration in line 5, והע]ושה ("and he who do[es]"), does not fit well with the context.[58]

L. 5 **ויס]גור אל בעדם]**. The words are taken from Gen 7:16b: ויסגר ה' בעדו ("And the Lord shut him in"). The editor notes that the Tetragrammaton, found in the biblical verse, was substituted here with the title אל (cf. also cols. ii 9; iii 11).[59] In addition, the scribe rewrote the preposition בעדו as בעדם, in order to adapt it to the preceding list of ark dwellers.

צו]הׄעליו את כׄו[לׄ]. The letter *he*, attached to the preposition עליו ("on him"), indicates that the scribe wrote the two adjacent words without a separating space (compare likewise cols. i 8; iii 9). Given the context, עליו refers to Noah. The biblical story states that Noah carried out all God's commands (Gen 6:22; 7:5–6). The verse reworked at the beginning of this line, Gen 7:16, employs the expression צוה אתו ("commanded him"). Thus it is proposed to restore here with a synonymous phrase צוה על (Gen 2:16; 12:20): צוׅוׅ]הׄעליו ("commanded him").

L. 6 **כול [אשר בחרבה אׄ]ׄשר**.[55] The scroll alludes here to Gen 7:22.

אׅׄרֻבֹּות השמיׄ]ם [○ **נפֹ[תׄ]חׄו**. This line reworks Gen 7:11. See *Comments* on frg. D.

---

58 As noted by Bernstein, "Review of DJD XIII," 111. In the corrected edition of 4Q422 ii the editor avoided restoring this word (Elgvin, *DSSR*, 3:571).
59 On this practice, see H. Stegemann, "Religionsgeschichtliche Erwägungen zu den Gottesbezeichnungen in den Qumrantexten," in *Qumrân: Sa piété, sa théologie et son milieu* (ed. M. Delcor; Paris-Gembloux: Duculout, 1978), 200–217.

גשם הרי[קו על הארץ]. The reconstruction גשם הרי[קו ("poured out rain") is based on Eccl 11:3: גשם על הארץ יריקו ("they will pour down rain on the earth").[60] Compare 4Q370 1 i 5: וארבות השמים הֹ[רי]קו סטר]). The rain is mentioned in Gen 7:12.

Ll. 7–8 ארבעים [יום וארב]עים] לילה היה הֹגֹּשם הארץ]. This formulation points to Gen 7:12.

L. 7 תחת כול הֹשמ]ים. The expression is taken from Gen 7:19.

לה[עלות מֹיֹם על הארֹ]ץ. Elgvin restores לֹעֲלוֹת[, an infinitive of עלה in the *Qal*, "to ascend."[61] However, a *Hifʻil* infinitive, לה[עֲלוֹת, "to cause to rise,"[62] may be preferred (cf. Ezek 26:3), placing the word מים as its direct object. Genesis 7–8 employs the verb גבר to describe the increasing waters of the flood (7:18, 19, 24).

L. 8 המי]ם גב]רו [עֹלֹ] הארץ. The expression is taken from Gen 7:24.

למען [טֹהֹר חיט. טהר is an infinitive of טהר in *Piʻel*, meaning "to cleanse, to purify" (for the expression למען טהר, see Ezek 39:12).[63] חיט is a phonetic spelling of חֲטָא ("sin") in which a *yod* was added after *ḥet* as a *mater lectionis* for *ṣere*, while the radical quiescent *alef* was dropped (compare הֹ[ט]ֹי [4Q381 33a, b + 35 9], חט, חטֹאֹ [11QTª XLVII, 1; LXIV, 9]).[64] For the flood as a purification baptism, see *Discussion*.

Ll. 8–9 ולמען דעתֹ בֹבוד עלֹ]יון. דעת is an infinitive of ידע in *Qal*, "to know."[65] The conjunction למען indicates that דעת is employed here in its verbal sense: "in order that [they] will know" (cf. Ezek 38:16; Mic 6:5; 4Q504 XV, 11).[66] The scroll's formulation echoes Hab 2:14 (see also 1QHª XIV, 15). The phrase דעת עליון ("a knowledge of the Most High") occurs in Num 24:16; 1QS IV, 22; 4Q378 26 1. For a string of infinitives with למען, see Deut 8:18; Jer 44:8. The scroll indicates that in addition to cleansing the earth, the flood bears witness to God's power as the Most High (cf. 4Q422 iii, 7).

---

60 Suggested by Bernstein, "Review of DJD XIII," 111.
61 *HALOT*, 828.
62 Ibid., 830.
63 Ibid., 368.
64 For the phenomenon, see Qimron, *Hebrew of the Dead Sea Scrolls*, 19, 23. On the *Ketiv* חט in the ancient sources, see also idem, "The Language of the Temple Scroll," *Leš* 42 (1978): 83–98 (85 n. 11) (Hebrew).
65 *HALOT*, 390–91.
66 For the usages of למען in the Hebrew Bible, see Joüon–Muraoka, *Grammar*, 634, 636.

L. 9 הִגִּישׁ לְפָנָיו. The verb הִגִּישׁ is a 3rd masc. sg. *qatal* of נגשׁ in *Hifʻil*, "to bring in close, to present."[67] The verb is best applied to Noah as subject with לפניו referring to God (instead of the reverse, as proposed by Elgvin[68]), for it fits the biblical sequence of events, in which the description of the sacrifice of Noah precedes the setting up of the rainbow as a sign of covenant with mankind (Gen 8:20–21; 9:12–19). Furthermore, in the Hebrew Bible, הגישׁ is frequently employed in relation to the sacrificial procedures (e.g. Exod 32:6; Lev 8:14; Amos 5:25).[69] In addition, in the Hebrew Bible, the verb הגישׁ is often related to grain offering (e.g., Amos 5:25; Mal 1:7, 2:12, 3:3). Although the flood story in Gen 8:20 speaks only of the animal burnt offerings (using the verb עלה), according to 1QapGen X, 16, Noah also presented grain offerings.

L. 10 וַיָּאֶר עַל [הַ]שָּׁמַ֫[יִ]ם. The verb וַיָּאֶר is to be parsed as a 3rd masc. sg. *wayyiqtol* of אור in *Hifʻil*, meaning "to shine, to illuminate."[70] According to some scholars, the subject of this verb is the rainbow.[71] However, the masculine singular verb does not tally with the feminine gender of the Hebrew noun קשׁת.[72] A better sense is obtained by taking God as the subject of this verb, depicting how he illuminated the heavens, as suggested by the DJD translation. However, given the reference to the rainbow preserved at the end of the line, the illumination may be effected by the rainbow. This may indicate that the scribe understood Gen 9:13 (את קשתי נתתי בענן) as an actual manifestation of a rainbow (as probably is the case also in Sir 44:18 and 4Q370 i 9), and not as an explanation of the significance of the rainbow (as in *L. A. B.* 3:12; 4:5).

הָאָ[רֶץ וְאָ]. The paucity of preserved text cautions against an elaborate restoration.[73]

Ll. 10–11 לְ[הָ]מָּה [] [אוֹת לְדוֹר]וֹת עוֹלָם. This is a clear reference to the rainbow since the phrase is an abbreviated version of the rainbow depiction in Gen 9:12, where

---

67 *HALOT*, 671.
68 As becomes clear from his translation in the DJD edition. Elgvin, *DSSR*, 3:572, restores: את הקשת] הגיש לפניו ("The bow] He set before him"). The same interpretation is reflected in M. Abegg, "A Commentary on Genesis and Exodus," in M. Wise et al., *The Dead Sea Scrolls: A New Translation* (San Francisco: Harper, 2005), 496.
69 See J. Milgrom, *Leviticus 1–16* (AB; New York: Doubleday, 1991), 186, 391.
70 *HALOT*, 24.
71 Abegg, "Commentary," 496; *DSSSE*, 885; Elgvin in *DSSR*, 3:572.
72 The only exception might be 2 Sam 1:22: קשת יהונתן לא נשוג אחור ("The bow of Jonathan never turned back"). See BDB, 905.
73 As did Elgvin: והיתה אות בין אל לבין הא[רץ וא]דם; idem in *DSSR*, 3:572.

the rainbow is given as "a sign of covenant" (אות ברית) between God, mankind, and the animals.

L. 11 ‎לחדא[. Probably the Aramaic word לְחֲדָא ("much"; 1QGenApoc XIII, 15; 4Q196 4 i 14 [= Tob 6:12]; 4Q544 1 2).[74] Given the fragmentary state of the manuscript, it is difficult to ascertain whether the word belongs to the previous sentence or opens the next one.

ולוא עוד] היות מֿבּוּל לשחת הארץ. The sequence of events suggests that the phrase היות מֿבּוּל alludes to God's promise from Gen 9:11, 15 to not flood the earth again. The proposed restoration follows that of Elgvin.

L. 12 מו[עַדֵי יום ולילה]○. The expression is based on Gen 8:22. However, the locution מועד לילה ("set time of night") is nonbiblical but is found in the Qumran Scrolls. See 1QHᵃ XX, 9; 4Q503 33 i + 34 21; 51–55 10.

עַ[ל שָׁמַיִם וארץ]. Since the context deals with the establishment of the day-night sequence, related in Gen 1:15 to the luminaries, perhaps the phrase alludes to them. This seems to be the motive behind Elgvin's restoration, מאורות להאיר עַ[ל שָׁמַיִם וָארץ ("the lights to shine o]n heaven and earth").

L. 13 הכו[ל נתן] לאדם   [הארץ ומ[לו]אֿהּ]. The editor restores here the biblical phrase ארץ ומלאה ("[the] earth and its fullness"; cf. Deut 33:16; Ps 24:1). The verb נתן ("gave"), a 3rd masc. sg. qatal of נתן in Qal, echoes Gen 9:2–3, where this verb occurs twice. Accordingly, it is restored here with Elgvin: הכו[ל נתן] לאדם.[75]

The editor assumed that the following two fragments relate to the flood story and numbered them frgs. 8 and 9.

Frg. 8

[ומות]	1
[כרת]	2
[○ ו ○ ח̇]ח̇	3
[○]	4

---

74 Sokoloff, *Dictionary of Jewish Palestinian Aramaic*, 280.
75 Ibid.

Comments

L. 1 וֹמות[. One may restore here with Elgvin תה[וֹמות (cf. Gen 7:11, 8:2). An alternative restoration would be וֹ]מות [.

L. 2]כרת[. The surviving letters may be read as a form of כרת. If the fragment indeed refers to the flood (thus Elgvin), perhaps it alludes to Gen 9:11, where the same verb appears to negate a future annihilation of mankind.

Frg. 9

1 [יעשו ידיו ואספ]
2 [○ ○○○]

Comments

The fragment perhaps refers to Noah, for the verb אסף is used in God's instructions to Noah in Gen 6:21 and עשה occurs in Gen 6:14–16, 22 with reference to the construction of the ark. Elgvin's proposal that both verbs have God as their subject and that they refer to the gathering of the primeval waters on the second day of creation (Gen 1:9) is less probable. Such a reference would be out of sequence in the outline displayed in the fragment. Also, the Hebrew Bible and the Qumran Scrolls never use the verb אסף in *Qal* with reference to water.

While frgs. 8–9 may indeed belong with the rewritten flood story in col. ii, their precise placement in this column must remain uncertain given its fragmentary state of preservation.

Col. iii (Frgs. 10a–e)[76]

			1 [ ]ם ולוא [
וישליכו את vac	] vac? [		2 [ש]תֹי המיל]דות
וישמע א[ותם	[או אֹת]		3 [ב]נֹיהם ליא]ר [○
[○	[במראת]		4 [ו]ישלח להמה את מו]שה
א[חֹיו חברֹה] [עֹמו	[סֹמכו וֹעֹ]	[○○	5 באותות ומופתים]
הֹ[ ] [ויביאו דבֹרו	[אות למצרים]	[נֹפֹל] [לצֹ]וֹות נגועים	6 וישלחם אל פרעוֹה]

---

[76] This is a reworked version of A. Feldman, "The Reworking of the Exodus Story in 4Q422," *Meghillot* 8–9 (2010): 373–91 (Hebrew).

7 אל פרעוה לשלח א̇[ת עמם ו]יחזק את לב[ו ל]ח̇טוא למען דעת א[ת כבוד [אל עד
דו]רות [עולם ויופכ לדם] מימ[י]ה̇מ̇ה
8 הצפרדעים בכול ארצ̇ם]וכנים בכול גבול[ם]ערוב בבתיהסה ו[נ]ג̇[ע בכול פ]רי[הסה
ויגוף בדב]ר את[
9 מקניהסה ובהמתם ל[מו]ת̇ הסגיר ישי[ת חו]שכ בארצם ואפלה ב̇[בתי]הסה בלירא[ה]
איש את אחיו̇] ויד[
10 בברד ארצם ואדמת̇ם̇ ב]חנמל לה̇[שחית כו]ל̇ פרי אוכ̇[ל]ם ויבא ארב̇ה לכסות עין
ה̇א̇]רצ[ ]חסל כבד בכול גבולם
11 לאכול כול ירוק בא[רצם ל̇[ ]ם̇ ויח̇[זק]אל את לב [פרעו]ה̇ לבלתו̇]
ש[לח]ם [ו]ל̇מ̇ען הרבות מופתים
12 [ויך בכורם]ר̇שית לכו[ל אונם]ל̇ל[ ]o[ ]ה̇א[ ]ל̇[ ]o ל[
[ ]o[

Notes on Readings

L. 2 ם̇[ ]. The DJD edition has here ת̇[ ]. The traces of a bottom horizontal stroke are visible on the fragment itself and in PAM 43540, identifying the surviving letter as a final *mem*.

L. 3]א̇ת̇. Tov reads here]או. However, the long upper horizontal stroke fits better with the roof of a *taw* than with the hook-shaped top of a *waw*.

L. 5]oo[. On the fragment itself, as well as in its photographs (e.g. IAA 375678), traces of two letters appear above the word לצ̇[וות in line 6. The long horizontal base line may belong to a *bet*, while the short base line, descending to the left, may be read as a medial *kaf* (the scribe of 4Q422 used medial *kaf* also in final position: ויופכ [col. iii 7], חו]שכ [col. iii 9], יארכ [frg. Q]).

ס̇מכו[. The editor reads ת̇מכו[. The concave upper horizontal stroke and the left vertical stroke curving to the right (PAM 40966) indicate that the first letter is a *samech* (cf. the *samech* in חסל [col. III, 10]) and not a *taw* (see the *taw* in במראת [col. iii, 4]).

א[ח̇יו̇. The DJD edition has here ooo[. As to the first letter, the remains of the two vertical strokes may belong to a *het*. The two vertical strokes with hooks on their tops should be read as *waw* and *yod*.

ע̇מו[. Tov reads מ̇ו[. On PAM 41478 and 42820, a trace of a letter that resembles the lower part of the right downstroke of an *'ayin* is visible preceding the medial *mem*. Of the last letter, the vertical stroke with a hook on its top is certainly a *waw* or *yod*, but not a *resh* (cf. *resh* in במראת [line 4]).

L. 6 לִזְ[וּ]חֹת. The editor reads לזו[. A vertical stroke with a hooked-shaped top, typical of *waw* or *yod*, is seen before the *waw* on PAM 43520 and is read here as a second *waw*.

L. 10 לְהַ[שְׁחִית]. This restoration is appropriate to the context. See Comments below.

Translation
1. [ ]. and not [   ]
2. the [t]wo mid[wives   ] vac? [and they threw] vac
3. their so[ns] to the Nil[e].[   ].. the[and he heard t]hem
4. [and] he sent them Mo[ses   ] in the vision of[   ].
5. with signs and wonders[   ]..[   ]he supported him ..[   ]his [b]rother he joined[ ] with him (or: joined[ ]him)
6. and he sent them to Pharaoh[to dec]ree plagues [ ] wo[n]ders for Egypt [ ]and they brought his word
7. to Pharaoh to let [their people] go. [And] he hardened [his] heart [so that he would] sin in order to make known God's [glory] for gene[rations] of eternity. And he turned their [waters] to blood.
8. The frogs in [their] entire land and lice throughout [their] territory, flies in their houses and [a plagu]e on all their b[ull]s. And he inflicted with pestilen[ce]
9. their livestock and their cattle he delivered to [deat]h. He broug[ht dark]ness on their land and gloom on their [houses] so that no one would be able to se[e] the other.[And he struck]
10. their land with hail and [their] land [with] frost to r[uin al]l the fruit which they ea[t]. And he brought locusts to cover the face of the ear[th], heavy locust in all of their territory,
11. to eat every plant in [their] la[nd,].[   ]. and God har[dened] the heart of [Pharao]h so as not to let [them] g[o] and in order to multiply wonders.
12. [And he smote their firstborn,]the prime of al[l their strength   ]..[ ]. .. [ ].[] ..[ ].[ ]

Comments

L. 2 [שׁ]תֵּי הַמְיַלְ[דוֹת]. This phrase indicates that the line alludes to the story of the midwives in Exod 1:15–21. Cf. the mention of the midwives in 4Q464 12 and the discussion there.

Ll. 2–3 וישליכו את[ב] / [ב]ניהם ליוא[ר. The phrase refers to Pharaoh's decree to throw the Israelites' sons into the Nile (Exod 1:22), and the restoration is proposed accordingly (following Tov).

L. 3 וישמע א[ותם. The 3rd masc. pl. pronominal suffix [ותם refers to the Israelites, as is suggested by the following phrase, [ו]ישלח להמה. The scroll perhaps alludes here to Exod 2:24: וישמע אלהים את נאקתם ("God heard their moaning") and the restoration is proposed accordingly. If correct, line 3 begins with Pharaoh's decree to kill the Hebrew newborns (Exod 1:22) and concludes with the cry of the suffering Hebrew slaves (Exod 2:23). The rest of line 3 is lost yet, given the size of the lacuna, it is doubtful that the author could fit here much of Moses' biography as told in Exod 2:1–22.

L. 4 [ו]ישלח להמה את מו[שה. Tov's restoration, [ו]ישלח, a 3rd masc. sg. *Qal wayyiqtol* of שלח, is retained here in line with the string of verbs of the same form occurring in the previous lines, all describing the divine actions. The verb שלח is used frequently in Exod 3:10–15 describing the calling of Moses.

[במראת]. This seems to be a reference to the vision of the burning bush (Exod 3:3a). Interestingly, the biblical episode employs for this extraordinary sight the masculine noun הַמַּרְאֶה, signifying "sight, appearance, vision," while the Qumran text chose a construct form of a feminine noun, מַרְאָה, used in the biblical parlance predominantly with reference to prophetic visions.[77] Both nouns are used interchangeably in Ezek 43:3 and in Dan 10:1, 7, 8, so the replacement of מַרְאֶה with מַרְאָה may be due to their synonymity.[78] In fact, a similar change, מַרְאֶה → מַרְאָה, is attested also in 1Q34[bis] 3 ii 6, which rewrites the biblical phrase ומראה כבוד (Exod 24:17) as במראת כב[ו]ד.[79] For מַרְאָה with the preposition ב-, see Gen 46:2; Ezek 8:3, 40:2; Dan 10:16. Tov restores here [במראת] הסנה הבוער, following Exod 3:2. But the construct form במראת may take another complement such as

---

[77] See BDB, 909; *HALOT*, 630; H. F. Fuhs, "ראה," *TDOT*, 13:239–40.
[78] See A. Brenner, "מַרְאָה and מַרְאֶה," *Beth-Mikra* 25 (1980): 373–74 (Hebrew). On the possible differentiation between מַרְאָה and מַרְאֶה in Num 12:6–8, see R. Fidler, *'Dreams Speak Falsely'? Dream Theophanies in the Bible: Their Place in Ancient Israelite Faith and Tradition* (Jerusalem: Magnes, 2005), 46 (Hebrew).
[79] On the other hand, 4Q160 1 5, reworking the story of God's revelation to Samuel at Shiloh (1 Samuel 3), employs the expression מראה האלוהים instead of the biblical הַמַּרְאָה (v. 15). Fidler, ibid., 282–83, deducing from Num 12:6, 8 that מַרְאֶה denotes a higher level of divine communication than מַרְאָה, suggests that this was done in order to bring Samuel closer to the special status enjoyed by Moses, to whom, according to Num 12:8, God revealed himself in מַרְאֶה. But this change may reflect the synonymity of the two Hebrew nouns.

מראֶה כבוד (Exod 24:17) or מראה אש (Num 9:16; Ezek 1:27). Cf. also the complement אלהים for the plural מראות (Ezek 1:1, 8:3, 40:2).

L. 5 **באותות ומופתים]**. In the Hebrew Bible, the phrase אותות ומופתים usually refers to the Exodus story. Sometimes it occurs with an instrumental -ב as in Deut 4:34 and Jer 32:20 as seems to be the case here. Tov suggested that the expression here refers in particular to the miracles performed by Moses before the Israelites (Exod 4:30). Yet, it is equally possible that it stands for all the signs that Moses was about to perform upon his return to Egypt (see Exod 4:21; compare *Jub.* 48:4).

סֿמכוֹ[. The word סֿמכוֹ is to be parsed as a 3rd masc. sg. *Qal qatal* of סמך with a 3rd masc. sg. pronominal suffix, סְמָכוֹ. In biblical parlance, this verb in the *Qal* denotes "to support, to sustain" (see Isa 59:16; Ps 3:6; 37:24; Sir 51:7. For the Qumran documents, see 1QH[a] X, 9; XV, 9).[80] The agent is probably God as in the preceding verb, וישלח[ו] (line 4), while the 3rd masc. sg. pronominal suffix refers to Moses, whom God strengthened by means of the miracles with which he was entrusted (Exod 4:2–8). By selecting the verb סמכו, the author may further indicate Moses' appointment as God's messenger, given the biblical usage of the expression סמך יד ("to lay hand on") to designate the impartation of authority (on Joshua by Moses, Num 27:18, 23; Deut 34:9; 1Q22 iv 9; see also 11QT[a] XV, 18) or consecration (of the Levites by the Israelites, Num 8:10).[81] However, since Aaron is mentioned in the following words, the verb may refer to the appointment of Aaron as Moses' assistant and companion (Exod 4:16) rather than to Moses.

א[חֿיוֹ חבֿרֿ] עָֿמוֹ. The word א[חֿיוֹ refers to Aaron, Moses' brother (cf. Exod 4:14).

חבֿרֿ] עָֿמוֹ. The verb חבר can be parsed as a 3rd masc. sg. *Qal qatal* of חבר ("to ally oneself"),[82] and understood as referring to Aaron's joining Moses. Since the preceding and following 3rd person verbal forms (סֿמכוֹ[and וישלחם) have God as their subject, it is also possible to parse חבֿרֿ as a 3rd masc. sg. *Pi'el qatal*, חִבֵּר, making God the subject. The locution חִבֵּר עם in the sense of "to make someone partner with oneself" is employed both by the Hebrew Bible (2 Chr 20:36) and the Qumran texts (1QS XI, 8).[83] עָֿמוֹ ("with him") most likely refers to Moses. If so, the preceding א[חֿיוֹ is the direct object of this verb and the entire phrase describes God's appointment of Aaron as Moses' companion before dispatching them to Pharaoh.

---

80 *HALOT*, 759; H.-J. Fabry, "סמך," *TDOT*, 10:278–86.
81 Note also the later rabbinic use of the locution with the meaning "to ordain" (e.g. *m. Sanh.* 4:4; *b. Sanh.* 14a–b).
82 *HALOT*, 287.
83 *HALOT*, 288.

L. 6 **וישלחם אל פרעוה**. The first word, a 3rd masc. sg. *Qal wayyiqtol* of שלח, וַיְּשַׁלְּחֵם, takes God as subject, while the 3rd masc. pl. pronominal suffix refers to Moses and Aaron (cf. Exod 4:14–15; Josh 24:5). The spelling פרעוה (MT: פרעה) reflects the practice of supplying a *waw* as a *mater lectionis* for the vowel "o."[84]

לצ[וֹ]ת נגועים. In Biblical Hebrew, the plural of נֶגַע is נְגָעִים. In the Qumran texts, however, a nominal pattern *qeṭulim*, נגועים, is attested (1QS III, 23; IV, 12; 4Q418 303 4; 4Q454 1 3).[85] The noun נֶגַע occurs in Exod 11:1 in relation to the plague of the firstborn in particular. Here, the term refers to all the plagues God was about to send on Egypt. One may perhaps restore here לצ[וֹ]ת נגועים (cf. Ps 44:5: צַוֵּה יְשׁוּעוֹת). Interestingly, the plural form of נגע is employed in Gen 12:17, when relating how God punished Pharaoh for seizing Sarai. 4Q422 may echo this biblical story.[86]

נֹפֹ[ל]אות למצרים]. The noun נֹפֹ[ל]אות ("wonders") refers explicitly in Exod 3:20 to the ten plagues. In biblical parlance, it often alludes to the wonders effected during the Exodus (e.g. Judg 6:13; Mic 7:5; Ps 106:7, 22; in the Qumran texts: 4Q185 1–2 i 14; 4Q370 ii 7). Tov compares the language of the passage here with that of Ps 135:9 and therefore suggests that frg. O, preserving as it does the word מופ[תים in the first line, may be placed here in the lacuna following the word למצרים].

Ll. 6–7 **ויביאו דֹבֹרֹוֹ אל פרעוה לשלח אֹ]ת עמם**. The formulation is based partly on Exod 18:19, 22, 26, where the phrase הביא דבר אֶל is found. The verb ויביאו, a 3rd masc. pl. *Hif'il wayyiqtol* of בוא, designates the action of Moses and Aaron. לשלח is a *Pi'el* infinitive of שלח, formulating the divine demand to Pharaoh to let Israel out of Egypt, a demand recurring frequently in Exodus 5–10 (e.g. 5:1, 7:14, 16, 26).

L. 7 **וֹ]יחזק את לבֹו**. Given the direct object את לבו, the verb יחזק[ו should be parsed as a transitive verb, וַיְחַזֵּק[, a 3rd masc. sg. *Pi'el wayyiqtol* of חזק. The same syntactical structure appears in several biblical statements of this detail (e.g. Exod 4:21; 9:12; 10:20). In this formulation, God is the agent while Pharaoh's heart is the object. A biblical variation of the same detail is formulated with the intransitive *Qal* form of the verb, חזק (וַיֶּחֱזַק), so that Pharaoh's heart becomes the subject

---

[84] Qimron, *Hebrew of the Dead Sea Scrolls*, 21.
[85] In the Qumran Scrolls, the forms נגעים (4Q368 10 i 8) and נגיעים (1QH[a] XVI, 28; XVII, 10) also appear. See Qimron, "A Grammar of the Hebrew Language," 256; idem, *Hebrew of the Dead Sea Scrolls*, 66, 118.
[86] For a similar tendency (suggested already in the Hebrew Bible itself) in the *Genesis Apocryphon*, see M. Segal, "The Literary Relationship between the Genesis Apocryphon and Jubilees: The Chronology of Abram and Sarai's Descent to Egypt," *Aramaic Studies* 8 (2010): 71–88 (76–79); idem, "Identifying Biblical Interpretation in Parabiblical Texts," in *The Dead Sea Scrolls in Context* (ed. A. Lange et al.; VTSup 140; Leiden, Boston: Brill, 2011), 296–308 (304–05).

(e.g. Exod 7:13, 22; 8:15). However, here the syntax of the Qumran fragment clearly shows that God is the subject. This also tallies with the fact that God is the agent of most of the 3rd masc. sg. verbs in this column (cf. וישלחם [line 6], ויופך [line 7]).

לחֹ[טוא. לחֹ[טוא is a *Qal* infinitive of חטא. חטא, with reference to Pharaoh, appears in Exod 9:27, 34. See Discussion.

למען דעת א[ת כבוד [אל עד דו[רות [עולם. The conjunction למען indicates that דעת (a *Qal* infinitive of ידע) is employed here in a verbal sense: "in order that [they] will know" (compare Ezek 38:16; Mic 6:5; 4Q504 XV, 11).[87] The supplement דעת א[ת כבוד [אל provides both an object for the infinitive דעת and a restoration similar to the expression found in col. ii 6–7, למען דעת כָּבוֹד על]יון. It is therefore preferable to other restorations such as למען דעת א[נשי ישר]אל (Tov) or למען דעת א[ת יד [אל (Qimron, quoted by Tov). The obtained sentence suggested here states that by hardening Pharaoh's heart God made his glory known to the future Israelite generations (cf. Exod 9:16; 10:1–2).[88]

ויופך לדם] מימ[יהמֹה. The verb ויופך should be parsed as a 3rd masc. sg. *Qal wayyiqtol* of אפך, which is a secondary root of הפך (thus Tov) attested in the Qumran documents (1QIsa[a] I, 9; XI, 27;[89] 4Q501 4),[90] in Palestinian Aramaic,[91] and in rabbinic Hebrew.[92] The quiescent *'alef* (ויואפך*) was dropped after a *waw* was added as a *mater lectionis* for "o."[93] The verb alludes here to the plague of blood. Yet, while Exod 7:17, 20 has the waters as the subject of the verb הפך (נהפכו לדם [v. 17], ויהפכו כל המים [v. 20]), 4Q422 presents God as the one who transforms the waters of Nile into blood, as in Ps 78:44 and 105:29. Perhaps the scroll is actu-

---

[87] The phrase למען דעת may indicate either a purpose or a result: "so that (he/they) will know" or "in order to make known" (for the phrase למען ידע, cf. Exod 8:6, 18; 9:29; 11:7). While it is frequently difficult to distinguish between the two (see Joüon–Muraoka, *Grammar*, 634, 636), here it is translated as denoting purpose in order to fit with the context.
[88] On the knowledge of God as one of the dominant motives of the plagues narrative, see M. Greenberg, *Understanding Exodus* (New York: Behrman House, 1969), 170; N. M. Sarna, *Exodus* (JPS Torah Commentary; Philadelphia: JPS, 1991), 38. Peters, *Traditions*, 141, notes that the usage of the expression עד דו[רות [עולם is reminiscent of לדרת עולם from Gen 9:12.
[89] Qimron, "A Grammar of the Hebrew Language," 98.
[90] M. Bar-Asher, "Qumran Hebrew and Mishnaic Hebrew," *Meghillot* 8–9 (2010): 288 (Hebrew).
[91] Sokoloff, *Dictionary of Jewish Palestinian Aramaic*, 71.
[92] See *m. Kil.* 2:3; 5:7; *m. Ter.* 9:1; *t. Ter.* 8:1. For discussions, see G. Haneman, *A Morphology of Mishnaic Hebrew* (Texts and Studies in the Hebrew Language and Related Subjects 3; Tel-Aviv: Tel-Aviv University, 1980), 224 (Hebrew); S. Luggassy, "New Verbal Roots and New Verbal Patterns in the Dead Sea Scrolls," (Ph.D. diss., Beer Sheva: Ben-Gurion University, 2004), 24–25 (Hebrew).
[93] Qimron, "A Grammar of the Hebrew Language," 99–100.

ally based on the language of these psalms. Accordingly, the restoration מִ[ימ יהמה, proposed by Tov, is adopted.

L. 8 הַצְפַרְדְעִים בכול אר[צָ]ם. This phrase refers to the plague of frogs (Exod 8:1–2). Perhaps the word אר[צָ]ם, as restored by Tov, is based on the formulation of this plague in Ps 105:30: שרץ ארצם צפרדעים.

וכנים בכול גבו[לָ]ם. The plague of lice is described in Exod 8:12–15 but the scroll appears to borrow the formulation of Ps 105:31b for the correspondiong plague: כנים בכל גבולם.

עָרוב בבתיהסה. This phrase, referring to the plague of *arov* ("flies"),[94] uses the language of Exod 8:17.

וָ[נג]ע בכול פ[רי]הסה. It is proposed to restore this phrase as a specific allusion to the plague of boils (Exod 9:8–12; similarly Qimron [quoted by Tov], וָ[היה נג]ע, rather than the general restoration of Tov, וָ[יפג]ע). This clause perhaps follows the parallel pattern of the first part of the line: הצפרדעים בכול ארצָ[ם // וכנים בכול גבולָ[ם. If so, the damaged word ע[ ]וָ should be a noun denoting a plague (as is עָרוב) and the phrase בכול פ[ ]הסה would signify the object of affliction (as does the noun בבתיהסה). It is therefore proposed to restore the first word as a noun וָ[נג]ע ("and a plague"; cf. Exod 11:1) referring to the plague of boils (שחין), and the following word as פָ[רי]הסה ("their b[ull]s"). It should be noted that נֶגַע is sometimes used in the Hebrew Bible, in particular in Leviticus, with reference to skin diseases.[95] According to Lev 13:18–23, שחין may prompt an appearance of צרעת,[96] frequently called נגע הצרעת or simply נגע (e.g. Lev 13:20, 22).[97]

Ll. 8–9 וַיִגוף בדב[ר את] מִקְנֵיהסה. The verb וַיִגוף, a 3rd masc. sg. *Qal wayyiqtol* of נגף "to strike,"[98] occurs in Exod 7:27; 12:23, 27 with reference to the plagues of frogs and of the firstborn. Here it describes the plague of pestilence. For the pestilence striking livestock (מקנה), see Exod 9:3, 4, 6.

---

[94] On the various interpretations of the difficult ערוב, see S. E. Loewenstamm, *The Tradition of the Exodus in its Development* (Jerusalem: Magnes, 1965), 37 n. 37 (Hebrew); W. H. C. Propp, *Exodus 1–18* (AB 2; New York: Doubleday, 1999), 328.
[95] Cf. L. Schwiehnhorst, "נָגַע, נֶגַע," *TDOT*, 9:207–09; Milgrom, *Leviticus 1–16*, 775–76.
[96] On the nature of שחין, see Milgrom, ibid., 787; Propp, *Exodus 1–18*, 332.
[97] On the use of נגע in the *Temple Scroll* XL, 18; XLVIII, 15 as signifying a disease differing from צרעת, see Milgrom, ibid., 789. He notes that in the rabbinic sources נגע serves as an inclusive term for various kinds of skin diseases (see *m. Neg.* 1:1).
[98] *HALOT*, 669.

L. 9 **הסגיר ובהמתם ל[מו]ת**. הסגיר is a 3rd masc. *Hifʿil qatal* of סגר. Unlike the preceding parallelistic patterns, both bicola, מקניהסה [את בדב]ר ויגוף and ובהמתם ל[מו]ת הסגיר, deal with the same plague, the pestilence, as does Ps 78:50. However, since the word דבר was already used by the text in the previous line, it was replaced here with מות ("death"). The introduction of the word בהמתם ("their cattle") here seems to be influenced by the formulation of this plague in Ps 78:50, וחיתם לדבר הסגיר, understanding חיתם as cattle as did LXX and *Tg. Ket*. Other Bible versions understood it as referring to animals in general (the Vulgate and the Peshitta) but later commentators interpreted the words as "their lives," parallel to נפשם in other verses (cf. Ps 143:3; Job 33:22).[99] In fact, חיה is not used in Exodus 7–12, but בהמה does appear in the account of the plague of boils (Exod 9:8, 10), listed here before pestilence. On the order of the plagues in the scroll, see Discussion.

יש[ית חו]שך בארצם ואפלה ב[בתי]הסמ. The phrase refers to the plague of darkness, depicted by Exod 10:21–29. However, the locution לשית חושך יש[ית] being a 3rd masc. sg. *Qal yiqtol* of שית, "to set, to cause to occur"[100]) is not found in either Exodus or the parallel descriptions in Psalms 78 and 105. However, it is attested elsewhere in a different context (cf. Ps 104:20). Here it replaces the formulation of Exod 10:22. The replacement thus emphasizes that it was God who brought the darkness on Egypt. However, some elements from Exod 10:22 did find their way into the scroll. The biblical hendiadys חשך אפלה has been split to create two parallel phrases, one using חו]שך ("darkness in their land") the other employing אפלה ("in their houses"). The word ב[בתי]הסמ, as restored by the editor, may refer to Exod 10:23.

בלירא[ה] איש את אחיו. This phrase reworks Exod 10:23. The replacement of the biblical *qatal* לא ראו with a jussive בלירא[ה] (= בל יראה), written without an intervening space, emphasizes the purpose served by the plague of darkness.

Ll. 9–10 **ויך] בברד ארצם**. The scroll deals here with the plague of hail (Exod 9:25). The restoration follows Tov's supplement. Unlike the biblical verse, where the hail is the subject, here God is the agent as he is in the formulation of Ps 78:47.

L. 10 **ואדמת[ם ב]חנמל**. The wording of Ps 78:47 influenced the entire Qumranic line, but while the first part of Ps 78:47 clearly refers to the plague of hail, the use

---

99 Thus medieval commentators Rashi and Radak ad loc., and also many modern interpreters. See e.g. M. Dahood, *Psalms III: 51–100* (AB; Garden City: Doubleday, 1968), 237; M. Tate, *Psalms 51–100* (WBC; Dallas: Word Books), 279; H.-J. Kraus, *Psalms 60–150* (trans. by H. C. Oswald; CC; Minneapolis: Fortress Press, 1993), 120. See *HALOT*, 310.
100 *HALOT*, 1485.

of the hapax word חנמל in the second part prompted two different interpretations. Dimant notes that LXX and the Vulgate understood the rare word as "frost," to fit with the hail in the first strophe of the verse,[101] whereas *Tg. Ket.* translates it "locust."[102] Since the present scroll reworks the plague of locusts in the following two parallel strophes, it seems appropriate to adopt here the interpretation of חנמל as "frost" (thus Dimant).

לה̇]שחית כו]ל̇ פרי אוכ̇]ל̇[ם. If חנמל assumes here the meaning of "frost," the restoration לה̇]שחית (a *Hif'il* infinitive of שחת; cf. Mal 3:11) is more appropriate, referring to plants (rather than Tov's restoration of לה̇]אביד). The nonbiblical expression פרי אוכ̇]ל̇ם designates the fruitage of "all the trees of the field" that according to Exod 9:25 was destroyed by the hail.

ויבא̇ ארבה̇ לכסות עין הא̇]רץ. The verb ויבא̇ should be read with Tov as 3rd masc. sg. *Hif'il* wayyiqtol of בוא, וַיָּבֵא, according to Exod 10:4 and not וַיָּבֹא as in Ps 105:34. This reading accords with the orthographic system used by 4Q422, which otherwise would have written here ויבוא. Also, it fits with the tendency in the scroll to present the plagues as enacted by God. The expression לכסות עין הא̇]רץ (לכסות being a *Qal* infinitive of כסה) is borrowed from Exod 10:5, 15.

חסל כבד בכול ג̇בולם. The noun חסל, "locust,"[103] is based on Ps 78:46. As noted by the editor, it appears here in a different nominal pattern, *qatal* (or *qattal*) and not as the biblical *qattil* (חסיל).[104] The phrase בכול גבולם is influenced by the formulation in Exod 10:4; 14.

L. 11 **לאכול כול פרי ירוק בא]רצם**. The scroll reworks here Exod 10:15 and Ps 105:35. Accordingly, Tov proposed a restoration here in line with Ps 105:35: לאכול כול ירוק בא]רצם [ל̇]אכול כל פרי אדמת̇ם. Notably, in describing the devastation of the vegetation by the locusts, the MT for Exod 10:15 employs the expression יֶרֶק ("greenery"), while the scroll has ירוק, probably a *qatull* noun.[105] As was noted by the editor, a similar phenomenon is also attested in 1QIsaᵃ (e.g., 1QIsaᵃ XIII, 13 [= Isa 15:6]), but it is also possible that 4Q422 read Exod 10:15 ירק (cf. Job 39:8). The

---

101 *HALOT*, 334 explains חנמל as "a devastating flood," an interpretation that is also closer to hail than to a type of locust.
102 Thus also Rashi ad. loc.
103 See the entry חסיל in BDB, 340; *HALOT*, 337–38.
104 E. Qimron, "Improvements to the Editions of the Dead Sea Scrolls," *ErIsr* 26 (1999), 142–46 (144) (Hebrew), suggests (with some hesitation) that the scroll might have read חסיל, yet the *yod* is damaged. However, close inspection of the fragment and its photographs does not support this suggestion.
105 See Kutscher, *Isaiah Scroll*, 152, 186.

influence of the Aramaic ירוק, synonymous with the biblical ירק, may also be taken into account.[106]

ויח[זק] [אל את לב [פרעו]הֹ לבֹלתֹיֹ] ש[לח]ם [ו]לֹמֹען הרבות מופתים. The scroll reworks here Exod 11:9–10 (cf. also 7:3; 10:1). It substituted the Tetragrammaton found in the biblical verse with the title אל (also in col. ii, 2, 9).

L. 12 **[ויך בכורם [ר̇שית לכו]ל אונם**. The restoration ויך בכורם, suggested by Tov, is based on Exod 12:2, 29. The noun ר̇שית, spelled without *alef* (as is frequently done in the Qumran documents[107]), takes up the formulation from Ps 105:36 (cf. also Ps 38:51). Tov restored accordingly לכו]ל אונם.

Unidentified Fragments

Frg. A

top margin

1   [ת תתנסו]

Translation

1.]You will be tested[

Comments

The verb תתנסו is a 2nd pl. *Hithpaʻel yiqtol* of נסה, a construction unattested for this verb in the Hebrew Bible and other Qumran documents, but it is thus employed by rabbinical sources with a meaning "to be tested."[108]

Frg. B

1   [ומה]
2   [vacat]
3   [ה̇יות ש̇]

---

106 Cf. *Tg. Onq.* to Exod 10:15. See further Kutscher, *Isaiah Scroll*, 152, 186; Sokoloff, *Dictionary of Jewish Palestinian Aramaic*, 244.
107 Qimron, "A Grammar of the Hebrew Language," 73.
108 For instance, *m. ʾAbot* 5:3; *Gen. Rab.* 87, 4. See Jastrow, *Dictionary*, 916; Luggassy, "New Verbal Roots and New Verbal Patterns," 174.

Frg. C

                                                  t]op margin[

1   [את דרכו]

      [עוֹד]

2   ]∘[

Notes on Readings

]עוֹד[

L. 2]∘[. Elgvin and Tov transcribed the word]עוֹד[as line 2, but PAM 41856 and 42820 show an extant trace of ink a few millimeters below]עוֹד[, which was not noticed by the editors. Moreover, the distance between דרכו and]עוֹד[is considerably shorter than the distance between]עוֹד[and the following line. Thus,]עוֹד[appears to be an addition inserted above line 2. DJD reads]עוֹד[. However, in PAM 42820, a tiny stroke resembling a serif of a *dalet* (cf. *dalet* in דרכו) is discernible to the left of the vertical stroke read as *nun*.

Translation

1.]its way[
   ]again[
2.]∘[

Comments

L. 1]את דרכו[. As suggested by the editors, this phrase may refer to Gen 6:12 and thus belongs with the first line of col. ii, dealing with the sins of the flood generation.

Frg. D

                                               מ[עֹינות רבה]

Notes on Readings

The DJD edition reads]∘ינות. A tiny stroke touching the vertical stroke of *yod* from the right is discernible on the fragment and in PAM 41478. It seems to be part of the left stroke of *'ayin*.

Translation
]great [fo]untains[

Comments
This fragment refers to a detail in the flood story (see Gen 7:11) and may belong to col. ii, 6, which reworks the same verse. As for the disagreement in number between the plural מ[עֹיָנות and the singular רבה, compare the similar combination in Ps 78:15: כתהמות רבה ("as if from the great deep").

Frg. E

top margin
[ור∘∘ב ∘]

Notes on Readings
The editors read]ידניב∘[. The first letter may be read as either *waw* or *yod*. According to PAM 40966, the second letter is a *resh* (cf. the *resh* in רע [col. i 12]). A short vertical stroke remains of the third letter, which is perhaps a *waw* or *yod*. An extant vertical stroke of the last letter may belong to *zayin* or *he*. Since it appears at some distance from *bet*, it is possible that this letter opens a new word.

Frg. F

      ]∘∘∘∘[1
      ]∘ או[2
   ]∘י הֹיֹוֹת[3

Notes on Readings
L. 2 או∘[. The editors read אי∘[. However, *waw* and *yod* are frequently indistinguishable in this scroll so a *waw* also may be read here.

L. 3 הֹיֹוֹת[. The DJD edition reads ה∘∘י[. However, an upper horizontal stroke of *he* followed by a hook-shaped top of *waw* (or *yod*) are seen in PAM 42820 and 43520. The third letter may be read as either *waw* or *yod*.

Frg. G

1   ה[תֹגֹוֹללו ו○]
2   [○יות את]
2a ה[תהלכֹ○]
3   [נוֹחֹ]

Notes on Readings

L. 1 **ה[תֹגֹוֹללו**. Wacholder and Abegg (perhaps following Strugnell's preliminary reading) read here]אֹיֹללו.[109] Elgvin and Tov suggested]○א יללו[. The bottom part of a *gimel* is visible at the beginning of the line in PAM 41478 and 42820. The following letter may be read as either *waw* or *yod*. A tiny stroke that slants down to the left appears before *gimel*. Given the context, it may be read as the left vertical stroke of a *taw*.

L. 2a **ה[תהלכֹ○**. This is a supralinear addition. In DJD, it is read]יצהלו[. Strugnell has here]ה[תהלכֹו.[110] An examination of the fragment and PAM 40966, 41478, and 42820 confirms his reading of *taw* and medial *kaf*. A trace of ink appearing after *kaf* is difficult to decipher (belonging to the vertical stroke of a *lamed* written in line 3?).

L. 3 **]נוֹחֹ[**. The editors read here ניו. The second letter may be read as either *waw* or *yod*. The following vertical stroke with a concave upper stroke (PAM 41478) suggests a *ḥet* (cf. the *ḥet* in וישכחו [col. i 11]).

Translation

1.   (they) w]allowed ..[
2.   ]…. the [
2a. w]alked[
3.   ]Noah[

---

[109] Wacholder–Abegg, *Preliminary Edition*, vol. 2, p. 251
[110] *Preliminary Concordance*, 2:656.

Comments

L. 1 ה[תְגֹּלֲלוּ. This verb is restored here as a 3rd masc. pl. perfect of גלל in *Hithpolel*, "to wallow."[111] The *Hithpolel* of גלל is used in the sectarian literature with the sense of wallowing in evildoing (cf. CD III, 17; 1QS IV, 19; 1QH[a] XIV, 25), as well as in nonsectarian texts (see Sir 12:14).

L. 2a]∘כֹּ֯לֲהִת[ה. The verb]∘כֹּ֯לֲהִת[ה is restored here as a perfect of הלך in *Hithpaʻel*. Given the practice of the present scribe to write a medial *kaf* instead of a final one, and the fact that the sign following this letter belongs to the line below (see *Notes on Readings* above), the legible letters may constitute a single word. Since the next line mentions Noah, the verb perhaps refers to the mention of the biblical patriarch in Gen 6:9, את האלהים התהלך נח ("Noah walked with God"). In that context, התהלך denotes intimacy and fellowship.[112] Col. ii 2a also refers to Gen 6:9 (see Comments). Thus, this fragment might have belonged to lines 1–3 of that column.

Frg. H

[כבית֯]

Notes on Readings

A long vertical stroke visible at the end of the line may alternatively be read as a downstroke of *dalet* (cf. *dalet* in בעדם [col. ii 5]), namely: [כבוד].

Frg. I

[ג֯ור֯] 1
[לֹומְקֹלֲלֹ] 2
[וכֹח֯] 3
[∘] 4

Notes on Readings

L. 1 [ג֯ור֯]. The editors read [ור֯]∘∘. However, traces of a *gimel* are visible on PAM 42820. They were transcribed as two separate letters in the DJD edition.

---

111 *HALOT*, 194.
112 BDB, 236.

L. 2]לֹומקלל[. Elgvin and Tov read]לֹ וֹמיֹלל[. The distance between *lamed* and *waw* is negligible and it seems that the scribe wrote these two words as one. Traces of a *qof* after the medial *mem* are clearly observable on PAM 42820.

Translation
1.]...[
2.]does not curse[
3.]...[
4.].[

Comments
L. 2]לֹומקלל[. The scribe wrote the negation לו (= לא in MT[113]) and the *Pi'el* masc. sg. participle of קלל, מְקַלֵּל, without an intervening space (cf. 4Q266 5 i 18).

Frg. J

[מג]   1
[וי̊]   2

Notes on Readings
L. 1 מג[. The editors read מ[, but a *gimel* is seen clearly on PAM 41478, 42820, and 43520.

L. 2]וי̊ [. The DJD edition reads]ooo[. However, the tops of the first two letters, which resemble those of *waw* and *yod*, are discernible in the aforementioned photographs.

Frg. K

[את]

---
113 See Qimron, "A Grammar of the Hebrew Language," 76–77.

Frg. L

                         top margin
                         [ואמר
1   [את צדקתו]

Notes on Readings
In the DJD edition, the word ואמר is transcribed as an addition written between lines 1 and 2. In line 2, the editors read]ה∘∘[. However, a close inspection indicates that the faint letters visible under the word את (PAM 41478) are not, in fact, letters, but an imprint of a word found on another layer of the scroll. The small space between the word ואמר and an expression]את צדקתו[suggests that the word ואמר is an addition that was inscribed above line 1.

L. 1 **ואמר**[. Given the similarities between *waw* and *yod* in 4Q422, one may read here]יאמר[and restore ו[יאמר].

Translation
     ]and he pronounced[
1.   ]his righteousness[

Comments
[ואמר
L. 1]**את צדקתו**[. It is possible that the verb ואמר was supposed to be introduced right before the phrase את צדקתו. A similar language is found in Isa 45:24: 'אך בה אמר צדקות (cf. ספר (את) צדקות [1QS I, 21, 23; 1QHª IV, 29]).

Frg. M

1   [∘[
2   ה[י]ה יועֵץ ∘[
3   [בני ישׂרׂ]אל
4   [י]דם ∘[

Notes on Readings

L. 3 בני יש֯ר֯]אל[. The editors read]בניו ֯ ○[. However, the fourth letter is situated at some distance from בני[and appears to introduce a new word. The letters *shin* and *resh* are seen on PAM 41478.

L. 4 ידם[. The reading ודם[is also possible.

Translation
1.].[
2. w]as a counselor [
3.]sons of Isr[ael
4.] ... .[

Comments

L. 2 ה[י֯ו֯ע֯ץ. The word יו֯ע֯ץ, a *Qal* masc. sg. participle of יעץ, may denote either the act of counseling (2 Chr 22:4) or a position of a counselor (see 2 Chr 22:3).

L. 3 בני יש֯ר֯]אל[. This expression may point to an affinity with col iii.

Frg. N

]○○[1
]ב֯ז֯ע֯ת֯ א֯פ[ו 2

Translation
1.]..[
2.]in the sweat of [his]face[

Comments

The phrase]בזעת אפ[ו is perhaps borrowed from Gen 3:19. Thus, the editors suggest that this fragment belongs with col. i, which is concerned with Adam's fall and punishment.

Frg. O

1 [מופ]תים ‏מׄ[
2]ׄ‏ׄ‏[

Translation
1.]. won[ders
2.]..[

Comments

L. 1 **מופ]תים**. The term appears also in col. iii 5. Tov suggested that this fragment belongs with col. iii 6 and should be placed after the phrase]אות למצרים[.[114]

Frg. P

The fragment published in the DJD edition as frg. P appears on PAM 41478 without a connection to the other fragments of 4Q422. However, on PAM 42820, 43540, IAA 375678, and 375680, it is joined to frg. 10e. It contains the first letters of col. iii, 7–9.

Frg. Q

[יארכ יׄ‏]

Comments

The surviving word may be parsed as a 3rd masc. sg. *yiqtol* of ארך ("to be long").[115]

Frg. R

[ׄ‏כבשו]

---

114 Elgvin–Tov, "Paraphrase," 432.
115 BDB, 73.

Notes on Readings

A short vertical stroke descending to the right is visible at the beginning of the line. The editors read it as final *nun* but the remains are too meager to propose a reading.

Translation

] (they) subdued [

Comments

כבשו is to be parsed as a 3rd pl. *Qal qatal* of כבש ("to subdue, master").[116] A *Qal* form of כבש appears in Gen 1:28: ומלאו הארץ וכבשה ("and fill the earth and master it") and the fragment may be related to it.

Frg. S

]∘∘[1
[אשר] 2
]∘∘א̊ל̊ ∘∘[3

Notes on Readings

L. 3]∘∘א̊ל̊ ∘∘[. The DJD edition reads]לא̊ב̊ל̊ ∘∘[, but the surviving traces following *alef* are illegible (PAM 41478).

Frg. T

]∘∘∘[1
[כ̊ א̊∘∘∘ש להימוג̊] 2
]∘ה∘י[ ]ה̊ואה̊[3

Notes on Readings

L. 2]ג̊להימו ש∘∘∘א̊ כ̊[. The editors read]∘הימי של ∘∘∘ כ[. However, PAM 41478 preserves the right and oblique strokes of an *alef*. The *lamed* introduces a new word.

---

116 Ibid., 461.

The last letter is *gimel*; its right stroke is clearly visible on PAM 41478. The preceding letter may be either *waw* or *yod*; the former is preferred for contextual reasons.

Translation
1.]...[
2.]. ..... to melt away[
3.]he [ ]....[

Comments
L. 2]להימוג. This is a *Nif'al* infinitive of מוג, which may denote "melting away (i.e., being helpless and disorganized), waiving, despairing."[117]

As noted above, the photographs of 4Q422 present two additional fragments that were initially associated with the scroll. They are not included in the DJD edition of 4Q422 and are missing from Mus. Inv. plates 165–166. Since these fragments may belong with this scroll, they are edited below.

Frg. U
This fragment is found on PAM 41478 along with frgs. O, R, and S. It appears below frg. S.

]ח̊[1
י̇ש̇ראל ב̊ו̊[2
]ת [3
]○[4

Translation
1.]. [
2. I]srael ..[
3.].[
4.].[

---

117 BDB, 556; *HALOT*, 555.

Comments

L. 2]ֹיִשְׂרָאֵ֣ל[י. Assuming that the fragment belongs with this scroll, the mention of ישרא[ל may perhaps link it to col. iii, which deals with the exodus story.

Frg. V
This fragment appears on PAM 40966, 41478, 42820, and 43520.

[גוב *vac*

Comments

If the surviving three letters constitute a separate word, it may signify either a type of locust, as in Nah 3:17,[118] or a den, as in biblical Aramaic (cf. Dan 6:8, 13, 14) and rabbinic Hebrew (e.g. *Exod. Rab.* 18, 9).

Discussion

The overall picture of 4Q422 as a work recasting biblical episodes emerges clearly from the above detailed analysis. However, the surviving passages concentrate only on three themes, Adam's sin, the flood, and the exodus story. The episodes appear without clear interconnections due, probably, to the fragmentary state of the scroll. But a closer inspection of the technique used in each episode may assist us in gaining an understanding of the general outlook and purpose of the original work, limited though it may be by the present state of preservation.

The Creation and Adam's Sin

Rewriting Genesis 1–3, the first column of 4Q422 deals with God's creational activities (lines 6–7), human rule over the animals and the plants (lines 8–9), the divine prohibition against eating from the Tree of Knowledge (line 10), and its violation (lines 11–12). Frg. N, alluding to Adam's punishment, seems also to belong here. While much is unclear due to the poor state of preservation, col. i reveals one of the most important features of 4Q422, namely, its selective approach to the biblical text. Thus, in lines 9–10, it juxtaposes the prohibition against eating from the Tree of Knowledge, found in Gen 2:16, 17, to the description of man's rule

---

[118] BDB, 146; *HALOT*, 173.

over the floral domain from Gen 1:29, skipping over many a detail of the garden of Eden narrative in Genesis 2. This seems to suggest that, for the author of our scroll, Genesis 1–3 is primarily a story of sin and punishment.

The Story of the Flood

The reworking of this episode is contained in col. ii, which opens with a description of the depravity of humankind (line 1 referring to Gen 6:5). Frg. C, alluding to another verse dealing with the antediluvians' sins, Gen 6:12, may also be fitted here (cf. also frg. G 1).[119] Col. ii 2a, preserving the word ב[דֹורו ("in] his generation"), alludes to Noah's righteousness (Gen 6:9[120]). Frg. G 3 also seems to deal with the same subject. The next two phrases refer to the salvation of the ark inhabitants (lines 2a–3). Notably, the expressions used here, "God kept alive with h[im" and "they were saved," precede the description of Noah boarding the ark and the flood (lines 4–8). Thus, presenting the delivery of the ark dwellers as an accomplished fact even before the catastrophe took place, the scroll proleptically underscores the conclusion of this great biblical event. Another instance of a proleptic reading appears in lines 6–8, where the description of the flood itself opens with a statement declaring that all those living were exterminated by the floodwaters, highlighting the destruction of the wicked.

One of the techniques utilized by the scroll while rewriting the biblical flood account is harmonization. Col. ii 4–5 depict the inhabitants of the ark using the language of Gen 7:7–8. Yet, while both humans and animals come into the ark on their own in these verses, the marker of the direct object, את, preceding the word בניו ("his sons," line 4) suggests that they are brought in there by someone. Apparently, the reading of Gen 7:7 in the scroll is influenced by Gen 6:19, where Noah is commanded to bring the animals into the ark. In light of this verse, the author of 4Q422 could have read the opening words of Gen 7:7 as וַיָּבֵא נח ("And Noah took") and not as וַיָּבֹא נח ("And came Noah"). Thus, he harmonized God's order with the mode of its execution.

---

119 Hence, the scroll might have reworked together Gen 6:5 and 12. Opening with the phrase "the Lord/God saw" and ending with the expression "on the earth," these two verses are also reworked together in other writings describing the wickedness of the antediluvian generation (see *1 En.* 8:2; *Jub.* 5:3; 4Q370 i 3 [see Comments ad loc.]).
120 4Q422 uses the singular ב[דֹורו instead of the plural בדרתיו of Gen 6:9. Such an understanding may have been influenced by God's address to Noah in Gen 7:1: "for you alone have I found righteous before me in this generation (בדור הזה)." Such an interpretative tradition is also reflected in the LXX and *Tg. Neof.* (marginal variant) to Gen 6:9, as well as *L. A. B.* 3:4.

Another technique typical of the present scroll is evident in lines 4–5. It retells the entrance of Noah and the animals into the ark, following Gen 7:7, 8, 16 but drops all the redundancies of Gen 7:10–15, producing a smoother and more coherent version than that of the biblical story.

A further interesting feature of the technique in the passage is seen in the depiction of the flooding waters. Only after describing the rising of the water in line 7 does 4Q422 allude to the forty days and nights of rain of Gen 7:12. It thus alters the order of the verse, specifying the entire length of the rainfall before depicting the event related to it, perhaps in order to emphasize its long duration.

While dealing at some length with the floodwaters (lines 6–8a), the scroll seems to omit the biblical details on how the floodwaters subsided and Noah left the ark (Gen 8:1). Instead, col. II states the purpose of the flood: "in order] to cleanse sin" (line 8). The flood is perceived, then, as a purifying bath, a notion well known from other ancient Jewish and early Christian sources.[121] The phrase "in order to make known the glory of the Most [High," alluding to Hab 2:14, makes it clear that the flood also revealed God's glory. An allusion to Habakkuk in this context might have been influenced by the prophet's comparison of the knowledge of God to the waters of the sea. Yet, while Habakkuk speaks of "the knowledge of the glory of the Lord," employing the Tetragrammaton, 4Q422 prefers the title "Most High." Indeed, the punishment of the wicked in the flood revealed God's supreme power as the Most High God.

Having referred to Noah's sacrifice in line 9, our passage follows with an allusion to the appearance of the rainbow (line 10). The biblical story mentions the rainbow while discussing God's covenant with Noah, but here it appears immediately after Noah's offering. This order of events may signify the acceptance of Noah's sacrifice. Moreover, in juxtaposing the rainbow to the offering, 4Q422 avoided the anthropomorphic language of Gen 8:21: "The Lord smelled the pleasant odor."[122] Additionally, called a "sign of the covenant" (Gen 9:12, 13, 16, 17), the rainbow fittingly appears here after the sacrifice that established the covenant.

Line 11 reworks God's promise never again to bring a flood on the earth (Gen 9:11). Here, 4Q422 again departs from the biblical sequence of events. It refers first to Gen 9:11 and in the following line reworks Gen 8:22 (line 12). A similar procedure is reflected in *Jub.* 6:4, where the promise not to bring the flood precedes

---

[121] Cf. *1 En.* 10:20; 106:17; Philo, *Det.*, 170; 1 Pet 3:20–21; Origen, *Cels.* iv, 21; *Ps.-Clem.*, *Homilies* VIII, 17). See the comments of Kugel, *Traditions*, 187–90, 199–200.
[122] For a similar tendency, see Philo, *Prelim. Studies*, 115; Josephus, *Ant.* i, 99; *L. A. B.* 3:8. Cf. also *Tg. Onq.*, *Tg. Ps.-J.* and *Tg. Neof.* ad loc.

the promise to establish the cycle of seasons.[123] Juxtaposing the covenant with the sacrifice, *Jubilees* presents Noah's offering as confirming the covenant between God and men.[124] Just as in *Jubilees*, the reworking of Gen 9:9 is followed by an allusion to Gen 9:11, so the mention of the rainbow right after Noah's sacrifice in 4Q422 might have prompted a reference to Gen 9:11.

Alternatively, this rearrangement of the biblical verses may be explained by the similarity between God's promise found in Gen 9:11: "and never again shall there be a flood to destroy the earth" and that of Gen 8:21: "nor will I again destroy every living being, as I have done." Thus, 4Q422 could have reworked Gen 8:21 employing the language of Gen 9:11. The rewriting of biblical verse with a synonymous expression found in its immediate context is another technique used widely in the contemporaneous sources.

Line 12 reworks Gen 8:22, as indicated by the phrase: [מו]עֲדֵי יוֹם וְלַיְלָה ○[("[the s]et times of day and night"). However, while Genesis says יוֹם וְלַיְלָה, implying that the sequence of days and nights will not be altered, 4Q422 introduces the notion of מוֹעֵד ("set time"). This addition suggests a precise temporal rhythm of days and nights. It is possible that the addition of the word [מו]עֲדֵי was influenced by the formulation of Gen 1:14. Elgvin proposed that the expression "o]n heaven and ea[rth," found further on in line 12, alludes to Gen 1:15.[125] Genesis itself draws numerous parallels between the creation and the flood (cf. Gen 1:28–30 // 9:1–3, 7) and these are further developed in various ways in the postbiblical literature (cf. *1 En.* 89:8–9;[126] Philo, *Mos.* 2.64–65; *QG* 2.56 [cf. 2.13]).

The reworking of Genesis 6–9 in 4Q422 ii, fragmentary as it is, concludes with the entrusting of the earth into human hands, alluding to Gen 9:1–3 (line 13). Although the bottom lines of col. ii are lost, given the scope of the flood story as presented in its thirteen extant lines, it seems that the major part of the flood narrative as retold in 4Q422 has been preserved.

---

123 J. C. VanderKam, *The Book of Jubilees* (CSCO: Scriptores Aethiopici 88; Leuven: E. Peeters, 1989), 37.
124 See J. Barr, "Reflections on the Covenant with Noah," in *Covenant as Context* (ed. A. D. H. Mayes and R. B. Salters; Oxford: Oxford University Press, 2003), 11–22 (21); J. van Ruiten, "The Covenant of Noah in *Jubilees* 6:1–38," in *The Concept of the Covenant in the Second Temple Period* (ed. S. E. Porter and J. C. R. de Roo; JSJSup 71; Leiden: Brill, 2003), 167–90 (174–76).
125 See further Peters, *Traditions*, 143–44.
126 F. Martin, *Le Livre d'Hénoch* (Paris: Letouzey et Ané, 1906), 205, noted that the reappearance of light after the flood in *1 En.* 89:8 may allude to Gen 1:1–5.

The Exodus Story

Although the text of 4Q422 iii is better preserved than that of the two preceding columns, much of its first six lines has been lost. Despite this, the expression "the [t]wo mid[wives," found at the beginning of its second line, points unmistakably to the midwives' story from Exod 1:15–21. Line 3 opens with Pharaoh's order to throw all the male Israelite infants into the Nile (Exod 1:22) and ends with the cry of the Hebrew slaves (Exod 2:23). It appears that the author skipped over the events of Moses' early life and juxtaposed the cry of the enslaved nation to Pharaoh's malicious order. Setting these two side by side, 4Q422 provides a justification for the severe punishment of the Egyptians described further on in lines 6–12.

Following the sequence of Exodus 3–4, line 4 speaks of the mission given to Moses, apparently alluding to the vision of the burning bush (Exod 3:3). In the book of Exodus, the description of the theophany precedes that of Moses' commission, but in 4Q422 the order of events is reversed (thus Tov). In this way, the scroll makes clear that the appointment of Moses is God's answer to their cry.[127]

Line 5 apparently refers to the signs that Moses was about to perform before the Israelites (Exod 4:1–9) and, following the exodus account, attaches a reference to the future role of Aaron as Moses' companion and assistant.

Line 6 elaborates on the mission of Moses and Aaron. While the biblical account describes in great detail how Moses and Aaron repeatedly presented Pharaoh with God's demand to release His people, this episode is stated only briefly in the scroll, and includes merely the demand of Moses and Aaron to let the Israelites leave Egypt and Pharaoh's refusal to comply. Yet, while several contemporary sources, such as *Jubilees* (48:16–17) and Josephus, *Ant.* (ii, 293, 295, 299, 302, 304, 305), tend to downplay God's role in Pharaoh's obstinate refusal to release the Israelites, leading to his punishment, 4Q422 states bluntly that "He hardened [his] heart [so that he would] sin in order to make known [   ] for gene[rations] of eternity."[128]

So, according to 4Q422, the punishment of the depraved antediluvians and the wicked Pharaoh attests to God's glory. The notion of punishment as the means for making known God's power fits well with the story of the exodus (e.g. Exod 10:1–2) but is not expressed overtly in the Genesis flood account. By introducing it

---

[127] A similar formulation is found in *L. A. B.* 10:1. See H. Jacobson, *A Commentary on Pseudo-Philo's Liber Antiquitatum Biblicarum* (AGAJU 31; Leiden: Brill, 1996), 1:106.

[128] See Kugel, *Traditions*, 548–51; L. H. Feldman, "The Plague of the First-Born Egyptians in Rabbinic Tradition, Philo, Pseudo-Philo, and Josephus," *RB* 109 (2002): 403–21 (405–06).

into the reworking of both stories, 4Q422 emphasizes their common message and reveals its didactic purpose.¹²⁹

A brief description of the ten plagues (lines 7–12) follows these statements. Notably, as observed by Tov, this passage employs poetical parallelism, and is influenced by two biblical psalms retelling the exodus story, Psalms 78 and 105. Tov argues that these lines depend primarily on Psalm 78 and to a lesser extent on Psalm 105 and Exodus 7–12.¹³⁰ However, a closer examination suggests that the passage relies mostly on Exodus 7–12 (the lexica borrowed from Exod 7–12 and Pss 78 and 105 are represented as follows: Exodus, Ps 78, *Ps 105*):

			ויופך לדם [מימ/]יהמה ¹³¹
	וכנים בכול גבול]ם		הצפרדעים בכול ארצ]ם ¹³²
	ו[נג]ע בכול פ[רי]הסה		ערוב בבתיהסה
	ובהמתם ל[מו]ת *הסגיר*		ויגוף בדב[ר את] מקניהסה
בלירא[ה] איש את אחיו	ואפלה ב[בתי]הסה		ישי[ת חו]שך בארצם
לה[]אביד כו[]ל פרי אוכ[ל]ם	ואדמת[ם ב]*חנמל*		[ויך] *בברד* ארצם
לאכול כול ירוק בא[]רצם	*חסל* כבד בכו[ל ג]בולם		ויבא ארבֹה לכסות עין הֹא[]רץ
	רֹשית לכו]ל אונם		[ויך בכורם

The suggestion that this passage is based first and foremost on Exodus 7–12 tallies well with the fact that the order in the scroll follows the order of the plagues in Exodus. Thus, although 4Q422 is heavily influenced by Psalms 78 and 105, its base text is Exodus 7–12.

A reworking of a biblical passage using terminology found in parallel biblical texts is a well-known technique. It is applied for different purposes in various contexts. Here it may reflect the author's preference for the concise and poetic formulation of the subject. In a similar way, the biblical account of creation seems

---

129 As noted by Chazon, "Creation and Fall of Adam," 17.
130 Elgvin–Tov, "Paraphrase," 429; Tov, "Paraphrase of Exodus," 362–63.
131 This phrase, as restored by Tov (see *Comments*), alludes to Ps 105:29. However, it is also possible that the scroll relies here on Ps 78:44: ויהפך לדם יאריהם.
132 It is difficult to determine whether the scroll reworks here Exod 8:1–3 or Ps 105:30. See *Comments* on col. III, 8.

to be recapitulated in 4Q422 i 6 by utilizing the language of Ps 33:6. Furthermore, the depiction of the plagues in Psalms 78 and 105, in which they are presented as the direct work of God with no human mediation accords with the description in cols. i and ii of the divine punishment.

As was shown by Tov, the order of the plagues in lines 7–12 follows, in general, that of Exodus 7–12:

Exodus 7–12	Psalm 78	Psalm 105	4Q422
Blood	Blood	Darkness	Blood
Frogs	Flies	Blood	Frogs
Gnats	Frogs	Frogs	Gnats
Flies	Locusts	Flies	Flies
Pestilence	Hail	Gnats	Boils
Boils	Pestilence	Hail	Pestilence
Hail	Firstborn	Locusts	Darkness
Locusts		Firstborn	Hail
Darkness			Locusts
Firstborn			Firstborn

Still, there are a few changes that deserve further examination. Thus, the plague of boils precedes the plague of pestilence in 4Q422 iii, while in Exodus the order is reversed. This is not the only case in which 4Q422 deviates from the sequence of the plagues in Exodus; the scroll mentions the plague of darkness before the plague of hail. In this case, one may point to the fact that the resulting order of the last triad of plagues in 4Q422, hail, locusts, and firstborn, is identical to that of Psalm 105. However, a comparison with Psalm 105 can hardly explain the displacement of boils in 4Q422, for this plague is omitted in this psalm. While omissions and displacements in the order of the plagues are frequent in contemporary sources,[133] placing the boils before the pestilence in 4Q422, as is done also in *Jubilees* (48:5), might have had an exegetical motive. According to Exod 9:3, the plague of pestilence struck "the livestock in the fields—the horses, the asses, the camels, the cattle, and the sheep." As a result, Exod 9:6 states that all the livestock of the Egyptians died. However, when describing the following plague

---

[133] See *Jub.* 48:5; Ezekiel the Tragedian, *Exagoge*, 132–48; Artapanus 3:28–902; Philo, *Mos.* 1, 98–134; Wis 11:5–8, 17–18; Josephus, *Ant.* ii, 294–313; *L. A. B.* 10:1. For the discussion, see Ginzberg, *Legends*, 1:525–26; S. E. Loewenstamm, *The Tradition of the Exodus in its Development* (Jerusalem: Magnes Press, 1965), 43–47 (Hebrew); H. Jacobson, *The Exagoge of Ezekiel* (Cambridge: Cambridge University Press, 1983), 114–16; S. Cheon, *The Exodus Story in the Wisdom of Solomon* (Sheffield: Sheffield Academic Press, 1997), 47–89.

of boils, Exod 9:10 reports that the boils were "on man and cattle." The author of 4Q422 perhaps mentioned the boils first in order to resolve this discrepancy. A similar sensitivity to this type of discrepancy is reflected in the description of the plague of hail that follows. According to Exodus 9, the hail struck man and cattle as well as all the grasses and the trees (9:25), but 4Q422 iii 10 refers only to all the fruits, perhaps because the cattle should have been destroyed already by the pestilence.

The poetic description of the plagues in 4Q422 is interrupted by a statement set in prose (line 11): "and God har[dened] the heart of [Pharao]h so as not to let [them] go and in order to multiply wonders." Its wording rests on God's words to Moses from Exod 11:9–10. Significantly, both in Exodus and in 4Q422, this statement precedes the plague of the firstborn. In the introduction to the plagues account, the author of 4Q422 had already explained the purpose served by them. Concerned with presenting God's punishment of Pharaoh and the Egyptians as being just, as he is, the author reclarifies the purpose of the plagues before introducing the most severe plague of all, that of the firstborn.

Conclusion

The scholars who have dealt with 4Q422 have pointed out the didactic aspect of this composition.[134] The foregoing analysis brings forth this characteristic. The paraenetic character of the work is expressed by the choice of biblical stories that feature sin and punishment, by their selective reworking with an emphasis on this aspect of the stories, and by the recurring theme of punishment as a means for making known God's glory and justice. Given the presence of a second person address in frg. A, the original work also may have included an admonition phrased in this style. Thus, 4Q422 is an example of a didactic reworking of Scripture.

---

134 Bernstein, "Interpretation," 139; idem, "Flood," 211–13; idem, "Contours," 74–75; idem, "Contribution," 229–30.

4Q464 (Exposition on the Patriarchs), 4Q464ᵃ, and 4Q464ᵇ

Literature

M. E. Stone and E. Eshel, "An Exposition on the Patriarchs (4Q464) and Two Other Documents (4Q464ᵃ and 4Q464ᵇ)," *Le Muséon* 105 (1992): 243–64; E. Eshel and M. E. Stone, "The Eschatological Holy Tongue in Light of a Fragment Found at Qumran," *Tarbiẓ* 62 (1993): 169–77 (Hebrew); idem, "464. 4QExposition on the Patriarchs," "464ᵃ. 4QNarrative E," "464ᵇ. 4QUnclassified Fragments," in *Qumran Cave 4.XIV: Parabiblical Texts, Part 2* (ed. M. Broshi et al.; DJD XIX; Oxford: Clarendon Press, 1995), 215–34 (referred below as "the editors"); M. Bernstein, "Three Notes on 4Q464," *Tarbiẓ* 65 (1996): 29–32 (Hebrew); M. Bernstein, "Contours of Genesis: Interpretation at Qumran: Contents, Context, and Nomenclature," in *Studies in Ancient Midrash* (ed. J. L. Kugel; Cambridge: Harvard University Press, 2001), 37–85 (73–74); idem, "The Contribution of the Qumran Discoveries to the History of Early Biblical Interpretation," in *The Idea of Biblical Interpretation* (ed. H. Najman and J. H. Newman; JSJSup 83; Leiden: Brill, 2004), 215–38 (228); S. Weitzman, "Why did the Qumran Community Write Hebrew," *JAOS* 119 (1999): 35–45; J. C. Poirer, "4Q464: Not Eschatological," *RevQ* 20 (2002): 583–87; J. Charlesworth and C. D. Elledge, "Exposition on the Patriarchs (4Q464 = 4QExPat)," "Midwives to Pharaoh Fragment (4Q464a)," "Unidentified Fragments (4Q464b)," in *Pesharim, Other Commentaries, and Related Documents* (ed. J. H. Charlesworth et al.; PTSDSSP 6B; Tübingen: Mohr Siebeck, 2002), 274–85, 351–57; C. Batsch, "Commentaires sur la vie des Patriarches (4QExposition on the Patriarchs) 4Q464," in *La Bibliothèque de Qumran: Torah: Genèse* (ed. K. Berthellot, T. Legrand, and A. Paul; Paris: Cerf, 2008), 389–97; A. Feldman, "A Note on 4Q464ᵃ," *Meghillot* 7 (2009): 299–304 (Hebrew).

Most of the fragments assigned to 4Q464 are concerned with events from the lives of Abraham and Jacob. Therefore, the final editors, Esther Eshel and Michael Stone, published it under the name "Exposition on the Patriarchs."[1] As to the general character of 4Q464, one should note the formula פשר עָ[ל, occurring in frg. 3 ii 7, which may suggest a sectarian provenance. However, the scroll lacks other sectarian markers such as the peculiar terminology of the Yahad writings.[2] Moreover, some of its fragments deal with biblical episodes in a manner similar to that of the rewritten Bible texts, for instance, frg. 6.[3] So the locution פשר עָ[ל

---

[1] Eshel–Stone "An Exposition on the Patriarchs (4Q464)" and DJD XIX, 215–34.
[2] E. Eshel and M. E. Stone, "The Eschatological Holy Tongue in Light of a Fragment Found at Qumran," *Tarbiẓ* 62 (1993): 169–77 (176; Hebrew), leave this question open.
[3] This scroll perhaps belongs with the writings that are close to the sectarian literature yet lack its peculiar characteristics, such as *Jubilees*, the *Temple Scroll*, and *Apocryphon of Jeremiah C*. On this intermediate category, see D. Dimant, "Between the Sectarian and Non-Sectarian: The Case

may indicate here a nonsectarian interpretation of a biblical passage, a usage also known from other Qumran documents (cf. 1Q30 1 6; 4Q159 5 5; 4Q252 IV, 5).[4]

The Manuscript

The DJD edition of 4Q464 contains eleven fragments written in a Herodian script.[5] John Strugnell, the first editor of the scroll, assigned three additional fragments to 4Q464 (seen on PAM 42819 and 43357) but they were treated separately and edited as 4Q464[a] and 4Q464[b] by Eshel and Stone.[6] The two fragments assigned to 4Q464[b] are very small and their original assignment to 4Q464 is indeed doubtful (see *Appendix*). However, the separation from 4Q464 of the fragment assigned to 4Q464[a] seems unwarranted since its script resembles that of 4Q464.[7] The same is true of the size of the letters, the interlinear spaces, and the color of the parchment. Although the editors point out that 4Q464[a] differs from 4Q464 in its language and literary style, a detailed study of the fragment leads to the opposite conclusion (cf. below). Thus, in the present edition it appears as 4Q464 12. At the same time, frg. 5 may not in fact belong to 4Q464. It differs from the rest of the manuscript in script,[8] its darker color, defective orthography (כֹּל), and the absence of the lengthened forms (כִּֿ, וְלֹאִֿ [frg. 5 ii 3, 5]) compared with the plene one of 4Q464 (ולוא [frg. 6 2]) and its lengthened forms (כיא, הואה [frg. 3 i 7]; ידכה [frg. 6 3]).[9] In addition, the extant text of frg. 5 lacks the division into paragraphs

---

of the *Apocryphon of Joshua*," in *History, Ideology and Bible Interpretation in the Dead Sea Scrolls: Collected Studies* (Tübingen: Mohr Siebeck, 2014), 113–33.

4 The noun פשר occurs in Eccl 8:1 and thus in itself is not a sectarian term. Scholars have already pointed out that pesher as an exegetical method did not originate in the Qumran community, but was appropriated and developed by it. See D. Dimant, "Pesher," in *Encyclopedia of Religion* (ed. L. Jones; Detroit: Thomson Gale, 2004[2]), 7065.

5 The fragments were studied by me anew in spring 2006 and spring 2007.

6 4Q464[a] appears in the earliest PAM photographs of the scroll, 41894 and 42819. The two fragments labeled 4Q464[b] appear only in its last photograph in the PAM series, 43357. 4Q464[a] is also treated separately in a recent French edition by T. Legrand, "Fragment mentionnant les sages-femmes de Pharaon (4QNarrative E)," in *La Bibliothéque de Qumran: Torah: 2: Exode-Lévitique-Nombres* (ed. K. Berthelot and T. Legrand; Paris: Cerf, 2008), 203–05.

7 This is the opinion of Ada Yardeni (private communication). I thank Dr. Yardeni for looking into this matter and sharing with me the results of her examination.

8 Thus Ada Yardeni in a private communication.

9 Many Qumran scrolls display inconsistency when it comes to orthography and morphology, yet in the case of 4Q464 all such inconsistencies occur in frg. 5. See the data culled by Tov, *Scribal Practices*, 339–43.

that is seen in several other fragments of 4Q464 (frgs. 3, 4, 7, 10).[10] All these distinctive features lead to the conclusion that frg. 5 belongs to a different scroll. It is, therefore, presented here as an unidentified fragment.

Text and Comments

The fragments of 4Q464 are presented in the DJD edition according to the biblical order of events to which they allude. The first three fragments deal with episodes from Abraham's life.

Frg. 1[11]

1]∘ אברהם ב[ן
2 ויש[ב̊ בחרן]

Notes on Readings

L. 1 **אברהם** ∘[. Eshel and Stone read ב̊אברהם. The oblique stroke descending to the left (seen on PAM 42819) resembles the base of a *bet* or medial *mem* (compare the medial *mem* in אמר in frg. 7 3). It appears at some distance from an *alef* and may belong to the preceding word.

L. 2 **ויש[ב̊**. An upper horizontal stroke with a short serif on its left extremity is visible at the beginning of the line, both on the fragment and in its photographs (especially PAM 42819). The editors noted that it may belong to a *resh*, yet proposed no reading; Charlesworth and Elledge read ר̊[. However, this short concave stroke does not accord with *resh* as it is inscribed in this fragment (see the *resh* in אברהם and בחרן), but rather with the roof of a *bet* (compare the *bet* in בחרן, בן).

---

10 On this practice, see Tov, ibid., 147–48.
11 This fragment was initially published in J. R. Davila, "4QGen[h-para]," in *Qumran Cave 4.VI: Genesis to Numbers* (ed. E. Ulrich et al.; DJD XII; Oxford: Clarendon Press, 1994), 62–63. However, since its script is identical to that of 4Q464, it was reassigned to this scroll. In addition to PAM 42819 and 43357, frg. 1 is also found on PAM 41996.

Translation

1. 　　　]. Abraham [　　]years old[
2. and he dwe]lled in Haran[

Comments

L. 1 ‏אברהם בן‎[. ○[. The editors understood the word ‏בן‎ as "son" and restored the nonbiblical formula ‏אברהם בן‎ ‏תרח‎.[12] However, given the reference in the next line to the sojourn in Haran, the expression may specify Abraham's age upon his arrival at this locality.[13] The Hebrew Bible does not supply this datum. Yet, 4Q252 II 9–10 states that on that occasion the patriarch was seventy years old. According to *Jub.* 12:12, Abraham was then sixty years old.[14] Note that the Qumran text designates the patriarch by his full name, Abraham, although the change of his name from Abram to Abraham (Gen 17:5) occurs long after the patriarch's sojourn in Haran.[15] Among the Second Temple sources dealing with Genesis 11–16, some have Abram (1QapGen XIX, 14–XXIV; 4Q180 2–4 i 4; 4Q252 II 10–13),[16] while others employ Abraham (4Q225 2 i 3–8, reworking Gen 15:1–6).[17]

L. 2 ‏וישׁ[ב בחרן‎. The restoration ‏וישׁ[ב‎, namely the 3rd masc. sg. *Qal wayyiqtol* of ‏ישׁב‎, relies on the formulation of Gen 11:31. Similar phrasing of the Haran episode appears in two Qumran Hebrew rewritten Bible texts, 4Q225 2 i 2 and 4Q252 ii 9–10.

---

12 This formulation is attested in late midrashim. See *Pirqe R. El.* 24; *S. Eli. Zut.* 24.
13 The use of the word ‏בן‎ to designate Abraham's age occurs in Gen 17:1.
14 4Q225 2 i 2 states, most probably with reference to Abraham, that he dwelt in Haran for twenty years. According to Gen 12:4, he left Haran when he was seventy-five years old. If the author of 4Q225 accepted this biblical datum, he might have thought that Abraham was fifty-five years old when he arrived at Haran. For the significance of this date to other events in Genesis, and consequently its importance, see A. Livneh, "How Long was Abraham's Sojourn in Haran? Traditions Regarding the Patriarch in Compositions from Qumran," *Meghillot* 8 (2010): 193–210 (Hebrew).
15 In describing the time spent in Haran, Genesis appropriately employs the name Abram (11:21; 12:1, 4, 5).
16 A similar differentiation seems to be reflected in *Jub.* 11:4–15:6 (not extant among the Hebrew Qumran fragments of *Jubilees*) and in *L. A. B.* 6:3–8:3 (but see 9:3).
17 The name Ἀβραάμ appears in Rom 4:3, Gal 3:6, and Heb 7:1–5, alluding to Gen 14:18; 15:6. In his *Jewish Antiquities*, Josephus consistently uses the form Ἄβραμος. See L. H. Feldman, *Judean Antiquities 1–4: Translation and Commentary* (Flavius Josephus: Translation and Commentary 3; Leiden: Brill, 2000), 72.

Frg. 2

top margin?

1 [ת֯פ֯ כיא אם *vac*[
2]ו֯ לשון הו֯א[
3]ד֯ב֯ק ע֯מ[

Notes on Readings

The blank space above the first line may be part of the top margin or a blank line between the paragraphs.

L. 1 ת֯פ֯[. The editors proposed no reading for the beginning of the line, but traces of two letters are visible there. An upper horizontal stroke and a trace of a right vertical stroke remain of the first letter (see PAM 41894). These may belong to a *taw*. The following letter is a final *pe*, its upper part being clearly visible on PAM 42819 and 43357.

L. 3 ד֯ב֯ק[. The editors read ○א֯ק[, but as seen on PAM 42819, the first letter may be read as *dalet* or *resh*, for it is represented by the upper part of a vertical stroke and a horizontal stroke descending to the right. However, since the horizontal stroke reaches beyond the vertical one, as it does usually in *dalet* in this scroll (cf. באחד [frg. 3 i 4]), it is preferable to read here a *dalet*. As for the second letter, on PAM 42819 one may see a vertical stroke with a convex base stroke. The upper stroke has the form of a right angle. This shape does not fit an *alef*, but perhaps that of a *bet*.

Translation
1.].. though[
2.]. tongue it[
3.]he joined to[

Comments

L. 1 ת֯פ֯ כיא אם[. In biblical Hebrew, the construction כי אם is usually used to denote a contrast (CD IV, 11; X, 22, 23; 1QSa I, 3).[18] I was unable to suggest a suitable restoration for the first word.

---

[18] On the biblical usages of כי אם, see Jouon-Muraoka, *Grammar*, § 164c, § 173c, § 174b.

L. 2]לשׁון הוֹאֹ ○[. The noun לשון occurs also in frg. 3 i 8: לשון הקודש. As the editors note, it seems probable that both fragments deal with the same topic. Syntactically, the 3rd masc. sg. pronoun הוא may open a new clause or function as a copula in a nominative sentence explicating the word לשון (in the Hebrew Bible, לשון may be used also in the masculine; see Josh 7:21). Alternatively, לשון may be a *nomen rectum* in a construct pair with a now-lost masculine *nomen regens*. See frg. 3 i 8.

L. 3]דֹּבֹק עֹםֹ[. The first word is perhaps a 3rd masc. sg. *Qal qatal* of דבק. For the locution דבק עם, see Ruth 2:8.[19]

Frg. 3 i

[	1
]םֹ[	2
]○ עבד	3
]ש באחד	4
]○תֹבלת	5
]םֹ לאברהום	6
[○עֹדֹ עולם כיא הואה	7
ה[וא לשון הקודש	8
אהפך] אל עמים שפה ברורה	9
] vacat [	10
]○תֹוֹ○[	11

Notes on Readings

L. 4 באחד. An examination of the fragment indicates that the reading of a *bet* (with the editors) should be preferred to a reading with a medial *kaf*, כאחד.

L. 5]תֹ○[. The editors read]נֹבלת ○[but, as Qimron suggests, the traces of ink preceding the *bet* seem to suit better a *taw*.[20] There is another illegible letter before this *taw*.

---

19 See *HALOT*, 209. For a discussion of the usages of דבק in ancient sources, see H. Dihi, "The Morphological and Lexical Innovations in the Book of Ben Sira" (Ph.D. diss., Ben-Gurion University of the Negev, 2004), 162–64.

20 Personal communication. I thank Prof. Qimron for sharing his observations on this fragment.

L. 6 לֹאברהום. The DJD edition reads לֹאברה{ר}ם. Qimron (quoted by the editors) proposed לֹאברהום, a reading followed here. While the top of the sixth letter does indeed resemble that of a *resh* (occurring in the same word), the upper horizontal stroke of a *resh* is a little longer. Further support for the reading לֹאברהום may be found in a form לאברוֹ[הם occurring in frg. 3 ii 3.

L. 8 ו[ה. The vertical stroke with a hook-shaped top, visible at the beginning of the line, is certainly a *waw* and not a *resh* (see PAM 43357), as read by Eshel and Stone.

L. 11]∘תֿ∘[. The DJD edition has here]∘כֿ[but a trace of a letter can be seen at the beginning of the line, unnoted by the editors. The upper horizontal stroke with a serif at its left extremity belongs to a *taw*. The left vertical stroke of a *taw* is still visible on PAM 41894. The following vertical stroke with a hook-shaped top is a *waw* or a *yod* (thus Charlesworth–Elledge, "New Edition").

Translation
1.]
2.]..
3.]. a slave
4.] on the first
5.]. confusion of
6.]. to Abraham
7.]. forever, since he/it
8. I]t is the sacred tongue
9. I will make] the peoples pure of tongue
10.]*vacat*
11.]... .[

Comments
L. 3 עבד. The lack of a context makes it impossible to decide whether the surviving word should be read as a verb, a 3rd masc. sg. *Qal qatal* of עבד, or as a noun עֶבֶד. The translation above renders it as a noun, following the editors.

L. 4 ש[באחד. The word באחד may be part of some chronological information, giving the precise date of an event. If so, it may denote a day in a month (see the formulations in Gen 8:5; Exod 40:2; 1Q22 i 2; 4Q252 i 4). Therefore, it may be restored לחודש] / ויע[ש באחד.²¹ Batsch suggests החוד[ש באחד בשבת, as in 4Q252 I, 17, 19.²²

L. 5 תֹּ̊בלת∘[. The word seems to be connected to the theme of the tongue appearing in lines 8–9. Qimron suggests that this is an otherwise unattested nominal form, תְּבְלָה, in construct. As a derivative of בלל, "to mix up, to confound," it probably denotes "confusion."²³ While the editors suggested a different reading here, they have correctly interpreted this line as referring to the confusion of languages related in Gen 11:7 וְנָבְלָה שם שפתם ("Let us ... and confound their speech there").²⁴ Compare the construct pair בלת לשון that describes the biblical "confusion of tongues" in the *War Scroll* (1QM X, 14).

L. 6 לאברהום ם̊[. If the proposed reading is correct, one may assume that the unusual orthography אברהום, with the vowel "o" after the *he* (indicated by a *waw*) instead of the vowel "a" (as in the MT), is influenced by a labial final *mem*.²⁵ See *Comments* on col. ii 3 of this fragment.

L. 7 עַ֯ד עולם כיא הואה. The phrase עד עולם occurs in God's promise to Abraham to give him and his offspring the land of Canaan "forever (עד עולם)" in Gen 13:15; see also Gen 17:7, 8, 13, 19. If so, the expression perhaps concludes the same promise here (not preserved), while הואה may refer to Abraham in a clause explaining why he was worthy of such a promise.

L. 8 ה[וא לשון הקודש. The supplement of a *he* is suggested at the beginning of the phrase, being preferable to the editors' restoration לקר[וא לשון הקודש. Supplying a pronoun lends the phrase coherence as the second part of an explicative nominal phrase, the beginning of which is lost. If correct, the noun לשון is treated here in the masculine, as it is in frg. 2 2.²⁶ The collocation לשון הקודש ("the sacred tongue") is nonbiblical and this is its only appearance in the Qumran documents.

---

21 If the date is connected to the "sacred language" mentioned in line 8, it is interesting to note that according to *Jub.* 12:16 the Hebrew language was revealed to Abraham on the first day of the seventh month.
22 Batsch, "Commentaires," 392.
23 Cf. *HALOT*, 134.
24 Eshel–Stone, "Holy Tongue," 173–74; "464. 4QExposition on the Patriarchs," 219, 221.
25 See Kutscher, *Isaiah Scroll*, 391–92; Qimron, "A Grammar of the Hebrew Language," 114–17.
26 The supplement creates the pronoun in a short form. However the interchange of long and short forms of this pronoun is evident in the present scroll. In line 7 of this fragment, the long form הואה occurs while the short one הוא appears in frg. 11 4. In some scrolls, both short and

However, it appears frequently in the rabbinic literature as a designation of the Hebrew language.²⁷ The fragment seems to allude to the tradition attributing to Abraham knowledge of Hebrew (thus the editors). This tradition is also known to *Jub.* 12:25–27, as well as to the rabbinic midrash (*Gen. Rab.* 42, 8).²⁸

L. 9 אהפך[אל עמים שפה ברורה. A quotation of Zeph 3:9–10 and the word אהפך is restored from this biblical verse. Since the locution שפה ברורה occurs here in close proximity to the expression לשון הקודש, referring as it does to Hebrew, it appears that the Qumran author understood the prophecy of Zephaniah as alluding to this sacred tongue (thus the editors).²⁹ Eshel and Stone suggest plausibly that 4Q464 also took up the eschatological context of this biblical prophecy, namely, that in the last days all the nations worshipping YHWH will speak Hebrew.³⁰ Poirer's suggestion that the quotation from Zephaniah serves here as a proof-text for the tradition that Abraham knew Hebrew is less convincing.³¹

Frg. 3 ii

1 הכ[ο
2 המשפט [   ]ο[   ] וברl
3 כאשר אמר לאברו[הם ידוע תדע כי גר יהיה זרעך בארץ לא להם]
4 ועבדום וענוֹ[אותם ארבע מאות שנה
5 וֹשׁכב עֹם [אבותיו
6 שמ[ο

---

longer forms appear side by side (see 1QIsaᵃ XXXII, 7, 11 [see Kutscher, *Isaiah Scroll*, 343–44]; 4Q251 9 3–4).

27 See, for instance, *m. Soṭah* 7:2, 8:2; *t. Ḥag.* 1:2. The Aramaic equivalent of this collocation occurs also in the Aramaic Targumim (e.g., *Tg. Ps.-J.*, *Frg. Tg.*, *Tg. Neof.* to Gen 11:1). Cf. A. Shinan, "לישן בית קודשא in the Aramaic Targums of the Pentateuch," *Beth-Miqra* 21 (1976): 472–74 (Hebrew).

28 Poirer assumes that the scroll depends on *Jubilees* 12 (idem, "4Q464: Not Eschatological," 586–87). However, the wording of the present Qumran fragment does not support the supposition of a literary dependence on *Jubilees*. A more plausible assumption is that both *Jubilees* 12 and 4Q464 reflect the same exegetical tradition.

29 A similar interpretation, though without an explicit link to the Hebrew, is found in *T. Jud* 25:3 and in the Aramaic Targum to Zeph 3:9. See further Eshel–Stone, "Holy Tongue."

30 Eshel–Stone, "464. 4QExposition on the Patriarchs," 220. Thus also E. Eshel, "Hermeneutical Approaches to Genesis in the Dead Sea Scrolls," in *The Book of Genesis in Jewish and Oriental Christian Interpretation* (ed. J. Frishman and L. Van Rompay; Traditio Exegetica Graeca 5; Leuven: A. Peters, 1997), 1–12 (5–7).

31 Poirer, "Eschatology," 586–87.

7 פשר ע]ל
8 לאב֯[ו]ל[

Notes on Readings

L. 5 **לאברו]הם**. The editors read לאברה֯]ם. However, PAM 42819 and 43357 show next to the *resh* a vertical stroke with a hook-shaped top, characteristic of *waw* or *yod*; see Comments.

L. 8 **לאב֯[ו]ל[**. The DJD edition has לא[ ]ל[ ]ל, but in PAM 41503 the vertical stroke and upper horizontal stroke of a medial *kaf* are visible.

Translation

1. ...[
2. the judgment [ ].[ ] and..[
3. as he said to Abrah[am, "You shall surely know that your seed will be a sojourner in a foreign land,]
4. and they will enslave them and oppress[them for four hundred years   ]
5. and (he) will lie down with [his fathers
6. ...[
7. an explanation conc[erning
8. to e[a]t[

Comments

L. 2 **ובר] [   ]o[   ] המשפט**. The immediate context of the noun הַמִּשְׁפָּט has not been preserved. The editors suggest that it is connected to the quotation in the next lines of the prophecy on the future servitude of Israel in Egypt, from Gen 15:13. Accordingly, they propose to restore here the conclusion of this prophecy from Gen 15:14 (ואחרי כן יצאו ברכוש גדול), which forecasts that following this servitude Israel will leave that country with much property, ובר]כוש. If correct, the word המשפט ("the judgment") may refer to the judgment to be meted to the enslaving people (see the verb דן ["judge"] in Gen 15:14).

L. 3 **כאשר אמר**. The phrase כאשר אמר appears frequently in the scrolls as an introductory formula to a biblical quotation, often as proof of a previous statement (CD VII, 8; XIX, 5; XX, 16). The wording כאשר אמר ל-, found here, occurs also in 4Q385 3a–c 4 (= 4Q388a 3 3); 4Q385 4 6.

L. 4 לאברו]הם. In col. i 6 of the fragment, the name is written אברהום. The change in the position of *waw* in relation to *he* suggests that *he* was not pronounced. This phenomenon is well attested in the Qumran texts, especially in relation to *alef*; compare, for instance, ויאׄומרו (4Q457b ii 7) with יואמרו (4Q158 10–12 10).[32]

Ll. 3–4 ידוע תדע כי גר יהיה זרעך בארץ לא להם] ועבדום ועֹנוּ֯] אותם ארבע מאוד שנה. The phrase ועבדום ועֹנוּ֯] is a unique biblical combination, taken from Gen 15:13. The reconstruction follows this biblical verse (with the editors).

L. 5 וּשׁכב עׄםׄ]אבותיו. In line with the preceding ועבדום ועֹנוּ֯, the verb וּשׁכב is to be read as a 3rd masc. sg. *Qal weqatal* of שכב. The scroll seems to allude here to Gen 15:15: "And for you, you shall go to your fathers in peace (תבוא אל אבתיך); you shall be buried at a ripe old age." The expression שכב עם אבתיו appears in Gen 47:30 in relation to Joseph's death.

L. 7 פשר עָ]ל. The noun פֵּשֶׁר ("meaning, explanation"), is found in Eccl 8:1,[33] but in the Qumran sectarian literature it is used as a technical term for introducing an actualizing interpretation of biblical prophecy. In such contexts, the locution פשרו על appears (e.g. 1QpHab IV, 5; V, 9; 1Q14 8–10 4).[34] However, the construction פשר על (without the pronominal suffix) appears only here and in 4Q180 1 1, 7, and 4Q171 1–10 iii 7, where it introduces interpretations of themes rather than specific biblical texts.[35] This may also be the case here. However, in the absence of other sectarian markers in the scroll, the term may not be sectarian. Moreover, given the fragmentary state of the text not much can be said of it.

L. 8 לאבֹ[ו]ל]. Only the word לאבֹ[ו]ל, a *Qal* infinitive of אכל, has been preserved without any context. Perhaps it is connected to the episode relating the visit of the three "men" in Gen 18:8. In this case, the phrase פשר עָ]ל in the previous line would refer to this entire biblical episode (compare 4Q180 2–4 ii 2–7) and not to a specific verse.

---

32 See Qimron, "A Grammar of the Hebrew Language," 72.
33 *HALOT*, 982–83.
34 For a discussion of the term, see M. Horgan, *Pesharim: Qumran Interpretations of Biblical Books* (CBQMS 8; Washington: Catholic Biblical Association of America, 1979), 239–44.
35 D. Dimant, "The 'Pesher on Periods' (4Q180) and 4Q181," in *History, Ideology and Bible Interpretation in the Dead Sea Scrolls: Collected Studies* (FAT 90; Tübingen: Mohr Siebeck, 2014), 385–404 (387).

Frg. 4

```
                           ]ṓ[ ]ọṃ[      1
             ] vacat שׁ̇מעו[              2
             ] לשמונים שנה[               3
```

Notes on Readings

L. 2 שׁ̇מעו[. The DJD edition reads ט[ ]קֹמ[. According to PAM 43357, the traces belong to two different letters, *'ayin* and *waw*. A trace of a letter is visible at the beginning of the line. The editors read it as a *qof*. However, given the context, it is suggested to read it as a *shin*.

Translation

1.]..[ ].[
2.] (they) heard *vacat* [
3.] for eighty years [

Comments

L. 2 שׁ̇מעו[. The absence of a context permits reading the surviving word in various ways. However, assuming a narrative passage, the word may be read either as a noun שֵׁמַע with the 3rd masc. sg. possessive suffix, שִׁמְעוֹ, or as a verb, the 3rd masc. pl. *Qal qatal* of שמע.

L. 3 לשמונים שנה[. The editors assume that the fragment belongs with the section concerned with the life of Abraham, of whom Gen 16:16 says that he was eighty-six years old when Hagar bore him Ishmael. There is some difficulty with such a straightforward link to Abraham's age, since the preposition -ל attached here to the number suggests that it is not concerned with the age of a person, but with the length of a period (cf. 2 Chr 11:17).[36] Since the scroll deals also with the Israelites' enslavement in Egypt (see frg. 12 below), the fragment perhaps alludes to Joseph's eighty years of service at Pharaoh's court, a chronological detail culled from the biblical data (Gen 41:46, 50:26; cf. *Jub.* 46:3).

---

36 BDB, 517.

Frg. 6

1　　　　　　　　　　　　　　[הא̊ו̊]
2　　　　　　　　　　　　[י̊דו ולוא ○]
3　　　　　　　　　　　[ה̊ א̊]ת̊ ידכה לנער]
4　　　　　　　　　　　　[עשהו עולה̊]
5　　　　　　　　　　　　[שני ○ [

Notes on Readings

L. 3 א̊[ת̊. The DJD edition reads ידכה, yet traces of an upper horizontal stroke with a small serif at its left extremity can be seen at the beginning of the line in PAM 42819. This is perhaps the roof of a *taw* (cf. *taw* in לתת [frg. 7 3]).

ה̊[. The editors read and restored ו̊א[ל. However, two vertical strokes are visible next to the word לנער in PAM 42819. The bottom part of the left downstroke bends leftwards. These two strokes do not fit *waw* and *alef*, but are consistent with *he*.

L. 5] שני ○[. The DJD edition has]שמ̊[. The convex stroke visible at the beginning of the line (PAM 42819) does not suit *waw*. It is clear in PAM 42819 that the letter that was read by the editors as a medial *mem* is in fact two letters, *shin* and medial *nun*, written close to one another.

Translation

1.]...[
2.]his hand and not .[
3.]your hand against the boy .[
4.]made it a burnt-offering[
5.]. two [

Comments

L. 2 י̊דו ולוא[. The surviving words relate to the Akedah account. Therefore, the word ידו probably refers to Gen 22:10: וישלח אברהם את ידו ("and Abraham reached out his hand").

L. 3 א̊]ת̊ ידכה לנער ה̊[. The words rewrite Gen 22:12: אל תשלח ידך אל הנער ("Do not lay your hand on the boy"). While the biblical verse reads אל תשלח ידך (without *nota accusativi*), 4Q464 has here א̊]ת̊ ידכה (for the expression שלח את ידו, see Exod

3:20, 9:15; 1 Sam 22:17).³⁷ It also reads לנער, instead of אל הנער. The change of ל- to אל is found in the Qumran texts (see 1QIsaᵃ to Isa 18:2, 37:6, 7).³⁸ One may perhaps restore here א[ת ידכה לנער ה]זה.

L. 4 **[עשהו עולֹהֹ**. The noun עולה points to Gen 22:13: ויקח את האיל ויעלהו לעלה תחת בנו ("So Abraham went and took the ram and offered it up as a burnt offering in place of his son"). Yet, while Genesis reads ויעלהו לעלה, the scroll employs the synonymous expression עשה עלה, found, for example, in Lev 5:10 and Num 15:8.

L. 5 **שני**. Perhaps שְׁנֵי (rather than שְׁנֵי) may be read here as a reference to the two servants who accompanied Abraham and Isaac on their journey to Mount Moriah (see Gen 22:3, 19). Alternatively, the number may refer to the two-day journey of Abraham to the place of the sacrifice (cf. Gen 22:4), namely to Mount Moriah, formulated by 4Q180 5–6 3 as דֹרך שני ימים ("a journey of two days").³⁹

Frg. 7

[היו בני חמש עשרא]	1
ויצא מבאר [שֹבע ללכת חרן וע]	2
כא[שֹר אמר לתת לו אֹ]ת הארץ	3
[vacat]	4
יֹ[עֹקוב ל∘]	5
[לֹבֹיא מאה צוא]ן	6
[∘ שנה יעקוֹ]ב	7
[אן בנות שכֹ]ם	8
[לֹ]	9

---

37 For the addition of את in Qumran biblical texts, see S. E. Fassberg, "The Syntax of the Biblical Documents from the Judean Desert as Reflected in a Comparison of Multiple Copies of Biblical Texts," in *Diggers at the Well* (ed. T. Muraoka and J. F. Elwolde; STDJ 36; Leiden: Brill, 2000), 100, 104.
38 See Kutscher, *Isaiah Scroll*, 310; Fassberg, "Syntax," 100, 104. The Samaritan version reads here על.
39 See Milik, *Books of Enoch*, 252; G. Barzilai, "Offhand Exegesis: Passing Allusions to Interpretation of the Book of Genesis, as Found in the Dead Sea Scrolls" (Ph.D. diss., Bar-Ilan University, 2002), 239–44; Dimant, "Pesher on Periods," 398.

Notes on Readings

L. 1 היו [. The DJD edition reads היו ○[, but no traces of writing are seen before היו on the fragment or in its photographs (PAM 41894; 42819; 43357).

L. 3 שׄ[כא. The tiny trace of ink visible at the beginning of the line may be read as the left stroke of a *shin*. Such a reading also lends itself to a restoration that fits the context of the surviving phrase (similarly the editors).

L. 5]ל○. The editors read and restored לע[שו. However, the tiny trace of a letter preserved at the end of the line is undecipherable.

Translation

1.   ] (they) were fifteen (years old)[
2. and he went from Beer]sheba to go to Haran and .[
3.   a]s (he) said to him to give him th[e land
4.   ]   *vacat*   [
5.   J]acob to .[
6.   ]to bring one hundred shee[p
7.   ]. years Jacob[
8.   ].. women of Shech[em
9.   ].[

Comments

L. 1 היו בני חמש עשרא. The *alef* in the word עשרא (עשרה in MT) is a *mater lectionis* for the vowel "e."[40] The fragment deals with the life of Jacob, so the phrase היו בני חמש עשרא refers to Jacob and Esau. According to the biblical chronology, the twins were fifteen years old when their grandfather Abraham died (Gen 21:5, 25:26, and 25:7), as noted by the editors.[41]

L. 2 ויצא מבאר]שׄבע ללכת חרן וע[. The surviving words rewrite the unique formulation of Gen 28:10, so the supplement restores the beginning of the phrase with the biblical wording. However, the Qumran author made a few changes to the biblical

---

[40] Qimron, "A Grammar of the Hebrew Language," 67, 69.
[41] Bernstein, "Three Notes," 31, remarks that according to the rabbinic sources Esau rebelled against God on that very day. See *b. B. Bat.* 16b; *Gen. Rab.* 63, 12. See also the note by Eshel–Stone, "464. 4QExposition on the Patriarchs," 277.

verse. He replaced the Genesis *wayyiqtol* וילך with the infinitive ללכת.⁴² Also the name of the city, חרן, appears here without *he* locale.⁴³ The same reformulation of the biblical phrase appears in a Qumran copy of *Jubilees*, 1Q17 2, which preserves the detail as retold in *Jub.* 27:19: ל[לכת חרן].

וע[. The scroll perhaps originally read here וע]שרים שנה, for Jacob stayed in Haran for twenty years (Gen 31:38).

L. 3 כא[שר אמר לתת לו א]ת הארץ. Perhaps 4Q464 alludes here to the promise of the land given to Jacob in Bethel on his way to Haran (Gen 28:13). The fragment may describe Jacob's return to Canaan after twenty years spent in Haran (Gen 31:13). The wording is, perhaps, influenced by 2 Chr 21:7.

L. 5 י]ע̊קוב ל[. The blank space left in line 4 may indicate that line 5 deals with a new subject. However, the mention of Jacob's name makes clear that he remains the topic of this line.

L. 6 ל̊ב̊יא מאה צוא]ן. The number "one hundred" connects the expression צוא]ן מאה ("hundred flocks") to the price paid by Jacob for the land he purchased from the Shechemites "for one hundred kesitahs" (במאה קשיטה [Gen 33:19]).⁴⁴ The author of 4Q464 was apparently familiar with the interpretative tradition, known from other ancient Jewish sources, that the difficult word קשיטה means "a sheep."⁴⁵ So the surviving word refers to the bringing of these flocks. The short phrase attests to two orthographic phenomena that are typical of the linguistic background of the Qumran scrolls. The word ל̊ב̊יא, a *Hifʿil* infinitive of בוא (להביא), is written without the *he*, a practice often observed in the scrolls that resulted from the weakening of the gutturals in contemporary Hebrew.⁴⁶ Another practice is seen in the orthography of the word צוא]ן (MT צאן), for the *waw* has been added as a *mater lectionis* to designate the vowel "o."⁴⁷

---

42 The Samaritan version also reads here ללכת.
43 For a similar phenomenon, see 1QIsaᵃ to Isa 8:23, 36:2. See Kutscher, *Isaiah Scroll*, 317.
44 Suggested by Bernstein, "Three Notes," 31–32.
45 The noun קשיטה occurs in the Hebrew Bible only three times (Gen 33:19; Josh 24:32; Job 42:11). The Septuagint, Vulgate, and Syriac render it (in all three instances) as "sheep." A similar interpretation is reflected also in *Tg. Neb.* to Josh 24:32 and in Qumran Aramaic Targum to Job 42:11 (11Q10 XXXVIII, 7). See also *Tg. Ket.* to Job 42:11, *Gen. Rab.* 79, 7 and *b. Roš Haš.* 26a. Cf. D. Sperber, "A Note on the Word *qśiṭa*," *Acta Antiqua* 19 (1971): 37–39; Y. Maori, *Peshitta Version of the Pentateuch and Early Jewish Exegesis* (Jerusalem: Magnes Press, 1995), 123 (Hebrew).
46 See Qimron, "A Grammar of the Hebrew Language," 148–49.
47 See idem, "A Grammar of the Hebrew Language," 72–75.

L. 7 שנה יעקו]ב. The word שנה ("year") implies a chronological datum. The mention of events related to Jacob's dealings with the inhabitants of Shechem (Genesis 43) in the surrounding lines suggests that this term is connected to the same circumstances. The scroll perhaps mentions the age of Jacob upon his arrival at Shechem (cf. Gen 33:18). Although not mentioned in Genesis, nonbiblical traditions recorded by the Jewish Hellenistic historian Demetrius (frg. 2, 9)[48] and *Jub.* 19:13, 30:1 state that he was ninety-seven years old at the time. Alternatively, one may suggest that the scroll refers here to the period of time that elapsed between his arrival at Shechem and Dina's rape (Gen 34:2), alluded to in the next line. According to the passage cited from Demetrius, twenty years had elapsed between these two events. The *Levi Aramaic Document* 12:6 (Geniza)[49] and the Greek *Testament of Levi* 12:5 relate that Jacob's return to Canaan and Dina's rape occurred in the same year.

L. 8 א[ן בנות שכֹ]ם. The expression בנות שכֹ]ם ("women of Shechem") must allude to Gen 34:1, telling as it does of Dinah association with the local women. But the Qumran author replaces the biblical construct pair בנות הארץ with בנות שכ]ם, an expression better adapted to the story. In addition, the structure of the construct is altered. In the biblical version it is an indirect object of the verb לראות, whereas in 4Q464 the pair בנות שכ]ם stands without a preposition and may well be the subject of the sentence. The preceding two letters, א[ן may in fact constitute the last letters of a 3rd per. pl. fem. *Qal qatal* short form of the verb יצא, וַתֵּצֶאןָ, as in Exod 15:20 (reworking this verse, 4Q365 (4QRP^c) 6b 6 has ו[תצינה]). Thus, the supplement ותצ[אן בנות שכֹ]ם may be suggested. If this is correct, the verb יצא would refer to the daughters of Shechem and not to Dina as in the biblical verse.[50]

Frg. 8

1   [יֹעֲקוֹב]
2   ]○ שנים [

---

48 Cf. C. Holladay, *Fragments from Hellenistic Jewish Authors: Volume I: Historians* (SBLTT 20, Pseudepigrapha Series 10; Chico: Scholars Press, 1983), 66–69.
49 The versification of the *Aramaic Levi Document* here follows that of J. C. Greenfield, M. E. Stone, and E. Eshel, *The Aramaic Levi Document: Edition, Translation, Commentary* (SVTP 19; Leiden: Brill, 2004). The relevant passage appears on p. 98.
50 A late midrash, *Pirqe R. El.*, 38, states that Dina was seduced to go out of her tent by the women of Shechem. It is based on the verbal similarity between Gen 34:1: ותצא, and Exod 15:20, noted above. Cf. Ginzberg, *Legends*, 309 n. 284.

Translation
1.]Jacob[
2.]. years [

Comments

L. 2 שנים. While the surviving word may also be read as שְׁנַיִם, given the interest in chronology in the scroll, the reading שָׁנִים seems to be preferable.

Frg. 9

]○[ ]○[1
[בֵּית אל]   2

Translation
1.].[ ].[
2.]Bethel[

Comments

L. 2 [בית אל]. Bethel played an important role in the biographies of Abraham (Gen 12:8, 13:3) and, particularly, Jacob (Gen 28:11–19; ch. 35; cf. also 31:13). So the present fragment may also be related to Jacob's life.

Frg. 10

] vacat שׁור[1
] vac מכרוהו [2
vacat [3
]וּיִֿ[4

Notes on Readings

The blank spaces in lines 1–2 are most likely the remains of the left intercolumnal margin (thus the editors). Therefore, the fragment comes from the left edge of one of the middle columns of a sheet. The *vacat* in the third line suggests that either the whole line or part of it was left uninscribed.

L. 4]ויִֿ[. PAM 41894, 42819, and 43357 show two vertical strokes with hook-shaped tops, fitting *waw* and *yod*, followed by the horizontal stroke of a *dalet*.

Translation
1.]bull [
2.] they sold him [
3.] *vacat*
4.]and a hand[

Comments

L. 1 שור[. The word שור may be read as a 2nd masc. sg. *Qal* imperative of שור ("to look at"; cf. Num 23:9; 24:17) or as the nouns שׁוֹר ("ox"; cf. Isa 1:3) or שׁוּר ("wall"; cf. Gen 49:22).[51] Alternatively it may represent the last part of a word, the beginning of which is lost.

L. 2 מכרוהו. The 3rd masc. pl. *Qal qatal* of מכר with an attached 3rd masc. sg. suffix suggests that this line deals with Joseph's story (Gen 37:27, 28, 36; 45:4, 5). The use of the word שור in the preceding line seems to give further support to this interpretation, for it occurs both in Jacob's and Moses' blessings of Joseph (Gen 49:22;[52] Deut 33:17[53]).[54]

Frg. 11

```
                        ]אֹיֹ○[    1
                    ] ]הכו[ ]לֹ[   2
                         ]שֹׁה מתֿ[  3
                       [ הוא מי○]  4
                           [ ○לֿ]   5
```

---

51 *HALOT*, 1450–52.
52 On the traditions that have developed on the basis of the various meanings of שור in this verse, see J. Kugel, "The Case against Joseph," in *Lingering over Words* (ed. T. Abusch et al.; Atlanta: Scholars Press, 1990), 279–83.
53 Influenced by this verse, in which Joseph is compared to an ox, *Frg. Tg.* and a marginal reading of *Tg. Neof.* to Gen 49:6 interpret Jacob's address to Simeon and Levi in Gen 49:6, which also speaks of an ox, as referring to Joseph.
54 Thus Bernstein, "Three Notes," 32.

Notes on Readings

L. 1]ֹאׄ[. The DJD edition reads]הֿאׄ, but the oblique stroke visible at the beginning of the line does not suit *he* (PAM 42819).

L. 2]לׄ[ ]הכו[. The editors read]הם[, but a close inspection shows that what the editors read as a final *mem* is in fact two letters, a medial *kaf* and a *waw*. As for the preceding letter, the reading is based on PAM 42819, in which a vertical stroke, probably of a *lamed*, is visible under the unidentified letter in the first line.

L. 3 **מתֿ**]. The DJD edition has]מׄ[. However, vertical strokes and the roof of a *taw* can be seen in PAM 42819 next to the medial *mem*.

Comments

L. 1]הכו[. One may read here הִכּוּ, a 3rd masc. pl. *Hifʿil qatal* of נכה ("to strike").

Frg. 12 (= 4Q464ᵃ)[55]

This fragment, which is similar to the other 4Q464 fragments in color and script, was separated from them and labeled 4Q464ᵃ by the DJD editors because of its supposedly distinct content: a. They rendered the word ברז (line 3) as "in a mystery" and suggested that this term indicates that the fragment is not a paraphrase of Exodus 1, but reflects a different composition; b. The editors interpreted the word קץ (line 4) as "a period" and concluded that the fragment deals with eschatological matters. However, both interpretations are questionable. The reading and interpretation proposed below suggest that the term ברז refers to Pharaoh's desire to keep his wicked plan secret. In addition, the term קץ may be understood to signify "end" without eschatological overtones. Finally, the present fragment rewrites its biblical models in a manner similar to that of 4Q464.

1]מׄ[ ]יׄ[
2 [ועׄשׂר ישבׄ]ו ם[
3 למי]לׄדות ברז להמי]תם
4 [מילדות לפרעוהׄ]
5 [עד קץ]
6]לׄ[

---

[55] I have discussed this fragment in A. Feldman, "A Note on 4Q464ᵃ," *Meghillot* 7 (2009): 299–304 (Hebrew).

Notes on Readings

L. 2 וְעֶשֶׂר. The DJD edition reads here וְעָמַד. However, three strokes of a *shin* are seen next to the *'ayin* in PAM 41894. The fourth letter may be read either as a *dalet* or a *resh* (compare these letters in לְמִ[יַ]לְּדֹת [line 3] and in ברז [line 3]). Given the context, it is proposed to read here a *resh*.

וַיֵּשְׁ[בוּ]. The editors read וַשְׁפ[ט. The short downstroke of the first letter indicates that this is a *yod* and not a *waw* (compare the *waw* in וְעֶשֶׂר). As for the last letter, PAM 42819 shows an upper horizontal stroke with a serif, a usual feature of the *bet* (compare ברז [line 3]).

L. 3 לְמִ[יַ]לְּדֹת. The editors read]ooדת, but PAM 42819 and 43357 indicate the presence of the vertical stroke of a *lamed* preceding the *dalet*. A vertical stroke with a hook-shaped top appears after *dalet*, as in *waw*.

לַהֲמִי[תָם. The editors read לַהֲמָ[ה]. However, the short vertical stroke of the last letter better suits a *yod* than a *he* (compare the *he* here with the *yod* of וַיֵּשְׁ[בוּ] [line 2]).

Translation

1.].[ ].[
2.]. and ten (they) dwell[ed
3. to the mid]wives in secret to kil[l them
4.]midwives to Pharaoh[
5.]until the end[
6.].[

Comments

L. 2]ם[. וְעֶשֶׂר וַיֵּשְׁבוּ. The extant text of lines 3–4 relates this fragment to the midwives episode from Exod 1:15–21. The surviving numeral וְעֶשֶׂר, with a *waw* indicating that it belongs to a compound number, suggests that this line might have included a chronological datum related to the Israelites dwelling in Egypt, as indicated by the verb וַיֵּשְׁבוּ. This verb may point to Exod 12:40, which states that the Israelites dwelled (ישבו) in Egypt for 430 years. Yet, clearly, the wording of the fragment does not suit the datum given in this verse. Since the 430 years of bondage in Egypt indicated in Exod 12:40 appear to contradict other chronological data found in Genesis and Exodus,[56] ancient Jewish sources offer alterna-

---

[56] While Exod 12:40 speaks of 430 years, Gen 15:13 states that Abraham's descendants will be enslaved for four hundred years "in a land not theirs." At the same time, the chronological data

tive calculations.⁵⁷ One of these calculations suggests that the Israelites dwelt in Egypt for 210 years (see *L. A. B.* 8:14, 9:3).⁵⁸ This number suits well the extant wording of this line, which can be restored as שנים מאתי[ם ועשׂר (for the formula "years x," instead of "x years" see Neh 5:14; and also CD I, 5, 6, 10; XX, 15).⁵⁹

L. 3 למי[לֹדות ברז להמיֹ]תם. The restoration למי[לֹדות is based on Exod 1:15–16 as is the restoration להמי]תם, a *Hifʻil* infinitive of מות with the 3rd masc. pl. suffix, referring to the male infants of the Hebrews. The wording ברז ("in secret") indicates that Pharaoh carried out his wicked scheme covertly. A similar usage of ברז, though in Aramaic, is found in 1QapGen V, 25: ועם למך ברה בֹרֹז מלל ("and he spoke in secret with his son Lemech").

L. 4]מיֹלדֹות לפרעוֹהֹ[. The formulation relies on Exod 1:19a (thus the editors): ותאמרן המילדת ("The midwives said to Pharaoh"). The change of the preposition ל- (אל פרעה) to ל- here (לפרעוֹהֹ) occurs also in frg. 6 3 (see *Comments*). The *waw* in לפרעוֹהֹ (MT פרעה) is added as a *mater lectionis* for the "o" vowel.⁶⁰

L. 5]עד קץ[. In the Qumran scrolls, the noun קץ denotes either "end" (e.g. 1QHᵃ XIII, 13) or "period" (e.g. 1QS IV, 16–17). Due to the fragmentary context it is impossible to ascertain which of the meanings is employed here.

---

found in Exod 6:16–20, 7:7 indicate that the sum total of the years lived by Qahat (one of those who went down to Egypt with Jacob), Amram, and Moses (until the Exodus) is 350 years.
57 See J. Heinemann, "210 Years of Egyptian Exile: A Study in Midrashic Chronology," *JJS* 22 (1971):19–30; O. Andrei, "The 430 Years of Ex. 12:40, From Demetrius to Julius Africanus: A Study in Jewish and Christian Chronography," *Hen* 18 (1996), 9–67 (9–34).
58 The calculation of 210 years is based on the assumption that the four hundred years mentioned in Gen 15:13 are counted from the birth of Isaac:
    60 years   age of Isaac at Jacob's birth (Gen 25:26)
    130 years   age of Jacob upon his arrival to Egypt (Gen 47:9)
    Total: 190 years
    400 years – 190 years = 210 years
The 210-year chronology is amply attested in the rabbinic sources (see, e.g., *S. ʻOlam Rab.* 1; *Tanḥ. Shemot*, 4). See further Heinemann, "210 Years."
59 The dates mentioned in frgs. 4 7 and 7 7 employ the formula "x years" while this fragment seems to use the formula "years x." If the fragment indeed belongs to 4Q464, then one would have to assume that the scroll employed several ways of presenting chronological data. Alternatively, the fragment might have read: עד שנת מאתי[ם ועשר ישבו].
60 Cf. Qimron, "A Grammar of the Hebrew Language," 72–75, 79.

Unidentified Fragment (previously Frg. 5)

This fragment differs in script, color, and orthography from the rest of 4Q464 (cf. the description of the manuscript above). Hence it may not belong with this scroll.[61]

Frg. 5 i

1   [
2   [מֹה
3   [יֹם
4   [סֹ את
5   [o

Notes on Readings

L. 3 יֹם[. DJD reads סo[. The vertical stroke preceding the *mem* belongs to *waw* or *yod*.[62]

Frg. 5 ii

1   וֹ[o]אֹץ [ ]oפֹוֹ[
2   וישֹם מים מבֹ]ול
3   יהיה שם יכלון כֹל הֹ[
4   להשחית הארץ כֹי הֹ[
5   [נ]פֹּתֹחוֹ ולא oo oooo[

Notes on Readings

L. 1 וֹפֹo. Traces of a medial *pe* are clearly observable on PAM 43357 and therefore the editors' reading וֹ[o can be supplemented. The next surviving vertical stroke descending to the right with an oblique base stroke descending to the left may be either a medial *kaf* or a medial *nun*.

אֹץ. The DJD edition reads oחֹץ[, but note that the right vertical stroke of *ḥet* is not visible on the parchment. An examination of PAM 41894, 42819, and 43357

---

[61] In the preliminary edition of the scroll, the editors assumed that the fragment deals with the story of Sodom and Gomorrah and placed it with the fragments concerned with Abraham. In the DJD edition, they interpreted it as referring to the flood story, yet retained its numbering.
[62] Thus Charlesworth–Elledge, "New Edition," 280.

points to two rather than the three letters noted by the editors (וֹמֹ[ץ]), an *alef* and a final *ṣade*.

L. 2 וישם. A trace of a vertical stroke is visible above the left stroke of the *shin* in PAM 41894, 42819, and 43357. The editors suggest that this is a *yod* added above the line.
מב]ול. The editors read only מ[ו, yet the horizontal upper stroke and base of a *bet* are seen in PAM 41894.

L. 3 יכלן. The DJD edition reads וכלון, but the editor later revised it to יכלון.[63] This reading is indeed supported by the physical data and is adopted here.
כֹל. The editors read מֹ, but the traces of the letters do not suit these two letters in the form in which they are written in מים in line 2. As to the first letter, the vertical stroke, roof, and base identify it as a medial *kaf* (cf. medial *kaf* in יכלון). The following vertical stroke, read by the editors as the upper horizontal stroke of a medial *mem*, resembles the lower part of a *lamed*. The short vertical stroke deciphered by Eshel and Stone as a *yod* is most likely the vertical stroke of a *lamed* (PAM 42819).

L. 4]הֹ. The editors read]דֹר, but noted that the reading of *resh* is doubtful. An examination of PAM 41894, 42819, and 43357 reveals that the two vertical strokes and bold upper horizontal stroke are more consistent with *he*.

L. 5 [נ]פֹתֹהֹ. There is a letter-sized lacuna before the medial *pe*.
לֹא. The editors read [ו]לא. The space between [נ]פֹתֹהֹ and לא is small and reveals no trace of ink. Above the *lamed* a trace of a vertical stroke is visible, perhaps a *waw* inserted above the line (see PAM 41894).
]oooo oo. Eshel and Stone read אֹooo]י. In a comment on this line, they suggest אבדן. However, the reading of these letters is extremely difficult and therefore no reading is proposed here.

Translation
1. ....[ ] he hastened and .[
2. and he put water, flo[od
3. will be there. All the[ ] will be destroyed[

---

63 Eshel–Stone, "4Q464 (4QExposition on the Patriarchs)," *DSSR* 3:586.

4. to corrupt the earth, for .[
5. were open[ed] and did not .. ....[

Comments

L. 1 אָץ. The word אץ may be parsed as a masc. sg. participle or as a 3rd masc. sg. *qatal* of אוץ in *Qal*, אָץ ("to hasten").[64] This verb does not appear in Genesis 6–9 and it is unclear to whom it refers.

L. 2 וישׂ̊ם מים מב̇]ול. The phrase alludes to Gen 6:17. The orthography וישׂ̊ם, with a superlinear *yod*, reflects a particular linguistic phenomenon. In biblical Hebrew, this form, a 3rd masc. sg. *Qal* imperfect of שׂים, both with *waw* inversive and *waw* conjunctive, is spelled without *yod* after *shin*: וַיָּשֶׂם / וְיָשֵׂם.[65] This is also the general rule in Qumran Hebrew (see 1QpHab IV, 9; 1QS III, 18; 4Q421 1a ii–b 16; yet cf. Sir 14:26 [Ms. A] has וישׂים קנו בעופיה). If the reading proposed here is correct, the supralinear *yod* may be interpreted as a *mater lectionis* for a *ṣere*.[66] However, the orthography וישׂ̊ם may be explained differently. Since such shortened *yiqtol* forms were no longer used in rabbinic Hebrew, the case here might constitute an instance of this phenomenon.[67] It is also unclear whether a form with *waw* conjunctive should be read here (וְיָשׂ̊ם, in line with יהיה, יכלון [line 3]) or one with *waw* inversive (וַיָּשׂ̊ם).

L. 3 יהיה שם יכלון כֹּל ה]. The entire phrase is related to the flood, which is mentioned in the preceding line. The fragment perhaps read כל אשר]יהיה שם, a synonym for the phrase כֹּל ה] found at the end of the line. Both phrases may point to Gen 7:21–22. The pair יכלון כֹּל appears to describe the total destruction of all living beings in the flood, with יכלון being a 3rd. pl. *yiqtol* of כלה ("to stop, to come to an end, to perish"; Isa 31:3; Jer 16:4; 1QS IV, 14).[68] It is less clear why the scroll employs here the *yiqtol* forms, יהיה and יכלון.

L. 4 להשחית הארץ כֹּי ה]. להשחית is the *Hifʿil* infinitive of שחת. The expression seems to be based on Gen 6:13, specifying the divine intention to annihilate all those living on earth.

---

64 *HALOT*, 23.
65 See *Gesenius' Hebrew Grammar* (ed. and enlarged E. Kautzsch; Oxford: Clarendon Press, 1960), § 73c.
66 Qimron, "A Grammar of the Hebrew Language," 57–58.
67 See Kutscher, *Isaiah Scroll*, 265.
68 *HALOT*, 477.

L. 5 ו֯ל֯א ו֯פ֯ת֯ת֯ו֯[ן]. The word ו֯פ֯ת֯ת֯ו֯[ן] (the restoration follows the editors) is to be parsed as the *Nif'al* 3rd pl. form of פתח, perhaps based on Gen 7:11, which describes the opening of the floodgates of the skies. It is thus a follow-up of lines 2–4, depicting the destruction to be brought about by the flood waters.

Discussion

The fragments of 4Q464 analyzed above reveal a composition reworking selected accounts from Genesis and Exodus. As is clear from the following chart, the surviving passages of the scroll cover events spanning from the lives of Abraham and Jacob to the servitude in Egypt.

4Q464	Event	Source
Abraham		
Frg. 1	Sojourn in Haran	Gen 11:31
Frg. 3 i (and Frg. 2?)	Abraham's knowledge of Hebrew with a link to the confusion of tongues	Nonbiblical
Frg. 3 ii	Covenant of Pieces	Gen 15:13, 15
Frg. 6	The Akedah	Gen 2:10, 12, 13, 19
Jacob		
Frg. 7	Jacob and Esau are 15 years old	
	Jacob's Journey to Haran	Gen 28:10
	Purchase of a land in Shechem	Gen 33:19
	Rape of Dinah	Gen 34:1
Joseph		
Frg. 10	Sold to Egypt?	Genesis 37
In Egypt		
Frg. 12 (= 4Q464ᵃ)	Midwives story	Exod 1:19

The picture emerging from the list is a type of compendium of episodes from Genesis and Exodus. The literary framework and the genre of this collection are less clear. The fragmentary state of the passages contributes to this ambiguity, along with the appearance of various literary forms.[69] Narrative rewriting of biblical episodes (see frg. 6, which reworks the story of the Akedah) occurs side by side with exegetical introductory terms such as כאשר אמר ל- (frg. 3 ii

---

[69] This fact is observed by Eshel–Stone, "464. 4QExposition on the Patriarchs," 215, 217. See also Charlesworth–Elledge, "New Edition," 275.

3–4; see also frg. 3 i 9)[70] and פשר עֹ[ל known form the sectarian commentaries.[71] There are other extant Qumran writings that include a similar mixture of forms, such as 4QCommentary on Genesis A (4Q252)[72] and 4QApocryphon of Joshua[b] (4Q379),[73] but since they are both unique[74] they do not help to clarify the nature of 4Q464.

The effort to understand the purpose of this composition is also hampered by its bad state of preservation. However, some major outlines do emerge from the detailed study offered above: the work frequently dates the various events it describes.[75] Most of the dates are nonbiblical additions, although they are often based on biblical data. This is the case with the age of Jacob and Esau when Abraham died (frg. 7 1; see also frg. 12 1). Also, while several stories, such as the events from Jacob's life (frg. 7), are presented very briefly, others, such as the Akedah (frg. 6), are discussed in more detail. Furthermore, the scroll seems to deal repeatedly with God's promises and their fulfillment (frgs. 3 i 7; 3 ii 3–4; 7 3). These final two features may indicate a didactic purpose. It is possible that the interest in biblical chronology may also be related to this tendency, for the author made use of it to show that God's promises are fulfilled in their appointed times.

---

[70] For this formula, see J. A. Fitzmyer, "The Use of the Explicit Old Testament Quotations in Qumran Literature and in the New Testament," in *Essays on the Semitic Background of the New Testament* (London: Chapman, 1971), 3–58 (10–12); M. Fishbane, "Mikra at Qumran," in *Mikra* (ed. M. J. Mulder; Assen: Van Gorcum, 1988), 339–77 (347–50).

[71] The phrases לשון הוא[(frg. 2 2) and ה]וא לשון הקודש (frg. 3 i 8) may be interpreted as identification formulae, which appear frequently in pesharim.

[72] Cf. the reworking of the Akedah story in 4Q252 iii, 6–9 with a pesher on Jacob's blessing of Judah in 4Q252 V. Also, the use of the formulae כאשר כתוב (col. III, 1) and כאשר דבר ל- (col. IV, 2) in 4Q252 are notable.

[73] A pesher on Joshua's curse of the rebuilder of Jericho (6:26) is found in this scroll (4Q379 22 ii 9–15). The same pesher appears in 4Q175 21–30. See D. Dimant, "Between Sectarian and Non-Sectarian: The Case of the *Apocryphon of Joshua*"; A. Feldman, *The Rewritten Joshua Scrolls from Qumran* (BZAW 438; Berlin: de Gruyter, 2013), 99–104, 119–25.

[74] On 4Q252, see M. Bernstein, "4Q252: From the Re-Written Bible to Biblical Commentary," *JJS* 45 (1994): 1–27 (17–18); G. J. Brooke, "4Q252 as Early Jewish Commentary," *RevQ* 17 (1996): 385–401 (395–401).

[75] Chronological data is found in frgs. 3 i 4; 4 3; 7 1; 8 2; 12 1.

Appendix

A Revised Edition of 4Q464ᵇ

These two fragments, originally assigned to 4Q464, were edited by Eshel and Stone as 4Q464ᵇ, apparently due to the fact that their script differs slightly from that of 4Q464.[76] Several improvements to Eshel and Stone's edition are suggested here.

Frg. 1

top margin

1   [ל[א]מֹר ל[

Frg. 2

1   וֹיֹשׁ[מֹעוֹ oo]
2   [בֹּאמתֹ] [ ] vac [
3   [לֹ]

Notes on Readings

L. 1]oo וֹיֹשׁ[מֹ. Eshel and Stone read]oוֹoֹo[. In PAM 43357, the first letter is clearly a medial *mem*.

L. 2 [בֹּאמתֹ]. The editors read] oאמרֹ [. In PAM 43537, one can see the base and the upper horizontal stroke of a *bet* at the beginning of the line. In the same photograph, the left leg of a *taw* is visible at the end of the word. Following *taw* there is a hole that could contain one letter and a blank space. This is perhaps the left margin of the column.

Translation
1.   and they he]ard ..[
2.   ]truly[ ] vac [
3.   ].[

---

76 Eshel–Stone, "464ᵇ. 4QUnclassified Fragments," 233.

Comments

L. 1 וִיּֽשְׁ[מֹֽעוּ. The surviving letters suggest that the fragment read a 3rd pl. form of שמע: שׁ[מֹֽעוּ or וִיּֽשְׁ[מֹֽעוּ.

L. 2]בֺּאמֺתֺ[. To be read בֶּאֱמֶת ("truly").

2Q21 (Apocrypon of Moses?)

Literature

M. Baillet, "Un Apocryphe de Moïse," in *Les 'Petites Grottes' de Qumrân* (ed. M. Baillet, J. T. Milik, and R. de Vaux; DJD III; Oxford: Clarendon Press, 1962), 79–81.

The Manuscript

Two fragments inscribed in a Herodian hand and assigned to the scroll 2Q21 were edited by Maurice Baillet. He named this scroll "An Apocryphon of Moses." His edition remains the only detailed discussion of this text. The larger fragment of this scroll contains remains of six lines, whereas only a single word is preserved in the small fragment. The state of preservation of these two fragments precludes any conclusions as to their placement within the original scroll.

Text and Comments

Frg. 1

נדב ו[אב]י̇[הוא אלע̇]זר ואיתמר	1 [
לעשות [לך משפט באמת ולהוכיח באמו[נ]ה̇ [	2 [
] vacat [	3 [
ויצא אל מחו[ץ למחנה ויתפלל לפני יהוה ויתנפ̇]ל לפניו	4 [
ויאמר יהוה אלוהי[ם̇ מה אביט אליך ואיך אש[א] פני [אליך	5 [
[לל̇]∘[עם אחר]∘∘יד̇[	6 [
[לה̇]	7 [

Notes on Readings

L. 6 **עם** ∘[   ]ל̇[. The editor read]ל[עשו]ת̇. The tiny trace of ink after the lacuna is illegible (PAM 41390). Therefore no reading is proposed here.

אחר. Baillet read אחד. The third letter may be read as either *dalet* or *resh*, yet the reading אחר seems to be preferable on contextual grounds. See *Comments*.

יד̇∘∘[   ]∘. The DJD edition has ב̇[מ]ע̇שׂי̇ד[. However, the traces of ink before and after the lacuna are indecipherable.

Translation
1. [Nadab and] Ab[i]hu, Elea[zar and Ithamar
2. [to work] justice for you in truth, and faith[fu]lly reprove [
3. [   ]   *vacat*   [
4. [and he went out]side the camp, and prayed before YHWH, and prost[rated] himself [before him
5. [and he said, "O, YHWH Go]d, how can I look upon you? And how shall I li[ft] my face [to you?
6. [   ].[ ] another nation .[   ]....[
7.   ]..[

The fragment consists of two sections, separated by a partly preserved blank space the length of several words or even an entire line. Lines 1–2 constitute the end of the previous pericope, while lines 4–7 form the beginning of the following section. The 2nd masc. sg. pronoun לך in line 2 suggests that the first two lines cite an address to someone. Perhaps it is a divine address (through Moses?) to Israel, clarifying the judicial functions of priests (thus Baillet). The second unit begins with a third person narrative statement and continues with a second person address to God, the speaker being perhaps Moses.

Comments

L. 1 נדב ו[אב]י[הוא אלעֿזר ואיתמר. The fragment lists the names of Aaron's sons, Abihu and Eleazar (cf. Exod 6:23; 24:1–9; 28:1; Num 3:2; 26:60; 1 Chr 5:29; 24:1). Since Eleazar's name is not preceded by a *waw* (conjunctive), it is likely that at least one more name followed. So it may be assumed, with Baillet, that the names of all four sons appear here and the names of the first and fourth, Nadab and Ithamar, are restored accordingly. While it is possible that this line deals with Abihu and Nadab's sin and their replacement by Eleazar and Ithamar (Leviticus 10; Num 3:4; 1 Chr 24:2; cf. 1QM XVII, 2–3), it may alternatively allude to the installation of Aaron and his sons as priests (Exodus 28).

L. 2 לעשות] לך משפט באמת ולהוכיח באמו[נ]ה [. The 2nd per. pronoun לך suggests an address to someone. Given that the second part of the fragment (lines 5–6) seems to contain the response (of Moses?) to this address, the present speech may be assigned to God. The surviving phrase seems to consist of two parallel expressions. Since באמת parallels באמו[נ]ה, the infinitive ולהוכיח also requires a counterpart. Baillet's restoration לעשות] לך משפט is therefore adopted here (cf. Ezek 18:8; Prov 29:14; but the restoration [לשפוט] לך משפט באמת, as in Zech 7:9, is also possible). In biblical parlance, the expression לעשות משפט may denote "doing what is right" (Jer 9:23; Ezek 18:5). However, its association here with the expression ולהוכיח באמו[נ]ה suggests that it refers to acting as a judge (e.g. 1 Kgs 3:28; Ezek 18:8).[1] The verb ולהוכיח is a *Hifʻil* infinitive of יכח, "to rebuke, decide."[2] Since it occurs here in parallel with a phrase that includes the noun משפט, perhaps it refers to a legal reproof (Lev 19:17; for the parallel שפט // הוכיח, see Isa 2:4, 11:3; for the construction הוכיח ב-, see 2 Sam 7:14).[3] The noun אמונה denotes "firmness, steadfastness, fidelity" (for the pair אמונה ... משפט, see Jer 5:1; cf. ונשפט באמונה [Isa 59:4]).[4] Yet, the expression הוכיח באמונה is not attested in the Hebrew Bible. Given the mention of Aaron's sons in the previous line, it is possible that the fragment refers here to one of the responsibilities of the priests, namely to serve as judges for the people (see Deut 17:8–12; 33:10; 2 Chr 19:8–11).

L. 4 ויצא אל מחו[ץ למחנה ויתפלל לפני יהוה ויתנפ]ל לפני. The blank space left in line 4 indicates a change of subject. Indeed, also the style is changed, for the second person address of the previous section is replaced here by a narrative third person singular narrative style set in the past (see the *wayyiqtol* forms ויתנפ]ל, ויתפלל). Baillet restored ויצא מושה אל מחו[ץ למחנה. While a more cautious textual restoration without the name of Moses is proposed here, several factors nevertheless suggest the assumption that these two verbs refer to Moses. Firstly, of the twenty-nine occurrences of the expression מחו[ץ למחנה in the Hebrew Bible, twenty-eight are from the Pentateuch, in connection with the Israelite camp in the desert (thus Dimant). More specifically, in connection with prayer, it appears in Exod 33:7, which reports that Moses pitched the Tent of Meeting "outside the camp." Secondly, the locution of התפלל לפני occurs elsewhere with reference to praying in the Tent of Meeting (1 Sam 1:12; see also Neh 1:4, 6; 1 Chr 17:25; 2 Chr 6:10). As for the *Hithpaʻel* of נפל, "to prostrate oneself," ויתנפ]ל,[5] out of the four occurrences of this form in the Hebrew Bible, three refer to Moses (Deut 9:18, 25; see also Ezra 10:1). Compare 1QH[a] VIII, 24; XX, 7. One may also note that in both Deut 9:25 and Ezra 10:1, the *Hithpaʻel* of נפל refers to a penitential prayer, which may also be the case here, as indicated by line 5. Thirdly, the wording of line 6 suggests that the address to God in lines 4–5 relates to the whole nation of Israel. Since the mention of Aaron's sons (line 1) sets the fragment in the context of events that took place

---

1 BDB, 1048.
2 *HALOT*, 410.
3 For reproof in the Qumran sectarian writings, see L. H. Schiffman, *Sectarian Law in the Dead Sea Scrolls: Courts, Testimony, and the Penal Code* (Chico: Scholars Press, 1983), 90–91.
4 BDB, 53.
5 *HALOT*, 711.

after the exodus, Moses seems to be the most fitting person to intercede on behalf of the people.

L. 5 ויאמר יהוה אלוהי[ם̊ מה אביט אליך ואיך אש[א] פני [אליך. Given the change of style from the third person narrative to a second person address, some introductory formula to the speech is required and, following Baillet, it is supplied by the verb ויאמר. Baillet supplies ויואמר, yet the extant fragments contain no other instances of the plene orthography employed by many Qumran scrolls. For the phrase ואיך אש[א] פני [אליך, implying a troubled conscience, cf. 2 Sam 2:22, as well as Job 22:26.[6] Both this expression and the previous one, מה אביט אליך, suggest that the speaker seeks God's forgiveness, either for himself or for others. The mention of Aaron's sons in line 1 may suggest that this prayer concerns the sin of Abihu and Nadab, who "offered alien fire before the Lord" (Num 3:4). Yet, the blank space left in line 3 may indicate that the fragment deals here with another issue. Indeed, that this may be the case is suggested by the wording of line 6, referring to "another nation."

L. 6 עם אחר. Since the second word may be read in two ways, two interpretations are possible. Retaining the reading with *resh*, the expression עם אחר ("another people") occurs in Deut 28:32, describing the future servitude to a foreign people as a result of Israel's sins. If this reading is retained here, it may be related to the penitentiary tone of the preceding prayer. However, if the reading עם אחד is adopted, אחד may be interpreted as "certain" (Esth 3:8) or "one," namely "unanimous" (Gen 34:16, 22).[7]

Frg. 2

[ ]◦ לבד י[

Translation

]. your heart .[

---

6 BDB, 670.
7 *HALOT*, 30–31.

Comments

If related to frg. 1, the 2nd sg. pronominal suffix in לבך may link it to a 2nd sg. address in frg. 1 2: לעשות] לך משפט.

Discussion

The scanty remains of 2Q21 contain a discourse perhaps by God, and a prayer probably by Moses. The prayer is preceded by a short narrative remark identifying the person offering the prayer (now lost) and the location in which this prayer is offered. By naming Aaron's sons and by situating the aforementioned prayer outside of the camp, the scroll places the described events at the time of the Israelites' wanderings in the desert. Since the wording of the scroll does not match any of the biblical speeches or prayers, the composition in question likely rewrites the biblical account of Israel's sojourn in the desert by expanding it with prayers and discourses, a method adopted by many rewritten Bible texts. Notably, 4Q368 and 4Q377 rework the same biblical episodes from Israelite history and apply similar rewriting techniques. While the name assigned to 2Q21, 2QapocrMoses?, may correctly identify the addressee of the speech in frg. 1 1–2 and the speaker in frg. 1 5, it is misleading. For, due to this title, the present scroll has been associated incorrectly with a pseudepigraphic work named by John Strugnell as the *Apocryphon of Moses*.[8] However, there are no contextual or linguistic links between this scroll and 1Q29, 4Q375, 4Q376, and 4Q408.[9] Neither is there a connection between 2Q21 and another text mistakenly associated with the *Apocryphon of Moses*, 1Q22 (*Words of Moses*) re-edited in this volume. Therefore, a different title should be considered for 2Q21.

---

8 Re-edited by Liora Goldman in this volume.
9 J. Strugnell, "Moses-Pseudepigrapha at Qumran: 4Q375, 4Q376, and Similar Works," in *Archaeology and History in the Dead Sea Scrolls* (ed. L. H. Schiffman; JSPSup 8; Sheffield: Sheffield Academic Press, 1990), 221–56; idem, "376. 4QApocryphon of Moses[b]?," in *Qumran Cave 4, XIV: Parabiblical Texts, Part 2* (ed. M. Broshi et al.; DJD XIX; Oxford: Clarendon Press, 1995), 129–36; A. Steudel, "408. 4QApocryphon of Moses[c]?," in *Qumran Cave4. XXVI: Cryptic Texts* (ed. S. Pfann et al.; DJD XXXVI; Oxford: Clarendon Press, 2000), 298–315.

4Q368 (4QApocryphal Pentateuch A)

Literature

J. C. VanderKam and M. Brady, "368. 4QApocryphal Pentateuch B," in DJD XXVIII, 131–49 (cited as "the editors"); H. Jacobson, "4Q368 Fg. 3," *RevQ* 21 (2003): 117–18; A. Feldman, "Reading Exodus with Deuteronomy in 4Q368 frg. 2," *JAJ* 3 (2012): 329–38.

The Manuscript

The fragmentary scroll 4Q368, given the title "4QApocryphal Pentateuch A," was edited by James VanderKam and Monica Brady and appeared in DJD XXVIII.[1] Its publication was initially entrusted to John Strugnell who prepared a preliminary transcription of the scroll,[2] which Brady and VanderKam consulted frequently. Besides the DJD edition and short contributions by Howard Jacobson and Ariel Feldman, 4Q368 has received no scholarly attention.

The 4Q368 scroll survived in fifteen pieces, which were joined by the editors into ten fragments.[3] The scroll is written in a Herodian formal script (50–1 BCE). It closely resembles the script of 4Q393 and at an earlier research stage, reflected in PAM 41865 and 42973, the fragments belonging to both scrolls were grouped together. It seems that for this reason frg. 8 was also edited as 4Q393 6.[4]

Text and Comments

Frg. 1

אֹ[ ]ֹ◦[ ]מֹתִי	1 [
עֹ[ם מֹשֶׁה הֹדבריֹם	2 [
פנים [אל פֹנֹם כֹאֹ[ש]רֹ	3 [
רא[ה א]ֹתֹה אֹוֹמר	4 [
אֹת אשר תשלח עמי[	5 [

---

[1] VanderKam and Brady, "368. 4QApocryphal Pentateuch B."
[2] Strugnell's edition may be recovered from the *Preliminary Concordance*. Indeed, this was done by Wacholder–Abegg, *Preliminary Edition*, 3:135–39.
[3] I re-examined the fragments at the Israel Museum in February-March, 2008.
[4] See D. Falk, "393. 4QCommunal Confession," in DJD XXIX, 47, 60.

| | 6 | ב[עֵי]נִי [וֹעתה אם |
| | 7 | [ ]ל[|

Notes on Reading
The fragment comes from the left edge of the column, as is indicated by the fact that the surviving words form the last sections of the lines.

L. 1 אo[. The DJD edition reads א̇[. An examination of the fragment and the photographs (PAM 43533; 42973) suggests an *alef*, preceded by an illegible trace of ink.

L. 3 אֹ֯ל פֹּנִֹים. The editors read here אֹלפֹּנִֹים. However, the fragment and the photographs (in particular PAM 42832) indicate that the two words are separated by a small gap. Therefore, the reading אֹ֯ל פֹּנִֹים, proposed by Strugnell, should be retained.[5]

Translation
1. [   ]...[ ]...
2. [wit]h Moses the words
3. [face] to face a[s
4. [se]e [y]ou say
5. [ ]whom you will send with me
6. [in my] ey[es.]And now if
7. [ ].[ ]

Comments
L. 1 מֹ֯תִ[. The surviving letters may be vocalized as מָתַי ("when") or מְתֵי ("men/people of"). Alternatively, they may be the final letters of a verb or a noun with a 1st per. sg. suffixed pronoun. However, since *waw* and *yod* in 4Q368 are frequently indistinguishable, מֹ֯תוֹ[(or מֹ֯תוֹ[י), a 3rd masc. pl. perfect (or imperfect) of the verb מות, "to die," is also possible.

L. 2 עֹ[ם מֹשֹׁהֹ הֹדבֹרֹיֹם. Lines 3–7 of the fragment quote Exod 33:11–13 (see below). In this context, the line perhaps alludes to Exod 33:9: ודבר עם משה. This is one

---
[5] *Preliminary Concordance*, 4:1614. His reading is adopted by the *DSSSE*, 2:726.

of the few instances in which the Pentateuch uses the expression דבר עם rather than דבר אֶל to describe divine communication with Moses (see also Exod 19:9; Num 11:17). Accordingly, Strugnell restored here וּדבר עָ[ם מֹשֶׁה הַדְּבָרִים הָאלה] / ‎.⁶ Usually, the determined noun הדברים and the phrase הדברים האלה are preceded by the *nota accusativi* את (e.g. Num 14:39; 16:31) and its absence here is remarkable. Still, both the Hebrew Bible and the Scrolls attest to cases that lack the expected את (see, for instance, וידברו הדברים in 1 Sam 11:4; for other possible examples of the omission of את in this scroll, see frgs. 2 5; 9 3).⁷ Given the fragmentary state of the line, it is impossible to ascertain whether הַדְּבָרִים or הַדְּבָרִים] / האלה refer to preceding events (as in Num 14:39) or introduce the following quotation from 33:11–13 (cf. Exod 20:1).

L. 3 ר[ש]ךָ בָּאֹם אֵל פָּנִים [פנים. The scroll quotes Exod 33:11.

L. 4 רָא[ה] הֻ[אָ]תָה אוֹמֵר. A quotation from Exod 33:12. Given the space limitations, it seems plausible to assume with the editors that 4Q368 did not include the second part of the verse concerning Joshua (Exod 33:11b). So, the phrase introduces the exchange between God and Moses in the following line, quoting Exod 33:12. See Discussion.

L. 5 ‎[אֵת אשר תשלח עמי. A quotation of Exod 33:12.

L. 6 ב[עֵי]נַי [וֹעתה אם. A quotation from Exod 33:12–13.

L. 7]לֹ[. This line perhaps contained a quotation from Exod 33:13.

Reconstruction
The reconstructed text follows that proposed by the editors. While there is a possibility that the wording of the non-extant sections diverged from the MT, as is the case in line 4, the editors adopted the Masoretic version, which fits well with the length of the lacunae.

---

6 *Preliminary Concordance*, 2:579.

7 Cf. T. Muraoka, *Emphatic Words and Structures in Biblical Hebrew* (Jerusalem: Magnes Press, 1985), 150–51; Joüon-Muraoka, *Grammar*, § 125 f; S. E. Fassberg, "The Syntax of the Biblical Documents from the Judean Desert as Reflected in a Comparison of Multiple Copies of Biblical Texts," in *Diggers at the Well* (ed. T. Muraoka and J. F. Elwolde; STDJ 36; Leiden: Brill, 2000), 100; T. Muraoka, "An Approach to the Morphosyntax and Syntax of Qumran Hebrew," ibid., 203–04.

```
[       ]                                               ]  1  [אֹ[ ]ο אֹ[ ]מֹתי
[       ]                                               ]  2  ע[ֹם מֹשֶׁה הֹדברֹיֹם
[       ]                                               ]  3  ודבר יהוה אל משה  פנים [ אל פנֹֹם כאֹ[שֹ]רֹ
[       ]                                               ]  4  ידבר איש אל רעהו ויאמר משה אל יהוה רא[ֹה ]אֹ[תֹה אֹומר
[       ]                                               ]  5  אלי העל את העם הזה ואתה לא הודעתני ]אֹת אשר תשלח עמי
[       ]                                               ]  6  ואתה אמרת ידעתיך בשם וגם מצאת חן ב[ֹעֹיֹ]נֹי [ועתה אם
[       ]                                               ]  7  נא מצאתי חן בעיניך הודעני נא את דרכך ואדעך [לֹ]מֹעֹןֹ]
```

Translation

1. [   ]...[   ]...
2. [wit]h Moses the words
3. [The LORD would speak to face] to face a[s]
4. [one man speaks to another. And Moses said to the LORD, "Se]e, [y]ou say
5. [to me, 'Lead this people forward,' but you have not made known to me] whom you will send with me
6. [And you have said, 'I have singled you out by name, and you have, indeed, gained favor in my] ey[es.]And now if
7. [I have truly gained Your favor, pray let me know Your ways so that I may know You]in[order]

Frg. 2

```
[       ]                                               ]  1  [ ]οο [ ]ο
[       ]                                               ]  2  [דך מֹ] [ ] הֹנֹני גֹוֹרֹשֹ מֹפניכם אתֹ
[       ]                                               ]  3  וה[ֹפרזי וֹ]       [הֹשמר לך פן תכרות
[       ]                                               ]  4  [ אתה ] פֹ[ןֹ] יהיה לך למוקש בקרבֹכם
[       ]                                               ]  5  תש[רֹפֹון באש ומצבותיהם
[       ]                                               ]  6  [יהוה קנא שמו אלקנא
[       ]                                               ]  7  [אֹחֹרֹי אלוהיהם ויזבֹחֹו
[       ]                                               ]  8  א[ת בניך אחרֹי אֹלוהיהם
[       ]                                               ]  9  תש[מֹרו שבעת הימים תאכלו
[       ]                                               ] 10  חודש הא[בֹיֹב כי בו יצאת ממצרים
[       ]                                               ] 11  הזכ[ֹרֹ פטרֹ שו]רֹ ו[ֹ]שה וֹפֹטֹר חֹמֹוֹרֹ
[       ]                                               ] 12  תפ[ֹדֹהֹ ולא יראו
[ֹפני ריקם]                                             ] 13  [
[       ]                                               ] 14  ה[ֹסֹוֹכֹוֹת
[       ]                                               ] 15  ה[ֹאֹדֹון
[       ]                                               ] 16  א[ֹת
[       ]                                               ] 17  [לֹוֹ תוֹדות
```

Notes on Reading

Frg. 2 is comprised of three pieces. All three appear to cite Exodus 34. The editors placed the fragments at some distance from each other in order to match their wording with that of Exodus 34. The largest piece, frg. 2b, preserves the majority of the extant text (lines 1–12). Frg. 2c contains the final sections of lines 14–17. Line 13, left blank by the editors, represents the text of Exod 34:21, which is not preserved in frgs. 2b and 2c. However, in order to make sense out of line 12 it is suggested that two words from Exod 34:21 be restored at the beginning of line 13. A small piece of leather, frg. 2a, seems to contain some of the wording of Exod 34:11–12. The editors placed it adjacent to the right edge of frg. 2b, in lines 2–4.

L. 1]∘∘[. The DJD edition reads]צ̊∘ [. The vertical stroke curving to the left at its bottom projects below the imaginary bottom line and thus may belong to a final *kaf*, final *ṣade* or *qof*, but not to a medial *ṣade*. Given the ambiguity, no reading is proposed here.

L. 7 **תֹוּדוֹת לֹ֯**[. The editors read here ל̊י̊[∘ירות. Since *waw* and *yod* are frequently indistinguishable in the present manuscript, it is proposed to read here לֹי. Only a short base stroke survives of the first letter of the second word. Perhaps it belongs to the left leg of a *taw*. The next letter could be read as a *waw*, whereas the shape of the third letter is more consistent with a *dalet* than with a *resh*.

Translation

1. [   ]..[   ]...[   ]
2. [   ].. [   ] I am now driving out before you
3. [and the] Perizzite and[   ]be careful lest you make
4. [   ] you [le]st it should become a snare for you among you
5. [you shall b]urn with fire and their pillars
6. [   ]LORD Elqana (= "a jealous God") is his name.
7. [   ]after their gods, and they will sacrifice
8. [   ]your sons after their gods
9. [ke]ep ᵗʰᵉ seven days you will eat
10. [the month of Ab]ib for during it you went out of Egypt
11. [from all your ma]le[livestock], first issue of a bul[l and] sheep, but the first issue of a donkey
12. [you shall re]deem and they shall not be seen
13. [before me empty-handed   ]

14. [the]booths
15. [the]Lord
16. [th]e
17. [   ]to him
   thanks

Comments

L. 2 אֵת מִפְּנֵיכֶם גֹּרֵשׁ הִנְנִי [ ]מ דך[. The phrase אֵת מִפְּנֵיכֶם גֹּרֵשׁ הִנְנִי is borrowed from Exod 34:11. It introduces an extensive quotation from Exod 34:11–20 in lines 2–22. The editors suggest restoring the first letters according to a parallel passage from Deut 7:4 [הר]מ דך[והשמי. Other instances of the Deuteronomic influences of Exod 34:11–20 on the text of the scroll lend some support to this reconstruction (see Discussion). Alternatively, the beginning of the line may rework the introductory statement from Exod 34:11: שמר לך את אשר אנכי מצוך היום.

מִפְּנֵיכֶם. While the MT has a sg. pronoun מפניך (Exod 34:11), the scroll employs the plural מִפְּנֵיכֶם, as does LXX (πρὸ προσώπου ὑμῶν). A similar change occurs in line 4. Unlike the MT reading a sg. בקרבך (Exod 34:12), it has the pl. בקרבכם (cf. below, Comments).

L. 3]וה[פרזי ו].   ]הִשָּׁמֶר לך פן תכרות[. A quotation from Exod 34:11–12.

L. 4]אתה [   ]פ[ן יהיה לך למוקש בקרבכם. A quotation from Exod 34:12. The quotation differs from that of the MT in two respects. First, it has לך after יהיה, as does also the Syr. (ܕܠܐ ܢܗܘܐ ܠܟ ܠܬܘܩܠܬܐ). Secondly, while the MT reads בקרבך, the scroll has בְּקִרְבְּכֶם. Similarly, LXX has here ἐν ὑμῖν[8] and *Tg. Neof.* reads ביניכון.

L. 5 תש[רֹפוּן באש ומצבותיהם. The scroll quotes Exod 34:13. The phrase תש[רֹפוּן באש is taken from the parallel passage in Deut 7:5: ומצבתם תשברו ואשריהם תגדעון ופסיליהם תשרפון באש (see also Deut 7:25; 12:3). However, the LXX to Exod 34:13 has a reading similar to that in the scroll: καὶ τὰ γλυπτὰ τῶν θεῶν αὐτῶν κατακαύσετε πυρί ("and the images of their gods burn in fire"). So the scroll may have had the same reading, ופסיליהם תש[רֹפוּן.[9] The scroll differs from MT in two further details.

---

[8] Several manuscripts (among them Codex Vaticanus) read here: μὴ σοι γένηται. See J. W. Wevers, *Exodus* (Göttingen: Vandenhoeck & Ruprecht, 1991), 378.
[9] Thus *Preliminary Concordance*, 4:1806 and *DSSSE*, 726.

It omits the particle את, and uses the long possessive pronominal suffix, ומצבותיהם (cf. Exod 23:24), frequent in later biblical books.[10] See Discussion.

L. 6 **יהוה קנא שמו אלקנא**[. A quotation from Exod 34:14. The scribe wrote the words אלקנא without an intervening space. The formulation (שמו) suggests that he treated it as a divine name.[11]

L. 7 **א̊ח̊ר̊י̊ אלוהיהם ויזב̊ח̊ו**[. The scroll quotes Exod 34:15, but instead of the *waw* inversive *yiqtol* וזבחו of the MT, the fragment has a *yiqtol* with *waw* conjunctive ויזב̊ח̊ו, as do *Tg. Onq.*, *Tg. Ps.-J.*, *Tg. Neof.*, and Syr. Most likely, the preceding word in the scroll was ויזנו instead of the MT וזנו. The editors note that in its reworking of Exod 34:15–16 the present scroll replaces the MT inversive forms with *yiqtol* with *waw* conjunctive forms.[12]

L. 8 **א[ת בניך אחרי א̇לוהיהם**. A quotation from Exod 34:16. The MT reads אלהיהן, the 3rd fem. pl. possessive suffix referring to the daughters of the indigenous inhabitants of Canaan. However, the Qumran fragment has a 3rd masc. pl. possessive suffix, probably alluding to the "inhabitants of the land" (יושב הארץ) mentioned in the previous verse. This alteration may have been influenced by the parallel phrase א̊ח̊ר̊י̊ אלוהיהם[in the preceding line, but alternatively it may stem from a text other than the MT. The editors note that the length of the surviving lines suggests that 4Q368 did not contain the clause ולקחת מבנתיו לבניך וזנו בנתיו אחרי אלהיהן :

MT	4Q368
פן תכרת ברית ליושבי הארץ וזנו אחרי אלהיהם וזבחו לאלהיהן וקרא לך ואכלת מזבחו ולקחת מבנתיו לבניך וזנו בנתיו אחרי אלהיהן והזנו את בניך אחרי אלהיהן	פן תכרות ברית ליושב הארץ ויזנו]א̊ח̊ר̊י̊ אלוהיהם ויזב̊ח̊ו / [לאלוהיהם וקרא לך ואכלת מזבחו והזנו א[ת בניך אחרי א̇לוהיהם

---

10 Jouön-Muraoka, *Grammar*, § 94g.
11 This was also suggested by Aryeh Amihai in a lecture "The Divine Names in the Qumran Scrolls" given at the 15th World Congress of Jewish Studies, August 3, 2009. On the writing of words without an intervening space in the Qumran scrolls, see Qimron, "A Grammar of the Hebrew Language," 121–27.
12 On the replacement of *qatal* with *waw* inversive with *yiqtol* with *waw* conjunctive, testifying to a gradual disappearance of the biblical inverted verbal forms, see further Kutscher, *Isaiah*, 273–74; Muraoka, "An Approach to the Morphosyntax and Syntax," 209.

According to this restoration, the subject of והזנו is יושב הארץ. While this solves the difficulty with the 3rd masc. pl. suffix of אֱלֹהֵיהֶם, it omits the issue of the intermarriage with the nations. Alternatively, one may propose that the scroll lacked both the expressions וזנו בנתיו אחרי אלהיהן and וקרא לך ואכלת מזבחו:

MT	4Q368
פן תכרת ברית ליושבי הארץ וזנו אחרי אלהיהם וזבחו לאלהיהם	פן תכרות ברית ליושב הארץ ויזנו [אַֽחֲרֵ֖י אֱלוֹהֵיהֶם וַיִּזְבְּחוּ֯ / [לֱאלוהיהם
וקרא לך ואכלת מזבחו	
ולקחת מבנתיו לבניך	ולקחת מבנתיו לבניך
וזנו בנתיו אחרי אלהיהן	
והזנו את בניך אחרי אלהיהן	והזנו א[ת בניך אחרי אֱלוֹהֵיהֶם

Support for this proposal may be found in 4QpaleoExod[m] (4Q22) XLI, 2, which also lacks the phrase וזנו בנתיו אחרי אלהיהן.[13]

L. 9 תש[מֹרו שבעת ימים תאכלו]. The scroll quotes Exod 34:18, referring to the Feast of Unleavened Bread (חג המצות). Unlike in the MT verse, here the verbs תש[מֹרו and תאכלו stand in plural, as in *Tg. Ps.-J.*, תינטרון, and in *Tg. Neof.*, תטרון and תאכלון. The definite article ה- added above the line makes the indefinite noun ימים (in MT) definite, specifying the identity of the festival days.[14]

L. 10 חודש הא[בֹּיב כי בו יצאת ממצרים]. A quotation from Exod 34:18, restored accordingly (חודש is restored in full orthography, as is the practice in the Qumran documents). The MT repeated the temporal note "the month of Abib" (חדש האביב), while it is replaced here with בו, as in the Samaritan Pentateuch, כי בו יצאת ממצרם, and in the *Sam. Tg.* הלא בה נפקת ממצרים.

L. 11 הזכ]ֹר פטֹר שוֹ[ר ו]שה ופטר חמור. The scroll quotes here Exod 34:19–20. The MT has a difficult verbal form תִּזָּכָר, frequently amended to a determinate noun הַזָּכָר.[15] A similar alteration is reflected in the ancient versions. The LXX reads here τὰ ἀρσενικά. The same expression is used in the LXX to translate הַזָּכָר in Deut

---

13 Cf. DJD IX, 128–29.
14 On the fluctuation in the use of the definite article in Dead Sea Scrolls, see Kutscher, *Isaiah*, 315; Fassberg, "The Syntax of the Biblical Documents from the Judean Desert," 99.
15 Thus BDB, 270; *HALOT*, 1715. See, for instance, B. Childs, *Exodus* (OTL; London: SCM, 1979), 604; J. I. Durham, *Exodus* (WBC; Waco: Word Books, 1987), 457.

15:19, הזכרים in Exod 13:15, and כל זכר in Num 1:20, 22; 3:43.[16] Similar renderings are recorded in the Vulgate (*generis masculini*) and the Aramaic Targumim (*Tg. Onq.* וכל בעירכון; *Tg. Neof.* וכל בעירך תקדיש דכרין; *Tg. Ps.-J.* וכל בעירך תקדיש מנהון דיכריא; *Tg. Yer. II* כל פיטרכון דיכריא דיכרייה).[17] While it is difficult to determine whether the versions reflect a *Vorlage* differing from the MT (הזכר) or a contextual exegesis of a difficult Masoretic form (תזכר), the editors' restoration of the more intelligible form הזכ[ר is followed here.

Ll. 12–13 תפ[דה ולא יראון] פניך ריקם. The scroll quotes Exod 34:20. Since the sequence and context follow this verse closely, the last word should be parsed just as it is in the biblical passage, namely, as a 3rd per. pl. *yiqtol Nif'al* of the verb ראה (יֵרָאוּ), and be supplemented by the following biblical words, as proposed here.

L. 14 ה]סֻּכּוֹת. The passage continues to quote Exodus 34 and takes up verse 22, which speaks of the Feast of Ingathering (חג האסיף). However, the scroll replaces the biblical name with the term ה]סֻּכּוֹת (probably to be restored חג ה]סוכות), taking up the name of this feast used in Lev 23:34 and Deut 16:13, 16 (cf. also Neh 8:16–17).

L. 15 ה]אָדון. The surviving word suggests a quotation of Exod 34:23.

L. 16 א]ת. Perhaps this line contained a quotation from Exod 34:24.

L. 17]לוֹ תוֹדוֹת. For the plural form of the Hebrew noun תודה, "thanksgiving,"[18] see, for instance, Ps 56:13: אשלם תודת לך. It may also refer to the thank-offerings (cf. 2 Chr 29:31; see further Lev 7:12, 13, 15). Perhaps the phrase]לוֹ תוֹדוֹת, "]to him thanks", which may be restored as לשלם]לוֹ תוֹדוֹת, "to render]thank offerings to him" or להביא]לוֹ תוֹדוֹת, "to bring]him thank offerings," paraphrases Deut 16:16–17.

Reconstruction

The reconstruction follows that of the editors with the slight alterations noted above. As with frg. 1, the reconstruction follows the MT with a few exceptions,

---

[16] See J. W. Wevers, *Notes on the Greek Text of Exodus* (SBLSCS 30; Atlanta: Scholars Press, 1990), 564–65.
[17] See B. Grossfeld, *The Targum Onkelos* (ArBib 7; Wilmington: Glazier, 1988), 97.
[18] BDB, 392–93.

since in most cases the Masoretic version fits well into the lacunae and with the surviving words.

1.] [oo[ ]o
2.] [מ דך] [הִנְנִי גֹרֵשׁ מִפְּנֵיכֶם אֶת
3. [האמרי והכנעני והחתי וה]פרזי ו[החוי והיבוסי]הִשָּׁמֶר לך פן תכרות
4. [ברית ליושב הארץ אשר] אתה [בא עליה פ]ן יהיה לך למוקש בקרבכם
5. [כי את מזבחותיהם תתוצון ואת פסיליהם תש]רְֹפוּן באש ומצבותיהם
6. [תשברון כי לא תשתחוה לאל אחר כי]יהוה קנא שמו אלקנא
7. [הוא פן תכרות ברית ליושב הארץ ויזנו]אַחֲרֵי אֱלוֹהֵיהֶם וְיִזְבְּחוּ
8. [לאלוהיהם ולקחת מבנתיו לבניך והזנו א]ת בניך אחרי אֱלוֹהֵיהֶם
9. [אלוהי מסכה לא תעשה לך את חג המצות תש]מֹרוּ שבעת הימים תאכלו
10. [מצות אשר צויתך למועד חודש הא]בִּ֗יב כי יצאת ממצרים
11. [כל פטר רחם לי וכל מקנך הזכ]ר פטר שו[ר ו]שה וּפֶטֶר חֲמוֹר
12. [תפדה בשה ואם לא תפדה ערפתו כל בכור בניך תפ]דֵּ֗ה ולא יראו
13. [פני ריקם ששת ימים תעבד וביום השביעי תשבות בחריש ובקציר]
14. [תשבות חג שבועות תעשה לך בכורי קציר חטים וחג ה]סֻכּוֹת
15. [תקופת השנה שלוש פעמים בשנה יראה כל זכורך את פני ה]אָדוֹן
16. [יהוה אלוהי ישראל כי אוריש גוים מפניך והרחבתי א]ת
17. [גבולך ולא יחמד איש את ארצך בעלתך]לוֹ תוֹדוֹת

Translation

1. [ ].. .[ ]...[ ]
2. [ ].. [ ] I am now driving out before you
3. [the Amorites and the Canaanites and the Hittites and the] Perizzite and[the Hivites and the Jebusites.]Be careful lest you make
4. [a covenant with the inhabitants of the land against which] you [are advancing, le]st it should become a snare for you among you
5. [You must tear down their altars and you shall b]urn[their images]with fire and [smash] their pillars;
6. [for you must not worship any other god, because]YHWH, his name is Qana (= "jealous"), [he is] Elqana (= "a jealous God").
7. [You must not make a covenant with the inhabitants of the land, for they will lust]after their gods, and they will sacrifice
8. [to their gods. And you will take from their daughters for your sons and (they) will cause]your sons[to lust] after their gods
9. [You shall not make molten gods for yourselves. You shall ke]ep [the Feast of Unleavened Bread.] For ᵗʰᵉ seven days you will eat
10. [unleavened bread as I have commanded you—at the set time of the month of Ab]ib for during it you went out of Egypt

11. [Every first issue of the womb is Mine, from all your ma]le[livestock], first issue of a bul[l and] sheep. But the first issue of a donkey
12. [you shall redeem with a sheep; if you do not redeem it, you must break its neck. And you shall re]deem [every first-born among your sons.] And they shall not be seen
13. [before me empty-handed. Six days you shall work, but on the seventh day you shall cease from labor; you shall cease from labor even at plowing time and harvest time.]
14. [You shall observe the Feast of Weeks, of the first fruits of the first harvest; and the Feast of]Booths
15. [at the turn of the year. Three times a year all your males shall appear before the]Lord
16. [YHWH, the God of Israel. I will drive out nations from your path and enlarge]
17. [your territory; no one will covet your land when you go up   ]to him thanks

Frg. 3

[	]ₒמ [	] 1
[	[וֹמִי]הֹ	] 2
[	[בֹּשר נהפֹּךֹ]	] 3
	[ₒת ואכֹמהֹ	] 4
	ת[רים קֹרן	] 5
	[עם הֹשׁכנתהֹ	] 6
	[לֹךֹ מלֹיֹץֹ	] 7

Notes on Reading

L. 2 הֹ[. The DJD edition reads here ה [. The right vertical stroke of *he* and the preceding letter have been blotted out. However, the *he* was certainly not written in isolation and therefore should be presented as הֹ[.

L. 4 תₒ[. The editors read תₒ [. The tiny trace of ink visible before *taw* (perhaps *waw* or *yod*) is preceded by a space of three letters. Since the letters תₒ most probably represent the ending of a word, the line should be transcribed as תₒ[.

ואכֹמהֹ. The editors read ואעֹמוֹדֹ. The upper horizontal stroke and the base stroke, observable below in the PAM photographs 41427; 43219 suggest a medial *kaf* (compare the *kaf* in הֹשׁכנתהֹ [line 6]; contrast *ʿayin* in עם [line 6]). As to the last letter, two vertical strokes are visible on the fragment and in the photographs. On the top of the right stroke a trace of a horizontal stroke is visible. Its shape does not fit the hook of *waw* (cf. *waw* in the same word), but fits with the upper bar of *he*. See Comments below.

L. 5 ת]רים. The editors read רים [. The *resh* is preceded by a blank space of three letters due to the surface damage (as noted by the editors). So the space was not intentional and therefore the transcription suggested here is ת]רים. See Comments below.

Translation
1. [   ]..[   ]
2. [   ]. and who[   ]
3. [   ]flesh was changed [   ]
4. [   ].. and I will strike them
5. [you will rais]e the horn
6. [   ] a people you settled
7. [   ] a mediator for you

Comments

L. 2]וּמִֿי. The surviving letters may be vocalized וּמִי ("and who") or וּמֵי[("and waters of").

L. 3] בָּשֹׂר נהפּךְ[. The editors suggest that the phrase בשר נהפך refers to Moses' transfiguration, described in Exod 34:29–35. They consider the occurrence of the word קרן in line 5, similar to Exod 34:29, as support for their suggestion. However, Exod 34:29–35 uses neither the noun בשר nor the verb הפך. Furthermore, the word קרן in line 5 seems to belong to a different expression, הרים קרן, and is not related to the verb קרן in Exodus 34. As was noted by Jacobson, the expression בָּשֹׂר נהפּךְ ("[the] flesh is/was turned") may concern leprosy, since it is used in the Lev 13:16 description of this disease. Jacobson suggests that the fragment alludes to Exod 4:6–7, where God renders Moses' hand leprous and then restores it as a sign intended to convince the Israelites of Moses' mission.

L. 4 וָאַכֵּמֹֿה. The word is best parsed as a 1st sg. imperfect (with *waw* conjunctive or *waw* inversive) of נכה, "to strike,"[19] in the *Hifʻil*, with a 3rd masc. pl. pronominal

---
[19] *HALOT*, 697.

suffix (long form [20]מה-). As a 1st sg. verb, it suggests that God is the speaker, referring to the Exodus plagues (cf., for instance, Exod 3:20). Such a context creates a link to the allusion to Moses' leprosy in the previous line.

L. 5 ת[רים קֶרן. The editors understood the word קֶרן as a perfect of קרן ("shine"),[21] but left the preceding three letters, רים, unexplained. Jacobson suggested plausibly that the scroll employs here the biblical phrase הרים קרן, literally "to raise horn" meaning "to strengthen" (cf. 1 Sam 2:10: וירם קרן משיחו; Ps 148:14: וירם קרן לעמו).[22] Since lines 6–7 seem to contain an address to God phrased in the 2nd sg., it is proposed to restore here ת[רים, namely the 2nd sg. imperfect of רום in *Hif'il*. However, given the 1st per. sg. verb of the previous line, ואבֹמה, the restoration of the similar 1st per. sg. verb א[רים is also possible.

L. 6 עם הֹשׁכנתֹה. הֹשׁכנתֹה is a 2nd masc. sg. perfect of שכן in *Hif'il*, "to cause to dwell, settle."[23] The editors leave the word עם unexplained. Yet, as Jacobson notes, it may be vocalized as עַם, "people." Assuming that עם is the direct object of הֹשׁכנתֹה, the line may be interpreted as referring to God's settling of his people in the promised land (cf. Ps 78:55). According to this interpretation, the addressee is God, perhaps in a liturgy pronounced by the Israelite people.

L. 7 מלִיץ לֹך. לֹך, with the 2nd per. sg. suffix, refers to God, as does הֹשׁכנתֹה in the previous line. מליץ, a *Pi'el* participle (or noun?) of ליץ, denotes "interpreter" (Gen 42:23), "envoy" (2 Chr 32:31; cf. Sir 10:2), "advocate" (Job 16:20; 33:23).[24] In the Scrolls, in particular in *Hodayot*, מליץ is used as a *nomen regens* in such constructs as מליץ דעת (1QH[a] X, 15), מליצי תעות (1QH[a] X, 16), מליצי כזב (1QH[a] X, 33) and מליצי רמיה (1QH[a] XII, 8).[25] The construction מליץ ל-, employed here, occurs also in 4Q374 7 2: מליץ לעמד, apparently a reference to Moses.[26] The context suggests that also here מלִיץ stands for Moses. So Moses is described here as an interpreter for God and the locution should be translated "an interpreter for you." The description of Moses as מלִיץ points to his role as a mediator between God and the people during the revelation at Sinai (cf. Exod 20:19) and as an intercessor before God on behalf of Israel (cf. Exod 32:11). *Pesiq. Rab.*, 10, *Ki Tissa* equates the "angel

---

20 On מה-, see Kutscher, *Isaiah*, 351; Qimron, "A Grammar of the Hebrew Language," 243, 245.
21 *HALOT*, 1144.
22 Ibid., 1146.
23 Ibid., 1499.
24 *HALOT*, 590; C. Barth, "ליץ," in *TDOT*, 7:550–52.
25 See ibid., 552.
26 See C. Newsom, "4Q374. 4QDiscourse on the Exodus/Conquest Tradition," in DJD XIX, 107.

advocate" (מלאך מליץ) of Job 33:23 with Moses: ואין מלאך אלא משה ("and 'an angel' is none but Moses").

Frg. 4

[ ]○ [ק]צָ̇ה א[ר]ץ אדום	]	1
[ה̇ אל משה לאמר	]	2
[○ל̇○○ ○	]	3

Notes on Reading

L. 1 [ק]צָ̇ה ○[. The trace of the first letter is probably the left vertical stroke of a *taw*, but *bet* is also possible. Strugnell suggested [ק]בָ̇צָ̇ה[²⁷ while the editors read [ק]○צָ̇ה. The letter is followed by a blank gap, large enough to be a space between words.

L. 3 [○ל̇○○ ○. On the fragment, as well as in its photographs (PAM 42973; 42832; 43219), traces of letters belonging to line 3 are visible (absent from the DJD transcription). A long vertical stroke indicates that one of them is a *lamed*.

Translation
1. [ ]. [e]dge of the l[an]d of Edom
2. [ ]. to Moses, saying
3. [ ].....

Comments

L. 1 [**ק**]**צָ̇ה א[ר]ץ אדום**. The phrase ק]צָ̇ה א[ר]ץ אדום is borrowed from Num 33:37, where it designates the area of the location of Hor Hahar, the place of Aaron's death. This may also be the context in this fragment.

L. 2 [**ה̇ אל משה לאמר**. The editors propose to restore the surviving text in line with the recurring formula: וידבר יהו]ה̇ אל משה לאמר (e.g. Exod 6:10; Lev 1:1; 10:8; Num 4:1; 14:26). Describing Aaron's death, Num 20:22–29 includes God's instructions to Moses and Aaron (v. 23). Perhaps 4Q368 refers to this passage. The actual scene of Aaron's death on Hor Hahar is partly preserved in frg. 5.

---

27 *Preliminary Concordance*, 4:1704.

Frg. 5

```
[ ]              [ש̇oo[ ]o                    1 [ ]
[שרי ה̇ש̇[בטים ו]כ̇ו̇ל̇[ ]ש[פ̇טיהם            2 [ ]
[ם̇ למספר̇ כ̇[ו]ל̇ בית אבותם                   3 [ ]
[מכיר ועליתה אתה ואהרן                          4 [ ]
[לא̇ה̇רן ולאלעזר בנו והפש̇ט̇ת̇[ה]              5 [ ]
[oo oo[ ]מ̇ש                                    6 [ ]
[o                                              7 [ ]
```

Translation

1. [ ]...[ ].
2. [ ]the chiefs of the t[ribes and] all their [j]udges
3. [ ]. to the number of a[l]l the houses of their fathers
4. [ ]Machir. And you are to go up, you and Aaron
5. [ ]to Aaron and to Eleazar his son, and you are to strip off
6. [ ].. ..[ ]..
7. [ ].

Comments

L. 2 [שרי ה̇ש̇[בטים ו]כ̇ו̇ל̇[ ]ש[פ̇טיהם. The surviving words in this and the following line are formulated in biblical terms (cf. Ps 148:11; Pr 8:16; 1 Chr 27:22; 28:1) but do not come from a specific biblical passage. Given the references to the scene of Aaron's death in lines 4–5 (Num 20:25–29), the extant words may describe the gathering of the entire people or the leaders who were present on that occasion, as referred to in Num 20:22, 29.

L. 3 [ם̇ למספר̇ כ̇[ו]ל̇ בית אבותם. Here again the formulation is a free one, but uses biblical nomenclature (cf. Num 2:32); the reference seems to continue the depiction of the entire people as in Num 20:29. On the possibility that the scroll reflects an attempt to model its account of Aaron's death on that of Moses, see Discussion.

L. 4 [מכיר. Apparently this is the name of Joseph's grandson, Machir (cf. Gen 50:23). The family of Machir, son of Manasseh, is mentioned several times in the book of Numbers (26:29; 27:1; 32:39, 40; 36:1). Its importance is highlighted in Judg 5:14: "from Machir came down leaders" (מחקקים, "commanders, rulers"); cf. line 2. The rabbinic midrash describes Machir as one of the pious Israelites who were faithful to Moses in the desert (cf. *Num. Rab.* 43, 6 *Ki-Tissa*). Perhaps a similar tradition underlies the mention of Machir here. He may have been one of the dignitaries who witnessed the departure of Aaron.

ועליתה אתה ואהרן. The phrase appears in Exod 19:24, dealing with God's revelation at Sinai. However, the mention of Eleazar in the following line, as well as the verb [ה]והפשׁטתׄ ("and you are to strip off"), indicates that the replacement of Aaron by Eleazar, described in Num 20:25, is alluded to here.

ועליתה. This is the 2nd per. sg. perfect *Qal* of עלה with *waw* inversive, meaning "you are to go up." It seems to continue an imperative not preserved in the fragment but present in its biblical model, Num 20:25 (קח).[28] The verb indicates a divine address to Moses, as does the verb [ה]והפשׁטתׄ in the following line. Both are taken from the ceremony inaugurating Aaron's replacement in Num 20:25–26, the scene being reworked in the present fragment.

L. 5 **[**לׄאׄהׄרון ולאלעזר בנו והפשׁטתׄ[ה]**]**. A reference to God's command to Moses to strip off Aaron's clothes in Num 20:26.

והפשׁטתׄ[ה]. A *waw* inversive 2nd per. sg. perfect *Hif'il* of פשט, meaning "and you are to strip off." Cf. Comments on ועליתה in line 4.

Frg. 6

]◦[		1
]ונׄשאׄוה[		2
]לׄאׄ ◦ארית[		3

Notes on Readings

L. 2 **ונׄשאׄו[**. The DJD edition reads here הׄנשארה. While the traces of the first letter suit both *he* and *waw* (or *yod*), the hook-shaped top of the fifth letter indicates a *waw* rather than a *resh* (compare the *resh* in the following line).

◦ארות. Strugnell read here תׄארית. The editors read ◦ארית. The traces of the first letter may be read as *taw* (see PAM 41865) or *he*. However, both readings, הׄארות and תׄארות, are difficult. Therefore, none is proposed here.

---

28 For this usage, see Joüon-Muraoka, *Grammar*, § 119j.

Translation
1. [   ].
2. [   ] and they carried her
3. [   ] no .....

Comments
L. 2 וֹנִשְׂאֻוֹהָ[. וֹנשׂאוה is the 3rd pl. perfect (with *waw* conjunctive or inversive) of נשא in *Qal*, "to carry,"[29] with a 3rd. fem. sg. pronominal suffix. Perhaps the plural refers to the people of Israel but it is less clear who or what is being carried. Perhaps it is a reference to Miriam's death (Num 20:1), which preceded Aaron's demise (Num 20:25–29).

Frg. 7

]ᵒᵒיה[1

Frg. 8[30]

] מᵒ[1
וי[עָנוּ וי]אמרו   2
]בְּעד [3
]אֹלᵒ[4

Notes on Readings
L. 1 מᵒ[. The DJD edition reads] מ[but a trace of ink before the final *mem* is still visible (thus Falk).[31]

L. 2 וי[עָנוּ וי]אמרו. The editors read]וי נני[. But the vertical stroke of the first letter projects below the base line, suggesting an *'ayin* (cf. *'ayin* in the following line) rather than a *nun*. Also Falk reads it as *'ayin*.

L. 3]בְּעד[. Thus the editors. Falk proposes]עד מֹ[. The traces of the first letter may indeed be read as the left upper corner of a final *mem*. Yet, the space between

---
29 *HALOT*, 724.
30 Published also as 4Q393 6 by D. Falk in DJD XXIX, 60 (see Introduction).
31 Cf. Falk, ibid.

it and the following letter is too small to be the interval between two adjacent words. Therefore, the editors' reading is to be preferred.

L. 4]אֹל∘[. DJD reads here]∘∘ל[. Falk suggests plausibly that the second letter is an *alef* (see PAM 42973) and mentions Strugnell's suggestion,]יִֹשְׂרָאֵל[.[32]

Translation
1.   ]..[
2.   and th]ey answered and s[aid
3.   ] for [
4.   ]...[

Comments

L. 2 וִ[עָנוּ וי]אמרו. The few letters preserved in this line may be restored as a frequently occurring biblical expression וי[עָנוּ וי]אמרו (e.g. Exod 19:8; Josh 9:24; Hag 2:13). Note that two plural inversive future verbs are stringed together here, perhaps referring to the people of Israel.

L. 3 בְּעַד[. The surviving letters may be read as the preposition בַּעַד, "behind, through, for the benefit of, for."[33]

Frg. 9

ם לֹא[ ]∘נִי[אל ת[ֹתְעָרְבֹוֹ בֹאלֹהֹיֹ]הם	] 1
אל תמרו[אֹת פי יהוה אלהיכם כבֹדוֹ אֹוֹתוֹ וחרדו מ]פניו	] 2
וימלא את ב[תיכם וֹאֹ[וה]לֹ[י]כֹם כבוד ועצ]ה [לחיים]∘	] 3
[כֹבֹוד יתן יהוה אלהים ל]עוש[ֹה דברי כבודו]	] 4
]∘∘∘[וֹמֹושֹ]ה [ ]∘∘∘[ ]וְעָלֹ[ ]∘∘∘[	] 5
]∘בֹ∘[ ]∘[ ]∘בֹ∘[	] 6
]∘∘[	] 7

---

32 4QCommunal Confession, 60.
33 *HALOT*, 141.

Notes on Reading

The blank space at the beginning of lines 2 and 3 (PAM 41579) may belong to the right margin.

L. 3 בֿ[תיכם. The editors read תוכמ[but the second letter may also be read as a *yod*.

וֹאֿ[וה]לֹ[יֹ]כֿם. The editors propose וֹאֿת]לֹבֿם. The lacuna next to the *lamed* can accommodate a *yod*, while the penultimate letter, represented by a base stroke, may belong to either a *bet* or a medial *kaf*.

לֹחיים. The editors read וחייםֿ[but PAM 41579 shows that a *lamed* is inscribed before the *ḥet*.

Translation

1. [ ]...[ ]...[do not de]file yourselves with [their] gods[
2. [do not disobey] YHWH your God. Honor him and tremble be[fore him
3. [and he will fill] your[ho]uses and your t[e]n[t]s with glory and coun[cil] for life .[
4. [ ]glory may YHWH God give to[the one do]ing the words of his glory [
5. [ ] ...[ ] and Mos[es]and upon[ ] [
6. [ ].[ ]....[
7. [ ]..[

Comments

L. 1 אל ת[תערֿבֿוֿ בֿאלהיהם. The surviving letters תֿערֿבֿוֿ[suggest a pl. form of ערב in the *Hithpa'el*, and are thus restored. The construction התערב ב- is used in biblical parlance with the general meaning of "to mingle with" (cf. Ps 106:35–36; Ezra 9:2; note also 1QS VI, 17; VIII, 23; 4Q397 IV, 8).[34] However, the locution התערב באלוהים is not biblical but appears to indicate a particular meaning used in the Qumran Scrolls. The verb התערב is employed by the Scrolls in contexts of ritual purity, in the sense of mingling with impurity thus defiling oneself (cf. CD XI, 4–5; 4Q274 1 i 5–6; 4Q397 IV, 8 [4QMMT[d]]; 11QT[a] XLV, 4). So the present phrase warns against mingling with idols for fear of contamination. The context may be related to the admonition against idolatry in frg. 2 4–8. The reconstruction אל ת[תערֿבֿוֿ is suggested by the paraenetic tone of the fragment (see the following line). Since line 5 mentions the name of Moses, this fragment may preserve the conclusion of Moses' exhortation that appears in frg. 2.

---

34 *HALOT*, 877.

L. 2 **ולא תמרו] אֵת פִּי יהוה אלהיכם**. The restoration ולא תמרו as a negated 2nd per. pl. *Hifʿil* jussive of the verb מרה follows the similar formulation in 1 Sam 12:14. It fits with the following 2nd per. pl. imperatives כבדו and חרדו.

כַּבְדוֹ אֹוֹתוֹ וחרדו מ]פניו. Both verbs, כבדו, "honor," and חרדו, "tremble," stand as 2nd per. pl. imperatives. For the restoration וחרדו מ]פניו, cf. Isa 19:16. The injunction to honor God is specified in Isa 24:15; Ps 22:24; 4Q418 81 + 81a 4.

L. 3 **וימלא את ב]תיכם וא[וה]ל[י]כֹם כבוד ועצ]ה**. The reconstruction וימלא את ב]תיכם takes its cue from Deut 6:11: ובתים מלאים כל טוב (see also Hag 2:7). For the pair בתים ואהלים, see Deut 11:6. The surviving letters [ועצ may be restored ועצ]ה ("and a coun[cil"). Compare the pair כבוד/עצה in Ps 73:24. This line describes the bounties awaiting the Israelites if they follow the exhortation in lines 1–2. It is probably influenced by Deut 6:11. However, unlike the Deuteronomic passage that speaks of houses full of material goods, here they are full of spiritual gifts (Dimant). See Comments, line 4.

לחיים. Perhaps a locution such as לחיים אורח (Prov 10:17) or דרך] לחיים (4Q185 1–2 ii 2) should be restored.

L. 4 **כְּבוֹד יתן יהוה אלהים ל]עוֹשֵׂהֹ דברי כבודו[**. For the phrase כבוד יתן יהוה אלהים, see Ps 84:12: חן וכבוד יתן ה' (see also 2 Chr 1:12). For the expression דברי עושה, see Joel 2:11; Ps 103:20 (עשי דברו). Compare the construct participle עושי, which is common in the sectarian literature (e.g. עושי התורה [1QpHab VII, 16; VIII, 1; 4Q171 1–10 ii 15] and עושי רצונו [4Q171 1–10 ii 5]). For דברי כבודו, see 4Q405 3 ii 3; 4Q504 XXIII, 5. The formulation plays on the previous mention of "houses full of glory."

L. 5 **וּמֹוֹשֹׁ[ה**. The name of Moses is preserved in this badly damaged line. If Moses is referred to in the speech, then he is not the speaker. However, if the line takes up a 3rd per. narrative sequence referring to Moses, he may be the person addressing this admonition to the people of Israel.

Frg. 10 i

[	]ח̇ה̇ ל̇[	]	1
[	עד [תוֹם ה]	]	2
[	]ק̇ [ ]ο[ ] יצוֹא [	]	3
[	]ο ο[ ]ת בֹשמים מתהלכות בֹּין כֹּ]וכבים	]	4
[	ובאות בחדרי בטן לדעת מחשב]וֹת	]	5
[עֹשה	ו]הֹם על משבבו ומה יתנדב ואתם	]	6
[מחלים	]οο̇[ ]ל̇ גֹדולים הֹמפלי לעיניכם בארץ]	]	7

8   רֹעִים וֹמַכֹּהֹ גד[ו]לֹהֹ ונגעים לאין [מרפא   ולאין]שִׁבֹּוֹת
9   ֹלֹ[ ]ֹo[   ]ooo יובחֹo[[
10]   ]ֹלֹ[[

Notes on Readings

L. 1]ֹלֹ חֹoחֹ[. The first letter should be read with the editors as *ḥet* since the two surviving parallel vertical strokes are typical of this letter, as is the straight horizontal roof (see the *ḥet* in מחשבֹ[ות in line 5). Next to it survived the tip of a short vertical stroke (a *yod*?), not marked by the editors but visible on PAM 42973, 43219, and 43533. The third letter is a *he*, clearly indicated by its two slightly slanting vertical legs (compare the *he* in ומה, line 6). The space left following this letter and the next stroke indicates a new word. Of this letter, only the slanted tip of a stroke in the middle of the line has survived, which fits with a *lamed*.

L. 2 חתֹוֹםֹ[. The editors read נִיםֹ[. However, it is clear on PAM 42973 that the left vertical stroke of the first letter, with its small protruding bottom peg, belongs to a *taw*.

Translation

1. [   ]... .[   ]
2. [until the] end of the .[   ]
3. [   ]..[ ] going out [   ]
4. [   ]. ... in the heavens, going about among s[tars   ]
5. and entering into the rooms of the abdomen to know thoug[hts   ]
6. [and] they upon his bed. And what will he offer voluntarily? And you [   ]he made
7. [ ] great things, who acts wonders before your eyes in the land[   ] bad sicknesses
8. and a gr[e]at blow and plagues without [a cure   and without a]return
9. ..[ ].[   ]... will be admonished.[   ]
10. [   ].[   ]

Comments

L. 3] יצוֹא [. This absolute infinitive of יצא in *Qal*, יצוֹא, was most likely followed by another absolute infinitive, for instance יצוא ושוב (Gen 8:7), or by a perfect or imperfect form of יצא, such as יָצֹא יָצָא (Gen 27:30) or יָצֹא יֵצֵא (Num 35:26).

L. 4 וּבשׁמיֹםׄ מֹתהלכות בֹּיֹן כֹּ]וכבים. The restoration follows that of the editors. The phrase speaks of beings moving about in the skies. Their wandering is designated by the verb מֹתהלכות, a fem. pl. *Hithpaʻel* participle of הלך. Since the subject of this participle has not been preserved, the reader must deduce it from the context. In biblical parlance, the fem. sg. participle of the same verb is used in Ezek 1:13, relating to the fire that went back and forth among the living creatures that carried the chariot Ezekiel saw in his vision. In the next line, another fem. pl. participle occurs, בֹאוֹת, describing the ability to penetrate the deepest parts and to know human thoughts. The depiction seems to have been influenced by the picture of God's eyes scanning to and fro throughout the world to watch the various occurrences taking place, an image drawn from Zech 4:10 and 2 Chr 16:9.[35] So perhaps the fem. pl. participles מֹתהלכות and בֹאוֹת also refer here to God's eyes. The restored end of the phrase takes up Obadiah 4: בין כֹּ]וכבים ("among stars"). The expression ties in with the mention of the skies (בשמים), where the unnamed beings (God's eyes?) are moving back and forth. The skies and the stars together with the internal human organs mentioned in the following line denote the two extremities of the world, its height and its depth, thus depicting its totality (Dimant). A similar way of depicting the entire universe is seen in Obadiah 4 and Job 28:29, which probably influenced the Qumran depiction here.

L. 5 וּבאוֹת בחֹדֹרֹיֹ בטן לדעת מחשב]וׄת. This phrase continues the thought of the previous line, for the fem. pl. participle וּבאוֹת has most likely the same subject as מֹתהלכות. So, here, God's eyes are described as penetrating the inner human thoughts. This is depicted in the image of entering the חדרי בטן, literally "rooms of the abdomen" (cf. Prov 18:8; 20:30; 26:22), referring to the internal human organs, in which, it was considered, thoughts are created and stored up.[36] In the present context, the formulation לבוא בחדרי בטן לדעת מחשב]ות ("entering into the rooms of the abdomen to know plan[s") reflects the notion of God's omniscience. The restoration is patterned on the similar formulation in Ps 94:11 (ה' ידע מחשבות אדם) and the general biblical notion that God is familiar with human actions and their innermost thoughts (cf. e.g. Jer 29:11; Ps 14:2; 139:4, 23).

מחשב]וֹת. The editors understand מחשב] as מַחְשָׁב, the plural form of מחשב*, a masculine by-form of מחשבה,[37] and translate it as "a plan." However, in several instances in the Scrolls, the plural of this noun designates the depths of the earth

---
[35] Note the feminine formulation of 2 Chronicles: כי ה' עיניו משטטות בכל הארץ. Note also Job 28:24.
[36] See D. N. Freedman and J. Lundbom, "בטן," *TDOT*, 2:96–97.
[37] Cf. Qimron, *Hebrew of the DSS*, 68–69.

and its designs (cf. 1QHᵃ XI, 33–34;³⁸ 4Q286 5 1; 4Q504 XX, 8; 4Q511 37 3–4). It also appears in reference to the heavenly structures (4Q427 7 ii 23) or skillfully crafted parts of the inner divine sanctum (e.g. 4Q403 1 ii 13; 4Q405 23 ii 10). But מחשב* is never used in reference to human thoughts. So the restoration מחשב[ות, a plural of the fem. noun ³⁹מחשבה in the sense of "a thought" (cf. Ps 94:11; Prov 19:21), accords better with the context and the general idea expressed here. Restoring this feminine noun is not necessarily at variance with the masc. pl. pronoun of הֹם in the next line, for its antecedent may have been another masculine (⁴⁰/שרעפים שעפים?⁴¹) noun, now lost.

L. 6 **[ו]הֹם עֹל מֹשכבו**. הֹ[ו] "[and] they" probably refers to a lost antecedent (cf. the previous comment). It is obviously connected to something occurring during sleep since the phrase specifies that it takes place עֹל מֹשכבו ("upon his bed"); the 3rd sg. pronoun seems to refer to man in general. In biblical parlance, the locution על משכב ("upon the bed") designates nighttime rest or sleep (Job 7:13; 33:15; Cant 3:1; compare Dan 4:2), and this is obviously the sense here. Thoughts occurring during night time rest (e.g. Ps 4:5) or evil schemes planned at that time (cf. Mic 2:1; Ps 36:5) provide the biblical background for the picture here.

ומה יתנדב. יתנדב is a 3rd masc. sg. imperfect of נדב in *Hithpa'el*, used in Late Biblical Hebrew with the meaning "to make a voluntary decision" (Ezra 2:68; Neh 11:2) or "contribution" (Ezek 1:6; 3:5; 1 Chr 29:5).⁴² In the Qumran sectarian literature, the use of the *Hithpa'el*, and at times the *Nif'al*, acquired the particular meaning of voluntary dedication to the life and practices of the Scrolls community.⁴³ So the use of this construct here is peculiar since, as a rule, the present scroll does not employ sectarian nomenclature. It is therefore safer to interpret the verb with the general sense of voluntary behavior or decision, as it is employed in Ezra and Nehemiah. Perhaps, after stating that God observes human actions and

---

38 J. Licht, *The Thanksgiving Scroll* (Jerusalem: Bialik Institute, 1957), 87 [Hebrew], suggests "deeps." *DSSSE*, 1:167 and *DSSR*, 5:25 translate "plotters," "schemers."
39 Cf. BDB, 364.
40 Cf. Job 4:13; 20:2; *HALOT*, 1343.
41 Cf. Ps 94:19. Compare Dan 4:2 (Aramaic). Cf. BDB, 972; *HALOT*, 1358
42 Cf. *HALOT*, 671.
43 For a detailed discussion of התנדב in the Dead Sea Scrolls, see Cf. D. Dimant, "The Volunteers in the Rule of the Community: A Biblical Notion in Sectarian Garb," *RevQ* 23 (2007): 233–45; eadem, "נדב," *ThWQ*, 2:879–83.

thoughts, the author presents a rhetorical question: "What is man able to do voluntarily?".[44]

ואתם [. The 2nd masc. pl. personal pronoun, found also in לעיניכם in the following line, indicates that the passage, perhaps in its entirety, is part of a paraenetic address (to the people of Israel?).

עָשָׂה[. The missing letters in the preceding lacuna permit more than one reading. The letters עשה[may be read as a 3rd masc. sg. perfect of עשה ("act, do") with God as subject or be restored as the noun מ]עשה ("deed, action"). Perhaps the phrase in lines 7–8 may be read and restored as מ]עשה [א]לוה גדולים. If so, מעשה would stand here for the construct plural מעשי (Dimant).[45] Compare זכרו נפלאותיו אשר עשה (Ps 105:5; see also Neh 9:17; 1 Chr 16:12; 4Q185 1–2 i 14–15).

Ll. 7–8 מַחֲלִים רָעִים וּמַכּוֹת גְּד[וֹ]לוֹת וּנְגָעִים לְאֵין [מרפא ולאין [שִׁבֹוּת. The scroll lists a series of plagues and diseases, probably as punishments for various sins. It is partly influenced by the similar list in the covenantal curses of Deut 28:59 (note the biblical formulation מכות גדלות ונאמנות וחלים רעים). Deuteronomy employs the combination וחלים רעים but the scroll uses מחלים רעים, which is found in other Qumran texts (1QpHab IX, 1–2; 4Q181 1 ii 1). For נגעים ("plagues") as the means of God's punishment, see Gen 12:17; 2 Sam 7:14; Ps 89:32–33. The negation לאין may allude to the biblical phrase לאין מרפא (2 Chr 21:18; 36:16), while the noun שִׁבֹוּת[may be restored as לאין [שִׁבֹוּת. The list of punishments continues in col. ii.

L. 7 [ ]לְ°° גְּדוֹלִים°°. The masc. pl. adjective גְּדוֹלִים°° most likely refers to the wondrous acts mentioned further on. Cf. e.g. Ps 136:4.

הַמַּפְלִי לְעֵינֵיכֶם בָּאָרֶץ[. The *Hifʿil* masc. sg. participle of פלא is written without the radical *alef*, a phenomenon attested also in other Qumran scrolls.[46] The line seems to allude to the wonders performed during the exodus. See Mic 7:15; Ps 106:22, which employ the term נפלאות of these actions.

L. 8 ולאין [שִׁבֹוּת. Perhaps meaning "without (the possibility of) returning." Compare the similar locution ואין להשב in frg. 10 ii 4.

---

44 This type of rhetorical question is also confined to the sectarian literature. It is particularly favored by the author of the *Hodayot* (e.g., 1QS XI, 25; 1QHª V, 31; IX, 25, 27).
45 On the interchange between the *yod* and *he* in construct nouns ending with *he*, see Qimron, *Hebrew of the DSS*, 20.
46 Qimron, *Hebrew of the DSS*, 23.

L. 9]∘**יוכח**. The surviving letters may be interpreted as an imperfect of יכח in the *Hifʿil*, "to rebuke" or the *Hofʿal*, "to be reproved,"[47] which would tally with the general admonitory atmosphere of the passage.

Frg. 10 ii

[ ]	1
[ ]	2
[ ]∘מ∘[ ]	3
[ ]∘∘∘[ ] בֿדֿ∘∘∘ ∘[ ]	4
[ ]ו ∘[ולשָׁמ]יר ול[שית ואין להשב יגע	5
[ ]ו[ל]ב[ ]המות בשדה ולעוברֿ ולֿשב וֿיֿ	6
[חיות וירמסוויו בהמות הכרֿת בלא]	7
[ ]ל[לבעֿר ושית ולו[ ]תֿ∘∘ ∘∘ עֿוֿן	8
[ ]∘∘ ∘∘∘∘[ ]	9
[ ]	10

Translation
1. [   ]
2. [   ]
3. [   ]...[   ]
4. [   ]. .....[   ]...[   ]
5. and to a thorn[bush and to] weeds, and there is no return from labor and.
   [ ]
6. [and] to the [c]attle in the field, and to one crossing over and to one returning and ..[ ]
7. animals, and the cattle will trample it, cut off without [   ]
8. to burn and to weeds and ..[ ]... .. ..[ ].[   ]
9. [ ].. ....[   ]
10. [   ]

Comments
L. 5 **ולשָׁמֹ[יר] ולשית**. In biblical parlance, the phrase שמיר ושית designates an uncultivated, desolate area abandoned to weeds (Isa 5:6; 7:23–25). The picture of desolation is continued throughout lines 4–7.

---

47 Cf. *HALOT*, 410.

ואין להשב יגע. Using the negation ואין, the scroll states that there is no return for the labor. להשב may be parsed as a *Hif'il* infinitive of שוב written defectively (in the MT, it always appears with a *yod* after the *shin*). The locution להשיב יגע appears in a slightly different form in Job 20:18, מֵשִׁיב יָגָע: "He (the impious man) will give back a product of labor not swallowed."[48]

L. 6 **[ו]ב[ל]ל֯הבמות בשדה**. For the expression בהמת (ה)שדה, see 1 Sam 17:44; Joel 1:20; Ps 8:8. For the phrase ב[המות בשדה, compare Exod 9:19.

ולעובר ולשב. The locution ע(ו)בר ושב, meaning "a passer-by",[49] occurs in Ezek 35:7 and Zech 7:14; 9:8 in prophetic forecasts that foretell desolation with no passers-by remaining. This also appears to be the context here.

L. 7 **חיות**. The animals mentioned here are linked to "the cattle of the field" in line 5 and the cattle in the following depiction. All relate to the description of an uninhabited and desolate area, not cultivated by humans but populated by wild animals (see Isa 34:13–15). For the attack of wild animals as a curse, see Deut 32:24.

וירמסווי בהמות. The peculiar form וירמסווי may be a scribal error for וירמסוהו, a 3rd masc. pl. imperfect (with *waw* conjunctive or inversive) of רמס in the *Qal*, "to trample with one's feet."[50] The verb refers to בהמות. Compare 2 Kgs 14:9 (= 2 Chr 25:18); Isa 7:25. Perhaps the line may be restored: ויעברוהו [חיות וירמסווי בהמות (cf. also עבר ורמס in Mic 5:7).

הכרת בלא]. הכרת may be parsed as a *Hif'il* imperative of כרת, הַכְרֵת: "Cut off without." Perhaps the scroll reads here something like הכרת בלא [שארית ופליטה (Ezra 9:14). This detail continues the picture of desolation.

L. 8 **לבעֵר ושית**. Perhaps to be restored והיה] לבעֵר ושית ("and it will be to burn and [to grow] weed," another detail in the scene of an uncultivated land, taking up the features from Isa 5:5–6. The Isaianic depiction includes both the locution "to burn down," והיה לבער[51] (5:5) and the growth of weeds, ועלה שמיר ושית (5:6).

---

48 Cf. *HALOT*, 386.
49 This is also the common meaning of the locution in rabbinic Hebrew (e.g. *t. Sanh.* 9:7; *b. Soṭah* 10b; *'Abot R. Nat.* A, 11).
50 Cf. *HALOT*, 1245.
51 Ibid., 146.

Discussion

The ten surviving fragments of 4Q386 yield a complex literary work dealing with various episodes from the period of Israel wandering in the desert. However, as is the case with many Qumran compositions, the fragmentary character of the evidence permits only a general impression of the writing copied in this manuscript.

Frgs. 1–2 quote from and rework Exodus 33–34, retelling a substantial section of the divine instructions given to Moses during his second sojourn on Mount Sinai. Frgs. 4–5 rework the account of the death and replacement of Aaron at Hor Hahar (Num 33:37; 20:25–26). Moses himself is mentioned twice by name (in frgs. 1 2; 9 5) and twice by allusion (frgs. 3 7; 5 4). The detailed Torah commandments in frg. 2 and the more general directive to obey and fear God in frg. 9 also belong to themes related to the desert wanderings, as are the threats of punishments in frg. 10 i–ii.

The structure of the work can be gleaned from the distinctive styles of the various fragments. The 3rd per. pl. narrative formulation in frg. 7 2 (וי[ענו וי]אמרו) is significant. A narrative style may also be present in frg. 4 3, אל משה לאמר. Such phrasing may point to an overall narrative framework containing the various surviving discourses. However, most of the extant pieces yield sections from diverse discourses. Frg. 2 contains some of the commandments addressed by God to the people of Israel. Frg. 3 may preserve a liturgical address of the Israelites to God, referring in line 7 to Moses as "a mediator" for God (cf. Comments, above). Frg. 1 includes some of Moses' words to God, while frg. 9 seems to offer part of another address to the people of Israel, perhaps pronounced by Moses. Frg. 5 contains part of the divine commandment to Moses related to Aaron.

Frg. 1 reworks Exod 33:11–13 and preserves the transition from a 3rd per. account of Moses' close contact with God to his direct address to the divine (lines 4–6). Frg. 2 quotes the following chapter, Exod 34:11–24. This string suggests that frgs. 1–2 came from adjacent columns that reworked a single biblical sequence. However, the only surviving words in the last line of frg. 2, לו תודות, are not biblical. Thus, the reworking of the biblical passages is apparently interlaced with other nonbiblical portions. Indeed, frgs. 3, 5, 9 and 10 i–ii contain such elaborations, albeit inspired thematically and stylistically by biblical sources. So the present composition is characterized by a combination of long, closely reworked sections of certain Torah passages together with citations from them, along with nonbiblical additions.

The Reworking of the Torah in 4Q386

Exodus 33–34 in Frgs. 1–2:

Frgs. 1 and 2 reproduce Exod 33:11–13 and 34:11–24. The extant wording of Exod 33:11–13 in frg. 1 is very close to the MT. Still, the size of the lacuna in frg. 1 4 suggests that the fragment did not contain the phrase: "Then he (Moses) would return to the camp; but his young assistant, Joshua son of Nun, would not leave the tent" (Exod 33:11b). By not including the mention of Joshua, the Qumran text yields a smoother version since the mention of Moses' faithful servant does not fit properly into this episode. It cannot be determined whether the Qumran reading reflects a biblical text circulating at the time or whether the omission is due to the reworking technique of the fragment.

Frg. 2 provides a version of Exod 34:11–24. It is notable that frg. 2, like frg. 1, closely follows the biblical text and sequence. At times, especially in frg. 2, the Qumran text deviates from the MT and adopts readings known from other textual witnesses, though it does not seem to follow any particular textual tradition. Most of the variants are alterations in gender, number, and tense. There are also variations in the use of the definite article, prepositions, and the short/long form of the pronominal suffix. The most frequent alteration, in relation to the MT, is the change from singular to plural forms (מִפְּנֵיכֶם, בקרבכם, שׁ[מ]רו, and תאכלו [frg. 2 2, 4, 7, 9]). However, the fluctuation between 2nd per. sg. and pl. is already embedded in the biblical model (cf. the 2nd pl. forms in Exod 34:13).

In three instances, the text in the scroll from Exod 34:11–24 appears to be influenced by parallel passages from Deuteronomy. The directive in Exod 34:13 prescribes the breaking of the altars of the idols, the smashing of their pillars and the tearing down of their sacred posts. The Septuagint adds the burning of the images to this threefold command, harmonizing this verse with a parallel text in Deut 7:25. A similar attempt to read Exod 34:13 with Deut 7:25–26 in mind is found in the *Temple Scroll* (11QT^a II, 6–8). 4Q386 effects the same combination. However, space considerations suggest that it uses the shorter formulation found in Deut 7:5 and inserts it before the command to break the pillars. 4Q386 also seems to omit the command to tear down the sacred posts (ואת אשריו תברתון).

A second example of Deuteronomistic influence is found in frg. 2 14. It preserved a single word, הסֻכּוֹת[. It evidently follows the sequence of the Exodus 34 quotation, which mentions this festival in verse 22. However, instead of the Exodus term, חג האסיף, the scroll uses the one from the parallel text in Deut 16:13 (cf. also Lev 23:34), חג הסכת.

A third case of Deuteronomic influence may be present at the end of frg. 2 17; according to the proposed reconstruction, it is likely that this line cites Exod 34:24. Yet, the phrase]לֹל תודות is missing from this biblical verse. While the

Hebrew noun תודה denotes "thanksgiving,"[52] it also refers to a thank-offering. Since the three yearly pilgrimages prescribed for the Israelites are mentioned in the Exodus reference, it seems that the thanks in line 17 are related to these festivals. Both Exod 34:23–24 and Deut 16:16–17 deal with the command to appear before God during the pilgrimage festivals.[53] However, while Exodus 34 records the divine promise to protect the land while the Israelites fulfill this command, Deut 16:16–17 postulates that they should "appear before the Lord ... each with his own gift."[54] So frg. 2 17 in 4Q386 may have been influenced by the Deuteronomic version.

The foregoing survey demonstrates that 4Q386 read the laws of Exodus 34 with the Deuteronomic legislation in mind. Therefore, 4Q368 offers a harmonistic reading of the legal sections of the Torah. In this respect, 4Q368 1 and 2 resemble 4QReworked Pentateuch[55] and the *Temple Scroll*.[56] The reproducing of Exodus 34 provides yet another example of the variety of harmonistic scriptural texts[57] in the Second Temple period.[58]

Rewritten Account of Aaron's Death

In addition to the extensive reproduction of Exodus 33–34, the scroll also features in frgs. 4 and 5 a reworking of the account of Aaron's death reported in Num 20:22–29 and 33:37. Frg. 4 conflates the wording from both pericopae. The

---

52 BDB, 392–93.
53 On Deut 16:16 as an elaboration on Exod 34:17, see N. Sarna, *Genesis: The Traditional Hebrew Text with New JPS Translation and Commentary* (Philadelphia: JPS, 1989), 219.
54 Paraphrasing Deut 16:16–17, Josephus also introduces the notion of "giving thanks to God" (*Ant.* iv, 203).
55 See M. Bernstein, "What Has Happened to the Laws? The Treatment of Legal Material in 4QReworked Pentateuch," *DSD* 15 (2008): 41–42 (on 4Q366 4 i). Several other examples have been discussed by D. Falk, *Parabiblical Texts: Strategies for Extending the Scriptures among the Dead Sea Scrolls* (Companion to the Qumran Scrolls 8; Library of Second Temple Studies 63; London: T & T Clark, 2007), 117–18.
56 G.J. Brooke, "The Textual Tradition of the *Temple Scroll* and Recently Published Manuscripts of the Pentateuch," in *The Dead Sea Scrolls: Forty Years of Research* (ed. D. Dimant, U. Rappaport; STDJ 10; Leiden/Jerusalem: Brill/Magnes Press, Yad Izhak Ben-Zvi, 1992), 263.
57 See the list compiled by E. and H. Eshel, "Dating the Samaritan Pentateuch's Compilation in Light of the Qumran Biblical Scrolls," in *Emanuel: Studies in Hebrew Bible, Septuagint, and Dead Sea Scrolls in Honor of Emanuel Tov* (ed. S. M. Paul et al.; VTSup 94; Leiden: Brill, 2003), 228–29.
58 Regrettably, 4Q368 2 is not mentioned in the recent survey of the Exodus texts from Qumran by R. S. Hendel, "Assessing the Text-Critical Theories of the Hebrew Bible after Qumran," in *The Oxford Handbook of the Dead Sea Scrolls* (ed. T. H. Lim and J. J. Collins; Oxford: Oxford University Press, 2010), 281–302.

geographic designation "[e]dge of the l[an]d of Edom," found only in Num 33:37, occurs in line 1, while line 2, reading "and YHW]H[spoke] to Moses, saying," points to Num 20:23. Frg. 5 alludes to the actual command to strip Aaron of his vestments, and to put them on his son Eleazar (lines 4b–5; cf. Num 20:25–26). However, the preceding lines 2–4a mention tribal chiefs, judges, and the heads of clans, details not found in the parallel biblical account. However, the wording of Num 20:27 may help elucidate this expansion of the biblical story: "they [Moses, Aaron and Eleazar] went up Mount Hor in the sight *of the whole congregation.*" Thus, it appears that lines 2–4b elaborate on the expression "the whole congregation." Interestingly, according to Deut 31:28, before his ascent to Mount Nebo, Moses summoned "all the elders of ... tribes and ... officials." Deut 32:50 compares the manner of Moses' death with that of Aaron. The wording of the scroll perhaps reflects an attempt to model the rewritten account of Aaron's demise on that of Moses.[59] This fact emphasizes the difference between the treating of the biblical sources in frgs. 1–2 and frgs. 4–5 and raises an interesting methodological question. The faithful reproduction of long biblical stretches in frgs. 1–2 may be defined as "quotations" of the biblical text, as indeed was done throughout the Comments above. However, in frgs. 4–5, the biblical source is not followed with the same fidelity and nonbiblical details appear. They exhibit the characteristic method used for reworking biblical texts in parabiblical works. So perhaps passages that are very faithful to biblical texts should be defined as "quotations," and freer adaptations of the biblical sources should be defined as the "reworking" of such sources. The differences between the two modes of treating the Bible merits further investigation; cf. Introduction. In any case, both types of approaches are adopted by 4Q368.

Paraenetic Discourses in 4Q368

While the previously discussed sections are clearly related to specific biblical passages, frgs. 9 and 10 contain freely composed admonitory expansions. Although employing biblical phraseology, they do not come from any specific biblical text. However, their sources of inspiration are relatively clear. Frg. 9 relates an exhortation against idolatry and, perhaps, intermarriage with foreign peoples (line 1). This links it to frg. 2, which cites the scriptural prohibition of intermarriage with the Canaanite nations cited in frg. 1. This fragment elaborates on the blessings

---

[59] On the symmetry between the biblical accounts of Aaron's and Moses' deaths see B. A. Levine, *Numbers 1–20* (AB; New York: Doubleday, 1993), 495.

that will be experienced by those who obey the divine commandments. At the same time, the exhortation in frg. 10 i employs the language of the covenantal curse in Deut 28:59. The theme of divine punishment is taken up also in frg. 10 ii, which alludes to various biblical passages that describe a desolation inflicted by God. While frg. 2 presents God's commandments (with frg. 1 introducing this presentation), it seems likely that frgs. 9–10 feature blessings and curses for complying with or breaking them, following the Deuteronomic model.[60] The 2nd pl. pronoun אתם in frg. 10 i 6 suggests that here, too, the admonition is addressed to the people of Israel and perhaps comes from the mouth of Moses. Finally, the reading in frg. 8 2, "and th]ey answered and s[aid," may be the people's response to these exhortations. However, it remains somewhat unclear as to whether Moses is the speaker of the admonition, yet, in light of the mention of his name in frg. 9, this seems to be quite likely.

Of particular interest is the passage in frg. 2 i 3–7. It seems to describe divine omniscience by way of a specific image, God's eyes that scan everything, above as well as below. It is a unique depiction, which evokes in a peculiar way the notion of divine Providence.

---

[60] On the use of biblical patterns in Second Temple writings, see D. Dimant, "Use and Interpretation of Mikra in the Apocrypha and Pseudepigrapha," in *Mikra* (ed. M. J. Mulder; CRINT II/1; Assen/Maastricht: Van Gorcum, 1988), 379–419.

4Q377 (4QApocryphal Pentateuch B)

Literature

J. C. VanderKam and M. Brady, "377. 4QApocryphal Pentateuch B," DJD XXVIII, 205–17 (referred to as "the editors"); J. Zimmerman, *Messianische Texte aus Qumran* (WUNT 2/104; Tübingen: Mohr Siebeck, 1998), 332–42; C. H. T. Fletcher-Louis, "Some Reflections on Angelomorphic Humanity Texts among the Dead Sea Scrolls," *DSD* 7 (2000): 292–312; idem, *All the Glory of Adam: Liturgical Anthropology in the Dead Sea Scrolls* (STDJ 62; Leiden: Brill, 2002), 141–49; G. G. Xeravits, *King, Priest, Prophet: Positive Eschatological Protagonists of the Qumran Library* (STDJ 47; Leiden: Brill, 2003), 124–27, 177–81; É. Puech, "Le fragment 2 de 4Q377, *Pentateuque Apocryphe B*: L'exaltation de Moïse," *RevQ* 21 (2004): 469–75; W. van Peursen, "Who Was Standing on the Mountain? The Portrait of Moses in 4Q377," in *Moses in Biblical and Extra-Biblical Traditions* (ed. A. Graupner and M. Wolter; BZAW 372; Berlin: de Gruyter, 2007), 99–113; P. Makiello, "Was Moses Considered to be an Angel by Those at Qumran?," in ibid., 115–27; H.-J. Fabry, "Mose, der 'Gesalbte JHWHs': Messianische Aspekte der Mose Interpretation in Qumran," in ibid., 130–42; A. Feldman, "The Sinai Revelation according to 4Q377 (*Apocryphal Pentateuch B*)," *DSD* 18 (2011): 155–72.

The Manuscript

The publication of 4Q377 was initially entrusted to John Strugnell. His preliminary transcription of the fragments[1] was utilized by the final editors in DJD XXVIII. Strugnell named this text "Apocryphal Moses C,"[2] but the editors published it as "4QApocryphal Pentateuch B."[3] Besides the commentary provided in

---

[1] Strugnell's transcription is embedded in the *Preliminary Concordance*. These readings were utilized by Wacholder–Abegg, *Preliminary Edition*, 3:164–66.

[2] Wacholder–Abegg, *Preliminary Edition*, 164. Following his lead, Vermes and Wise call it "A Moses Apocryphon C" and "A Moses Apocryphon," respectively. See G. Vermes, *The Complete Dead Sea Scrolls in English* (London: Penguin Press, 1997), 542; M. Wise, "A Moses Apocryphon," in idem et al., *Dead Sea Scrolls: A New Translation* (New York: Harper, 2005), 427.

[3] By labeling the scroll as "4QApocryphal Pentateuch B," the editors (VanderKam–Brady, "4Q377," 208) associate it with yet another scroll re-edited in this volume, 4Q368, entitled "4QApocryphal Pentateuch A." Although they note that the two works do not overlap and point to their distinctive features, these similar titles are misleading. No less problematic is the attempt to link 4Q377 to the rewritten sections of the book of Joshua among the Qumran scrolls (4Q123, 4Q378, 4Q379, and 4Q522), as has been suggested by Zimmermann, *Messianische Texte*, 341; Van Peursen, "Portrait," 99. With the exception of the phrase איש החסידים, applied to Moses by both 4Q377 2 i 8 (see *Comments*) and 4Q378 26 2, there are no affinities between 4Q377 and any of the rewritten Joshua scrolls.

the DJD edition, different aspects of 4Q377 were discussed by various scholars.[4] However, since these scholars focused primarily on frg. 2 ii, the present study is the first attempt to re-examine the entire scroll since its first publication in 2001. 4Q377 consists of five fragments. An imprint of the letters inscribed on an upper layer of the scroll is visible on the verso of the largest fragment. Under the assumption that the scroll was rolled from its end, Strugnell designated this "mirror-image" of the text as frg. 1 and the text found on the recto of this fragment as frg. 2. Based on their shape and contents, the editors made a plausible join of frgs. 5 and 6 to form a single unit.

The script is formal Hasmonean, dated between 100–50 BCE. 4Q377 reveals no traces of the terminology and worldview peculiar to the sectarian literature from Qumran[5] and therefore it is not considered to have been produced by the sectaries.

Text and Commentary

Frg. 1 i

[ ] ל[הם לב להבדי]ל   בין   ] 1
[ ]ο מ̇ο[ ] ת̇ ο ל̇ [ ]כ̇עצם השמים[   ] 2
[ ]ο[   ]צדקתי לעיני כול ה̇[גויים   ] 3
[ ]ש̇מ̇ונת̇]   [ ]ק̇[ ]לעמ̇ו̇[ο לה]נחיל   ] 4
[ ]בין ה[   ]οοο ת̇[ ]ο פ]הגו̇יים   [ ] 5
[ ]ו̇[שפט]תי ב[י̇]ן̇ איש לרעהו ובין אב לבנו ובין איש לג̇ר̇[ו   ] 6
[ ]ο̇ל̇צ̇[ ]ο̇יοי[ ]ο[ ]ל̇[רא]י̇ש̇ לכול אב בנכה כי οοο]ο[ ]οοο כ̇י̇א̇[ ]ור̇[אה 7
οοοοο[ה]ח̇וי הכנעני החתי האמרי הי̇ב̇[ו]ס̇[י̇] הגר̇גש̇[י   ] 8
οο οοοοοοοο   οοοοο οοοοο [מא]ר̇צ̇ות ורחב̇ה̇ [טובה] ארץ   ] 9
[   ] 10
[   ] 11

bottom margin

---

4 Most recently in Kristine Ruffatto, "The Exaltation of Moses in 4Q374 and 4Q377: A Divinized Moses at Qumran?," an unpublished paper presented at the Second Enoch Graduate Student Conference held on June 16–18, 2008 at Princeton Theological Seminary.

5 Zimmermann, *Messianische Texte*, 341–42; Fletcher-Louis, *Glory*, 148; Xeravitz, *King, Priest, Prophet*, 124.

Notes on Readings

The DJD edition has nine lines of text in frg. 1 i. The illegible traces of ink visible on the photographs (e.g., PAM 41973) seem to indicate that there were two more lines in this column.

L. 1 **לְ[הֵם**. Following Strugnell's preliminary transcription, the editors read [o הֵ בְ. Following an examination of the fragment and photographs, it is impossible to establish whether there are any traces of ink before *he*. The editors read the second letter as a *bet* rather than a final *mem*. However, the fragment shows that the surviving left vertical line is in fact an imprint of a vertical stroke, apparently of a final *mem*.

לְבֿ. The editors read here]ב[ ]o. The photographs (PAM 41903; 41973; 42241; 43154) reveal faint traces of a *lamed* before *bet*. There is no space between the two letters. The space left between the words לְבֿ and לְהַבְדִּי֯ל] is not a lacuna, as suggested in DJD, but an interval between two adjacent words.

L. 2 **כְֹעֲצַ֯ם[**. Strugnell and DJD read here עֲצַ֯ם[.[6] On PAM 41973, a trace of an upper horizontal stroke seems to be visible before the *'ayin*. It is read here as a medial *kaf*. See Comments.

הֿo[. DJD reads הֿוֹ[. The traces of ink visible on the fragment itself, as well as on the photographs (PAM 41903; 41973; 43154), are illegible. Thus, no reading is proposed here.

מֿo]oלֿo. The editors read הֿ[ ]o[. On PAM 41973, traces of the vertical and horizontal strokes of a *lamed* are visible. Next to it there are illegible remains of another letter (unnoted by the editors). After a blank space there are traces of three more letters. The shape of the second letter is consistent with a medial *mem*.

L. 3 **כול הֿ[**. PAM 41903 and 41973 reveal traces of a *he* after the word כול.

L. 4 o]. The editors read הֿ[. Yet, its shape does not match that of *he* as inscribed in 4Q377 (cf. *he* in the following להנחיל). It resembles a *samech* (cf. *samech* in הֿחֿסידים [frg. 2 8]). Still, given the uncertainty, no reading is suggested here.

לִעְמֿ]. DJD reads לְעֵינֵי֯. The traces read by the editors as a *yod* and a medial *nun* may belong to a medial *mem*.

L. 6 **בֿ[**. The editors offer no reading for the letter visible before the *waw* of וֿ]שפט[תי. Based on its appearance in PAM 41973 and 43154, it is most likely a *bet*.

---

6 *Preliminary Concordance*, 4:1559.

L. 7]ooo כִֿאָ. The editors read here ooooכ[ ]. In PAM 41973 and 43154, the traces of ink appearing after medial *kaf* are consistent with *yod* and *alef*. The medial *kaf* is preceded by a blank space that may contain two letters; it is possibly the right margin of this column. Next to *alef*, traces of three more letters are visible (unnoted by the editors).

וּרְ[אָה]o[. The DJD edition has הo[but the photographs (PAM 41973, 42241, 43154) reveal the left stroke and the top of an oblique stroke of *alef* before *he*. An illegible trace of ink can be seen several letter-spaces to the right of *alef*, which was unnoticed by the editors (PAM 43514).

בנכֿה. The editors read בֿoחֿה. However, remnants of a vertical base stroke following the *bet*, seen clearly on PAM 41973, 43154, suggest a medial *nun* (cf. the *nun* in הכנעני, line 8). A trace of a base line from a third letter, seen on these photographs, suggests a medial *kaf*. The trace of ink that the editors read as a left vertical stroke of *ḥet* may be a left tip of an upper bar of *kaf* (cf. medial *kaf* in the word לכול).

אָב. The DJD edition reads oב but the traces of ink before *bet*, seen on PAM 41973, are consistent with *alef*.

יִֿעִיֿ[o. The DJD edition reads וִיֿעִיֿ [. The traces of the first and last letters are difficult to read. There seems to be no blank space between the traces of the first letter and the lacuna.

לְלֿצֿo[. The editors read וֿלֿoעo. However, what they understood as the top of a *waw* is, in fact, the right extremity of the horizontal stroke of *lamed*. There is no letter between the second *lamed* and the medial *ṣade*.

L. 9 oooo ooooo oo ooo [מאֿ]רְצֿוֹֿתֿ. Following Strugnell, the editors read [מאֿ]רְצֿוֹֿתֿ עֹמִֿ[י]סֿ[אֿ]חֿרִיםֿ.[7] Yet they note that the traces of ink following [מאֿ]רְצֿוֹֿתֿ are nearly illegible.

Translation
1. [to]them a heart to distingui[sh between   ]
2. [ ]like the very heavens [   ].. .. ...[   ]
3. [ ]my righteousness before the eyes of all the[nations].[   ]
4. [ ] to give as a possession to my people[ ]..[   ]eight [   ]
5. [ ] the nations ..[   ]. ...[   ]between the .[   ]
6. [ ]. and I [will judge] be[tw]een a man and his fellow, and between a father and his son, and between a man and [his] sojourner[   ]

---

7 *Preliminary Concordance*, 1:67, 216.

7. [ ]for [ ].[and] your son [will s]ee that ... a father to all Is[rae]l to ..[ ]. [ ].... ....[ ]
8. [the] Hivite, the Canaanite, the Hittite, the Amorite, the Jeb[u]s[ite], the Girgash[ite   ]
9. [a land]better and wider [than the la]nds ... .

Comments

The surviving lines appear to be a part of a divine address. That God is the speaker is suggested by the context and the 1st per. sg. pronoun attached to the forms צדקתי in line 3 and וֹ[שפט]תי in line 6. The 3rd masc. pl. pronoun לָהֶם (line 1) and 2nd masc. sg. suffix in בנךֹ (line 7) may indicate that the subject of the discourse is Israel, while its addressee is Moses, whose role as God's spokesman at Sinai is highlighted in frg. 2 ii.

L. 1 **לְ[הֶם לֵב לְהַבְדִּי]ל בין**. לְ[הַבְדִּי]ל is a *Hifʻil* infinitive of בדל, "to separate, to make distinction between."[8] The verb appears in Gen 1:14, Lev 10:10, 11:47, and Ezek 42:20 with the sense of separating two different things. Solomon's request to be given "an understanding heart ... to distinguish between good and evil" (...לב שמע להבין בין טוב לרע [1 Kgs 3:9]) is perhaps echoed here. Note also the locution אתי לב לדעת, "a heart to know me" in Jer 24:7; 32:39.

L. 2 **כְּעֶצֶם הַשָּׁמַיִם[**. The expression appears only once in the unique vision of the Deity in Exod 24:10. The vision scene occurs in the context of the giving of the Torah on Mount Sinai, described here in frg. 2 ii 5–12. Given the sporadic allusions to Torah commandments in the present fragment, this expression may indeed refer to the same scene.

L. 3 **צָדַקְתִּי לְעֵינֵי כֹל הַ[גוייִם**[. The editors read צדקתי as a noun with the 1st sg. possessive suffixed pronoun, צִדְקָתִי, "my righteousness."[9] Yet, it may also be parsed as a 1st sg. form of צדק in *Qal*, צָדַקְתִּי, "I was right/just" or the *Nifʻal*, נ[ִצְדַּקְתִּי, "I was justified."[10] The 1st sg. suffix, as well as the context, particularly in line 6, suggests that God is the speaker. The scroll may allude here to Ps 98:2: לעיני הגוים גלה צדקתו, "he revealed his righteousness before the eyes of the nations"; cf. also 1QH^a VI, 27. If correct, it expands this biblical phrase by introducing an emphatic

---

8 Cf. *HALOT*, 110.
9 Cf. BDB, 842.
10 *HALOT*, 1003.

כּוֹל, "all," before the word הַ[גּוֹיִים, thus including the recurring biblical locution כל הגוים (see Exod 34:10; Deut 11:23, 26:19). The line may be restored as [וגיליתי צדקתי (with Ps 98:2) or as]צדקתי ונגלתה [(with 1QHª VI 27, paraphrasing Ps 98:2). While the context is lost, an allusion to the events of Israel's sojourn in the wilderness in line 2 may indicate that the scroll refers here to the events of the Exodus (cf. the usage of צדקות in 1 Sam 12:6–7). Alternatively, since lines 4, 8, and 9 deal with Israel's taking possession of the promised land, perhaps it is by fulfilling his promise to the patriarchs in this respect that God reveals his righteousness to all nations.

L. 4 לְהַנְחִיל לְעַמּ[וֹ]. The construction הנחיל ל-, "to give as an inheritance to" (Num 34:17; 1 Chr 28:8), seems to be part of a divine discourse.[11]

]שְׁמוֹנַת [. The reading of the word is dubious and due to the fragmentary context it is difficult to determine its precise meaning. It may be related to the "nations" (הַגּוֹיִים) mentioned in the following line and the Canaanite peoples listed in line 8. This list includes six such nations, but a similar list in Ezra 9:1 names eight nations. If so, the reference may be connected to the allusion to inheritance, לְהַנְחִיל לְעַמּ[וֹ], at the beginning of the line. Note that according to Exod 23:27–33 the promise of the inheritance of Canaan and the expulsion of its indigenous peoples is given at the conclusion of the Sinai scene. This may also be the background of the present reference, as well as that of the list in line 8 (cf. Comments, line 8).

L. 5 הַגּוֹיִים. The same orthography of הגויים with a double *yod* (גוים in MT) appears in 1QM XIV, 5; XV, 1; 4Q158 14 4.[12] The nations (הַגּוֹיִים) mentioned here are probably those listed in line 8.

L. 6 וֹ]שפט[תי ב]י[ן אִישׁ לרעהו ובין אָב לבְנוֹ וּבֵין אישׁ לגֵר]וֹ. With a typical rewriting technique, the sentence combines phrases from various biblical contexts: ו]שפט[תי ב]י[ן אִישׁ לרעהו from Exod 18:16 (cf. Jer 7:5), ובין אָב לבְנוֹ from Num 30:17, and וּבֵין אישׁ לגֵר]וֹ from Deut 1:16.[13] By combining them, the Qumran text creates a more inclusive list of those to whom the judicial act mentioned at the beginning

---

[11] *HALOT*, 686.
[12] For a discussion, see Qimron, "A Grammar of the Hebrew Language," 55; idem, *Hebrew of the Dead Sea Scrolls*, 24.
[13] Note that while Exod 18:16 and Deut 1:16 employ a construction בין ... ובין, the fragment consistently uses a construction בין ... ל-, common in later biblical Hebrew. See G. Haneman, "The Particle בין in the Mishna and in the Hebrew Bible," *Leš* 40 (1976): 43–45 (Hebrew); J. Barr, "Some Notes on *Ben* "Between" in Classical Hebrew," *JSS* 23 (1978): 10–12.

of the line applies. Compare a similar inclusive roster in CD VII, 8–9; XIX, 5: בין איש לאשתו ובין אב לבנו.

L. 7 **ור[אָ̊ה בנכה כי**. The first word is best parsed as a 3rd masc. sg. *Qal weqatal* וְרָאָה, "and (your son) will see," as ו[שפט]תי̊ in the previous line. The discursive tone is expressed by the 2nd sg. suffix of בנכה, "your son," of the divine address to Moses. That Moses may be the addressee and that Israel is the subject of the exchange is indicated by the 3rd masc. sg. suffix attached to ל[הם̊ in line 1.

אָ̊ב לכול יש̊]רא[ל̊. The formulation is influenced by Jer 31:9: כי הייתי לישראל לאב, depicting the compassionate attitude of God towards Israel. So it continues the divine speech in which God describes his actions. The image of father links the locution to the preceding "your son" and to the biblical citation in line 6, "between father and his son" (ובין אָ̊ב לב̊נ̊ו̊).[14]

L. 8 **ה[ח̊וי הכנעני החתי האמרי הי̊ב̊]ו̊[ס̊]י̊[ ] הג̊רגש̊]י**. The fragment lists six Canaanite nations. Similar lists are found elsewhere in the Hebrew Bible with some variations in order and number of the names.[15] It seems that the list found here does not follow a particular biblical passage. The list belongs with the promise of the land in the next line. Cf. Discussion.

L. 9 **ארץ [טובה ורחבה̊ [מא̊]ר̊צות̊**. The expression ארץ [טובה ורחבה̊ is taken from the promise of the land in Exod 3:8. This biblical source refers to the land of Canaan as the land of the six Canaanite peoples, some of whom appear in line 8. Lines 8–9 of the present Qumran text may have been influenced by this biblical formulation.

---

[14] On God as Israel's father in Second Temple literature, see J. Kugel, "4Q369 "Prayer of Enosh" and Ancient Biblical Interpretation," *DSD* 5 (1999): 119–48; idem, "Biblical Interpretation at Qumran," in *The Qumran Scrolls and Their World* (ed. M. Kister; Jerusalem: Yad Ben Zvi Press, 2009), 392–94 (Hebrew).

[15] The number of the nations varies as following: five (Exod 13:15), six (e.g. Exod 3:8, 17; 23:23; Deut 20:17; Josh 9:1; Neh 9:8), seven (Deut 7:1; Josh 3:10; 24:1), eight (Ezra 9:1), and ten (Gen 15:19–21). For a detailed discussion of these lists, both in the MT and the ancient versions, see K. G. O'Connell, "The List of Seven Peoples in Canaan: A Fresh Analysis," in *The Answers Lie Below: Essays in Honor of Lawrence Edmond Toombs* (ed. H. O. Thompson; Lanham: University Press of America, 1984), 221–41.

Frg. 1 ii

[		] 1–7
[	[וֹגֹםׄ [	] 8
[	תשיׄר נׄפׄלאֹ[ות	] 9
[		] 10
[		] 11

bottom margin

Notes on Readings

If the suggestion that col. i contains eleven lines of text is correct, it would imply that this column also had at least eleven lines. In fact, on PAM 41973 one may observe some traces of ink below line 9.

L. 5 The DJD edition reads]פֹנֹיׄםׄ עֹםׄ אֹל פֹנֹיׄםׄ כֹאשר[. The traces of the letters visible both on the fragment and the photographs are virtually illegible. Hence no reading is proposed here.

L. 7 The editors suggest]טֹ[ל]יׄוֹ [ד]וׄיׄוׄ[. However, the traces of ink are illegible.

Translation

8. [ ]and also[ ]
9. [ ] you will sing wonder[s]

Comments

L. 9 **תשיׄר נׄפׄלאֹ[ות**. Compare Ps 98:1. The form תשיׄר may be parsed either as a 3rd fem. sg. or a 2nd masc. sg. *yiqtol* of שיר in *Qal* ("she/you will sing"). While the extant text leaves the referent of the verb תשיׄר[unknown, either Moses or Miriam mentioned in frg. 2 i 8 and 9 might be considered. In that case, the scroll may refer here to the past events of the crossing of the Read Sea (Exod 15:1–21).

Frg. 2 i

[		] 1
מֹהׄ○[		] 2
למ[טֹה		] 3
למ[טֹה בנימין רפיה		] 4
עׄ[וֹמרי למטה גד אליו		] 5

[ ] 6		[ל֯ המאסף מבן עֶשׂרים שנה
7 [ומעלה		] vacat [
8 [ ]	]ο[	[ל איש הֿחֿסידים וישא קולו
9 [ ]		וֿיֿשוב חרון אֿ[פו ותסגׄ]רׄמרים מעיני ?vac בֿנׄי
10 [ישראל		]הׄ עׄלׄינו ונהגה עׄלׄינו כיא
11 [ ]	]ο[	[שׄοοο
12 [ ]		[

bottom margin

Notes on Readings

L. 2 מֿהֿο[. The DJD edition reads יֿοο[. Zimmermann suggests οο[.[16] However, a reading proposed by Puech, מהο[, seems to better fit the evidence.[17] According to Puech, the first letter might be a *shin*, yet the tiny extant trace of ink is illegible.

L. 3 למׄ[טֿה. The DJD edition reads זֿה[. Indeed, the vertical stroke visible on the fragment and its photographs may be read as a *zayin*, yet, in view of the context, Puech's reading and restoration, למׄ[טה, seem to be preferable.[18]

L. 5 עַ[וֹׄמׄרי. The editors, with Strugnell, read יֿמׄרי[.[19] The *DSSE* suggests זמרי[.[20] However, on PAM 43372, the hook-shaped top, which identifies the first letter as a *waw* or a *yod*, is clearly visible. In the Qumran scrolls, a short "i" in a closed unaccentuated syllable is usually not represented by a *yod*.[21] It is therefore proposed to read here a *waw*.

L. 9 וֿ[יׄשוב. VanderKam and Brady read וֿ[יֿשיב. Strugnell suggested יֿשיב[.[22] The vertical stroke following *shin* may be read both as a *waw* and a *yod*. See *Comments*.

מעיני. The editors follow Strugnell in reading מעינו.[23] In the present manuscript, the *waw* and *yod* are quite similar but contextually the *yod* is preferable. See *Comments*.

---

16 *Messianische Texte*, 334.
17 "L'exaltation," 475. Puech's transcription provides no diacritic marks.
18 "L'exaltation," 475.
19 *Preliminary Concordance*, 3:1248.
20 *DSSR* 2:744.
21 Qimron, "A Grammar of the Hebrew Language," 100.
22 *Preliminary Concordance*, 2:743.
23 *Preliminary Concordance*, 4:1491.

בֹּ֯נִ֯י. The editors, with Strugnell, read שֹׁנִי֯, as do Zimmermann and *DSSSE*. On PAM 43372, a vertical stroke of *bet* is visible. What others interpreted as strokes of a *shin* are in fact a base and an upper bar of *bet*. בֹּנִי֯ seems to be preceded by a blank space (two or three letter-spaces), which is now partially destroyed by a hole in the leather.

L. 10 ה֯[. The editors suggest no reading for the traces of the first letter. However, the left vertical stroke and left extremity of an upper bar of *he* are visible on PAM 43372.

עלינו ונהגה עלינו. Strugnell read עלינו ונהגה אלינו.[24] Zimmermann suggests: עֹלִינֹוּ ונהגה אֹלִינֹוּ. The DJD edition has עלינו ונהגה אלינו. Puech proposes ונהגה אלינו עלינו. A close examination of the fragment and its photographs (especially PAM 41942, 43372) suggests that the first letter in both words is *'ayin*.

L. 11 ooo. The illegible traces of two or three letters next to *shin* appear on PAM 43372.

Translation
2. [   ]...[
3. [to the tri]be [
4. [to the tr]ibe of Benjamin Rephaiah
5. [O]mri to the tribe of Gad Elyo
6. [   ] the rearguard from twenty years of age
7. [   ] vacat
8. [   ] one of the pious ones and he lifted his voice
9. [and] the anger of [his] fu[ry] abated. [And] Miriam [was shu]t from the eyes *vac?* of the sons of
10. [Israel   ] upon us and we pleaded on our behalf, because
11. [   ].[   ]....

Comments
L. 4 למ[טה בנימין רפיה. It appears that this is part of a list of tribal chieftains. In the Hebrew Bible, the name רְפָיָה is borne by several individuals (Neh 3:9; 1 Chr 3:21, 4:42, 7:2, 9:43 [= 8:37: רָפָה]). Assuming that the scroll employs here a biblical formula "to the tribe X + a name of a person" (cf. Num 13:4–15; 34:17–29), Rephaiah

---

24 *Preliminary Concordance*, 3:1386.

belongs to the tribe of Benjamin. 1 Chr 9:43 also refers to a certain רפיה, alternatively named רפה (1 Chr 8:37), a descendant of Benjamin. The editors suggest that the present fragment alludes to the list of the twelve spies from Numbers 13, mentioning Palti son of Rafu from the tribe of Benjamin (Num 13:9). However, besides the difference in spelling (רפוא/רפיה), the name Rafu in Numbers 13 is a patronymic. Furthermore, none of the other names listed in frg. 2 i corresponds to those of the spies. The formula "to the tribe X + a name of a person" is used by the book of Numbers for tribal chieftains (Num 1:5–15; 2; 10:14–28; 34:18–28), but nowhere do we find the order of Benjamin-Gad. It seems that the author compiled his own list of tribal chiefs. The list of chieftains perhaps relates to the march of the tribes in the desert, a context suggested by the mention of the rearguard (המאסף) in line 6.

L. 5 ע[ומר]י. The name Omri is borne by a few individuals in the Hebrew Bible (1 Kgs 16:15–28; 1 Chr 7:8, 9:4, 27:18). From the meager remains of the text it is unclear to which tribe Omri belongs.

למטה גד אליו. According to the formula "to the tribe X + a name of a person," אליו is the name of a man from the tribe of Gad, probably its chieftain. Perhaps it is connected to the name Elyasaf (אליסף), the chieftain of the tribe of Gad, mentioned in several biblical passages (e.g. Num 1:14; 7:42). The name אליו appears once on an ostracon from Kuntillet Ajrud (ninth to eight centuries BCE).[25] In *Jub.* 7:22 (Ge'ez), this name is given to a race of primordial giants fathered by the sinful Watchers.[26]

Ll. 6–7 [.כ]ל המאסף מבן עשרים שנה / [ומעלה. The Hebrew noun מאסף means "a rearguard."[27] The restoration follows Num 1:3. Twenty years age was the minimum age for Israelites to bear arms (Num 1:3, 26:2; 2 Chr 25:5).

---

[25] R. Zadok, *The Pre-Hellenistic Israelite Anthroponymy and Prosopography* (OLA 28; Leuven: Peeters, 1988), 279. For late examples of names with the theophoric ending יו, see M. Ohana and M. Heltzer, *The Extra-Biblical Tradition of Hebrew Personal Names* (Studies in the History of the Jewish People and the Land of Israel 2; Haifa: University of Haifa, 1978), 120–21 (Hebrew); J. D. Fowler, *Theophoric Personal Names* (JSOTSup 49; Sheffield: Sheffield Academic Press, 1988), 35. In Masada ostraca 881, 883–890 (66–73 CE), the name שביו is recorded. See R. Hachlili, "Names and Nicknames at Masada," in *These are the Names: Studies in Jewish Onomastics* (ed. A. Demsky; Ramat-Gan: Bar-Ilan University, 2002), 93–108 (97).
[26] Cf. J. C. VanderKam, *The Book of Jubilees: A Critical Text* (CSCO 510; SA 87; Leuven: Peeters, 1989), 46. The tradition is also recorded in a Greek version of *1 En.* 7:2, preserved by the Byzantine chronographer Syncellus. Cf. G. W. E. Nickelsburg, *1 Enoch: A Commentary on the Book of 1 Enoch, Chapters 1–36; 81–108* (Hermeneia; Minneapolis: Fortress Press, 2001), 185.
[27] *HALOT*, 541.

L. 6 המאסף. This term is used in Num 10:25 with reference to the entire tribal division of Dan (consisting of the tribes of Dan, Asher, and Naphtali) placed at the rear of the Israelites' camp on the march.[28] In Josh 6:9, 13 it stands for the particular military unit that brought up the rear in the procession that marched around the walls of Jericho. The precise nature of the rearguard here, as well as its relation to the preceding list of tribal chiefs, remains unclear. Perhaps one may restore here ע[ל המאסף and conjecture that the scroll named here the person (from the tribe of Dan?) leading the rearguard. In the Scrolls, the term appears chiefly in texts related to the final eschatological war (e.g. 1QM III, 2; VII, 13).[29]

L. 7 *vacat* [. A blank of at least several words and perhaps the entire line has been left here, a usual scribal practice in the Qumran manuscripts to mark the conclusion of a paragraph and the transition to a new one. The transition is clear also from the content. Lines 2–6 seem to deal with a list of tribes and their chieftains, whereas lines 8–11 mention Moses and Miriam.

L. 8 ל̇ אי̇ש הֺח̇סידים [. The epithet איש החסידים refers to Moses, as does the appellation איש חסדים in frg. 2 ii 12. It is probably influenced by the blessing of Levi in Deut 33:8, where Levi is called איש חסדך.[30] For a discussion of the epithet איש חסדים, see *Comments* to frg. 2 ii 12. Since line 9 alludes to Num 12:15, the scroll may record here a verbal interchange between Aaron and Moses.

וישא קולו. וישא is a 3rd masc. sg. *Qal wayyiqtol* of the verb נשא and, in conjunction with the word קול, it means "to raise one's voice."[31] Since the following line mentions Miriam's leprosy, referring to the account in Numbers 12, the expression וישא קולו may paraphrase the biblical statement that Moses prayed on behalf of

---

[28] See S. Ahituv, *Joshua: Introduction and Commentary* (A Bible Commentary for Israel; Tel Aviv: Am Oved, Jerusalem: Magnes Press, 1995), 114 (Hebrew).
[29] 4Q491 1–3 14 uses the noun המאסף to describe troops placed at the rear of the battle formation. In the Qumran War literature one also finds an expression חצוצרות המאסף, which, however, seems to describe the trumpets signaling a return of the troops from the battle (1QM III, 2; VII, 13; 4Q493 12). See Y. Yadin, *The Scroll of the War of the Sons of Light against the Sons of Darkness* (Jerusalem: Bialik Institute, 1955), 88 (Hebrew).
[30] The MT reads חֲסִידֶךָ, "your pious/faithful one," in singular, as it is rendered by LXX, *Tg. Yer. II*, *Tg. Neof.* ad loc. Cf. also *Tg. Onq.*, *Frg. Tg.*, *Tg. Ps.-J.*, Syr. and the commentary by Ibn Ezra ad loc. The 4Q175 14 version of this Deuteronomy verse is identical to the MT. Note also *Lev. Rab.* 1, 4 and *Pesiq. Rab Kah.* 5, 4, which employ both חסידיך and חסידך. The present Qumran text produces the plural הֺחסידים, perhaps reading the biblical title חֲסִיד(י)ךָ. Some Aramaic Targums (*Tg. Ps.-J.*, *Frg. Tg.*, *Tg. Neof.*) interpret this passage as referring to Aaron as does *Sif. Deut.* 349. Yet, *Lev. Rab.* 1:4 applies it to Moses.
[31] *HALOT*, 725.

Miriam (Num 12:13). The *wayyiqtol* form indicates that the line is set in a narrative style, relating events that occurred in the past.

L. 9 **וֹ]יָּשׁוּב חרון אָ[פּו**. Graphically, the first word may be read as both יָּשׁ[יב, a 3rd masc. sg. *Hifʿil yiqtol* of שוב, and יָּשׁו[ב, a 3rd masc. sg. *Qal yiqtol* of שוב. The phrase takes up the biblical locution שוב/השב חרון אף, "to turn away anger." In view of the highly plausible restoration ותסג[ר, based on Num 12:15, one would expect here a *wayyiqtol* form. Yet, the reconstruction וָיָּשׁ[יב, "and he returned" (DJD; *DSSSE*) is difficult, for the 3rd masc. sg. *Hifʿil* imperfect of שוב with *waw* conjunctive/inversive are written without a *yod*, וישב, in both biblical and Qumran Hebrew.[32] The alternative reading, יָּשׁו[ב, is also not without problems, as 3rd masc. sg. *Qal yiqtol* forms of שוב with *waw* conjunctive/inversive are short in biblical Hebrew. However, a few deviations from this rule are attested in Qumran Hebrew, e.g. ילד וישוב (11Q19 LXII, 3) and וישוב להודיע (4Q254a 3 4),[33] so this form is adopted above. The divine anger against Aaron and Miriam is mentioned in Num 12:9. Yet, the phrase יָּשׁוב חרון אָ[פו] seems to follow Num 25:4 (וישב חרון אף ה'); cf. also Jer 23:20; 2 Chr 29:10). While the biblical story does not say explicitly that God's anger abated after Moses' intervention on behalf of Miriam, it seems to be implied by the fact that her punishment by leprosy had been replaced by seven days of isolation.

בָּנֵי֯ [/ (?)vac מרים מעיני ותסג[ר֯. The editors restore the extant text (with Strugnell) as two words written without an intervening space ותסג[ר֯ מרים. ותסג[ר֯ is a 3rd fem. sg. *Nifʿal wayyiqtol* of סגר, "to be shut out." This verb is used to describe Miriam's isolation in Num 12:15. Although a blank space separates the words מעיני and בָּנֵי֯, the two words are syntaciacally linked as a construct locution, perhaps מעיני בני [ישראל. Therefore, the reading מעיני is preferable to מעינו. The space between מעיני and בני was probably left blank due to a defect in the leather.

L. 10 **ה֯[עָ֯לינו ונהגה עָ֯לינו כיא**. The 1st pl. pronominal suffix in עָ֯לינו indicates that it is a direct speech and the speakers, perhaps Moses and Aaron or the people of Israel, are referring to themselves. Dimant suggests that the context favors parsing the word ונהגה as the 1st pl. *Qal wayyiqtol* of הגה in the sense of "to speak, mutter" (cf., e.g., Ps 37:30; Prov 8:7).[34] This interpretation befits the prayer of Moses mentioned in line 8. Such an understanding lends the passage coherence and therefore is better than parsing ונהגה as a form of נהג, "to drive, to lead" (thus

---

[32] Qimron, "A Grammar of the Hebrew Language," 183, 206.
[33] Qimron, "A Grammar of the Hebrew Language," 201.
[34] *HALOT*, 237.

the editors and Zimmermann[35]). Dimant observes that the Qumranic description here seems to be inspired by Isa 59:11 וכיונים הגה נהגה, taken from a communal prayer.[36] The conjunction כיא at the end of the line suggests that an unpreserved clause followed that elaborated the reasons for the speech.

Frg. 2 ii

1   א̇[ותותיכה] ומופתיכה]ooo[   ]
2   יבינו בחוקות מושה   *vacat*   [   ]
3   ויען אליב֯ח̇[וי]אמר שמ̇[עי]עדת יהוה והקשב כול הקהל הג̇ד̇ו̇ו̇ל[כ]י̇ [
4   ל[ ]ooo[ ]י̇[ ] ֯o֯שוֹ*vac* ארו֯ר האיש אשר לוא יעמוד וישמור ויע]שה[
5   לכול מצ[וות י]ה֯וה בפי מושה משיחו וללכת אחר יהוה אלוהי אבותינו המ̇[ooo
6   לנו מהר סינ[י   *vac* וי֯ד֯ב֯ר ע֯[ם]קהל ישראל פנים עם אל פנים כאשר ידבר
7   איש עם רעהו וכא[ש]ר את ג̇דלו הראנו באש בוערה ממעלה [מ]שמים [*vac*
8   ועל הא̇רץ עמד על הה̇ר להודיע̇ כיא אין אלוה מב֯לעדיו ואין צור כמוהו [וכו]ל
9   הקהל{ הע̇ד̇[ה] }ע̇נו ורעדודיה אחזתם מלפני כבוד אלוהים ומקולות הפלא
10 ויעמודו מרוחק   *vacat*   ומושה איש האלוהים עם אלוהים בענן ויכס
11 עליו הע̇נן כיא]o[   ]בהקדשו וכמלאך ידבר מפיהו כיא מי מבש[ר]כ֯מ̇ו̇ה̇ו֯
12 איש חסדים ויצ̇[או]ם אשר לוא נבר̇או]ל{מעולם ולע̇ד̇[ ]oooo[ ]oo
                           bottom margin

Notes on Readings

L. 1 [ותותיכה]א̇. The editors offer no reading for the tiny oblique stroke visible at the beginning of the line. Puech plausibly proposes that it belongs to an *alef*.[37]

]ooo. Strugnell read]ooא̇.[38] Puech suggested]לכול. Yet, the tiny traces of the letters are illegible. Therefore, the reading in DJD,]ooo, is followed here.

L. 3]אליב֯ח̇. As is clearly seen in PAM 43372 and PAM I-342901, only the right vertical stroke and part of the horizontal stroke of the last letter have survived. They fit with either a *ḥet* (thus the editors, followed here) or a *dalet*.

שמ̇[עי. Puech suggests that the lacuna is large enough to contain another word שמ̇[עי לי לי. However, since the spaces between the adjacent words in this

---

35 Cf. DJD XXVIII, 212; Zimmermann, *Messianische Texte*, 334.
36 A similar sense is also surmised in *DSSSE*, 745, "and we will bemoan," perhaps based on Nah 2:8: מנהגות כקול יונים.
37 "L'exaltation," 470.
38 *Preliminary Concordance*, 3:1233.

column are relatively large (cf. בחוקות מושה [line 2]), there is no need to assume that the lacuna contained another word.

הֹגֹּדֹוֹ]לֹ[כֹּי]. The DJD edition reads] מֹ[ ]∘∘∘∘. On PAM 41892, 41492, and 43372, traces of *he*, *gimel*, *dalet*, and *waw* are visible. Accordingly, Puech reads הגדו]ל.[39] As to the next word, he suggests correctly that a base stroke and the lower end of a vertical stroke may belong to a medial *kaf* and a *yod*. Yet, while Puech reads [כ]יא, a blank space next to the *yod* indicates that the scroll reads here כי.

L. 4 Most of the letters at the beginning of the line cannot be read.

L. 5 לכול מצֹ]ווֹת יֹהוֹה. The reading follows Strugnell[40] and Puech.
הֹמֹ[ ]∘∘. Thus reads the DJD edition.

L. 7 אֹת גֹּדֹוֹ. Strugnell read יֹרֹאֹה אֹיֹשׁ אֹ[ו]רֹ.[41] VanderKam and Brady suggest ∘∘שׁ ∘[ ]רֹ. Puech proposes תפארתו. The first letter is represented by a tiny trace of ink in PAM 41942 and 43372. It appears above the hole in the parchment and may well be the right stroke of an *alef*. The following horizontal stroke with a serif at its left extremity suits a *taw*. Next to it, traces of a *gimel* are visible on PAM 41942. *Dalet* is represented by a vertical stroke and the trace of a horizontal stroke. The following vertical stroke may belong to a *lamed*. The last letter, read by Strugnell and the editors as a *resh*, seems to be a *waw*, as Puech suggests.

L. 9 הקהל {הֹעֹדֹ]ה}. The editors note that העד]ה was erased by the scribe.

L. 11 כֹיֹא]∘. Thus DJD. Puech proposes כיא נ]כבד, yet notes that the trace of a vertical stroke visible before the lacuna may be interpreted in various ways.[42]

L. 12 ויֹצֹו]ן. The third letter is clearly a *waw* or a *yod*, and not a *dalet* as read in *DSSSE*, 774. The right extremity of a horizontal stroke (interpreted as a *lamed* by Puech) and a vertical stroke curving to the left at its bottom (Puech's *dalet*) are consistent with a medial *ṣade*; cf. the *ṣade* in צור (line 8).
∘∘∘[ ]∘∘∘∘. Thus Strugnell and the editors. Puech suggested מי כמ]והו [מבני. However, only faint illegible traces of ink have been preserved. The last letter may perhaps be read as a final or medial *kaf* (PAM 41892).

---

39 His transcription in "L'exaltation," 470, reads כ]יא, yet the lemma on p. 472 has "ky[′."
40 *Preliminary Concordance*, 3:1335.
41 *Preliminary Concordance*, 1:46.
42 "L'exaltation," 472, 474.

Translation

1. [your] s[igns] and your wonders [so that]
2. they may understand the statutes of Moses. *vac* [   ]
3. And Elibaḥ[ ]answered [and s]aid, 'He[ar], congregation of YHWH, and pay attention, all the grea[t] assembly for [ ]
4. to [ ].. [ ].....[ ] *vacat* Cursed is the man who will not arise and keep and d[o]
5. all the com[mandments of Y]HWH through the mouth of Moses, His anointed one, and to follow YHWH, the God of our fathers, who is.. [ ]
6. to us from Mount Sin[ai.] *vac* And he spoke wi[th]the assembly of Israel face to face as a man speaks
7. with his fellow and wh[e]n he showed us his greatness in a burning fire from above, [from] heaven. *vac* [ ]
8. And on the earth he stood, on the mountain, to make known that there is no god beside him and there is no rock like him. [And the entire]
9. assembly {the congrega[tion}]answered. And a trembling seized them before the glory of God and because of the wondrous sounds, [ ]
10. and they stood at a distance. *vacat* And Moses, the man of God, is with God in the cloud. And the cloud covered
11. him because [ ]when he was sanctified, and as an angel he spoke from His mouth. For who is a mess[enger]like him,
12. a man of pious acts. And he comman[ded   ] that were not created {to}from eternity and forever [ ]

Comments

L. 1 א̇[ותותיכה] ומופתיכה. The expression אתות ומופתים is used frequently in the Hebrew Bible and in the Qumran Scrolls with reference to the miracles performed by God during the exodus from Egypt (Exod 7:3; Deut 4:34; Ps 78:43; 4Q392 2 2; 4Q422 iii 5). The 2nd masc. sg. possessive suffix in ומופתיכה suggests that this line preserves an address to God, but it is not pronounced by Moses, since he is later referred to in the 3rd person.

L. 2 ***vacat* מושה בחוקות יבינו**. יבינו is a 3rd pl. *Qal yiqtol* of בין. As Zimmermann notes, the construction ב- הבין, "to perceive,"[43] occurs predominantly in the late biblical books (see Dan 1:17; 9:2; 10:11; Neh 8:8, 12) as it does in the Scrolls (CD I, 1;

---

43 *HALOT*, 122.

II, 14; 1QH[a] XI, 28; 1Q34 + 1Q34[bis] 3 ii 4).[44] According to the editors, the *yiqtol* יבינו denotes future action,[45] yet it seems that Zimmermann's rendering: "sie sollen achtgeben," taking יבינו as a jussive, should be preferred. Perhaps, the fragment read למען] / יבינו בחוקות מושה. The formula "חקות + name" appears several times in the Hebrew Bible: חקות העמים (Jer 10:3), חקות עמרי (Mic 6:7). However, the expression חוקות מושה is peculiar to 4Q377, but compare similar biblical formulations (Num 27:11; 31:21). The *vacat* following the clause may indicate a change in the train of thought and a new paragraph. Its size cannot be determined due to the tear in the skin, so it may have occupied the entire line or covered only a few word-spaces.

L. 3 וי[אמר] אליבֹחֹ[וי]אמר. If the new paragraph started in the preceding line, the surviving words in line 3 continue a narrative depiction. If the *vacat* occupied the remaining space in the preceding line, the present words open a new section with a recurring biblical formula ויען . . . וי[אמר]. The speaker is a certain [אליבֹחֹ]. There is no name beginning with אליב[ח] (אֱלִיבָ֫חַ?) attested in the Hebrew Bible or in the extrabiblical sources. Others read and restore here אליבוא].[46] However, this reading is problematic, and the name אליבו[א is also unattested.[47] Puech interprets אליבוא as a verbal negation אל with a jussive יבוא, written in one word. However this interpretation is unacceptable since a direct speech cannot stand between the verbs ויען . . . ויאמר.

שמֹ[עי עדת יהוה והקשב כול הקהל הֹגֹּדֹ[וֹ]ל]. From here on, the fragment quotes the words of "Elibaḥ[." The phrase is a mosaic of biblical locutions. For the pair שמע and הקשב see Isa 28:23; Jer 18:19; Hos 5:1. The wording שמֹ[עי עדת יהוה is reminiscent of Num 27:20. The phrase עדת ה' occurs in Num 27:17; 31:16; Josh 22:16. The expression הקהל הגדול is found in 1 Kgs 8:65; Jer 31:8; 44:15. For the word pair קהל . . . עדה, see Prov 5:14 (cf. also קהל עדת ישראל [Exod 12:6; Num 14:5]).

Ll. 4–5 אָרוֹר האיש אשר לוא יעמוד וישמור ויע[שה] לכול מצֹ[וות י]הֹוֹהֹ בפי מושה משיחו. The scroll paraphrases a covenantal curse from Deut 27:26: ארור אשר לא יקים את דברי התורה הזאת לעשות אותם. It employs a synonymous formula ארור האיש (see, e.g., Jer 11:3), replaces יקים with יעמוד וישמור, rewrites דברי התורה as an emphatic

---

44 *Messianische Texte*, 335.
45 Thus also the translations of Vermes, *Scrolls*, 542 and Puech, "L'exaltation," 470. *DSSSE*, 744, renders: "they understand."
46 *DSSSE*, 744–45. Vermes, *Scrolls*, 554, proposes "Eliab [?]." Wise, "Moses Apocryphon," 427, reads "Eliba [?]."
47 A similar name, אלבא, appears in the 8th century BCE Samarian ostraca. See Zadok, *Anthroponymy*, 279 (#72129.5).

כֹּ֯ל מִצְֿ[וות י]ְהֹ֯וֹ֯הֹ, and introduces Moses as the divine agent transmitting the commandments to Israel.

L. 4 **יעמוד וישמור ויע]שה**. These are 3rd masc. sg. jussives. The phrase יעמוד וישמור seems to paraphrase the Deuteronomic יקים in 27:26. Second Temple sources attest to a tendency to replace קום with עמד.[48] By introducing the verb ישמור, the scroll explicates the biblical יקים את דברי התורה as keeping the precepts of the Lord (for the word pair שמר and עשה, see Lev 25:18; Deut 4:6; 7:12).

L. 5 **לכול מִצְֿ[וות י]ְהֹ֯וֹ֯הֹ**. The preposition -ל signifies a direct object (cf. Lev 4:2, 13, 22, 27; Num 15:39).[49] In biblical Hebrew, the expression מצות ה' appears with both שמר (e.g. Deut 8:6) and עשה (e.g. Num 15:39).

בפי מושה משיחו. The Hebrew Bible never refers to Moses as "an anointed one." Given the following description of his role as God's messenger, this title may relate to his prophetic office.[50] While the Hebrew Bible only rarely refers to the prophets as God's anointed ones (1 Kgs 19:16; Isa 61:1; Ps 105:15; 1 Chr 16:2),[51] this usage is attested in other Qumran texts (see CD II, 12; VI, 1[= 4Q267 2 6; 6Q15 3 4]; 1QM XI, 7–8).[52] The language and stance of this passage, threatening those who do not obey the divine commandments given by way of Moses with a curse, may echo the description of the future prophet from Deut 18:18–19.

---

[48] See A. Hurvitz, "The Linguistic Status of Ben Sira as a Link between the Biblical and the Mishnaic Hebrew: Lexicographical Aspects," in *The Hebrew of the Dead Sea Scrolls and Ben Sira* (ed. T. Muraoka and J. F. Elwolde; STDJ 26; Leiden: Brill, 1997), 78–85; H. Dihi, "The Morphological and Lexical Innovations in the Book of Ben Sira" (Ph.D. diss.; Ben-Gurion University of the Negev, 2004), 514–16 (Hebrew).
[49] BDB, 511–12.
[50] Thus Zimmermann, *Messianische Texte*, 339–40; M. Wise, "A Moses Apocryphon," 427; P. E. Hughes, "Moses' Birth Story: A Biblical Matrix for Prophetic Messianism," in *Eschatology, Messianism, and the Dead Sea Scrolls* (ed. C. A. Evans and P. W. Flint; Grand Rapids: Eerdmans, 1997), 10–22 (13); Xeravitz, *King*, 125, 179; Van Peursen, "Portrait," 113; Makkiello, "Angel," 123; Fabry, "Mose," 136–38, 141–42; idem, "Die Messiaserwartung in den Handschriften von Qumran," in *Wisdom and Apocalypticism in the Dead Sea Scrolls and in the Biblical Tradition* (ed. F. García Martínez; Leuven: University Press, 2003), 357–84 (381); A. P. Jassen, *Mediating the Divine: Prophecy and Revelation in the Dead Sea Scrolls and Second Temple Literature* (STDJ 68; Leiden: Brill, 2007), 100–102. J. E. Bowley, "Moses in the Dead Sea Scrolls: Living in the Shadow of God's Anointed," in *The Bible at Qumran: Text, Shape, and Interpretation* (ed. P. W. Flint; Grand Rapids: Eerdmans, 2001), 159–81 (175–76), prefers a more general approach, suggesting that the title משיח indicates "the special status and significance of Moses."
[51] See the recent discussion of Jassen, *Mediating*, 88–90.
[52] Ibid., 85–86, 90–103.

וללכת אחר יהוה אלוהי אבותינו. For the phrase יהוה אלוהי אבותינו, see Exod 3:15, 16; Deut 1:11, 4:1; 11QT^a LIV, 12–13. In biblical Hebrew, a construction הלך אחרי is frequently used with reference to following other gods (Deut 6:14; 1 Kgs 18:18; Jer 7:9) but it may also refer to the worship of YHWH (1 Kgs 14:8; 2 Kgs 23:3; 2 Chr 34:31; 11QT^a LIV, 12–14), as is the case here.

Ll. 5–6 **לנו מהר סינ]י** [ ]ooהֹמֹ. The reading]ooהֹמֹ is difficult (see Notes on Readings). The surviving letters, as well as the context, suggest that it is a participle. Strugnell read and restored here [המצֹוֹ[ה] (for ל- צוה, see Num 9:8; cf. also Lev 7:38; Amos 9:3–4). Puech proposed המת]גלה.[53] However, a *Hitpaʿel* of גלה, "to reveal one's self," with reference to God is not attested in the Hebrew Bible or the Qumran Scrolls. These corpora employ *Nifʿal* forms of גלה to describe a theophany (Job 38:17; Dan 10:1; 1QS IX, 19).[54] Other possible readings and restorations would be [המֹוֹפֹ[יע] (cf. הופיע מהר פארן [Deut 33:2]; for ל- הופיע, see 1Q33 XVIII, 10: והיום הופיע לנו), המֹוֹדֹ[יע] (for ל- הודיע, see Exod 18:20; Deut 4:9), or המֹדֹבֹ[ר] (for דבר -ל, see Deut 11:25; for מ- דבר, see Exod 20:19). The wording of the scroll indicates that the audience of "Elibaḥ[" consists of those who were present at the time of the Sinai revelation. Thus it suggests that the event described here took place sometime after the giving of the Torah at Mount Sinai and before the entrance to the Promised Land.

L. 6 **וֹיֹדֹבֹּרֹ עֹ[ם] [ק]הל ישראל פנים עם אל פנים כאשר ידבר / איש עם רעהו**. The 3rd sg. *Qal wayyiqtol* of דבר, וידבר, appears to refer to God. This is suggested by the locution "face to face," referring to God in the model biblical verse, Exod 33:11, and by the entire context. While, in Exod 33:11, the phrase "face to face" describes the intimate relations between God and Moses, here it is reworked and applied to God's communication with the entire nation of Israel (for the phrase קהל ישראל, see Lev 16:17; Deut 31:30; Josh 8:35).[55] In this respect, the scroll may be influenced by Deut 5:4, which describes God's revelation at Sinai, where the phrase "face to face" (פנים בפנים) is applied to the entire people of Israel.

---

[53] "L'exaltation," 470.
[54] This usage is recorded only in later rabbinic Hebrew. Cf., e.g., the rabbinic midrash *Tanhuma, Devarim* 1: מה הקב"ה עושה מתגלה להם קמעא קמעא, "what the Lord does is revealed to them gradually."
[55] Noted also by Zimmermann, *Messianische Texte*, 338. Puech, "L'exaltation," 472; Van Peursen, "Portrait," 101.

פנים עם אל פנים. The unusual combination of prepositions עם אל has been explained as a reflection of a tendency to accumulate prepositions observed in late biblical and rabbinic Hebrew.⁵⁶ However, such a combination is unattested in both biblical and rabbinic sources. Still, one may observe that while paraphrasing Exod 33:11 the scroll consistently replaces the preposition אל (employed several times in this verse) with the preposition עם. This may perhaps account for the formulation פנים עם אל פנים.

L. 7 וכא[ש]ר את גׄדׄלׄוׄ הראנו באש בעורה. This line reworks Deut 5:20 and therefore the form הראנו, "[he] showed us," should be parsed as a 3rd masc. *Hifʿil qatal* of ראה, as הֶרְאָנוּ of the biblical verse, rather than as a 3rd masc. *qatal* of *Hofʿal* (cf. הָרְאֵתָ לָדַעַת in Deut 4:35), as proposed by the editors. בעורה, "burning" is a fem. sg. *Qal* participle of בער, "to burn."⁵⁷ A similar form seems to be found in the same expression in 4Q381 46a + b 9:]וׄאש בעוׄרׄ, "and a burn[ing] fire."⁵⁸ In the Hebrew Bible, various *Qal* participle forms of בער are recorded: בערת (Jer 20:29), בֹּעֵרָה (Isa 30:33), and בֹּעֵרָה (Isa 34:9). Perhaps בעורה is another case of Qumran orthography, in which the position of a *waw* with gutturals varies.⁵⁹ However, it is possible to parse the form as a *Qal* passive participle of בער, used in an active sense, although such a form is unattested in the Hebrew Bible.⁶⁰ The detail "a burning fire" (אש בעורה) is influenced by the descriptions of Mount Sinai in Deuteronomy (4:11, 5:23, 9:15).

ממעלה [מ]שמים. "From above, [from] heaven"; the expression is added to the depiction of Deut 5:20. Indeed, the preposition ממעלה, "from above," is not attested in biblical Hebrew; instead, the biblical parlance employs two forms,

---

56 Van Peursen, "Portrait," 103 n. 20. See Poltzin's note on the usage of עד ל- before a substantive in Chronicles and Ezra (R. Poltzin, *Late Biblical Hebrew* [Missoula: Scholars Press], 69). On the accumulation of prepositions in rabbinic Hebrew, see M. Pérez Fernández, *An Introductory Grammar of Rabbinic Hebrew* (trans. J. Ewolde; Leiden: Brill, 1997), 160.
57 *HALOT*, 145.
58 E. Schuller restores בעור[ת. See E. Schuller "381. 4QNon-Canonical Psalms B," in *Qumran Cave 4.VI: Poetical and Liturgical Texts, Part 1* (ed. E. Eshel et al.; DJD XI; Oxford: Clarendon Press, 1998), 137. However, in light of the form in the present text it seems preferable to restore בעור[ה with 4Q377 2 ii 7.
59 Thus Schuller, "381. 4QNon-Canonical Psalms B," 137, in her comment on 4Q381 46 a + b 9. This phenomenon is well attested in the case of quiescent *alef*, yet cf. ואתועדדה (4Q382 23 1). See further Qimron, "A Grammar of the Hebrew Language," 71 f; idem, *Grammar*, 20 f.
60 Joüon-Muraoka, *Grammar*, § 50d. Perhaps it was also understood in this way by Strugnell, as indicated by his remark "qâtôl," בְּעוֹרָה in the *Preliminary Concordance*, 1:512.

either ממעל or ממעלה. ⁶¹ מלמעלה appears in another Qumran text (4Q405 31 3; see also 1Q22 II, 10), as well as in the rabbinic Hebrew.⁶² The phrase ממעלה [מ]שמים, "from above, [from] heaven," with [מ]שמים as an apposition to ממעלה, alludes to a description of the Sinai theophany in Deut 4:36. It contrasts with the term הארץ, "the earth," in the following line. See Discussion.

ועל הָאָרֶץ עמד על ההר. Some scholars understand the verb עמד, "he stood," as applying to Moses, thus taking the passage here as speaking of him.⁶³ However, the entire section in lines 6–8 seems to speak of God as is made clear by the phrase "he showed us his greatness in a burning fire from above, [from] heaven" (line 7). The description in these lines fits better with a divine theophany (cf. Hab 3:6). The distinctive character of Moses' role in the event is underlined by the *vacat* in line 10 that precedes the introduction of Moses' actions, thus separating it from the previous description of the theophany. The expression על ההר, "on the mountain" (cf. Exod 19:20; Neh 9:13), is an apposition clarifying the preceding ועלה ארץ, "on the earth" (cf. Exod 19:20; Deut 4:36).

להודיעֵ כיא אין אלוה מִבַּלְעדיו ואין צור כמוהו]. This line possibly reworks Deut 4:35: אתה הראת לדעת כי ה' הוא האלהים אין עוד מלבדו, "It has been clear to you that the Lord alone is God; there is none beside Him" (cf. also Deut 4:39), utilizing the similar language in 2 Sam 22:32 (= Ps 18:32, reading אלוה instead of אל).⁶⁴ For the phrase ואין . . . כמוהו, "there is...none like Him," see Exod 9:14; 2 Sam 7:22. Thus, the purpose of the divine revelation at Sinai is להודיעֵ, "to make known,"⁶⁵ that YHWH is the only God. See Discussion.

Ll. 9–10 **ורעדודיה אחזתם מלפני כבוד אלוהים ומקולוֹת הפלא ויעמודו מרוחק**. The scroll depends here on Exod 20:14. The noun רעדודיה is not attested in the Hebrew Bible or in the later sources. Perhaps, it should be understood as a noun *רעדוד derived from רעד, "to quake,"⁶⁶ in *qatlul*,⁶⁷ with יה for יהוה. It has been suggested that the ending -יה in such Hebrew words as שלהבתיה (Cant 8:6) serves as an intensifi-

---

61 On *he locale* in the Qumran Scrolls, see Qimron, *Grammar*, 69.
62 See *t. Yoma* 3:1; *b. 'Erub.* 101a.
63 Fletcher-Louis, *Glory*, 143–44, suggest that the wording in the scroll points to Moses' divine status. Similarly, A. Orlov, "Moses' Heavenly Counterpart in the Book of Jubilees and the Exagoge of Ezekiel the Tragedian," *Bib* 88 (2007): 153–73 (167–68), interprets Moses' standing as an indication of his status as a celestial being. For a detailed critique of their arguments, see van Peursen, "Portrait," 104–06; Ruffatto, "Exaltation."
64 Thus Zimmermann, *Messianische Texte*, 338.
65 Cf. *HALOT*, 392.
66 *HALOT*, 1258.
67 On this nominal pattern in the Hebrew Bible, see Joüon-Muraoka, *Grammar*, § 88a.

er.[68] Thus, while the translation "a trembling of Jah" is possible, the rendering "a great trembling" should be preferred. אחזתם is a 3rd fem. sg. *Qal qatal* of אחז, "to seize."[69] For the wording ורעדודיה אחזתם, cf. רעדה אחזתם (Ps 48:7), יאחזמו רעד (Exod 15:15), and אחזה רעדה (Isa 33:14).[70] For the phrase כבוד אלוהים, see Exod 24:16–17. The unique expression קוֹלוֹת הפלא, "wondrous sounds" elaborates on the word הקולת, "the sounds" in Exod 20:14 (cf. also 19:16). See Discussion.

L. 9 וְעֻ]נוֹ [הָעֵדָ]ה {הקהל} / וכול. Since the second part of this line reworks Exod 20:14, this formulation may refer to the Israelites' request that Moses mediate between them and God, spelled out in v. 15. However, the wording also echoes Exod 19:8, which formulates the people's acceptance of the divine commandments (cf. also Exod 24:3). The reconstruction follows Puech (for the phrase וכול / [הקהל see, e.g., Deut 5:19(22); a sg. קהל is followed by a pl. verb in Exod 12:6; 1 Sam 17:47).[71] The fragment does not quote the people's answer: "All that Lord has spoken we will do." See *Discussion*.

Ll. 10–11 ומושה איש האלוהים עם אלוהים בענן ויכס עליו הֶעָנֶן. A *vacat* preceding the word ומושה suggests a change in the train of thought. Having described the manner of God's communication with Israel on Mount Sinai, as well as their reaction, the fragment turns now to the role played by Moses during the Sinai theophany. Moses is called איש האלוהים in biblical parlance (e.g. Deut 33:1; Josh 14:6; Ezra 3:2) as well as in another Qumran text, 4Q378 26 2.[72] For the phrase עם אלוהים, see Deut 5:28(31). For the wording "and the cloud covered him," see Exod 24:15–18.

ויכס עליו הענן. The phrase is influenced by the description of the event in Exod 24:16, ויכסהו הענן. The biblical expression refers either to Mount Sinai or to Moses. In the above formulation it is applied to Moses. As a result of being covered by the cloud of the divine presence, Moses was "sanctified and as an angel ... spoke from His mouth" (line 11). Similar exegetical traditions pertaining to Exod 24:16 are found in the rabbinic sources.[73] An interpretative tradition cited by *b. Yoma* 4a agrees with the scroll in applying the verb ויכסהו in Exod 24:16 to Moses and

---

68 Joüon-Muraoka, *Grammar*, § 142n.
69 *HALOT*, 32.
70 In an attempt to explain the difficult word רעדודיה, Puech, "L'exaltation," 473, suggests that the scribe misread רעדודיה for רעדת יראה, ורעד יראה, or ורעה ויראה (cf. ורעד ורעד [וירעה וירא Ps 55:6]), but without convincing arguments.
71 Puech, "L'exaltation," 470.
72 See Jassen, *Mediating*, 113–21.
73 See *b. Yoma* 4a–b; *Mek. R. Shim.*, *Yethro* (to Exod 19:9); *'Abot R. Nat.* (A, B), 1.

interprets his being covered with a cloud as an act of sanctification. Also, according to both sources, Moses' sanctification relates to his role as the bearer of the divine words. Finally, R. Nathan (middle of the second century CE), also cited there, considers that Moses purging to become as one of the ministering angels (כמלאכי שרת) is reminiscent of the comparison in the scroll of the sanctified Moses to an angel, כמלאך. Note, however, that the scroll does not actually identify Moses as an angel, but only states that he was "like an angel."[74]

L. 10 **ויעמודו מרוחק**. This phrase is borrowed from Exod 20:14 (cf. also v. 17). Yet instead of the expected ויעמדו, a 3rd masc. pl. Qal wayyiqtol of עמד, the scroll uses a pausal form ויעמודו, as is frequently done in Qumran Hebrew.[75] While the MT has here מֵרָחֹק, the fragment reads מרוחק. It is perhaps the same adjective but in a different pattern, qātal,[76] or an otherwise unattested Hebrew noun רוחק* (cf. Aramaic רוחקה).[77]

L. 11 **בהקדשו]** [○ **כיא**. בהקדשו is a Nif'al infinitive of קדש with a 3rd masc. sg. pronominal suffix referring to Moses. For the sanctification of the people and the priests at Sinai, see Exod 19:10, 14, 22. The biblical story says nothing of Moses being sanctified. However, the rabbinic tradition (quoted by the editors) does speak of it (b. Yoma 4a; cf. also 'Abot R. Nat. [a, B], 1; Mek. R. Shim. 19, 9; Num. Rab. 12). See the preceding Comment.

וכמלאך ידבר מפיהו. The Hebrew מלאך denotes both "messenger" and "angel."[78] Since the scroll uses the preposition כ-, one may assume that מלאך here means "angel." The preposition כ- also indicates that Moses is not an angel, but is compared to an angelic messenger, for he speaks what God has told him. Compare similar formulations in Judg 13:16; 1 Sam 29:9; 2 Sam 14:17, 19:28; Zech 12:8; 1QSb IV, 25. A comparison to an angel emphasizes Moses' privileged role as a mediator who declares the pronouncements of God, מפיהו.[79]

כיא מי מבש̇ר] [כמ̇ו̇ת̇ו̇. While some read the word מבשר as מִבְּשַׂר, i.e. "from flesh," the reading מְבַשֵּׂר, a masc. sg. Pi'el participle of בשר, "to bring good news"

---

74 See Brooke, "Moses in the Dead Sea Scrolls," 221.
75 Qimron, "A Grammar of the Hebrew Language," 155, 161–67; idem, Grammar, 50–51.
76 Joüon-Muraoka, Grammar, § 88a.
77 Sokoloff, Dictionary of Palestinian Aramaic, 518.
78 HALOT, 585–86.
79 Puech, "L'exaltation," 474. Interestingly, according to the Aramaic Visions of Amram (4Q545 1a i 9), the Hebrew name of Moses is מלאכיה, "Messenger of YH." See R. Duke, "Moses' Hebrew Name: The Evidence of the Vision of Amram," DSD 14 (2007): 34–48.

(1 Sam 4:17; 2 Sam 18:26),[80] suits the context better.[81] In fact, in the Hebrew Bible and in the Qumran Scrolls there are no examples of the use of מן + בשר to denote 'to be made of flesh/to be of flesh.'

L. 12 אִישׁ חֹסְדִים. This expression is borrowed from Deut 33:8: וּלְלֵוִי אָמַר תֻּמֶּיךָ וְאוּרֶיךָ לְאִישׁ חֲסִידֶךָ. It refers to Moses both here and in frg. 2 ii 8. Yet, while frg. 2 i 8 reads אִישׁ הַחֲֿסִידִים, this line has אִישׁ חֹסְדִים. It is unclear whether one should read here אִישׁ חֲסִדִים, "man of pious people," as in frg. 2 i 8 (defective spelling), or, more likely, אִישׁ חֳסָדִים, "man of pious acts" (cf. זכור [את]דֳֿוִד שהיא איש חסדים [4Q398 14–17 ii 1]). If the second reading is correct, then the scroll attests to two different readings and interpretations of the biblical לְאִישׁ חֲסִדְךָ. Such a reading might have been influenced by the locutions אִישׁ חֶסֶד (Prov 11:17) and אַנְשֵׁי חֶסֶד (Isa 57:1; Sir 44:1).

וַיְצַ[וּ . וַיְצַ[וּ]ו∘[ם∘ אשר לוא נברֳאו {לְ}מעולם וְלֳעַֿד. וַיְצַ[וּ is a Qal wayiqtol form of צוה, "to command/to decree." The phrase אשר לוא נברֳאו, "which have not been created" alludes to Exod 34:10. While in the biblical passage it is God who performs the wonders, here the verb וַיְצַ[וּ seems to have Moses as the subject. The editors suggest that the scroll read here מופת[ים, "wonders, signs."[82] However, since in both biblical and Qumran Hebrew צוה never occurs with מופתים, it seems more likely that the scroll refers here to משפט[ים or חוק[ים, e.g., those mentioned in Deut 5:28. Perhaps the language of the scroll reflects the notion that the Torah and its commandments are eternal.[83]

מעולם וְלֳעַֿד. While both מעולם, "ever since, from old,"[84] and לֳעַֿד, "forever,"[85] appear frequently in the Hebrew Bible and in the Qumran scrolls, the combination מעולם ולֳעַֿד is not attested in these corpora.

Frg. 3

]∘[ ]∘ בם ∘[	1
]ם ואלוהים [	2
] ישראל ∘[	3

---

80 *HALOT*, 163.
81 Xeravitz, *King*, 179; Wise, "Moses Apocryphon," 428.
82 BDB, 68–69. Zimmermann, *Messianische Texte*, 339, also mentions this possible restoration.
83 On this exegetical motif in the ancient sources, see J. L. Kugel, *Traditions of the Bible: A Guide to the Bible as It Was at the Start of the Common Era* (Cambridge, MA: Harvard University Press, 1997), 44, 47, 54.
84 *HALOT*, 799.
85 *HALOT*, 786.

Notes on Readings
L. 1]ο[ ]ο בּׄםׄο[. DJD reads] ο תׄםׄο[. Puech proposes בכב[ו]ד[. Only the bottom parts of the letters are preserved and it is extremely difficult to propose a reading. In any case, the trace of the first letter is at a distance from the next one and seems to belong to another word, as suggested by the editors. A long base line of the next letter survives, better suiting a *bet* than a *taw*. The traces of the following letter are consistent with a final *mem*. The next letter is represented by a short base line, followed by a blank space and a trace of another letter.

Translation
1.].…[ ].[
2.] and God [
3.] Israel .[

Frg. 4

[כׄבוׄדׄ]

Notes on Readings
The editors read] וׄבׄο[. The trace of the first letter may be read as the upper bar of a medial *kaf*. As to the last letter, its remains may be read both as a *dalet* and as a *resh*. There is no space after *dalet*.

Translation
]glory[

Frgs. 5–6

1   [οממׄהׄ]ο [בכוׄ]לׄο[
2   [תהלה לישׂרׄאׄלׄ]
3   [οרׄ לו כלבׄבׄם הפοο]

Notes on Readings
L. 3 לוׄ רׄο[. The DJD edition reads וׄדׄο[. The upper stroke of the second letter, which widens a little at its left extremity, resembles that of *resh* but not of *dalet*.

According to PAM 41942 and 43372, the space between *resh* and *lamed* is of the same size as the space between לו and כלבבם. Strugnell also reads כלבבם לו ר֯[ו.[86]

Translation
1.]...[ ]. In al[l] [
2.]praise to Israel[
3.].. to him as their heart [

Comments
L. 2]תֹּהלה לישׂרׂאֹלֹ[. The first word may be vocalized as תְּהִלָּה, "praise, song of praise."[87] The phrase תהלה לישראל is not found in the Hebrew Bible, but note תהלות ישראל in Ps 22:4.

Discussion

The extant fragments of 4Q377 contain various themes related to the events that took place during the Israelites' sojourn in the desert: a divine discourse featuring the theme of inheriting the promised land (frg. 1 i), a list of tribal chiefs (frg. 2 i), a reworked account of Miriam's and Aaron's criticism of Moses (Numbers 12; frg. 2 i), and a second person admonition focusing on the Sinai revelation (frg. 2 ii). A closer look at the treatment of the latter two episodes in the scroll illuminates the exegetical outlook of its author.

The Reworking of Numbers 12 in Frg. 2 i 8–12

The references to Numbers 12 appear in the second section of frg. 2 i, following a *vacat* in line 7. In the present scroll, long and short *vacats* indicate different literary units and signal changes of topics; cf. frgs. 2 i 7 and 2 ii 2. The *vacat* in frg. 2 i 7 separates the list of the tribal chiefs from the reworking of the story of Miriam's leprosy. Space considerations suggest that the scroll omits large portions of the biblical account in Numbers 12. Particularly notable is the absence in the extant text of any reference to the nature of Aaron's and Miriam's complaint against

---

[86] *Preliminary Concordance*, 3:1192.
[87] *HALOT*, 1692.

Moses.[88] At the same time, the scroll expands the biblical story. For instance, it states that God's anger abated following Moses' intervention (frg. 2 i 8–9). While this detail is not explicit in the biblical account, it seems to be implied by the fact that Miriam's consignment to a lifetime of leprosy was replaced by seven days' isolation (vv. 13–14). By calling Moses by a nonbiblical appellation, איש הֽחֹסידים (frg. 2 i 8), as well as by making explicit the immediate effect of his plea on Miriam's behalf, 4Q377 highlights Moses' unique position that had been challenged by his siblings. Another embellishment of the biblical narrative seems to be found in line 10, which contains a prayer not appearing in Numbers 12.[89]

The Admonitory Speech by Elibaḥ[

The admonition by Elibaḥ in frg. 2 ii 3–12 comprises five paragraphs marked by four small *vacats*. The first paragraph, lines 3–4a, contains the speaker's summons to "all the grea[t] assembly" to listen to his words. In the second paragraph, lines 4b–6a, Elibaḥ[pronounces a curse on those who will not observe all of God's commandments transmitted by Moses. Such an adjuration suggests that the speaker is a man of considerable authority. The curse concludes with a reference to the Sinai revelation (line 6); the remaining section of Elibaḥ['s speech is concerned with this event.

The biblical accounts of the giving of the Torah at Sinai intertwine both the direct and mediated divine speeches to Israel.[90] One of the best examples of the juxtaposition of the two is Deut 5:4–5.[91] The scroll seems to deal separately with

---

[88] The intriguing absence of these details has been explained by Tervanotko as a reflection of the author's uneasiness with Moses' marriage to a Cushite. See H. Tervanotko, "'The Hope of the Enemy Has Perished': The Figure of Miriam in the Qumran Library," in *From Qumran to Aleppo: A Discussion with Emanuel Tov about the Textual History of Jewish Scriptures in Honor of his 65th Birthday* (ed. A. Lange, M. Weigold, and J. Zsengellér; FRLANT 230; Göttingen: Vandenhoeck & Ruprecht, 2009), 156–75 (161–64).

[89] Contra Tervanotko, ibid., who assumes that this line does not belong to the reworking of Numbers 12.

[90] See J. Licht, "The Sinai Theophany," in *Studies in the Bible and the Ancient Near East* (ed. I. Avishur, J. Blau; Jerusalem: Rubinstein, 1978), 251–67 (Hebrew); M. Greenberg, "The Decalogue Tradition Critically Reexamined," in *The Ten Commandments in History and Tradition* (ed. B.-Z. Segal, G. Levi; Jerusalem: Magnes Press, 1985), 83–119 (84–87) (Hebrew); M. Z. Brettler, "'Fire, Cloud, and Deep Darkness' (Deuteronomy 5:22): Deuteronomy's Recasting of Revelation," in *The Significance of Sinai* (ed. G. J. Brooke et al.; Themes in Biblical Narrative 12; Leiden: Brill, 2008), 15–28 (17–20).

[91] See M. Weinfeld, *Deuteronomy 1–11* (AB; New York: Doubleday 1991), 212–13; J. Tigay, *Deuteronomy* (JPS Torah Commentary; Philadelphia: JPS, 1996), 61–62.

these two modes of divine communication. First it describes the Deity's direct speech to Israel and then Moses' role as God's messenger. The divine direct communication with Israel is described in the third and fourth paragraphs, lines 6b–7 and 8–10a. Paraphrasing Exod 33:11, depicting Moses speaking with God in the Tent of Meeting, the scroll states that God spoke to the Israelites "face to face as a man speak with his fellow" (lines 6–7). By applying this passage to the Sinai revelation, the scroll draws a parallel between God's direct communication with Moses in the Tent of Meeting and his direct speech to Israel at Sinai.

Next, 4Q377 describes God's whereabouts while addressing Israel (lines 7–8). The biblical Sinai accounts differ on the question of God's location at the time of the revelation.[92] Thus, Exod 19:18 reads: "Now Mount Sinai was all in smoke, for the Lord had come upon it in fire" (cf. vv. 11, 20). Yet, in Exod 20:18, God says: "You yourselves saw that I spoke to you from the very heavens." Utilizing the language of Deut 4:36 and 5:20, the scroll attempts to reconcile these different biblical views. First, it speaks of God addressing Israel "face to face" while the divine glory is manifested in fire coming down from above (line 7). Next, it depicts the Deity standing on Mount Sinai (line 8) in order "to make known that there is no god besides him and there is no rock like him" (line 8), a statement paralleling the first of the Ten Commandments (Exod 20:3; Deut 5:7).

The Qumran text proceeds to describe the people's reaction to this divine pronouncement. The phrase "[and the entire] assembly answered" (lines 8–9) points to the people's request to Moses in Exod 20:15: "'You speak to us ...'"[93] The expression "and a trembling seized them" expounds the verb וינעו of Exod 20:14. The author of 4Q377 understood it not as a movement ("they fell back"), but as a trembling. A similar interpretation is found in the later Jewish sources.[94] According to the scroll, people trembled "because of the wondrous sounds" (ומקולות הפלא). The adjective "wondrous" may point to the puzzling feature of the sounds during the Sinai revelation: according to Exod 20:14 they were seen, not heard.[95]

In Exodus 20, the people's fear and request of Moses are mentioned after the giving of the Ten Commandments (vv. 14–15), but in the Qumran text they are jux-

---

92 See Brettler, "Fire, Cloud, and Deep Darkness," 17–19.
93 Alternatively, 4Q377 may allude to the people's response in Exod 19:8 and 24:3: "All the people answered as one, saying, 'All that the Lord has spoken we will do.'"
94 See, for instance, Aramaic Targums (*Tg. Onq.*, *Frg. Tg.*, *Tg. Neof.*) ad loc. and *Mek.*, *Baḥodesh*, 9. See the discussion by Y. Maori, *The Peshitta Version of the Pentateuch and Early Jewish Exegesis* (Jerusalem: Magnes Press, 1995), 66–67 (Hebrew).
95 For the ancient interpretations of this verse, see Kugel, *Traditions*, 676–77; S. D. Fraade, "Hearing and Seeing at Sinai: Interpretive Trajectories," in *The Significance of Sinai* (ed. G. J. Brooke et al.; Themes in Biblical Narrative 12; Leiden: Brill, 2008), 247–68.

taposed to an allusion to the first of the Ten Commandments. The author perhaps noticed the change in the voice of the speaker from the first person in Exod 20:2–5 to the third person in vv. 6–13 and concluded that God announced to Israel only the first two Commandments (summarized in line 8 as "there is no god besides him and there is no rock like him"), while the remaining eight were given through Moses.[96] In this case, the people's fear and request that Moses speak to them would have to be transposed after v. 5.[97] In fact, this interpretation of Exodus 20 is found in the rabbinic sources.[98]

Nevertheless, one also has to consider the possibility that the phrase "to make known that there is no god besides him" (line 8) refers to the Ten Commandments as a whole. In that case, by reworking Exod 20:14–15 right next to it, the scroll simply followed the order of the events as outlined in Exodus 20. According to this interpretation, 4Q377 concurs with other ancient Jewish sources claiming that all of the Ten Commandments were given to Israel directly by God.[99]

Having described the people's fearful reaction (lines 9–10), the present text, after another small *vacat*, turns to Moses' role during the Sinai revelation. It depicts him as being with the Deity in the cloud (lines 10b–11). The wording of the scroll here is based on Exod 24:15–18.

Having said that Moses spoke from God's mouth as an angel, the scroll further highlights his role as God's emissary by posing a rhetorical question (line 11): "who is a mess[enger]like him?" It also refers to Moses as "a man of godly acts." Finally, it depicts him as the one entrusted with commanding God's eternal laws.

This emphatic description of Moses' role during the Sinai revelation may be understood in light of the reworking of Numbers 12 in the preceding column. According to Num 12:2, Miriam and Aaron challenged Moses' leadership, saying: "Has the Lord spoken only through Moses? Has he not spoken through us as

---

[96] This interpretation is found in the rabbinic literature, e.g., b. Mak. 24a and b. Hor. 8a. See Kugel, *Traditions*, 636–37. Michael Segal suggests that it may also underlie the formulation of 4Q158 frgs. 6 and 7–8 (idem, "Biblical Exegesis in 4Q158: Techniques and Genre," *Text* 19 [1998]: 45–62 [56–58]).

[97] According to this interpretation, the phrase "to make known that there is no god besides him" stands here for the entire passage found in Exod 20:2–6. On the various approaches to the counting of the commandments in these verses, see Greenberg, "Decalogue," 96–99; M. Breuer, "Dividing the Decalogue into Verses and Commandments," in *The Ten Commandments in History and Tradition* (ed. B.-Z. Segal and G. Levi; Jerusalem: Magnes Press, 1985), 314–26; Kugel, *Traditions*, 641–43.

[98] *Song of Songs Rab.*, 22. Cf. *Pesiq. Rab.*, Ten Commandments, 22.

[99] See Philo, *Decalogue*, 175; Josephus, *Ant.* iii, 90, 93; *L. A. B.* 11:6–14; *Mek., Baḥodesh*, 4, 9. See further Kugel, *Traditions*, 636–37.

well?"[100] Elibaḥ's address, noting God's direct communication with Israel at Sinai while emphasizing Moses' unique role as God's messenger, provides an ample reply to this challenge. The scroll perhaps reflects the same exegetical move as found in Josephus' reworking of Numbers 12. According to him, among those criticizing Moses was one who admonished the people not to forget Moses' past merits (*Ant.* iii, 297).

In summary, one may note the associative manner in which the author of this scroll deals with his biblical sources. As characteristic of many "rewritten Bible" Qumran texts, the present author considers the Torah to be a single consecutive text and so associates different verses that share similar themes and formulations. At the same time, it supplies nonbiblical additions that reflect an advanced interpretation of the biblical material. This is illustrated, for instance, by the angel-like sanctification of Moses, based on his sojourn on Mount Sinai.

---

[100] H. Tervanotko, "Miriam's Mistake: Numbers 12 Renarrated in Demetrius the Chronographer, 4Q377 (Apocryphal Pentateuch B), Legum Allegoriae and the Pentateuchal Targumim," in *Embroidered Garments: Priests and Gender in Biblical Israel* (ed. D. Rooke; Hebrew Bible Monographs 25; Sheffield: Sheffield Phoenix Press, 2009), 131–50 (137), also links Elibaḥ's speech to the challenge presented to Moses in Num 12:2. However, she highlights the statement in 4Q377 that God spoke to the entire nation (frg. 2 ii 6–7) at Sinai and finds this inconsistent with Miriam's punishment.

1Q22 (Words of Moses)

Literature

J. T. Milik, "Dires de Moïse," in *Qumran Cave I* (ed. D. Barthélemy and J. T. Milik; DJD I; Oxford: Clarendon Press, 1955), 91–97; J. Carmignac, "Quelques détails de lecture dans la 'Règle de la Congrégation', le 'Recueil des Bénédictions' et les 'Dires de Moïse'," *RevQ* 4 (1963–1964): 83–96 (88–96); E. J. C. Tigchelaar, "A Cave 4 Fragment of Divre Mosheh (4QDM) and the Text of 1Q22 1:7–10 and Jubilees 1:9, 14," *DSD* 12 (2005): 303–12; E. Qimron, *The Dead Sea Scrolls: Hebrew Writings* (Jerusalem: Yad Ben-Zvi, 2013), 2:104–06 (Hebrew); A. Feldman, "Moses' Farewell Address according to 1QWords of Moses," *JSP* 23 (2014): 201–14.

The Manuscript

1Q22, inscribed in a mid- to late Hasmonean hand, is preserved in forty-nine fragments.[1] Milik incorporated most of these fragments into the first four columns of the scroll. Some of the forty-nine fragments no longer appear on the plates as seen in the recent AWS photographs.[2] At the same time, the early photographs of 1Q22 display several fragments that were not included in the DJD edition. Since it is difficult to determine whether they have been identified as belonging to a different scroll(s), these fragments are edited here under Unidentified Fragments.

With a few exceptions (see Notes on Readings), the present edition follows the DJD reconstruction of cols. I–IV, which seems to be supported by the early photographs of the scroll.[3] However, in many cases the present edition adjusts that in DJD in order to present the spaces between the fragments comprising cols. I–IV more accurately. As a result, the spaces between the words are uneven. In

---

[1] Milik, "Dires de Moïse," 91–97. Milik offered no dating for 1Q22, but Tigchelaar observes that while most letters take a form typical of the mid-Hasmonean script, a few take a form typical of the late Hasmonean period (idem, "Divre Mosheh," 311–12 n. 16). This scroll is now in the possession of the Department of Antiquities of Jordan. Since it was not possible to inspect the fragments themselves, the reader is referred to the physical description of 1Q22 in the introduction to the DJD edition.

[2] These were made available by the West Semitic Research Project of the University of Southern California and are accessible on the InscriptiFact online database (http://www.inscriptifact.com/).

[3] See especially PAM 40508 and 40511. For a photograph 1Q22 prior to its unrolling, see G. Lankester Harding, "The Dead Sea Scrolls," *PEQ* 81 (1949): 112–16, plate XXI fig. 2. For the identification of the detached fragments in this photograph, see Tigchelaar, "Divre Mosheh," 303 n. 2.

numerous cases, this represents the idiosyncrasy of the scribe who copied 1Q22,[4] yet sometimes it may serve as an indication that the proposed restoration is too short and that an alternative should be sought. Given the fragmentary state of the scroll, it is frequently difficult to determine which of the two is appropriate.

Milik labeled the scroll *Words of Moses* (דברי משה), as the majority of the remaining text (cols. II–IV) contains Moses' farewell address to Israel. But 1Q22 is sometimes also referred to as *Apocryphon of Moses* (1QapocrMoses[a]),[5] following the study by John Strugnell in which he proposed that 1Q22, 1Q29, 4Q375, and 4Q376 are copies of the same pseudepigraphic work, *Apocryphon of Moses*.[6] In addition to these two scholars, several others contributed to the study of 1Q22. Jean Carmignac offered improvements to Milik's edition.[7] Eibert Tigchelaar identified a fragment that may belong to another copy of the *Words of Moses* from cave 4 at Qumran.[8] Mats Eskhult studied several aspects of the Hebrew of the scroll.[9] Finally, Elisha Qimron revised Milik's text of cols. I–IV in significant ways.[10] Nevertheless, no detailed study of the entire scroll has been undertaken since its initial publication in 1955 and this is the first endeavor to do so.

---

4 As observed by Tigchelaar, "Divre Mosheh," 311–12 n. 16.
5 See, for instance, E. Tov (ed.), *The Dead Sea Scrolls Electronic Library* (Leiden/Boston: Brill, 2006).
6 J. Strugnell, "Moses-Pseudepigrapha at Qumran: 4Q375, 4Q376, and Similar Works," in *Archaeology and History in the Dead Sea Scrolls* (ed. L. H. Schiffman; JSPSup 8; Sheffield: Sheffield Academic Press, 1990), 221–56 (233, 245–47); idem, "4QApocryphon of Moses[b]?" in *Qumran Cave 4XIV: Parabiblical Texts, Part 2* (ed. M. Broshi et al.; DJD XIX; Oxford: Clarendon Press, 1995), 129–36 (129–31). Another copy of this composition was later identified in 4Q408. See A. Steudel, "408. 4QApocryphon of Moses[c]?" in *Qumran Cave 4.XXVI: Cryptic Texts* (ed. S. Pfann et al.; DJD XXXVI; Oxford: Clarendon Press, 2000), 298–315. All these manuscripts are re-edited in the present volume.
7 Carmignac, "Quelques détails," 88–96; see also his translation and notes in J. Carmignac et al., *Les textes de Qumran: Traduits et annotés* (Paris: Letouzey et Ané, 1963), 247–78.
8 Tigchelaar, "Divre Mosheh," 303–12.
9 M. Eskhult, "Some Aspects of the Verbal System in Qumran Hebrew," in *Conservatism and Innovation in the Hebrew Language of the Hellenistic Period* (ed. J. Joosten and J.-S. Rey; STDJ 73; Leiden: Brill, 2008), 33–35.
10 Qimron, *Hebrew Writings*, 2:104–06.

Text and Comments

Col. i

top margin

1. [ויצו]על מֹוֹשֶׁהֹ] בשנֹת [ארבעים]השנה לצֹאֹ]ת בני יֹשֹֹר]אל מארץ מ[צרים בחוֹד]ש ע[שׁתי

2. עשֹר] [בֹאֹחֹד לֹ]חוֹ]דֹש לאמורֹ [הקהל אֹ]ת כול הֹעֹ]דֹ]ה ועלה אֹ]ל הר נבו] ועמדתהֹ] שמ[ה אתה

3. ואלע[זר] בן אהרן]ן *vac* ופשֹ]ור לראשי הא[בות ללו]י[ים וכול הֹ]כוהנים [וצויתהֹ] א[ת בני

4. ישרא]ל דֹבֹֹרֹי התֹֹו]רה אשר צויתֹי אותך [בֹהר ס]י[ני לצוות את] העם [בֹאוזניהֹם [את הכול

5. היט]ב למען] אשר אֹצֹד]ק מהם ו]העידותה ב]ם אֹת] הֹ]שמים ואת [הארץ] ולוא] יעז]וֹבו

6. בֹרֹי]תי אשר [צויתי [אותם]הֹ]מה [ה]מה] ובניֹ]הם כול [הֹ]ימים [אשר המה [חיים על האד[מה כי] מגיד

7. אנו]כי אשר יעזבֹו]ני ויזנו אֹ[חֹרֹ]י שקוצי ה[ג]וֹ]ם וכול תו[עבותיהם]וכול גלֹ]וֹליהם] ועבדו [את

8. אלוהיה]ם והיו לפ[ח ול[מוקש ויש]כחו חוק ומועד וחו[דש ושבת [ויובל וֹ]ברית [ויפרו] אֹת אשר

9. אנו]כי מֹצוֹד היום] לצֹ]וֹות אותם]וקרא]ת אותם [רעה] רבה בקרבֹֹ] הֹ]ארץ א]שר המֹ[ה עוברים

10. את] הי]רדן שמה] לרש]תה והיהֹ] כא]שֹר יבואו עֹ]לֹ]יהם כול הקללֹ]וֹת] והשיגום עֹ]ד [אוֹבדם ועד

11. הש]מֹד]ם וידעו [כי] אמת נע]שתה [עמהם] [*vacat*] ויקרא [מושה] [לאלעזר בן

12. אהרן] ולישוֹ]ע בן נון וידבֹ]ר דֹבֹֹרֹי [התורה [לֹכֹלות] א]ותם הסכת

Notes on Readings

L. 1 בשנֹת. Milik read אֹ[לוהים. However, the trace of a horizontal stroke visible on PAM 40530 (unnoticed by Qimron) may also belong to a *taw*, which seems contextually more plausible.

L. 2 עשֹר]. The DJD edition has עש]ר, but a trace of a vertical stroke, perhaps of a *resh*, is visible after *shin* in PAM 40530.

L. 3 בֹן. Milik read and restored ב]ן, but faint traces of a *bet* are visible in PAM 40474.

ופש[ור vac. The DJD edition reads פש[ור. However, in a recent infrared photograph, J5928 R ir, the *pe* is preceded by a *waw*.

L. 4 אֹת[. The DJD edition disregards the vertical trace of ink following the *alef*, visible in PAM 40530. It may belong to a *taw*. However, Qimron reads it as a *waw* (אֹו[תם), but his reconstruction is too short for the lacuna (see Comments).

L. 5 אֶצֶ[ד]ק. Read with Qimron, and similarly Carmignac, אצדק,[11] rather than with Milik א[עשו]ק.

   ]לֹוא. Milik read]לוא יֹ[כ. The first letter, either a *waw* or a *yod*, is preceded by a blank space and seems to belong with the word לוא.

   וֹ[ז]יֹעבו. The short diagonal stroke preceding the *bet* fits better with a *waw* or *yod* (thus Carmignac and Qimron) than a *he* (read by Milik).

L. 6 בֹּרִ[י]תי. This is Qimron's reading (see PAM 40530). The editor read כֹּאֹשֹׁ[ר.

L. 7 הֹ[גו]םֹ. Milik suggested ה[גו]ים. A trace of a vertical stroke resembling that of a *waw* or *yod* is visible in PAM 40532 and J5928 R ir.

   גל[וליהםֹ]. This is Milik's reading, retained here. Qimron reads שקוצֵיהֹםֹ. An examination of PAM 40532 indicates that both readings are possible.

L. 8 ויש[כחו. Qimron's reading is retained here, since the extant trace of ink accords with the right stroke of a *shin* and not with that of an *'ayin*, as read in the DJD edition (ויעֹ[זבוני).

   ושבת [ויובל]הֹברית. Milik read ושבת הֹברית, but the physical evidence places the two words at a distance, since they appear on two different fragments (frgs. 3 and 28 respectively) and the shapes of the edges of the fragments do not match. In fact, there is a relatively large space between them. Tigchelaar suggests [יובל]ו.[12] However, no traces of a *waw* are seen in PAM 40530 and J5928 R ir.

   וֹברית[. PAM 40532 indicates that the first visible letter should be read as a *waw* rather than the *he* of the DJD edition (הֹברית), since the upper part of its vertical stroke with a hook-shaped top accords with this letter.

   אֹת[. This is Milik's reading. Qimron reads the oblique vertical stroke of the first letter as the hook of a *waw* and restores the word המצו[ות. Both readings are possible. However, Qimron's restoration, המצו[ות וכול, is too long for the length of the lacuna.

---

11 Carmignac, "Quelques détails," 89.
12 Tigchelaar, "Divre Mosheh," 305.

L. 9 לח[וֹת. Milik has לע[שׂוֹת. However, as Carmignac observed, the vertical stroke with a hook-shaped top is most likely a *waw*, and not the left stroke of a *shin*.[13]

L. 12 וַיֵדַב[רֹ. Contrary to the DJD reading]חֹם, the horizontal upper stroke of the surviving letter, with a serif at its left extremity, may belong to a *resh*. No traces of a *he* are visible in PAM 40508 and J5928 R ir.
   דְּבָרָיו. Milik read דבריו. The trace of the last letter suits both a *waw* and a *yod*. The proposed reading better suits the context.

Translation
1. [And he commanded] Moses[in]the [fortieth ye]ar after the [children of I]sra[el] lef[t the land of E]gypt, in the [el]eventh mo[nth,]
2. on the first day of the [mo]nth, saying, "[Convene] the entire cong[rega]tion and ascend t[o Mount Nebo] and stand[ther]e, you
3. and Elea[zar] son of Aar[on]. *vac* And ex[plain to the heads of the fa]milies, to the Lev[i]tes and all the[priests] and command the children of
4. Israe[l] the [w]ords of the L[a]w that [I] have commanded[you]on Mount S[i]nai to command [the people]in the[ir] ears, everything
5. thorou[ghly, so] that I may be[found more in the]rig[h]t than them. *vac* And[call as witnesses against th]em the heaven and [the earth] so that they [may not for]sake
6. [my]covenant[which]I have commanded [them], t[hey] and [their]sons, all]the days that they [live on the ear]th. [For] I declare
7. that they will abandon[me and will pursue adulterously the detestable things of the]nation[s, and all] their [abo]minations, [and all]their [id]ols[. And they will worship] the[ir]
8. go[d]s. And (they) will become a tr[ap and] a snare. And they will f[orget statute, and appointed time, and mo]nth, and Sabbath, [and jubilee,]and covenant. [And (they) will violate] what
9. I [am]commanding you today[to com]mand them. [And] a great [calamity will come upon] them in the midst[of the]land t[hat the]y are about to cross
10. [the J]ordan there [to poss]ess. And [wh]en all the curs[es] will come upon th[e]m and reach them un[til]they perish and until
11. they are des[troy]ed, then they will know [that] a just judgment has been pa[ssed] on them. [ ] *vacat* [ ]And Moses called Eleazar son of

---

[13] Carmignac, "Quelques détails," 91.

12. [Aaron] and Joshu[a son of Nun   and he spo]ke the words [of the Law   ]to complete t[hem, "Be quiet,]

Comments

Milik interpreted the unusually large right margin in col. i, taken, according to his reconstruction, from the first sheet of the scroll, as indicating that the first column was left blank. He suggested that it served as a "page de garde."[14]

Ll. 1–2 בשנ[ת [ארבעים] השנה] מ[צרים ... בחו̇[ד]ש ע[ש̇תי עשר̇] [ ] בא̇ח̇ד̇ ל̇[חו]ד̇ש. The scroll paraphrases the opening of Deuteronomy (here, Deut 1:3 in particular), creating a narrative framework for Moses' speech, modeled on this biblical book and Moses' final address before his death. However, the text rewrites the biblical account with slight variations. Unlike the MT and other ancient textual witnesses, it reads השנה and places the word בחו̇[ד]ש before the numeral ע[ש̇תי עשר̇. While the biblical statement provides only the date "in the fortieth year" for the discourse in question, the scroll supplies a further detail in stating that the number forty is the time elapsed since the exodus. This datum is taken from Num 33:38, in which this date is given as the time of Aaron's death.

L. 1 [ויצו עַל מֹש̇ה̇]. The restoration [ויצו עַל מֹש̇ה̇] is based on Deut 1:3, which is reworked further on in this line. It also connects syntactically to the infinitive לאמור preserved in line 2. Milik's restoration, [ויקרא עַל מֹש̇ה̇], based on Lev 1:1 (Qimron similarly restores [ויקר עַל מֹש̇ה̇]), is less appropriate. In biblical Hebrew, קרא על usually denotes "to cry against, to proclaim,"[15] and therefore Milik's reconstruction requires the presupposition that the scroll displays an אל/על interchange (cf. ויקרא אל משה [Exod 24:16; Lev 1:1]).[16]

Ll. 2–3 [הקהל א]ת̇ כול הע̇[ד]ה ועלה א̇[ל הר נבו]ועמדתה̇] שמ[ה אתה ואלע[זר] ב̇ן אהרן[ן]. The command to summon the entire congregation is not mentioned in Deuteronomy 1, although it is implied in verses 1 and 3 (cf. also Deut 31:1, 30). For the expression [הקהל א]ת̇ כול הע̇[ד]ה, see, e.g., Lev 8:3; Num 20:8. The command to ascend Mt. Nebo follows Deut 32:49. See, further, Discussion.

---

14 Milik, "Dires de Moïse," 91. See ibid., plate XVIII.
15 BDB, 895.
16 On this interchange in the Qumran scrolls, see Kutscher, *Isaiah Scroll*, 404–05; Qimron, "A Grammar of the Hebrew Language," 88.

L. 2 לֵאמוֹר. This term introduces a divine address to Moses, reported in lines 2–11.

Ll. 3–5 [וְצִוִּיתִהּ]. [א]ת בני ישראל ד[בְּרֵי הַתּ[וֹ]רה ... [את הכול היט]ב. The scroll reworks here Deut 1:3b. It identifies "the instructions that the Lord had given" that are mentioned in the biblical verse as those that were revealed at Sinai (for the expression דברי התורה, see, e.g., Deut 17:18, 28:58, 29:28).

L. 3 אתה ואלע[זר] בֶּן אהר[ן]. The inclusion of Eleazar son of Aaron here indicates that the scene took place after Aaron's death. Significantly, this nonbiblical addition depicts two figures presiding over the gathering, Moses and the senior priest at the time. This duality is well known from other Qumran texts, both sectarian and non-sectarian (Dimant).[17]

ופשׁ]ור לראשי הא[בות ללו[י]ים וכול הֹ[כוהנים. A small *vacat* precedes the next series of divine commands to Moses, starting with the verb ופש[ור, a 2nd masc. sg. *Qal* imperative of פשר. While the noun פשר ("meaning, explanation")[18] is found in Eccl 8:1, the verb פשר is not attested in biblical Hebrew. It appears in the Aramaic sections of Daniel (Dan 5:12, 16) with reference to interpreting dreams.[19] In the sectarian 1QpHab II, 7–9, this verb refers to the sectarian exegetical method applied to the biblical prophecies. Here, it most likely implies an elucidation of the law to the leaders of Israel. The restoration of an imperative ופש[ור is imposed by the second surviving verb,]וְצִוִּיתִהּ[, a *wayyiqtol* 2nd masc. sg. *Pi'el* of צוה. Both verbs are part of the divine commandment to Moses. The surviving letters suggest that Moses was commanded to elucidate the law to three groups: the heads of the families, the Levites, and the priests. The *lamed* attached to the term "Levites" connects this group to the restored imperative פש[ור and the heads of the families are similarly supplemented. This syntax shows that these two groups are distinct.[20] So although no *lamed* is attached to the third term ("all the [priests?]"), it is plausibly another distinct group.[21] Compare the various lists of dignitaries, including the "heads of the congregation," in the sectarian texts (1Q28a I, 24; 1QM I, 1, 3; III, 4).

---

17 Compare CD XIX, 9–10; XX, 1; 1QS IX, 11; 1QSa II, 12–14; 4Q522 9 ii. See D. Dimant, "The Apocryphon of Joshua – 4Q522 9 ii: A Reappraisal," in *History, Ideology and Bible Interpretation in the Dead Sea Scrolls: Collected Studies* (FAT 90; Tübingen: Mohr Siebeck, 2014), 335–53 (349–51).
18 *HALOT*, 982.
19 BDB, 1109.
20 Thus J. Maier, *Die Texte vom Toten Meer* (Munich: Ernst Reinhardt, 1960), 1:168; *DSSSE*, 1:59; E. Cook, "Words of Moses," in *Dead Sea Scrolls: A New Translation* (ed. M. Wise, M. G. Abegg, and E. M. Cook; rev. ed.; New York: Harper, 2005), 106.
21 The phrase לראשי הא[בות ללו[י]ים can also be interpreted as "to the family] heads *of* the Lev[i]tes" (cf. 1 Chr 9:33, 34; 15:12). For the restoration "and all the[priests," וכול הֹ[כוהנים, see Jer 29:25;

Ll. 4–5 מהם אֹצ̇[ד]ק אשר [למען]ב היט[ב הכול את] [בֹּאזניה]ם העם] אֹתֹ̇ם [לצוות. These lines imply the legal principle of warning, the prerequisite for establishing the intentional character of an offence, which therefore needed to precede the verdict and punishment. In the Qumran sectarian legal system, it acquired the form of a reproof, which necessitated that the sectaries "reprove" someone committing an offence before he was punished (Dimant).[22]

L. 4 לצוות אֹתֹ̇ם [העם. The restoration proposed here, which is in accordance with the Deuteronomistic formulations (Deut 2:4, 27:11), fits the size of the lacuna. Milik's restoration (followed by Qimron) לצוות א[ותם is, as Carmignac noted, too short for the size of the lacuna.

Ll. 5–6 האד[מה על חיים] המה [אשר ... תי] בֹּרֹיֹ̇[ובו יעז]וֹאל. The exhortation that Moses is instructed to pronounce paraphrases Deut 31:13a (cf. also Deut 4:10). The restoration יעז[ובו is that of Qimron.

L. 5 מהם אֹצ̇[ד]ק אשר [למען. The construction צדק מן denotes "to be more in the right than."[23] God instructs Moses to command the words of the law to the people "well" (היט[ב). Hence, if the people choose to forsake His commandments, God will still be found in the right.

ואת [הארץ] ה[שמים אֹתֹ ב]ם ב[העידותה]ו. The scroll is based on the formulation in Deut 31:28.

Ll. 6–7 כי] מגיד אנו]כי. From this point on, the scroll rewrites Mosaic prophetic warnings from Deuteronomy 31. The *Hifʿil* of נגד ("to declare, make known")[24] is sometimes used in the Hebrew Bible with reference to the foretelling of future events, as is the case here (cf. Isa 41:26, 46:10; see also 4Q216 I, 12 [= *Jub*. 1:5]).

L. 7 [וליהם]גל [וכול ה]עבות[יהם ותו] וכול ה[גוי]ם א[חר]י שקוצי ה[גוי]ם ויזנו נ[י יעזבו]אשר. This formulation expands on Deut 31:16 using formulations from other biblical passages, such as Ezek 5:11; 6:9.

---

2 Chr 5:11; 26:20. However, the last mentioned group may be reconstructed differently, וכול הֹ[זקנים (cf. 1 Kgs 20.8; see also Deut 31:1, 9).
22 For an analysis of this legal procedure, see L. H. Schiffman, *Sectarian Law in the Dead Sea Scrolls: Courts, Testimony and the Penal Code* (BJS 33; Chico: Scholars Press, 1983), 89–109.
23 BDB, 842.
24 BDB, 616; *HALOT*, 666.

Ll. 7–8 ‏ועבדו [את / אלו[הי]ם̇ והיו לפ[ח ול[מוקש‎. The scroll goes on to describe Israel's future apostasy, echoing Deut 31:20. The expression ‏והיו לפ[ח ול[מוקש‎ is taken from Joshua's farewell address, warning Israel of the obstacles to be caused by the Canaanites remaining in the land (Josh 23:13).

Ll. 8–9 ‏ויש̇[כחו ... אנו] כי [מ̇צוך היום] לצ[ו̇ות אותם‎. This formulation expands on Deut 31:16b.

‏ויש̇[כחו חוק ומועד וחו]דש ושבת [ויובל]ו̇ברית‎. The reconstruction ‏ויובל]ו̇ברית‎ follows the wording of a fragment identified by Tigchelaar as another copy of the same work (‏ויובל וב̇ר̇]ית‎ [frg. 30, DJD XXXIII]).[25] He also drew attention to the similar rosters of the divine precepts forsaken by Israel in 4Q390 1 7–8 (‏ישכחו חוק‎ [4Q216 ‏וש̇כ]חו חודש ושבת]‎ / [‏ומועד ויובל וברית‎) and *Jub.* 1:14 (‏ומועד ושב̇ת וברית ויפרו הכל‎ 2 17]). Qimron's reconstruction adopted here follows 4Q390 1 7–8. Compare also the similar list in CD III, 14–15.

‏ויפרו [א̇ת אשר‎. This restoration is supported by Deut 31:16b and 4Q390 1 7–8 (thus Tigchelaar).

Ll. 9–10 ‏ו̇קרא[ת אותם [רעה] רבה ... לרש[תה‎. The scroll intertwines phraseology borrowed from Deut 31:29b (‏וקראת אתכם הרעה‎ [Qimron]) and Deut 30:18 (‏על האדמה אשר אתה עבר את הירדן לבא שמה לרשתה‎). It reworks ‏הרעה‎ of 31:29 as ‏רעה] רבה‎ (perhaps, influenced by the emphatic ‏רעות רבות‎ in vv. 17, 21) and replaces the expression ‏על האדמה‎ of 30:18 with ‏[ה̇א̇רץ]ב̇קרב̇‎ (cf. Exod 8:18).

Ll. 10–11 ‏.והיה̇] כא[ש̇ר יבואו ע̇]ל̇י]הם כול הקלל[ות] והשיגום ע̇]ד [א̇ובדם ועד הש[מ̇ד[ם‎. This formulation is based on Deut 28:15b, 20.

Ll. 11–12 ‏[ו̇יקרא משה לאלעזר בן [אהרון] ולישו̇[ע בן נון‎. In line with the divine command in lines 2–3, Moses now summons Eleazar. In addition, he also calls for Joshua. The scroll may allude here to Deut 31:7, which depicts Moses appointing Joshua as his successor (cf. also Deut 3:28), and Num 27:21, in which Joshua is commanded to obey Eleazar. Joshua is named here next to Eleazar, as is the case in all the instances in which the Hebrew Bible mentions these two figures (Num 32:28, 34:17; Josh 14:1, 19:51, 21:1; cf. also CD V, 3; 4Q522 9 ii 13), reflecting Joshua as being subordinate to Eleazar (Num 27:18–21). Cf. Discussion.

---

25 Cf. *Qumran Cave 4.XXIII: Unidentified Fragments* (ed. D. M. Pike and A. C. Skinner; DJD XXXIII; Oxford: Clarendon Press, 2001), 200–201.

ול[ישו]ע. Joshua's name is spelled here without *he*, as is the case in Neh 8:17 and in multiple Qumran texts (CD V, 4; 4Q175 21; 4Q378 21 i 2, 3; 4Q379 22 ii 7; 4Q522 9 ii 14; 5Q9 1 1).

L. 11 וידעו [כי] אמת נע[שתה] עמהם. This clause concludes God's address to Moses. The locution עשה אמת with reference to divine punishment is taken from Neh 9:33. This verse also contains a justification of the divine punishment (ואתה צדיק; "and you are just"), here taken up in line 5 (למען אצדק), announcing proleptically the future justification of God (Dimant).

L 12 וִיְדבֵּ̊֯ר דִּ֯בְ֯רֵ֯י֯ [התורה] [לכלות א]ותם הסכת]. The verb וִיְדבֵּ̊֯ר, if restored correctly, refers to Moses. From now on, the scroll quotes his address to Israel. In agreement with the divine command in line 4, the noun דִּ֯בְ֯רֵ֯י֯ is restored here as דִּ֯בְ֯רֵ֯י֯ [התורה] (cf. also col. II, 9). The phrase לכלות א]ותם ("to complete t[hem]"),[26] as reconstructed by Milik, concerns the "words of [the Torah," התורה] דִּ֯בְ֯רֵ֯י֯. Following the editor, the end of the line, הסכת], is restored on the basis of Deut 27:9, since the first line of the next column paraphrases the same verse.

Col. ii

top margin

1 [י]שראל ושמ̊ע̊[ו] היו̊[ם הזה] נהייתה לע[ם לאלוהי [אלוהי]ך וש̊[מרתה חוקיו] ועדוותי[ו] ומצוותיו א[שֹ̊ר]

2 [אני] מצוך הי[ום אשר ת]עשה אותם כא[שֹר א]תה [עֹובר את ה̊]ירדן [לשֹ̊מ̊ה] [לרשת אר]ים גדולות

3 [וטובו]ת ובת[י]ֹם מלאים כֹו]ל טוב כרמים וזיתים] אשר[]ל]וא נטעתה ובו]רֹות חצוב]ים א[שר ל̊ו]א̊

4 [ח]צֹבתה ואכל[ת]ה ושבעתה [השמר לך] למה ירום [לב]בכה ושכ̊]חתה את כול א[שֹר אנוכי [מצו]ך היום

5 [כי [הוא חי]יך [וֹאורך ימ]יך [vac] ויוסף [מושה ו]יאמר אל בני י̊שֹראל [זה]ארבעים

6 [שנה מ]יום צ[את]ֹנו מארץ [מצרים היום] הזה [ ] אלו[הי אלוהי]ך השמיע את כול הדב[רים] הא[לה מפיה]ו̊]

7 [את כול חוקיו וא̊]ת כול מש]פטיו [הֹ[ ] [וֹ]טרחכם [ומש]א[כ]ם [ויהיה

8 [ה]ברית ולצוו̊]ת לכם את [הֹד]רך אש]ר תלכו בה] ואת המעשה אשר ת]עשו לבאר

---

[26] BDB, 478.

9 [באוזני]כֹּם̇ את [כול דברי הת]ורה הזא[ת ᵛᵉᵗʰ הש]מרו מא[ו]דה לנפשותיכם [ ]
   ○[ד]בּ̇ר וחרה אף
10 [אלוהים [בכמֹ]ה ו]עצר את השמימֹ [ל]בֹּלֹתֹי המטר ל[כ]ֹם מטר ואת ה[אדמה] לבֹּ[ל]תֹ[י]
   תת לכם את
11 [יבו]לֹה vac [ ]ו̇[ ] ויאמ[ר מושה אל כ]ול העם [אל]ה [ה]מֹצֹ[ו]ות אשר] צוה
   אֹ[ל]ל לעשות אותֹם
12 [ ]]○○[[

Notes on Readings

L. 1 ושׂ]מרתה. The reading follows Milik and is confirmed by PAM 40529, which shows traces of the middle and right strokes of *shin* rather than *'ayin*, as read by Qimron (וע̇שיתה).

ועדוותיּ]ו. Milik read ועדוותי. Qimron suggested restoring (with Deut 27:10 underlying this line) ועדוותי]ו (see *Comments*).

L. 2 תֹ]עשה. Qimron reads תֹ[ע]שׂהֹ but does not specify on what evidence he bases the reading of the last two letters. They are not visible in the photographs.

[לֹשׁמֹה]. Only one *lamed* is visible on the parchment (see PAM 40473, 40511, and as observed by Carmignac).[27] Therefore, Milik's reading of [תת] לֹבֹה] is unsubstantiated. Qimron does not read this *lamed*.

L. 7 The editor read and restored את כול מש[פטיו] at the beginning of the line. The letters]פטיו[are found on frg. 29. The placement of this fragment here is supported by PAM 40532,[28] in which it appears together with frgs. 27, 28, 30, and 31. It seems that they represent a single wad (and so they are numbered frgs. 27–31). Yet, the placement of this fragment in lines 5–6 creates an awkward Hebrew text. Qimron also avoided placing this fragment here; therefore, this fragment is treated separately below.

[○ה. Milik reads א[יֹ]כֹה, but the traces of the first letter do not yield a clear letter.

[וֹטרחכם. PAM 40529 and J5928 R ir present a trace of ink before *tet*, which is perhaps the top of a *waw* or *yod*, not marked in the DJD edition.

ויהיה. Qimron has ויהוה. However, Milik's reading followed here is preferable on contextual grounds. See *Comments*.

---

27 Carmignac, "Quelques détails," 92.
28 It is missing from the new AWS photographs (the fragment numbered frg. 29 there is, in fact, frg. 36 of the DJD edition).

L. 8 Milik read and restored [אשר בכלו̇תנ̇ ל] at the beginning of the line. The letters]תנ̇ ל[are preserved on frg. 29. As is mentioned in the note on line 7, its placement here is doubtful.

L. 9 ה̇[אה ⁱᵉˢʰ̇ʷ. הזא[ת̇. This is Qimron's reading; it suits better the extant traces of ink than that of Milik, הא̇לה̇.

]ο [. The editor read and restored here [לעשו]ת̇. Qimron reads this trace of a letter as a medial *mem*, but the remaining traces are difficult to decipher.

ד[ב̇ר. The relatively long base stroke of the first letter more closely resembles that of a *bet* than an *ʿayin*. Therefore, Milik's reading ע̇[יב is unsubstantiated and is also difficult in the context. See *Comments* ad loc.

L. 10 בכמ̇[ה]. The third letter, as seen clearly in PAM 40508, is undoubtedly a medial *mem*, unlike Milik's reading of it as a final *mem*.

ל[ב̇לתי̇. This is Qimron's reading, which accords better with the surviving traces than Milik's reading, ממ[על̇ה̇.

ל[כ]ם. The trace of a letter visible in PAM 40508 may be read as the diagonal stroke of a *lamed* rather than Milik's reading, ע̇[ליכ]ם.

ל[ת̇ל̇ב̇]י̇. This is Qimron's reading, which is preferable contextually to that of Milik, למ̇[טה. A trace of a *taw* seems to appear on the scrap of leather forming the left part of frg. 38 (unnoticed by Qimron).

L. 11 ל̇ה[יבו]. The diagonal stroke of the first letter suits a *lamed* (with Qimron) and so it is preferable contextually to Milik's reading of an *alef*, [התבו]א̇ה.

ב̇[ול. Traces of either a *bet* or medial *kaf* are visible in PAM 40508 and J5928 R ir. Therefore, the reading of the first two letters in the DJD edition, ב̇[ני ישרא]ל̇, has no firm basis. The last *lamed* is also unsubstantiated by the photographs.

המצ̇וות. Qimron's reading is retained here instead of Milik's, מצ̇[ווה, as PAM 40529 displays a trace of ink before the *mem* that may belong to the upper horizontal stroke of a *he*.

א̇[ל. A trace of an *alef* is visible on the scrap of leather forming the left section of frg. 38 (see PAM 40508, where it appears as frg. 6).

Translation
1. [I]srael, and hear! This very [da]y [you became a peo]ple of your God of [Gods]. And [you should] o[bserve his laws], and his statute[s, and his commandments th]at
2. [I am] commanding you [to]day, that [you shall] d[o them wh]en y[ou]will cross the[Jordan]there [to inherit citi]es large

3. and [flourishin]g and hou[s]es full of eve[ry good thing, vineyards, and olive trees] that [you did]n[ot plant and hewed-[out cis]terns [that you] did no[t]
4. [c]ut. And you will e[a]t and become satisfied. [Be careful lest your hea]rt grow proud and you fo[rget all th]at I [command]you today.
5. [For]it is [your l]ife and length of [your] day[s."   ] vac [   ] And Moses continued and [said to the sons of I]srael. ["It is now]forty
6. [years from the]day we ca[me out of] the land of [Egypt.] This very [day your Go]d of Gods [has announced all the]se [wor]ds from [his] mouth
7. [all his laws and] all [his] judg[ments]..[   ]and your burden [and your lo]a[d   ] [   ] And it shall be,
8. [the]covenant and to comman[d you] the w[ay tha]t you should walk in[and the deed that]you [should] do, in order to explain
9. [in]your[ears] all the words of [thi]s L[aw]. ^(And now,) be [very careful] of yourselves [a thi]ng and the wrath of [God] will ignite
10. against yo[u. And] he will shut the heavens[so] that they will not give y[o]u rain and the[earth] so that [it will]n[ot] give you
11. its [produ]ce. *vacat* [   ].[and] Moses [spok]e to [the] en[tire people,] "The[se] are the com[mandments that]G[od]commanded to observe them
12. [   ]..[   ]

Comments

L. 1 הסכת[ ]י[שראל ושמע] הי[ום] הזה[נהייתה לע]ם לאלוהי[ ] אלוהי[ך. This line follows Deut 27:9. Replacing the Tetragrammaton with a construct form of אלהים, the scroll obtains a construction לאלוהי[ ] אלוהי[ך.²⁹

Ll. 1–2 וש[מרתה חוקיו] ועדוותיו[ומצוותיו א[שר [אני] מצוך[הי]ום. The scroll continues to paraphrase Deut 27:10. It apparently replaced the biblical ועשית with the synonymous וש[מרתה and (building on 2 Kgs 23:3) it expanded the phrase את מצותו ואת חקיו with ועדוותי]ו (for חוק, מצוה, and עדות as an object of שמר, cf. 1 Kgs 2:3; 1 Chr 29:19). Milik restores with the MT מצוך [אנוכי], yet the short [אני], suggested by Carmignac, better fits the size of the lacuna.³⁰

---

29 See the recent discussion of this and similar divine names by J. Ben-Dov, "The Elohistic Psalter and the Writing of Divine Names at Qumran," *Meghillot* 8–9 (2010): 53–80 (72 n. 70) (Hebrew).
30 Thus also Carmignac, "Quelques details," 92.

Ll. 2–4 [לרשת ער]ים גדולות ... ואכל[ת]ה ושבעתה. The scroll paraphrases Deut 6:10–11. The reconstruction [לרשת ער]ים follows Deut 6:1, as the space seems to be too short for לתת לך in Deut 6:10. The scroll re-orders the biblical verse, mentioning the vines and olives before the cisterns.

L. 2 אשר ת[עשה אותם כא]שׁר א[תה] עׄובר את הׄ[ירדן]לׁשׁׄמה. The formulation seems to follow Deut 6:1, replacing the biblical שמה with the unusual לשמה.

L. 4 [השמר לך] למה ירום [לב]בכה ושכׁ[חתה את כול א]שׁרׄ אנוכי [מצו]ׄך היום. The scroll combines phrases borrowed from Deut 8:11 and 8:14, but while these verses warn against forgetting God, the scroll reworks them as a warning against forgetting the commandments.

L. 5 ואורך ימ[יך] [הוא חי]ׄיך כי. This clause is based on Deut 30:20. As with the preceding formulation, the Qumran text reformulates it as referring to the divine commandments, and not to God himself (cf. Deut 32:47; Prov 4:13).[31]

[יקרא] מושה ו[יאמר. Milik restores ויאמר מושה [ויוסף. Qimron suggests ויאמר מושה [ויל]. The proposed reconstruction follows the biblical formula, ויוסף ... ויאמר (see 2 Sam 18:22; Job 36:1).

Ll. 5–6 זה [ארבעים שנה מ[יום צ]את]ׄנו מארץ [מצרים. Following Deut 1:3, the author of this text dates Moses' address to Israel to the fortieth year after the exodus. Cf. col. i 1 and Comments ad loc.

Ll. 6–7 היום [הזה] אלו[הי אלוהי]ׄך השמיע ... את כול חוקיו וא[ׄת כול מש]פטיו. Moses is here referring to the divine address to him earlier on this day in col. i 1–11. For the phrase היום הזה, employed also in line 1, see Deut 5:24, whereas the reconstruction השמיע את כול הדב[רׄיׄםׄ] is based on Deut 4:10, 36. Both passages describe the Sinai revelation. For the word pair חקים ומשפטים, cf., e.g., Deut 4:5, 8, 14.

L. 7 [ׄוׁטרחכם ומש[א]כם [ ]הׄ[. The scroll alludes to Moses' complaint in Deut 1:12. Milki (followed by Qimron) restores the line according to this verse: אי[כׁה אשא לבדי] טרחכם ומש[א]כם וריבכם. However, the waw preceding the noun טרחכם may perhaps indicate that this is a paraphrase rather than an exact quotation.

---

[31] As observed by J. Tigay, *Deuteronomy* (JPS Torah Commentary; Philadelphia: JPS, 1996), 288, 400 n. 22, a similar interpretation is reflected in the Jewish morning liturgy ("For they are our life and the length of our days").

ויהיה. In biblical and Qumran Hebrew, the short form יהי is usually preferred, yet cf. ויהיה לבבכם in 4Q175 1 3.[32] Qimron reads ויהוה, but this would be the only instance of the use of the Tetragrammaton in the extant remains of this scroll. Elsewhere, the Tetragrammaton found in its biblical sources is replaced with other divine names.

L. 8 ה[ברית]. As the following text paraphrases Exod 18:20, Qimron restores here a formulation based on this verse: ויהוה [צוני להודיע את ה]ברית.

ולצוו̇]ת לכם את [ה̇ד̇]רך אש[ר תלכו בה] המעשה אשר ת[עשו. The scroll paraphrases Exod 18:20 with some changes. As in 4QpaleoExod^m, Sam. Pent., and LXX, it seems to read הדרך אשר instead of the הדרך of MT. It also appears to replace the biblical והודעת with ולצוו̇ת]. Exod 18:20 quotes Jethro's advice to Moses, but the same locution, צוה דרך, is used in Deut 5:33 of following the divine commandments delivered by Moses (cf. also the use of צוה in Deut 1:16, 18 dealing with the same event as in Exodus 18). So undoubtedly the Deuteronomic phraseology and context influenced the present Qumranic formulation. This connection provides a fine example of the association of different verses that are similar in wording and context, a technique seen throughout various Qumran texts as well as in other contemporary works.

Ll. 8–9 לבאר [באוזני]כֹ̇ם] את [כול דברי הת]ורה הזא[ת̇. Beside transmitting the divine commandments, Moses is also commissioned to explain (לבאר)[33] "all the words of the La[w." The use of לבאר points to Deut 1:5, in which Moses' farewell speech is described as an expounding (באר) of the Torah (cf. Comments on col. i 3). Milik's restoration, לכם ולבני]כם, appears to be a little too long for the available space. Hence, Qimron's reconstruction, באוזני]כֹ̇ם, is followed here.

L. 9 [ ]ו̇[ ] ד[בֹ̇ר ̇ע̇ת̇ה̇. השׁ]מרו מא[דה לנפשותיכם. A similar exhortation appears earlier on in this column, in line 4. For the formulation, see Deut 4:15. For the second part of the phrase, Qimron offers the restoration: פן תסירו] מֹ[מנה ד]בֹ̇ר.

Ll. 9–11 וחרה אף [אלוהים]בכמ̇]ה ... לבלתי [ ] תת לכם את [יבו]לֹ̇ה. The scroll paraphrases here Deut 11:17. The biblical לא תתן את יבולה and ולא יהיה מטר have been recast here using the negation לבלתי, לבֹ̇לֹ̇תֹ̇י המטר and [ ]תֹ̇[ל̇]י̇ תת. The phrase ל̇]בֹ̇לתֹ̇י המטר ל̇]כ̇]ם מטר may be influenced by the formulation of Isa 5:6.

---

32 Exod 20:18 is quoted in 4Q175 1 3 according to the Sam. Pent., which corresponds to MT Deut 5:23.
33 באר in the *Pi'el* means "to explain, elucidate, clarify." Cf. *HALOT*, 1:105; *DCH*, 2:87.

[וֹ]   ויאמ[ר מושה אל כ]וֹל העם [אל]ה הֿמצֿ[וות אשר] צוה אֿ[ל] [לעשות L. 11
אותֿםֿ   ]. For the reconstruction ויאמ[ר מושה אל כ]וֹל העם, cf. Josh 24:2. The rest of the line follows Deut 28:1. Milik's restoration, וֹ[יוסף   לדב[ר מושה, is difficult, as the subject, מושה, usually precedes the infinitive, לדב[ר, in biblical Hebrew (cf. Deut 20:8; Judg 9:37; Isa 8:5).

Col. iii

top margin

1   [   ] את שבתֿ] הארץ   [ooֿ] והיתה שבת הארץ לכם [לאכלה ל]ך לבהמתך ולחית [הש]דה]
2   [בארצך ואשר יו]תֿר ל]אביוני עמ]כֿה אשר בֿ[ארץ   שדהו לוֿ]אֿ יזֿ[רע וכרמו לוא [יזמור אי]ש]
3   [את ספיח קצירו לוֿ]אֿ] יקצור ולוא י]אסוף ל]וֿ   ושמרתה א]ֿת כוֿ]ל דברי ה]בֿרֿיֹתֿ] האֿ[ל]ה]
4   [לעשות אותם וה]יֹה כי [תשמור] לעשות [את כול המצוה הזואת] ושמטתה [ידך בש]נֿה הזואֿ[ת]
5   [כול בעל משה ידו א]שֿר] ישה   [איש o]ישה בר]עהו כי   בֿ[ל   יש]ה
6   [קרא שמטה ל]אֿ[ל]והי אלוהיכֿ]מֿ את הנֿ]וכרי תגוש ואשר יהיה לך את אחידֿ[לֿ]וֿ]אֿ תגוש] כי בשנ]ה]
7   [הזואת יברכך אלוֿ]הֿיֹםֿ] ויכפר] את עווֿנֿ]ותיך בעשו]תֿך את הדֿ[בר]
8   [   ]   [ooֿ]   שנ]ה בשנה]   לחודש [
9   [   ]   בֿ]אֿהֿלֹיֿה]ם ותשבו]ת ביום הזה]   הי]וֿ שטים
10 [ולוקטים אבו]תֿיכם עד יומֿ] oֿ] עש]וֿר לחודש] הֿ[וביום ע]שר לחודש]
11 [כול מלאכה ת]אסר וביום עֿ]שור ל]חודש יכופר]   לחודש]
12 [   ]   קחו [   ]   [

Notes on Readings

L. 1 At the beginning of this line, Milik placed a small scrap of leather reading:

1   שֿ[נֿים
2   [לֿ

The reconstructed line reads as following: [מקץ שבע שׁ[נֿים את שבת]. Although this fragment appears in the early photographs of frg. 20 (see especially PAM 40511), there are no physical or contextual grounds for placing it here. It is edited here under Unidentified Fragments.

L. 1]∘∘[. Milik read and restored here ‏ה[ר̊א̊]ץ‎. However, the bottom tips of the two letters visible on the fragment are illegible.

L. 3 ‏ל[ו]א̇‎]. Traces of an *alef* are visible (unnoticed by the editor) in PAM 40505.

L. 5]∘. The editor read and restored ‏ו̊[אש]ר‎. The vertical stroke visible in the photographs may belong to one of several letters and therefore no reading is offered here.

‏ב[ל̊‎. In PAM 40511 and J5928 R ir a tip of the vertical stroke of a *lamed* is clearly visible (not noted in the DJD transcription).

L. 7 ‏הד̊[בר]‎. This is Qimron's reading. Milik read and restored ‏הז[את]‎. The curving vertical stroke extant on the fragment is more consistent with a *dalet* than with that of a *zayin* (cf. *zayin* in ‏יזמור‎[[line 2]; ‏הזואת]‎[[line 4]).

L. 9 ‏ב̊א̊ה̊ל̊ל̊י̇ה[ם‎. The DJD edition reads ‏ה̊ה̊ל̊∘ב‎[. The faint traces of the second letter conform with an *alef* (PAM 40488). A trace of a vertical stroke, perhaps from a *waw* or *yod*, is observable next to the *lamed*.

L. 10 ‏לחודש‎ ∘ˆ]. There is a vertical stroke right before the lacuna. Milik read it as a *he*, while Qimron thinks it is a *waw*. However, as this trace could belong to one of several letters, no reading is proposed here. Three dots forming a triangle appear above the line right before the aforementioned letter. The words inscribed at the end of the line seem to have been erased. Milik assumed that this is a scribal mark (which is unattested elsewhere in the Qumran documents), noting a text that has to be deleted.

‏ה̊[‎. Milik placed a tiny scrap of leather, frg. 40 (not extant in the PAM and AWS images), between frgs. 8 and 9. This placement is suggested by its physical resemblance to frg. 38 (similarly located in col. ii).

L. 12] ‏קחו‎ [. The editor read] ‏קחו[ו‎, but a blank space is visible before *qof* in PAM 40488.

Translation
1. [   ] the Sabbath[of the land   ]..[and the (produce of the) Sabbath of the land will be for]y[ou and your cattle and] the wi[ld beast] to eat

2. [in your land. And whatever is le]ft (is) fo[r the needy among]your[people] who are in[the land   his field] he shall[n]ot s[ow and his vine he shall not] prune. He
3. [shall n]o[t reap the aftergrowth of his harvest and shall not]gather for[himself and you shall keep] al[l t]h[ese words of the]covenant
4. [to observe them. And]it will come to pass that [you will] observe [all this commandment   ] and you will release [your hand in]thi[s y]ear,
5. [every creditor w]ho[lends   ] a man .[a man should no]t cl[aim from] his [fell]ow, for
6. [a remission]of [G]o[d you]r [God has been proclaimed.] Of a f[oreigner you may exact it; but whatever of yours is with your brother you should] n[o]t [exact.] For in [this] yea[r]
7. [G]od[will bless you and will forgive your]iniqu[ities   when]you[d]o th[is[
8. [   ]...[an]nually [   ] of the month
9. [   ]in[their]tents [and you will observe a sabbath] on this day[we]re wandering
10. [and gathering,]your [fathe]rs, until the [te]nth day of the month ([on the t]enth[day] of the month)
11. [all work shall be]forbidden and on the t[enth of the] month shall be atoned[ ] of the month
12. [   ] take [   ]

Comments

L. 1 האר]ץ שבת[את. The phrase שבת] הארץ occurring in Lev 25:6 refers to the produce of the land during the Sabbatical Year. Perhaps, a form of אכל preceded this phrase.

והיתה שבת הארץ לכם] לאכלה ל[ך ולבהמתך ולחית] הֹשֹׂ[דה] [בארצך. The reconstruction follows Lev 25:6–7. The scroll rewrites לחיה as הֹשֹׂ[דה ולחית], an expression found in the parallel passage in Exod 23:11.

Ll. 2–3 שדהו לו[אֹ יוֹ]רע ... לו[אֹ] יקצור. The formulation takes up Lev 25:4–5.

L. 2 ואשר יו[תר ל]אביוני עמ[כה אשר ב]אֹרץ. The text alludes here to Exod 23:11: ואכלו אביני עמך ויתרם תאכל חית השדה ("Let the needy among your people eat of it, and what they leave let the wild beast eat"). The proposed reconstruction is that of Qimron. If correct, it prescribes that the needy ones receive whatever is left from the Sabbatical Year produce, whereas the biblical verse dictates that they are entitled to eat from the entire produce of that year while what remains is left for the beasts. See also Deut 15:9.

Ll. 3–4 ‏ושמרתה א[ת כ̇ו̇]ל דברי ה[ב̇ר̇י̇ת̇] הא[ל̇]ה [לעשות אותם]‎. For the phrase ‏דברי הברית‎, see Comments on col. i 3–5.

L. 3 ‏ולוא י̇[אסוף ל]ו‎. Perhaps to be restored with Lev 25:3: ‏ולוא י[אסוף ל]ו את תבואת הארץ‎. Milik reconstructs here: ‏ולוא י[אסוף ל]ו מאומה‎.

Ll. 4–5 ‏וה[]ה̇ כי [תשמור] לעשות ... [כול בעל משה א[שר] ישה‎ The scroll turns now to the regulations pertaining to the remission of debt during the fallow year. The reconstructions follow Deut 15:2, 5.

‏ושמטתה [ידך‎. The verb ‏ושמטתה‎, a 2nd masc. sg Qal qatal of ‏שמט‎ ("to let go, remove"),[34] is based on ‏תשמט ידך‎ in Deut 15:3. If the reconstruction is correct, it suggests that the scroll did not read the verb ‏תשמט‎ as a Hif'il form (as vocalized in MT) but as a Qal form (cf. LXX ad loc.; see also Jer 17:4).

L. 5 ‏ב̇[ל̊ יש]ה איש בר[עהו כי [קרא שמטה [ל]א[ל]והי אלוהיכ[ם̊‎. The reconstructions are based on Deut 15:2–3. The scroll seems to have replaced the Tetragrammaton with ‏ל̊[א]ל[ו]הי אלוהיכ[ם̊‎.

‏את הנ̇[ו]כרי תגוש ואשר יהיה לך את אחיד̇] ל[ו]א [תגוש‎. The text is restored according to Deut 15:3.

Ll. 6–7 ‏כי בשנ[ה הזאת יברכך אלו[ה̊י̊ם̊‎. The reconstruction echoes Deut 15:4.

‏[ויכפר] את עוו̇נ̇]ותיך‎. Milik restores similarly (see Isa 27:9; Ps 78:38; Dan 9:24), yet ‏סלח/מחה] את עוו̇נ̇]ותיך‎ (Exod 34:9; Ps 51:11) is likewise possible. The association of the forgiveness of sins with the remission of debts during the fallow year fits with the context.[35] Less appropriate is Qimron's linking of the forgiveness of sins with the Jubilee Year (cf. his restoration: ‏כי בשנ]ת היובל אלוהי אלוהיכם יעזוב לכם] את עוו̇נ̇]ותיכם‎, similar to 11Q13 ii 6).

L. 7 ‏[בעשו]ת̇ך את הד̇]בר‎. This is Qimron's reconstruction.

---

34 HALOT, 4:1557.
35 On the link between the remission of debts and forgiveness of sins in the ancient sources, see M. Weinfeld, "The Day of Atonement and Freedom (Deror): The Redemption of the Soul," in idem, Normative and Sectarian Judaism in the Second Temple Period (London: T & T Clark, 2005), 227–31 (229–28).

L. 8 ‏לחודש‎ [‏שנ[ה בשנה‎]. The extant words, particularly ‏שנ[ה בשנה‎ (cf. Deut 15:20), appear to belong with the following section dealing with the Day of Atonement. Most likely, a numeral, probably ‏עשר‎ or ‏עשור‎, preceded the word ‏לחודש‎.

Ll. 9–10 ‏הי[ו שטים]ולוקטים אבו[תֹ֯יֹ֯כם עד יוֹ֯ם] עשֹ[וֹ֯ר לחודש‎. Milik restores ‏הי[ו שטים‎ ‏במדבר אבו[תֹ֯יֹ֯כם‎],[36] but the masc. pl. Qal participle of ‏שוט‎ ("to rove about")[37] points to Num 11:8, which describes the collecting of the manna: ‏שטו העם ולקטו‎ ‏וטחנו ברחים‎ ("The people would go about and gather it, grind it between millstones"). So, by adopting the biblical term from this episode, the present text suggests that the Israelites observed the Day of Atonement in the desert by refraining from collecting the manna on that day, which in turn implies fasting.[38]

L. 9 ‏בֹ֯אֹ֯הֹ֯לֹיהֹ[ם‎. In light of the preceding allusion to the gathering of manna, the mention of the tents suggests the backdrop of the desert wanderings, perhaps in connection with the halachic regulations pertaining to the Day of Atonement.

‏ותשבו[ת ביום הזה‎]. The first word is restored as a form of the verb ‏שבת‎, e.g., ‏לשבות‎ or ‏ותשבות‎, as inferred from the context.

L. 10 ‏עד יוֹ֯ם] עשֹ[וֹ֯ר לחודש‎. The formulation ‏יוֹ֯ם] עשֹ[וֹ֯ר לחודש‎ is taken from Lev 16:29, which prescribes the laws pertaining to the Day of Atonement. For the formula "‏עד יום‎ x," see Ezra 10:17.

‏לחודש‎]o^. Milik notes that the phrase ‏ע[שר לחודש‎ at the end of the line may have been erased. He proposes that the entire section to the left of the scribal mark composed of three dots placed above the line was erased, perhaps due to a homoioteleuton (‏עש[וֹ֯ר לחודש ... ע[שר לחודש‎).

L. 11 ‏כול מלאכה ת[אסר‎]. In biblical Hebrew, the verb ‏אסר‎ denotes "to bind, to tie,"[39] but here, as Milik notes, it means "to prohibit, to forbid," a meaning attested in rab-

---

36 Milik, "Dires de Moïse," 95, commented that this formulation provides a midrashic explanation of the origins of the Yom Kippur festival.
37 *HALOT*, 1440.
38 In the Second Temple sources, the biblical injunction "and you shall practice self-denial" (Lev 16:31; cf. 23:27; Num 29:7) is commonly understood as fasting. See L. H. Schiffman, "The Case of the Day of Atonement Ritual," in *Biblical Perspectives* (ed. M. E. Stone and E. G. Chazon; STDJ 27; Leiden: Brill, 1998), 181–88 (183–84); N. Hacham, "Communal Fasts in the Judean Desert Scrolls," in *Historical Perspectives: From the Hasmoneans to Bar Kokhba in Light of the Dead Sea Scrolls* (ed. D. Goodblatt, A. Pinnick, and D. Schwartz; STDJ 37; Leiden: Brill, 2000), 127–46.
39 BDB, 63–64; *HALOT*, 75.

binic Hebrew.[40] The editor restores כול עבודה ת[אסר, yet perhaps כול מלאכה ת[אסר, in line with Lev 23:28 and Num 29:7, should be preferred (cf. also the *Temple Scroll* [11QTª] XXVII, 7, 10: ולוא תעשו כול מלאכה).

וביום עֹ[שור ל]חודש יכופר]. The formula ביום ... לחדש (or: לחדש ...-ב), in contrast to ב-... יום לחודש, is more frequent in late biblical Hebrew (cf. Hag 1:1; Ezra 10:16; Neh 8:2).[41] The *Puʻal* of כפר, יכופר], appears frequently in the Hebrew Bible with the noun עון. This verbal form occurs also in col. iv 3.

L. 12] קחו [. The only word surviving here suggests that this line dealt with the sacrificial procedures related to the ceremony of the Day of Atonement, as prescribed in Leviticus 16 and Numbers 29. It is phrased as a second person command. Milik's restoration, וי]קחו [הכוהנים את שני השעירים, is based on Lev 16:5, but all the appearances of לקח in Leviticus 16 are singular.

Col. iv

top margin

[ ]o אלים [	כ]בֹשים וב]	לכפ]רֹ בעדֹ] בני ישר]אל ובעד הא]רץ]	1
[ ]o[הד הנ]שפך בארץ [לטהרם] מן		[ ]ושׁ]פך	כֹּי ת]	2
[ ]o[]oo[] צנ]o[וי]כֹופר להם ב]o		[ ]תעשו	אלה]	3
[ ]ם חוקו]ת עול]ם לדורות]יכם		[ ]וביו]ם	אֹתֹ]	4
[ ]לֹ[ ]הכֹ]פורי]ם יקח ה]כוהן		[בֹני ישֹׂר]אל	5
[ ]וכו]ל אשר]		[שֹמם לבֹ]ול	6
[ ]ֹם לשנה [		[הנפש אשר חֹ]טאה	7
[ ]על ספר [		[יבי]אנו הכוהן [	8
[ ]וסמך את יד]יו		[o את כול אלהֹ	9
[ ]ובשנה הֹ]		[הדבר]ֹם האלהֹ]	10
[ ]שֹ שֹהֹ הש]		[	11
[ ]		[	12

---

40 See, e.g., *m. Demai* 6:11. See also Jastrow, *Dictionary*, 98; Sokoloff, *Dictionary of Jewish Palestinian Aramaic*, 68.

41 See E. Qimron, "The Vocabulary of the Temple Scroll," *Shnaton* 4 (1979–1980): 239–61 (244) (Hebrew).

Notes on Readings

Milik reconstructs this column from frgs. 22, 10, 23, and 11 (from left to right). Qimron replaces frg. 23 with frg. 24.⁴² This placement is supported by the physical features of frg. 24 (its shape resembles that of frgs. 22 and 23 and it also has an upper margin), as well as by its content, which relates it to the description of the Day of Atonement.

L. 1 Milik read וּבֹעדת אלים [ובסוד ק]דֹ[ו]שים at the beginning of the line. This reading is obtained by placing here a small fragment presumably reading וּבֹעדת, but the shapes of the edges of the fragments do not match, as can be seen from the comparison of PAM 40511 and PAM 40474, and its color is significantly darker than frg. 22. Neither does the trace of a letter appearing before the word אלים fit the shape of a *taw*, as Milik suggests (in PAM 40474 and plate XIX in the DJD edition). This small fragment is edited below under Unidentified Fragments.

כ]בשים. The DJD edition has קד[ושים, but a tip of a base stroke resembling that of a *bet* is visible at some distance to the right of the *shin* in PAM 40529 and J5928B R ir.

L. 2 Milik read [ו]ל[קח] at the beginning of this line. The trace of ink interpreted as the tip of a *lamed* may have appeared on the small fragment attached to frg. 22 (see previous comment).

L. 3]∘צו[. The remains of the third word are difficult to read. Milik read it as a *he*, as does Qimron (צנהֹ[יר), but it may also be read as a *waw* or *yod* (PAM 40474, 40511, J5928B R ir).

[וֹ]כֹופר. PAM 40529 and J5928B R ir display the trace of a base fitting with *kaf*.

ב]∘. The vertical stroke next to the *bet* may belong to one of several letters. Qimron reads בֹדֹ[ם.

L. 7 חֹ[טאה. The vertical stroke seen on PAM 40529 may belong to a *het* (cf. *het* in יקח [line 5]); *he* is also possible as read by Milik, ה[ואה.

L. 11]שׁ שׁהֹ[. The DJD edition has]מֹן שׁוֹ[, but what Milik read as a medial mem and a final nun is, in fact, the three strokes of a shin (J5928B R ir). The upper bar of a *he* is seen clearly next to the *shin* of the second word in PAM 40530.

---

42 The suggestion that frg. 24 belongs in this column was made by Carmignac, "Quelques details," 95, who proposed placing it between frgs. 23 and 11.

Translation

1. [ ] rams .[s]heep ..[to ato]ne for[the sons of Isra]el and for the la[nd]
2. [to purify them] from [the blood s]hed on the earth [ ] for .[ ]. and it shall be po[ured]
3. [ ].[ ]..[]...[and it shall be a]toned for them ..[ ]these[ ]you shall do [ ]
4. [ ].[eterna]l statut[es] throughout[your] generations [ ]..[ ] and on the day [ ]
5. [ ]the at[onmen]t the [priest] shall take[ ]sons of Isra[el]
6. [and al]l that[ ]... for a[ll]
7. [ ].. for the year[ ]the person who s[inned]
8. [ ] on a scroll[ ] the priest [will bri]ng it [ ]
9. [ ] and he shall lay [his] hand[s]. all these
10. [ ]and in the[ ]year [ ] these [word]s[ ]
11. [ ]. a lamb ..[ ]

Comments

Ll. 1–2 לכפ[ר בעד] בני ישר[אל ובעד הא]רץ לטהרם] מן [הדם הנ]שפך בארץ. This is Qimron's reconstruction based on Lev 16:17, 24, 33–34. The atonement for the land is absent from the biblical descriptions of the Day of Atonement but is found in Num 35:33 (cf. Deut 32:43).[43] The notion of the atonement for the land is further developed in 1QapGen X, 13 and *Jub.* 6:2, in which Noah's sacrifice after the flood is interpreted as an atonement for the land (cf. also *Jub.* 4:26).[44] One may also note several sectarian texts (1QS VIII, 6, 10; IX, 4–5; 1QSa I, 3; 4Q265 7 9) that depict the Qumran community functioning to atone for the land. However, 1Q22 seems to be the only known Second Temple source that includes an actual procedure for the atonement of the land in its description of the Day of Atonement.

L. 1 אלים. This is, apparently, a phonetical reading of the plural of איל ("ram"; cf. the *Temple Scroll* [11QTª] XV, 12: אילים; XVII, 15: ולאלים; XXII, 4: לאלים[ו]). Leviticus

---

[43] On the defilement of the land in the Hebrew Bible, see C. E. Hayes, *Gentile Impurities and Jewish Identities: Intermarriage and Conversion from the Bible to the Talmud* (New York: Oxford University Press, 2002), 43–44; J. Klawans, *Purity, Sacrifice, and the Temple, Symbolism and Supersessionism in the Study of Ancient Judaism* (New York: Oxford University Press, 2005), 55–56.

[44] The description of Noah's sacrifice in *Jubilees* suggests a close affinity between Noah's act and the Day of Atonement (see *Jub.* 5:18). For an analysis of Noah's sacrificial procedures, see D. K. Falk, *The Parabiblical Texts: Strategies for Extending the Scriptures among the Dead Sea Scrolls* (Companion to the Qumran Scrolls 8; Library of Second Temple Studies 63; London: T & T Clark, 2007), 69–71.

16 mentions two rams, one brought by the high priest (v. 3) and another given by the people (v. 5). The additional sacrifices offered on this day, as outlined in Numbers 29, included yet another ram (Num 29:8, 9).[45]

כ[ב]שׂים. Num 29:8 mentions seven sheep among the Day of Atonement offerings. If correct, this line lists the sacrificial animals mentioned in both Leviticus 16 and Numbers 29.

ותש[פך]. This is Milik's restoration, but it is uncertain as the context is lost. Since the verb שפך does not appear in the biblical passages dealing with the Day of Atonement, it may perhaps be related to the preceding section dealing with the nonbiblical atonement for the land.

L. 3 **ו[י]כופר להם ב[o**. יכופר is the *Pu'al yiqtol* 3rd per. masc. sg. of כפר. The form occurs also in col. III, 11. The pronoun להם apparently refers to the Israelites (for כפר ב-, see Lev 7:7; Num 5:8).

L. 4 **חוקו]ת עול[ם לדורות]יכם**. This phrase occurs in a passage concerned with the Day of Atonement in Lev 23:31: חקת עולם לדרתיכם (cf. also Lev 16:34). For the plural חוקו]ת עול[ם, cf. Ezek 46:14. A similar change from singular to plural occurs in the description of the Day of Atonement in the *Temple Scroll* (11QT^a) XXVII, 4–5: חֻוקו]ת [עֹו]לם לדורותיהמה.

L. 5 **[הכ]פֻורים**. Another possible restoration is [הכ]והני[ם.

יקח ה[כוהן. Milik restores in line with the recurring phrase in Leviticus 16, in which לקח appears several times with reference to the High Priest.

L. 6 **שֻׁמם לב[ול**. The surviving letters may be read as either the plural of שֵׁם ("name") or a verbal form of the verbs שׂים or שׁמם. They may also form the final part of a longer word, the beginning of which is lost.

L. 7 **הנפש אשר חֹ[טאה]**. Cf. the phrase נפש כי תחטא בשגגה (Lev 4:2, 27; Num 15:27), which has been rephrased in 4Q266 11 2 as נפש אשר תחטא בשיגגה (= 4Q270 7 i 17).

---

[45] The sages disagreed regarding whether the ram mentioned in Numbers 29 and that given by the people are, in fact, the same (*Sifra Aḥarei Mot*, 2; *b. Yoma* 70b). The *Temple Scroll* states that the ram mentioned in Numbers 29 is an additional one (11QT^a XXXV, 12–16). A similar interpretation is found in Philo (*Spec. Laws* 1, 188) and Josephus (*Ant.* iii, 240). The position of the author of 1Q22 on this matter is unclear. See Y. Yadin, *The Temple Scroll* (Jerusalem: Israel Exploration Society: 1983), 1:132–34; L. H. Schiffman, "The Case of the Day of Atonement Ritual," *Biblical Perspectives* (ed. M. E. Stone and E. G. Chazon; STDJ 27; Leiden: Brill, 1998), 181–88 (184–87).

L. 8 על ספר. In the Hebrew Bible this phrase always appears with the verb כתב (cf. Deut 17:18, 31:24; Josh 10:13; cf. *Temple Scroll* [11QT[a]] LVI, 21). However, neither a book nor the act of writing is mentioned in the biblical passages concerned with the Day of Atonement.[46]

יבי[אנו הכוהן. The verb יבי[אנו may refer to the scapegoat, alluded to in line 9. Qimron restores יקר[אנו הכוהן. Milik read here אני הכוהן[, i.e. a direct speech, presumably by the high priest (cf. the confession uttered by the high priest upon the sacrifice of the bull and the sending away of the scapegoat in *m. Yoma* 3:8, 4:2, 6:2).

L. 9 וסמך את יד[יו. This is most likely an allusion to the laying of hands on the head of the scapegoat in Lev 16:21.

L. 10 ובשנה ה̊]. Perhaps to be restored here ובשנה ה̊[זואת. Alternatively, a numeral followed (cf. Lev 19:25, 25:4).

L. 11 [ש̊ שׂה̊ הש]. Probably read שֶׂה ("small livestock beast, a sheep or a goat").[47]

The precise placement of frgs. 12, 13, 23, 25, 29 and 41–49 are difficult to determine.

Frg. 12

top marg[in[

ויק[ח̊ו להם]	1
]וּבוֹ[	2
]ooo[	3
[אל כול]	4
[עמה]ם	5
חט[אותיך̇]	6
[כי]	7

---

46 In light of the preceding phrase "]the person who s[inned," one may recall the tradition according to which on this day the names of those destined for life are written in the Book of Life. While this tradition is best known from the rabbinic sources (e.g., *b. Roš Haš.* 16b; *b. 'Arak.* 10b), the notion of the divine judgment taking place at the beginning of the year is found already in *L. A. B.* 13:7. See H. Jacobson, *A Commentary on Pseudo-Philo's Liber Antiquitatum Biblicarum* (Leiden: Brill, 1996), 1:113. See also T. Elgvin, "Qumran and the Roots of the Rosh Hashanah Liturgy," in *Liturgical Perspectives: Prayer and Poetry in Light of the Dead Sea Scrolls* (ed. E. Chazon et al.; STDJ 48; Leiden; Brill, 2003), 49–67.
47 *HALOT*, 1310.

Notes on Readings

This fragment is an assemblage of several scraps of leather. Some of them seem to fit well together. However, the two scraps placed on the top do not seem to join well (the second scrap itself is comprised of two pieces). Moreover, the shapes of their edges do not match (despite the attempt to join the second scrap to the assemblage of scraps below, as can be seen in the image J5928B R ir). The scrap placed as the second from the top preserves traces of three letters:] וּבֹ[. If placed correctly, it constitutes the second line. The blank piece of leather visible above the first line is most likely the top margin.

L. 2 The DJD edition reads in line 2:]ooo[. However, the traces of ink most likely belong to line 3.

L. 4 כול. The DJD edition reads כרל. However, according to PAM 40505 and J5928B R ir, the second letter is clearly a *waw*.

L. 6]חט[אותיךָ. Milik read and restored] חט[אותיךָ, but there is no blank space visible after the final *kaf* in PAM 40505 and J5928B R ir.

Translation

1. and]they [too]k for themselves [
2.]and in it[
3.]...[
4.]to all [
5.] with th[em
6.]your [si]ns[
7.] because [

Comments

L. 6]חט[אותיךָ. Milik suggests that this fragment belongs with col. v. If correct, the term indicates that col. v also dealt with the Day of Atonement.

Frg. 13

t]op marg[in

]ע [	1
] איש[	2
]ל[	3

Notes on Readings

Frg. 13, as it appears on plate XIX in DJD I and in PAM 40505, is comprised of three tiny scraps of leather placed one above the other. The scrap placed on top bears no traces of writing and seems to be large enough to belong to a top margin and not to a *vacat* in the middle of a line.

L. 1]ע [. The DJD edition reads]∘[, but a blank space (two letter-spaces) is observable before the traces of writing in PAM 40505 and J5928B R ir. The remaining traces resemble the right and middle strokes of an *'ayin* (cf. *'ayin* in ע]מה ס[[frg. 12 5]).

L. 3]ל[. The top of the vertical stroke of a *lamed* (unnoted by Milik) is clearly visible in PAM 40505 and J5928B R ir.

Translation
2.]a man [

Frg. 23

```
                                top margin
                                ]הם[      1
                                ]דׄותמ[ׄי    2
                                ]מׄושה [    3
                                ]אׄתׄ[       4
```

Translation
1.]they [
2. h]andles [
3.]Moses [
4.]..[

Comments

L. 1]הם[. This might be either a 3rd masc. pl. demonstrative pronoun or the pronominal suffix of a word that has been lost.

L. 2]דׄותמ[ׄי. Restored here as]דׄותמׄ[י, a plural of יד. In the Hebrew Bible, the form ידות appears in the description of the support (מכונה) of the basins in Solomon's temple (1 Kgs 7:32, 33, 35, 36). In 4Q397 1–2 2 (= B 22), the expression כ]לים ידות appears with ידי denoting "handles."[48] If this fragment belongs to the section of the scroll dealing with the Day of Atonement, י[דׄות here perhaps refers to the basins or the vessels used during the ceremony of this holy day.[49]

Frg. 25

to]p mar[gin

[ׄדׄ ולוא]	1
[ל◦]	2
[יה]	3

Notes on Readings
The blank space left above line 1 is probably the top margin. As seen on plate XIX in DJD I, as well as in PAM 40511 and J5928B R ir, a tiny scrap of leather has been joined to frg. 25. There are illegible traces of writing on this fragment. On plate XIX, it is placed so that it belongs with line 2, thus reading:]◦   [ל◦. In PAM 40511, it is attached above line 1. Both placements are difficult, for the shapes of the edges of the two fragments do not match.

L. 1 [דׄ. The DJD edition offers no reading here. The trace of ink visible in PAM 40511 and J5928B R ir fits with the upper stroke of a *dalet*.

Translation
1.] and not[

Frg. 29

מש[פטיו]	1
[לת]	2

---

48 Cf. DJD X, 48.
49 In *m. Yoma* 3:10, it is reported that "King Monobases had handles (ידות) made of gold for all the vessels used on the Day of Atonement."

Notes on Readings
Milik placed this fragment under frg. 17, forming a section of lines 7–8 in col. ii. This placement seems to be supported by PAM 40532,[50] where it appears together with frgs. 27, 28, 30, and 31. These fragments probably came from a single wad and were therefore numbered 27–31. However, its placement in lines 5–6 produces an awkward reading, and therefore it is treated separately here.

L. 2 **]לת**   [. Milik read]ל בכלו̇[תנ̇י. Traces of *lamed* and *taw* are visible in PAM 40532.

Translation
1.]his[la]ws[
2.   ] ..[

Frg. 41

]א̇ת [	1
ש[בועות]	2
[מקד]ש	3
]ל[	4

Notes on Readings
The dry lines of this fragment have been drawn (see PAM 40505, J5928B R ir [numbered there as frg. 34]), a feature shared by frgs. 42–44.

Translation
1.]..[
2. w]eeks [
3.] sanctu[ary of
4.   ].[

---

[50] It is missing from the new AWS photographs, in which frg. 29 there is in fact identified as frg. 36 in the DJD edition).

Comments

L. 2 ש[בועות. The restoration is that of Milik. The noun ש[בו֯עות ("weeks"), may refer to a certain time period, such as that elapsing between Passover and the Festival of Weeks (Deut 16:9) or to the Festival of Weeks itself (חג שבעת [Exod 34:22; Deut 16:10, 16).

L. 3 מקד]ש. This is Milik's restoration. It is either a noun, "a sanctuary" (perhaps in a construct state), or a *Pi'el* participle of קדש ("to sanctify"; Ezek 37:28).

Frg. 42

1	[֯o]
2	הב[רית ה]זואת
3	בכ[ול שנֽה֯]
4	[֯o ֯o]

Notes on Readings

Here too the dry lines have been drawn (see PAM 40.505, J5928B R ir [identified there as frg. 35]), a feature also shared by frgs. 41, 43, and 44.

L. 3 שנֽה֯[. The DJD edition has ש[נה, but the bottom part of the right vertical stroke of a *he* is visible in PAM 40505 and J5928B R ir.

Translation

1.   ].[
2.   th]is[co]venant
3.   eve]ry year[
4.   ]..[

Comments

L. 2 הב֯[רית ה]זואת. Perhaps restore as the recurring expression, הב֯[רית ה]זואת (cf. Deut 29:13).

L. 3 כ[ול שנֽה֯]. This phrase can be reconstructed as בכ[ול שנֽה֯] or as בכ[ול שנֽה֯] ושנה; cf. Esth 9:21, 27; 11QT^a XLII, 13 (with reference to the Festival of Booths).

Frg. 43

```
[ב̇]                    1
מא[ד̇ה להש]מר           2
ה[ו̇א נ○]               3
```

Notes on Readings
Also in this fragment the dry lines are drawn (see PAM 40505, J5928B R ir [identified there as frg. 36]), as they are in frgs. 41, 42, and 44.

Translation
1.   ].[
2.   mu]ch to kee[p
3.   h]e ..[

Comments
L. 2 **מא[ד̇ה להש]מר**. Thus restored by Milik. In biblical Hebrew, the adverb מאד usually follows a verb; therefore, the infinitive להש]מר most likely opens a new clause.

Frg. 44

```
[ל̇יה ב]                1
א[ת אש]ר                2
[○○]                    3
```

Notes on Readings
This fragment appears in J5928B R ir as frg. 37.

Frg. 45

```
[○]                     1
י[שראל ק]               2
[אשר צל̇]               3
```

Notes on Readings

L. 1]∘[. A trace of ink, not noticed by the editor, is clearly visible above the *lamed* of ‏[י]שראל‎ in PAM 40505 and J5928B R ir. In the latter photograph, this fragment is labeled as frg. 38.

L. 3 ‏צֿ]ל‎. Milik read ‏צ[וה‎. A trace of a long vertical stroke, as in *lamed*, is seen next to the *ṣade* in PAM 40505 and J5928B R ir.

Translation
1.].[
2. I]srael .[
3.]that ..[

Frg. 46

1 [∘‏מיד ה‎]
2 [∘ ‏ב חֿ‎ ∘∘]

Notes on Readings
This fragment is missing in J5928B R ir.

Translation
1.]from the hand of ..[
2.]. .. ..[

Frg. 47

1 [∘∘]
2 [∘‏לֿבֿ‎∘]

Notes on Readings
On the DJD plate XIX, as well as in PAM 40505 and J5928B R ir (mistakenly designated in the latter as frg. 40), frg. 47 appears as an assemblage of several scraps of leather. Without direct access to the fragment itself, it is difficult to ascertain whether the scrap joined on the right has been placed correctly, for the traces of the letter visible at its right extremity resemble a *shin* placed on its left side.

L. 2]∘בל∘[. Milik read]מלב[, but the traces of ink that he read as a medial *mem* are inconsistent with this letter. It appears that the edges of the two scraps of leather converge at this place. If our suggestion regarding the placement of one of the pieces is correct, then what remains is a vertical stroke. Until the placement of the right scrap is clarified, no reading can be proposed. Illegible traces of another letter are visible next to the *bet* in PAM 40505 and J5928B R ir.

Frg. 48

]לה

I was unable to locate this fragment in the PAM photographs of 1Q22. It has been designated as frg. 41 in J5928B R ir.

Frg. 49

]∘∘∘[

I was unable to locate this fragment in the PAM photographs of 1Q22. It has been designated as frg. 42 in J5928B.

Unidentified Fragments

Frg. A

] שׁ[נִֽים	1
]ל[	2

Milik joined this scrap of leather to frg. 20. According to his reconstruction, it should be placed in the first two lines of col. III. However, as was noted in Notes on Readings ad loc., this placement is unwarranted.

Translation
1. y]ears[
2.].[

Frg. B

]בֿדתֿ[∘∘[

Notes on Readings

Milik attached this piece to frg. 22 so that it formed a part of col. IV, line 1. As was explained above (see Notes on Readings ad loc.), this placement is unsubstantiated.

Milik read here וּבְעדת. Traces of two illegible letters are visible in PAM 40474, 40511, and J5928B R ir, followed by an interval. The letter preceding *dalet* is most likely a *bet*. All three of its strokes can still be seen in the photographs.

Frg. C

[בו]

This relatively large but badly shrunken fragment appears in PAM 40488 together with frgs. 34, 35, 37, and 39.

Frg. D

[○שׁבֹ]	1
[פֿי אֹ]	2
[לוֹ○]	3

This fragment appears in the upper left corner of PAM 40505.

Frg. E

This fragment is the leftmost in the first row in PAM 40532. Dark and shrunken, it does not appear to preserve any traces of ink.

Frg. F

[שׁ]

This fragment is the leftmost in the second row in PAM 40532.

Frg. G

[וֹשֹׁה]

Notes on Readings
Frg. G is found in the upper right corner of PAM 40532. The remains of the third letter may also be read as a *dalet*.

Discussion

The extant fragments of 1Q22 contain two discourses. First, God instructs Moses (col. i 1–11). Then, following his command, Moses exhorts Israel to remain faithful to God and recites the law (cols. ii 11–iv 11). The scroll dates these two discourses to the day when, according to Deut 1:3, Moses began addressing Israel in the plains of Moab. Not only does 1Q22 assume the temporal framework of Deuteronomy, but it also borrows its overarching literary structure of admonitions (Deuteronomy 1–11) followed by an exposition of the laws (Deuteronomy 12–26:15). Furthermore, cols. i–iii 7 rely heavily on Deuteronomy for their wording.[51]

However, the account in 1Q22 of what took place on "the first day of the eleventh month" (Deut 1:3) differs in several respects from that in Deuteronomy. Firstly, 1Q22 claims that God spoke to Moses at length on that day, whereas Deut 1:3 states that Moses spoke to Israel in accordance with the divine instructions. Secondly, as Deut 1:1 introduces Deuteronomy as "the words that Moses addressed to *all* Israel," the scroll reports that Moses convened the entire congregation.[52] Thirdly, it rearranges the order of events in Deuteronomy and Moses is commanded to ascend Mount Nebo before his address to Israel. Fourthly, instead of presenting Moses as expounding the law to the entire nation as in Deut 1:5, the scroll relates that Moses expounded the Torah to the heads of the families, Levites, and priests alone.[53] This may have been inspired by Deut 31:28, in which Moses speaks to "all the elders of your tribes and your officials";[54] here, this occasion is envisioned as having taken place before his speech to the people. At least some of the

---

51 As was observed also by Milik, "Dires de Moïse," 92.
52 This transposition could have been suggested by Deut 3:27: "Go up (עלה) to the summit of Pisgah." Compare a similar interpretation of the events in chapter 7 of the late Samaritan work frequently referred to as the Arabic *Book of Joshua*. For the English translation, see O. T. Crane, *The Samaritan Chronicle or the Book of Joshua, the Son of Nun* (New York: John Alden, 1890), 29.
53 For the role of the Levites as expounders of the law, see Deut 33:8–11; Mal 2:7. G. J. Brooke, "Levi and the Levites in the Dead Sea Scrolls and the New Testament," in *Mogilany 1989: Papers on the Dead Sea Scrolls offered in Memory of Jean Carmignac* (Krakow: Enigma Press, 1993), 105–29 (109), observes that the mention of the Levitical chiefs may point to the Levitical orientation of this scroll. A similar comment was made by Tigchelaar, "Divre Mosheh," 311.
54 LXX and, apparently, 4QDeut[b] add here the heads of the tribes and the judges.

features of the reworking of Deuteronomy in 1Q22 may have been influenced by the biblical accounts of the giving of the Torah at Sinai. Indeed, God's address to Moses, the gathering of the entire congregation (cf. Deut 4:10), Moses' ascent to the mount (cf. Exod 19:3, 20, 24; 24:1, 9, 12, 13, 15, 18; Deut 9:9; 10:1, 3), his "standing" there while addressing Israel (cf. Deut 5:4–5), and Eleazar's presence (cf. Exod 19:24; 24:1, 9–11[55]) seem to point to the Sinai revelation. Even Moses' explanation of the law first to the leaders echoes Exod 19:7, according to which he transmits the divine commands first to the elders (cf. Exod 24:9, 14).[56]

The legal section of the Mosaic discourse in 1Q22 (cols. iii–iv) also deviates from the Deuteronomic Code (Deuteronomy 12–26:15). Its treatment of the laws seems to have been selective, apparently focusing on the commandments related to the appointed times, as well as to the land. The laws pertaining to the Sabbatical Year become operational only upon entrance into the promised land (cf. Lev 25:2), just as the atonement for the land featured in the treatment of the Day of Atonement in the scroll. The scroll seems to arrange these regulations according to their calendrical order, beginning with the month of Tishre.[57] In addition, 1Q22 appears to present a harmonistic exposition of a given legal topic, bringing together the relevant passages from the different books of the Torah, and not from Deuteronomy alone.[58] In the Hebrew Bible, the agricultural regulations pertaining to the Sabbatical Year are outlined in Leviticus 25, while the laws regulating the remission of debts taking place during this year are found in Deuteronomy 15. In 1Q22, both aspects of the fallow year are treated within the same section concerning the fallow year (the agricultural laws are mentioned first).[59] Moreover, it includes laws that are not dealt with in the book of Deuteronomy, as is the

---

[55] See also the Samaritan version of Exod 24:1, 9 and the pre-Samaritan 4QpaleoExod^m XXVI, 20; XXVII, 31, which add the names of Eleazar and Ithamar. For Joshua's presence on Mount Nebo along with Eleazar (col. i 11–12), cf. Exod 24:13, 15 (LXX); 32:17–18; 4Q364 14 4–5.
[56] See further Feldman, "Moses' Farewell Address."
[57] Cf. a similar ordering of the festivals by Josephus in *Ant*. iii, 239 f. See further L. H. Feldman, "Rearrangement of Pentateuchal Material in Josephus' Antiquities, Books 1–4," in idem, *Judaism and Hellenism Reconsidered* (JSJSup 107; Leiden: Brill, 2006), 361–412 (388–89). On the rabbinic view that the Shemitah year begins on the 1st of Tishre, see *m. Roš. Haš.* 1:1. The fact that the discussion of the Shemitah in 1Q22 precedes that of the Day of Atonement may imply that the author of the scroll shared this view. See the recent discussion by J. Ben-Dov, "Jubilean Chronology and the 364-Day Year," *Meghillot* 5–6 (2007): 49–60 (Hebrew), and the literature cited there.
[58] On the topical arrangement of laws in other Qumran texts, see L. Schiffman, "Codification of Jewish Law in the Dead Sea Scrolls," in idem, *Qumran and Jerusalem* (Grand Rapids/Cambridge: Eerdmans, 2010), 170–83 (181).
[59] As has been noted by J. Licht, "Review of D. Barthélemy, J. T. Milik et alii: Qumran Cave 1 (Discoveries in the Judean Desert 1) Oxford, 1955," *Tarbiẓ* 26 (1956–1957): 472–73 (473) (Hebrew).

case with the Day of Atonement. Furthermore, reworking the Pentateuchal laws, 1Q22 introduces exegetical traditions that are not found in the Hebrew Bible. Thus, the section dealing with the Sabbatical Year seems to link the forgiveness of sins to the remission of debts, while the columns concerned with the Day of Atonement appear to mention Israel's avoidance of collecting the manna on the 10th of Tishre and a provision for the atonement of the land.

How does the work preserved in 1Q22 relate to the other four scrolls assembled under the title *Apocryphon of Moses*? In spite of it fragmentary state, it can be observed that none of its extant fragments deal with topics appearing in the *Apocryphon of Moses*, such as the identity of the false/true prophet (4Q375) and the voluntary war (4Q376). Neither does it contain liturgy, as is the case in 1Q29 and 4Q408. Strugnell was well aware of the fact that the text of 1Q22 does not overlap with that of 1Q29, 4Q375, and 4Q376. However, in his view that was "not a grave obstacle," as the identification of 1Q22 with the *Apocryphon of Moses* "would give us in 1Q22 column i the historical or pseudepigraphical setting of 1Q29, 4Q375 and 4Q376."[60] Yet, there is nothing in these four scrolls that implies a "historical and pseudepigraphical setting" similar to that of 1Q22.[61] Furthermore, if our observation regarding the preoccupation of 1Q22 with the commandments related to the appointed times of Israel's calendar and the land is correct, it is unlikely that this scroll would have dealt with the aforementioned halachic issues.[62] Therefore, it seems appropriate to abandon the designation of 1Q22 as 1QapocrMoses[a], allowing 1QWords of Moses to be studied as a composition in its own right.[63]

---

60 Strugnell, "Moses-Pseudepigrapha," 247.
61 As Schiffman notes, the extant text of these scrolls does not mention Moses. L. H. Schiffman, "The Temple Scroll and the Halakhic Pseudepigrapha of the Second Temple Period," in idem, *The Courtyards of the House of the Lord* (ed. F. García Martínez; STDJ 75; Leiden/Boston: Brill, 2008), 174.
62 Tigchelaar, "Divre Mosheh," 309–10, observes that 1Q22, unlike 1Q29, 4Q375, and 4Q408, does not employ the Tetragrammaton, but refers to God as לאלוהי֯ [אלוהי֯] (col. II, 1), אלו[הי אלוהי]נו (col. II, 6), and כ֯ל[א]ל֯[ו]הי אלוהיכ֯ם (col. III, 6). He also notes that while 1Q29 and 4Q408 speak of כל ישראל, 1Q22 uses the expression בני ישראל.
63 For a similar conclusion, see G. Brin, *Studies in Biblical Law: From the Hebrew Bible to the Dead Sea Scrolls* (Sheffield: JSOT Press, 1994), 158.

Liora Goldman
Rewritten Scripture: Law and Liturgy
with contributions by Devorah Dimant

The Qumran *Apocryphon of Moses* (4Q375, 4Q376, 1Q29, 4Q408):

General Introduction

The composition known as the *Apocryphon of Moses* is one of the rewritten Scripture texts whose content and character have yet to be examined and understood fully; very little scholarly attention has been paid to them to date. Based on the common usage of the phrases לשונות אש (1Q29 1 3; 2 3; 4Q376 ii 1; 4Q408 11 2), נביא and לדבר סרה (4Q375 i 9; 4Q376 i 1), and הכהן המשיח (4Q375 i 9; 4Q376 i 1) and the overlap of several lines of the prayer in 1Q29 3–4 and 4Q408 2, four manuscripts are regarded as belonging to this work: 1Q29, 4Q375, 4Q376, and 4Q408.[1]

The first to suggest that these manuscripts constitute copies of a single composition was John Strugnell. After publishing 4Q375 and 4Q376 in the 1990s, he then noted their affinity with 1Q29, published by Milik in 1955, suggesting that all three scrolls deal with the same subject, namely how the "anointed priest" distinguishes between true and false prophets.[2] While Steudel recognized the links between 4Q408 and the aforementioned three scrolls and the similarities they displayed to one another when she published this scroll in 1994, she was tentative in presenting it as a copy of the *Apocryphon of Moses*.[3] In his recently published edition of these texts, Qimron accepts the identification of all four

---

[1] For 1Q29, see J. T. Milik, "Liturgie des 'trois longues de feu'," in *Qumran Cave 1* (ed. D. Barthélemy; Oxford: Clarendon Press, 1955), 130–32. For the initial publication of 4Q375, see J. Strugnell, "Moses-Pseudepigrapha at Qumran: 4Q375, 4Q376, and Similar Works," in *Archaeology and History in the Dead Sea Scrolls* (ed. L. H. Schiffman; JSPSup 8; Sheffield: Sheffield Academic Press, 1990), 221–56 (221–25); for the official edition, see idem, "Apocryphon of Moses," in *Qumran Cave 4.XIV: Parabiblical Texts, Part 2* (ed. M. Broshi et al.; DJD XIX; Oxford: Clarendon Press, 1995), 111–36 (111–19); for my edition, see L. Goldman, "The Law of the Prophet as Reflected in 4Q375," *Meghillot* 5–6 (2007): 61–84 (Hebrew). Strugnell published 4Q376 together with 4Q375: "Moses-Pseudepigrapha," 221–25; idem, "Apocryphon of Moses," 121–36. For my edition, see L. Goldman, "The Rules Regarding fighting a Permitted War in 4Q376," *Meghillot* 8–9 (2010): 319–41 (Hebrew). For the initial publication of 4Q408, see A. Steudel, "4Q408: A Liturgy on Morning and Evening Prayer – Preliminary Edition," *RevQ* 16 (1994): 313–34; for the official edition, see eadem, "4Q408: 4QApocryphon of Moses^c?" in *Qumran Cave 4. XXVI: Miscellanea, Part 1* (ed. P. Alexander et. al.; DJD XXXVI; Oxford: Clarendon Press, 2002), 298–315.

[2] Strugnell, "Moses-Pseudepigrapha," 221–25; idem, "Apocryphon of Moses," 111–19.

[3] Steudel, "Liturgy," 313–34; eadem, "Apocryphon of Moses," 298–317. The same tentative determination appears in *DSSR*, 3:104, the question mark there (98–109) indicating a degree of doubt that all the copies belong to the same composition.

manuscripts as belonging to a single composition, and offers a reconstruction of the entire text.[4]

However, a close examination of the four manuscripts evinces a complex set of data. While the congruence between the expressions "tongues of fire" and "and the left-hand stone" in three of the scrolls is clear and unequivocal (4Q408 11; 4Q376 1 ii; 1Q29 1 2–4), each scroll includes sections that have no parallels in the other scrolls. The content of the scrolls also differs. Strugnell regarded 4Q376 as a continuation of the rewriting of the law regarding the true prophet in 4Q375. While 4Q375 appears to be based on the biblical laws concerning true and false prophets in Deut 13:2–6, 18:15–20, 4Q376 reworks the biblical laws regulating fighting a permitted war and 4Q408 (as noted in the preliminary publication and early edition) is a liturgical text for morning and evening worship.[5] The fragmentary nature of 1Q29 has precluded precise determination to date of its content and nature; Milik suggested that it is a liturgical fragment, possibly a copy of a prayer.[6] This supposition was subsequently strengthened by the parallels between 4Q408 2 1–3 and 1Q29 3–4.

An independent examination of each of the four scrolls attributed to the composition elucidated the subject, literary style, scriptural texts reworked, relationship between the sections of each manuscript, and relationship between each of the scrolls. This reveals that we have in our hands partially overlapping copies of a single halachic document whose intention is to establish the high priest as the supreme judicial authority in cases that require a divine decision, such as whether a prophet is true or false or engaging in a permitted war.

---

4 E. Qimron, *The Dead Sea Scrolls: The Hebrew Writings* (Jerusalem: Yad Ben Zvi Press, 2013), 2:311–15 (Hebrew).
5 For 4Q375, see Goldman, "Law." For 4Q376, see Goldman, "Permitted War." For 4Q408, see Steudel, "Liturgy."
6 Milik, "Liturgie," 130–32.

4Q375: The Identification of True and False Prophets

Literature

J. T. Milik, "Liturgie des 'trois longues de feu'," in *Qumran Cave 1* (ed. D. Barthélemy; Oxford: Clarendon Press, 1955), 130–32; J. Strugnell, "Moses-Pseudepigrapha at Qumran: 4Q375, 4Q376 and Similar Works," in *Archaeology and History in the Dead Sea Scrolls* (ed. L. H. Schiffman; JSPSup 8; Sheffield: Sheffield Academic Press, 1990), 221–56; idem, "Apocryphon of Moses," in *Qumran Cave 4.XIV: Parabiblical Texts, Part 2* (ed. M. Broshi et al.; DJD XIX; Oxford: Clarendon Press, 1995), 111–36; É. Latour, "Une Proposition de Reconstruction de l'Apocryphe de Moise (1Q29, 4Q375, 4Q376, 4Q408)," *RevQ* 22 (2006): 575–91; L. Goldman, "The Law of the Prophet as Reflected in 4Q375," *Meghillot* 5–6 (2007): 61–84 (Hebrew); eadem, "The Apocryphon of Moses: A Composition Representing the High Priest as the Supreme Judicial Authority," *Meghillot* 10 (2013): 181–200 (Hebrew); E. Qimron, *The Dead Sea Scrolls: The Hebrew Writings* (Jerusalem: Yad Ben Zvi Press, 2013), 2:311–15 (Hebrew).

The Manuscript

Despite Strugnell's determination of 4Q375 as a single fragment, it appears to be two.[1] The manuscript is written on a tiny piece of leather (7 cm in height), is well preserved. It contains two columns with top, bottom, and intercolumnar margins. Col. i has nine lines. Although the beginning of most of the lines is missing, line 8 lacks only the first letter of the first word. This line, having forty-three letter-spaces, forms the basis of Strugnell's reconstruction of the remainder of the text. The second column contains the remains of seven lines. The scroll is dated paleographically to the beginning of the Herodian period.[2]

Inspection of the photographs demonstrates that Strugnell's frg. 1 consists of three scraps of leather sewn together, referred to herein as a, b, and c:[3]

a contains the right and middle sections of the first column. The right-hand edge having been damaged, the right margin and the beginning of the lines are missing.

b contains the middle section of the first column, the intercolumnar margin, and the beginning of lines 3–9 of col. ii. The sequential text obtained by juxtaposing a and b indicates that Strugnell's reconstruction is correct.

---

[1] Strugnell's numbering and terminology are retained here to avoid ambguity.
[2] Strugnell, "Apocryphon of Moses," 111–12.
[3] See Goldman, "Law," 64.

c is a small, mutilated piece of leather containing the remnants of four lines. Exhibiting no physical continuity (connection) with a or b, it forms a separate fragment, the second of the scroll. As the parchment, script, and spaces between the lines resemble those of a and b, it would appear to belong to the same manuscript. Its textual relation to a and b is less certain, however. Strugnell views it as a continuation of lines 5–8 of col. ii, arguing that its (alleged) reworking of Leviticus 16 makes this the most logical arrangement. However, as discussed below, several linguistic considerations cast doubt on both these assumptions. While accepting Strugnell's proposal in his new edition of *ApocrMoses*, Qimron proposes more plausible arguments for the textual sequence between b and c. I follow these herein.[4]

Text and Comments

Col. i (a+b)

top margin

1 [את כול אשר] יצוה אלוהיכה אליכה מפי הנביא ושמרׄתה
2 [את כול החוׄ]קׄים האלה ושבתה עד יהוה אלוהיכה בכול
3 לבבכה ובכוׄ[ל] נפשכה ושב אׄלוהיכה מחרון אפו הגדול
4 [להושיעכ]הׄ ממצוקותיכה והנביא אשר יקום ודבר בכה
5 [סרה להש]יׄבכה מאחרי אלוהיכה יומתׄ *vac* וׄכיא יקום השבט
6 [אשר] הואה ממנו ואמר לוא יומת כי צדיק הואה נביא
7 [נ]אׄמן הואה ובאתהׄ עם השבט ההואה וזקניכה ושופטיכה
8 [א]לׄ המקום אשר יבחר אלוהיכה באחד שבטיכה *vac* לפני
9 [הכו]הן המׄשיח אשר יוצקׄ עׄל רׄ[ו]אשו שמן המשוחה

bottom margin

Notes on Readings

L. 9 [הכו]הן. Strugnell reads [ה]כׄוׄהן. As the medial *kaf* and *waw* are not visible in PAM I-342890, this should rather be read [הכו]הן.

המשוחה. The photographs (PAM I-342889, I-342890) clearly show that the fourth letter is a *waw*, as also evidenced by comparison with the word ממצוקותיכה in line 4, where these two letters have distinctively different forms. Strugnell

---

4 Qimron, *Hebrew Writings*, 2:313.

reads המשיחה, but in his notes he admits that paleographically the word should be read with a *waw*.⁵

Translation⁶
1. [all that] your God will command you by the mouth of the prophet, and you will keep
2. [all] these [sta]tutes, and you will return unto YHWH your God with all
3. [your heart and with al]l your soul then your God will turn from the fury of his great anger
4. [so as to save yo]u from your afflictions. But the prophet who rises up and speak against you
5. [rebellion so as to make] you turn away from your God, he shall be put to death. *vacat* But, if there stands up the tribe
6. [which] he comes from, and says, "Let him not be put to death, for he is truthful, a
7. [fai]thful prophet," then you shall come, with that tribe and your elders and your judges,
8. [t]o the place which your God shall choose from one (of the territories of) your tribes, *vacat* into the presence of
9. [the] anointed [p]riest, upon whose h[e]ad will be poured the oil of anointing

Comments
Part 1: Lines 1–4a
Ll. 1–3 The first part of the column is a conditional clause. Lines 1–3a (to the word נפשכה) contain the protasis stating the conditions the addressee must meet in order to ensure the fulfillment of the promise elaborated in the apodosis, namely, the mitigation of God's anger.⁷

Ll. 1–2 **את כול אשר [יצוה אלוהיכה אליכה ושמרׄתה [את כול החוׄ[קׄים האלה**. Although the beginning of the conditional clause has not been preserved, the context makes the conditions clear. The people—addressed as a collective—must obey God's words given in his laws and through his prophets in order to avoid his wrath.

---

5 Cf. Strugnell, "Apocryphon of Moses," 115.
6 The translation follows Strugnell, ibid, with minor modifications.
7 For the two-part conditional clause in biblical Hebrew, see Joüon–Muraoka, *Grammar*, § 167 b–c.

מפי הנביא. While this phrase is not attested in the biblical texts (Zech 8:9 referring to מפי נביאים in the plural), the idea that the prophet speaks God's words is prevalent.[8] The closest parallel to our line, both linguistically and conceptually, is Deut 18:18, which describes the true prophet who will speak only what he was commanded by God. The scroll employs two of the words in this verse (פי and a verbal form of צו"ה) and conveys the same thought, that is, that the prophet transmits God's words and therefore must be heeded. The same stipulation occurs in Deut 18:15: אליו תשמעון ("him you shall heed)." As discussed below, the scroll reworks the laws with respect to the prophet in Deut 18:15–20. This clause, a paraphrase of Deut 18:18, opens the passage.

This section also alludes to Deut 13:1. Both Deut 13:1 and the scroll use the roots צו"ה and שמ"ר and share a similar substantive sequence (cf. col. i 4b–5a).

L. 2 את כול החו[קי]ם האלה. This is Strugnell's restoration, followed here. Cf. Deut 4:6, 6:24: את כל החקים האלה.

Ll. 2–3 ושבתה עד יהוה אלוהיכה בכול [לבכה ובכו]ל נפשכה. This formulation is also typically Deuteronomistic, the formulation בכל לב ובכל נפש occurring in Deut 6:5, 11:13, 13:4. While its affinity with Deut 13:4 suggests that this passage is still based on Deut 13:2–6, the wording also closely corresponds to Deut 30:2: ושבת עד יהוה אלוהיך ושמעת בקולו ככל אשר אנוכי מצוך היום ("and return to the LORD your God, and you and your children heed His command with all your heart and soul, just as I enjoin upon you this day"; cf. also v. 10). Stylistically, both passages represent the first part of a conditional clause (protasis), indicating the people's obligation via the roots צו"ה and שו"ב and the expressions לשוב עד ה' אלהיך and בכל לבד ובכל נפשך.

Ll. 3–4 ושב אלוהיכה מחרון אפו הגדול [להושיעכ]ה ממצוקותיכה. This forms the apodosis of the conditional clause, indicating that God will forgive the people if they listen to his prophet. As in many biblical texts, it opens with a *waw*.[9] This sentence continues the reworking of Deut 13:2–6 and 18:15–18. The expression ושב אלוהיכה מחרון אפו recalls Num 25:4 (cf. also Deut 30:3; Jer 30:24; Job 9:13) and constitutes the apodosis of the conditional clause, God pledging to forgive the people if they

---

[8] Cf. 1) בפי כל נביאיו Kgs 22:22; 2 Chr 18:22, 23); 2) בפי ירמיהו Chr 36:21, 22). Note also Exod 4:12; Isa 59:21; Jer 1:9; Hos 12:10.
[9] In the majority of cases in which the apodosis opens with a *waw*, the protasis also begins with one, as in Deut 30:2–3: see Joüon–Muraoka, *Grammar*, 628, 647–48.

return wholeheartedly to Him.[10] The phrase חרון אפו also appears in Deut 13:18. The fact that this verse also constitutes the apodosis of a conditional clause suggests that this is the most likely source here, as no other usages of the phrase in a conditional clause occur in the biblical texts despite the prevalence of the phrase itself. The addition of the adjective הגדול (חרון אפו הגדול) appears only once in the Hebrew Bible, in reference to Manasseh's sins (2 Kgs 23:26). Its insertion here stresses the danger in which the people stand if they do not heed God through His prophet.

L. 4 להושיעכ]הֿ ממצוקותיכה[. The reconstruction, suggested by the size of the lacuna, is that of Strugnell. It is based on Psalm 107, wherein the noun מצוקה occurs four times, twice in the similar construction ממצקתיהם יושיעם (vv. 13, 19) and twice with the roots נצ"ל and יצ"א (vv. 6, 28).[11]

The first part of the first column is a conditional clause that stipulates that God's forgiveness of his people is contingent upon them heeding his prophet. The section reworks and interweaves three passages from Deuteronomy—13:1–6, 18:15–20, and 30:2–10—together with phraseology from other biblical texts. The following table presents the text of the fragment and the biblical sources underlying it, the phrases and roots occurring both in the Bible and in the scroll being set in bold:

4Q375	MT
[את כול אשר]יֿצוה אלוהיכה אליכה	את כל הדבר אשר אנכי **מצוה** אתכם (Deut 13:1)
	ודבר אליהם את כל אשר **אצונו** (Deut 18:18)
	ושמעת בקולו ככל אשר אנכי **מצוך** היום (Deut 30:2)
מפי הנביא	ונתתי דברי ב**פיו** ודבר אליהם (Deut 18:18)
ושמרתה [את כול החו]קים האלה	את כל אשר אנכי מצוה אתכם אתו **תשמרו** לעשות (Deut 13:1)
ושב אֿלוהיכה מחרון אפו הגדול	**ויֿשב חרון אףֿ** יהוה מישראל (Num 25:4)
	למען יֿ**שוב** יהוה **מחרון אפו** (Deut 13:18)
	ו**שב** יהוה **אלהיך** את שבותך ורחמך (Deut 30:3)
[להושיעכ]הֿ ממצוקותיכה	ויזעקו אל יהוה בצר להם **ממצקותיהם** יושיעם (Ps 107:13, 19)

---

10 For the root שו"ב in the Hebrew Bible, see W. L. Holladay, *The Root Šûbh in the Old Testament* (Leiden: Brill, 1958). For the use of this root in the Qumran literature, see H. J. Fabry, *Die Wurzel šûb in der Qumran-Literatur: Zur Semantik eines Grundbegriffes* (Cologne: P. Hanstein, 1975).
11 Strugnell, "Apocryphon of Moses," 114. The noun occurs elsewhere in Zeph 1:15; Job 15:24; Ps 25:17.

By interweaving Deut 13:1, 4 with 18:18 and 30:2, the scroll links the injunction to obey the prophet with the covenantal blessings imparted for obedience to the law in Deut 30:2–10.

Part 2: Lines 4b–5a

Ll. 4–5 והנביא אשר יקום ודבר בכה [סרה להש]יבכה מאחרי אלוהיכה יומת. The second part of the column adduces the punishment meted out to the prophet who speaks falsehood (סרה, meaning literally "turning aside"), the antithesis of the prophet who delivers God's laws in line 1. The wording of the scroll here is based on the laws regarding the prophet in Deut 13:2–6, as the phrases יקום נביא and דבר סרה indicate. The sequence also follows that of Deut 18:15–20, which first refers to the necessity of heeding the prophet (vv. 15–18) and then describes how the false prophet is to be identified (vv. 19–20). Lines 1–4a thus require that the people obey the true prophet and lines 4b–5a deal with the false prophet.

ודבר בכה [סרה. Strugnell, positing that this reworks Deut 13:6, reconstructs סרה. This restoration—followed here—is supported by a similar formulation in CD V, 21–VI, 1, which employs the phrases לדבר סרה and להשיב מאחר אל.[12] The biblical locution לדבר סרה bears two complementary meanings. Its first signification is "to speak falsely," as in Isa 59:13, where it is synonymous with the phrase דברי שקר, and Jer 28:15–16 and 29:31–32, in which the false prophet is accused of speaking falsehood.[13] It also denotes "to cause to rebel"—in parallel with the phrase להשיב מאחר אל—the rebellion customarily being caused by the false speech.[14] In Deut 13:2, the prophet prompts people to engage in false worship, thereby leading them to rebel against God. In contrast to the biblical formulation, wherein the prophet speaks falsehood against God, here the object of his attention is בכה, namely "you, the people." [15]As the first part of the text makes clear, the prophet must be heeded because he proclaims God's word. If he speaks falsely, he delivers erroneous laws, ordinances that God has not ordained. Thus, the text refers here to deviant observance of the divine commandments. The prophet causes the people to rebel by means of falsehood (סרה), inducing them to forsake God's laws. In so doing, he is acting against the people (בכה), the *bet* signifying "against"

---

[12] J. M. Baumgarten and D. R. Schwartz, "Damascus Document (CD)," in *PTSDSSP* 2:23. The phrase לדבר סרה in the Qumran texts occurs primarily in the copies of CD: see 4Q267 2 5; 4Q267 4 13; 4Q271 5 i 18. Cf. also 1Q29 1 6; 4Q177 1–4 14; 11QTª LIV, 15; LXI, 8.

[13] *HALOT*, 769.

[14] See L. Ruppert, "סרר *srr*," *TDOT*, 10:353–57.

[15] Thus G. Brin, "The Laws of the Prophets in the Sect of the Judaean Desert: Studies in 4Q375," *JSP* 10 (1992): 19–51 (22).

(cf. Num 12:8, 21:5, 7).[16] The import of this act is highlighted by the fact that the people can only hope for forgiveness if they obey the true prophet and the laws of the Torah and repent wholeheartedly.

L. 5 להש[יבכה מאחרי אלוהיכה. Strugnell posited that the fragment reworks the phrase להשיב מאחרי אל. The phrase להשיב מאחר אל—the opposite of לדרוש אל—that refers to abandoning God or rebelling against him in the biblical texts,[17] carries the same meaning in the Qumran sectarian texts (cf. CD V, 1; 1QS I, 17). It also occurs in the nonsectarian *Apocryphon of Jeremiah C* (4Q383 2 1–2).[18]

יוּמָת. The scroll describes the punishment the false prophet receives in the language of Deut 13:6: יומת ... והנביא ההוא ("As for that prophet ... he shall be put to death").[19] The same sentence is adduced in Deut 18:20: ומת הנביא ההוא ("that prophet shall die"). While Deut 13:6 employs the *Hof'al* form of the root מו"ת, Deut 18:20 uses the *Qal*, possibly signifying a divinely enacted punishment;[20] cf. Jeremiah's prophecy against Hananiah in Jer 28:16–17. The fact that the false prophet is punished by a human court is of particular relevance with respect to 4Q375, which modifies the biblical law by allowing the presentation of testimony on behalf of a person suspected of being a false prophet, and thus the possibility of his acquittal (see Comments on Part 3). Therefore, this is clearly a judicial case

---

16 *HALOT*, 104. Aharon Shemesh understands the Aramaic phrase נבי[אי ש]קרא די קמו [בישראל, included in the Qumran text known as *List of the False Prophets* (4Q339 1 1), as denoting the "false prophets that stood up against Israel", given the fact that the list includes Balaam, a non-Israelite. See idem, "A Note on 4Q339 'List of False Prophets'," *RevQ* 20 (2001): 319–20 (320).
17 Cf. Num 14:43; Josh 22:16, 18, 23, 29. The phrase מאחר אל appears also with other verbs that bear the same meaning: cf. 2 Kgs 17:21; Hos 1:2; Zeph 1:6. See *HALOT*, 1:35–36.
18 Cf. D. Dimant, *Qumran Cave 4.XXI: Parabiblical Texts, Part 4: Pseudo-Prophetic Texts* (DJD XXX; Oxford: Clarendon Press, 2001), 120.
19 Unless otherwise noted, scriptural quotations follow the NJPS.
20 Rabbinic sources interpret the death sentence in Deut 17:12, 18:20, 22:25 as being administered by a human court, the root כר"ת being reserved for divine retribution: see See J. H. Tigay, *Deuteronomy* (Philadelphia: JPS, 1996), 177. A similar interpretation is reflected in the *Temple Scroll*, where the verb מת, which occurs in several Deuteronomistic passages, is systematically replaced with והומת: see 11QT[a] LXI, 1–2 (on Deut 18:20); LXVI, 5 (on Deut 22:25); and יומת in col. LVI, 10 (on Deut 17:12). Aharon Shemesh posits that these alterations reflect a tendency to add capital punishment to the Pentateuchal ordinance and interpret capital punishment in the Pentateuch as a human judicial responsibility. He also draws attention to the fact that the Sages transform the false prophet into a sage, זקן ממרא, with the statements of the false prophet being assessed on the basis of whether they correspond to the ruling halacha; if they are proved "false," he is punishable by a human court rather than by God. See idem, *Punishments and Sins: From Scripture to the Rabbis* (Jerusalem: Magnes, 2003), 113–23 (Hebrew); idem, *Halakhah in the Making* (Berkeley: University of California Press; 2011), 49–52.

that must be determined by human judges rather than a case that is subject to divine punishment.

Part 3: Lines 5b–9

Ll. 5–7 הואה נ]אמן[נביא הואה צדיק כי יומת לוא ואמר ממנו הואה [אשר] השבט יקום וכיא.
At this juncture, the scroll inserts a nonbiblical stipulation. Stylistically, the language remains reminiscent of Deut 13:2: נביא בקרבך יקום כי.[21] The wording of lines 4–6 recalls the biblical casuistic laws that first state the general law and then list exceptions. The scroll allows the person suspected of false prophecy to be acquitted if his tribe testifies to his uprightness and faithfulness, הואה צדיק כי. The noun צדיק denotes "righteous," "upright," "truthful," and "trustworthy" in the biblical texts, this also appearing to be its meaning here.[22] The adjective נאמן is used twice in reference to a prophet in the biblical texts: once it is said of Moses (Num 12:7) and once of Samuel (1 Sam 3:20). The tribe thus testifies that the person who belongs to it is both trustworthy and upright before men, and faithful to God and His commandments. Tribal affiliation does not customarily form a significant element with respect to prophetic figures in the prophetic, historiographical, or legal literature in the Hebrew Bible.[23] While the account of Jeremiah's unfair trial (Jeremiah 26) refers to the "elders," these are more likely to have been older men endowed with knowledge, experience, and memory in legal matters rather than tribal heads.[24] As the tribal arrangement had ceased to exist prior to the period in which 4Q375 was composed, the allusion appears to exemplify the use of anachronistic biblical language, a characteristic feature of the rewritten Bible genre.[25] Here, it may serve to present the text as authentic biblical law. Gershon Brin suggests that the reference elucidates the word בקרבך in Deut 13:2; the same phrase also appears in Deut 18:15 (מאחיך מקרבך נביא) and 18:18 (אחיהם מקרב).[26] If so, the tribe is the group to whom the prophet belongs, their personal acquaintance with him enabling them to testify to his character.[27]

---

21 Brin, "Laws of the Prophets," 26, suggests that the scroll is reworking Deut 13:2 here.
22 BDB, 109, 842; *HALOT*, 1:125, 1002.
23 Brin, "Laws of the Prophets," 27.
24 Y. Hoffman, *Jeremiah: Introduction and Commentary* (*Mikra Leyisrael*; Tel Aviv/Jerusalem: Am Oved/Magnes, 2001), 1:523 (Hebrew). The term שבט also recalls the authority wielded by figures of authority (cf. Gen 49:10; Num 24:17; Judg 5:14; Ezek 19:11; Ps 2:9).
25 For the geo-tribal notation in line 8, see there.
26 Brin, "Laws of the Prophets," 27.
27 Aharon Shemesh adduces numerous rabbinic sources that reflect a similar concept, according to which false prophets had acquired a reputation locally as true prophets prior to utter-

The section may possibly reflect a sectarian controversy over how to determine the identity of true and false prophets, the modification allowing a suspected person's community to testify on his behalf (see below).

Ll. 7–9 ובאתֿה עם השבט ההואה וזקניכה ושופטיכה [א]ל המקום אשר יבחר אלוהיכה באחד שבטיכה לפני [הכו]הן המֿשיח. The scroll continues to rework passages from Deuteronomy, here from Deut 17:8–9; 21:2 and 12:14.

4Q375	MT
ובאתֿה עם השבט ההואה וזקניכה ושופטיכה	ובאת אל הכהנים הלוים ואל השפט (Deut 17:9) ויצאו זקניך ושפטיך ומדדו אל הערים אשר סביבות החלל (Deut 21:2)
[א]ל המקום אשר יבחר אלוהיכה באחד שבטיכה	כי יפלא ממך דבר למשפט בין דם לדם בין דין לדין ובין נגע לנגע דברי ריבת בשעריך וקמת ועלית אל המקום אשר יבחר יהוה אלהיך בו (Deut 17:8) כי אם במקום אשר יבחר יהוה אלהיך באחד שבטך שם תעלה עולותיך (Deut 12:14)
לפני [הכו]הן המֿשיח	ובאת אל הכהנים הלוים ואל השפט אשר יהיה בימים ההם ודרשת והגידו לך את המשפט (Deut 17:9)

As this table shows, the central biblical text here is Deut 17:8–9, which lays out the procedure for settling difficult legal cases.[28] The judges of the field cities (שערים) must inquire of the highest judicial authority (the priest or judge, according to the severity of the case) at "the place that the LORD your God will have chosen."[29] The people, tribe, elders, and judges would thus go to the anointed priest in the temple at Jerusalem to settle the issue of the prophet's status as true or false. The

---

ing false prophecies. See idem, "Halacha and Prophecy: The False Prophet and the Rebellious Elder." in *Renewing Jewish Commitment: The Work and Thought of David Hartman* (ed. A. Sagi and T. Zohar; Tel Aviv: Hakibbutz Hemeuchad, 2001), 2:923–41 (932, 936) (Hebrew).

28 For the implications of the phrase בין דם לדם בין דין לדין ובין נגע לנגע דברי ריבת בשעריך ("... be it a controversy over homicide, civil law, or assault—matters of dispute in your courts ..."; Deut 17:8), see A. Rofé, *Deuteronomy: Issues and Interpretation* (Edinburgh: T & T Clark, 2002), 109; Tigay, *Deuteronomy*, 164.

29 Tigay (*Deuteronomy*, 164–65) suggests that the priests were instituted as judges in secular matters because they were involved in settling unsolved cases via the Urim and Thummim; R. D. Nelson, (*Deuteronomy: A Commentary* [OTL; Louisville: Westminster John Knox, 2002], 221) suggests that the phrase יפלא ממך / נפלאות refers to things beyond human capacity to understand, and argues that resolution of the difficulty demanded the priest's use of sacral texts, adjurations, or the Urim and Thummim.

sole biblical passage that refers to the tribe in this context is Deut 12:14, which states that "the place that the LORD your God will choose" lies "in one of your tribal territories" (cf. v. 4). As 4Q375 was composed during the Second Temple period, when the tribal territories no longer possessed any practical significance, the relevance of this religio-geographical notation is obscure. While the addition באחד שבטכה ("in one of your tribes") may reflect a regular biblical usage, it is evidently introduced by the Qumran text to reinforce the link between the prophet and his tribe. The place God chooses "amidst all your tribes as His habitation, to establish His name there ... in one of your tribal territories" is the locus at which His worship as the only God must be performed rather than as in the general Deuteronomistic formulation (Deut 12:2).

L. 7 וּבָאתָה. As above, the singular verb refers to the collective, here comprised of the people, elders, and judges, that is, the representatives of the community (cf. Josh 8:33; 23:2) whose presence guaranteed impartiality.

זקניכה ושופטיכה. This phrase, taken from Deut 21:2, which lays out the regulations regarding cases in which a murderer's identity is unknown, highlights the public nature of the procedure prescribed here for determining whether a person is a false prophet.[30] The elders may have been assigned a role in the ceremony, such as laying of hands on the sacrifice (cf. Lev 4:15; see below).

Ll. 8–9 לפני [הכו]הן המשיח אשר יוצק על ר[ו]אשו שמן המשוחה. The prophet's status is to be determined by "the anointed priest" (הכו[הן המשיח]) in the temple. The text refers here to Deut 17:9. However, Deuteronomy names the Levitical priests or the magistrate as the authorities to whom the case should be brought, whereas the present Qumran text replaces it by "the anointed priest." This change reflects the purpose of the composition, namely, to establish the high priest's status as the supreme legal authority in the land. The identification of a prophet as true or false is thus regarded as falling under the category of cases too difficult for local authorities and therefore needing to be settled before the high priest in the temple.[31] The line stresses the priest's status by calling him "the anointed priest"

---

[30] According to Shemesh ("Halacha," 936), the false prophet was judged by a court of seventy-one members, indicating the importance attached to the issue within the community.

[31] Shemesh notes ("Halacha," 929, 935–40) that the scroll differs in this respect from the rabbinic view, with the Sages transforming the false prophet into a theoretical issue by accentuating the analogy between him and the rebellious elder, whom they regarded as a sage who took a stance and taught in such a way that undermined the authority of the high court. 4Q375, in contrast, outlines a practical test to determine whether a prophet is true or false.

(הכוהן המשיח) and describing the nature of the anointing.³² The reference to the anointing recalls Aaron's investiture in Lev 8:12. The wording here closely corresponds to Lev 21:10, thereby signifying the importance of determining whether a prophet is true or false by stipulating that this decision can only be made by the anointed high priest.³³

שמן המשוחה. The biblical phrase has שמן המִשְחה but the reading with *waw* is clear (see *Notes on Readings*). In the texts, the designation הכהן המשיח is restricted to the high priest whose head is anointed with oil (Lev 4:3, 5, 16), while the ordinary priest (כהן הדיוט) is merely sprinkled with oil. This distinction vanishes in Second Temple Jewish literature.³⁴

Col. ii (b+c)

The second column of 4Q375 has been preserved on two scraps of leather (b and c). Under the assumption that col. ii describes the ceremony depicted in Leviticus 16, Strugnell joined them together, regarding the separated scrap c as a part of col. ii, and interpreted the text on the basis of this reconstruction. However, both the presupposition and restorations are problematic. As there is no physical continuity between the two scraps, their juxtaposition must be justified convincingly. Although the small left-hand scrap (c) most likely belongs to this composition—as indicated by its content and form—its precise placement is difficult to determine. While accepting Strugnell's determination that c forms the continuation of lines 5–8 of col. ii, Qimron in his new edition proposes a variant set of reconstructions that sever the link Strugnell perceived between col. ii and Leviticus 16.³⁵ He also maintains that 4Q376 i parallels 4Q375 i 8–ii 2. The present edition incorporates certain features from the respective editions of Strugnell and Qimron. However, unlike Strugnell, Leviticus 16 is not perceived as having a connection to col. ii (cf. below).

Col. ii elaborates the details of a certain ceremony, but the damaged condition of the scroll makes it difficult to perceive its character. Strugnell, followed

---

32 The high priest is only designated הכהן המשיח in P (cf. Lev 4:3, 16; 6:12). Jacob Milgrom (idem, *Leviticus 1–16* [AB; New York: Doubleday, 1991], 231) notes that this usage was characteristic of the pre-exilic period. The scroll reads שמן המשוחה (cf. 1QM 9:8, 4Q365 9 ii 2, 12 ii 6) rather than the biblical שמן המִשְחה (Lev 8:2, 10). For the appellation הכהן המשיח, see N. Mizrahi, "The Lexicon and Phraseology of the Songs of the Sabbath Sacrifice" (Ph.D. diss.; Hebrew University of Jerusalem, 2008), 134–35 (Hebrew).
33 Brin, "Laws of the Prophets," 37.
34 See Mizrahi, "Lexicon and Phraseology," 134–35, 138.
35 Qimron, *Hebrew Writings*, 2:313.

by Latour and Qimron, regards 1Q29, 4Q375 and 4Q376 as copies of a single composition dealing with the method for identifying a false prophet. He therefore posited that the high priest's inquiry via the Urim and Thummim in 1Q29 1–2 and 4Q376 i–ii illustrates the way in which he determined whether a person was a true or false prophet. However, the composition represented by the various copies is viewed here as addressing various halachic issues. Thus, the inquiry via the Urim in the other copies of the composition is not necessarily related to the issue of the true/false prophet. In fact, the high priest may use other procedures to decide whether a person is a false prophet, such as the entrance through the veil. So the nature of the ceremony referred to by the present Qumran text cannot be ascertained conclusively (see also Comments on col. ii below). As a matter of fact, the present 4Q375 manuscript, dealing as it does with the identification of true and false prophets, does not mention a query by way of the Urim, but an entrance through the veil, whereas 4Q376, which does mentioned the Urim, deals with a different topic, namely, going to war. Strugnell and his followers have not noticed these differences, nor have they taken into account the different biblical sources lying at the base of 4Q376.

```
1  [                                                  ]
2  [                                                  ]
3  ולקח [פר בן בקר          והזה [
4  באצב]עו את הדם
5  בשר האי̊]ל           [ ו̇שעיר עז̊]ים אחד]
6  לחטאת יק̊]ח     וכפ[ר̊ ב̊ע̊ד̊ כול העדה ואח̊]ר יבוא[
7  לפני פרוכת [הקודש אש[ר̊ לארון העדות ודרש את̂ [ ]
8  יהוה לכול [הנפלאות והנסת]ר̊ות ממכה ויצא לפני כ̇]ול [
9  העדה וזה vac [                                    ]     [
                           bottom margin
```

Notes on Readings

L. 9 *vac*. The three-letter-long blank space between the words is not represented in Strugnell's transcription.

Translation

1. [   ]
2. [   ]
3. and he shall take [a bull of the herd,   and he shall sprinkle]
4. with [his] finge[r the blood   ]

5. the flesh of the ra[m] and [one] hairy go[at]
6. shall he ta[ke] for a sin offering [and he shall make at]onement on behalf of all the assembly. And af[terwards he shall come]
7. before the veil [of the shrine] that is [o]n the Ark of the Pact, and shall inquire [ ]
8. YHWH about all [the matters wondrous and hidd]en from you. And he shall [co]me forth before a[ll]
9. the congregation. And this [ ]

Comments

The extant text of col. ii indicates that here the scroll is reworking Lev 4:21–23, a passage dealing with sin committed inadvertently by the congregation. As all the words in this column except "the flesh of the ra[m" (בשר האי]ל) in line 5) appear in Leviticus 4, this chapter rather than Leviticus 16, as suggested by Strugnell, should be regarded as forming the biblical basis of the text.

Ll. 1–2 These lines have not been preserved. As noted above, Qimron inserts 4Q376 i 2–3 here, a reconstruction that implies that the sacrifice depicted here is related to the inquiry via the Urim and Thummim mentioned in 4Q376, suggesting that this column precedes such an inquiry. However, as no connection between the offering and the Urim and Thummim has been preserved, and no such offering is known from the biblical texts, no connection between the two is assumed here. It is proposed that the sacrifice in question here constitutes a sin offering on behalf of the congregation, given its similarity to the depiction of such an offering in Leviticus 4 (see Comments on lines 3–7 below).

Ll. 3–4 והזה [באצב]עו את הדם. This is a reworking of Lev 4:17, which describes the purification ceremony when a sacrifice is offered for a wrong done inadvertently by the community. The Qumran text appears to describe the same act of purification depicted in Leviticus.

L. 3 ולקח [פר בן בקר. The restoration is based on Lev 4:14. This phrase does not appear in Leviticus 4, but the verb ולקח is one of the three verbal forms found in the biblical account, referring to sacrificing by the high priest.

L. 5 בשר האי]ל. This phrase alludes to the consumption of the ram of ordination offered at the priests' investiture (Exod 29:32). In the parallel description in Leviticus 8, only "the flesh" is adduced (v. 31), with vv. 22 and 29 indicating that the reference is to the ram of ordination. As the biblical texts only refer to the flesh of a sacrifice when it is consumed, this appears to be the meaning here, too, the flesh of the ram perhaps being eaten by the high priest. *Contra* Strugnell, who regards col. ii as reworking Leviticus 16, the phrase בשר האיל does not derive from this biblical text, for Leviticus 16 prescribes that the ram be burnt completely on the altar. The present scroll also refers to Leviticus 8 (in col. i 9) but in connection with the pouring of the anointing oil on the priest's head (cf. Lev 8:12). While such echoes of Leviticus 8 suggest that this text also reworks this biblical chapter, the precise relation between Leviticus 4 and 8 (or Exodus 29) here and the nature of the ceremony conducted in the temple remain obscure.

וּשְׂעִיר עִזִּ[ים אחד] [. Here, the text resumes its reworking of Leviticus 4, with this line apparently relating to Lev 4:23 and the chieftains' sin offering. The reworking is clearly attached to Leviticus 4 rather than Lev 16:5–7, the latter text speaking of two goats and its context being the Day of Atonement.

Ll. 6–7 וְאָ[ח]ר יבוא] לפני פרוכת [הקודש אש]ר לארון העדות. This line reworks Lev 4:17. According to Lev 4:1–21, a sin committed inadvertently by the congregation or high priest defiles the altar in front of the veil in the sanctuary, necessitating its purification via the sprinkling of the blood of the bull of the sin offering.[36] The words באצבֹ]עו and לפני פרוכת in lines 4 and 7 point to a similar purification ceremony.

L. 6 לחטאת יקֹ[ח] וכפ]ר בֹּעַֹד כול העדה. According to Leviticus, the congregation's sin is to be atoned for by the offering of a bull as a sin offering (Lev 4:14, 20). Apart from Leviticus 16, Leviticus 4 is the only text that speaks of the sin offering as atoning for a sin rather than serving as a form of physical purification.[37] As the scroll does not deal with the latter issue, this is evidently not the meaning of the phrase here. The community's sin appears to be related in some way to the uncertainty regarding a prophet's identity: it refers either to a person pretending to be a true prophet who leads them astray, or to their failure to recognize someone as a true prophet. The fact that the priest performs the act within the sanctuary but not within the Holy of Holies is also significant for our understanding of the text and determination of its biblical background. This passage forms additional proof that the scroll reinterprets Leviticus 4 as a ritual for the atonement of a sin committed inadvertently by the congregation—and perhaps the chieftains—rather than Leviticus 16 and the ceremony related to the Day of Atonement performed within the Holy of Holies. Strugnell and Shemesh regard the procedure

---

36 Milgrom, *Leviticus*, 257. Milgrom distinguishes between three types of defilement of the temple based on the type of impurity or sin committed by the person presenting the sin offering.
37 See *ibid*, 253.

to determine whether a prophet is true or false as being performed in the Holy of Holies in front of the curtain of the Ark of the Pact, with God revealing Himself above the *kapporet* (כפרת), the golden cover on the top of the ark (Exod 25:17; 36:6), and indicating whether the prophet is true or false.[38] However, according to Lev 16:3, the high priest is only allowed to enter the Holy of Holies when sacrificing the bull of the sin offering or the ram of the burnt offering. Lev 16:29–34 states that the single occasion on which he is permitted to enter the Holy of Holies is the Day of Atonement. The discrepancy between these two texts is customarily explained as deriving from a conflation of the Priestly and Holiness Code sources (Lev 16:1–28 and Lev 16:29–34). The presence of the two manuscripts of Leviticus in the Qumran library indicates that the *Vorlage* that lay before the author of 4Q375 was the same as the extant MT.[39] Thus, they were faced with the prohibition against entering the Holy of Holies except on the Day of Atonement. The restriction on the high priest's entry within this sanctum precludes the assumption that the ceremony described in the second column took place in this holy place.

L. 7 פרוכת. The noun perhaps forms part of a construct phrase and thus is restored as פרוכת [הקודש], following Lev 4:6 (thus Strugnell). Qimron restores פרוכת [המסך]; cf. e.g. Exod 35:12 and repeatedly in Exod 25:1–27:19 in the description of the erection of the Ark. While the Ark was placed within the Holy of Holies, our text stresses—in line with Lev 4:17—that the high priest does not enter within the veil that separates it from the sanctuary.

Ll. 7–8 ודרש את [ ] יהוה לכול [הנפלאות והנסת]רֹות ממכה. Strugnell's reconstruction הנפלאות והנסת[רֹות] is based on Deut 17:8. Our text hints at this verse in the first column when it states that the people must go to "the place which thy God shall choose from one (of the territories of) thy tribes … into the presence of [the]

---

38 Strugnell, "Apocryphon of Moses," 116; Shemesh, "Halacha," 939; Shemesh, *Halakhah*, 53–55.
39 In 4QLev-Num[a] (4Q23 8–14 i 1–16), Lev 16:15–29 appears as a single continuous passage. Ulrich's reconstruction of v. 29 is based on the length of the lacuna at the end of v. 28: E. Ulrich, "4QLev-Num[a]," in *Qumran Cave 4.VII: Genesis to Numbers* (ed. E. Ulrich et al.; DJD XII; Oxford: Clarendon Press, 1996), 159. 11QpaleoLev[a] preserves Lev 16:16 and 34 in two separate fragments of the same manuscript: see D. N. Freedman and K. A. Mathews, *The Paleo-Hebrew Leviticus Scroll from Qumran* (Winona Lake: Eisenbrauns, 1985); É. Puech, "Notes en marge de 11QPaléoLévitique: Le Fragment L, des fragments inédits et une jarre de la grotte 11," *RB* 86 (1989): 161–83. The text in these fragments is very close to MT. So the author of 4Q375 was probably aware of the biblical prohibition against entering the Holy of Holies, except for the High Priest on the Day of Atonement.

anointed [p]riest" (lines 7–9). This restoration appears to strengthen the link with Deuteronomy 17, highlighting the purpose of the anointed priest's acts by describing how he inquired of God in a case "too baffling" for him to reach a decision. This line depicts the way in which the high priest received God's answer regarding whether someone was a true or false prophet, a case too difficult for him to determine without divine assistance. Strugnell's reconstruction הנסת[רוֹת ("hidden things") is plausible in this context and in light of the preserved letters. The term is taken from Deut 29:28, where it forms the reverse of the "revealed things" (נגלֹת).[40] In the Qumran sectarian writings, נגלות represent the injunctions given to Israel as a whole at Sinai, while the נסתרות are those given exclusively to the Qumran community.[41] However, in the present text, the latter term appears to bear the biblical sense of the commandments and interpretations known only to God. As he is not being able to determine whether a person is a true or false prophet, the anointed priest must seek divine revelation in order to deliver a verdict. In its extant state, the scroll gives no indication of the method of inquiry employed by the high priest. The terminology in lines 7–8 differs from that in the remainder of col. ii. While the majority of the allusions in this column are to Leviticus 4 and 8, here the text resumes its reworking of Deuteronomy, specifically Deut 29:28 and, if the reconstruction is correct, Deut 17:8. The fact that the root ד"רש also appears in 1Q29 5–7 suggests that the present scarp (4Q375 ii c) may belong with 1Q29 5–7 (see the comments on 1Q29 5–7).

Ll. 8–9 ויצא לפני כ[ו]ל [העדה. Having received an answer from God on a case that was too difficult for him to reach a decision, the priest then leaves the sanctuary and announces the verdict to the awaiting people. The scroll seems to allude here to Lev 4:13–21, which deals with the sin offering made on behalf of the com-

---

40 The biblical verse is customarily understood to distinguish between "concealed" and "overt" sins, the former being hidden from human beings but known to God and the latter being those punishable by a human court. Alternatively, the נסתרות ("hidden things") signify the reason for and purpose of the commandments, which are known only to God, the נגלות ("revealed things") being the ordinances themselves. See Tigay, *Deuteronomy*, 283.
41 Cf. CD III, 14; 1QS V, 11–12; 4Q266 2 i 3–6. Cana Werman suggests that the Qumran sectarians understood the vocalization points above the words in Deut 29:28 as signs indicating that the letters should be deleted, affording a dual reading of the verse: "the concealed things are God's concern" or "the concealed and overt things are for us and our children." According to her, the dual reading led the Qumranites to advance a new interpretation of the "hidden things," which were transferred from God to the community. Cf. eadem, "The Authorization for the Development of Halakhah," in *Revealing the Hidden: Exegesis and Halakha in the Qumran Scrolls* (ed. C. Werman and A. Shemesh; Jerusalem: Bialik Institute, 2011), 72–103 (81–82) (Hebrew).

munity of Israel for inadvertent transgressions (v. 13). Such an understanding is supported by the fact that the scroll deals with a community, as seen in the reference to the tribe, elders, and judges in the third part of col. i (line 9), and the fact that the case is determined by the anointed priest rather than an ordinary priest serving in the temple. The question of whether a person is a true or false prophet is of great interest and import to the whole congregation, who may have been led astray, advertently or inadvertently, if he was a false prophet. The high priest's exit from the temple to deliver God's answer to the awaiting people is a recurring theme in this scroll (see also the comments on 4Q376 ii and 1Q29 1–2) and thus forms a key element within it.

L. 9] חזה *vac.* This word introduces a new subject, as indicated by the small uninscribed space separating it from the preceding word עדה. The continuation may have detailed the divine answer received by the anointed priest, or the author may have moved on to a reworking of another Deuteronomic injunction.

Discussion

A detailed analysis of 4Q375 reveals that it centers upon the procedure employed to distinguish between true and false prophets. It does so by reworking various passages from Deuteronomy (Deut 13:1–6; 17: 8–9; 18:15–20; 29: 28; 30:2–3).

Col. i

Part 1: The Obligation to Heed the Prophet (lines 1–4 a)
The interweaving of Deut 13:2 and 18:18–20 in the present column indicates that the author made no distinction between the prophet who leads the people into idolatry and the false prophet.

The reworking of Deut 13:1, 4 together with 18:18 and 30:2–3 offers a new interpretation of the prophet's functions, suggesting that heeding him (Deut 18:18) takes the form of observing God's commandments without adding to or detracting from them (Deut 13: 1). Doing so faithfully with all one's heart and soul (Deut 13:4, 30:2) secures the covenantal blessings (Deut 30:2–10) and God's forgiveness (Deut 30:3), withdrawing his wrath. Therefore 4Q375 regards the heeding of the prophet as playing a key role in bringing the time of judgment to an end and introducing the fulfillment of the covenantal blessings.

The theme of heeding the true prophet because he delivers God's commandments is treated by other Qumran writings, both sectarian and nonsectarian, so it is interesting to see how 4Q375 fits into this picture. In the *Rule of the Community* (1QS), the sectaries are to devote themselves to serving God by observing his laws and statutes: "In order to seek God with [all the heart and soul] doing what is good and right before him, as he commanded through Moses and through all his servants the prophets."[42] The *Pesher of Hosea* and the nonsectarian *Apocryphon of Jeremiah C* both reprove the people for failing to observe God's laws as given by the prophets (4Q166 ii 4–5; 4Q390 2 i 4–5). Thus, the injunction to heed the prophet who transmits God's statutes appears to be a prevalent theme in sectarian as well as in rewritten Bible texts. However, the view that a person can only obtain the covenantal blessings by obedience to the prophet seems to be unique to the composition embodied in 4Q375 and its other copies.

The *Words of the Luminaries* reworks Deut 30:2–10 in a slightly different fashion: "You have shown covenant mercies to your people Israel in all [the] lands to which You have exiled them. You have again placed it in their hearts to return to you, to obey your voice [according] to all that you have commanded through Your servant Moses" (4Q504 XVIII, 12–15).[43] In contrast to 4Q375, this text implies that the punishment and mercy described in Deuteronomy 30 have already occurred.[44] Like 4Q375, it also regards the covenantal blessings as being given independently of obedience to the prophet. According to both these texts, God's mercy prompts the people to repent and observe the commandments delivered by Moses.[45]

Part 2: The False Prophet (lines 4b–5a)

The second part of col. i describes the false prophet as the antithesis of the prophet who is to be heeded. Although the scroll reworks Deut 13:2, 6, which deals with the prophet who leads the people into idolatry, the passage in the present text relates to the false prophet. The application to the false prophet of the phrase לדבר סרה (Deut 13:6), which describes the behavior of the prophet who leads people to commit idolatry, suggests that as early as the biblical period itself the two laws of Deut 13:2–6 and 18:15–20 were regarded as relating to the false

---

42 *PTSDSSP* 1:7.
43 *DSSR* 5:253.
44 Esther Chazon suggests that the *Words of the Luminaries* relates Leviticus 26 and Deuteronomy 30 to the return from the Babylonian exile. See eadem, "A Liturgical Document from Qumran and its Implications: Words of the Luminaries" (Ph.D. diss.; Hebrew University of Jerusalem, 1992) 269, 276 (Hebrew).
45 According to Chazon (ibid, 277–89), in contrast to other prayers that rework Deuteronomy 30, that in the *Words of the Luminaries* states that God's mercy precedes the people's repentance.

prophet; cf. Jer 28:16, 29:32. ⁴⁶The same tradition is also found in later rabbinic literature.⁴⁷ 4Q375 thus constitutes further ancient evidence that both Deut 13:2–6 and 18:15–20 address the issue of the false prophet. The author of the scroll may have preferred the terminology used in Deuteronomy 13 to that in Deuteronomy 18 because of the use of the verb יומת in the former. For the present context, it is important to note that Deut 13:6 stipulates that the false prophet is to be sentenced by a human court, thus facilitating the possibility of bringing testimony on behalf of the person suspected of false prophecy.

Part 3: The Decision Delivered by the High Priest (lines 5b–9)

As the scroll makes clear, establishing whether a prophet is true or false was a matter of vital importance to the community. Thus, the case is judged in the temple by the high priest in the presence of the elders and judges. As Jeremiah's unfair trial (Jer 26:7–24) demonstrates, the charge of being a false prophet was decided via judicial proceedings. While Jeremiah defended himself before the acting magistrates, testifying of himself that "It was the LORD who sent me to prophesy against this house and this city all the words you heard" (Jer 26:12), in 4Q375 it is the tribe who testifies of the faithful and true character of the person who belongs to it, the issue being settled by the high priest in a ceremony performed in the temple. The difficulty posed by the mention of the prophet's "tribe" has been noted in the Comments above, where it is suggested that perhaps it is the interpretation of the word מקרבך in the relevant biblical verse (Deut 18:15) and that it may allude to the prophet in question being a member of the (Qumran?) community. If the term שבט ("tribe") hints at the controversies of the Qumranites, the preoccupation with the issue of false/true prophets may reflect the sectarian practice of labeling their opponents as false prophets and their concern in establishing a procedure by which one of their own speakers may be proven to be a true prophet.

According to the Mishnah, the case of a false prophet was to be judged by a court of seventy-one judges (m. Sanh. 1:5). This view appears to correspond to that reflected in 4Q375, which regards the matter of the false prophet as a "hidden" issue to be settled by the highest authority in Jerusalem.⁴⁸ Both the Qumran text and the Mishnah seem to reflect an interpretative tradition of the phrase כי יפלא

---

46 See Rofé, *Deuteronomy*, 215
47 Shemesh, "Halacha," 159–65.
48 As Tigay (*Deuteronomy*, 163–64) notes, rabbinic halachic texts understand Deut 17:8–13 as referring to the Great Sanhedrin in Jerusalem.

ממך דבר למשפט (Deut 17:8). This suggestion is further evidence of the combining of Deut 17:8 with Deut 29:28 made by col. ii, whereby the "hidden things" are identified as "baffling" legal issues that can only be resolved by going up to the court in Jerusalem. The major divergence of the scroll from the ruling of Deut 17:9 in this matter is in its provision that the anointed priest rather than the magistrates possess the supreme judicial authority in the Jerusalem temple. This theme is a key element in the present Qumran composition, apparently reflecting the intention to establish that the high priest holds authority over both prophets and judges.

Thus, the reworking in 4Q375 of the laws regarding the false prophet in Deut 13:2–6, 18:15–20, and 17:8–13 shows that the matter of whether a person is a true or false prophet was regarded as a legal issue to be settled by the highest legal authority in Jerusalem.

Col. ii

Sacrificing a Sin Offering and Inquiring of God

The affinity between col. ii and Lev 4:13–21 suggests that several of the details in col. i (such as the "anointed priest" and the "elders") may also be based on this biblical text. The "anointed priest" as an appellation for the high priest (col. i 9) corresponds to Lev 4:16. The elders referred to in col. i as being amongst those who accompany the party to Jerusalem (4Q375 i 7) may also be required for the laying of hands on the sin offering mentioned in col. ii (cf. Lev 4:15). If this scriptural passage lies at the center of col. ii, the fragment describes a ceremony of atonement conducted by the anointed priest in the temple, which included the sacrificing of a sin offering to atone for the sin of the entire congregation. In commenting on Lev 4:21, Milgrom proposes that perhaps the high priest himself inadvertently misled the people. He suggests that in the case of 4Q375 the false prophet misled his own tribe.[49]

However, despite the fragmentary state of 4Q375, its focus on how a prophet is identified as true or false suggests that here the sin offering is due to the offence of being misled by a false prophet. Alternatively, it may have been the failure to obey a true prophet whom they erroneously believed to be a false prophet.

As noted above, col. i 7–8 deals with a difficult legal case such as those addressed in Deut 17:8 (כי יפלא ממך דבר למשפט); "if a case is too baffling for you to

---

[49] See Milgrom, *Leviticus*, 242. However, if this was true the prophet would have "wittingly" represented himself as a true prophet.

judge") while col. ii adduces the sin offering that atones for a sin committed inadvertently by the congregation (Lev 4:13–21). Thus, both texts deal with things that are "unknown": a legal uncertainty and an unwitting transgression. If the scroll interlinks these two themes, it suggests that failure to identify a false prophet may fall under the category of inadvertent sin. The prophet's responsibility for delivering God's commandments (4Q375 i 1–2) demonstrates his crucial role in instructing them to obey them "with all their heart and soul" in order to receive the divine blessings.[50]

In reworking a priestly-cultic section of the Pentateuch, col. ii betrays its priestly agenda, suggesting the authorship of a priestly group. This comes out clearly in col. ii, which details the way in which legal decisions are to be resolved by the offering of sacrifices and conducting of ritual ceremonies by the high priest in the Jerusalem temple.

This composition highlights the socio-religious significance of identifying whether a prophet is true or false, and presents the prophet as being responsible for delivering the divine commandments whose observance is requisite for averting God's wrath and obtaining the covenantal promises. In contrast to the rabbinic notion that "After the later prophets Haggai, Zechariah, and Malachi had died, the Holy Spirit departed from Israel" (*b. Yoma* 9b), the present Qumran text deals with prophecy as a real phenomenon since it offers a practical method for ascertaining whether a prophet is true or false. Not only does the scroll assert that prophecy continues, but it also assigns to the prophet a crucial role in the observance of the covenantal prophecies. This may form the context of the list of false prophets given in the nonsectarian 4Q339; a group that does not believe in the current existence of prophecy would be unlikely to record a roster of false prophets.[51]

The scroll may possibly reflect a sectarian polemic with its opponents, each accusing the other of being misled by a false prophet. This view is supported by the fact that the pesharim designate the community's opponents via sobriquets borrowed from biblical passages dealing with false prophets. While it does not contain sectarian terminology, the question of the relationship of 4Q375 to the Qumran literature remains unresolved.

---

50 Cf. 1QS I, 2–3; 4Q166 ii 4–5.
51 See M. Broshi and A. Yardeni, "4QList of False Prophets," *Qumran Cave 4.XIV: Parabiblical Texts, Part 2* (ed. M. Broshi et al.; DJD XIX; Oxford: Clarendon Press, 1995), 77–79.

4Q376: The Rules Regulating Permitted Wars

Literature

J. Strugnell, "Moses-Pseudepigrapha at Qumran: 4Q375, 4Q376, and Similar Works," in *Archaeology and History in the Dead Sea Scrolls* (ed. L. H. Schiffman; JSPSup 8; Sheffield: Sheffield Academic Press, 1990), 221–56; idem, "Apocryphon of Moses," in *Qumran Cave 4.XIV: Parabiblical Texts, Part 2* (ed. M. Broshi et al.; DJD XIX; Oxford: Clarendon Press, 1995), 111–36; É. Latour, "Une Proposition de Reconstruction de l'Apocryphe de Moïse (1Q29, 4Q375, 4Q376, 4Q408)," *RevQ* 22 (2006): 575–91; L. Goldman, "The Rules Regarding fighting a Permitted War in 4Q376," *Meghillot* 8–9 (2010): 319–41 (Hebrew); eadem, "The *Apocryphon of Moses*: A Composition Representing the High Priest as the Supreme Judicial Authority," *Meghillot* 10 (2013): 181–200 (Hebrew); E. Qimron, *The Dead Sea Scrolls: The Hebrew Writings, Volume Two* (Jerusalem: Yad Ben-Zvi Press, 2013), 311–15 (Hebrew).

The Manuscript

4Q376 consists of one fragment containing three columns, in which the three upper lines have been preserved, the top margins being 12 mm in width. The margin between the first and second columns is 20–25 mm wide, and that between the second and third columns measures 15 mm. The first and third columns are fragmentary, the right margin of the first column and the left margin of the third column being missing. Only the second (middle) column has been preserved in its original width. The dimensions of the fragment cannot be estimated precisely due to the shrinkage and wrinkling of the leather. The average space between the lines is 7.5 mm. The middle column is the most complete, with its 10-cm width containing space for approximately fifty letters. The third column is 11 cm wide and in its fragmentary state has room for fifty-five letters. No indication of the number of letters which could complete the end of this third column is available.[1]

Strugnell's paleographic dating of the scroll places it between the end of the Hasmonean period and the beginning of the Herodian period. The spelling is mostly full, and the pronominal endings (אוריכה, אליכה, etc.) follow the practice in many Qumran scrolls.

---

[1] Strugnell's data ("Apocryphon of Moses," 121) differ slightly. According to his estimation, the second column contains space for forty to forty-five letters, with the third column containing space for at least fifty-four letters.

Text and Comments

Col. i

top margin

[	]o̊נ̊י הכ׳הן המשיח	1
[	פר אח[ד̊ בן בקר̊ ואיל [אחד]	2
[	ooo לא̊ו̊רים	3

Notes on Readings

L. 1 המשיח. With Strugnell. The reading of a *yod* rather than a *waw* is preferable due to the slightly curved head of the letter, which is typical of a *yod*.

L. 2 פר אח[ד̊. Of the last letter, only the edge of the upper horizontal stroke, and the bottom tip of a right perpendicular stroke are seen. They match either *dalet* or *resh*. Strugnell reads a *resh* (פ]ר), but a *dalet* is preferred here given the context (see Comments).

L. 3 ooo[. Two black dots that form the upper end of one or two letters are visible at the right end of line 3, alongside the tear in the scroll. The leather has been twisted, making it difficult to ascertain whether they belong to a word in line 3 —as suggested here—or to a word in line 4.

Translation

1. [   ]... the anointed priest
2. [on]e [bull] of the herd and [one] ram [ ]
3. [   ]... for the Urim

Comments

Strugnell judged that this column belongs at the end of the first column and beginning of the second column of 4Q375, which also contains the phrase לפני הכוהן המשיח ("before the anointed priest"). He thus regards the description of the acts performed by the high priest and the testing of the prophet as sequential units.[2] However, the lack of thematic and contextual continuity between the

---

[2] Ibid., 123. Both Latour ("Proposition," 585) and Qimron (*Hebrew Writings*, 2:312–13) accept this reconstruction and integrate 4Q376 i into the end of the first and beginning of the second columns of 4Q375. However, this reconstruction subsumes the לאורים in 4Q376 i 3 within the descrip-

columns of this scroll (4Q376) and the second column of 4Q375 militate against this reading. Herein, it is proposed that the text of 4Q376 does not overlaps the text of 4Q375 and deals with a different topic: the rules governing engaging in a permitted war.

L. 1 ‏נ]ו הכוהן המשיח‎. The beginning may be reconstructed ‏לפני‎ ("before the anointed priest"; cf. 4Q375 i 8–9). The "anointed priest" is referred to on four occasions in the biblical texts, three times in Leviticus 4 (vv. 3, 5, 16) and once in Lev 6:15. The person in question is the high priest, who is described as being anointed with oil in Lev 8:10–13.[3]

L. 2 ‏פר אח]ד בן בקר ואיל [אחד‎. This and the preceding line form part of a ritual text describing the sacrifices offered by the "anointed priest."[4] Bullocks and rams are frequent objects of sacrifice in the biblical cult. The closest example to 4Q376 is the burnt offering of "one young bull, one ram, one male lamb a year old" made by the tribal chieftains at the dedication of the tabernacle in the wilderness (Num 7:15–81). The ‏נשיא‎ is mentioned in col. iii and therefore he might be the figure alluded to here (see below). The textual affinities with Numbers 7, which speaks of a single ram, suggest that the reconstruction ‏פר אח]ד בן בקר ואיל [אחד‎ is preferable.[5] Although this accentuates the offering made by the chieftain (Num 7:10), the identification is not complete because Numbers 7 also speaks of a one-year-old lamb for a burnt offering, a male goat for a sin offering, and additional thanksgiving sacrifices. Likewise, the discussions of warfare in the *War Scroll* and *Temple Scroll* contain no recognizable parallel to sacrifices offered by a chieftain or king before going out to battle. As noted above, Qimron regards 4Q376 i as a parallel to 4Q375 i 9–ii 2, thus positing that the bullock and ram formed part of the sacrifices offered by the anointed priest in the temple prior to inquiring about the status of the prophet. However, only the phrase ‏לפני הכהן המשיח‎ appears in both texts, the other lines being absent. The reference to the ram's flesh in 4Q375 ii 5 also indicates that this was not a burnt offer-

---

tion of the sprinkling of blood by the anointed priest in 4Q375 ii 2–4. As the inquiry of God and sprinkling of blood are two unrelated issues, they cannot be conjoined.

3 See Comments on 4Q375 i 9.

4 Qimron, *Hebrew Writings*, 2:312–13.

5 Strugnell ("Apocryphon of Moses," 123) noted that an empty space is clearly visible after the *lamed*, and therefore his reconstruction ‏ואיל]ים‎ must be rejected. While the missing section of the third line allows for the description of other offerings, space must be left for the beginning of the new subject of the Urim. For the Second Temple understanding of the Urim and Thummim, see the Discussion below.

ing. Thus, this text must refer to another event/sacrifice. The most probable reference here is therefore to the freewill offering brought to the priest by the chieftain before he inquires via the Urim whether the people should engage in war.

L. 3 לאׄוׄרים. This is the only remaining word in this line, appearing at the end. The anointed priest is associated with the offering brought by the chieftain and the inquiry made via the Urim. Notably, in its extant state, this column concludes with the word לאׄוׄרים ("Urim") while the first word of the second column, ואוריׄכה, is also connected with the Urim. The first and second columns are thus substantively sequential. The missing lines may also have dealt with the Urim. The word Urim occurs with the preposition *lamed* in Ezra 2:63 and Neh 7:65: עד עמד כהן לאורים ותמים ("until there should arise a priest to consult the Urim and Thummim"). The Urim and Thummim are referred to together five times in the biblical text, with the Urim appearing twice alone (Num 27:21; 1 Sam 28:8). They were holy lots embedded in the high priest's breastplate whereby he inquired of God concerning whether to engage in war (Num 27:21; 1 Sam 28:6), how to allot the tribal inheritances, and how to identify figures chosen by God.[6] The biblical sources neither provide us with a physical description of the Urim and Thummim nor describe how the inquiry was made.[7] According to Exod 28:30 and Lev 8:8, the high priest placed the Urim in his breastplate over his heart. The scrolls contain two examples of inquiry via the Urim prior to going out to war. The *Temple Scroll* (11QT[a] LVIII, 15–21) reworks Num 27:21 in a section describing the obligations imposed upon the king when engaging in a permitted war, one of which was to ask the high priest for a decision via the Urim and Thummim.[8] In the *Apocryphon of Joshua*, the phrase "Urim and Thummim" has been reconstructed in a fragment that speaks of Joshua being rebuked for failing to inquire of the Urim regarding how to deal with the Gibeonites (4Q522 9 ii 10–11).[9] I suggest that the reference to the Urim here relates to the same matter. 4Q376 iii alludes to the "chieftain" who is the military commander, the "camp" set opposite the enemy, and the "siege of a city."[10]

---

6 Cf. H. J. Tigay, *The JPS Torah Commentary: Deuteronomy* (Philadelphia: JPS, 1996), 324.
7 Jacob Milgrom suggests that they were stones, arrows, or sticks. Cf. idem, *The JPS Torah Commentary: Numbers* (Philadelphia: JPS, 1990), 485.
8 See Y. Yadin, *The Temple Scroll* (Jerusalem: IEJ, 1983), 2:182–86 (Hebrew).
9 See D. Dimant, "The Apocryphon of Joshua – 4Q522 9 ii: A Reappraisal," in *History, Ideology and Bible Interpretation in the Dead Sea Scrolls: Collected Studies* (FAT 90; Tübingen: Mohr Siebeck, 2014), 335–52 (46–52).
10 Christophe Batsch also interprets the Urim and Thummim in 4Q376 as being linked to the chieftain's inquiry as to whether or not to engage in battle. See idem, *La Guerre et les Rites de Guerre dans le Judaïsme du Deuxième Temple* (JSJSup 93; Leiden: Brill, 2005), 329–30.

Col. ii

top margin

1 ואוריׄכה ויצא עמו בלשונות אש האבן השמאׄלׄית אשר על צדו
2 השמאלי תגלה לעיני כול הקהל עד כלות הכוהן לדבר ואחר נעלה
3 [הענן]לׄ לׄ[ooo] [ו]אתה תשמור וׄעׄ[שיתה כו]לׄ[אשר] יׄדׄבׄרׄ[א]לׄיׄכׄהׄ

Notes on Readings

L. 1 ואוריׄכה. Strugnell reads יׄאיׄרוׄכׄהׄ. However, in spite of the similarity between *yod* and *waw* in this manuscript, they may be distinguished. The *waw* is slightly thinner and has a more pointed head (see PAM 41421, 43478). Accordingly, the word is read here with a *waw* at the beginning.

השמאׄלׄית. With Qimron. Strugnell has השמאלית. The scroll is torn in the middle of this word and the words are thus preserved in two parts.

Translation

1. and your Urim. And he shall go out with him, with tongues of fire. The left-hand stone which is on his left-hand
2. side shall shine forth before the eyes of all the assembly until the priest finishes speaking. And afterwards [the cloud] lifts
3. [ ].. you shall keep and per[form al]l[that] he shall tell [y]ou

Comments

The principal difficulty in this column lies in determining the number and identity of the persons to which it refers. Two figures are explicitly adduced in the second line: the "congregation"—a collective designation for the whole of Israel—and the "priest" (see Discussion).

L. 1 ואוריׄכה ויצא עמו בלשונות אש. This sentence contains several difficulties. Not only it is unclear how the word ואוריכה is linked to the continuation but the line has no parallel in the biblical texts. Two subjects are indicated, "your light" (אוריׄכה), 2nd pers. sg. pronoun, and יצא, 3rd pers. sg. verb. The phrase ויצא עמו ("and he shall go out with him") adduces two figures, one of whom accompanies the other when he "goes out." I suggest that the text originally comprised two sentences, the first concluding with ואוריׄכה, and the second opening with ויצא.

ואוריׄכה. Strugnell reads here the form יׄאיׄרוׄכה (see Notes on Readings), parsing it as a *Hif'il yiqqtol* masc. pl. verb, with a 2nd pers. sg. pronominal suffix ("they shall give you light").[11] Nevertheless, he notes that the reading ואוריכה is also possible on the basis of Deut 33:8. Indeed, the physical evidence, the syntax, and the context support this reading, which links back to col. i. The 2nd per. pronominal suffix may be taken from or reflect the language of Deut 33:8, namely, referring to God. The conjunctive *waw* indicates the presence of a previous noun that is now lost. Perhaps it was תומיכה ("your Thummim"), modeled on the Deuteronomistic pair תמיך ואוריך (Deut 33:8). The following words, ויצא עמו ("and he shall go out with him") plausibly begin a new sentence in the proceedings. The first stage of the ceremony described here takes place in the temple, the second is constituted by the (high priest's) "going out" to the assembled people. So the first sentence concludes the theme of the Urim that began in line 3 of the previous column. The close thematic links between the columns is best explained by the assumption that each column was comprised of merely three to five lines.[12]

ויצא עמו. The identity of the person going out and the one who accompanies him, the place they are leaving, and where they are going are difficult to determine. Various scholars maintain that the principal subject is the anointed priest who is referred to in the first column and appears again in the following line.[13] Strugnell and Latour propose that the priest is accompanied by the prophet whose status the priest is seeking to determine.[14] However, 4Q376 and 4Q375 display different sequences. The three columns of 4Q376 display a clear continuity while the two columns of 4Q375 are linked by sequentiality. Therefore, 4Q376 cannot be regarded as a continuation or parallel of 4Q375 as there is insufficient space for the insertion of the three columns of 4Q376 at the end of the first column and beginning of the second column of 4Q375.[15] Instead, the context demands that the

---

11 Strugnell, "Apocryphon of Moses," 125
12 The linkage proposed here differs from Latour's ("Proposition," 585–86) and Qimron's (*Hebrew Writings*, 2:312–14) reconstruction, which regards 4Q376 i as belonging to the end of the first column and beginning of the second column of 4Q375, with 4Q376 ii belonging to the second column of 4Q375. Latour inserts 4Q376 iii following the three sections of 1Q29 (frgs. 1, 2. 5–7). According to this reconstruction, no conceptual continuity exists between the three columns of 4Q376 other than inquiry of the Urim.
13 Strugnell ("Apocryphon of Moses," 124) tentatively suggests that the priest is the person who goes out with the tongues of fire. Cf. also Latour, "Proposition," 590.
14 Strugnell, ibid.,126; Latour, ibid, 590–91. This suggestion is based on the parallel formulation in 1Q29 1, which refers to the "priest" in line 4 and the "prophet" and "the one speaking rebellion" in lines 5–6. The principal problem derives from the lack of clarity regarding the relationship between 1Q29 1–2 and 4Q376 ii and the fact that, while the two fragments of 1Q29 partially overlap with 4Q376 ii, they are not identical to it. See Comments on 1Q29.
15 Cf. Latour, "Proposition," 585–86 and Qimron, *Hebrew Writings*, 2:312–14.

person who accompanies the high priest as he exits the temple to the people is the "chieftain" (נשיא), mentioned in the third column of the present manuscript, and it is perhaps he who offered a sacrifice in col. i. We may thus reconstruct the event portrayed as follows: the high priest enters the temple in order to inquire via the Urim whether the people should go out to war. Having received an answer from God, he goes out to deliver it to the people assembled outside, accompanied by the chieftain as the commander of the troops. Num 27:12–23 describes a similar circumstance at the appointing of Moses' successor.

בלשונות אש. The phrase "tongues of fire" is unique to the three manuscripts belonging to the *Apocryphon of Moses*, recurring in them four times (4Q376 ii 1; 1Q29 1 3; 1Q29 2 3; 4Q408 11 2) and providing the basis for the argument that they represent copies of the same composition. 1Q29, in which the phrase occurs twice, states that they were three in number (1Q29 2 3). The expression occurs nowhere in the biblical texts. Isa 5:24 refers to a "tongue of fire" consuming straw, a literal description used as a simile for the demise of the wicked. The "cloven tongues like as of fire" in Acts 4:2–4 symbolize the Holy Spirit descending upon the apostles and enabling them to prophesy. However, they are in a private house rather than the temple and no association appears to exist with either the high priest or the Urim. As Strugnell notes, the closest parallel lies in Josephus' description of the high priest's garments.[16] Josephus describes how one of the stones on the high priest's ephod "shone out" and emitted "bright rays" despite such a quality not being natural to its constitution, its "splendor" being so great that it was visible even to "those that were most remote." The image of "tongues of fire" corresponds closely to this depiction. For the link between the tongues of fire and the Urim, see below.

Ll. 1–2 השמאלי. האבן השמאלית אשר על צדו. These lines appear to refer to the onyx stone on the shoulder piece of the high priest's ephod (Exod 28:9–12). On the basis of Josephus' account (*Ant.* iii, 214–216) and 1Q29 2 2, Strugnell suggests that this represented the first stage in determining whether a prophet was true or

---

[16] *Ant.* iii, 214–216: "For as to those stones, which we told you before, the high priest bare on his shoulders, which were sardonyxes ... the one of them shined out when God was present at their sacrifices; I mean that which was in the nature of a button on his right shoulder, bright rays darting out thence, and being seen even by those that were most remote; which splendor yet was not before natural to the stone ... for so great a splendor shone forth from them before the army began to march, that all the people were sensible of God's being present for their assistance ... Now this breastplate, and this sardonyx, left off shining two hundred years before I composed this book, God having been displeased at the transgressions of his laws."

false; ¹⁷as it was not sufficiently conclusive for this purpose, the right-hand stone was thus invoked, this being the phase depicted in 1Q29 2 2.¹⁸ However, contra Strugnell line 2 continues with the following words "it shall shine forth to the eyes of all the assembly" (תגלה לעיני כול הקהל), implying that the left-hand stone was sufficient proof for the congregation.¹⁹

L. 2 תגלה לעיני כול הקהל. This line describes how the left-hand stone on the high priest's ephod shone for the congregation to see. As the common meaning of the root גל"ה in the *Nif'al*, "to be shown, exposed" fits the text, Strugnell interprets the verb תגלה as "will shine," making reference to Sir 42:16, 1Q27 1 6, and CD XX,20.²⁰

עד כלות הכוהן לדבר. This is a subordinate temporal clause defining the length of time that the stone shone, namely, from the moment the priest went out to the congregation until he finished speaking. His speech was undoubtedly related to the matter concerning which he had inquired of God via the Urim and the response that was evinced through the shining of the onyx. The text may perhaps have cited the scriptural regulations for battle from Deut 20:2–4. Rabbinic and later sources give the title "priest anointed for battle," כהן משוח מלחמה, to this figure.²¹ 4Q376 i 1 calls him "the anointed priest" (הכוהן המשיח). The phrase "until the priest finishes speaking" (עד כלות הכוהן לדבר) recalls the Deuteronomistic verse in the same context (Deut 20:9): "When the officials have finished addressing the troops" (והיה ככלות השטרים לדבר אל העם). Here, as in Deuteronomy, the troops are then organized for battle, with 4Q376 iii giving regulations for conduct during war. The text thus links the priest's speech prior to

---

17 See Josephus' statement: "I will now treat of what I before omitted, the garment of the high priest: for he [Moses] left no room for the evil practices of [false] prophets; but if some of that sort should attempt to abuse the Divine authority, he left it to God to be present at his sacrifices when he pleased, and when he pleased to be absent. And he was willing this should be known ... For as to those stones ... the high priest bare on his shoulders ... the one of them shined out when God was present at their sacrifices" (*Ant.* iii, 214). His formulation makes it difficult to determine whether he understands that the shining of the stones demonstrated whether a person was a true or false prophet. Also understanding "prophecy" in the sense of foretelling future events, he includes the high priests amongst the "prophets": cf. *Ant.* v, 120, 159; vi, 115, 254, 257. See also L. H. Feldman in *Flavius Josephus, Translation and Commentary* (ed. S. Mason; Judean Antiquities 1–4; Leiden: Brill, 2000), 288–89.
18 Strugnell, "Apocryphon of Moses," 126.
19 The difference between the description in 4Q376 ii, which is related to the left-hand stone, and that of 1Q29 2 2 related to the right-hand stone points to the difficulty in seeing 1Q29 as an overlapping copy of 4Q376 (see Comments on 1Q29).
20 Strugnell, "Apocryphon of Moses," 126.
21 Cf. *m. Soṭah* 8:1; Maimonides, *Laws of Kings and Wars*, 7:1–3.

battle to his inquiry of the Urim (as Num 27:18–20). This interpretive move reflects the conviction that, having enquired of the Urim, the priest knows that God will grant his people victory and can thus encourage them to engage in battle. 11QT^a LXI, 12–15 and 1QM X, 2–5 also refer to the priest's address to the people prior to war.[22] In contrast to the *Temple Scroll*, and apparently also 4Q376, the *War Scroll* makes no allusion to the priest's inquiring of the Urim and Thummim, instead associating the regulations for battle in Deuteronomy 20 with the obligation to sound the war trumpet in order to prompt God to remember and save his people (Num 10:9).

Ll. 2–3 ואחר נעלה [הענן]. This line alludes to the cloud that accompanied the Israelites in the wilderness (cf. Exod 13:21–22, 14:19–20; Num 9:15–23, 10:11–12). Covering the tabernacle, it symbolized God's presence with the people, its "lifting" signaling to the people that they should resume traveling.[23] The context of Numbers 10 is clearly military, with Moses' statement to his father-in-law, "We are setting out for the place of which the LORD has said, 'I will give it to you'" (v. 29) indicating that this journey formed part of the campaign to conquer Canaan.[24]

L. 3 ואתה תשמור וֹעֹ[שׁ]יתה כו[ל] אשר יֹדֹבֹּרֹ [א]לֹיֹכֹהֹ[. At this juncture, the text moves from narrative description to direct speech, the addressee being a singular person (or collective?), who is exhorted to "keep and per[form al]l [that] he shall tell [y]ou." The identities of both the speaker and those addressed are unclear. Plausibly the address is directed to the whole people, modeled on similar biblical instructions/warnings (cf. Deut 7:11; 16:11; 30:8, 10 and in particular those in which the inheritance of the promised land is conditional upon the performance of God's statutes, such as Deut 6:1–3, 20–25; 8:1). Perhaps the closest example is Deut 6:3.

---

22 See Yadin, *Temple*, 2:196; idem, *The Scroll of the War of the Sons of Light against the Sons of Darkness* (trans. B. and C. Rabin; Oxford: Oxford University Press, 1962), 190–91, 315–16. 4Q491 11 ii 11 (a copy of the *War Scroll*) also alludes to the "chief priest" (כהן הרואש) who motivates the soldiers before battle. The epithet "the chief priest" is synonymous with "the high priest," the choice of this designation in the *War Scroll* being intended to emphasize his role as leader of the congregation in the eschatological war. The title "the appointed priest" (הכהן החרוץ) is also given to the priest who encourages the troops following the first battle in 1QM XV, 6 and 4Q491 10 ii 13: see R. Yishai, "The Model for the Eschatological War Description in Qumran Literature," *Meghillot* 4 (2006): 121–39 (132–36) (Hebrew).
23 Cf. Exod 40:34–36; Milgrom, *Numbers*, 70–71.
24 In interpreting Num 1:2, the medieval commentator Rashbam (R. Samuel ben Meir), also links the lifting of the cloud above the tabernacle on the twentieth day of the month to setting off to battle.

Another less plausible possibility is that these words are spoken to the chieftain, referred to in col. iii 1, speaking of someone who accompanies the priest as he "goes out." In this reading, the chieftain is cautioned that divine aid and salvation are dependent upon his conduct. As in Deut 17:18–20, regarding the king, they are intended to stress upon him that he must "learn to revere the LORD his God, to observe faithfully every word of this teaching as well as these laws" (Deut 17:19). The speaker is most likely the priest. The difficulty posed by the fact that line 2 indicates that he had already finished speaking can be explained either by understanding that, having encouraged the people to go out to battle, he then moves on to the conditions under which they will receive divine aid, or, having addressed the people he then turns to the chieftain. Alternatively, the speaker is not the priest but a gloss by the author of the scroll clarifying that the help promised by God via the Urim is dependent upon observance of all the commandments. This composition, as at the beginning of 4Q375, appears to require that Israel heeds the prophet.

Col. iii

top margin

1   כבול המשפט הזה ואם במחנה יהיה הנשיא אשר לכול העדה וֹנלֹ[חם]
2   א'יבו וישראל עמו או כי ילכו לעיר לצוֹר עליה או לכול דבר אשׁר[ ]
3   לנשיא֯[ ]לֹ[   ]∘∘[ ] ∘ [   ]הׁשדה רחׁוֹקׁהֹ[ ]

Notes on Readings

L. 1 [חם]וֹנלֹ. Read with Qimron.[25] The flag of the *lamed*, although faded, is still recognizable in PAM I-440120.

Translation
1. ...in accordance with this regulation. And if there shall be in the camp the chieftain for all the congregation, and fou[ght?]
2. his enemies, Israel being with him, or if they march to a city to besiege it, or regarding any matter that[ ]
3. to the chieftain [ ] the field is distant[ ]

---

25 Qimron, *Hebrew Writings*, 2:314.

Comments

L. 1 ככול המשפט הזה. This phrase appears to be the ending of a sentence stipulating that the addressees must conduct themselves according to the regulations and instructions just given (cf. Exod 21:31; Deut 17:9, 11).[26] The term משפט means here "a precept" or "a regulation."[27] The injunction is formulated in terms of the biblical law.[28]

ואם במחנה יהיה הנשיא אשר לכול העדה וֹנִלְ[חם]. This line introduces a new regulation, presented in characteristic casuistic formulation: הנשיא אשר לכול העדה. The title נשיאים (pl.) refers in the Pentateuch to the leaders of the people/tribes, who perform various functions, and the heads of foreign people or tribes (cf. Gen 17:20).[29] In the singular (נשיא), the term recurs thirty-six times in Ezekiel, where it serves to designate the current ruler or king (cf. 19:1) and the messianic king (cf. 34:24, 37:25, 40–48).[30] In the Qumran literature, the term also carries several different meanings. In the sectarian scrolls, it is applied to the community's messianic (military) leader (cf. CD VII, 20; 1QSb V, 20; 1QM XVI, 1). On several occasions in 4QSefer ha-Milhamah, the נשיא represents the military commander (4Q285 4 2, 6, 10), who is also called the "Prince of the Congregation, the Bran[ch of David]" (4Q285 7 4).[31] In the *Damascus Document*, the title signifies "king," since it quotes Deut 17:17, said of the king, but replaces this title with the term נשיא(CD V, 1–2).[32]

---

[26] This type of formulation is common in the scrolls; cf. e.g. CD III, 3; VII, 7; 1QS VIII, 19.
[27] Cf. *HALOT*, 2:651.
[28] For this way of reworking biblical laws, see L. H. Schiffmann, "The Temple Scroll and the Halakhic Pseudepigrapha of the Second Temple Period," in *Pseudepigraphic Perspectives: The Apocrypha and the Pseudepigrapha in the Light of the Dead Sea Scrolls* (ed. E. G. Chazon and M. E. Stone; STDJ 31; Leiden: Brill, 1999), 121–31; M. Bernstein, "Pseudepigraphy in the Qumran Scrolls; Categories and Function," in ibid, 19–22.
[29] Cf. Exod 34:31 (leaders of the people), Num 1:16 (military commanders of the tribes), Numbers 3 (heads of the ancestral houses of the families of the tribe of Levi), Num 27:2, 31:13 (some of the juridical authorities in the wilderness with Moses and Eleazar the priest), and Numbers 10 (representatives of the tribes).
[30] Cf. H. Niehr, "nāśî," *TDOT*, 10:44–53.
[31] P. Alexander and G. Vermes, "4QSefer ha-Milhamah," in *Qumran Cave 4.XXVI: Miscellanea, Part I* (DJD XXXVI; Oxford: Clarendon, 2000), 235–41.
[32] Alexander Rofé suggests that the replacement of the title "king" (מלך) with that of "chieftain" (נשיא) in Pentateuch quotations in the Qumran texts reflects a different biblical text in use by the Qumranic authors, similar to that of the Septuagint, in which such a replacement is recorded. See idem, *Deuteronomy: Issues and Interpretation* (Edinburgh: T & T Clark, 2002), 42–46. For the issues related to whether the title נשיא in the scrolls attests to the messianic nature of its bearer, namely, that the laws in question relate to the future messianic age, and whether the scroll is a sectarian work, see the General Conclusion to the four manuscripts.

The *Temple Scroll* (11QT^a LVI, 12–LVIII, 21) reworks the laws of the king in Deuteronomy 17 and incorporates them into the regulations for battle due to the fact that the observance of the biblical regulations for war are the king's responsibility.[33] 4Q376 may reflect a similar interpretive perspective with respect to the chieftain.

L. 2 **א‏י‏ב‏ו וישראל עמו**. The first word, אויבו ("his enemies"), continues a phrase from the previous line, perhaps as restored by Qimron, וֹנִלֹ]חם עם[איבו. The sentence may thus be understood as relating to the chieftain's war against his enemies. Strugnell prefers to read אויבו as a phonetic spelling of the plural, as is clear from his translation "his enemies."[34] The situation described here may allude to that in Deut 23:10: "When you are encamped against your enemies." Therefore, according to the parallel biblical context and the sequence of the present scroll, this line appears to describe deployment for battle in an open area prior to besieging a city, such as in the depiction of the conquest of Ai (Josh 8:11–13) or those of Makkedah, Libnah, Lachish, Eglon, Hebron, and Debir, against which Joshua set out from his base camp at Gilgal (Josh 10:15–43).

וישראל עמו. The word עמו is preferably vocalized עִמּוֹ ("with him") rather than עַמּוֹ ("his people"), for the phrase seems to allude to the repeated expression "and all Israel with him" in the description of the conquest of the southern cities by Joshua (e.g. Josh 10:15, 31, 34).[35]

או כי ילכו לעיר לצֹור עליה. This line continues the reworking of the regulations for battle from Deuteronomy (Deut 20:10, 12). In contrast to the biblical text, 4Q376 omits any reference to the two-stage process, the offering of terms of peace and the laying of the siege if the terms of surrender are not accepted. The *Temple Scroll* (11QT^a LXII, 5–16) also quotes Deut 20:10–18.

Ll. 2–3 **לנשׁיֹא**[ ] **[או לכול דבר אשׁרׄ**]. This line adds a generalized supplement to the biblical law, possibly alluding to further obligations laid on the chieftain. Formulations of this type occur in various Qumran sectarian laws such as וכן ישאלו למשפט ולכול עצה ודבר אשר יהיה לרבים ("they shall be questioned about any judgment, deliberation or matter that may come before the general membership"; 1QS VI, 9; cf. V, 3) and לכל דבר אשר יהיה לבל האדם ("Anything that any man might have to say"; CD XIV, 11; IX, 16). These parallel formulations demonstrate that our line should be read לכול דבר אשר [יהיה] לנשיא ("any matter which pertains to

---

33 Yadin, *Temple*, 1:264–77; 2:177–86.
34 Strugnell, "Apocryphon of Moses," 127–28.
35 Cf. also 2 Sam 17:24; 1 Kgs 16:17.

the chieftain"). This usage may suggest that the regulations or matters were well known.

L. 3 [ ]הֹ֯קֹ֯וֹהֹ֯ הֹ֯שדה רחֹ֯וֹקֹ֯הֹ֯. The syntactical relation between the two surviving words is awkward and cannot be resolved even if they belong to two separate sentences. While the latter might explain the lack of agreement between the gender and presence/absence of the article, it might also be a scribal error or reflect current linguistic usage in which the noun שדה ("field") was regarded as feminine, a common practice in rabbinic and later literature.[36] This word also appears in the feminine form in 4Q251 14 2: הכוהן [אחזת תהיה החרם והשדה. Alternatively, the adjective "far/distant" (רחוקה) may form the *nomens rectum* of a feminine word as in the construct עיר השדה (ה)רחוקה (cf. 1 Sam 27:5). Here, it may represent חלקת השדה רחוקה. However, these suggestions do not resolve the absence of the definite article in the adjective רחוקה ("far off"). If this sentence is understood in terms of the entire fragment, a continuation of the reworking of Deut 20:15 is plausible: "Thus you will deal with all towns that lie very far from you, towns that do not belong to nations hereabout."

Discussion

An examination of 4Q376 and its reworking of biblical passages evinces that this text deals with the regulations for fighting a battle led by the chieftain as ruler and commander of the army. While the first and second columns describe general regulations and ceremonies to be performed prior to engaging in war, the third column lays down the regulations for the battle itself. The first column describes the sacrifice offered by the high priest, possibly the freewill offering made before he entered the temple to inquire of the Urim and Thummim. The second column depicts the priest, accompanied by the chieftain, going out to the people assembled outside the temple awaiting the divine response as to whether or not they should go to war. The latter is signified by the shining of the stones on the priest's ephod as "tongues of fire" and the cloud, indicating the divine presence, lifting from up from above the tent of meeting/temple. The priest also gives them verbal confirmation of God's answer by encouraging their spirits in the knowledge that God will fight on their behalf. The third column contains the regulations for warfare. Its fragmentary condition only allows us to deduce the general gist of

---

[36] See E. Ben-Yehuda, *A Complete Dictionary of Ancient and Modern Hebrew* (ed. N. H. Tur-Sinai; Jerusalem, 1959), 16:7527 (Hebrew).

the column: laying a siege against a city, possibly going out against a distant city or land, and additional matters for which the chieftain is responsible.

The conceptual connection between the lines suggests that the original complete scroll closely resembled the extant text, only one or two lines being missing from the end of each column. This being the case, the suggestion that 4Q376 forms the continuation of 4Q375 and deals with the same subject, namely the identification of a true or false prophet (thus Strugnell), is untenable. In fact, the two texts deal with two separate matters. 4Q375 is concerned with the identification of true/false prophets while 4Q376 addresses the laws concerning the fighting of a permitted war. Despite the difference in subject matter, the two nonetheless form part of the same composition for they share terminology, approach to biblical interpretation, and the central issue relating to the role and status of the high priest in judicial and practical matters. The larger composition appears to have reworked a series of Pentateuchal laws, possibly employing a method similar to that of the *Temple Scroll*, which rewrites Deuteronomy by inserting additional harmonizing expansions.

The subjects addressed in 4Q376 include the offering by the priest—entitled in this fragment the "anointed priest" (col. i 1) or simply "the priest" (col. ii 2)—of the freewill sacrifice and inquiry of God via the Urim. Col. ii clearly indicates that this figure is identified with the priest who speaks to the people in Deut 20:2–4, known in rabbinic and later literature as "the priest anointed for battle" (cf. *m. Soṭah* 8:1). The central question here is whether the priest anointed for battle also inquires of God via the Urim and whether in our text the designation (הכוהן המשיח) refers to the high priest or the priest anointed for war. From the Babylonian Talmud, it may be gathered that the "priest anointed for war," who wore all the eight items of the high priest's garments, was permitted to enquire of the Urim and Thummim (*b. Yoma* 73a). This similarity suggests that the same or a similar priest is alluded to by the Talmud. Here, the Talmud questions the claim that the priest anointed for battle does not wear the eight items comprising the high priest's garments (cf. Exod 29:5–9). From this, it may be understood that, when wearing this vestments, he is authorized to inquire of the Urim.[37] Also one of the copies of the *Pesher of Isaiah* from cave 4 may indicate that when the priest wore these garments he could thus inquire of the Urim and Thummim: "One of the priests of renown will go out, and in his hand the garments of [ ]" (4Q161 8–10 29).

---

[37] Cf. "Urim and Thummim," in *Encyclopaedia of the Talmud Concerning Matters of Halachah* (ed. M. Berlin and S. A. Zevin; Jerusalem, 1952), 1:295 (Hebrew), contra Milgrom (*Numbers*, 485), who maintains that only the high priest used the Urim and Thummim.

Despite the fragmentary state of this text, it clearly implies that the king must be guided by the priest. While the Babylonian Talmud attests to an understanding that the priest anointed for war inquired of God via the Urim, the "anointed priest" of our text (4Q376) relates to the high priest in precisely the same way as in 4Q375 i 9: הכו[הן] המשיח אשר יוצק עַל רֹ[ו]אשו שמן המשיחה. Thus, in our text, the high priest instructs the king as to when he should go out to war, in line with its intention of establishing the high priest as the supreme judicial authority in the land. It is thus implausible that the priest referred to herein as the "anointed priest" could be an ordinary priest with the authority to initiate a war.

Although Exod 28:30 and Lev 8:8 describe the Urim and Thummim as being embedded in the high priest's breastplate, in Second Temple and later Jewish literature the Urim and Thummim and the stones of the breastplate merge. This idea is reflected in the LXX in Exod 28:30, which translates "Urim and Thummin" as δήλωσις καὶ ἀλήθεια ("vision and truth") and the "breastplate" as λογεῖον (Exod 28:15, 30; Lev 8:8). In contrast, when Josephus and Philo refer to the Urim and Thummim, they regularly use the term λογεῖον, i.e., the "breastplate."[38] In its description of the high priest's garments based on Exodus 28, the *Letter of Aristeas* (96–99) only alludes to the stones of the breastplate in the ephod on which the names of the tribes of Israel are engraved as shining in indication of the divine answer. 1 Maccabees depicts how the people assembled at Mitzpah to seek God's counsel by means of the book of the Law and the priestly garments, first fruits and tithes also being brought, before Judas went out against Nicanor.[39] The bringing of the priestly garments is thus associated with receiving a divine answer via the high priest's breastplate. Josephus' account of the illumination of the breastplate and onyx stones also implies that he makes no distinction between the Urim and Thummim, the stones of the breastplate, and the onyx stones on the high priest's shoulder pieces (*Ant.* iii, 214–216).[40]

4Q376 appears to reflect a similar view regarding all matters concerning the Urim and Thummim, referring explicitly to the tongues of fire and the left-hand stone in conjunction with the Urim. The prevailing understanding that all three objects shone corresponds closely to Josephus' description. Such an understanding appears to have been a type of interpretative midrash once the real nature of the Urim was no longer known. This midrash is based on the significance of

---

38 Cf. Josephus, *Ant.* iii, 163, 166, 185; Philo, *Spec.* 1.151.
39 1 Macc 3:46–54. See also U. Rappaport, *The First Book of Maccabees* (Jerusalem: Yad Ben-Zvi, 2004) (Hebrew), 141, who posits that these items were taken to Mitzpah because the temple had been defiled.
40 See Comments on 4Q376 ii.

the name Urim (אורים; "lights/lightened; illuminations/illuminated"), which suggests that the stones "lit up" with the divine response. The "tongues of fire" in 4Q376 thus appear to refer to the brilliant light flashing from the stones of the breastplate, the Urim also possibly being linked with fire.[41]

This interpretation occurs in two additional texts from Qumran. 4QTestimonia (4Q175 17) states: "They shall cause your ordinances to shine for Jacob."[42] This appears to be a midrashic interpretation of Deut 33:10 that takes the directives and regulations of the priest as based on the divine response obtained from inquiry of God via the Urim. The *Pesher of Isaiah* on Isa 54:11–12 similarly reads: "This refers to the twelve [ ] who make the Urim and Thummim shine in judgment (מאירים במשפט)" (4Q164 1 5). Numerous suggestions have been made regarding the identity of the "twelve" in the pesher who employ the Urim to convey a verdict.[43] Although it remains unclear whether they are objects or people, this text also clearly asserts that the Urim "shone." A similar interpretation is reflected in some of the Greek and Aramaic translations of the Bible.[44]

In the harmonizing adaptation of the biblical text in 4Q376, the duty of inquiring of God via the Urim and Thummim before going out to war in Num 27:21 is linked to the laws of warfare in Deuteronomy 20 and 23:10–15. A juxtaposition occurs in the *Temple Scroll* (cols. LVIII–LXII), which seems to associate the law of the king with the regulations for warfare, apparently due to its view that the king is the supreme commander of the army and responsible for the decision to lead

---

[41] The Syriac Peshitta translates the word "Urim" as both light (Exod 28:30, Deut 33:8) and fire (1 Sam 28:6).

[42] The similar rendition in the LXX of Deut 33:10 suggests the existence of an early interpretative tradition in which Levi is associated with the teaching of the Torah via light: see M. Kister, "Levi = Light," *Tarbiz* 45 (1976): 327–30 (Hebrew).

[43] See J. M. Allegro, *Qumran Cave 4: 4Q186* (DJD V; Oxford: Clarendon Press, 1958), 28. According to David Flusser, the reading should be: "Its interpretation is the twelve [stones of carbuncle which] shine with the judgment of the Urim and Thummim." See idem, "The Isaiah Pesher and the Idea of the Twelve Apostles at the Beginning of Christianity," *ErIsr* 8 (1967): 52–62 (Hebrew). Menachem Kister reconstructs: "Its interpretation is the twelve [chief priests who are] illuminated with the judgment of the Urim and Thummim." See idem, "Olalot mi-sifrut Qumran (Gleanings from the Qumran Literature)," *Tarbiẓ* 57 (1988): 315–25 (321–24) (Hebrew). Joseph Baumgarten suggests "the twelve stones of the breastpiece"; see J. M. Baumgarten, "The Duodecimal Courts of Qumran, Revelation and Sanhedrin," *JBL* 95 (1976): 59–63. However, as Flusser and Kister noted, the grammatical disagreement between "twelve" (masc.) and "stones" (fem.) makes this proposal implausible.

[44] Cf. LXX Ezra 2:63 and Neh 7:65, which read the MT "until a priest with Urim and Thummim should arise" as: "until the priest should arise to enlighten," with the verb φωτίζω replacing the phrase "Urim and Thummim." See also the Greek translation of Sir 45:17 (ἐν νόμῳ αὐτοῦ φωτίσαι Ἰσραήλ), in which the connection between teaching (*Hifʿil* of ירה) and light (אור) is made explicit.

the people into war. 4Q376 may thus possess a corresponding conception, attributing the regulations for warfare to the chieftain (4Q376 1 iii 2).

According to Ezra 2:63 and Neh 7:65 (cf. *b. Yoma* 21a), the Urim was not in use in the Second Temple period. However, the various references to it and/or the breastplate in Second Temple literature suggest that the high priest continued to use the Urim and Thummim until the death of John Hyrcanus (104 BCE).[45] 4Q376 provides additional support for this thesis.

Three aspects concerning the use of the Urim and Thummim are prominent in the interpretative reworking of the Hebrew Bible in this scroll. Firstly, it associates the obligation to inquire of God via the Urim with going out to war, a link also made in 11QT^a LVIII, 15–21 and the *Apocryphon of Joshua* (4Q522 9 ii 10–11). Secondly, it highlights the public nature of the divine response. While the biblical text does not elaborate how the people knew God's answer, the scroll states that it was given both to the priest inside the temple and publicly to the assembled people via the flashing of the (stones on the) high priest's garments and the lifting of the cloud. The inquiry of God via the Urim and Thummim when Joshua was invested as military commander before the whole assembly of Israel (Num 27:15–23) is similarly connected with the cloud that indicated God's presence in the tabernacle during the wandering in the wilderness (Exod 40:34–38; Num 9:15–23) and Josephus' interpretive tradition that the onyx stones on the shoulder pieces of the high priest's ephod shone (*Ant.* iii, 215–218). Thirdly—and unique to this composition—is its understanding of the nature of the Urim and the way in which the divine answer was obtained, namely via light. Echoes of this tradition also appear in some of the Greek and Aramaic traditions and Josephus' description, as well as in 4QPesher Isaiah and 4QTestimonia.

---

[45] See L. S. Fried, "Did the Second Temple High Priest Possess the Urim and Thummim?," *JHS* 7 (2007): article 3. This suggestion accords with Josephus' assertion (*Ant.* iii, 218) that the use of the stones of the breastplate and the onyx stones had ceased two hundred years before the writing of the *Antiquities* (ca. 94 CE). Fried contends that the fact that the Urim and Thummim are mentioned in Second Temple literature—even though these accounts describe Aaron—is evidence that they were still in use. Among the evidence she adduces is a copy of the book of Exodus in 4Q17 (4QExod-Lev). Dated to the mid-third century BCE, this reads Exod 39:21 as: "and he will use the Urim and [Thummim as the Lord commanded] Moses" (4Q17 1 ii), an emphasis upon the actual practice of the commandment that is absent from the MT (cf. also the Sam. Pent. to Exod 39:21). According to Fried, the Urim and Thummim were in use in the mid-third century BCE, when the SP and 4Q17 were copied, MT being a later text. She also refers to allusion to the Urim in the description of the high priest in Sir 45:7–13 (beginning of the second century BCE), the description of the bringing of the priestly garments in order to inquire the will of God before engaging in war in 1 Macc 3:49, and the *Temple Scroll* (11QT^a LVIII, 15–21, around mid-second century BCE).

1Q29: Law and Ceremony

Literature

J. T. Milik, "Liturgie des 'trois longues de feu'," in *Qumran Cave 1* (ed. D. Barthélemy; Oxford: Clarendon Press, 1955), 130–32; J. Strugnell, "Moses-Pseudepigrapha at Qumran: 4Q375, 4Q376 and Similar Works," in *Archaeology and History in the Dead Sea Scrolls* (ed. L. H. Schiffman; JSPSup 8; Sheffield: Sheffield Academic Press, 1990), 221–56; E. J. C. Tigchelaar, "A Cave 4 Fragment of *Divre Moshe* (4QMD) and the Text of 1Q22 1:7–10 and Jubilees 1:9, 14," *DSD* 12 (2005): 303–12; É. Latour, "Une Proposition de Reconstruction de l'Apocryphe de Moïse (1Q29, 4Q375, 4Q376, 4Q408)," *RevQ* 22 (2006): 575–91; L. Goldman, "The Apocryphon of Moses: A Composition Representing the High Priest as the Supreme Judicial Authority," *Meghillot* 10 (2013): 181–200 (Hebrew); E. Qimron, *The Dead Sea Scrolls: The Hebrew Writings* (Jerusalem: Yad Ben Zvi Press, 2013), 2:311–15 (Hebrew).

The Manuscript

This manuscript was originally published by Józef Milik in 1955 in DJD I under the title "Liturgy of Three Tongues of Fire." The seventeen fragments included in Milik's edition are small and fragmentary, the leather being worn, the ink faint, and the photographs dark. The poor preservation makes reading very difficult; the edition also suffers from the fact that it was published when the majority of the material from Qumran was still unknown. These problems are compounded by the uncertainty regarding their sequence. For these and perhaps other reasons, the manuscript has remained relatively neglected, a state of affairs that the current edition hopes to redress in some measure.

The script of frgs. 1–12 is comparatively large, and the letters were written in a clear hand by a competent scribe who also left a wide space between the lines. Milik deliberated over whether frgs. 13–17 belong to the same manuscript as the writing in them is smaller although the ends of the lines resemble those of frgs. 5–7.[1] A new examination of sections of the script demonstrates that frgs. 13–17 were in fact penned by a different scribe; they differ from the other fragments in both letter and space size. As Tov's updated lists of scrolls adopted Tigchelaar's proposal that frgs. 13–17 should be entitled "1Q29a," they are excluded from this edition.[2] Tigchelaar and Qimron have both suggested that frgs. 13–17 constitute

---

[1] Milik, "Liturgie," 130.
[2] E. J. C. Tigchelaar, "'These are the Names of the Spirits of ...': A Preliminary Edition of 4QCatalogue of Spirits (4Q230) and New Manuscript Evidence for the Two Spirits Treatise (4Q257 and

copies of the Treatise of the Two Spirits in cols. III–IV of the *Rule of the Community*.³

Neither Milik nor the listing in DJD XXXIX provides a paleographic date for these fragments.⁴ Milik's title, "Liturgy of Three Tongues of Fire," derives from the appearance of this expression in frg. 2 2. While not fully cognizant of the content of the scroll, Milik considered it to be a liturgical text of some type, possibly associated with a battle and related to Num 10:36 ("Return, O Lord, You who are Israel's myriads of thousands").⁵ The fourth manuscript of this composition, 4Q408, indeed proved to be principally a liturgical text comprising a prayer of praise to God, the creator of the luminaries and light, and therefore Milik's original identification remains at least partially valid.⁶ The interpretation of 4Q376 proposed here also substantiates Milik's association of the "tongues of fire" with military warfare.

Most significantly, 1Q29 is the only text to contain all the phrases that occur in the manuscripts identified with this composition: "the prophet speaking rebellion," "the tongues of fire," and a liturgical fragment.

Text and Comments

Frg. 1

1   [ת̇ ת̇]
2   [האבן כאשר̇]
3   [ת̇מו בלשונות א̇ש̇]
4   עד [כלות הכוהן לד̇ב̇ר̇]
5   יד[בר אליכה והנב̇]י̇א
6   [ ]ל[ ] [המדבר סר̇ה]
7   [ ]ל̇[ ] י[הוה אל]והיכה

1Q29a)," *RevQ* 21 (2004): 529–47 (545); E. Tov, *Revised Lists of the Texts from the Judaean Desert* (Leiden: Brill, 2010), 14.

3 Tigchelaar, "Names," 543–45; Qimron, *Hebrew Writings*, 3.

4 E. Tov, ed., *The Texts from the Judaean Desert: Indices and an Introduction to the Discoveries in the Judaean Desert Series* (DJD XXXIX; Oxford: Clarendon, 2002).

5 Milik, "Liturgie," 130.

6 Although the fragments congruent with 4Q408 and several additional fragments are liturgical, those in which the "tongues of fire" appear are not, being rather an adaption of laws from the Pentateuch (see below).

Notes on Readings
L. 3]תֹּמוּ. With Milik. The straight protruding tip of the horizontal lower stroke, as well as the surviving left vertical stroke, suggest a *taw*. The left edge of the upper horizontal stroke that is connected to this vertical stroke can still be seen on PAM 40539.

Translation
1.   ]. .[
2.] the stone, when[
3.]... with tongues of fire[
4. until] the priest has finished speaking [
5.   sp]eaks to you and the proph[et
6.   ].[ ]who speaks rebellion [
7.   ].[Y]HWH yo[ur God

Comments
While lines 3–5 parallel 4Q376 ii and the description of the "prophet who speaks rebellion" and lines 5–6 resemble the text in 4Q375 i 4–5, no full parallel exists with either of these two scrolls. See the discussion below.

L. 2]האבן כאשר[. "The stone" is one of the precious stones set in the shoulder pieces of the high priest's ephod (Exod 28:9–12). While 1Q29 2 refers to the right-hand stone and 4Q376 ii speaks of the left-hand stone, here the sequence of the two words in the line leaves no room to indicate on which side it was placed. The use of the article ("the stone") suggests that the stone was already identified in text that is no longer extant.

L. 3]תֹּמוּ בלשונות אֹשׁ[. In light of the parallelism with 4Q376 ii, this line appears to depict the high priest as he goes out to the people to tell them God's answer. However, unlike the parallel text in 4Q376, no mention is made in the present fragment of a person who accompanies the priest, identified there as the "Prince" / "Chieftain." The fact that the phrase "tongues of fire" is unique to the three manuscripts belonging to the *Apocryphon of Moses*—recurring in them four times (1Q29 1 3, 1Q29 2 3, 4Q376 ii 1, and 4Q408 11 2)—is largely responsible for the scholarly proposal that they constitute copies of the same composition. 1Q29, in which the phrase appears twice, speaks of "three" tongues of fire (1Q29 2 3). Strugnell noted that the closest parallel to the description here is to be found in Josephus' presentation (*Ant.* iii, 214–216).[7]

L. 4 [כלות הכוהן לדבר] עד. This is a subordinate temporal clause defining the duration of the shining of the stone, from the moment the high priest went out to the congregation until he finished speaking. The high priest's utterance presumably constituted his delivery of the divine response to his inquiry of God via the Urim. If the context is that of warfare, as suggested in 4Q376, the speech presumably accorded with Deut 20:2: "Before you join battle, the priest shall come forward and address the troops." Although the precise content appears in neither this text nor 4Q376, it is detailed in Deut 20:3–4. Encouraging the people prior to going out to war, the priest assures them of God's providence.

הכוהן. As in Deuteronomy, this text refrains from bestowing a special title upon this priest; however, the composition as a whole speaks typically of the "anointed priest" (cf. 4Q375 i 9; 4Q376 i 1). Later rabbinic Jewish texts also refer to "the priest anointed for battle" (כהן משוח מלחמה).[8]

L. 5 יד[בר אליכה. This clause continues the section parallel to 4Q376 ii 3. The fragmentary text appears to contain a command to pay heed to God's words delivered via his emissary, in this case the high priest just as stated in 4Q376 ii 3: "and you shall observe and do everything he shall say to you." As in 4Q376, the object of direct appeal, "to you," appears to be the assembly gathered outside the sanctuary to receive God's answer to the priest's inquiry via the Urim and Thummim, the shining of the stones on the priest's garments indicating that the response has been given. The speech of encouragement having been delivered, this issue is now concluded with a directive to listen to the priest or to God. The style adopted in the fragment is borrowed from Deuteronomy, wherein the people (addressed in the second person singular) are commanded to observe and do as God has spoken (cf. Deut 6:3, 17:10, 18:19). These references appear to be designed to indicate that divine assistance is conditional upon the fulfillment of his commandments. The same pattern occurs in Moses' speeches regarding the inheritance of Canaan (cf. Deut 6:1–3, 20–25; 8:1).

---

[7] See Comments on 4Q376 ii. The locution "tongues of fire" appears only in one biblical text (Isa 5:24), in a metaphorical sense, and is irrelevant to the matter under discussion. The fact that the "tongues of fire" in Acts 4:2–4 are linked to the giving of the Torah and prophecy suggests a possible association with inquiring of God via the Urim and Thummim.

[8] Cf. *m. Soṭah* 8:1; *b. Soṭah* 43a; *b. Naz.* 43b; *Lev. Rab.* 20, 2; Maimonides, *Laws of Kings and Wars*, 7:1–3.

Ll. 5–6 ‏והנב̇[יא]ל̇[ ]ה̇מדבר סרה‏. The biblical locution ‏לדבר סרה‏ means "to speak falsely" (Isa 59:13; Jer 28:16, 29:32) or "to cause to rebel (against God)," usually by false speech (Deut 13:2).[9] This phrase resembles 4Q375 i 4–5. However, it differs in context and meaning. In the events described in 1Q29 1, the depiction of the priest's shining appearance before the assembled people, indicating the divine response to his inquiry of the Urim, is followed by a reference to the prophet speaking rebellion. This is a different order from that given in 4Q375 i, wherein the prophet first speaks rebellion and subsequently the priest offers a sacrifice and enters behind the veil to receive the divine answer regarding the prophet.[10] The textual sequence in 1Q29 1 may suggest that the prophet speaking rebellion is mentioned because he casts doubt on the authority of the priest and the validity of the answer the latter receives via the Urim. Given the similarity to 4Q376, it may be concluded that the answer received by the priest concerned going to war. If so the objection of the person who is labeled "a prophet who speaks rebellion" probably related to this answer.[11] If so, this text may represent a reworking of Deut 17:8–13. Deut 17:8–11 refer to the necessity of going up to Jerusalem to the judge or Levitical priest in the case of a difficult case, vv. 12–13 then relating to the ordinance regarding the person who disregards the verdict, "that man shall die. Thus you will sweep out evil from Israel." On this reading, 1Q29 describes the defiant man who acts presumptuously in refusing to accept the priest's authority as analogous to the false prophet who speaks rebellion.[12]

---

9 See *TDOT* 10:353–57; *HALOT*, 769.

10 If the order of events is reversed, the texts do not overlap and may not even treat the same matters. Therefore, these divergences form an additional argument for rejecting Strugnell's thesis ("Apocryphon of Moses") that 4Q375 and 4Q376 are continuous and deal with the same subject. According to the analysis of 4Q376 proposed in the present volume, it addresses the regulations for engagement in permissible warfare, exhibiting an independent existence characterized by textual sequentiality throughout its three columns. Following Strugnell, Qimron (*Hebrew Writings*, 2) argues for a continuity between all the fragments, with the reference to the prophet speaking rebellion at the end of 1Q29 1 closing the section regarding the law of the prophet. This reconstruction relies heavily on numerous proposed supplements of the text, and therefore must remain tenuous. For the impossibility of combining 4Q375 and 4Q376 into a continuous sequence, see Goldmam, "Apocryphon of Moses," 192–95.

11 See 1 Kings 22, where the role false prophets played in connection with going to war is treated.

12 For the linguistic links between the pericopae dealing with the false prophet (Deut 18:20–22), the prophet who speaks rebellion (Deut 13:2–6), and the defiant elder (Deut 17:2–7), see A. Shemesh, "Law and Prophecy: The False Prophet and the Rebellious Elder," in *Renewing Jewish Commitment: The Work and Thought of David Hartman* (ed. A. Sagi and T. Zohar; Tel Aviv: Hakibbutz Hemeuchad, 2001), 2:923–41 (924–26) (Hebrew). Shemesh argues that the biblical text employs the same root (‏ז"ד‏, "to act presumptuously/willfully") in both Deut 17:12–13 and 18:20,

Frg. 2

1 [כֹּל]
2 הא[בן הימנית בצאת הכו]הן
3 [שֹׁלוש לשונות אש מ]
4 [ואחר יעלה וננעֹלֹ]
5 [אִיֹּ ֯֯]

Notes on Readings

L. 4 וננעֹלֹ[. With Qimron. The surviving strokes of the fourth letter fit with the upper ends of the two arms of an *'ayin* rather than with a *shin* as read by Milik, וננשׁ֯ל].[13] The fifth letter is read correctly as a *lamed* by Qimron.[14] The remains of its upper horizontal stroke and some of its vertical flag can be seen on the new, better photograph B-365076. The parallel passage in 4Q408 15 1 does indeed read ננעֹל[.[15] Cf. the Comment on this line in the following chapter on 4Q408.

L. 5 אִיֹּ ֯֯[. The first letter should be read as *yod* rather than *waw* (read by Qimron), indicated by its wider head (Milik read ֯א[יֹ֯]).

Translation

1.]..[
2. the] right-hand [s]tone when the pri[est] comes out [
3.]three tongues of fire from[
4.]and after he/it shall go up and shall be determined[
5.].. ..[

---

the shared characteristics (and fate) of the rebellious elder and false prophet being those of undermining the authority of the king, judge, and true prophet. This understanding accords with the interpretation of the prophet speaking rebellion in 1Q29 as acting in defiance of the priest/judge. See also B. M. Levinson, *Deuteronomy and the Hermeneutics of Legal Innovation* (Oxford: Oxford University Press, 1998), 102–04.

13 But in his notes, Milik suggests the reading וננע[ל (idem, "Liturgie," 131), which indicates that he considered also the possibility of reading an *'ayin*.

14 Cf. Qimron, *Hebrew Writings*, 2:313.

15 See Tigchelaar, "Cave 4 Fragment," 308, n. 8.

Comments

L. 1 ‎]כל[‎. The letters must form part of a longer word, now lost. They cannot be read as the single word meaning "all," this term being written כול in frgs. 5–7 1 and 2, in line with the full orthography of this scroll.

L. 2 ‎הא]בן הימנית בצאת הכו]הן‎. This fragment appears to deal with the onyx stone set on the right-hand shoulder piece of the high priest's ephod (cf. Exod 28:6–12). 4Q376 ii 1–2 refers to the left-hand stone in a similar context: ויצא עמו בלשונות אש האבן השמאלית אשר על צדו השמאלי ("and he shall come forth with him with the tongues of fire and the left-hand stone"). Both contexts relate to the high priest's public revelation of the divine response to his inquiry of God via the Urim, all the stones on the high priest's garments—including the twelve on the breastplate and the two onyx stones on the shoulder pieces of the ephod—being understood as representing the Urim and Thummim. The divine response was given either via the flashing of the stones on the breastplate like "tongues of fire" or the shining of the onyx stones whose radiance was visible to the assembled congregation.[16]

בצאת הכו]הן. The priest's going out to the congregation is stated explicitly in 4Q376 ii 1–2. 1Q29 1 may depict an analogous event, although formulated differently and no mention is made of a person accompanying the priest or the verb יצא. All three fragments (1Q29 1, 1Q29 2, and 4Q376 ii) reflect a similar view of the public revelation of the divine response to the priest's inquiry of the Urim.

L. 3 שׁלוש לשונות אש. This is the only fragment to identify the number of the tongues of fire: three. For an interpretation of the phenomenon and a discussion of the number three, see the comments on 4Q376 ii 1.

L. 4 ‎[ואחר יעלה וננעל]‎. The literal sense of these three words is clear: "and after he/it shall go up and shall be locked." However, the broken lines make it difficult to understand who or what is referred to and how this statement fits into the context, fragmentary as it is. None of the proposed reconstructions quite resolves these difficulties.

וננעל[. The form is a *wayyiqtol* 3rd per. sg. *Nif'al*, the *waw* being the conversive of the verb נעל, in the sense of "to lock, close." Qimron suggests that the verb may mean here "the sealing of the lot," namely the "determining" of the divine answer given through the Urim.[17] This meaning fits here better than the sense "to

---

[16] See Discussion on 4Q376.
[17] Cf. Qimron, *Hebrew Writings*, 2:313.

wear shoes" (cf. *HALOT*, 705; *DCH*, 5:705),[18] for the *Nif'al* form does not accord with the act of wearing shoes; therefore the suggestion that it may refer to this action carried out by the priest is to be discarded.[19] The *Nif'al* of this verb does not occur in the Hebrew Bible but is current in rabbinic sources; cf. e.g. *m. 'Ed.* 5:6. The usage here may reflect the development of the sense "determine" into metaphorical imagery.

Frgs. 3–4
Parallel: 4Q408 2 (underlined)

1   ]○[
2   את י[הֹוֹהֹ אלוֹהֹיכה]
3   ויענו כו[ל ישראל vac]
4   יהוה] בכול מֹשֹׁפֹטֹ]יכה
5   הנאדר ב[רוב כוח הנכבדֹ]
6   [ל]   [ל]

Notes on Readings
Frgs. 3–4 are poorly preserved, the leather being worn and the ink faint. Nevertheless, with the help of the photographs (see PAM 40437), they appear to match and complement one another. Frg. 3 consists of lines 1–3 and the upper part of line 4 (the upper horizontal lines and the flag of the *lamed*). Frg. 4 contains the lower part of lines 4 and 5 and the upper end of the flags of two *lamed*s in line 6.

L. 2 הֹוֹהֹ[י. With Qimron. Taking into account the parallel text in 4Q408 2 1, which contains the *taw* of the את marking the direct object, the reading of the word as a verb here (for instance, יהיה) is excluded.

L. 3 ***vacat***. The six-letter space following the word "Israel," as far as the tear, requires the insertion of a *vacat*, not marked by Milik.

L. 4 מֹשֹׁפֹטֹ]יכה. With Qimron, rather than Milik's שֹׁמֹכֹה. The lower part of *mem* can still be recognized but the letter should be attached to the following group of

---

[18] Perhaps there is a word play here between the two verbs, for they are formed of similar roots על"ה ("go up") and נע"ל ("close, decide").
[19] Strugnell considered that the verb יעלה ("he/it will go up"; 1Q29 2 4) refers to the priest rather than to the cloud, as is the case in 4Q376 ii 3–4. See idem, "Apocryphon of Moses," 126.

characters. The following pointed bottom of the *shin* is also visible. The next letter is better read as a *pe* than a *kaf*. The final letter is certainly not a *he* (read by Milik), its lower section being a closed square, fitting with the lower part of a *ṭet* (see PAM 40437 and its improved visibility in B-277254). This reading also matches the parallel text in 4Q408 2 3 ‏בכלמ‎[with a *mem*, which is rightly supplemented by Steudel, ‏בכלמ‎]‏שפטיכה‎.

Translation
1.   ].[
2.   Y]HWH your God [
3.   al]l of Israel [shall answer] *vacat* [
4.   YHWH,] in all [your] judgmen[ts
5.   the exalted in] great strength, honored [
6.   ].[   ].[

Comments
This fragment comprises a prayer whose formulation partly parallels that preserved in 4Q408 2. The supplements are based on this congruence. The text includes the command to bless God (line 2), a formulation marking a communal prayer recited by the congregation (line 3), a blessing, and praises (lines 3–5).

L. 2 ‏יְ]הֹוֹה אֱלֹוֹהֹיכֹה‎. The expression seems to stand as the direct object of an unpreserved verb, as suggested by the parallel in 4Q408 2 1 [‏אלוהיכם‎] ‏א‎[‏ת יהוה‎. If so, the phrase may be restored ‏לברך את יְ‎[‏הֹוֹה אֱלֹוֹהֹיכֹה‎.

L. 3 ‏ויענו כו‎[‏ל ישראל‎] *vac*. This line suggests that the fragment contains a congregational prayer, the formula ‏יענו כל ישראל‎ being preserved in the parallel in 4Q408 2 2:- ‏[‏ונ‎]‏יֹענ‎ [‏כֹל ישראל‎. The prayer in 4Q408 3 5 also preserves part of the same formula: ‏יֹ‎]‏ענו כֹל‎. The daily prayers specified in 4Q503 contain the recurrent phrase [‏ואו‎]‏מרוֹ בֹרוּך א‎]‏ל ישראל‎ ‏יברכו וענו‎ (cf. 4Q503 1–6 III 1–2, 6, 18 and 4Q503 7–8 IV 6).[20] The blessing of God follows the formula marking congregational participation in 4Q408 and 4Q503. So perhaps the response of Israel here consisted of the blessing ‏ברוך אתה אדני‎ (thus also Qimron) as in 4Q408 3 6, where the

---

[20] For the daily prayers and their formulation, see D. K. Falk, *Daily, Sabbath and Festival Prayers in the Dead Sea Scrolls* (STDJ 27; Leiden: Brill, 1998), 35–38.

scribe deleted the Tetragrammaton and corrected it above the line to ברוך אתה אדני ("Blessed are you, O Lord").

Ll. 4–5 In the two prayers in 4Q408 2 and 3, the blessing is followed by praises. The lines here should probably be understood within the same context. The fragmentary formulae of three sentences of blessing and praise are preserved here, one in line 4 and two in line 5, and they may be reconstructed as follows (see Comments on 4Q408 2 and 3). Each sentence of praise probably consisted of an adjective depicting God and its expression in divine quality or actions.

יהוה [ ] בכול מֹשׁפֹּטֹ]יכה
[הנאדר ב]רֹוב כוח
הנכבדֹ[ ] באורך אפכה[²¹

L. 4 יהוה [ ] בכול מֹשׁפֹּטֹ]יכה. The divine epithet is missing in this first praise phrase. The Tetragrammaton is restored according to the parallel passage in 4Q408 2 3, where it is found. It should perhaps be restored with Qimron צדיק אתה יהוה [ ] בכול מֹשׁפֹּטֹ]יכה²². on the basis of Ps 119:137: צדיק אתה ה' וישר משפטיך.

L. 5 [הנאדר ב]רֹוב כוח. The restoration (with Qimron) הנאדר ("the exalted"; cf. DCH, 1:136) is proposed here on the basis that the same expression is used to describe God in the Song of the Sea (Exod 15:6), הנאדרי בכח.

הנכבדֹ[. This is the beginning of the third expression of praise. Here only one of the divine attributes is preserved. Recognition of the recurring praise pattern precludes Milik's reconstruction הנכבדֹ]ים ("the honorable ones/men") in the plural (followed by Steudel), since it breaks this pattern. It is more appropriate to leave the visible letters in the singular (thus Qimron). The epithet נכבד is applied to God in several Qumran sapiential texts; cf. 4Q299 9 3; 4Q301 3 4–6; 4Q403 1 i 4. Therefore, the expression הנכבד may be supplemented here with one of those formulations, for example [הנכבדֹ] באורך אפכה, based on 4Q301 3 4–5: [א]וֹנֹכֹבֹד בֹּא[ו]רך אפיו.²³

---

21 Milik ("Liturgie," 131) reads line 5 as one sentence rather than two as suggested here, proposing the reconstruction: רֹוב כוח הנכבדֹ]ים[. The reasons for finding this reconstruction unconvincing are noted above.
22 Qimron, *Hebrew Writings*, 2:315
23 See L. H. Schiffman, "4QMysteriesᶜ?," in *Qumran Cave 4.XV: Sapiential Texts, Part 1* (DJD XX; Oxford: Clarendon Press, 1997), 117–18.

As noted, the version of the prayer in the parallel text of 4Q408 2 4–5 is slightly fuller. However, it remains fragmentary and therefore it is difficult to form a precise idea of the prayer and its subject. The remaining lines yield only a general idea of the section recited: the formula preceding its utterance and a number of epithets in praise of God. Nevertheless, the prayer adds to our information on the liturgical customs the Qumran community may have practiced.

Frgs. 5–7

top margin

1   ה[דּברִים האלה על פי כול הֹ]
2   ואחֹ[רֹ ידרוֹשׁ הכוהן לכול רצונו כֹ]וֹל
3   [הקהֹל vacat]
4   [ֹכֹ]ל שמורו את הדֹּבֹרִיֹּם האלה]
5   לעֹ[שׂוֹת כוֹ]ל
6   [ֹם ספר המשֹׁ]פטים
7   [○ ○○]

Notes on Readings

Frgs. 5–7 are comprised of four scraps. Frg. 5 is formed out of two torn fragments. The large left-hand fragment includes the top margins and major part of lines 1–4 (see PAM 40442); the right-hand fragment includes the opening words of lines 1–3 and a small dot of the first letter in line 4 (PAM 40481). Frg. 6 (PAM 40476) is small and contains only one word, האלה ("these"); Milik placed it at the end of the fourth line of frg. 5. Milik joined frg. 7 (PAM 40538) here as lines 5–7. Qimron does not position it with frg. 5.[24]

L. 2 ידרושׁ. The *shin* is split between the two pieces.

L. 3 הקהֹל. This word is split between the two fragments, the *qop* and *he* lying in the right-hand fragment and the flag of the *lamed* in the left-hand fragment.

L. 6]ֹם ספר. PAM 40538 clearly shows that the first letter after the lacuna is a final *mem* and is separated by a space of one letter from the following letters, so it belongs to the previous word.

---

24 Qimron, *Hebrew Writings*, 2:314.

L. 7]o oo[. Only the upper horizontal strokes of three letters remain in this line. The space of one letter left between them indicates that they come from two separate words.

Translation
1.   ] these words, according to all [
2.   and the]n the priest shall seek according to his complete will, a[ll
3.   ] the congregation. *vacat* [
4.   ]. keep these words [
5.   to d]o al[l
6.   ]. the book of la[ws
7.   ]oo o[

Comments

L. 1]הֹ[הֹדְּבָרִים הָאֵלֶה עַל פִּי כוֹל. The expression הדברים האלה ("these words"), which is found in both biblical and Qumran texts, recurs again in line 4 of this fragment.[25] Its customary signification is an appeal to pay heed to the words that follow. Frequently, "the words" refers to God's words, laws, and/or commandments. Notably, the expression [כֹּ]ל הַדְּבָרִים הֹ[אלה] ("all these words") appears in 4Q408 1 2, regarded as an additional copy of the *Moses Apocryphon* and displaying parallels with 1Q29. This constitutes additional evidence of the connection between the two manuscripts.[26]

עַל פִּי. This locution meaning "according to," used here in a construct relationship with the noun "words" (דברים), appears in the Hebrew Bible only in Gen 43:7 and Exod 34:22 (cf. also Deut 17:10). In each of these examples, the sentence order differs from that in 1Q29 in which the phrase "according to" precedes the noun "word/s."[27] In his edition, Qimron reconstructs הֹדְּבָרִים הָאֵלֶה עַל פִּי כוֹל [הֹ]כתוב בספר תורת משה] on the basis of Deut 17:11. If this supplement is close to the original, it is consistent with the view proposed here that the composition reworks the laws of Deuteronomy, particularly those in 17:8–13.

---

25 Cf. Exod 4:30, 19:7; Deut 4:30; 1Q22 ii 6; 1QS VI, 24; 1QM XVII, 10.
26 Qimron does indeed suggest that the words הֹדְּבָרִים [ה]אלה in line 4 parallel those in 4Q408 1 2 (cf. idem, *Hebrew Writings*, 2:314–15.
27 As noted by Qimron, ibid, 314.

L. 2 ואח[ר]. It is unclear whether this constitutes a literary formula linking two issues, as is the case in the phrase "after these things" in Gen 15:1; 22:1, 20, or whether the word conjoins two events, a preceding one (no longer extant) and the inquiry of the priest described in the following text.

ידרוש הכוהן לכול רצונו כ[ו]ל. The priest seeks God's "complete will." The state of the fragment prevents us from knowing whether the reference is to an act of seeking God's will or an interpretation according to his will. "His will" (רצונו) undoubtedly refers to God's specifications, regulations, and instructions.[28] The text possibly constitutes an indirect allusion to Deut 17:8–13, wherein the complexity of the legal case necessitates turning to the judge/priest in Jerusalem. Although the person seeking to know how to proceed in the biblical passage is a layman, the decision is delivered by the priest/judge (Deut 17:9). The final verse in this pericope makes it clear that the priest is responsible for announcing how matters should proceed (Deut 17:12).[29] The *Rule of the Community* refers to the community's leaders as the "sons of Zadok and preservers of the covenant, seekers of his will" (1QS V, 9), those who oppose the separatist group being accused of not seeking God or fulfilling his commandments—revealed or hidden—in proper fashion: "They have not sought him nor inquired of his statutes" (1QS V, 11).[30] Seeking God with a perfect heart constituted one of the community members' fundamental obligations (1QS I, 1–2; CD VI, 6). However, while the sectarian designation "seekers of his will" (דורשי רצונו; 1QS V, 9) relates to all members of the community, our text here stresses that the act of "seeking God's will" is confined to the priest. Here we see a continuation of the tendency evident in 4Q375, in which the priest is responsible for resolving difficult cases, but only here, in 1Q29, is explicitly stated that the solution must be found by seeking God's will.

---

[28] The biblical texts employ the root רצ"ה and noun רצון in sentences in which God is the subject, or in requests that the speaker's words will be in accordance with his will. This usage is particularly prevalent in Isaiah and Psalms (cf. Isa 49:9; Ps 19:15, 30:6, 69:13). The same phenomenon is also evident in the scrolls: cf. the expressions חפצי רצונו ("the desires of His will"; cf. CD III, 15) and כל אשר צווה לרצונו ("all that He commanded by His good will"; 1QS V, 1). See *TDOT* 13:618–30.

[29] As Rofé notes, the fact that the priestly stratum of Deuteronomy gives no indication of the way in which the priest received the divine response to his inquiry leaves open the possibility that he could have inquired via means other than the Urim and Thummim. Deut 17:8–13 does reveal priestly influences, however, identifying the priest as a judge at "the place which the LORD shall choose" (Deut 17:10) and distinguishing "between one kind of assault and another" (Deut 17:8). See A. Rofé, *Deuteronomy: Issues and Interpretation* (Edinburgh: T&T Clark, 2002), 109.

[30] 1QS, which defines the obligations of the sectaries, appears to be a reworking of Deut 17:8–13. For 1QS I, 15 contains an implicit reference to Deut 17:11: "You must not deviate from the verdict that they announce to you there either to the right or to the left."

L. 3 הקהל. The term, meaning "the congregation," is one of the most common designations of the people of Israel in the priestly literature in the Pentateuch and later biblical books (Ezekiel, Psalms, Chronicles), frequently occurring in construct form: "the congregation of the Lord" (Num 16:3), "the congregation of Israel" (Lev 16:17), "the congregation of the assembly of Israel" (Exod 12:6).[31] In the biblical texts, the noun regularly refers to events involving the public assembly of the people (cf. Deut 5:19). It appears that in the present Qumran text the assembly is of the entire people, as it is in the biblical parlance. Here, the priest mentioned in line 2 addresses the people or goes out to them from the temple. If the congregation is in fact associated here with the priest's going forth, this matter would be alluded to once or twice in 1Q29 (cf., 1Q29 2 2 and perhaps also 1Q29 1 3), thus comprising the fourth or fifth reference to it in the composition as a whole (see 4Q376 ii 1 and 4Q375 ii 8–9).[32]

L. 4]ל֯ שמורו את הדברים האלה[. The imperative expressed in this phrase "to keep these things" may refer to the "words" with which the priest addresses the congregation when he goes out to them. See Comment on line 1. Qimron suggests that the line parallels 4Q408 3 1–2.[33]

שמורו. This is a 2nd per. pl. *qatol* imperative, a form prevalent in the scrolls.[34] The text possibly alludes to Deut 17:10: "You shall carry out the verdict that is announced to you from that place that the Lord chose, observing scrupulously all their instructions to you." Similar commands combining the verbs "keep/observe" and "do" (see the following line) occur in the biblical texts, most commonly in Deuteronomy (13:1 [12:32]).[35] They also appear in the scrolls; see, for instance, 1Q22 ii 9: "all [these] words of the [Law.] Be [very careful] of yourselves [to do them." A similar formulation also occurs in 4Q376, another copy of the present composition: "And you shall observe and [do al]l [that the prophet] shall speak [t]o you" (4Q376 ii 3).

---

31 See *TDOT* 12:546–57, wherein it is suggested that the term קהל in Deuteronomy refers to those present at the giving of the Torah on Sinai, being synonymous in the priestly literature with עדה. In Ezra-Nehemiah, the term denotes the returnees from exile. Rabbinic literature exhibits virtually no usage of either קהל or עדה in reference to all Israel or the people's assembling, these terms being replaced by כנסת and ציבור (ibid, 560).
32 4Q375 ii 8–9 employs עדה rather than קהל.
33 Qimron does not perceive any clear overlap, but simply notes that the end of 1Q29 5 is linked to 4Q408 3. He thus considers the prayer in 4Q408 to be a continuation of this fragment. Cf. idem, *Hebrew Writings*, 2:314.
34 Qimron, *Hebrew of the Dead Sea Scrolls*, 53–54.
35 Cf. e.g. Deut 15:5: 24:8; 28:1.

L. 5 לֹ[עֲ]שׂוֹת בֹּל. These words may also form part of the priest's address to the congregation, a continuation of the previous injunction. Formulae such as these are standard in both the biblical and Qumran texts, most frequently forming part of an exhortation to the people to keep the laws of the Torah. Similar formulae are also found in the sectarian scrolls (cf. 1QS I, 16–17). According to the priest's inquiry of God's will (see Comments on line 2 above): "You shall carry out the verdict that is announced to you from that place that the LORD chose, observing scrupulously all their instructions to you" (Deut 17:10 עד־עולם לעשות את־כל־דברי התורה הזאת). This verse may be detected in 4Q375 ii 7–8, describing the priest as seeking the "concealed matters" via the Ark of the Pact (עֹ[ד֯ לארון העדות ודרש אתֹ הנסת[רֹוֹת ממכה). In the Comments on lines 7–8 in 4Q375 ii, it is proposed that the text constitutes a reworking of Deut 17:8–11 and Deut 29:28.[36] The present line in 1Q29 may similarly represent a continuation of the joint reworking of these two texts indicated by the common use of the root דר"ש in 4Q375 ii 7–8 and 1Q29 5–7 2. Both appear to reflect the view of the priest as being responsible for seeking God's will and revealing to the people the proper way to observe the divine commandments.[37]

L. 6 מֹ[ספר המש֯]פטים. The meaning of the surviving phrase is unclear due to its fragmentary state. The word ספר is clearly the *nomen regens* in a construct pair while the three remaining letters of the following word belong to the *nomen rectum* of this combination. The proposed restoration ספר המש֯]פטים ("the book of laws") is provided accordingly. Although this expression appears in neither the biblical nor Qumran texts, it may be understood as being synonymous with the expression ספר התורה ("the book of the Law/Torah"), which occurs in the *Temple Scroll* (col. LVI, 4) in a paragraph reworking Deut 17:10–11 (col. LVI, 3–6).[38] It possibly constitutes a continuation of the priest's address to the congregation in which he exhorts them to "keep and do" all the laws of the Torah. If so, frgs. 5–7 comprise an adaptation of Deut 17:8–13 in a distinctive reworking that gives the priest—rather than the judge—supreme authority.

---

36 See the chapter on 4Q375 in the present volume.
37 In my previous edition of 4Q375, I suggested that 4Q375 c and 1Q29 5–7 constitute parallel copies of the same text, however, without proposing a reconstruction. See L. Goldman, "The Law of the Prophet as Reflected in 4Q375," *Meghillot* 5–6 (2007), 61–84 (63–64, 77) (Hebrew). It should be stressed that while 4Q375 c is retained in the current edition in the place assigned to it by Strugnell, it provides additional evidence of the similar way in which the various copies of this composition rework the same biblical text.
38 Qimron (*Hebrew Writings*, 2:314) suggests reconstructing line 1 of this fragment on the basis of the reference to Deut 17:10 in 11QT[a] LVI, 3–4.

Frg. 9

]o[1
]ל[2

Frgs. 10

הכו[הן

Translation
the p]riest

Frg. 11

א[שׁר בו]

Translation
th]at is in it[

Frg. 12

[ויום]

Translation
]and a day[

Discussion

The analysis of the large fragments of 1Q29 evinces that they address various legal problems on which decisions are reached by the high priest (frg. 5) or via his inquiry of God using the Urim (frgs. 1–2). While the poor preservation of these fragments prevents any precise elucidation of the questions posed by the high priest, his status and role in the settling of legal matters is clear. Consequently, the scroll appears to have originated in priestly circles that regarded the high priest as the supreme authority in judicial affairs rather than the magistrates or elders. It thus accords with the description given in 4Q375–4Q376, wherein the issues of the prophet's legitimacy and whether to engage in a battle are described as being

brought before the "anointed priest" for a decision.³⁹ Frg. 1 may present a figure—
the prophet who speaks rebellion—who opposed the authority of the priest and
the answers the latter received from his inquiry of God via the Urim. This interpretation explains the order of the contents: the priest and the shining of the stones in his garments being mentioned first (lines 3–4), followed by the false prophet (lines 5–6). In other words, a false prophet is challenging the divine answer that had been revealed to the priest who had inquired of God via the Urim.⁴⁰

The issue of the authority of the priest who delivers a verdict based on his inquiry of God is linked to his going out to the congregation, which is referred to explicitly in frg. 2. The congregation is also mentioned in frg. 5. This act constituted the public demonstration of the divine response to the priest's inquiry that apparently was conducted inside the temple, the shining of the stones on his shoulder pieces indicating that he had received an answer. Challenging this answer was, by definition, the action of a false prophet or disobedient figure. The above analysis indicates that 1Q29 1 and 5 rework Deut 17:8–13, and therefore this scroll deals with the establishment of the status of the priest as the supreme juridical authority.

Our understanding of the relationship of this theme to the prayer in frgs. 3–4 is hampered by the poor preservation of the fragments. Conjecturally, it may be a prayer of thanksgiving to God who has revealed the answer to the priest's inquiry or possibly a prayer offered by the priest prior to the inquiry.⁴¹ The analysis presented here elucidates the relationship between 1Q29 and 4Q375–4Q376. As noted above, Strugnell proposes that the three scrolls deal with the question of identifying true and false prophets. In my opinion, it is a halakhic composi-

---

39 For the view that the priests should constitute the supreme juridical and halakhic authority, a prevalent view amongst the priestly circles in the Jerusalem temple, see C. Werman, "The Authorization for the Development of Halakhah," in *Revealing the Hidden: Exegesis and Halakha in the Qumran Scrolls* (ed. C. Werman and A. Shemesh; Jerusalem: Bialik Institute, 2011), 72–103 (74–83) (Hebrew). See also A. Finkel, "The Oracular Interpretation of the Torah and Prophets as Reflected in the Temple Scroll and Pesharim of Qumran," in *Proceedings of the Eleventh World Congress of Jewish Studies, Jerusalem, June 22–29, 1993* (Jerusalem: World Union of Jewish Studies, 1994), 179–84. The latter accentuates the difference between the rabbinic midrash, based on the authority of interpreting the Torah, and priestly interpretation, drawing on the authority of divine revelation.

40 This order refutes Strugnell's proposal that the priest must determine whether he is faced by a true or false prophet, the reference to the prophet necessarily preceding that to the priest as in 4Q375. For further arguments against Strugnell's thesis, see L. Goldman, "The Rules Regarding fighting a Permitted War in 4Q376," *Meghillot* 8–9 (2010), 319–41 (335–36) (Hebrew).

41 Cf. *b. Ber.* 32a: "A man should always first recount the praise of the Holy One, blessed be He, and then pray."

tion that reworks various laws in Deuteronomy in order to establish the high priest as the supreme judicial authority in the land (see the summary of the four manuscripts).[42] Each of these relates to a different matter but all are resolved in a similar manner, i.e., a "baffling" legal case is determined by the high priest who seeks God's will or inquires of Him via the Urim.

---

[42] For a detailed discussion of the difficulties attendant on Strugnell's theory and the problems they raise for reconstructing the structure of the composition, see Goldman, "Apocryphon of Moses," 192–95.

4Q408: Prayers

Literature

A. Steudel, "4Q408: A Liturgy on Morning and Evening Prayer – Preliminary Edition," *RevQ* 16 (1994): 313–34; eadem, "408: 4QApocryphon of Moses^c?," in *Qumran Cave 4.XXVI: Miscellanea, Part 1* (ed. P. Alexander et. al.; DJD XXXVI; Oxford: Clarendon Press, 2002), 298–315; J. M. Baumgarten, "Some Notes on 4Q408," *RevQ* 18 (1997): 143–44; E. Qimron, *The Dead Sea Scrolls: The Hebrew Writings, Volume Two* (Jerusalem: Yad Ben-Zvi Press, 2013), 311–15 (Hebrew).

The Manuscript

4Q408 contains seventeen fragments and was published officially by Annette Steudel in DJD XXXVI.[1] Apart from frg. 3, all the fragments are miniscule, containing at most three lines out of which no more than two incomplete words are visible. The leather is very thin and cracked in many places. The color varies across the fragments, ranging from red to bright yellow, constituting a key factor in the reconstruction of the order of the fragments. According to Steudel, they comprise a single document consisting of four or five columns.[2] She posits the following order: first column: frgs. 1 and 2;[3] second column: frgs. 3 + 3a, 4, 5, 6, and perhaps 8; third column: frg. 7 and perhaps frg. 8; fourth column: frgs. 10, 11, 13, and perhaps frgs. 12, 14–16; fifth column (if it existed): frgs. 14, 15, and 16. Steudel notes that the place of frgs. 9, 17 cannot be determined conclusively. The present edition is based on that of Steudel.

Steudel dates the manuscript, which displays features characteristic of the early Hasmonean period, to the end of the second century BCE.[4] If correct, this is the earliest copy of the *Apocryphon*. The letters differ in size, as do the spaces between the lines, probably due to the absence of dry lines that regulate the spacing of the script. The orthography is remarkably defective: כל (frg. 3 5), קׄדֿ[ש] (frg. 3 5), מׄארי (frg. 3 5, 7), כח (frg. 3 6), בֹּקר (frg. 3 8), לׄהֿפֿיׄעׄ (frg. 3 8), and בראתם (frg. 3 9, 11). It also contains phonetic spelling, such as ברתה (frg. 3 8) for the *qatal* 2nd sg. of בר"א. Also, a medial *mem* occurs in the final position (שמ קדשך

---

[1] Steudel, "Apocryphon," 298–315.
[2] Ibid, 299–300.
[3] Qimron (*Hebrew Writings*, 2:315) joins frg. 1 to frg. 3 8–9, thus rejecting Steudel's reconstruction, which is based on material and formal considerations.
[4] Steudel, "Apocryphon," 301.

in frg. 3 9).[5] In addition, there are short forms of the 2nd per. pl. such as לעבדתם (frg. 3 9) and the 2nd per. sg. קדשך (frg. 3 9). The Tetragrammaton is written in full, with evidence of scribal deletion above and below indicated by dots (frg. 3 6). On occasion, two words are conjoined: אתהאדני (frg. 3 6a). Corrections in the text are frequent. Steudel assigns them to the scribe who copied the scroll.[6]

Text and Comments

Frg. 1

1 [בְּנֵי הָאדָֹם]
1a   ̊   ̊
2 [כ]ל̇ הׄדברׄים̇ הׄ[א]לה

Notes on Readings
L. 1a Remains of letters are clearly visible above the preserved line 2, but they are not noted by Steudel. See PAM 43543.

Translation
1.]the people[
1a. ...
2. a]ll th[ese] words[

Comments
It is difficult to classify frg. 1 and to place it within the sequence of the column. On the basis of its content, Steudel assigned it to col. 1, suggesting that it forms part of the opening section of the scroll.[7] Qimron regards it as a continuation of lines 8–9 of frg. 3.[8] This proposal does not derive from an overlap between the words or textual sequence among the fragments, and thus cannot be verified.

---

5 Steudel, ibid, suggests that this reflects the fact that the two words in question were regarded as a single unit.
6 Ibid, 302.
7 Ibid, 299.
8 Qimron, *Hebrew Writings*, 2: 315.

L. 1]בֹּנֵי האדֹם[. This is a common phrase ("men/mankind") but its meaning here is difficult to ascertain due to the fragmentary state of the line.

L. 2 [כ]ל הֹדברֹים הֹ[אלה]. The phrase "all these words" is widespread in both biblical and Qumran texts, customarily occurring in a command to heed the frequently divine words that follow.[9] It recurs twice in 1Q29 5–7 1, 4. This constitutes further evidence for the linguistic parallel between 1Q29 and 4Q408.[10]

Frg. 2
Parallel: 1Q29 3–4 (underlined)

1 לברך א[ת יהוה]אלוהיך
2 ו[יע]נו [כל ישראל ו]ֹיאמרו
3 יה[וה בכלמ]שפטיך
[4] הנאדר ב[רוב כוח הנכבד]
[5] [ ]ל[ ]ל[

Notes on Readings
The fragment contains three lines; the absence of any margins makes it difficult to ascertain its position within the column and the original length of the lines. Its text is paralleled in 1Q29 3–4. Lines 4–5 are reconstructed here according to the parallel fragment from cave 1. Steudel's edition and *DSSR* also contain lines 4–5.[11]

L. 2 ו[יאמרו. Remains of the possible pointed head of a *waw* can be seen on PAM 43543.

L. 3 שפטיך[בכלמ. Only four letters are visible, written without any spacing (see PAM 43543), so there is no evidence for Steudel's reading of a *shin* (פטיך[כל מש]). See the Readings and Comments on the parallel lines in 1Q29 3–4 4–5.

Translation
1. to bless] YHWH [your God   ]
2.   and] all of Israel shall ans[wer] and[say   ]

---

9 See Comments on 1Q29 5–7.
10 Thus also Qimron, *Hebrew Writings*, 2:314.
11 Steudel, "Apocryphon," 304; *DSSR* 3:104.

3. YH]WH in all [your] ju[dgments   ]
[4]. the exalted in] great strength, the honored [   ]
[5].   ].[   ].[   ]

Comments

The reconstruction here is based on the premise that the fragment constitutes a prayer, a fact suggested by the extant text, the liturgical parallel in 1Q29 3–4, and the similar language in frgs. 3 + 3a. See Comments on 1Q29 3–4.[12]

L. 2 ו[יע]נו [כל ישראל o[. This line may be continued with the restoration ו֗יאמרו ברוך אתה to connect it with the restoration לברך in the previous line. It supplies a blessing that was recited at the beginning of the prayer, linking this line with the Tetragrammaton in the following line.

L. 3 This line introduces the praise. The structure of the prayer appears to resemble that in frgs. 3 + 3a, the blessing being followed by praise of God's attributes and traits in various modes of action. The praise appears to follow a fixed pattern: a divine title depicting His qualities, a particle denoting inclusivity (all/much), and the area in which the divine attribute manifests itself (see below on frgs. 3 + 3a). It is impossible to ascertain the length of the prayer or how many encomia it contained.

L. 4 הנאדר ב]ר֗וב כוח הנכבד֗]. The adjective נכבד ("honored") is often used in praise of God in various contexts (cf. e.g. 1QS VI, 27; 4Q293 9 3; 4Q301 3 4–5). Therefore, the preceding word, now lost, may also have been a similar adjective, perhaps הנאדר ב]ר֗וב כוח הנכבד֗] באורך אפך (as suggested for 1Q29 3–4 5; see Comments ad. loc.). The restoration הנאדר ("the exalted"; Cf. *DCH*, 1:136) is proposed here on the basis that the same expression is used to describe God in the Song of the Sea (Exod 15:6) הנאדרי בכח. Cf. Comments on 1Q29 3–4.

Frgs. 3 + 3a

The fragment consists of three pieces, the largest one, frg. 3, a smaller one, frg. 3a, and a small unnumbered scrap. They are still separate in PAM 43543 and earlier photographs, as well as on plate XXI of Steudel's publication. Frg. 3a has been positioned to complete the end of lines 5–7 in frg. 3. However, in the absence of

---

[12] Only particular points, specific to 4Q408, are discussed here.

evidence regarding the original line length, the size of the lacuna to be calculated between frgs. 3a and 3 is a matter of conjecture, and estimates vary from one scholar to another (see Comments below). The scrap, which contains most of the words הערב and בראתם, is attached to the bottom of lines 10–11. In PAM 41515, frg. 3 appears without the small scrap that was subsequently attached to lines 10–11 as seen in later photographs.

1	[ ]	[שׁ]מֹ[	
2	[ ]	כל אשר דבר [א]ליכם שׁמֹרֹו לעֹשׂוֹת אֹ[ת]
3	[ ]	א[ל ישראל] [ ]דֹ[הוא ליחד]
4	[ ]	[ה אל כל ישראל בֹּראתֹם]
5	[ ]	ב[הֹפיע מֹארי כבדו מזבול קדׁ[ש ועם האספם למעון כבוד וי]ענו כל]
6a		אתהֹאדני
6	[ישראל ויאמרו בר]וך יהוֹה [ה]צדיק בכלדרכיך הר֗ כח הֹ] מש[פטיך
	הנאמן]	
7	בֹ[ל דבריך] המבֹין בֹכֹ[ל ש]כֹל הנעו] ב[כֹל גֹבורה וצֹוֹה להוצי את] האור [ºלוֹ]
	[לֹ]	
8	אשר ברתה אֹת הֹבקר אות להֹפֹיע ממשלת אור לגבול יומֹם בֹּ[ן]
9	לעֹבדתם לברך את שם קדשׁך בראתם כי טוב האור וב]ו [ ] [כי בכל]
10	] כֹ[ל הֹבֹרֹאֹים אשר בֹרֹ[ת]ה אֹת הערב אות להופיע ממשלתן חושך לגבול לילה
11	] [וֹ מֹעֹמל לברך [את שם קדשך ב]רֹאתמֹ [ ]ᵒ [ ]ᵒים כֹ[ל] מעשיך

Notes on Readings

L. 2 שֹׁמֹרֹו. The reading follows Qimron.[13] The third letter is a slightly bent *resh*, rather than the *he* read by Steudel (שמה). Although faded, the final letter is clearly a *waw*, seen on the good copy of PAM 43543, available at the IAA website. Note the similar formulations in 1Q29 5–7 4–5.

L. 3 דֹוֹ. Of the first letter only a small bent upper stroke has survived. It does not accord with Steudel's reading בֹרא[ה. Neither is Qimron's reading הדֹ supported by these data.[14]

L. 5 מֹארי. The first *mem* is clear (see PAM 43543). Thus also Qimron. Steudel's פארי is not supported by the physical evidence.[15]

---

13 Qimron, *Hebrew Writings*, 2:315.
14 Qimron, ibid; Steudel, "Apocryphon," 304.
15 Qimron, ibid; Steudel, ibid.

L. 6a אתהאֹדני. This is a supralinear correction intended to replace the Tetragrammaton below it. The Tetragrammaton is canceled by dots above and below the letters, which are preserved for the two first letters, *yod* and *he*.[16] The two words are written without an intervening space, unlike Steudel's presentation.

L. 6 בכלדרכיך. These two words are also written without an intervening space, *contra* Steudel.

הֹרֹּ כח. Thus also Qimron.[17] The reading tallies with the parallel line in 1Q29 3–4 5. Steudel's reading ה[ג]בֹּרֹ does not fit with the surviving traces.

ה]. The letter should be read as *he*, with Steudel (see PAM 42916, 43543). Compare the *he* in the words האור (line 9) and הער[ב (line 10). The reading of a *bet* (thus Qimron) is excluded by the surviving diagonal stroke descending from the horizontal upper roof. The following lacuna must contain several letters since the next words מש[פטיך הנאמן are placed below the words וי[ענו כל in the preceding line.

L. 7 הנעֹ[. Only a lower dot of the third letter has survived. It may fit with a number of letters (*waw*, *resh*, *taw*, and *ḥet*). Qimron reads and restores הנעֹ[ז], suggesting two thin letters to fit the narrow space,[18] perhaps following 1QH^a XIV, 28, but there the text relates this *Nifʿal* form to the human author. So his proposal remains conjectural.

וֹצֹוֹה. Following Qimron's וֹצֹוֹה and not Steudel's reading הֹנחֹה.[19] Of the *he*, only two tips at the bottom of the line remained. The reading of the second letter as *ṣade* is preferable since its surviving lower angle is curved and not pointed as that of a *nun* (compare the *ṣade* in להוצי in this line).

]לֹ[   ]ֹהֹ∘[. These letters come from the small fragment attached to lines 5–7. The scanty remains of a letter after the lacuna cannot be read. The two upper case letters, including the *lamed*, are written above the line, apparently as a correction. Of the *lamed* at the end, only part of its flag has survived. Qimron's]לֹ[בדי]לֹֹ [is therefore imprecise and conjectural, entailing the restoration of longer lines.

---

16 This is a well-known method of deletion practiced by the Qumran scribes (cf. e.g. 1QIsa^a XXIX, 3, 8 where this method is used).
17 Qimron, *Hebrew Writings*, 2:315.
18 Ibid.
19 Ibid; Steudel, "Apocryphon," 305.

L. 9]בכל. The two first letters are almost intact in PAM 41515 and 41860. Steudel and Qimron read]בכֹוֹל. However, there is insufficient space for a *waw* between the *kaf* and *lamed*, neither are there any remains of a long vertical stroke typical of this letter. From the orthographic point of view, the full orthography כול would be strange in this very defective manuscript (see the defective spelling of this word in line 6 and in frg. 2 2, 3).

L. 10 הֹבּרֹאֹים. Read with Qimron (cf. PAM 41515 and 41860, wherethere are sufficient remains of the upper strokes to permit an identification of the letters). Steudel reads מֹתֹים.

L. 11 מֹעְמל וֹ[. These letters are seen clearly on PAM 41515. Thus, also Qimron.

   ם׳ו[ ]ו. Steudel's reading of כֹ[י טוֹבִים cannot be supported by the physical data.

Translation
1.   ]..[
2. Everything he spoke]to you be careful to perform th[e
3. [ ] to Israel [ ].. is for joining[
4. [ ]. to all Israel, when they see[
5. [   ] when the luminaries of his glory appear from his hol[y] heaven [and when they are gathered back into his glorious habitation, and will]answer all[
6. [Israel and shall say: "Bles]sed ~~(is) YHWH~~ (are) You, O Lord, [who] (are) righteous in all your ways, who (are) mighty in power , who (are)[   ]your [jud]gments, who (are) trustworthy
7. in a[ll your words], who have understanding in a[ll in]sight, who (are) [in] all strength, and he commanded to bring out [the light], to ..[   ].
8. that you have created the morning as a sign for the appearance of the rule of light, as the boundary of the day ..[   ]
9. for their work, to bless your holy name you created them, "for the light is good" ...[   ] for in every[   ]
10. [a]ll the creatures that you have cre[a]ted the evening as a sign for the appearance of the rule[of darkness, as the boundary of the night]
11. [ ]. from labor, to bless [your holy name, you] created them[   ] .[ ]... [al]l[your deeds]

Comments

This is the largest section of the manuscript to have been preserved, comprising eleven lines. It consists of two fragments, numbered 3 and 3a, Steudel placing the latter as the conclusion of lines 5–7a. Although no left margin has been preserved in frg. 3a to indicate the end of the line, the content exhibits sequentiality between the ends of the lines in frg. 3a and the beginning of those following. Thus, a substantive continuity exists between the ends of the lines in frg. 3a and those that continue in frg. 3. This confirms the correctness of Steudel's placement. Therefore, it is feasible that the words preserved at the end of frg. 3a constitute the conclusion of the lines. The two pieces being separate, it remains unclear how far apart they should be placed and what line length should be assumed. The beginning of the line is determined by the right-hand margins preserved before lines 7–9. Line 7, preserving the right-hand margin and the conclusion of the sentence on the left side, provides the full line length of the fragment, around seventy letter-spaces. According to Steudel, this fragment belongs to the second column of the composition, apparently constituting its upper section (see the General Introduction to this manuscript).[20]

The fragment contains no line indicators, the script is sloppy, and the size of the letters is uneven. Some evidence exists of phonetic spelling (ברתה, להוצי), a medial *mem* in place of the final one (שמ קדשׂך), words without intervening spaces (אתהׂאׂדני), scribal corrections above the line, and the deletion of the Tetragrammaton by five dots, two above and below the first two letters and one before the word.

L. 2 א]ת אׂ[ליכם שׁמרׂו לעׂשׂוׂת דבר [אׂליכם שׁמרׂו לעׂשׂוׂת א]ת כל אשר דבר. This is a direct second person plural address, indicated both by the pronoun אׂליכם and the imperative שׁמרׂו, commanding the addressees to "be careful to perform ...." The latter may be the Israelites who are referred to explicitly in lines 3–4. The surviving phrase is supplemented here with the biblical formula דבר אליכם ("he spoke to you"), generally signifying a divine command to the people, usually given by Moses (cf. Deut 4:12, 15, 10:4; Josh 20:2, 23:15). The variant ואדבר אליכם ולא שמעתם also occurs (with slight variations; cf. Deut 1:43; Jer 7:13, 25:3, 35:14), attesting that God's words were understood as an unfulfilled injunction. Although the expression "speaking and doing" is prevalent in the biblical text (cf. Exod 23:22, 32:14), no precise parallel to our text exists. The purpose of the address may be to command the fixed recital of prayer or set its time. The prayer itself opens with the blessing in lines 6 + 6a.

---

[20] Steudel, "Apocryphon," 300.

L. 3 א]ל ישראל. This phrase may be understood either as a continuation of the general address to the people that commences in line 2, אל serving as a preposition ("to"). Less fitting with the context is Steudel's suggestion to read "God" and thus to understand the expression as "the God of Israel," based on its occurrence in the *Daily Prayers* (4Q503) and the *War Scroll*.[21]

[ ]◦הדׄר הוא ליחד]. The link between this clause and the preceding line depends on the understanding of the syntax of the clause. In connection with her reading of the first letters as הׄבֹּרֵאׄ[, i.e., the definite *qal* participle of the root ברא", Steudel reads the sentence to mean "the God of Israel, the Creator for (the sake of) the Yaḥad."[22] Therefore, for her, the term יחד is the well-known sectarian designation of the Qumran community, the Yaḥad.[23] Qimron, more plausibly, suggests the reading הׄדר הוא ליחד ("majesty is he to the Yaḥad").[24] The assertion that the text refers to the Qumran community is problematic because the address is made to all Israel (line 4) and there is no other distinctively sectarian terminology in the fragment.[25] Rather than reading ליחד as a preposition + noun, it may be parsed as a *Hifʻil* or *Piʻel* participle or infinitive of the root יח"ד ("to join/enter") a group/alliance, as in Gen 49:6: בקהלם אל-תחד כבדי ("Let not my being be counted in their assembly"). This meaning is also used by the scrolls: ליסד מוסד אמת לישראל, ליחד ברית עולם ("To establish a foundation of truth for Israel and distinguish an eternal covenant"; 1QS V, 5); להיחד בעצת קודש ("To become joined to the congregation of holiness"; 1QS V, 20).[26] Both of these texts employ the root as a verb. The first contains a parallelism, making ליחד synonymous with ליסד. Another alternative is to read the entire line as a nominative sentence, in which הוא is the copula and ליחד is the predicate. Even so, the broken line remains enigmatic.

L. 4 ה[. ה אל כל ישראל בֹּרֹאתםׄ]. This line mentions an address to all Israel, apparently related in the third person. This is indicated by the word בֹּרֹאתם. In line with the context and the following details, it should be parsed as the *Qal* infinitive of the verb ראה, with the attached 3rd per. pl. pronoun and the temporal *bet* (בְּרָאתָם, "when they see"), rather than the *qatal* 2nd per. sg. of ברא with the attached 3rd per. pl. pronoun (בְּרָאתָם, "you created them."; but see line 9, where this is the

---

21 Cf. e.g. 4Q503 14 2; 15–16 8; 33 i 20; 1QM X, 9; XIII, 1.
22 Steudel, "Apocryphon," 306.
23 Cf. e.g. 1QS I, 16; III, 2; V, 1–2.
24 Qimron, *Hebrew Writings*, 2:315.
25 For the question of whether the present composition is sectarian, see Discussion below.
26 My translation of both these texts. See S. Talmon, *The World of Qumran from Within* (Jerusalem: Magnes, 1989), 58–59.

correct reading). The reference appears to be to the seeing of the luminaries, mentioned in the following line and alluded to in the formula the "light is good" in line 9.[27] The determining of the visibility of the luminaries is important for establishing the time at which the prayer is to be recited. The line plausibly relates to the time at which the prayer should be recited daily, namely, when the luminaries make their appearance. Less likely is Steudel's reconstruction יקרא מש[ה אל כל ישראל], indicating that Moses is the person addressing Israel.[28] Nothing in this text is specifically connected with Moses, and he is not mentioned in any of the other fragments belonging to this composition. Therefore, reconstructing a historical occasion on which Moses addressed the people, during which the latter saw the luminaries, is awkward.

L. 5 ב[ה]פיע מאורי כבדו מזבול קד[ש ועם האספם למעון כבוד. The restoration is proposed based on the very similar lines in 1QS X, 2–3.[29] As indicated by the phrase ב[ה]פיע, a *Pi'el* infinitive of the root יפ"ע (written defectively), this is a temporal clause denoting the time at which the prayer is to be recited. A similar description appears in 1QH[a] XX, 7–10.[30] The *Hodayot* passage also prescribes that prayer is to be recited when the luminaries rise in the heavens, i.e., twice a day, in the morning and evening.[31]

מזבול קד[ש. In the biblical texts, זבול designates the temple as God's abode in the "heights" (cf. 1 Kgs 8:13; 2 Chr 6:2).[32] The phrase here reflects Isa 63:15; cf. also Hab 3:11.[33] The idea appears on several occasions in the Qumran literature, the various usages indicating two principal senses: a) the heavenly temple as the

---

27 Baumgarten ("Notes," 143–44) suggests that this phrase is a reworking of Qoh 11:7; cf. also Gen 1:18.
28 Steudel, "Apocryphon," 305.
29 The restoration fits with the reconstructed length of the line since, according to my calculation based on line 7, its maximum length is 70–75 letter-spaces.
30 Cf. 1QS X, 1–14. See Licht, *Rule Scroll*, 204–09.
31 For the morning and evening times of prayer/praise at Qumran see J. Licht, *The Thanksgiving Scroll* (Jerusalem: Bialik Institute, 1965), 204–08 (Hebrew); B. Nitzan, *Qumran Prayer and Religious Poetry* (STDJ 12; Leiden: Brill, 1993), 55–56; E. G. Chazon, "When Did They Pray? Times for Prayer in the Dead Sea Scrolls and Associated Literature," in *For a Later Generation: The Transformation of Tradition in Israel, Early Judaism and Early Christianity* (ed. R. A. Argall et. al.; Harrisburg, PA: Trinity Press International, 2000), 42–51.
32 See M. Held, "The Root ZBL/SBL in Akkadian, Ugaritic and Biblical Hebrew," *JAOS* 88 (1968): 90–96, who notes that since the Ugaritic parallels suggest that the biblical root should be regarded as synonymous with נש"א, זבול should be understood as signifying a high, lofty place.
33 *HALOT*, 263; *DCH*, 3:81. Gamberroni argues that Hab 3:11 preserves an echo of an (Ugaritic?) mythological tradition regarding the status of the moon, El's adversary. In the biblical context,

abode of God and his close angels (1QM XII, 1//4Q491 5–6 1; 4Q405 6 2; 4Q405 81 2); and b) closer to Habakkuk, the site of the stars 1QS X, 2–3.³⁴ An otherwise unidentified fragment also depicts the זבול as the place from which the sun appears (4Q468b 4). One of the sectarian *Hodayot* parallels the "holy habitation" with the "host of heaven" (1QHª XI, 35–36). It carries here the dual sense of the heights/heaven as God's habitation and the abode of the luminaries.

מֹאֲרֵי כְבוֹדוֹ. The expression describes the luminaries (מֹאֲרֵי = מאורי). The luminaries are regarded as expressing the glory of God who created them, being described metaphorically as elements of the heavenly temple.

Ll. 5–6 וֹ[עָנוּ כֹל] יִשְׂרָאֵל. The end of the line contains an injunction to recite a blessing, in a formulation familiar from other Qumran texts (see Comments on 1Q29 3–4 3, 4Q408 2 2). The formula precedes the prayer itself and notes the public recital of the blessing by all the people. The reconstruction ישראל is in line with the same formulation in frg. 2 2, and appears also in 1Q29 3–4 3, see Comments ad. loc.

Ll. 6 + 6a בָּר[וּךְ יְהוָה̇. This is the blessing formula that opens the prayer. The originally written ברוך יהוה was deleted by a scribe with upper and lower dots (see Notes on Readings) and replaced with the word אדני, obviously to avoid pronouncing the Tetragrammaton. Notably, the Tetragrammaton was replaced by אדני only in this prayer; in other sections, it appears in full (4Q408 2 1, 3; 1Q29 1 7; 3–4 2; 4Q375 ii 8). The formula appears three times elsewhere in the Qumran scrolls, all in the thanksgiving hymns (1QHª VIII, 26; XIII, 22; XVIII, 16). This forms an early testimony to the use of the formula ברוך אתה אדוני known from later prayers.³⁵

Ll. 6–7 [הַ]צַּדִּיק בְּכָל דְּרָכֶיךָ הֲ֗לֹ֗א כֹּחַ הֹ֗] מַשׁ[פִּטֶיךָ הַנֶּאֱמָן בְּכֹ]ל דְּבָרֶיךָ] הַמֵּבִ֗י֗ן בְּכֹ]ל שֶׂ[כֶל הַנֵּעָ[ור]בְּ[כֹל גְּב֗וּרָה. This forms part of the praise in the prayer, expressed via five or six similarly constructed phrases depicting God's attributes. The full formulaic pattern consisting of three words has been preserved in most of the praise phrases: a divine title, an object that defines the field in which the divine trait manifests itself, and the preposition בכל emphasizing the comprehensive and inclusive nature of the trait. The phrase is apparently influenced by the similar

---

the term denotes God's supremacy in line with the use of the root ZBL in Ugaritic: J. Gamberroni, "zᵉbhul," in *TDOT* 4:29–31.

34 Cf. 4Q256 19 1; 4Q258 8 12.
35 Baumgarten, "Notes," 144.

construction in Ps 145:17: צדיק יהוה בכל דרכיו וחסיד בכל מעשיו ("The LORD is beneficent in all His ways and faithful in all His works"). However, the biblical text has two clauses while our text has five/six. In the psalm, the pronominal suffix is in the third person singular, in our text it is in the second person singular, adapted to the direct address. In the biblical text, the titles are non-determined while in our text they are. Although the divine attributes adduced here are well known from the biblical texts, the final four of the five/six do not appear in this particular title and trait combination in either the Hebrew Bible or the Qumran scrolls.

L. 6 [ה]צדיק בכלדרכיך. This is the sole designation that alludes to and reworks a biblical phrase of Ps 145:17. A similar formula occurs in another sectarian text, the *Ritual of Purity*: הצדיק בכול מע[שי]כ[ה] (4Q512 34 16).[36]

הֹרֹ֗ב כח הֹ֗ [ ] מש[פטיך. Due to the fragmentary state of the phrase, it is difficult to ascertain whether one or two praise expressions are involved here. However, the surviving *he*, suggesting a definite article, is perhaps introducing an additional divine attribute, so two praise expressions may be assumed here. A similar but not identical formulation—ב]רוב כוח—appears in the prayer in 1Q29 3–4 5 (cf. also 4Q408 2 [4]). As noted in the comments on 4Q408 2 and 1Q29 3–4, the prayers therein are structured in a similar fashion to this one: a denoting of inclusivity, a command to recite a blessing, the blessing itself, and a series of praises. While the expression in frg. 2 depicts God's attribute and the way in which it is exemplified, here it constitutes a divine title. The formulation is apparently influenced by Ps 147:5, which depicts God as being גדול אדונינו ורב כח ("Great is our LORD and full of power").

Ll. 6–7 הנאמן בכֹ[ל דבריך]. Qimron's reconstruction, retained here, is based on the cave 11 psalms formulation of Ps 145:13: נֶאמן בכֹל דברֹי[ו] (11QPs^a XVII, 2–3), and the phrase נאמן אלוהים בדבריו in 4Q379 18 7.[37] It is preferable to Steudel's הנאמן [בכֹ]ל פקודיד], based on Ps 111:7 נאמנים כל פקודיו ("all his precepts are trustworthy"), since the biblical verse speaks of God's precepts being trustworthy rather than he himself.[38]

---

36 M. Baillet, "Rituel de Purification," in *Qumrân Grotte 4.III: (4Q482–4Q520)* (DJD VII; Oxford: Clarendon, 1982), 265. Baillet suggests that the formulation in this text is a reworking of Dan 9:14, which also resembles Baruch's prayer in Bar 2:9.
37 Qimron, *Hebrew Writings*, 2:71, 315.
38 Steudel, "Apocryphon," 307.

L. 7 הַמֵּבִ֗ין בְּכֹ[ל שֵׂ]כֶל. The *Hifʿil* participle (מבין) is here a divine title, a usage not customary in the Hebrew Bible.[39] The term is common in the Qumran sapiential work, *Instruction*, to designate the addressee, the wise and understanding student. However, perhaps once in this writing it is attributed to God: הואה מבין (4Q417 1 ii: 10).[40] As for the word שׂכל, here standing as a noun, in both biblical and Qumran literatures it signifies "understanding, insight," (see *HALOT*, 3:1329). So here it constitutes a praise of the divine understanding and wisdom.

הַנְעֶ[ה]בְּ[כֹל גְּ֗בוּרה. The first word, only partly preserved, seems to be patterned on the previous determinate participle. Qimron's reading and supplement [ז]הנעוֹה is difficult, for the form is extremely rare and does not apply to the divine in the biblical usage or in the Qumran texts. Steudel's reading הַנֹּעֵ֗ר[from the root נע"ר, i.e., "shaking," is even more problematic since it does not accord with the context or with the biblical parlance.

וַצִוָּ֗ה לְהוֹצִי [את] האור. Syntactically, this phrase opens a new section of the prayer, as it breaks away from the pattern of the preceding text. The two first words, וַצִוָּ֗ה לְהוֹצִי, are a 3rd sg. *qattal* (with *waw* consecutive) *Piʿel* and an infinitive. The infinitive להוצי (written defectively [= להוציא]) with the direct object marker את suggests that God is the one performing the action, just as he is in the previous lines. The phrase refers to the first creative act, that of the light, and thus to the setting of day and night (Gen 1:2-3), described in the following line. Consequently, the restoration וַצִוָּ֗ה לְהוֹצִי את] האור is proposed. As is clear from the following text, the light is interpreted both literally and metaphorically in this prayer. In the literal sense, it is the divinely created physical light. Its presence or absence establishes the temporal sequence (morning and evening). Metaphorically, the light represents the illumination of truth and justice by which the people are enabled to walk in God's paths, a usage known from the biblical parlance (e.g. Ps 37:6; 43:3). We may understand the phrase as relating to God who brings out his light, perhaps including that which shines from the Urim. Such an interpretation may explain the relationship between the prayer and the reworking of the laws dealing with the high priest's inquiring of God.[41]

---

[39] The closest biblical parallel is Ps 119:130: פתח דבריך יאיר מבין פתיים ("The words You inscribed give light, and grant understanding to the simple"). The root שכל takes God as its subject only twice in the Hebrew Bible, Job 28:23 and 1 Chr 28:9. See H. Ringgren, "bîn," *TDOT*, 2:102–03.

[40] It is understood thus by the editors, who point out that here the participle מבין is presented by a 3rd per. sg. pronoun (הואה), whereas when addressed to a human interlocutor it stands mostly in the 2nd per. sg. See J. Strugnell and D. Harrington, *Qumran Cave 4.XXIV: Sapiential Texts, Part 2: 4QInstruction* (DJD XXXIV; Oxford: Clarendon, 1999), 224.

[41] See also Discussion below.

L. 8 [בֹּ֯ן יֹומָ֯ם לגבול אור ממשלת להֹ֯פִ֯יע אות הבקר אֵ֯ת ברתה אשר. This marks a new section of the prayer, containing a series of praises to God. The first praise, introduced by the formula אשר בראת, concerns the creation of the light. This topic occupies the remaining lines of the fragment. Notably, the expression הב[קר אות] appears again in frg. 5 line 1.[42] The line is based on Gen 1:1–2, but reworks the biblical passage with its own phraseology. The term אשר indicates a relative clause; the main clause on which it is dependent has not been preserved. Containing a direct address, ברתה ("you created"), it is addressed to God the Creator, and thus suggests that the main clause may have been a blessing. Therefore, it may be reconstructed: [ברוך אתה אדוני] אשר ברתה. The term "morning" (בֹקר) serves as a temporal indicator of either the time of the rising of the sun or in the sense of "tomorrow (in the morning)."[43] The morning constitutes the sign of the appearance of the dominion of light, i.e., the period of light. While Genesis employs the root בד"ל to denote the separation of day and night, the scroll uses the root ג.ב"ל (לגבול).[44] In Genesis 1, the lights are created to dominate the day and night (Gen 1:16). The light/sun and the darkness/moon and stars distinguish between day and night, their appearance denoting the beginning of each period. Our text—which defines morning (בוקר) as the item created, signaling the advent of the dominion of the light—thus reverses the biblical concept, the appearance of the "dominion of light" following the creation of the morning.[45] In addition, the author replaces the biblical ממשלת היום ("rule of the day") with ממשלת אור ("rule of light"). The pairing "dominion of light"/"dominion of darkness" (ממשלת אור/ממשלת חושך) is well known in the Qumran literature, appearing both in 1QS and the *Daily Prayers*: ממשל אור היומם (4Q503 15–16 6).[46] Regulation of

---

[42] Steudel suggests that frg. 5 forms part of the prayer found here and should thus be placed in proximity to it. She argues that the two are not overlapping fragments but merely a repetition of the phrase in the same text. See eadem, "Apocryphon," 309.

[43] See C. Barth, "bōqer," in *TDOT*, 2:222–28, who notes that around half of the occurrences of the noun in the biblical texts are preceded by a preposition, most frequently ב- (בבוקר). Our text attests to the use of the word as a temporal indicator. See also the biblical phrase אור הבוקר, which links the light with the day: cf. Josh 16:2; 1 Sam 14:36; 25:34; Mic 2:1. Cf. *HALOT*, 1:151.

[44] Cf. *HALOT*, 1:171; *DCH*, 2:300–301.

[45] The phrases ממשלת יום/לילה also appear, with a slight variation, in a praise to God for his creation of the luminaries offered in Ps 136:7–9.

[46] The usage of sectarian terms in the *Daily Prayers* (4Q503) attests to its sectarian provenance, as shown by Daniel Falk and Devorah Dimant. See D. K. Falk, *Daily, Sabbath and Festival Prayers in the Dead Sea Scrolls* (STDJ 27; Leiden: Brill, 1998), 21–29 (note also B. Nitzan, *Qumran Prayer and Religious Poetry* [Leiden: Brill, 1994], 55–56) and D. Dimant, "The Vocabulary of the Qumran Sectarian Texts," in *History, Ideology and Bible Interpretation in the Dead Sea Scrolls: Collected Studies* (FAT 90; Tübingen: Mohr Siebeck, 2014), 57–100 (65–67).

the light is, of course, one of the central tasks of the luminaries (Gen 1:14). In this biblical context, the term "sign" (אות) denotes that the luminaries "set times" in their monthly/annual orbits. This fact has a special importance since this temporal rhythm determines the festival calendar.[47] In 4Q503, the noun occurs in association with the luminaries. While the text is fragmentary, it seems to relate to the appearance of the moon and stars as signifying the commencement of the evening: ד[מֹוֹעֵד ב לנו ללילה אֹות] ("[ ] sign for us at night at the appoin[ted time]"; 4Q503 64 4).

L. 9 בראתם לעבדתם לברך את שם קדשׁך. לעבדתם is the noun עבודה ("work, labor, service"[48]) suffixed by a 3rd per. pl. pronoun and prefixed by the preposition -ל. It belongs to the preceding lost sentence, plausibly dealing with the creation of the morning/domain of the light. Compare 1QH[a] IX, 14, where the same term denotes the functioning of the celestial beings and God's creation (nature) according to the rules God has set to govern them.[49] Both Steudel and Qimron associate the term with human activity, which is also possible.[50] Qimron combines the previous line and this with frg. 1 of this manuscript, reading lines 8–9 as: אשר ברתה אֹת הבֹּקֶר לעבדתם [יצאו למען] האדֹם ל[בני בר]אתו יוֹמָם לגבול אור ממשלת להֹפִיע אוֹת ("who created the morning as a sign for the appearance of the domain of light, as a boundary for the day he created it for the sons of man so that they may go out and serve their duty"). However, the combination of fragments proposed by Qimron is hypothetical and the text may be interpreted differently (see Comment below). Following the depiction of the regularity of the appearance of the light, the present line prescribes the duty of reciting a blessing over this divinely created phenomenon.[51] According to this context, the form בראתם should be parsed as a *qatal* 2nd per. sg. of ברא with the attached 3rd per. pl. pronoun (בְּרָאתָם; "you created them"). This expression perhaps refers to the luminaries or to the heavenly bodies and the natural elements in general, which praise God (see Ps 19:2).

---

47 See *HALOT*, 1:26; F. J. Helfmeyer, "ôth," in *TDOT*, 1:170. The latter argues that the word denotes "an object, an occurrence, an event through which a person is to recognize, learn, remember, or perceive the credibility of something," the "signs" in Gen 1:14 and 9:12–13 constituting the signs of the order of the created world and nature.
48 Cf. *HALOT*, 2:776–77; *DCH*, 6:209–14; H. Ringgren, "ªbōdâ," in *TDOT*, 10:403–05.
49 Cf. also the terms appearing in a similar context in 4Q286 3 a–d 2–5.
50 Steudel, "Apocryphon," 308; Qimron, *Hebrew Writings*, 2:315.
51 For similar blessings of creation, see 4Q216 V 10; 11QPs[a] XXVI, 11–12; 4Q364 30 3–5; 4Q365 6a i 2–3. Cf. also the blessing of God as part of the divine plan of creation in 4Q215a 1 ii 7–9; 4Q287 3 2–4.

[כי בכל] [ ]ו[ ]ב. **כי טוב האור וב**[ ]. The conjunction כי opens a causal clause, explaining why the light should be blessed, "because the light is good." The expression echoes God's statement at the conclusion of the first day of creation (Gen 1:4).

ובֿ[ ]. [כי בכל] The *waw* (consecutive) introduces a second causal clause, probably explaining why the light, or God, should be blessed. Steudel's reconstruction, [וב]הכירם כֿיֿ בכֿוֹלֿ], reads the verb as an infinitive of נכ"ר with pl. suffix, but this is conjectural.

L. 10 **כ]ל הֿבֿרֿאֿיֿםֿ**. This seems to connect the first praise, that of creating the light signaled by the morning, described in lines 8–9, with the second praise in lines 10–11. However, Qimron suggests that the transition is effected here to the evening blessing. Apparently "all the creatures" referred to here are linked to the light by the fact that they take advantage of it.

אשר בר[ת]אֿ את הערב. The formula אשר בר[ת]אֿה, used in line 8 to introduce the creation of the morning, is employed again here to introduce the creation of evening. It thus is related to the evening blessing, referred to in the following line. Qimron reconstructs along these lines [ברוך יוצר כ]ל הֿבֿרֿאֿיֿםֿ ("Blessed be the creator of all the creatures").

אות להופיעֿ ממשלתֿ[חושך לגבול לילה]. The formulation is parallel to that of the creation of the light in line 8 and is supplemented accordingly. Both lines are built on Gen 1:4–5. Here, too, the evening is the item being created, constituting the sign for the appearance of the dominion of darkness. The night is described in similar terms in two copies of the same hymn from the *Hodayot* (1QH^a XX, 9 and 4Q427 8 ii 12), בראשית ממשלת חושך למועד לילה ("at the beginning of the rule of darkness"). These passages also determine the times of prayer according to the rising and setting of the sun (1QH^a XX, 4–5).[52] In other words, the evening prayer is to be recited when darkness falls, this constituting the commencement of the period of the dominion of the night. Although the expression ממשלת חושך also occurs in the thanksgiving hymns—indisputably sectarian in provenance—the usage is not necessarily dualistic in the style characteristic of the community. In both the *Hodayot* and the present text, the reference is to the determination of the beginning of the evening/night—the dominion of darkness—without any moral/ ideological connotation.

L. 11 **[וֿ מֿעֿמֿל לבֿרך [את שם קדשך ב]רֿאתֿםֿ[ ] [ ]o[יֿ]oים[כ]ל[מעשיך**. This line continues the second half of the praise to God as the creator of the morning and night. As noted above, it is constructed of two parallel halves, the first describing the crea-

---

52 See J. Licht, *The Thanksgiving Scroll* (Jerusalem: Bialik Institute, 1965), 172–73 (Hebrew).

tion of the morning as the sign of the commencement of the rule of light and the second portraying the creation of the evening as the sign of the commencement of the rule of darkness. The second clause in each part relates to the benediction to God. In the first section, the luminaries, the heavenly bodies and perhaps the entire created world bless God because they were created for this purpose and because the light is good. However, in contrast to the term עבודה ("service, work"), which may be applied also to the regular functioning of the heavenly bodies and the interchange of day and night, the term עמל ("toil") is linked exclusively to humanity, usually in connection to working for a livelihood. Therefore, it appears that the blessing here relates to human beings. Linked to the previous rather than following sentence and assuming that man is the subject here, Qimron suggests that the allusion is to the blessing in the evening at the conclusion of the man's workday and thus reconstructs lines 10–11 as: אשר בר[ת]הֿ אתֿ הערב אות להופיעֿ לגבול לילה ממשלתֿ [חושך לגבול לילה בראתו/ לנוח ב]וֿ מֿעֿמל ("that you created the evening as a sign for the appearance of the rule of darkness, as a boundary for the night he created it/ to rest in it from labor").

מעשיך [ ]∘[כ]ל[ ]∘**ים**. Here, the cause has not been preserved, as the sentence breaks off precisely before the identification of what the people see and understand to be good. Steudel reconstructs ב[רֿאתםֿ [ ] כֿ]י טו[בֿים] כו[ל] כוכבים ("[when] they see th[at go]od [are al]l[the stars]") apparently in an attempt to create a parallelism with the "light" in the first part, but this is an unattested Hebrew formulation. Moreover, the combination טובים כוכבים could have an idolatrous association.[53] Steudel's reconstruction is plausible, based on the blessing of the light in the first part. Therefore the reconstruction proposed here is כֿ]י טו[בֿים כ]ל[מעשיך.

מעשיך. This is the plural of the noun מעשה ("work, deed, labor"[54]), with a masc. sg. possessive pronoun, assigning it to God. In biblical and Qumran literature, the term sometimes refers to the "works of creation" (Ps 8:4–7; 19:2; 102:26; 1QH[a] XV, 35; XVIII, 13).[55] *Jub.* 2:3 uses the root עשה to describe God's creative activity and מעשה to represent the work of creation: ראינו מעשיו ונֿ[ברכהו] / על כל [מ]עֿשיו וֿ[נהללה לפניו כי שבעה] מֿעשים גדוֿלים עֿ[שה ביום הראשון] ("Then we saw his works and we [blessed him] regarding all his [wo]rks, and [we offered praise

---

[53] However, some scrolls do mention the light of the stars; cf. 4Q299 5 1. See also the reference to the stars in the context of the creation (Ps 8:4; 4Q392 1 6). While Ps 148:3 states: הללוהו שמש וירח הללוהו כל כוכבי אור ("Praise him, sun and moon, praise him all the bright stars"), it does not single out the stars or speak of them as "good."
[54] *HALOT*, 2:616–17.
[55] Cf. H. Ringgren, "ma'aśeh," in *TDOT*, 11:400.

before him because he] had ma[de seven] great works [on the first day]"; 4Q216 V 10–11).

Structure of the Prayer

Line	Text	Function
5–6	[will]answer all [Israel]	Introductory formula
6	[and shall say Bles]sed (are) you, O Lord	Blessing
6–7	[who] are righteous in all your ways who (are) mighty in power, who (are)[ ] your [jud]gments who (are) trustworthy in a[ll your words] who have understanding in a[ll in]sight who (are) [in] all strength	Five/six praise sentences
7	And He commanded to bring out [the light]	Description of the creation
7–9 10–11	(A) [(Blessing? Blessed be You, O Lord?)] that you have created the morning as a sign for the appearance of the rule of light, as the boundary of the day [ ] (B) for their work, to bless your holy name you created them, "for the light is good" (A1)[(Blessing?)] A]ll the creatures, that you have cre[a]ted, the evening as a sign for the appearance of the rule[of darkness, as the boundary of the night] (B1) from labor, to bless [your holy name you] created them ....."f[or al]l[your deeds are go]od"	Praise to God for is creation of the light, morning and evening, constructed of two parallels halves devoted to the morning and evening respectively

Frg. 4

               ∘∘[1a
                אׄםׄ[1
              ל[ולבקׄר   2

No margins have been preserved in this fragment. The color of the leather and the word "morning" led Steudel to suggest that it forms the left-hand conclusion of lines 7–8 of frg. 3, on the left side underneath frg. 3a. Another plausible conjecture is that it forms the end of lines 8–9.[56]

Translation
1a.   ]..
1.   ]..
2.   ]. and to the morning

Comments
The text seems to relate to the morning prayer, as does frg. 5 (thus Steudel). However, due to its smallness, it cannot be established whether the fragment belongs to the prayer in frg. 3 or is independent.

Frg. 5

1   הב[קֹר אות]
2   [לֹ]

Notes on Readings
This is another fragment without margins, and therefore its position within the column/sequence remains unclear. The color of the leather and content led Steudel to posit that it belongs either to frg. 3 as a continuation of line 7 or to frg. 6. Both options are feasible and whichever is adopted frgs. 3–7 consist of a prayer that mentions the commencement of the morning and evening.

L. 1 הב[קֹר. Here the *qof* differs from the form it typically takes in this scroll. While the long descender in most of the incidences does not lie on a very diagonal angle, here it is written with a much greater slant—almost curved—resembling the left arm of the letter *shin*.

---

[56] Steudel, "Apocryphon," 308–09. She also notes that the insertion of the fragment at the end of lines 8–9 would yield the sentence: ולבקר לעבודתם לברך את שם קדשך. However, this is to be ruled out since it creates a syntactically awkward construction. Also implausible is the possibility she advances that the word בקר is to be read as "cattle," thereby associating the text with 4Q376 i 2, as frgs. 4–7 are now recognized as part of a prayer on the basis of their distinctive terminology.

Translation
1. the mo]rning is a sign[
2.   ].[

Comments
For the phrase אות הב[קֹר, see Comments on frg. 3 8.

Frg. 6

[מֹ[1
[מוצ]א 2

Translation
1.   ].[
2.]departu[re

Comments
This fragment has no margins, and therefore its place in the column/sequence is unclear. On the basis of its color, Steudel suggests that it should be placed in proximity to frg. 3. However, it fits better with line 11 of frg. 3, which relates to the evening and night.[57] Steudel's proposal to join frgs. 5 and 6 and read [מוצא הב[קֹר]אות ("The departure of the morning is a sign") is plausible; cf. Ps 65:9.

[מוצ]א. In biblical parlance, the term signifies "departure, exit" as well as "coming forth, appearance."[58] In the scrolls, however, מוצא designates the departure of the sun and the appearance of the moon/stars (1QH[a] XX, 8–9; 1QS X, 10). The term is thus used to signify the time of prayer, in this case that of the evening.[59] This seems to be the context of the term here.

---

[57] Cf. the similar usage in 1QM XIV, 13–14: עם מ[בו]א יומם ולילה / ומוצאי ערב ובוקר ("at the be[ginn]ing of day and night and at dawn and dusk") and 4Q299 5 4: [ומוצא לילה] מבוא יום ("the coming in of day] and the going out of night").
[58] Cf. *HALOT*, 2:559.
[59] Cf. Steudel, "Apocryphon," 310. The phrase באופיע מאורות מזבול קודש in 1QS X, 2–3 forms a parallel to the times presented in the prayer in frg. 3.

Frg. 7

1 בְּ[עֶרב בער]ְב
2 יְ[שביתוּ]

Translation
1. e]very evenin[g
2.]they [shall] cease[

Comments

It is tempting to regard these lines as the conclusion of lines 10–11 of frg. 3, but Steudel argues that the color of the leather precludes this placement. Instead, she ascribes the fragment to the right hand of line 2 of the following column, i.e., the third column according to her reconstruction.[60]

L. 1 בְּ[עֶרב בער]ְב. This phrase occurs twice in 2 Chr 13:11 in connection with the temple service. If the fragment alludes to this verse, it may point to an association between the time of the sacrificial offerings (in the temple) and the times of the prayer mentioned in this manuscript.

L. 2 יְ[שביתוּ]. This verb is a *Hifʻil* 3rd pl. *yiqtol* of שב"ת, perhaps used in an impersonal sense. It signifies a cessation of activity.[61] The reference may well be to stopping work on the Sabbath or a festival. In Lev 23:32, the commandments relating to the observance of the Day of Atonement include the statement: שבת שבתון הוא לכם ועניתם את נפשתיכם בתשעה לחדש בערב מערב עד ערב תשבתו שבתכם ("It shall be a Sabbath of complete rest for you, and you shall practice self-denial; on the ninth day of the month at evening, from evening to evening, you shall observe this your Sabbath"). This verse links the root שב"ת to the time of "evening" as the beginning and end of the Day of Atonement. If this forms the framework of our text, it reflects a similar view that defines the beginning of the day with sunset rather than sunrise.[62]

---

60 Ibid, 300, 310.
61 Cf. *HALOT*, 4:1407–08.
62 This theme is linked to another issue, namely, that of when the day begins according to the Qumranites. Talmon has proposed that it began in the morning whereas Baumgraten suggested that the evening marked the beginning. See S. Talmon, "The Calendar Reckoning of the Sect from the Judaean Desert," ScrHier 4 (1958): 162–99 (192–93). Talmon readdressed the issue in "The Reckoning of the Day in the Biblical and the Early Post-Biblical Periods: From Morning or

Frg. 8

oo[1
vacat [2
אַ֯תה[3

Translation
1.]..
2.] vacat [
3.] you

Comments
See Steudel's notes on the reading. The placement of this fragment is unclear, although the difference in line-spacing precludes its attachment to frg. 3. While the text is too fragmentary to be given any meaningful interpretation, the second singular pronoun (אַ֯תה) may refer to God, the fragment thus possibly constituting a continuation of the prayer in frg. 3 (see there).

Frg. 9

]ה֯שׂo[1
]oo[2

Notes on Readings
L. 1 ה֯שׂo[. A very small lower tip of a letter may be observed before the *shin* (see PAM 43543). Steudel reads עֹ֯שׂה[or מֹ֯שׁה[, but the *'ayin* and *mem* are equally unlikely.

From Evening?," in *The Bible in the Light of its Interpreters: Sarah Kamin Memorial Volume* (ed. S. Japhet; Jerusalem: Magnes, 1994), 73–108. For a critique of this view, see J. M. Baumgarten, "The Beginning of the Day in the Calendar of Jubilees," *JBL* 77 (1958): 355–60; idem, "4Q503 (Daily Prayers) and the Lunar Calendar," *RevQ* 12 (1987): 399–407. Perhaps the present work, found among the Qumran documents, reflects the view adopted by the sectaries that the day began in the evening. However, a definite conclusion cannot be obtained due to the fragmentary nature of the evidence.

Frg. 10

]א̇ש[	1
] ת̇[	2
?vac[	3
]∘[	4

The bright color of this fragment led Steudel to conclude that it does not belong to frg. 3 and should rather be placed at the end of lines 2–5 of the fourth column.⁶³

Frg. 11

האבן כ[אשר ∘]	1
ויצא עמו [בלשׁונות א̇שׁהא̇]בן	2
עד כלות ה[כ̇ה̇ן לד̇]בר	3

Notes on Readings
Frg. 11 contains the phrase לשונות אש, which appears in two of the other copies attributed to the *Apocryphon of Moses* (4Q376 ii 1 and 1Q29 1 3; 2 3) and has been influential in assigning the various copies to the present composition. According to Steudel, the fragment should be regarded as lines 7–9 of the fourth column.

L. 2 א̇ש. The word "fire" has been added as a correction above the line. The *shin* survived only in a small dot, but the reading is confirmed on the basis of the parallels in other copies.

Comments
This fragment parallels 1Q29 1 2–4 and 4Q376 ii, relating to the high priest's shining garments as he leaves the sanctuary. In the comments to 4Q376 ii, it was suggested that the high priest is accompanied by the chieftain, with the tongues of fire representing the shining of the stones on the high priest's breastplate/shoulder pieces, as a public answer to his inquiry of God via the Urim as to whether or not to engage in a permissible war.

---

63 Steudel, "Apocryphon," 300–311.

Frgs. 12–17

The remainder of the fragments are extremely fragmentary, none of their content being legible. Steudel is uncertain whether they all form one column—the fourth—or whether some (frgs. 14–16) belong to a fifth column. She suggests that frg. 17 may not in fact belong to this manuscript.

Frg. 12

1 [ׄ[
2 [תתיׄ] ׄ[
3 [לׄ]
4 [ׄ[

Notes on Readings

L. 1]ׄ[. A small tip of a letter may be seen on PAM 43543 that was not noted by Steudel.

L. 3]לׄ[. The flag of the *lamed* may be observed beneath the first *taw* (see PAM 42916, 43543). Steudel read it as a supralinear *shin*, but the stroke does not fit with a left arm of this letter.

L. 4]ׄ[. Only the trace of an upper horizontal stroke has been preserved. It may fit with a *he* or a final *mem*. Steudel opted for the latter possibility.

Frg. 13

1 [וׄלה ׄ]
2 [לׄ]

Frg. 14

1 [ׄ[וׄכלמׄ]

Frg. 15

1 [וׄנׄעׄלׄ]
2 מעׄ[רׄכה וׄעׄ]

Notes on Readings

L. 1]נׄעׄל[. Steudel reads ה[.צׄנע לׄ]כת.[64] However, the space between the *lamed* and *'ayin* does not seem to be as long as that between two words. Tigchelaar read נגעל, noting the parallelism with 1Q29 2 4;[65] see Comments on 1Q29 2 4.

Translation
1.   ] is determined [
2.   ba]ttle ..[

Comments

L. 1]נׄעׄל[. If this is the correct reading, this fragment appears to be close in content to frg. 11, which refers to the "tongues of fire" and the receipt of verdicts. See the discussion on 1Q29 2 4.

L. 2]מעׄרׄכה וׄעׄ[. Steudel suggests that this may read מעׄ]רׄכה or ב[.רׄכה. The former, adopted here, would support the proposal that the tongues of fire are linked to going out to "battle."

Frg. 16

]*vac*[	1
]מׄרׄו[ ]	2
]מׄלׄפׄנׄ]יׄ	3

Notes on Readings

L. 3]מׄלׄפׄנׄ]יׄ. Remains of the left strokes of a *mem* may be seen on PAM 42916 as well as on PAM 43543.

Frg. 17

]∘אׄ[ ]∘[	1
] *vacat* [	2

---

64 Ibid, 314.
65 Cf. E. J. C. Tigchelaar, "A Cave 4 Fragment of *Divre Moshe* (4QMD) and the Text of 1Q22 1:7–10 and Jubilees 1:9, 14," *DSD* 12 (2005): 303–12 (308, n. 8).

Discussion

Of the seventeen fragments belonging to this scroll, only three—frgs. 2, 3, and 11—can be properly understood since the remainder are very small and fragmentary. Frgs. 2 and 3 are prayers. Frg. 11 parallels 4Q376 ii and 1Q29 1 2–4, as it deals with the shining of the priest's garments. Nevertheless, frgs. 4–7 display various links to the prayer in frg. 3 and apparently form a continuation of this text. Frg. 15 appears to be a reworking of a law in this scroll. The words נֻעֲלֹ and possibly מֵעֲ[רֹכֹה suggest a link with going out to war after having inquired regarding victory via the Urim. Six of the seventeen fragments are prayers (frgs. 2–7), two (frgs. 11, 15) form part of a reworking of Pentateuchal laws, and the remainder (eight) are unidentifiable.

This analysis reveals the central element of this manuscript to be prayer. Although the prayer in frg. 2 is too brief to indicate its nature, the parts that have been preserved in frg. 3 tally with a prayer of thanksgiving and praise to God, the creator of the light and the luminaries. While it has not been preserved in its entirety, its structure and components are discernible (see the table above).

This structure is unique. Having no parallels in the Qumran liturgical literature, it is closer to fixed prayers such as those included in the Amida (Eighteen Benedictions), which contains similar structured and defined elements. The blessing constitutes an early attestation of the use of a fixed formula for liturgical purposes. In contrast to the structure of the blessing determined by the rabbinic sages, which must include God's name and adduce His kingship (cf. *b. Ber.* 40b), the blessing here only contains God's name. The pronouncement at the beginning that it must be recited at the appearance of the luminaries in the sky supplements the evidence in other Qumran prayers that the sectarians prayed twice a day, at sunrise and sunset.[66] As noted, the essential emphasis of the prayer is on praising God as creator of the light and the luminaries. The luminaries are referred to metaphorically as illuminating from the heavenly temple. Of the light, it is said explicitly that "it is good" (echoing Gen 1:4) and this is a reason for blessing the divine. Apparently, the characterization of the light as "good" is understood here as an expression of the divine management of the world, which is carried out in goodness, justice, and truth. This understanding provides a connection between the light created by God and the light of the Urim, revealing God's judgment.

In light of the above observations, the association between the light and the divine answer via the Urim perhaps echoes biblical statements, such as that of Zeph 3:5, which depicts God's righteousness as being as consistent and perpetual

---

[66] See Nitzan, *Qumran Prayer*, 55–56; Chazon, "When Did They Pray?," 42–51.

as the light at dawn. Frg. 7 may also form part of the elaborate praises to God for the creation of light in frg. 3, which contain the phrase ב[עֶׂרֶב ב ("every evening"). The section of elaborate praises in frg. 3 is constructed of two parallel halves describing respectively the creation of the morning and the evening. The expression ב[עֶׂרֶב ב may suggest the existence of the parallel בבקר בבקר ("each morning"), which may (also) rework Zeph 3:5.[67] The *Pesher of Isaiah*, which has been referred to in the discussion of 4Q376, also connects light with the Urim. The passage may be read as follows (*pace* Kister): "Its interpretation concerns the twelve[heads of the priests who] illuminate through the judgment of the Urim and Thummim [to Israel all the commandments] that they lack, like the sun in all its light" (פשרו על שנים עשר[ראשי הכהנים אשר המה[מאירים במשפט] האורים והתומים [לישראל את כל המצוות] הנעדרות מהמה כשמש בכול אורו]; 4Q164 1 4–6).[68] The *Pesher* interprets Isa 54:11–12, which refers to precious stones. It also alludes to Zeph 3:5 in combining the words נעדר, אור, and משפט. The *Pesher of Isaiah* thus appears to rework these two verses to say that God's righteousness is like the light of the sun and is revealed to Israel by the high priest via the Urim and Thummim. This connection may lie behind the texts under discussion and helps explain why the present prayer appears within a halakhic composition alongside a passage describing how the high priest receives answers to his inquiries of God.

Our prayer may also reflect the comparison of the high priest with the sun in 1QSb IV, 27–28: וישמכה קוד[ש] בעמו ולמאור [גדול לאור] לתבל בדעת ולהאיר פני רבים [בשכל חיים] ("and may he establish you as hol[y] among his people, as a [great] luminary [to illuminate] the world with knowledge and to shine upon the face of many [in intelligence of life]"). The blessing accorded to the eschatological high priest may also be based on the association between the high priest and the celestial light, the divine light being expressed by the luminaries in the heavenly sphere and by the priestly Urim and Thummim in the human sphere.

The analysis of frg. 3 and the context of the composition raises questions concerning the identity of those who recited it. Was it recited by all Israel, or by a specific group? Is it a sectarian prayer or one recited by all Israel? In contrast to the remainder of the composition, the prayer in frg. 3 contains a large number of terms or formulations that have affinity with those employed in sectarian scrolls. The closest resemblance is to the hymns relating to times of prayer recorded in

---

[67] In the commentary on frg. 7, it has been proposed that the phrase בערב בערב refers to 2 Chr 13:11. This verse also contains the parallel expression בבקר בבקר, both standing in cultic context.
[68] Cf. M. Kister, "Gleanings from the Qumran Literature," *Tarbiẓ* 57 (1988): 315–25 (321–24) (Hebrew).

the *Rule of the Community* (1QS X, 1–4) and the *Hodayot* (1QH^a XX, 6–10). They include such expressions as ממשלת אור ("rule of light"; 1QS X, 1), ממשלת חושך ("rule of darkness"; 1QH^a XX, 9), and באופיע מאורות מזבול קודש ("when luminaries appear from the holy abode"; 1QS X, 2–3). In addition, the blessing found in the present prayer, ברוך אתה אדוני ("blessed are you, O Lord"), appears on three other occasions in the *Hodayot* (1QH^a VIII, 26; XIII, 22; XVIII, 16).

Devorah Dimant has proposed assigning sectarian provenance to texts that display explicit sectarian terminology.[69] On the basis of this criterion, she determines that the *Daily Prayers* (4Q503) is a sectarian document. The foregoing analysis has revealed that some terms are shared by the present prayer and the *Daily Prayers*, such as ממשלת אור and ממשל אור היום. Adopting Dimant's criterion, it may be observed that while the number of sectarian phrases appearing in our prayer is significant, it is small in the *Apocryphon* as a whole. Thus, one may conjecture that the halakhic document as a whole stems from priestly circles related to the Qumran community, and that the prayer itself may have been extracted from a sectarian source. However, in the absence of substantiating evidence, the issue must remain open.

---

69 Cf. Dimant, "Vocabulary," 65–67.

General Conclusion:
The Nature of the *Apocryphon of Moses*

1Q29, 4Q375, 4Q376, and 4Q408 attest to a complex and unique literary composition. As they share common interests and formulations they are considered correctly in the research to be copies of a single composition, whose primary concern is a reworking of the Pentateuchal laws in order to establish that the high priest constitutes the supreme judicial authority in the land. At the same time, these manuscripts differ in several respects and the overlaps between them are only partial. The following list reviews the common elements shared by all four manuscripts, as well as the small variations displayed by them:

לשונות אש ("tongues of fire"): This phrase appears four times in three copies (4Q376 ii 1, 4Q408 11 2, 1Q29 1 3, and 1Q29 2 3). In 1Q29 2 3, the expression is cited differently than in the other three examples in that it gives the number of the tongues as three and does not use the preposition *bet*. Together with the different sequence of events described in 1Q29 1, these differences attest to slight variations among the copies with the two fragments of 1Q29 each offering a particular version. The fragment of 4Q408 possibly overlaps the fragment of 4Q376 but due to its fragmentary state this cannot be ascertained.

The expression "tongues of fire" nonetheless constitutes a unique and key motif in this composition. Appearing in the context of diverse laws, it highlights the high priest's inquiry of God via the Urim and the conveyance of the divine answer to the people assembled outside the temple by the shining of the stones on his breastplate. The context in which the phrase occurs in 4Q376 ii 1 relates to whether or not the people should engage in a permitted war. Although fragmented, the formulation of 4Q408 11 may parallel that in 4Q376. Although the sequence of 1Q29 1 2–4 parallels 4Q376 ii, the continuation of the former text does not overlap with the latter and is not consistent with the continuation of 4Q376 ii–iii. It is therefore suggested that the phrase in 1Q29 1 relates to another law that also requires that the high priest inquire of God for an answer via the Urim. As proposed in the comments to this fragment, the different circumstance referred to in 1Q29 1 is, perhaps, the "prophet ... who speaks rebellion" who refuses to recognize the high priest's authority or the divine answer he receives via the Urim.

האבן: This term appears four times in three scrolls and is reconstructed once. It displays a usage unique to the present writing. It appears in three phrases: האבן (1Q29 1 2, 4Q408 11 1 [reconstructed]), האבן השמאלית (4Q376 ii 1, 4Q408 11 2), and האבן הימנית (1Q29 2 2). In each case, the allusion is to one of the two stones on the shoulders of the high priest's garment. The various fragments of the composition evince a belief that both the stones of the high priest's breastplate and the "stones for remembrance" shone as he went out of the temple. In the Discussion on 4Q376, it is noted that the Urim came to be identified with the stones on the breastplate and the stones on the shoulders in Second Temple Jewish literature. As remarked there, Josephus' account is one of the clearest testimonies of this trend.

עד כלות הכהן לדבר: The phrase appears in three of the copies (4Q376 ii, 4Q408 11, and 1Q29 1 2–4) in varying states of preservation. While this suggests parallelism among the manuscripts, the continuation of 1Q29 1 5–7 does not correspond to the content of 4Q376 ii–iii. This complex relationship is a key issue in understanding the structure and reconstruction of the composition. Strugnell, Latour, and Qimron contend that the four scrolls are parallels, thus maintaining that the document deals with how the true/false prophet is to be recognized. However, as remarked in the Comments on 4Q376 and 1Q29, no sequentiality can be reconstructed between 4Q375 and 4Q376.[1] Qimron's proposal requires too many reconstructions to be plausible.[2] It is herein posited that no complete overlap exists between 4Q376 ii and 1Q29 1, and that the usage of the same expressions in the copies relates to diverse difficult laws that require inquiry of God via the Urim. However, 4Q408 11 probably does overlap with 4Q376 ii.

The root **יצ"א**, associated **with קהל or עדה** to depict the high priest's activity: The high priest's exit—apparently from the temple to the people assembled outside in order to convey God's answer to his inquiry via the Urim—is adduced on three occasions: ויצא לפני כ[ול] העדה (4Q375 ii 8–9), ויצא עמו (4Q376 ii 1), and (בצאת הכו[הן] 1Q29 2 1). Most likely, 1Q29 5–7 3 also employed the same root: הקהל [ ], as the context of this fragment also possibly relates to the high priest's exit. The theme of the high priest leaving the temple to publicly deliver God's answer to his inquiry via the Urim is, in fact, characteristic of the composition as a whole. The three (or four) extant accounts of these circumstances may attest to the fact that this document reworks various laws and describes diverse cases in which the high priest inquired of God and was given an answer, which he conveyed to the people. Were this to have been merely a determination of whether a prophet was true or false, no need would have existed for the occurrence of the repeated exits to the assembly.

הכהן המשיח: This expression appears twice (4Q375 i 9 and 4Q376 i 1), with the term כהן also being employed on its own elsewhere (4Q376 ii 2; 1Q29 1 4; 1Q29 5–7

---

[1] See also L. Goldman, "The Apocryphon of Moses: A Composition Portraying the High Priest as Supreme Juridical Authority," *Meghillot* 10 (2013): 181–200 (192–94) (Hebrew).
[2] Qimron, *Hebrew Writings*, 2:314.

2). In this writing, it designates the person known as the high priest in the biblical priestly source. The references highlight the acts performed by this figure, the composition as a whole presenting the ritual ceremonies he conducts in order to receive God's answer to "baffling" legal cases.

נביא together with לדבר סרה: The phrase, comprised of the noun נביא ("prophet") and the verb לדבר סרה ("to speak rebellion"), occurs twice in the composition (4Q375 i 4–5; 1Q29 1 5–6). In this case, too, the two copies do not overlap, apparently addressing two separate cases. The first (4Q375) is that of a person suspected of being a false prophet. The second (1Q29) seems to be that of a person who refuses to accept the answer the priest receives through his inquiry of God via the Urim, and is consequently described as a false prophet.

נגעל: This verb does not occur in this form in either the biblical or post-biblical literature but appears twice in this composition (1Q29 2 4; 4Q408 15 1). Although the root carries various meanings, the sense of "determine" appears to be the most appropriate here, indicating the answer given via the Urim. While the context in which the word appears is fragmentary in both texts, the presence of the term מע[ר]כה in 4Q408 15 2 may suggest that the line refers to determining whether or not to go out to war.

דר"ש: The root also appears twice in the composition (4Q375 ii 7; 1Q29 5–7 2). On both occasions—neither of which overlap—the content relates to the way in which the high priest seeks an answer from God. The document thus indicates clearly that the high priest was regarded as possessing various methods through which to inquire of God rather than being restricted solely to the use of the Urim.

הדברים האלה: This general expression whose formulation is typical of biblical law codes occurs twice in the composition (1Q29 5–7 1 and 4Q408 1 2). 4Q408 is too fragmentary to allow us to determine whether the repetition of the expression attests to overlapping texts or to the appearance of this characteristic feature in two separate contexts.

A parallel prayer unit preserved in 1Q29 3–4 and 4Q402 2 **and a long prayer** in 4Q408 3 + 3a: Both include the instruction to bless and the assembly's response, and several praises to God built around a distinctive syntactical pattern. The parallel prayer is very fragmentary, the remaining lines rendering it impossible to know what precise purpose it served. However, these lines undoubtedly demonstrate that the two prayers possessed a similar structure. The presence of two prayers in a text that reworks legal material suggests that they form part of the key theme of the composition, namely, the establishment of the high priest as the supreme judicial authority in the land. As proposed in the comments, these prayers may have been recited by the priest in praise and thanksgiving for God's revelation to his people.

The Nature of the Composition

The recurrence of the above-listed phrases, expressions, and motifs indicates that the four manuscripts belong to a single composition that employs distinctive terminology and presents diverse legal cases in order to establish that the high priest is the supreme legal authority in the land who receives answers from God by his inquiry via the Urim and other measures. The composition is thus not solely devoted to the issue of identifying true and false prophets but reworks several other laws: whether the people should engage in a permitted war and perhaps also to establish the person who refuses to accept the high priest's authority as a "prophet who speaks rebellion." Additional laws have been preserved very fragmentarily (in 1Q29 frgs. 2, 5–7) and their nature cannot easily be ascertained.

The composition is characterized by a unique reworking of laws from the book of Deuteronomy that stress the ritual role the high priest plays in elucidating and deciding on legal issues.[3] The biblical basis for the exegetical viewpoint reflected in the document is Deut 17:8-11. According to the biblical text, if "a case is too baffling for you to decide" (v. 8), the local magistrates must go up to the temple in Jerusalem "and appear before the Levitical priests, or the magistrate in charge at the time" (v. 9). Already in Deuteronomy, the reference to the Levitical priests as being responsible for clarifying complicated legal matters appears to be a later, secondary addition.[4] The scroll continues this development, transforming the high priest into the person in whose hands all legal authority resides.

The priest to whom the matter is brought for determination conducts a ritual ceremony and offers a sacrifice. Fragmentary descriptions of these ceremonies have been preserved in the second column of 4Q375 and the first column of 4Q376. The principal—but not exclusive—method of inquiry is via the Urim. In the latter case, the divine answer is delivered through the shining of the stones on the high

---

[3] B.M. Levinson, *Deuteronomy and the Hermeneutics of Legal Innovation* (Oxford: Oxford University Press, 1998), 114–16 observes that the tradition of the priest's ritual resolution of civil judicial matters is earlier than Deuteronomy, this course of action being taken in the absence of evidence or witnesses, as in Exod 22:7.

[4] Cf. A. Rofé, *Deuteronomy: Issues and Interpretation* (Edinburgh: T & T Clark, 2002), 79. Levinson (*Deuteronomy*, 112–16, 129–30) analyzes the historical-editorial process that led to the involvement of the priest in the resolution of legal cases in the temple, noting the existence of early traditions of a judicial-ritual resolution via a ceremony, oaths, and inquiry of the Urim on the one hand and the conventional method of going to the local altar when no evidence was available (in either a civil or criminal case) on the other. See also C. Werman, "The Authorization for the Development of Halakhah" in *Revealing the Hidden: Exegesis and Halakha in the Qumran Scrolls* (ed. C. Werman and A. Shemesh; Jerusalem: Bialik Institute, 2011), 72–103 (72–75) (Hebrew).

priest's breastpiece—a glowing that resembles tongues of fire—and the illumination of the onyx stones on his shoulder pieces. At the same time, other ritual procedures are adduced. Col. ii of 4Q375 alludes to entrance beyond the curtain veiling the Ark, an act that does not involve the Urim. 1Q29 5 also refers to the priest's seeking to know God's intention by way of a proper interpretation of God's laws. But this general statement does not detail the precise method by which he received the verdict. Interestingly, the ceremonial-ritual act performed by the priest to obtain God's answer in the composition differs essentially from that described in the *Damascus Document*: "A priest knowledgeable in the Book of the Hagi should always be present; by his command all shall be ruled" (אל ימש איש כהן מבונן בספר ההגי על פיהו ישקו כולם; CD XIII, 2–3). According to CD, the priest's rulings are based on his study of the "Book of the Hagi."[5] Our texts, on the other hand, indicate that the priest delivers the divine answer following his inquiry of God via the Urim, or within the curtain veiling the Ark, or by seeking God's intention.

The reworking of the laws in Deuteronomy in the composition is also marked by a harmonistic approach that combines various biblical sections on the basis of their content, a technique well known from other contemporary writings. The identification of the prophet in 4Q375 reworks the laws concerning the false prophet in Deut 13:1–6, 18:15–20 and the rules of the judicial system in Deut 17:8–13; it reworks promises for the future in Deut 30:1–3, and laws regarding a *ḥaṭṭa't* sacrifice for an inadvertent communal offence in Lev 4:13–21. The regulations concerning engaging in a permitted war in 4Q376 rework the ordinances relating to war in Deuteronomy 20, 23:10–15, and the obligation to inquire via the Urim in Num 27:21. 1Q29 is too fragmentary to allow ascertainment of the nature of the laws it interprets. If the hypothesis proposed herein is correct, namely, that frg. 1 alludes to a person who refuses to accept the high priest's authority, it may perhaps be regarded as a reworking of Deut 17:12, 13:6, 18:20.

The extant manuscripts of this composition make it difficult to determine its full scope: did it contain other laws, including some not found in Deuteronomy— as does the *Temple Scroll*—or is it reworking only certain specific laws? It clearly constitutes a reworked Bible scroll devoted to leading figures, a prophet (Deuteronomy 13, 18), the king (responsible for leading the people to war; Deuteronomy 20, 23[6]), and judges (Deut 17:8–13). The high priest, the highest authority in the

---

[5] The meaning of this term is uncertain. It is plausible to assume that it derives from the root הג"ה and that its usage is based on Josh 1:8 and Ps 1:2, which refer to reciting/studying the Torah day and night. Various identifications have been suggested, the Torah, the Torah with certain interpretations, or possibly a sectarian composition perhaps resembling the *Temple Scroll*.
[6] Cols. LVI–LIX of the *Temple Scroll* also combine the laws of the king with those of going to war.

land, decides difficult legal cases, identifies true and false prophets, and tells the king whether God will support him in battle.

As the priest's verdict in the various legal cases is a matter of interest to the people at large because divine blessing is dependent upon their obedience to his commandments, the writing also describes his going out to the assembly as the stones on his garments shine brightly.[7] The recurrent accounts of his exit from the temple to the people gathered outside constitute further evidence that the fragments do not comprise a consecutive unit dedicated to one theme. Were this to be the case, there would have been no need for repeated descriptions of the high priest leaving the temple. It should thus be regarded as a document of several laws. In each case or matter in which the priest required a verdict, he would go out to the people in order to show them that the answer he had received and was delivering to them came from God himself.

The importance attributed to the priest in this composition is also reflected in the lengthy prayer in 4Q408. A prayer of praise to the Creator of the light and luminaries, it also appears to extol the priests, suggesting a metaphorical linkage between the light of the celestial entities and the light that shines through the Urim (אורים).

The placement and role of the prayers in the composition raise numerous questions. The complete document evidently contained a reworking of the constitutional laws in Deuteronomy together with prayers. The long prayer in 4Q408 links the luminaries in the sky to the priests in the Jerusalem temple, thereby reflecting the view that divine judgment is exemplified in the cosmos through light, the light of the luminaries and the light of the Urim. However, this interpretation only provides a partial understanding of the role played by the prayer in the document. It remains uncertain whether the prayer was attached to the halakhic composition in order to express poetically the grandeur of God, the creator of light, who metes out justice in the world via the Urim, or whether it was added for halakhic reasons, such as establishing the obligation to pray twice a day.

Another issue concerns the praise of the Creator of the light and the luminaries and how it relates to the sectarian documents. The analysis conducted herein indicates that the terminology of the prayer differs considerably from that of the other sections of the composition. This prayer employs many expressions

---

[7] Note the depiction of Simon the High Priest in the "Praises of the Fathers" in Sirach: "How splendid he was with the people thronging round him, when he emerged from the curtained shrine, like the morning star among the clouds, like the moon at the full, like the sun shining on the Temple of the Most High, like the rainbow gleaming against brilliant clouds ... like fire and incense in the censer" (Sir 50:5–8).

that echo or comprise sectarian language and phraseology, known particularly from the *Hodayot* and the *Rule of the Community* but also from other texts. It also reflects the sectarian view that prayers must be recited twice daily, at sunrise and sunset. In discussing 4Q408, it is proposed that the prayers may have originated in sectarian circles while the halakhic sections may have derived from a priestly group. As with other Qumran texts of questionable provenance, whether sectarian or non-sectarian, such as the *Temple Scroll*, the nature of the present writing has yet to be clarified.

The *Apocryphon of Moses* evinces close affinities with the *Temple Scroll* in respect to the reworking of biblical laws, primarily those in Deuteronomy, in combination with numerous other ordinances. An additional correspondence exists with regard to the significance of the composition and the period during which its laws were followed. Were the injunctions in the *Apocryphon of Moses*—as those in the *Temple Scroll*—intended for the community's own days or for the eschaton? Does the *Apocryphon of Moses* present a future vision of a priestly theocracy whose center of power in the temple would rest on various ceremonies to be performed by the high priest in order to receive divine instruction? Or is the composition merely a reworking of biblical laws with a priestly/ritual-focused interpretation due to its origin in priestly circles? Are the descriptions of the high priest inquiring of God via the Urim a reworking, elucidation, and interpretation of the Pentateuch or a messianic vision of the establishment of a kingdom centered on the temple and the high priest? Notably, questions about the nature of the present composition and its purpose, and whether it offers a legal interpretation for contemporary days or for the eschaton, parallel the same questions raised about the *Temple Scroll*. This evinces another aspect of similarity between the two documents.

The two issues, the association of the composition with sectarian literature and our understanding of its present or future orientation, are themselves linked. Defining the *Apocryphon of Moses* as a sectarian document or one closely connected to sectarian literature may suggest that it relates to the eschaton. Moreover, beyond the terminological and ideological affinity of the prayer in 4Q408 to sectarian texts, the *Apocryphon of Moses* as a whole reveals clear links to sectarian eschatological notions. Firstly, the idea that the divine answer to the priests queries via the Urim is shown in light is also recorded in two messianic sectarian texts, *Testimonia* (4Q175 17) and the *Pesher of Isaiah* (4Q164 1 5). Secondly, the analogy between the sun and the high priest receiving divine revelation via the Urim is stated explicitly in the blessing for the high priest in the *Rule of Benedictions* (1QSb IV, 27). Thirdly, labeling the king as נשיא in 4Q376 ii corresponds to the title of the messianic king in several sectarian texts (CD VII, 20; 1QSb V, 20; 4Q285 4 2, 6, 10). The identification of a true or false prophet is itself closely linked to sectarian ideas, since a central theme of the sectaries' polemics is the attempt to portray the community members as true prophets and its opponents as false prophets.[8]

This cluster of examples attests to a particular affinity between the *Apocryphon of Moses* and sectarian ideas, especially in eschatological contexts. Therefore, it is possible that the work was authored by a priestly circle close to the Qumran community, or perhaps even by the sectarian priests themselves. In any case, the connections indicated above relate to the ideological sphere of the community. None of the distinctive sectarian nomenclature appears here. The *Apocryphon of Moses* is, then, a special specimen of rewritten scripture that displays proximity to the Qumran community's ideas but without the typical sectarian markers.

---

[8] See the discussion of 4Q375 and L. Goldman, "Biblical Exegesis and Pesher Interpretation in the Damascus Document" (Ph.D. diss.; University of Haifa, 2007), 98–103, 200–07, 265–66 (Hebrew).

Index of Sources

Hebrew Bible

Genesis

Gen 1:1 125, 336
Gen 1:2 88, 335
Gen 1:4 338, 348
Gen 1:9 101
Gen 1:14 125, 199, 337
Gen 1:15 100, 125
Gen 1:16 336
Gen 1:18 332
Gen 1:20 49, 89
Gen 1:24 89
Gen 1:26 89
Gen 1:28 89, 120, 125
Gen 1:29 61, 89, 123
Gen 1:31 88
Gen 2:1 88
Gen 2:7 89
Gen 2:10 155
Gen 2:16 90, 97, 122
Gen 2:17 90
Gen 3:2 90
Gen 3:11 90
Gen 3:19 118
Gen 5:28 42, 75
Gen 6:1 15, 66, 67, 75
Gen 6:3 21, 39, 60
Gen 6:4 19, 24, 53, 60, 68
Gen 6:5 18, 49, 51, 58, 59, 61, 63, 66, 67, 77, 80, 91, 123
Gen 6:7 80
Gen 6:9 96, 115, 123
Gen 6:11 36, 38, 66, 78
Gen 6:12 19, 35–38, 51, 59, 80, 112, 123
Gen 6:13 154
Gen 6:14 101
Gen 6:17 78, 154
Gen 6:18 53
Gen 6:19 78, 96, 123
Gen 6:21 101
Gen 6:22 77, 80, 97
Gen 7:1 96, 123
Gen 7:3 96
Gen 7:4 52
Gen 7:5 80
Gen 7:7 93, 97, 123, 124
Gen 7:8 97
Gen 7:10 124
Gen 7:11 51, 53, 60, 63, 65, 97, 101, 113, 155
Gen 7:12 52, 98, 124
Gen 7:13 53
Gen 7:14 60, 96
Gen 7:16 97
Gen 7:17 78
Gen 7:18 19
Gen 7:19 98
Gen 7:21 154
Gen 7:22 53, 58, 60, 68, 97
Gen 7:23 53
Gen 7:24 98
Gen 8:1 124
Gen 8:5 136
Gen 8:7 184
Gen 8:20 99
Gen 8:21 124, 125
Gen 8:22 100, 124, 125
Gen 9:1 125
Gen 9:2 100
Gen 9:3 61
Gen 9:6 49
Gen 9:9 53, 125
Gen 9:11 53, 79, 100, 101, 124, 125
Gen 9:12 53, 58, 60, 99, 107, 124
Gen 9:13 53, 99
Gen 9:15 58
Gen 11:1 138
Gen 11:5 80
Gen 11:7 137
Gen 11:30 25
Gen 11:31 133, 155
Gen 12:4 133
Gen 12:8 147

Gen 12:17 106, 187
Gen 13:15 137
Gen 14:1 22
Gen 14:13 68
Gen 14:18 133
Gen 14:19 47
Gen 15:1 133, 317
Gen 15:2 76
Gen 15:13 139, 140, 150, 151, 155
Gen 15:14 139
Gen 15:15 140
Gen 15:19 201
Gen 16:16 141
Gen 17:1 133
Gen 17:5 133
Gen 17:7 79, 137
Gen 17:20 298
Gen 18:8 140
Gen 18:21 19
Gen 18:25 75
Gen 21:5 144
Gen 22:3 143
Gen 22:4 143
Gen 22:10 142
Gen 22:12 142
Gen 22:13 143
Gen 25:26 151
Gen 26:1 32
Gen 27:30 184
Gen 28:10 144, 155
Gen 28:11 147
Gen 28:13 145
Gen 31:13 145
Gen 31:38 145
Gen 33:18 146
Gen 33:19 145, 155
Gen 34:1 146, 155
Gen 34:2 146
Gen 34:16 162
Gen 37:27 148
Gen 41:46 141
Gen 42:23 176
Gen 43:7 316
Gen 46:2 104
Gen 47:9 151
Gen 47:30 140
Gen 49:6 148, 331

Gen 49:10 274
Gen 49:22 148
Gen 50:23 178

Exodus

Exod 1:15 103, 126, 150, 151
Exod 1:19 155
Exod 1:22 104, 126
Exod 2:1 104
Exod 2:23 104, 126
Exod 2:24 104
Exod 3:2 104
Exod 3:3 126
Exod 3:8 201
Exod 3:9 19
Exod 3:10 104
Exod 3:15 213
Exod 3:20 106, 176
Exod 4:1 126
Exod 4:2 105
Exod 4:6 175
Exod 4:12 270
Exod 4:14 105, 106
Exod 4:16 105
Exod 4:21 105, 106
Exod 4:30 53, 105, 316
Exod 6:10 177
Exod 6:16 151
Exod 6:23 10, 160
Exod 7:3 210
Exod 7:12 127
Exod 7:13 107
Exod 7:17 107
Exod 7:27 108
Exod 8:1 108, 127
Exod 8:6 107
Exod 8:12 108
Exod 8:17 108
Exod 8:18 233
Exod 9:3 108, 128
Exod 9:6 128
Exod 9:8 108, 109
Exod 9:10 129
Exod 9:14 215
Exod 9:16 107

Exod 9:19 189
Exod 9:25 109, 110
Exod 9:27 107
Exod 10:1 126
Exod 10:4 110
Exod 10:5 110
Exod 10:15 110, 111
Exod 10:21 109
Exod 10:22 109
Exod 10:23 109
Exod 11:1 106, 108
Exod 11:9 111, 129
Exod 12:2 111
Exod 12:6 211, 216, 318
Exod 12:40 150
Exod 13:3 62
Exod 13:15 172, 201
Exod 13:21 296
Exod 15:1 67, 202
Exod 15:5 65
Exod 15:6 21, 314, 326
Exod 15:10 10, 52, 58, 65
Exod 15:11 76
Exod 15:15 216
Exod 15:20 146
Exod 16:13 50
Exod 18:1 64
Exod 18:16 200
Exod 18:19 106
Exod 18:20 213, 239
Exod 19:3 260
Exod 19:7 260
Exod 19:8 181, 216, 222
Exod 19:9 166, 216
Exod 19:10 217
Exod 19:18 222
Exod 19:20 215
Exod 19:24 179, 260
Exod 20:1 166
Exod 20:2 223
Exod 20:3 222
Exod 20:14 215–217, 222, 223
Exod 20:15 222
Exod 20:18 222, 239
Exod 20:19 176, 213
Exod 21:31 298
Exod 22:7 354

Exod 23:7 55
Exod 23:11 242
Exod 23:22 330
Exod 23:24 170
Exod 23:27 200
Exod 24:1 260
Exod 24:3 216
Exod 24:9 260
Exod 24:10 199
Exod 24:13 260
Exod 24:15 216, 223
Exod 24:16 216, 230
Exod 24:17 104, 105
Exod 25:1 281
Exod 25:17 281
Exod 28:2 32
Exod 28:6 311
Exod 28:9 294, 307
Exod 28:15 302
Exod 28:30 291, 302, 303
Exod 29:5 301
Exod 29:32 279
Exod 31:10 56
Exod 32:6 99
Exod 32:10 52
Exod 32:11 176
Exod 33:7 161
Exod 33:9 165
Exod 33:11 8, 165, 166, 190, 191, 213, 214, 222
Exod 33:12 166
Exod 33:13 166
Exod 34:9 243
Exod 34:10 200, 218
Exod 34:11 8, 168–190, 191
Exod 34:12 169
Exod 34:13 169, 191
Exod 34:14 170
Exod 34:15 170
Exod 34:16 170
Exod 34:17 192
Exod 34:18 171
Exod 34:19 171
Exod 34:20 172
Exod 34:21 168
Exod 34:22 254, 316
Exod 34:23 172, 192

Exod 34:24 172, 191
Exod 34:29 25, 175
Exod 34:31 298
Exod 35:12 281
Exod 39:21 304
Exod 40:2 136
Exod 40:34 296, 304

Leviticus

Lev 1:1 177, 230
Lev 4:1 280
Lev 4:2 212, 248
Lev 4:3 277
Lev 4:6 281
Lev 4:13 282, 286, 287, 355
Lev 4:14 279, 280
Lev 4:15 276, 286
Lev 4:16 286
Lev 4:17 279, 280, 281
Lev 4:21 279, 286
Lev 4:23 280
Lev 5:10 143
Lev 6:15 290
Lev 7:7 248
Lev 7:12 172
Lev 7:38 213
Lev 8:2 277
Lev 8:3 230
Lev 8:8 291, 302
Lev 8:10 290
Lev 8:12 277, 280
Lev 8:14 99
Lev 10:10 199
Lev 13:16 175
Lev 13:18 108
Lev 13:20 108
Lev 16:1 281
Lev 16:3 281
Lev 16:5 245, 280
Lev 16:15 281
Lev 16:16 281
Lev 16:17 213, 247, 318
Lev 16:21 249
Lev 16:29 244, 281
Lev 16:31 244

Lev 16:34 248
Lev 19:17 161
Lev 19:25 249
Lev 21:10 277
Lev 23:28 245
Lev 23:31 248
Lev 23:32 343
Lev 23:34 172, 191
Lev 25:2 260
Lev 25:3 243
Lev 25:4 242
Lev 25:6 242
Lev 25:18 212

Numbers

Num 1:2 296
Num 1:3 205
Num 1:5 205
Num 1:14 205
Num 1:16 298
Num 1:20 172
Num 2:32 178
Num 3:2 10, 160
Num 3:4 10, 160, 162
Num 4:1 177
Num 5:8 248
Num 6:25 76
Num 7:10 290
Num 7:15 290
Num 8:10 105
Num 9:8 213
Num 9:15 296, 304
Num 9:16 105
Num 10:9 296
Num 10:25 206
Num 10:36 306
Num 11:8 244
Num 11:17 166
Num 11:31 50
Num 12:2 223, 224
Num 12:6 104
Num 12:7 274
Num 12:8 104, 273
Num 12:9 207
Num 12:13 207

Num 12:15 206, 207
Num 13:4 204
Num 13:9 205
Num 13:33 68
Num 14:5 211
Num 14:39 166
Num 14:43 273
Num 15:8 143
Num 15:27 248
Num 15:39 212
Num 16:3 318
Num 20:1 180
Num 20:8 230
Num 20:22 177, 178, 192
Num 20:23 193
Num 20:24 50
Num 20:25 178–180, 193
Num 20:26 179
Num 20:27 193
Num 20:29 178
Num 23:9 148
Num 24:16 98
Num 24:17 274
Num 25:4 207, 270, 271
Num 27:2 298
Num 27:5 20
Num 27:11 211
Num 27:12 294
Num 27:15 304
Num 27:17 211
Num 27:18 105, 233, 296
Num 27:20 211
Num 27:21 233, 291, 303, 355
Num 29:7 9, 244, 245
Num 29:8 248
Num 30:14 90
Num 30:17 200
Num 32:13 49
Num 32:28 233
Num 33:37 177, 190, 193
Num 33:38 230
Num 34:17 200
Num 35:26 184
Num 35:33 247

Deuteronomy

Deut 1:1 259
Deut 1:3 230, 238, 259
Deut 1:5 239, 259
Deut 1:11 213
Deut 1:12 238
Deut 1:16 200, 239
Deut 1:28 68
Deut 1:39 55
Deut 1:43 330
Deut 2:4 232
Deut 3:11 68
Deut 3:24 74
Deut 3:27 259
Deut 3:28 233
Deut 4:5 238
Deut 4:6 212, 270
Deut 4:9 213
Deut 4:10 232, 238, 260
Deut 4:12 330
Deut 4:15 239
Deut 4:25 49
Deut 4:30 316
Deut 4:34 105, 210
Deut 4:35 214, 215
Deut 4:36 215, 222
Deut 4:39 215
Deut 5:4 213, 221, 260
Deut 5:7 222
Deut 5:19 216, 318
Deut 5:20 214
Deut 5:23 239
Deut 5:24 238
Deut 5:28 216, 218
Deut 5:33 239
Deut 6:1 238, 296, 308
Deut 6:3 296, 308
Deut 6:5 270
Deut 6:10 238
Deut 6:11 183
Deut 6:14 213
Deut 7:1 201
Deut 7:4 169
Deut 7:5 169, 191
Deut 7:11 296
Deut 7:25 169, 191

Deut 8:5 62
Deut 8:6 212
Deut 8:7 65
Deut 8:10 48, 52, 58, 61–63, 67
Deut 8:11 63, 238
Deut 8:18 98
Deut 8:19 52
Deut 9:9 260
Deut 9:18 161
Deut 9:25 161
Deut 10:17 22
Deut 10:18 75
Deut 11:6 183
Deut 11:17 239
Deut 11:23 200
Deut 11:25 213
Deut 12:2 276
Deut 12:14 275, 276
Deut 12:16 49
Deut 13:1 270–272, 283, 355
Deut 13:2 266, 270, 272, 274, 283–286, 309
Deut 13:4 270, 283
Deut 13:6 272, 273, 284, 285
Deut 13:18 271
Deut 15:2 243
Deut 15:3 243
Deut 15:4 243
Deut 15:5 318
Deut 15:9 243
Deut 15:20 244
Deut 16:9 254
Deut 16:10 254
Deut 16:13 172, 191
Deut 16:16 172, 192
Deut 17:2 309
Deut 17:8 9, 161, 275, 281, 282, 285, 286, 309, 317, 319, 321, 354, 355
Deut 17:9 275, 276, 286, 298, 317
Deut 17:10 316, 317, 318, 319
Deut 17:11 316, 317
Deut 17:12 273, 309, 317, 355
Deut 17:17 298
Deut 17:18 231, 249, 297
Deut 17:19 297
Deut 18:15 270, 272, 274, 285
Deut 18:18 212, 270, 271, 283
Deut 18:20 273, 309

Deut 20:2 295, 301, 308
Deut 20:3 308
Deut 20:9 295
Deut 20:10 299
Deut 20:15 300
Deut 20:17 201
Deut 21:2 275, 276
Deut 22:25 273
Deut 23:10 299
Deut 27:9 34, 237
Deut 27:10 235, 237
Deut 27:26 211
Deut 28:32 162
Deut 28:59 187, 194
Deut 29:13 254
Deut 29:28 282, 286, 319
Deut 30:1 355
Deut 30:2 270–272, 283, 284
Deut 30:3 270, 271, 283
Deut 30:18 233
Deut 30:20 238
Deut 31:1 230, 232
Deut 31:7 233
Deut 31:16 232
Deut 31:20 233
Deut 31:21 91
Deut 31:28 193, 232, 259
Deut 31:30 213
Deut 32:13 61
Deut 32:15 63
Deut 32:24 189
Deut 32:41 57
Deut 32:43 247
Deut 32:47 238
Deut 32:49 230
Deut 32:50 193
Deut 33:1 216
Deut 33:2 213
Deut 33:8 206, 218, 259, 293, 303
Deut 33:10 303
Deut 33:16 100
Deut 33:17 148
Deut 34:9 105

Joshua

Josh 1:8 355
Josh 3:10 201
Josh 6:9 206
Josh 7:21 135
Josh 8:11 299
Josh 8:33 276
Josh 8:35 213
Josh 9:1 201
Josh 9:24 181
Josh 10:12 27
Josh 10:13 249
Josh 10:15 299
Josh 11:22 68
Josh 14:1 233
Josh 14:6 216
Josh 14:10 27
Josh 16:2 336
Josh 20:2 330
Josh 22:16 211, 273
Josh 23:13 233
Josh 24:5 106
Josh 24:32 145

Judges

Judg 5:14 178, 274
Judg 6:13 56, 106
Judg 6:17 53
Judg 13:16 217

1 Samuel

1 Sam 1:12 161
1 Sam 2:10 176
1 Sam 3:20 274
1 Sam 4:17 218
1 Sam 7:6 49
1 Sam 7:10 51, 63
1 Sam 9:16 19
1 Sam 11:4 166
1 Sam 12:6 200
1 Sam 12:14 183
1 Sam 14:36 336
1 Sam 16:14 26
1 Sam 17:13 57
1 Sam 17:44 189
1 Sam 17:47 216
1 Sam 22:17 143
1 Sam 27:5 300
1 Sam 28:6 291, 303
1 Sam 28:8 291
1 Sam 29:9 217

2 Samuel

2 Sam 1:22 99
2 Sam 2:22 162
2 Sam 7:13 34
2 Sam 7:14 161, 187
2 Sam 7:22 215
2 Sam 14:17 217
2 Sam 17:24 99
2 Sam 18:22 238
2 Sam 18:26 218
2 Sam 19:36 55
2 Sam 20:15 49
2 Sam 22:5 26
2 Sam 22:14 51
2 Sam 22:32 215

1 Kings

1 Kgs 2:3 237
1 Kgs 3:9 199
1 Kgs 3:28 75, 161
1 Kgs 6:1 32
1 Kgs 7:32 252
1 Kgs 8:13 332
1 Kgs 8:32 55
1 Kgs 8:39 60
1 Kgs 8:65 211
1 Kgs 14:8 213
1 Kgs 16:15 205
1 Kgs 16:17 299
1 Kgs 18:18 213
1 Kgs 19:16 212

2 Kings

2 Kgs 14:9 189
2 Kgs 17:21 273
2 Kgs 19:32 49
2 Kgs 23:3 213, 237
2 Kgs 23:26 271

Isaiah

Isa 1:3 148
Isa 2:4 161
Isa 2:10 57
Isa 3:8 51
Isa 5:5 189
Isa 5:6 188, 239
Isa 5:24 294, 308
Isa 6:1 33
Isa 7:25 189
Isa 8:23 145
Isa 15:6 110
Isa 18:2 143
Isa 19:16 183
Isa 22:12 49
Isa 22:16 77
Isa 23:8 25
Isa 24:15 183
Isa 24:18 10, 51, 58, 63
Isa 27:9 243
Isa 28:15 52
Isa 28:18 52
Isa 28:23 211
Isa 29:6 64
Isa 29:16 91
Isa 30:33 214
Isa 31:3 154
Isa 33:14 216
Isa 34:9 214
Isa 34:13 189
Isa 37:33 49
Isa 40:6 55
Isa 41:26 232
Isa 45:18 34
Isa 45:24 117
Isa 49:9 317
Isa 51:9 22
Isa 51:10 65
Isa 54:8 55
Isa 54:11 303, 349
Isa 57:1 218
Isa 59:4 161
Isa 59:11 208
Isa 59:13 272, 309
Isa 59:16 23, 105
Isa 59:21 270
Isa 61:1 212
Isa 63:10 88
Isa 63:13 65
Isa 63:15 332

Jeremiah

Jer 1:9 270
Jer 5:1 161
Jer 7:5 200
Jer 7:9 213
Jer 7:13 330
Jer 9:23 161
Jer 10:3 211
Jer 10:13 53
Jer 11:3 211
Jer 16:4 154
Jer 17:4 243
Jer 18:19 211
Jer 20:29 214
Jer 23:20 207
Jer 24:7 199
Jer 26:7 285
Jer 26:12 285
Jer 28:15 272
Jer 28:16 273, 285, 309
Jer 29:11 185
Jer 29:25 231
Jer 30:24 270
Jer 31:8 211
Jer 31:9 201
Jer 32:18 22
Jer 32:20 105
Jer 33:8 55
Jer 42:6 81
Jer 44:8 98
Jer 46:6 69

Jer 46:9 53
Jer 46:10 69
Jer 51:34 81

Ezekiel

Ezek 1:1 105
Ezek 1:6 186
Ezek 1:13 185
Ezek 1:27 105
Ezek 4:1 77
Ezek 5:11 232
Ezek 7:3 51
Ezek 8:3 104
Ezek 14:14 96
Ezek 18:5 161
Ezek 18:8 160, 161
Ezek 19:11 274
Ezek 26:3 98
Ezek 28:22 33
Ezek 35:7 189
Ezek 36:8 48
Ezek 36:19 67
Ezek 36:30 61
Ezek 36:33 55
Ezek 37:28 254
Ezek 38:16 9 8, 107
Ezek 39:12 98
Ezek 42:20 199
Ezek 43:3 104
Ezek 46:14 248

Hosea

Hos 1:2 273
Hos 5:1 211
Hos 11:6 91
Hos 12:10 270

Joel

Joel 1:20 189
Joel 2:2 64
Joel 2:11 183

Joel 3:3 74
Joel 4:12 64
Joel 4:18 48

Amos

Amos 2:14 53, 69
Amos 2:16 69
Amos 5:25 99
Amos 9:3 213
Amos 9:13 48

Habakkuk

Hab 2:14 98, 124
Hab 2:18 91
Hab 3:6 215
Hab 3:11 332

Zephaniah

Zeph 1:6 273
Zeph 1:15 64, 271
Zeph 3:5 348, 349
Zeph 3:9 138

Haggai

Hag 1:1 245
Hag 2:7 183
Hag 2:13 181

Zechariah

Zech 1:4 51
Zech 1:17 51
Zech 4:10 185
Zech 7:9 160
Zech 7:14 189
Zech 8:9 270
Zech 9:14 64
Zech 12:8 217

Malachi

Mal 1:7 99
Mal 2:7 259
Mal 3:11 110

Psalms

Ps 1:2 355
Ps 2:9 274
Ps 3:6 105
Ps 4:5 186
Ps 7:10 34
Ps 8:4 339
Ps 8:6 32, 48
Ps 8:7 89
Ps 8:8 189
Ps 9:8 34
Ps 10:2 91
Ps 11:7 55
Ps 14:2 185
Ps 18:32 215
Ps 19:2 337
Ps 19:15 317
Ps 22:4 220
Ps 22:24 183
Ps 24:1 100
Ps 25:17 271
Ps 29:3 51, 63
Ps 33:6 88, 128
Ps 33:16 69
Ps 36:5 186
Ps 36:9 81
Ps 37:6 335
Ps 37:30 207
Ps 38:51 111
Ps 41:2 76
Ps 44:5 106
Ps 44:8 57
Ps 48:7 216
Ps 51:11 243
Ps 51:13 88
Ps 55:6 216
Ps 56:13 172
Ps 65:9 342
Ps 71:16 57
Ps 72:16 48
Ps 73:24 183
Ps 78:15 113
Ps 78:17 50
Ps 78:18 50
Ps 78:38 243
Ps 78:43 210
Ps 78:44 107, 127
Ps 78:46 110
Ps 78:47 109
Ps 78:50 109
Ps 78:55 176
Ps 78:56 50
Ps 84:12 183
Ps 86:4 57
Ps 86:17 53
Ps 89:32 187
Ps 93:4 52, 65
Ps 94:2 33
Ps 94:11 185, 186
Ps 94:19 186
Ps 96:6 32
Ps 98:1 202
Ps 98:2 199, 200
Ps 103:1 76
Ps 103:15 55
Ps 103:20 183
Ps 104:13 49
Ps 104:20 109
Ps 105:5 56, 187
Ps 105:15 212
Ps 105:28 57
Ps 105:29 127
Ps 105:30 108, 127
Ps 105:34 110
Ps 105:35 110
Ps 105:36 111
Ps 105:40 57
Ps 106:2 56
Ps 106:7 56, 106
Ps 106:9 65
Ps 106:22 187
Ps 106:29 51
Ps 106:35 182
Ps 107:13 271
Ps 111:7 334
Ps 113:6 74

Ps 119:130 335
Ps 119:137 314
Ps 135:9 106
Ps 136:3 22
Ps 136:4 187
Ps 136:7 336
Ps 143:3 109
Ps 143:4 23
Ps 145:13 334
Ps 145:16 49, 58, 61, 62, 67
Ps 145:17 334
Ps 147:5 334
Ps 148:3 339
Ps 148:11 178
Ps 148:14 176
Ps 149:8 25

Proverbs

Prov 3:19 34
Prov 3:20 65
Prov 4:13 238
Prov 5:14 211
Prov 5:16 51
Prov 8:7 207
Prov 10:17 183
Prov 11:17 218
Prov 15:8 6
Prov 18:8 185
Prov 19:21 186
Prov 29:14 160

Job

Job 4:13 186
Job 7:13 186
Job 7:14 26
Job 9:13 270
Job 14:1 55
Job 15:24 271
Job 16:20 176
Job 20:18 189
Job 21:7 67
Job 22:26 162
Job 28:23 335

Job 28:24 185
Job 28:29 185
Job 33:22 109
Job 33:23 177
Job 36:1 238
Job 37:5 63
Job 37:6 52
Job 38:17 213
Job 39:8 110
Job 41:22 25, 26
Job 42:11 145

Song of Songs 3:11 48

Ruth 2:8 135

Lamentations 2:22 52

Ecclesiastes

Eccl 8:1 131, 140, 231
Eccl 11:3 52, 98

Daniel

Dan 1:17 210
Dan 3:19 24
Dan 4:2 186
Dan 5:6 32
Dan 5:12 231
Dan 6:8 122
Dan 7:26 64
Dan 7:28 24
Dan 9:14 55, 334
Dan 9:24 21, 243
Dan 10:1 104, 213
Dan 10:16 104

Ezra

Ezra 2:63 291, 303, 304
Ezra 2:68 186
Ezra 3:2 216
Ezra 9:1 200, 201

Ezra 9:2 182
Ezra 9:14 189
Ezra 10:1 161
Ezra 10:16 245
Ezra 10:17 244

Nehemiah

Neh 1:4 161
Neh 3:9 204
Neh 5:14 151
Neh 7:65 291, 303, 304
Neh 8:2 245
Neh 8:8 210
Neh 8:16 172
Neh 8:17 234
Neh 9:8 201
Neh 9:13 215
Neh 9:17 56, 187
Neh 9:25 63, 81
Neh 9:26 63
Neh 9:32 22
Neh 9:33 234
Neh 11:2 186
Neh 11:9 57

1 Chronicles

1 Chr 3:21 204
1 Chr 5:29 160
1 Chr 7:8 205
1 Chr 8:37 205
1 Chr 9:33 231
1 Chr 9:43 205

1 Chr 16:2 212
1 Chr 16:12 56, 187
1 Chr 17:25 161
1 Chr 24:2 160
1 Chr 27:22 178
1 Chr 28:8 200
1 Chr 28:9 59, 335
1 Chr 29:5 186
1 Chr 29:15 55, 56
1 Chr 29:18 59
1 Chr 29:19 237

2 Chronicles

2 Chr 1:12 183
2 Chr 5:11 232
2 Chr 6:2 332
2 Chr 6:10 161
2 Chr 6:23 55
2 Chr 11:17 141
2 Chr 13:11 343, 349
2 Chr 16:9 185
2 Chr 18:22 270
2 Chr 19:8 161
2 Chr 20:36 105
2 Chr 21:7 145
2 Chr 21:18 187
2 Chr 22:3 118
2 Chr 22:4 118
2 Chr 25:5 205
2 Chr 25:18 189
2 Chr 29:10 207
2 Chr 29:31 172
2 Chr 32:31 176
2 Chr 34:31 213

Samaritan Pentateuch

Gen 22:12 143
Gen 28:10 146
Exod 18:20 239

Exod 20:18 239
Exod 24:1, 9 260
Exod 34:29 25

Septuagint

Gen 6:9 96
Gen 7:1 123
Gen 33:19 145
Exod 18:20 239
Exod 24:13, 15 260
Exod 28:30 302
Exod 34:11-13 169
Exod 34:11–24 191
Exod 34:29, 30, 35 25

Deut 15:3 243
Deut 31:28 259
Josh 24:32 145
Hos 11:6 91
Ps 10:2 91
Ps 78:47 110
Ps 78:50 109
Job 42:11 145

Vulgate

Gen 33:19 145
Exod 34:19-20 172
Josh 24:32 145
Ps 78:47 111

Ps 78:50 109
Ps 145:16 61
Job 42:11 145

Aramaic Targums

Gen 1:2 88
Gen 6:3 21, 60
Gen 6:9 96, 123
Gen 8:21 124
Gen 11:1 138
Gen 14:13 68
Gen 49:6 148
Gen 49:22 148
Exod 20:14 222
Exod 34:12 169

Exod 34:18 171
Exod 34:19-20 172
Exod 34:29 25
Deut 3:11 68
Deut 33:8 206
Josh 24:32 145
Zeph 3:9 138
Ps 78:47 110
Ps 78:50 109
Job 42:11 145

Apocrypha and Pseudepigrapha

1 Maccabees

1 Macc 3:46-54 302
1 Macc 3:49 304

3 Maccabees

3 Macc 2:4 53, 69

Sirach (Ben Sira)

Sir 6:31 48
Sir 10:2 176
Sir 12:14 115
Sir 14:26 154
Sir 15:14 91
Sir 16:7 53, 63, 69
Sir 42:15 88
Sir 42:16 295
Sir 43:8 24
Sir 43:24 23
Sir 44:1 218
Sir 44:4 91
Sir 44:5 30
Sir 44:17 97
Sir 44:18 99
Sir 45:7-13 304
Sir 45:17 303
Sir 50:5-8 356
Sir 51:7 105

Judith

Jdt 16:14 88

Wisdom of Solomon

Wis 14:6-7 68, 69
Wis 9:1 88
Wis 9:2-3 89
Wis 11:5-8, 17-18 128

Baruch

Bar 2:9 334
Bar 3:26 68

Jubilees

Jub 1:5 232
Jub 1:14 8, 233
Jub 2:2 88
Jub 2:3 339
Jub 2:14 89
Jub 2:21 62
Jub 4:26 247
Jub 5:1 68
Jub 5:3 18, 59, 123
Jub 5:9 68
Jub 5:11 60
Jub 5:12 64
Jub 5:13 77
Jub 5:18 247
Jub 6:2 247
Jub 6:4 124
Jub 7:22 205
Jub 8:11 16
Jub 11:4 133
Jub 12:4 88
Jub 12:12 133
Jub 12:16 137
Jub 12:25 138
Jub 19:13 146
Jub 22:6 48, 62
Jub 25:11 47
Jub 27:19 145
Jub 35:9 91
Jub 46:3 141
Jub 48:4 105
Jub 48:5 128

1 Enoch

1 En 6-11 15
1 En 6:2 66
1 En 7:1 66
1 En 7:2 36, 37, 53, 68, 205
1 En 7:3 36, 37
1 En 7:6 19, 36
1 En 7:10 35
1 En 7:15 66
1 En 8:1 37–39
1 En 8:2 19, 38, 39, 59, 123
1 En 8:3 37, 39
1 En 8:4 19, 37, 39
1 En 9:1 21
1 En 9:2 20
1 En 9:3 20, 21, 39
1 En 9:4 21, 22, 39

1 En 9:9 37, 38
1 En 10:9 68
1 En 10:16 64
1 En 10:20 124
1 En 54:6 66
1 En 65:10 60
1 En 86:2 66
1 En 86:4 66
1 En 88:2 68
1 En 89:4 64
1 En 89:8 125
1 En 93:2 77
1 En 93:4 64
1 En 106:2 25, 26, 28
1 En 106:4 26
1 En 106:5 25
1 En 106:7 28
1 En 106:13 66
1 En 106-107 15

2 Enoch

2 En 34:1 69

2 Baruch

2 Bar 21:4 88

Testament (Assumption) of Moses

As. Mos. 10:4 63

Sibylline Oracles

Sib. Or. 1.217–220 64
Sib. Or. 3.669, 675 63

Testaments of the Twelve Patriarchs

Testament of Levi 12:5 146
Testament of Judah 25:3 138
Testament of Levi 18:2 16

Biblical Antiquities

L.A.B. 3:4 96, 123
L.A.B. 3:8 124
L.A.B. 3:12, 4:5 99
L.A.B. 6:3-8:3 133
L.A.B. 8:14, 9:3 151
L.A.B 10:1 126, 128
L. A. B. 11:6–14 223
L.A.B. 12:1 25
L. A. B. 13:7 249

New Testament

Acts 4:2-4 294, 308
Rom 4:3 133
2 Cor 3:7 25
Gal 3:6 133
Heb 7:1-5 133
Heb 11:4 88
1 Pet 3:20-21 124
2 Pet 3:5 88

Qumran

Damascus Document (CD; Geniza)

CD I, 1 210
CD I, 2 75
CD I, 5, 6, 10 151
CD II, 12 88
CD II, 20 53
CD II, 16 59
CD II, 19-21 68
CD II, 20-21 69
CD III, 14-15 8
CD III, 3 298
CD III, 14 282
CD III, 14-15 233
CD III, 15 317
CD III, 17 115
CD IV, 11 134
CD V, 1 273
CD V, 1-2 298
CD V, 3 233
CD V, 4 234
CD V, 21-VI, 1 272
CD VI, 1 212
CD VI, 6 317
CD VII, 8 139
CD VII, 7 298
CD VII, 20 298, 357
CD VIII, 2-3 355
CD XI, 21-22 6
CD XIII 355
CD XIV, 11 299
CD XV, 16 90
CD XVI, 3-4 6
CD XIX, 12 30
CD XIX, 9-10 231
CD XX, 1 231
CD XX, 15 151
CD XX, 20 295
CD XX, 26 32

Aramaic Levi Document

ALD 12:6 146

Cave 1

1Q20 (*Genesis Apocryphon*)
1QapGen II, 1 24
1QapGen II, 3 66
1QapGen II, 7 22
1QapGen II, 12 24
1QapGen II, 23 28
1QapGen IV, 11 41
1QapGen V, 7 26
1QapGen V, 12 26
1QapGen V, 25 151
1QapGen V, 29 16
1QapGen X, 13 247
1QapGen X, 16 99
1QapGen XIX, 14 133
1QapGen XIII, 15 100

1QH^a (*Hodayot*)
1QH^a IV, 29 117
1QH^a V, 20 92
1QH^a V, 31 187
1QH^a V, 34 81
1QH^a VI, 27 199, 200
1QH^a VIII, 24 161
1QH^a VIII, 26 350
1QH^a IX, 14 337
1QH^a IX, 23 91
1QH^a IX, 26 74
1QH^a IX, 30 30
1QH^a X, 5 92
1QH^a X, 9 105
1QH^a X, 15 176
1QH^a X, 16 91, 176
1QH^a X, 33 176
1QH^a XI, 28 211
1QH^a XI, 33 186
1QH^a XI, 35 51, 63
1QH^a XII, 8 176
1QH^a XII, 34 47
1QH^a XIII, 13 151
1QH^a XIV, 15 98
1QH^a XIV, 25 115
1QH^a XIV, 28 328
1QH^a XIV, 38 53

Qumran — 375

1QHª XV, 35 339
1QHª XVI, 28 106
1QHª XVIII, 10 25
1QHª XIX, 33 57
1QHª XX, 4 338
1QHª XX, 6-10 350
1QHª XX, 7-10 332
1QHª XX, 8-9 342
1QHª XX, 9 100, 338, 350
1QHª XX, 18 32

1QM (*War Scroll*)
1QM I, 1 231
1QM I, 11 57
1QM II, 1 57
1QM III, 2 206
1QM VII, 3 52
1QM X, 1 22
1QM X, 2 296
1QM X, 9 331
1QM X, 14 137
1QM XI, 7 212
1QM XII, 1 333
1QM XIV, 5 200
1QM XIV, 11 25
1QM XIV, 13-14 342
1QM XV, 6 296
1QM XVI, 1 298
1QM XVII, 2 160
1QM XVII, 10 316

1QpHab (*Pesher Habakkuk*)
1QpHab II, 7 231
1QpHab IV, 2 25
1QpHab IV, 5 140
1QpHab IV, 9 154
1QpHab V, 3 52
1QpHab VII, 13 74
1QpHab VII, 16 183
1QpHab VIII, 6 52
1QpHab IX, 1 187
1QpHab X, 10 30

1QS (*Community Rule*)
1QS I, 1-2 317
1QS I, 2-3 287
1QS I, 15 317

1QS I, 16-17 319, 331
1QS I, 17 273
1QS I, 21 117
1QS III, 7 55
1QS III, 18 154
1QS III, 23 106
1QS IV, 14 154
1QS IV, 16 151
1QS IV, 19 115
1QS IV, 22 98
1QS IV, 24 57
1QS V, 1 317
1QS V, 4 59
1QS V, 5 92, 331
1QS V, 8 90
1QS V, 9 317
1QS V, 11 317
1QS V, 11-12 282
1QS V, 20 331
1QS VI, 9 299
1QS VI, 17 182
1QS VI, 24 316
1QS VI, 27 326
1QS VIII, 6 247
1QS VIII, 9 52
1QS VIII, 19 298
1QS IX, 11 231
1QS IX, 19 213
1QS X, 1 74, 332, 350
1QS X, 2 332, 333, 342, 350
1QS X, 9 32
1QS X, 10 342
1QS X, 15 81
1QS XI, 8 105
1QS XI, 25 187

1QSa (*Rule of the Congregation*)
1QSa I, 3 134, 247
1QSa I, 10 55
1QSa II, 12 231

1QSb (*Rule of Blessings*)
1QSb II, 22 76
1QSb IV, 25 217
1QSb IV, 27 357
1QSb IV, 27-28 349
1QSb V, 20 298, 357

Index of Sources

1QIsaª 23, 47, 85, 107, 110, 138, 143, 145, 328
1Q14 140
1Q17 145
1Q18 91
1Q19 (*Book of Noah*) 14–42
1Q22 (*Words of Moses*) 8, 9, 11, 105, 136, 163, 215, 225–261, 305, 316, 318, 347
1Q27 295
1Q29 9, 163, 226, 261, 265–267, 272, 278, 282, 283, 288, 293–295, 305–322, 325–328, 333–345, 347, 348, 351–355
1Q30 131
1Q34 211
1Q34[bis] 104, 211

Cave 2

2Q18 48
2Q21 (*Apocryphon of Moses?*) 9, 159–163

Cave 4

4QpaleoExod[m] 171, 239, 260
4QDeut[b] 259
4QDeut[j] 62
4QDeut[n] 62
4Q158 4, 140, 200, 223
4Q159 131
4Q160 104
4Q166 284, 287
4Q17 304
4Q171 140, 183
4Q175 156, 206, 234, 239, 303, 357
4Q177 77, 272
4Q180 24, 53, 77, 133, 140, 143
4Q181 140, 187
4Q185 10, 55, 56, 57, 71, 72, 106, 183, 187
4Q186 303
4Q196 100
4Q215a 337
4Q216 89, 232, 233, 337, 340
4Q225 7, 76, 133
4Q251 138, 300
4Q252 2, 21, 131, 133, 136, 137, 156
4Q256 333
4Q258 32, 333
4Q265 247
4Q266 74, 75, 116, 248, 282
4Q267 212, 272
4Q268 74, 75
4Q270 59, 248
4Q271 272
4Q274 182
4Q285 298, 357
4Q286 59, 186, 337
4Q287 337
4Q293 326
4Q299 57, 314, 339, 342
4Q301 89, 314, 326
4Q339 273, 287
4Q364 260, 337
4Q365 146, 277, 337
4Q366 192
4Q368 (*4QApocryphal Pentateuch A*) 8, 106, 163, 164–195
4Q370 (*Admonition on the Flood*) 10, 24, 42–72, 98, 99, 106, 123
4Q372 22, 48, 52, 75
4Q374 34, 51, 176, 196
4Q375 9, 163, 226, 261, 265–290, 293, 297, 301, 302, 305, 307–309, 317–321, 333, 351–355, 358
4Q376 9, 163, 226, 261, 265–277, 278–304, 305–309, 311, 312, 318, 320, 321, 341, 345, 348, 349, 351–355, 357
4Q377 (*4QApocryphal Pentateuch B*) 8, 163, 195, 195–224
4Q378 98, 195, 216, 234
4Q379 156, 195, 234, 334
4Q381 22, 51, 88, 89, 98, 214
4Q385 139
4Q386 190, 191, 192
4Q388a 139
4Q390 8, 49, 233, 284
4Q392 210, 339
4Q393 49, 164, 180
4Q396 25
4Q397 182, 252
4Q400 25
4Q401 25
4Q402 21, 353
4Q403 186, 314

4Q405 57, 183, 186, 215, 333
4Q408 9, 11, 163, 226, 261, 265–288, 294, 305–307, 310, 312–316, 318, 323–353, 356, 357
4Q417 59, 85
4Q418 106, 183
4Q421 154
4Q422 (*Paraphrase of Genesis and Exodus*) 10, 11, 52, 59, 83–129, 210
4Q423 85, 89
4Q424 55
4Q427 186, 338
4Q434 52, 62, 76
4Q437 30, 76
4Q448 52
4Q454 106
4Q462 32
4Q464 (*Exposition on the Patriarchs*) 10, 103, 130–158
4Q464a 130–134, 136, 138, 140, 142, 144, 146, 148–150, 152, 154–156, 158
4Q464b 130–132, 134, 136, 138, 140, 142, 144, 146, 148, 150, 152, 154, 156–158
4Q468dd 74
4Q491 206, 296, 333
4Q493 206
4Q501 107
4Q503 100, 313, 331, 336, 337, 344, 350
4Q504 88–90, 98, 107, 183, 186, 284
4Q508 90
4Q511 57, 186
4Q522 92, 195, 231, 233, 234, 291, 304
4Q531 32
4Q534 34, 40
4Q544 100
4Q577 11, 73–76, 78, 80, 82

Cave 5

5Q9 234

Cave 6

6Q15 212
6Q8 40

Cave 11

11QpaleoLev^a 281

11Q5 (11QPsalms^a)
11QPs^a XVII, 2 334
11QPs^a XIX, 7 48
11QPs^a XIX, 14 55
11QPs^a XXII, 15 57
11QPs^a XXVI, 11 337
11QPs^a XXVI, 13 48, 61, 67, 70
11QPs^a XXVII, 1 26

11Q13 30, 243
11Q14 47
11Q17 57

11QT^a (*Temple Scroll*)
11QT^a II, 6 191
11QT^a XV, 12 247
11QT^a XV, 18 105
11QT^a XXIII, 6 47
11QT^a XXVII, 4 248
11QT^a XXVII, 7 245
11QT^a XXXI, 4 57
11QT^a XXXV, 12 248
11QT^a XLII, 13 254
11QT^a XLV, 4 182
11QT^a XLVII, 1 98
11QT^a XLVIII, 3 47
11QT^a LIV, 12 213
11QT^a LIV, 15 272
11QT^a LVI, 3-4 319
11QT^a LVI-LIX 303
11QT^a LVI, 12-LVIII, 21 299
11QT^a LVI, 21 249
11QT^a LVIII, 15-21 291, 304
11QT^a LXI, 1 273
11QT^a LXI, 8 47
11QT^a LXI, 11 47
11QT^a LXI, 12-15 296
11QT^a LXII, 5-16 299
11QT^a LXVI, 4 47

Jewish Hellenistic authors

Artapanus 3:28-902 128
Demetrius 146, 224
Exagoge 132-148 128

Letter of Aristeas 96-99 302
Pseudo-Eupolemus 68

Philo

De vita Mosis
Mos. 1, 98-134 128
Mos. 2.263 64
Mos. 2.53 67
Mos. 2.64-65 125
Quod deterius potiori insidiari solet
Det. 170 124
De congressu quarendae eruditionis gratia
Prelim. Studies 115 124
De specialibus legibus

Spec. Laws 1.151 302
Spec. Laws 1.188 248
De decalogo
Decal. 175 223
Quaestiones et solutiones in Genesin
QG i, 89, 96 67
QG i, 91 21
QG ii, 13 125
QG ii, 16 60
QG ii, 56 125

Josephus

Jewish War
J.W. ii, 131 62
Jewish Antiquities
Ant. i, 27 88
Ant., i, 70-71 64
Ant. i, 72 66, 68
Ant. i, 99 124
Ant. i, 100 66
Ant. ii, 294-313 128
Ant. iii, 90, 93 223
Ant. iii, 163 302

Ant. iii, 166 302
Ant. iii 185 302
Ant. iii, 214 295
Ant. iii, 214-216 294, 302, 308
Ant. iii, 215-218 304
Ant. iii, 239 260
Ant. iii, 240 248
Ant. v, 120 294
Ant. v, 159 294
Ant. v, 254 294
Ant. v, 257 294

Christian Writings

Origen, *Cels.* iv, 21 124
Ps.-Clem. *Homilies* viii, 15 67
Ps.-Clem., *Homilies* viii, 17 124

Rabbinic Literature

Mishnah

m. *Demai* 6:11 245
m. *Yoma* 3:10 252
m. *Yoma* 3:8, 4:2, 6:2 249
m. *Soṭah* 7:2 138
m. *Soṭah* 8:1 295, 301, 308
m. *Soṭah* 8:2 138
m. Sanh 1:5 285
m. *Eduyyot* 5:6 312
m. *Kelim* 2:5, 4:1, 3 26

Toseftah

t. *Ber.* 6:1 62
t. *Ḥag.* 1:2 138
t. *Soṭah* 3:6 67
t. *Yoma* 3:1 215
t. *Ta'anit* 2:13 64
t. *Sanh.* 9:7 189

Babylonian Talmud

b. *'Arak.* 10b 249
b. *'Arak.* 16b 24
b. *B. Bat.* 16b 144
b. *Ber.* 32a 321
b. *Ber.* 40b 348
b. *Ber.* 48b 62
b. *Beṣah* 15b 24
b. *Hor.* 8a 223
b. *Ḥul.* 67b 26
b. *Mak.* 24a 223
b. *Meg.* 15a 21
b. *Naz.* 43b 308
b. *Niddah* 61a 68
b. *Roš Haš.* 16b 249
b. *Sanh.* 108a 21
b. *Soṭah* 10b 189
b. *Soṭah* 12a 26
b. *Soṭah* 35a 24
b. *Soṭah* 43a 308
b. *Yoma* 4a–b 216, 217
b. *Yoma* 9b 287
b. *Yoma* 21a 304
b. *Yoma* 70b 248
b. *Yoma* 73a 301
b. *Zebaḥ.* 113b 68
b. *Zebaḥ.* 116a 64

Midrashim

Mek. *Beshalaḥ* (*Shira*), 5 21
Mek. *Baḥodesh*, 4, 9 223
Mek. *Baḥodesh*, 9 222
Mek. R. Shim. Bar Yoḥai, *Beshalaḥ* to Exod 15:6 21
Mek. R. Shim. Bar Yoḥai, *Yethro* to Exod 19:9 216
Sifra Aḥarei Mot, 2 248
Sif. Deut. 349 206
Gen. Rab. 26, 7 67
Gen. Rab. 34, 1 67
Gen. Rab. 36, 1 67
Gen. Rab. 38, 1 67
Gen. Rab. 42, 8 138
Gen. Rab. 63, 12 144
Gen. Rab. 79, 7 145
Exod. Rab. 1, 20 26
Lev. Rab. 1, 4 206
Lev. Rab. 4, 1 67
Lev. Rab. 20, 2 308
Num. Rab. 9, 24 67
Num. Rab. 43, 6 178
Song of Songs Rab., 22 223
'*Abot R. Nat.* (A, B), 1 216
'*Abot R. Nat.* (A), 11 189
'*Abot R. Nat.* (A), 31 22
S. *'Olam Rab.* 1 151
Tanḥ. *Shemot*, 4 151
Tanḥ, *Beshalaḥ*, 15 21
Pesiq. Rab., 10, *Ki Tissa* 176
Pesiq. Rab., Ten Commandments, 22 223
Pesiq. Rab Kah. 5, 4 206
Pesiq. Rab Kah., *Parasha Aḥeret* 26
Pirqe R. El. 24 133
S. *Eli. Zut.* 24 133

Index of Names and Subjects

Aaron 50, 105, 106, 126, 160, 177–179, 190, 193, 206, 207, 223, 230, 231, 304
Abode 327, 332, 333, 342, 350
Abihu 9, 160, 162
Abraham 10, 130, 133, 136–138, 141–144, 147, 152, 155, 156
– Abram 106, 133
Ai 210, 299
Akedah 142, 155, 156
Amida (Eighteen Benedictions) prayer 348
Amram 40, 151, 217
Angels 8, 15, 19–22, 25, 36, 37, 39, 40–42, 66, 68, 69, 88, 176, 177, 195, 210, 212, 216, 217, 223, 224
Anointed, anointing 210, 212, 265, 269, 275–277, 280–283, 286, 289–291, 293, 295, 301, 302, 308, 321
– see also Messiah, messianic
Ark of the Covenant 279, 281, 319
– Kapporet (Ark's cover) 281
Asael 15, 18, 20, 21, 35, 37–39
Assembly / Congregation (קהל, עדה) 67, 193, 210, 221, 222, 230, 231, 259, 260, 278, 279, 280, 282, 283, 286, 287, 292, 295–298, 308, 311, 313, 316, 318, 319, 321, 331, 345, 352
Atonement 9, 242–250, 252, 260, 261, 280, 281, 286, 287, 343
– Day of, see "Day of Atonement"
Baraqel 37, 38
Benjamin, tribe of 204, 205
Birkat Ha-Mazon (Grace before the meal) 62
Blessing 41, 43, 48, 61, 62, 148, 156, 193, 194, 206, 272, 283, 284, 287, 313, 314, 326, 330, 333, 334, 336–340, 348–350, 356, 357
– see also "Covenantal curses and blessings"
Breastplate (High Priest's garments) 291, 294, 302–304, 311, 345, 351, 354
Bull 278, 280, 281, 289, 290
Calendar 2 60, 261, 337
Canaanites 173, 193, 199, 200, 201, 233
Canonization 6

Chiefs, chieftains 178, 193, 204–206, 220, 259, 280, 290, 291, 294, 296–298, 300, 301,303, 304, 307, 345
– Chieftain / Prince (נשיא) 280, 290, 291, 294, 297–299, 301, 304, 307, 308, 345, 357
Chronology 106, 136, 141, 144, 146, 147, 151, 156, 260
– Duration of the Israelites' stay in Egypt 150–151
Court 273, 275, 276, 282, 285, 286, 303
Covenant 8, 46, 53, 58, 60, 65, 79, 82, 83, 99, 100, 124, 125, 155, 173, 229, 237, 242, 284, 317, 331
Covenantal curses and blessings 187, 194, 211, 272, 283, 284, 287
Curtain / veil (פרוכת) 278–281, 309, 354, 355
David 26
Day of Atonement 240–250, 280, 281, 343
– Regulations pertaining to 240–250
– Atonement for the Land 247
Day of the Lord
– Depicting Flood using elements of the biblical descriptions of Day of the Lord 64, 69
Darkness
– Dominion of 336, 338
– Rule of 329, 338–340, 350
Debt, remission of 243, 260, 261
Dinah 146, 155
Divine 272–274, 282, 287, 295, 297, 300, 303, 304, 308, 309, 311, 314, 317, 319, 321, 325, 326, 330, 333–335, 337–349, 355, 356, 357
– Divine answer 283, 302, 304, 309, 311, 321, 348, 351, 354, 355, 357
Edom 177, 193
Egypt, Egyptian 10, 103, 105, 106, 109, 126, 128, 129, 139, 141, 150, 151, 155, 168, 173, 210, 237
Elder(s) 193, 259, 260, 269, 274, 275, 276, 283, 285, 286, 309, 310, 320
– Rebellious elder 275, 276, 309, 310

Eleazar 9, 160, 178, 179, 193, 229, 231, 233, 260, 298
Elisha 226
Elyo 204
Enoch, 1 Book of, 15–42
– Relation to Genesis Apocryphon and 1Q19 (Book of Noah) 35–42
– see also "Index of Sources, 1 Enoch"
Ephod 294, 295, 300, 302, 304, 307, 311
Esau 144, 155, 156
Eschatology 63, 64, 69, 130, 138, 149, 195, 206, 296, 349, 357, 358
– Eschatological High Priest 349
– Eschatological war 296
– Flood depicted as an eschatological war 69
Evening 265, 266, 329, 332, 335, 337–339, 340–344, 349
Evil inclination 91
Festival(s) 62, 171, 191, 192, 244, 254, 260, 313, 336, 337, 343
Flood 10, 11, 19, 41, 43, 44–48, 50–54, 56, 58–70, 72–84, 91, 92, 95–101, 110, 112, 113, 122–126, 129, 152, 154, 155, 247
– Antediluvians' ingratitude for God's generosity 66–68
– Cleansing sin 98
– Causes of 67–68
– Human rebellion against God 67–68
Gabriel 20, 21
Gad, tribe of 204, 205
Garments (priestly) 224, 294, 301, 302, 304, 308, 311, 321, 345, 348, 351, 356
Giants 6, 10, 15, 19, 25, 31, 36–40, 53, 60, 63, 66–69, 205
Gibeonites 291
Gilgal 299
Goat 280, 290
Gomorrah 67, 152
Hagar 141
Halakhah 244, 261, 266, 273, 278, 281, 282, 285, 298, 301, 321, 349, 350, 354, 356, 357
Hananiah 273
Haran 133, 144, 145, 155

Harmonization 4, 123, 191, 192, 260, 301, 303, 355
Hasmonean period 288, 323
Hebrew language
– As "the Holy tongue" 137–138
Herodian period 267, 288
Hidden (things, matters) 282, 285, 286, 317
Hittites 173
Hivites 173
Holiness Code 281
Holy of Holies 280, 281
Hor HaHar 177, 190, 193, 223
Idolatry 182, 193, 283, 284, 339
Ithamar 160, 260
Jacob 10, 130, 144–146, 147, 151, 155, 156, 277, 291, 303
Jericho 156, 206
Jerusalem 22, 56, 59, 69, 91, 104, 108, 145, 166, 186, 192, 201, 206, 221–223, 225, 248, 260, 266, 267, 273–275, 277, 282, 284–288, 291, 300–302, 305, 309, 317, 321, 323, 332, 338, 344, 354, 356
John Hyrcanus I 304
Jonathan 99
Jordan (river) 236
Joseph 10, 148, 155, 303
Jubilee 229, 243
Judas Maccabaeus 302
Judge(s) 269, 274–276, 283, 285–287, 289–310, 317, 319, 355
Justice 335, 348, 356
Kapporet see Ark of the Covenant
King 290, 291, 297, 298, 299, 302, 303, 310, 355, 357
Kokabel 37, 39
Light
– Dominion/rule of 329, 336, 339, 340, 350
Luminaries 9, 90, 100, 284, 306, 329, 332, 333, 336, 337, 339, 348–350, 356
Machir 178, 179
Magistrates 276, 285, 286, 320, 354
Messiah, messianic 298, 357
– Moses as anointed one 210, 212
Methuselah 28, 40
Michael 21

Midwives (Shiphrah and Puah) 103, 126, 130, 150, 151, 155
Miriam 202, 204, 206, 207, 221, 223
Mitzpah 302
Moriah 143
Morning 266, 329, 332, 335–343, 349, 356
Moses 6, 8, 9, 10, 11, 25, 26, 50, 64, 67, 104–106, 126, 129, 148, 151, 159–163, 165, 166, 175–179, 182, 183, 190, 191, 193–196, 199, 201, 202, 206, 207, 210–213, 215–218, 220–226, 228–234, 236–239, 242, 244, 246, 248, 250–252, 254, 256, 258–261, 265–267, 269, 271, 274, 281, 284, 288, 290, 293–295, 296, 298, 299, 304, 305, 307–309, 312, 316, 322, 330, 332, 345, 351–354, 357, 358
Nadab 10, 160, 162
Nathan, Rabbi 217
Nebo, Mount 193, 229, 230, 259, 260
Nephilim 36, 75
Nicanor 302
Noah 15, 24, 25, 26, 28, 30, 32–34, 36, 38, 40–43, 53, 54, 58, 60, 75, 77, 79, 80, 82, 96, 97, 99, 101, 114, 115, 123–125, 247
– Birth of 22–26
– Noah, Book of 15, 40, 41
Offerings, sacrifices 99, 124, 125, 142, 143, 163, 172, 192, 276, 279, 280, 287, 290, 291, 295 299–301, 309, 343, 351, 354, 355
– Burnt offering 281, 290
– Freewill offering 291, 300
– Sin offering 279–282, 286, 287, 290
– Thanksgiving offering / sacrifice 276–280, 287, 290, 291, 294, 295, 300, 301, 309, 354, 355
Onyx 294, 295, 302, 304, 311, 354
Palti 205
Passover 254
Perizzite 168, 173
Pesher, pesharim 77, 130, 131, 140, 143, 156, 284, 287, 301, 303, 321, 349, 357, 358
Pharaoh (of Exodus) 103, 105, 107, 126, 129–131, 150, 151
Prayer 9, 10, 21, 37, 39, 82, 91, 161–163, 201, 207, 208, 221, 249, 265, 266, 284, 306, 313–315, 318, 321, 323, 326, 328, 330, 332–336, 338, 340–350, 353, 356, 357
Predestination 74, 82
Priest 9, 32, 160, 161, 195, 196, 217, 224, 229, 231, 247–249, 265–267, 275–278, 287, 279–283, 285–298, 300–305, 307–312, 316–322, 345, 349–358
– Anointed Priest 265, 275, 276, 282, 283, 286, 289–291, 293, 295, 301, 302, 308, 321
– High Priest 266, 276–283, 285–291, 293–296, 300–302, 304, 307, 308, 311, 320, 322, 335, 345, 349, 351–357
– Priest anointed for battle 295, 301, 308
– Priestly circle / group 287, 320, 321, 350, 356, 357
– Priestly garments 302, 304
Priestly source (P) 353
Prophecy 3, 138–140, 212, 273–275, 285, 287, 294, 295, 308, 309
Prophet 3, 4, 6, 9, 65, 195, 196, 212, 261, 265–278, 280–289, 290, 293–295, 297, 301, 306, 307, 309, 310, 318, 319, 321, 351–355, 357
– False Prophet 9, 265–267, 272–276, 278, 282–287, 295, 301, 309, 310, 321, 322, 352–355, 357
– True Prophet 9, 266, 270, 272–274, 280, 283, 286, 288, 310, 322, 357
Qumran community / sect 282, 285, 315, 331, 350, 358
Qumran library 1, 68, 281
Qumran literature 271, 298, 332, 335, 336, 339
Rafu 205
Ram 279–281, 289, 290
Rearguard 204–206
Rebellion 50, 63, 66, 67, 70, 269, 272, 307, 309, 310, 321, 351, 353, 354
– speaking rebellion / speaking falsehood (לדבר סרה) see "Speaking"
– of antediluvians, see "Flood"
Rephaiah 204
Reproof 160, 161, 232, 284
Rewritten Bible 1–11, 163, 224, 274, 284

Index of Names and Subjects

Rule of the Community (1QS) 284, 306, 317, 350, 356
- see also "Index of Sources, Rule of the Community (1QS)"

Sacrifices see Offerings
Sabbath 8, 62, 229, 241, 242, 277, 313, 336, 343
Sabbatical Year 9, 240–243, 260, 261
Sage(s) 91, 131, 193, 248, 273, 276, 348
Sahriel 37, 39
Sanctuary 280–282, 308, 345
Sardonyx 294
Sariel 21
Sectarian literature 11, 59, 85, 115, 130, 140, 183, 186, 187, 196, 357
Seeking God (לדרוש אל) 273
Seeking God's will (לדרוש את רצונו) 317, 319
Septuagint 48, 91, 145, 191, 192, 298
see also "Index of Sources, Septuagint"
Scapegoat 249
Shamsiel 37, 39
Shechem, Shechemites 145, 146, 155
Shemihazah 15, 18, 20, 21, 35, 37, 38
Shiloh 104
Simeon 148
Simon, High Priest 356
Sin 10, 36, 37, 58, 60, 66–68, 70, 83, 86, 91, 96, 98, 103, 122–124, 126, 129, 160, 162, 210, 279–282, 286, 287, 290
- Inadvertent 279, 280, 283, 286, 287, 355
- Sin offering 287, 280–282, 286, 287, 290
Sinai 8, 176, 179, 190, 195, 199, 200, 213–217, 220–224, 231, 238, 260, 282, 300, 318
- Sinai revelation 221–224
Sirach (Ben Sira) 355
Sodom 67, 152
Solomon 199, 251
Speaking
- Rebellion 269, 293, 306, 307, 309, 310, 321, 351, 353, 354
- Falsehood 272
Tabernacle 290, 296, 304

Temple 1, 2, 5–9, 11, 42, 43, 53, 60, 62–64, 66–68, 86, 91, 98, 108, 125, 130, 133, 191, 192, 194, 201, 212, 243–245, 247–249, 252, 261, 273, 275–277, 280, 283, 285–287, 290, 291, 293, 294, 296, 298–304, 318, 319, 321, 332, 333, 343, 348, 351, 352, 354–357
- Heavenly Temple 322, 333, 348
- Second Temple period 42, 66, 67, 192, 276, 304, 322, 333, 348
Temple scroll (11QT^a) 273, 290, 291, 296, 299, 301, 303, 304, 319, 321, 355, 356, 357
- see also "Index of Sources, Temple scroll (11QT^a)"
Ten Commandments 221–224
- Order of giving 222, 223
- Some given directly by God and some through Moses 222–225
Ten Plagues 10, 101–111, 127–129
Tetragrammaton 49, 76, 86, 97, 111, 124, 237, 239, 243, 261, 314, 324, 326, 328, 333
Theophoric name 21, 205
Tongues of fire 266, 292–294, 300, 302, 303, 305–308, 310, 311, 345, 347, 351, 355
Tree of Knowledge 10, 90, 122
Tribe(s) 193, 204–206, 259, 269, 274–276, 281, 283, 285, 286, 298, 302
- see also by individual tribal name
Truth, truthful 269, 274, 302, 331, 335, 348
Urim (and Thummim) 9, 275, 278–297, 300–304, 308, 309, 311, 317, 320–322, 335, 345, 348, 349, 351–357
War(s) 288, 290, 292, 294–296, 298, 300, 302, 304, 308
- Permitted war 266, 288, 290, 291, 301, 321, 351, 354, 355
War Scroll (1QM) 290, 296, 331
- see also "Index of Sources, War Scroll (1QM)"
Yaḥad 327, 331
Zadok 317
Ziqel 37, 39

www.ingramcontent.com/pod-product-compliance
Lightning Source LLC
Chambersburg PA
CBHW071810230426
43670CB00013B/2414